OXFORD WORLD'S CLASSICS

LE MORTE DARTHUR

THE greatest English version of the stories of King Arthur, the *Morte Darthur* was completed in 1469–70 by Sir Thomas Malory, 'knight prisoner'. His identity is uncertain, but he is likely to have been the lord of the manor of Newbold Revel, in Warwickshire. After initially leading the life of a responsible member of the gentry, this Sir Thomas Malory turned to a career of spectacular lawlessness; he spent a number of years in prison, was excluded from two general pardons, and died in 1471.

Malory's text collects, combines, and abbreviates the key French thirteenth-century prose romances of Arthur, many of which were themselves based on earlier verse originals, and supplements them with English Arthurian material. The 'historical' Arthur had been given a biography of pan-European conquest by Geoffrey of Monmouth early in the twelfth century, and Malory incorporates a later version of this story too. The *Morte* thus channels all the important Arthurian legends into a single source that itself stands at the head of the whole later Arthurian tradition in English, from Tennyson's *Idylls of the King* and T. H. White's *The Sword in the Stone* to *Camelot* and *Monty Python and the Holy Grail*.

This edition, slightly abridged from the original, is the first designed for the general reader to be based on the 'Winchester manuscript' of the *Morte Darthur*, now British Library MS Additional 59678. This manuscript represents what Malory wrote more closely than the version edited and printed by William Caxton, the only version known until earlier this century, which has been used as the basis for most other editions of the work.

HELEN COOPER is Professor of English Language and Literature in the University of Oxford, and Tutorial Fellow, University College, Oxford. She is the author of *Oxford Guides to Chaucer: The Canterbury Tales* (Clarendon Press) and has edited Keith Harrison's translation of *Sir Gawain and the Green Knight* for Oxford World's Classics (1998).

W9-AJY-725

OXFORD WORLD'S CLASSICS

For over 100 years Oxford World's Classics have brought readers closer to the world's great literature. Now with over 700 titles—from the 4,000-year-old myths of Mesopotamia to the twentieth century's greatest novels—the series makes available lesser-known as well as celebrated writing.

The pocket-sized hardbacks of the early years contained introductions by Virginia Woolf, T. S. Eliot, Graham Greene, and other literary figures which enriched the experience of reading. Today the series is recognized for its fine scholarship and reliability in texts that span world literature, drama and poetry, religion, philosophy and politics. Each edition includes perceptive commentary and essential background information to meet the changing needs of readers.

OXFORD WORLD'S CLASSICS

SIR THOMAS MALORY

Le Morte Darthur

THE WINCHESTER MANUSCRIPT

Edited and abridged
with an Introduction and Notes by
HELEN COOPER

OXFORD
UNIVERSITY PRESS

OXFORD
UNIVERSITY PRESS

Great Clarendon Street, Oxford OX2 6DP

Oxford University Press is a department of the University of Oxford.
It furthers the University's objective of excellence in research, scholarship,
and education by publishing worldwide in

Oxford New York

Auckland Bangkok Buenos Aires Cape Town Chennai
Dar es Salaam Delhi Hong Kong Istanbul Karachi Kolkata
Kuala Lumpur Madrid Melbourne Mexico City Mumbai Nairobi
São Paulo Shanghai Singapore Taipei Tokyo Toronto

with an associated company in Berlin

Oxford is a registered trade mark of Oxford University Press
in the UK and in certain other countries

Published in the United States
by Oxford University Press Inc., New York

British Library Cataloguing in Publication Data

Data available

Library of Congress Cataloging in Publication Data

Malory, Thomas, Sir, 15th cent.
Le morte Darthur : the Winchester manuscript/Sir Thomas Malory;
edited and abridged with an introduction and notes by Helen Cooper,
(Oxford world's classics)
Based on the 'Winchester manuscript' of the Morte Darthur held by
the British Library.
Includes bibliographical references (p.   ) and index.
1. Arthurian romances.   2. Knights and knighthood—Romances.
3. Kings and rulers—Romances.   I. Cooper, Helen.   II. Title.
III. Series
PR2043.C63   1998   823'.2—dc21   97–18955
ISBN 0–19–282420–1

7 9 10 8 6

Typeset by Jayvee, Trivandrum, India
Printed in Great Britain by
Cox & Wyman Ltd.
Reading, Berkshire

CONTENTS

INTRODUCTION

The Story of Arthur

At the battle of Camlann, Arthur and Medraut fell.

That cryptic line is not quite the earliest reference to Arthur, but it is the first that lays claim to historical plausibility. It is also the first to name Mordred together with Arthur in their last battle—though whether as opponents or associates is not clear. The *Annales Cambriae*, which contains the entry, dates the battle to the early sixth century. Between that date, whether legendary or historical, and the first full account of Arthur written 600 years later, legends about him were widespread, as we know from tantalizingly allusive references in Welsh poetry, from recurrent appearances of Arthur as a Christian name, and from the record of a fracas in Cornwall early in the twelfth century between a local man and the servant of a visiting ecclesiastical dignitary over the issue of whether Arthur was still alive.

It was Geoffrey of Monmouth, however, writing his *History of the Kings of Britain* in the 1130s, who first made Arthur into the great British hero, and who provided him with the biography that remained current in accounts of the English past down to the time of the sixteenth-century historian Holinshed. Like the writers of much of the best fiction, Geoffrey claims to be deriving his work from an ancient book that he was lent, written in the British language; neither its existence nor its non-existence can be proved. His Arthur is a conqueror (both within the British Isles and on the continent of Europe) who is supported by a group of warriors, notable among them Gawain and Kay; it is while he is campaigning on the continent that his nephew Mordred, left as regent in his absence, attempts to usurp the throne, resulting in their final internecine battle. The Round Table makes its first appearance in a French verse redaction of Geoffrey made some fifteen years later, the *Roman de Brut* of Wace. Shortly after that, probably starting in the 1160s, Chrétien de Troyes composed the first French verse romances devoted to the exploits of individual knights of the Round Table. It is in these that Lancelot first achieves prominence, as the lover of Guenivere and as Arthur's best knight, displacing Gawain.

The fashion started by Chrétien initiated an extraordinary literary flowering of Arthurian material across Europe. New romances were composed; French ones were translated and adapted into a multiplicity of languages, from Norse to Portuguese and Hebrew. Early in the thirteenth century in France, the stories contained in the verse romances of Arthur were given a new and extended form in prose. A connected series of these written by various authors, known as the Vulgate Cycle, covered the whole history of the Round Table from the pre-history of the Grail in the generation after the Crucifixion down to Arthur's death in battle against Mordred, who by this time had become his illegitimate son unwittingly begotten on his sister. In this cycle, divine retribution for sexual sin—Arthur's incest with his sister, Lancelot's adultery with Guenivere—brings about the fall of the Round Table, and the Grail knights are accordingly upgraded into being warriors of God, pure of any sexual contact, and with the new figure of Galahad replacing the earlier and more worldly Grail hero Perceval. Tristan and Isolde, whose story had originally been independent of any Arthurian connections, were also drawn within the great magnetic field of the Round Table, and Tristan, in a huge prose romance of his own, became the only knight of medieval romance to rival Lancelot in both prowess and popularity.

In England, the history of Arthurian romance followed a slightly different path. The 'historical' story of Arthur, ultimately derived from Geoffrey of Monmouth, was retold several times in poetic form, notably in the alliterative *Morte Arthure* of the late fourteenth century. There are a number of English metrical romances of individual Arthurian knights: a version of the original Tristan story, a translation of Chrétien's *Yvain*, a *Percival of Gales* without the Grail. The most striking feature of the English tradition, however, is that Gawain remains the most popular Arthurian knight, eleven surviving metrical romances being devoted to his exploits besides the magnificent alliterative *Sir Gawain and the Green Knight*. Lancelot never received the kind of attention that he did in France: only a verse adaptation of the last part of the Vulgate Cycle, the stanzaic *Morte Arthur*, accords him any significant space before Malory himself.

The stanzaic *Morte Arthur*, probably composed around the same time as the alliterative *Morte*, is typical in translating French prose into English verse. Prose romance arrived late in England, well into the fifteenth century. To us, Malory's decision to write in prose looks inevitable; at the time he was writing, in the 1460s, it was by no means such an obvious choice. Only one English translation of Vulgate Cycle material out of the five that precede Malory uses prose; and his English sources are all in verse, stanzaic or alliterative. His choice of prose may have been influenced by the fact that the earliest English prose romances tend to be stories of disaster or tragedy—stories such as Oedipus or the fall of Troy—rather than of wish-fulfilment and happy endings. That Malory gives his whole work the title of the *Morte Darthur*, the death of Arthur, insists that this too is a story in which things go irrevocably wrong.

Although Malory was writing over two centuries after the composition of the French prose romances that form the bulk of his sources, he was neither old-fashioned nor anachronistic in turning back to them. They were enjoying a new surge of popularity in the fifteenth century, with new manuscript copies being made and a cult of chivalry to encourage their reading. A number are known to have been owned by readers in England, and Malory would probably not have needed to go to the continent to find copies of his source works.[1] England's first printer, William Caxton, who printed Malory's work in 1485, was both cashing in on the fashion for Arthurian material and setting the pace for its broader dissemination: the first French Arthurian prose romance to be printed, the *Lancelot*, appeared in 1488, the *Tristan* in 1489.

It was Malory's work, however, that survived. After tastes changed in the course of the sixteenth century the French romances ceased to be reprinted, and in so far as they have been known at all since then it is largely as works for study by academics, despite recent translations of some of them. Malory, by contrast, was reprinted several times down to 1634; he passed into some obscurity after that, but since the revival of interest in the *Morte* that started early in the nineteenth century, he has served as the direct or indirect basis for almost every Arthurian work in any medium: poems, novels, children's books, science fiction, films, advertisements, cartoons, modern heritage paraphernalia—everything from epics to T-shirts.

[1] See Carol M. Meale, 'Manuscripts, Readers and Patrons in Fifteenth-Century England: Sir Thomas Malory and Arthurian Romance', *Arthurian Literature*, 4 (1985), 93–126.

Sir Thomas Malory

Who was Sir Thomas Malory? The strong likelihood is that he was a man who at first sight appears distinctly unpromising, at least if one believes that writers' lives should accord with the principles of their work. The career of Sir Thomas Malory of Newbold Revel, in Warwickshire, reads more like an account of exemplary thuggery than chivalry.[2] His date of birth and early years are obscure; he may possibly have served in France in the later stages of the Hundred Years War. He first enters the records in 1439, and had been knighted by 1441. With the exception of an episode of grievous bodily harm, until 1450 he lived the life of a socially responsible member of the gentry, holding various public offices including that of Member of Parliament. After this, however, he turned to a career of crime and violence, interspersed with long periods of imprisonment. He began with a spectacular outburst that included attempted assassination, cattle-rustling, extortion, abbey-breaking, and rape. (He was indeed accused of raping the same woman on two separate occasions; in his favour, it should be noted that at this date a charge of rape of a married woman could be a husband's way of going on the offensive over his wife's adultery.) Unprecedentedly large forces were sent to arrest him; he twice escaped from imprisonment—once by swimming the moat, once with the help of swords and long knives—and his jailers were threatened with record-breaking penalty clauses in the event of a further escape. He had the unique distinction of being exempted by name from two separate general pardons. In his periods of liberty, various of the magnates who had interests in the Warwickshire area made gestures towards recruiting him into their affinities (political and, if necessary, military interest groups), but none showed any enthusiasm about either holding on to him or offering him support. A number of comments in the course of his Arthurian work inform us that he wrote it in prison; he completed it, he tells us, in the year 1469–70. He died in March 1471.

The mismatch between this life and the golden ideal of chivalry that the *Morte Darthur* promotes has led to a series of attempts to find other candidates for its authorship, but none has been convincing. There

---

[2] The following account is indebted to P. J. C. Field, *The Life and Times of Sir Thomas Malory* (Cambridge, 1993), modified in the light of Christine Carpenter, 'Sir Thomas Malory and Fifteenth-century Local Politics', *Bulletin of the Institute of Historical Research*, 53 (1980), 31–43.

were other Malory families in the fifteenth century, but none contained a Thomas known to have been knighted, nor one known to have been imprisoned for anything like the length of time necessary for producing such a huge work. Claims have been made for a Yorkshire Malory and, less convincingly, for a Cambridgeshire Malory, but supporting evidence is no more than circumstantial.[3]

The contrast between the ethics promoted in the *Morte Darthur* and those evinced by Malory's life is huge, but it is not so greatly different in kind from the contrast shown by the age in which he lived. The fifteenth century witnessed a cult of chivalry such as had never been known before: its practitioners seem to have thought of it as a revival, but it is hard to find actual precedents. Tournaments and individual chivalric combats, the latter often based on the model of the prose romances, reached new heights of elaboration on the continent of Europe. Noblemen and other gentlemen would sometimes set up a pillar or a shield or a basin at a crossroads or some comparable place, to be struck by challengers who wished to engage in combat with them—a process known as the *pas d'armes*, the passage of arms. A Burgundian gentleman named Jacques de Lalaing acquired fame for conducting his life on the model of a knight errant, travelling Europe in a search for chivalric combatants. Orders of knighthood flourished: one of the earliest, Edward III's Order of the Garter, had been established in 1348, in a conscious imitation of the fellowship of the Round Table, but the majority of such orders were fifteenth-century foundations. Malory himself apparently modelled the oath sworn by the fellows of the Round Table on the charge laid on the neophyte knights in the ceremony for creating Knights of the Bath.

Chivalric orders, however, were founded in order to set standards of aspiration in a world that was less than ideal. Local and national disorder in England increased in intensity in the course of the fifteenth century, more or less in line with Malory's own career of violence. The weak adult rule of Henry VI culminated in civil war between his house of Lancaster and the rival dynasty of York; but the battle for the throne was only the extreme form of a more general feuding and civil

[3] See William Matthews, *The Ill-Framed Knight: A Skeptical Enquiry into the Identity of Sir Thomas Malory* (Berkeley, California, 1966); and Richard R. Griffith, 'The Authorship Question Reconsidered: A Case for Sir Thomas Malory of Papworth St Agnes, Cambridgeshire', in *Aspects of Malory*, ed. Toshiyuki Takamiya and Derek Brewer (Cambridge, 1981), 159–77.

disturbance, which a stronger king could have controlled. It is much too easy to imagine the Wars of the Roses as a simple struggle between Yorkists and Lancastrians: in practice it was more like a series of faction-fights in which participants might on occasion change sides, not just over the question of which king they supported, but according to baronial enmities and local disputes that could in turn draw members of rival magnate affinities into larger feuds.

Malory's work may ostensibly be set in a legendary age in which chivalric behaviour was lived most fully, but not the least interesting thing about his own redaction of his Arthurian material is the way it intersects with the conditions of his own era. In the French Vulgate Cycle, it is the failure of earthly knighthood, as shown up by the standards of religious perfection set by the quest for the Holy Grail, that causes the downfall of Arthur. In Malory's version, the fellowship of the Round Table is split from within by warring factions. Gawain and his brothers (always excepting the 'good knight' Sir Gareth) acquire a hatred of Lancelot grounded on envy; and they murder Sir Lamorak because of a blood-feud deriving from their father's death in battle at the hands of Lamorak's father Pellinore. Arthur, bound to Gawain by close ties of kinship, appears helpless to stop the violence; and after Lancelot accidentally kills Gareth while he is unarmed and on the King's service, Gawain demands revenge from the King that Arthur cannot legally or feudally refuse.

All these episodes are present in his French sources, but Malory's changes of emphasis amount to an ethical restructuring of the whole history of Arthur. His version is not a clash between earthly and divine focused on the issue of sexual sinfulness, but a study of the personal rivalries that underlie political disintegration. His awareness of the connections between the story he is recounting and his own times becomes on occasion explicit: as he notes that in Arthur's days justice was exercised regardless of the rank of the accused and without miscarrying for 'favour, love, nor affinity'—the last being a reference to the system of magnates' packing of juries in support of their retainers; or in his outburst attacking 'all ye Englishmen' who are prepared to exchange one king for another, 'and men say that we of this land have not yet lost that custom'. Malory's *Morte Darthur* is not an exercise in nostalgia for a golden age: it is an account of the destruction of an ideal.

Malory's Arthurian World

Malory's 'whole book of King Arthur and of his noble knights of the Round Table' gives a complete history of the Arthurian world. In part it comprises a life of Arthur himself, from the mysterious circumstances of his begetting and birth, through his mighty conquests, to his downfall and death. Integrated with and inset within that is a series of individual histories of the most famous members of the fellowship of the Round Table. Some are given space of their own—Gareth, Lancelot, Tristram, Galahad; others are told of in the course of other stories—Gawain, Mordred, Pelleas, Bors, Palomides, Dinadan, Lamorak. The important thing, however, is that they do make up a *fellowship*. They support each other, rescue each other, 'enfellowship' with each other—the verb is Malory's own coinage. If they engage in combat in anger (as distinct from sport), it is because of mistaken identity, or because of an explicit failure of fellowship: a failure that becomes increasingly evident as the whole history progresses, and which finally destroys the fellowship from within.

The ideal of knighthood that Malory presents is summarized in the oath sworn by the Round Table knights: to avoid treason and wrongful quarrels; to show mercy; never to offer violence, especially sexual violence, to gentlewomen (the aristocratic social basis is a premiss almost universal in medieval romance, not least in Arthurian material) and to fight on their behalf. Later he adds that the quarrels in which a knight fights should come from God or his lady; and he repeats many times and in many forms that true love should be faithful and unchanging. It is, in fact, an ideal of secular Christian chivalry, that incorporates physical prowess, an observance of one's duties to God—his knights are generally meticulous about attending Mass—and faithful heterosexual love.

None of these, however, is unproblematic. Secular romance gave primacy to love—most often, to courtship and sexuality that leads to marriage; less often, though more famously, to love independent of marriage, such as proved its absoluteness by its inability to be constrained by the social taboos against adultery in general, or, in particular, with the wife of one's overlord. The medieval church, by contrast, had a tendency to define spiritual perfection in terms of sexual intactness, virginity, in a manner directly at odds with the ethos of secular romance. Malory seems perfectly happy to give examples of all three

attitudes: Gareth's winning of Dame Lyonesse as his wife, the illicit
passion of Lancelot and Guenivere or Tristram and Isode, the elevation of virginity in the knights of the Grail quest. He is notably free of
the anxieties about sexuality that are often ascribed to medieval culture; he takes it as natural and unthreatening, for instance, that women
have sexual desires, reserving his disapproval for women such as Morgan le Fay who try to impose their desires by force or blackmail in a
female equivalent of rape. His villains in his presentation of love are
those men or women who are promiscuous, jealous, or violent, or who
betray lovers in order to destroy them. Hermits and other confessors
who try to impose the standards of the Church are accepted without
fuss: they are, after all, only doing what holy men are supposed to do.

The knight's position in regard to God can none the less be rendered
untenable by the demands of a different ethical system. The clash of
the two becomes the engine that drives Malory's version of the Grail
quest. The French prose romance of the Grail may have been written
to offer a religious counterbalance to the attraction of secular romance;
it insists on the positive damage done by sexuality, by the desire for
honour, by all those things that elsewhere in the Arthurian stories con-
stitute the essence of knighthood. Lancelot, accordingly, becomes the
exemplary failure, the knight who is foiled by his own sinfulness, his
inability to change from a worldly ethic to a spiritual one. Malory's
Lancelot, by contrast, comes close to being the hero of the quest, precisely because he will not give up: because he will not abandon his
desire for the Grail, and cannot ultimately abandon his desire for
Guenivere.

It is only in the course of the Grail quest, when the episodes function
less as narratives of knightly adventure than as allegories of moral
temptation or theological signification, that Lancelot can be overcome.
Elsewhere, his prowess is absolute. His physical superiority and his
faithfulness to the terms of the Round Table oath together make him
the paragon of knightliness; by the time of Malory's great lyric
encomium on love, his devotion to Guenivere is included as a part of
that excellence. Might does not always or necessarily indicate right,
however. Good knights will frequently be defeated and mistreated by
stronger wicked ones, and rely on the most powerful figures, Lancelot
or Tristram, for rescue. King Mark generally relies on the underhand
methods of plotting rather than open combat to further his own interests and defeat his enemies, but he has the good fortune to defeat in

combat an opponent who has justly charged him with murder—God does not always, as Malory notes, intervene to support the right. And in the final stages of the work, even Lancelot's prowess becomes problematic.

Malory designs the last two sections of his work around Lancelot's three successive rescues of Guenivere from the threat of judicial execution. In the first, when she is charged with murder, she is innocent. In the second, given its place here by Malory himself and not by his sources, the charge is of adultery with one of the wounded knights lying in her chamber, and she is innocent only on a technicality: it is Lancelot himself who has slept with her. On the third occasion, when Lancelot is taken in her chamber and fights his way out, even Malory acknowledges that her innocence is problematic. He will not commit himself as to 'whether they were abed or at other manner of discourse', but he recognizes the inevitability of the position taken by both Lancelot and his kin, that he must fight in her defence: 'In so much as ye were taken with her, whether ye did right or wrong, it is now your part to hold with the Queen.' 'Whether right or wrong' becomes almost a leitmotiv phrase of the end of the work; and Arthur and Lancelot both know that if the issue comes to individual combat, then, whether right or wrong, Lancelot will be the victor.

There is a strong sense, however, in which Lancelot is in the right: not necessarily over the question of what happened that night in the Queen's chamber, which Malory avoids specifying, but because he, in contrast to his accusers, is (paradoxically) faithful to Arthur as his lord. Malory's Arthurian world operates by the principles of a shame culture, where worth is measured in terms of reputation, 'worship', rather than by the principles of a guilt culture, of what one's conscience may declare to be right or wrong. So long as Arthur's honour is not spoken against, his kingship is untouched. Agravain and Mordred insist on bringing the affair into the open, regardless of its direct damage to the King and the consequences to the fellowship and the realm. Lancelot, by contrast, does his best to restore 'worship' to Arthur by offering to fight (and therefore to overcome) all those who are prepared to accuse the Queen, and to restore the fellowship to its wholeness by his offers of reparation to Gawain. His refusal to fight with Arthur himself is consistently presented as due to love and loyalty rather than a guilty conscience. As author, Malory blames Agravain and Mordred for the downfall of the Round Table; both Gawain and

Guenivere blame themselves. Lancelot bitterly laments his misfortune in accidentally killing Gareth and his failure to arrive in time to assist Arthur in his final battle, but if Malory targets him for blame, it is only through his disposition of material, never by direct statement. Moreover, any guilt that might attach to the sin of the lovers in the eyes of God is strongly countered in two passages, apparently original to Malory, that occur on either side of the second accusation of Guenivere, the only occasion in the work when they do explicitly sleep together: first, when he insists that 'she was a true lover, and therefore she had a good end'—a phrase implying that her faithfulness to Lancelot wins her acceptance into Heaven; second, when God allows Lancelot to perform his own personal miracle, in the healing of Sir Urry.

Good knighthood in Malory is presented in terms of models and counter-models, led by Lancelot, Gareth, and Tristram. Opposing them are characters such as the brutal Sir Tarquin; the outright villain Sir Breunis sans Pité, who is an expert in violence but who flees as soon as he is offered serious opposition; and Mordred, the traitor within Arthur's own household. Malory deploys a rigorously limited vocabulary to define the two groups, in a resonating repetition that serves to associate all good or all bad knights with each other: *noble*, *worshipful*, *good*, against *shameful*, *false*, *traitorous*, or (most commonly used by his knights rather than himself as narrator) *recreant* or *recrayed*. This does not mean, however, that all good or all bad knights are interchangeable. Dinadan, whose worth Malory consistently stresses, is as much Tristram's sidekick as follower, a knight who has no more than the ordinary measure of physical courage or prowess and knows that he can get hurt; he is the direct ancestor of Don Quixote's Sancho Panza. Yet he too is a knight of the Round Table, and his courage is all the more notable for not being sustained by the casual self-confidence that marks Tristram or Lancelot; and his unhesitating clarity of moral vision makes him a touchstone for measuring knightliness in others. Other knights swing between the opposing poles of fellowship and treachery, often very consciously. Palomides' hopeless love for La Belle Isode makes him lurch between jealous hatred of Tristram and respect for his worthiness. Gawain, too, veers sharply between extremes, largely according to the source Malory is following at any given moment: the English hero is inconsistent with the French Gawain of the prose *Tristan* and the Grail, which present him as an antitype of knightliness. By the end, however, Malory can turn these contradictions into a source of power: the two readings of him become a psychological conflict within Gawain himself, when his principles of knightliness are defeated by his desire for revenge after the death of Gareth, and are only recovered on his deathbed, when the action he takes to save the kingdom comes too late.

'Psychological conflict' may appear to be the wrong sort of term to use about Malory's narrative: he presents speeches and actions, not thoughts or motives, and the inner life of his characters has to be deduced from those. Only very rarely does he report an unspoken thought (and most of those are given to Dinadan, the knight least effective in outward action). Yet the effect of the narrative is extraordinarily powerful. The spareness of Malory's style constantly invites the reader to fill in the gaps, to supply the motives that produce the recorded reaction of aggression, or tears, or passion, or an answer at cross-purposes, or on rare occasions a smile. The hinterland of Malory's characters requires active imaginative participation from the reader; his paratactic style, the juxtaposition of event and response with the causal connections omitted, invites such participation in every sentence, to turn a 'then' into a 'therefore'.

The effect is very different from that of a novel, and all the indications are that Malory would not have wanted to write one even if the form had been available to him. His style has been compared to that of a chronicle, and indeed he repeatedly insists on the fact that the Arthurian adventures were a matter of record: that first Merlin, then Arthur, had written accounts made to document the deeds of the Round Table for posterity. Malory takes up the position of a latter-day historian to Arthur's court. It shows, not only in his deferral to his sources (many of such references, it should be noted, being rhetorical strategies designed to suggest authoritativeness rather than footnotes of strict accuracy), but also in his pervasive additions of the details of names and places, and in his insistence on the protocol of giving all his characters titles. Kings are always designated as such; knights' names are always prefixed by Sir, even the more villainous (no other medieval writer, of fiction or chronicle, makes such a consistent habit of this); women are designated as Queen or Dame or by some more individual title.

In contrast to the writers of French romances, but in keeping with his Middle English sources, Malory seems to have assumed a primarily male readership for his work: readers who would share his own

fascination with battle-strategy and chivalric league tables. He tends
to cut out the elements conventionally associated with women readers,
such as the analysis of emotion. Women do, however, play a crucial role
in his work. Without Igraine, Dame Lyonesse, Guenivere, Isode, or
Elaine the mother of Galahad, almost none of the events of the *Morte
Darthur* would happen. Most of them, moreover, are active agents, not
mere passive damosels: Isode falls in love with Tristram before he does
with her, and later travels in his company almost as a fellow-knight;
Elaine has to scheme to get her man; Guenivere controls Lancelot's
passion for her for better and for worse. There are no women warriors
in Malory, as there are in the prose *Merlin* or many of the Renaissance
romantic epics, the *Orlando Furioso* or the *Gerusalemme Liberata* or the
Faerie Queene; his women have to make their mark in other ways. Their
separation from the military world makes them, for instance, much
more fully social beings than the male characters. Knights in armour
are recognized, or pass unrecognized, because of the shields they
carry; with the exception of Dinadan, one of the few knights who has
to any notable degree what recruitment agencies would call interper-
sonal skills, they are remarkably bad at recognizing each other face to
face. The women are much better: their space is primarily indoors, in
the hall or chamber where the knights are unarmed, not the forest of
adventure or the battlefield, and they can identify members of the fellowship with much more assurance than its members themselves can.

   The women who are presented most closely and sympathetically are
the ones who love, whether that love is reciprocated or not: the two
Elaines are a leading example. In themselves, they have nothing except
beauty and their own faithfulness by way of resources. Guenivere can
add rank and power, but those are presented as a liability, in making her
a target for scandal or in enabling her to put her anger against Lancelot
into practice, and are of no help when it comes to her love for him.
Around them are a group of other, more shadowy women, led by Morgan le Fay, who employ enchantments or other supernatural devices:
the Lady of the Lake; Isode's mother, with her access to poison and the
love-potion; the enchantress Hallewes, who tries to entrap Lancelot;
Dame Brusen, who succeeds in doing so on behalf of her mistress; or
the fiendish temptresses who try to seduce the knights of the Grail.
Morgan, Hallewes, and the fiends apart, such women are not necessarily presented as evil; many exploit learning or esoteric knowledge, of
herbs or potions, in a manner parallel to the knights' exertion of

physical strength. Not all of Malory's women, however, have access to such knowledge, and the contrast makes all the more poignant the plight of those who have nothing but love to offer in a world where love is unlikely to be enough.

Malory's Sources

Malory worked with four principal French sources, supplemented by at least two others, and two major English sources.[4] For the four connected stories that comprise the opening section of his work, he used the French *Suite du Merlin*: as its name indicates, this was intended as a sequel to the Vulgate Cycle *Merlin*, though it is much more condensed in its treatment of its material than the expansive Vulgate romances. The next section, the war against the Emperor Lucius, is taken from the English alliterative *Morte Arthure*: this poem, following the historical tradition deriving from Geoffrey of Monmouth, has Arthur leave Mordred in charge of the kingdom while he pursues his military ambitions on the continent, and Mordred's seizure of the crown takes place while Arthur is overseas for that purpose. Malory accordingly changes the details of the poem and cuts it off short, with Arthur returning to rule his kingdom while his knights undertake their various adventures.

The first section describing these, *The Tale of Sir Lancelot*, is based on extracts from a version of the French prose *Lancelot*. The later *Tale of Sir Lancelot and Queen Guenivere* incorporates a further episode from this, Meliagaunt's abduction of Guenivere and his accusation of adultery. The prose *Tristan* is the largest work used extensively by Malory, and this supplies the huge middle of his Arthuriad. The original verse redactions of the story, with their close concentration on the progress of the love affair of Tristan and Isolde, would have been useless for his purposes, but the prose romance gave him just what he needed: an extensive space in which the nature of Arthurian knighthood can be explored, free from the more serious political demands of war or dynastic struggles. That Tristram himself comes from outside the élite circle of Arthur's fellowship means that the Round Table itself is seen initially from an outsider's point of view, as

---

[4] Edward D. Kennedy, 'Malory and his English Sources', gives a more extended study of these (in *Aspects of Malory*, ed. Takamiya and Brewer, 27–55).

something to be admired and striven for, a secular equivalent of the Grail fellowship—though increasingly, and especially in Malory's treatment, one that carries within itself the potential for disaster.

The Grail quest again has a French prose original, the *Queste del Saint Graal* from the Vulgate Cycle. Malory also had access to the following, and final, book of the Cycle, *La Mort le Roi Artu*, though in fact his primary source for the *Tale of Sir Lancelot and Queen Guenivere* and the *Death of Arthur* would appear to be the stanzaic *Morte Arthur*, an English verse adaptation of the same French romance. Malory incorporates only a single one of the many episodes in the French that the English had already excluded; all verbal resemblances are to the English, and increase strikingly in density in the *Death*.

Less important sources include, in French, the *Perlesvaus*, another non-Vulgate prose romance; and perhaps, in English, the mid-fifteenth-century chronicle in seven-line stanzas of John Hardyng. Hardyng is the only person apart from Malory to declare that Arthur was actually crowned as emperor in Rome (a risky claim, since it is so signally lacking in support from all continental historical sources); but it is of course possible that if Hardyng could invent such a triumphant climax to the European campaign, so could Malory.

Two major episodes have no known sources: the *Tale of Sir Gareth* and the healing of Sir Urry. There may have been romances of these stories that are now lost (*Gareth*, indeed, has elements in common with some surviving romances, though nothing resembling Malory's customary process of translation and adaptation); but both must have been invented by somebody at some stage, and there is no strong reason why that person should not have been Malory.

Even where Malory is working with a source book in front of him, however, he will not merely translate or 'reduce', but invent. Those characteristic similes for combat that resonate across the work, for instance, of knights fighting like boars or rams, are Malory's own; so are many of the aphoristic speeches given to his laconic knights. More surprisingly, some of the passages that express most emotion—Elaine the mother of Galahad's complaint to Guenivere that Lancelot cannot love her, Elaine of Ascolat's dying defence of her love—are original to Malory. So is the longest speech of the work, Lancelot's defence of Guenivere; and so are the passages on the flourishing of love in the month of May, and on the hatred that cuts down the flower of chivalry like 'winter's rasure'. Sir Ector's final threnody over the corpse of

Lancelot doubles as Malory's own elegy for the passing of Arthurian knighthood.

The 'whole book'

For four-and-a-half centuries, the only version of Malory's work known was that printed by Caxton. It has no title page; the traditional title of *Le Morte Darthur* is announced at the very end of the work, in Caxton's own colophon rather than as part of Malory's text. It is retained in this edition, partly on account of its familiarity, but also because the defensiveness with which Caxton cites it suggests that he found it incorporated in some form in his copy-text, rather than that he made it up himself: 'Thus endeth this noble and joyous book entitled Le Morte Darthur. Notwithstanding it treateth of the birth, life, and acts of the said King Arthur, of his noble knights of the Round Table, their marvellous quests and adventures, the achieving of the Sangrail, and in the end the dolorous death and departing out of this world of them all.'

Then, in 1934, a manuscript was discovered in the library of Winchester College. Known on that account as the Winchester Manuscript, it is now housed in the British Library, and forms the basis of this edition. It divides its history of Arthur into several large sections (the number varying between four and eleven depending on the scholar who does the counting), in contrast to Caxton's division into twenty-one books. This division led Eugène Vinaver, who first produced an edition of the text that incorporated Winchester, to insist that the work was not a 'whole book', as Malory claims in his request for prayer at the very end of the work (in a passage taken from Caxton's print, since the opening and closing leaves of the manuscript are missing), but a series of eight separate Arthurian romances. He accordingly entitled his own edition *The Works of Sir Thomas Malory*.

The ensuing debate led to a more detailed examination of the structure of Malory's work than had hitherto been undertaken, and there are probably few scholars now who would take up as extreme a position as Vinaver did. Although there is some evidence that Malory may have thought of the various parts of the work as autonomous—he signs off the first linked series of four stories, for instance, with an invitation to his readers to seek out other books for themselves if they want to know more about Arthur—there is far more that suggests that he was actively seeking to make connections between sources that were themselves originally independent from each other, in order to make his own version a single history of Arthur and his fellowship. He accordingly inserts cross-references to show how the various stories relate to each other chronologically, or mentions forthcoming episodes in the course of previous ones, or reminds his readers of events of the past.

It is especially interesting, in this context, that two of the narratives that operate most strongly to forge links between the early and late parts of the whole story may be Malory's own inventions. One of these is the *Tale of Sir Gareth*, which gives the early history of one of Lancelot's most loyal supporters; it is his death at Lancelot's hands that precipitates the final tragedy—a tragedy that is especially poignant on account of the love between them shown in that first story. The other narrative is the healing of Sir Urry, in the course of which Malory gives a great roll-call of the whole fellowship of the Round Table, recalling moments from their past and completing stories earlier left half-told. As the sense of doom in the last stages of the book becomes more pervasive, so do recollections of the past: in the repeated references to the fact that it was Lancelot who knighted Gareth, or to the murder of Lamorak by Gawain and his brothers; or in Lancelot's reminders to Gawain and Arthur of how much they owe to him. Adventures that had seemed when they happened to float in a romance world free of time and space, are suddenly re-visioned as milestones on the one-way road to the 'day of destiny' on Salisbury Plain.

NOTE ON THE TEXT

This edition takes for its base text the Winchester Manuscript, housed in the British Library, shelfmark Additional MS 59678. The only full editions of Malory to use this manuscript are those by Eugène Vinaver, in the form of a three-volume scholarly version (recently revised by P. J. C. Field) and a one-volume student version. These are not, however, editions of Winchester: Vinaver's aim was to get as close as possible to what he believed Malory wrote, or should have written, and he therefore emended the Winchester text, not only from Caxton's print (a procedure that is sometimes unavoidable), but also by reference to the French originals. He also occasionally misrepresented both the sentence division and the larger text divisions and layout of the manuscript. My own aim is to re-create for modern readers something of the experience of the original readers of the Winchester manuscript—an aim that includes making the text more user-friendly than a full scholarly edition could be, through modernized spelling and punctuation. I have accordingly followed the manuscript as closely as is consistent with presenting a slightly abbreviated text, and with making sense of what it contains.

Although Winchester appears to preserve a text generally closer to what Malory wrote than the Caxton print, it is impossible to edit it without some reference to Caxton. The print is the only evidence we have for the opening and closing sections, where the outer leaves of the manuscript have been lost, and for the occasional missing or torn leaves in the middle. Just occasionally there are muddles or miscopyings by the scribes (there were two working on the manuscript), where the obviously correct reading, such as supplying a missing negative or changing a name, is confirmed by Caxton. Winchester also contains a number of short omissions of the sort known as eyeskip errors—that is, where the scribe has looked at his copy-text as far as one usage of a particular word, and then picked up his copying again at the next usage, leaving out the words in between: as if, for instance, all the words between those two occurrences of 'usage' had been omitted—'as far as one usage, leaving out the words in between'. I have supplied from Caxton all instances of such missing words and of any other omissions where they are essential for the sense.

These examples of eyeskip errors are especially interesting for proving that Caxton had his printed version set from a manuscript other than Winchester—one that contained the missing phrases. This is somewhat surprising, since it seems that Caxton had Winchester itself in his workshop at some stage: Lotte Hellinga has identified certain smudges on the manuscript as coming from Caxton's types,[1] and the claim has been generally accepted. The precise nature of the relationship between the two versions of the text, however, continues to be a matter of debate. Vinaver believed that there were at least two intermediate copyings of the work between Malory's own original and each of Caxton and Winchester; but few of the explicable variants between the texts require so complicated a model, while others are hard to explain in terms of textual descent.

The preparations for setting a text in type included making small marks on the manuscript to indicate how much text would fill a printed page, so that several typesetters could work on different parts of the text at the same time—a process known as 'casting off'. There are none of these marks on Winchester. Toshiyuki Takamiya has noticed, however, that the numerous small variants in wording between the Winchester and the Caxton versions increase in frequency towards the end of each page of Caxton.[2] This suggests that his copy-text was not so different in detail from Winchester as might at first appear: that the typesetters, following normal printing practice, would expand or shrink phrases to whatever small degree was necessary to get the required amount of text on to each printed page.

The biggest difference between the texts—apart from Caxton's division into books and chapters, which he tells us he supplied himself—lies in the very different versions of the story of Arthur's war against the Emperor Lucius, which comprises Caxton's Book V. For a long time it was assumed that Caxton himself, who often played an active part in producing the texts of the works he published, had written an abbreviated version of this whole episode. Now some scholars are arguing that perhaps it was Malory himself who did the

[1] 'The Malory Manuscript and Caxton', in *Aspects of Malory*, ed. Takamiya and Brewer, 127–41.

[2] 'Editor/Compositor at Work: The Case of Caxton's Malory', in *Arthurian and Other Studies presented to Shunichi Noguchi*, ed. T. Suzuki and T. Mukai (Cambridge, 1993), 143–51.

reworking.[3] The account of the war in both versions is very different in style, vocabulary, and tone from the rest of the work: it is based on the alliterative *Morte Arthure*, and preserves many northern language-forms as well as a specialized alliterative vocabulary and the structure of many of the original lines. The derivation of the poem from the historical rather than the romance tradition of Arthur also shows in its priorities of interest, in massed battles rather than personal combat. In keeping with the rest of this edition, I have followed Winchester, though with considerable abbreviation of the detail of Arthur's campaigns and of the more digressive episodes.

Caxton describes Malory as 'reducing' his huge French sources, so producing a text that fitted into a single large volume. I have in turn 'reduced' Malory, for exactly the same purpose. Few readers now are likely to share Malory's passionate interest in the details of battle tactics and tournaments, and I have cut these generously; this in turn enables a focus on the battles and tournaments that are of particular importance for the whole story. The crucial importance of the final sections of the work has required some slimming of the opening sections and the cutting of a number of self-contained episodes that occur as digressions within larger individual stories. All omissions are signalled in the notes.

Winchester presents its text in long blocks of continuous prose, broken up by occasional large capitals, by formal incipits and explicits—that is, announcements of a new start or of the completion of a story—and sometimes by leaving half a page or more blank. I have followed these indications of narrative division by announcing new stories with separate titles where Malory provides them, by leaving a line of white space where the scribe gives a large capital (except where it seems to represent a scribal quirk rather than something real about the structure of the narrative in hand), and, in the longer stories such as *Sir Tristram*, by supplying occasional page-breaks where the manuscript itself indicates some kind of breathing-space in the narrative. Caxton's subdivision into books and chapters was his solution to the problem presented by the massive blocks of prose; his numbering system for these still provides the most convenient means of referring to points in the text across different editions, and is retained here.

---

[3] *Arthuriana* 5: 2 (Summer 1995) and 7: 1 (Spring 1997) are devoted to this issue.

Punctuation within the manuscript takes two forms: small capital letters, and two short oblique lines (//). I have generally provided semicolons or full stops at the capital letters, full stops or paragraph breaks for the double lines. Commas are supplied in accordance with modern usage. Malory's prose is a wonderfully flexible medium, that moves with none of our required rigidity of division between speech and the action it initiates, or between reported and direct speech; in moments of intensive action, such as combat, he will dispense with punctuation altogether for several lines at a time. Close imitation would make a reading of the text so difficult as to falsify the effect of the original, but I have tried, so far as is compatible with ease of comprehension, to preserve both Malory's rhythms and his fluidity of sentence movement.

Modernizing spelling may appear to be an easier matter, but this too involves hard choices. Malory's language, to his original readers, was familiar and lucid. My aim has been to get as close to this familiarity as is possible without either misrepresenting what he wrote or losing any of his rhythms. This has required replacing some archaic forms of words, verbs in particular, with their modern spellings: 'helped' and 'bore' for 'holpen' and 'bare', for instance. I have retained all forms that carry a charge of meaning even if their connotations now are more with poetic diction than with Malory's everyday speech: to eliminate 'thou' and 'thee', for instance, would be to lose the crucial distinctions that Middle English, like modern French and German, can make between the insulting, familiar or intimate form of the second person and the formal and courtly 'you'. On a tiny number of occasions I have altered a preposition to make an idiom comprehensible, or modernized word order—object–verb–subject to subject–verb–object, for instance, in the very rare instances where Malory's form is seriously misleading. I provide a Glossary of recurrent words before the main text, and would urge readers to take note of it, particularly of false friends such as 'and' in the sense of 'if', and 'or' in the sense of 'before'. First occurrences of all these are signalled by ° in the foot-of-page glossing of unfamiliar words; these glosses are not repeated unless a phrase is particularly obscure.

SELECT BIBLIOGRAPHY

Arthurian Literature

The New Arthurian Encyclopedia, ed. Norris J. Lacy (updated edition, New York and London, 1996), contains an abundance of information on all matters Arthurian.

Arthurian Literature in the Middle Ages, ed. Roger Sherman Loomis (corrected edition, Oxford, 1979), gives a general survey of the numerous medieval Arthurian texts and their relationships.

The Romance of Arthur: An Anthology of Medieval Texts in Translation, ed. James J. Wilhelm (extended edition, New York and London, 1994), includes extracts from the early chronicles, the Arthurian section of Geoffrey of Monmouth, and a number of other Arthurian romances in whole or in part. The full text of Geoffrey's *History of the Kings of Britain* is translated by Lewis Thorpe for Penguin Classics (Harmondsworth, 1966).

Lancelot-Grail: The Old French Vulgate and Post-Vulgate in Translation, general editor Norris J. Lacy (5 vols., New York, 1992–6), is a full translation of the Old French Vulgate Cycle.

Periodicals devoted to Arthurian studies include the annual *Arthurian Literature* and the quarterly *Arthuriana*. An annual bibliography is published by the International Arthurian Society.

The Text of Le Morte Darthur: Editions and Studies

The text of the Winchester manuscript used for the preparation of this edition is the facsimile published by the Early English Text Society, *The Winchester Malory*, introduction by Neil Ker, EETS ss 4 (1976).

Supplementary material from Caxton comes from the Scolar Press facsimile, *Sir Thomas Malory: Le Morte D'Arthur printed by William Caxton 1485*, introduction by Paul Needham (London, 1976).

Modern editions of Malory include:

The Works of Sir Thomas Malory, ed. Eugène Vinaver, 3 vols., 3rd edn. revised by P. J. C. Field (Oxford, 1990). This is the major scholarly edition, primarily based on the Winchester manuscript. There is a one-volume student version, *Malory: Works* (2nd edn. first published London and Oxford, 1971).

Caxton's Malory, ed. James W. Spisak, 2 vols. (Berkeley and Los Angeles, 1983). An edition of Caxton's print.

Sir Thomas Malory: Le Morte D'Arthur, ed. Janet Cowen with an introduction by John Lawlor, 2 vols. (Penguin English Library; first published
Harmondsworth, 1969). A modern-spelling edition of Caxton, with a
useful introduction and foot-of-page glossing.

Sir Thomas Malory and his Culture

The major study of the life of Sir Thomas Malory of Newbold Revel is by
P. J. C. Field, *The Life and Times of Sir Thomas Malory* (Cambridge, 1993).

Two critical works that incorporate extensive and informative back-
ground material are Larry D. Benson, *Malory's Morte Darthur* (Cambridge,
Mass., 1976), and Felicity Riddy, *Sir Thomas Malory* (Leiden and New
York, 1987). Elizabeth T. Pochoda, *Arthurian Propaganda: Le Morte
Darthur as an Historical Ideal of Life* (Chapel Hill, 1971), makes a case for the
work as a political study of kingship.

On chivalry in general, see Richard Barber, *The Knight and Chivalry*
(revised edn. Woodbridge, 1995); and Maurice Keen, *Chivalry* (New
Haven and London, 1984).

Le Morte Darthur: *Critical Studies*

The critical literature is extensive, and very little can be cited here. Two
useful multi-author surveys of all aspects of the work are the *Companion to
Malory*, ed. Elizabeth Archibald and A. S. G. Edwards (Cambridge, 1996),
and *Aspects of Malory*, ed. Toshiyuki Takamiya and Derek Brewer (Cam-
bridge, 1981). Interesting material is also found in *Studies in Malory*, ed.
James W. Spisak (Kalamazoo, 1985), and in two older collections, *Essays on
Malory*, ed. J. A. W. Bennett (Oxford, 1963), and *Malory's Originality*, ed.
Robert M. Lumiansky (Baltimore, 1964).

On Malory's style, see P. J. C. Field, *From Romance to Chronicle: A Study
of Malory's Prose Style* (London, 1971), and, in particular, Mark Lambert,
Malory: Style and Vision in 'Le Morte Darthur' (New Haven and London,
1975).

Other useful studies include two by Terence McCarthy, *An Introduction
to Malory* (1988; reprinted under this title, Cambridge, 1991), and '*Le Morte
Darthur* and Romance', in *Studies in Medieval English Romance*, ed. D. S.
Brewer (Cambridge, 1988); two by Jill Mann, *The Narrative of Distance, the
Distance of Narrative in Malory's Morte Darthur* (William Matthews
Lectures, London, 1991), and the chapter on Malory in *Medieval Litera-
ture: Chaucer and the Alliterative Tradition*, ed. Boris Ford, New Pelican
Guide to English Literature (Harmondsworth, 1982); and Andrew Lynch,
Malory's Book of Arms (Cambridge, 1997).

Sources

The most important of Malory's sources are edited as follows:

Robert de Boron: Merlin, ed. Alexandre Micha, Textes littéraires français (Geneva, 1980), covers the events of Arthur's life down to his coronation; *La Suite du roman de Merlin*, ed. Gilles Roussineau (Geneva, 1996) underlies the rest of the first four connected tales. Robert is translated in volume 1 of Lacy's *Lancelot-Grail*, and the *Suite* in volumes 4–5 (see 'Arthurian Literature' above).

King Arthur's Death, ed. Larry D. Benson (1974; reprinted Exeter, 1986). Contains texts of both the alliterative *Morte Arthure* and the stanzaic *Morte Arthur*.

Lancelot ed. Alexandre Micha, Textes littéraires français, 9 vols. (Geneva, 1978–83). Malory uses only a handful of episodes from this huge work. The only complete translation is included in the *Lancelot-Grail* series cited under 'Arthurian Literature'. More accessible are two versions of the *Lancelot* material analogous to Malory's: the non-cyclic prose version is translated for World's Classics by Corin Corley, with an introduction by Elspeth Kennedy, *Lancelot of the Lake* (Oxford, 1989); and Chrétien's original of the 'Knight of the Cart' story is translated by William W. Kibler in *The Romance of Arthur*, above, and the Penguin Classics *Chrétien de Troyes: Arthurian Romances* (Harmondsworth, 1991).

Le Roman de Tristan en prose: an initial three volumes under this title are edited by Renée L. Curtis, reprinted as Arthurian Studies 12–14 (Cambridge, 1985; a fourth volume of annotation is under way). Succeeding volumes under the same title are edited by Philippe Ménard and others, Textes littéraires français (Geneva, 1987–97). The later volumes part increasingly from the text Malory appears to have known; closer to his version, though presenting difficulties for casual use, is the facsimile of the first printed version, *Tristan: 1489*, with an introduction by C. E. Pickford (London, 1978). The parts directly relevant to the love story are translated for World's Classics by Renée L. Curtis, *The Romance of Tristan* (Oxford, 1994).

La Queste del Saint Graal, ed. Albert Pauphilet, Classiques français du moyen age (Paris, 1923; repr. 1978). There is a translation for Penguin Classics by P. M. Matarasso, *The Quest of the Holy Grail* (Harmondsworth, 1969).

La Mort le roi Artu, ed. Jean Frappier, Textes littéraires français (2nd edn., Geneva, 1954). The French source for the last two sections of the work, alongside the English stanzaic *Morte Arthur*. There is a translation for Penguin Classics by James Cable, *The Death of King Arthur* (Harmondsworth, 1971).

The Chronicle of Iohn Hardyng, ed. Henry Ellis (London, 1812). Likely to be a further English source.

CHRONOLOGY

OF ARTHURIAN MATERIAL TO 1500

?late 5th–early 6th cent. The period of the 'historical' Arthur.

*c.*545   Gildas' account of recent British history refers to some possibly Arthurian events.

*c.*600   The northern poem *Gododdin* cities Arthur as being a familiar hero.

*c.*800   Nennius' chronicle lists twelve battles fought by Arthur against the Saxons.

*c.*960   The *Annales Cambriae* mentions the death of Arthur and Medraut at Camlann.

*c.*1000   Origins of the earliest Welsh Arthurian story, *Culhwch and Olwen*.

*c.*1136   Geoffrey of Monmouth compiles the basic outline of Arthur's biography in his *History of the Kings of Britain*.

*c.*1155   Wace's French adaptation of Geoffrey, the *Brut*, contains the first mention of the Round Table.

*c.*1160–90   Chrétien de Troyes' French Arthurian verse romances.

*c.*1200   Robert de Boron begins the spiritualizing of the Grail.

*c.*1210   Layamon's *Brut* contains the first account of Arthur in English.

*c.*1215–25   French prose Vulgate Cycle (*Lancelot-Graal*).

*c.*1240   French prose *Tristan* brings the Tristan story into the Arthurian orbit.

*c.*1300   First Arthurian verse romances in English.

*c.*1380   *Sir Gawain and the Green Knight*.

*c.*1390   Alliterative *Morte Arthure*.

*c.*1400   Stanzaic *Morte Arthur*.

*c.*1450   First English Arthurian prose romance (*Merlin*).

1469–70   Malory completes the *Morte Darthur*.

1485   Caxton prints the *Morte Darthur*.

1488–9   First printing of French prose *Lancelot* and *Tristan*.

GLOSSARY OF RECURRENT WORDS

This list contains only words that recur frequently in the text; they are marked in the foot-of-page glosses with a ° on their first occurrence, and the gloss is not repeated unless there is some special difficulty. Less common words and phrases are glossed on the page where they occur.

and	if
anon	immediately
astoned, astonied	stunned; astounded
avoid	get clear of, dismount from
beseen	equipped; dressed
big	strong
boot	remedy; **no boot**, no use
brachet	hunting-dog
brast	broke, burst
but, but if	unless
deal	part
defend	forbid, prevent
deliver (adj.)	agile; **deliverly**, agilely
divers	various
do (+ infinitive)	have (something) done
dole	grief
dress	set in place, set one's self
fain	glad
fewter	lay (a spear) in its rest ready for combat
foin	thrust
forthink (me forthinks)	(I) regret
gentle	noble; **gentleness**, of high descent; nobility
gramercy, grantmercy	thank you (French *grand merci*)
hight	[was] named
leech	doctor
liever	rather
list	pleases
long	belong, pertain
maugre	despite; **maugre** [my] **head**, against [my] will
or	before
passing	surpassingly
pavilion	ornamental tent

rased	pulled (of pulling off a helmet)
rede	counsel, advise
repents me (them)	I (they) regret
samite	rich silk
siege	seat
sith, sithen	since
stint	cease
truncheon	butt, broken stump
uneath	scarcely
undern	about 9 a.m.
unhappy	fateful, accursed
ween	think, believe
wist	knew, known
wit	know
wood	mad, furious
worship	honour; **worshipful**, honourable
wot	know
yede, yode	went

Le Morte Darthur

FROM THE MARRIAGE OF KING UTHER UNTO KING ARTHUR

How Uther Pendragon begot the Noble Conqueror King Arthur

It befell in the days of Uther Pendragon, when he was king of all Eng- [I.I]*
land and so reigned, that there was a mighty duke in Cornwall that
held war against him long time; and the duke was called the Duke of
Tintagel. And so by means King Uther sent for this duke, charging
him to bring his wife with him, for she was called a fair lady, and a passing wise; and her name was called Igraine.

So when the duke and his wife were come unto the King, by the
means of great lords they were accorded both. The King liked and
loved this lady well, and he made them great cheer out of measure,
and desired to have lain by her. But she was a passing good woman, and
would not assent unto the King.

And then she told the duke her husband, and said, 'I suppose that we
were sent for that I should be dishonoured; wherefore, husband, I counsel you that we depart from hence suddenly, that we may ride all night
unto our own castle.' And in like wise as she said so they departed, that
neither the King nor none of his council were ware of their departing.

As soon as King Uther knew of their departing so suddenly, he was
wonderly wroth. Then he called to him his privy council, and told them
of the sudden departing of the duke and his wife. Then they advised the
King to send for the duke and his wife by a great charge: 'And if he will
not come at your summons, then may ye do your best; then have ye
cause to make mighty war upon him.'

So that was done; and the messengers had their answers, and that was
this shortly, that neither he nor his wife would not come at him. Then
was the King wonderly wroth. And then the King sent him plain word
again, and bade him be ready and stuff him and garnish him, for within
forty days he would fetch him out of the biggest castle that he hath.

passing°] surpassingly (° see Glossary, p. xxxii)   accorded both] brought
to agreement   stuff him and garnish him] furnish himself with men and
provisions   biggest°] strongest

When the duke had this warning, anon he went and furnished and garnished two strong castles of his, of the which the one hight Tintagel, and the other castle hight Terrabil. So his wife Dame Igraine he put in the castle of Tintagel, and himself he put in the castle of Terrabil, the which had many issues and posterns out. Then in all haste came Uther with a great host and laid a siege about the castle of Terrabil, and there he pitched many pavilions. And there was great war made on both parties, and much people slain.

Then for pure anger and for great love of fair Igraine the King Uther fell sick. So came to the King Uther Sir Ulfius, a noble knight, and asked the King why he was sick.

'I shall tell thee,' said the King. 'I am sick for anger and for love of fair Igraine, that I may not be whole.'

'Well, my lord,' said Sir Ulfius, 'I shall seek Merlin, and he shall do you remedy, that your heart shall be pleased.'

So Ulfius departed. And by adventure he met Merlin in a beggar's array, and there Merlin asked Ulfius whom he sought; and he said he had little ado to tell him.

'Well,' said Merlin, 'I know whom thou seekest, for thou seekest Merlin; therefore seek no further, for I am he. And if King Uther will well reward me, and be sworn unto me to fulfil my desire, that shall be his honour and profit more than mine, for I shall cause him to have all his desire.'

'All this will I undertake,' said Ulfius, 'that there shall be nothing reasonable but thou shalt have thy desire.'

'Well,' said Merlin, 'he shall have his intent and desire. And therefore,' said Merlin, 'ride on your way, for I will not be long behind.'

[2] Then Ulfius was glad, and rode on more than apace till that he came to King Uther Pendragon, and told him he had met with Merlin.

'Where is he?' said the King.

'Sir,' said Ulfius, 'he will not dwell long.'

Therewith Ulfius was ware where Merlin stood at the porch of the pavilion's door. And then Merlin was bound to come to the King. When King Uther saw him, he said he was welcome.

'Sir,' said Merlin 'I know all your heart every deal. So ye will be sworn unto me, as ye be a true king anointed, to fulfil my desire, ye shall have your desire.'

anon°] immediately   hight°] was called   ado] concern   there shall be . . . desire] you shall have whatever you want within reason   deal] part

Then the King was sworn upon the four Evangelists.*

'Sir,' said Merlin, 'this is my desire: the first night that ye shall lie by Igraine ye shall get a child on her, and when that is born, that it shall be delivered to me for to nourish there as I will have it; for it shall be your worship, and the child's avail as mickle as the child is worth.'

'I will well,' said the King, 'as thou wilt have it.'

'Now make you ready,' said Merlin, 'this night ye shall lie with Igraine in the castle of Tintagel; and ye shall be like the duke her husband, Ulfius shall be like Sir Brastias, a knight of the duke's, and I will be like a knight that hight Sir Jordanus, a knight of the duke's. But wait ye make not many questions with her nor her men, but say ye are diseased, and so hie you to bed and rise not on the morn till I come to you; for the castle of Tintagel is but ten miles hence.'

So this was done as they devised. But the Duke of Tintagel espied how the King rode from the siege of Terrabil, and therefore that night he issued out of the castle at a postern for to have distressed the King's host. And so, through his own issue, the duke himself was slain or ever the King came at the castle of Tintagel.

So after the death of the duke, King Uther lay with Igraine more than three hours after his death, and begot on her that night Arthur; and, or day came, Merlin came to the King and bade him make him ready, and so he kissed the lady Igraine and departed in all haste. But when the lady heard tell of the duke her husband, and by all record he was dead or ever King Uther came to her, then she marvelled who that might be that lay with her in likeness of her lord; so she mourned privily and held her peace.

Then all the barons by one assent prayed the King of accord betwixt the lady Igraine and him. The King gave them leave, for fain would he have been accorded with her; so the King put all the trust in Ulfius to entreat between them. So by the entreaty at the last the King and she met together.

'Now will we do well,' said Ulfius. 'Our king is a lusty knight and wifeless, and my lady Igraine is a passing fair lady; it were great joy unto us all and it might please the King to make her his queen.'

Unto that they all well accorded and moved it to the King. And

---

worship°] honour   the child's avail . . . worth] to the child's advantage, as noble
as he is   wait] be careful   slain or° ever] slain even before   fain°]
gladly   and° it might] if it might

anon, like a lusty knight, he assented thereto with good will, and so in all haste they were married in a morning with great mirth and joy. And King Lot of Lothian and of Orkney* then wedded Morgause that was Gawain's mother, and King Nentres of the land of Garlot wedded Elaine. All this was done at the request of King Uther. And the third sister Morgan le Fay was put to school in a nunnery, and there she learned so much that she was a great clerk of necromancy; and after she was wedded to King Uriens of the land of Gore, that was Sir Uwain le Blanchemains' father.

[3]   Then Queen Igraine waxed daily greater and greater. So it befell after within half a year, as King Uther lay by his queen, he asked her, by the faith she owed to him, whose was the child within her body; then was she sore abashed to give answer.

'Dismay you not,' said the King, 'but tell me the truth, and I shall love you the better, by the faith of my body.'

'Sir,' said she, 'I shall tell you the truth. The same night that my lord was dead, the hour of his death, as his knights record, there came into my castle of Tintagel a man like my lord in speech and in countenance, and two knights with him in likeness of his two knights Brastias and Jordanus, and so I went unto bed with him as I ought to do with my lord. And the same night, as I shall answer unto God, this child was begotten upon me.'

'That is truth,' said the King, 'as ye say; for it was I myself that came in the likeness, and therefore dismay you not, for I am father to the child.' And there he told her all the cause, how it was by Merlin's counsel. Then the queen made great joy when she knew who was the father of her child.

Soon came Merlin unto the King, and said, 'Sir, ye must purvey you for the nourishing of your child.'

'As thou wilt,' said the King, 'be it.'

'Well,' said Merlin, 'I know a lord of yours in this land that is a passing true man and a faithful, and he shall have the nourishing of your child; and his name is Sir Ector, and he is a lord of fair livelihood in many parts in England and Wales; and this lord, Sir Ector, let him be sent for, for to come and speak with you, and desire him yourself, as he loveth you, that he will put his own child to nourishing to another woman, and that his wife nourish yours.* And when the child is born, let it be delivered to me at yonder privy postern unchristened.'

purvey you] provide   privy postern] secluded gate

So like as Merlin devised it was done. And when Sir Ector was come he made affiance to the King for to nourish the child like as the King desired; and there the King granted Sir Ector great rewards. Then when the lady was delivered, the King commanded two knights and two ladies to take the child, bound in a cloth of gold, 'and that ye deliver him to what poor man ye meet at the postern gate of the castle.' So the child was delivered unto Merlin, and so he bore it forth unto Sir Ector, and made a holy man to christen him, and named him Arthur; and so Sir Ector's wife nourished him with her own pap.

Then within two years King Uther fell sick of a great malady. And in the meanwhile his enemies usurped upon him and did a great battle upon his men, and slew many of his people. [4]

'Sir,' said Merlin, 'ye may not lie so as ye do, for ye must to the field though ye ride in a horse-litter; for ye shall never have the better of your enemies but if your person be there, and then shall ye have the victory.'

So it was done as Merlin had devised, and they carried the King forth in a horse-litter with a great host toward his enemies; and at St Albans there met with the King a great host of the north. And that day Sir Ulfius and Sir Brastias did great deeds of arms, and King Uther's men overcame the northern battle and slew many people, and put the remnant to flight. And then the King returned unto London, and made great joy of his victory.

And then he fell passing sore sick, so that three days and three nights he was speechless; wherefore all the barons made great sorrow, and asked Merlin what counsel were best.

'There is no other remedy,' said Merlin, 'but God will have his will. But look ye all, barons, be before King Uther tomorrow, and God and I shall make him to speak.'

So on the morn all the barons with Merlin came before the King; then Merlin said aloud unto King Uther, 'Sir, shall your son Arthur be king, after your days, of this realm with all the appurtenance?'

Then Uther Pendragon turned him, and said in hearing of them all, 'I give him God's blessing and mine; and bid him pray for my soul, and righteously and worshipfully that he claim the crown, upon forfeiture of my blessing.'

made affiance to] promised   but° if] unless   battle] battalion
appurtenance] associated rights and privileges   worshipfully°] honourably

And therewith he yielded up the ghost; and then was he interred as longed to a king, wherefore the queen, fair Igraine, made great sorrow, and all the barons.

[5] Then stood the realm in great jeopardy long while, for every lord that was mighty of men made him strong, and many weened to have been king. Then Merlin went to the Archbishop of Canterbury, and counselled him for to send for all the lords of the realm, and all the gentlemen of arms, that they should to London come by Christmas, upon pain of cursing; and for this cause: that Jesus, that was born on that night, that He would of His great mercy show some miracle, as He was come to be king of mankind, for to show some miracle who should be rightwise king of this realm. So the archbishop, by the advice of Merlin, sent for all the lords and gentlemen of arms that they should come by Christmas even unto London. And many of them made them clean of their life,* that their prayer might be the more acceptable unto God. So in the greatest church of London (whether it were Paul's or not the French book maketh no mention*), all the estates were long or day in the church for to pray. And when matins and the first Mass was done, there was seen in the churchyard, against the high altar, a great stone four square, like unto a marble stone; and in the midst thereof was like an anvil of steel a foot on high, and therein stuck a fair sword naked by the point, and letters there were written in gold about the sword that said thus: 'Whoso pulleth out this sword of this stone and anvil, is rightwise king born of all England.'

Then the people marvelled, and told it to the archbishop.

'I command,' said the archbishop, 'that ye keep you within your church and pray unto God still; and that no man touch the sword till the High Mass be all done.'

So when all Masses were done all the lords went to behold the stone and the sword. And when they saw the scripture, some assayed, such as would have been king. But none might stir the sword nor move it.

'He is not here,' said the archbishop, 'that shall achieve the sword, but doubt not God will make him known. But this is my counsel,' said the archbishop, 'that we let purvey ten knights, men of good fame, and they to keep this sword.'

---

longed°] pertained, was appropriate to　　　　　　　weened°] intended, thought
cursing] excommunication

So it was ordained, and then there was made a cry that every man should assay that would, for to win the sword. And upon New Year's Day the barons let make a jousts and a tournament, that all knights that would joust or tourney there might play. And all this was ordained for to keep the lords together and the commons, for the archbishop trusted that God would make him known that should win the sword. So upon New Year's Day, when the service was done, the barons rode unto the field, some to joust and some to tourney.

And so it happed that Sir Ector, that had great livelihood about London, rode unto the jousts, and with him rode Sir Kay his son, and young Arthur that was his nourished brother; and Sir Kay was made knight at All Hallowmas before. So as they rode to the jousts-ward, Sir Kay had lost his sword, for he had left it at his father's lodging, and so he prayed young Arthur for to ride for his sword.

'I will well,' said Arthur, and rode fast after the sword. And when he came home the lady and all were out to see the jousting. Then was Arthur wroth, and said to himself, 'I will ride to the churchyard, and take the sword with me that sticketh in the stone, for my brother Sir Kay shall not be without a sword this day.'

So when he came to the churchyard, Sir Arthur alit and tied his horse to the stile, and so he went to the tent, and found no knights there, for they were at jousting; and so he handled the sword by the handles, and lightly and fiercely pulled it out of the stone, and took his horse and rode his way until he came to his brother Sir Kay and delivered him the sword. And as soon as Sir Kay saw the sword, he wist well it was the sword of the stone, and so he rode to his father Sir Ector, and said: 'Sir, lo here is the sword of the stone, wherefore I must be king of this land.'

When Sir Ector beheld the sword, he returned again and came to the church, and there they alit all three and went into the church. And anon he made Sir Kay to swear upon a book* how he came to that sword.

'Sir,' said Sir Kay, 'by my brother Arthur, for he brought it to me.'

'How got ye this sword?' said Sir Ector to Arthur.

'Sir, I will tell you. When I came home for my brother's sword, I found nobody at home to deliver me his sword, and so I thought my brother Sir Kay should not be swordless; and so I came hither eagerly and pulled it out of the stone without any pain.'

All Hallowmas] All Saints' Day (1 November)   wist°] knew

'Found ye any knights about this sword?' said Sir Ector.

'Nay,' said Arthur.

'Now,' said Sir Ector to Arthur, 'I understand ye must be king of this land.'

'Wherefore I,' said Arthur, 'and for what cause?'

'Sir,' said Ector, 'for God will have it so, for there should never man have drawn out this sword, but he that shall be rightwise king of this land. Now let me see whether ye can put the sword there as it was, and pull it out again.'

'That is no mastery,' said Arthur, and so he put it in the stone; therewith Sir Ector assayed to pull out the sword and failed.

[6]   'Now assay,' said Sir Ector unto Sir Kay. And anon he pulled at the sword with all his might, but it would not be.

'Now shall ye assay,' said Sir Ector to Arthur.

'I will well,' said Arthur, and pulled it out easily. And therewith Sir Ector knelt down to the earth, and Sir Kay. 'Alas,' said Arthur, 'my own dear father and brother, why kneel ye to me?'

'Nay, nay, my lord Arthur, it is not so, I was never your father nor of your blood, but I wot well ye are of a higher blood than I weened ye were.'

And then Sir Ector told him all, how he was betaken him for to nourish him, and by whose commandment, and by Merlin's deliverance. Then Arthur made great dole when he understood that Sir Ector was not his father.

'Sir,' said Ector unto Arthur, 'will ye be my good and gracious lord* when ye are king?'

'Else were I to blame,' said Arthur, 'for ye are the man in the world that I am most beholden to, and my good lady and mother your wife, that as well as her own hath fostered me and kept. And if ever it be God's will that I be king as ye say, ye shall desire of me what I may do, and I shall not fail you—God forbid I should fail you!'

'Sir,' said Sir Ector, 'I will ask no more of you, but that ye will make my son, your foster brother, Sir Kay, seneschal of all your lands.'

'That shall be done,' said Arthur, 'and more, by the faith of my body, that never man shall have that office but he, while he and I live.'

Therewith they went unto the archbishop, and told him how the sword was achieved and by whom. And on Twelfth-day all the barons

is no mastery] needs no great skill   wot°] know   weened°] believed, thought
betaken] given, entrusted   dole°] grief   Twelfth-day] i.e. Twelfth
Night (6 January)

came thither, and to assay to take the sword, who that would assay. But there before them all, there might none take it out but Arthur; wherefore there were many lords wroth, and said it was great shame unto them all and the realm, to be over-governed with a boy of no high blood born. And so they fell out at that time, that it was put off till Candlemas,* and then all the barons should meet there again; but always the ten knights were ordained to watch the sword day and night, and so they set a pavilion over the stone and the sword, and five always watched.

So at Candlemas many more great lords came thither for to have won the sword, but there might none prevail. And right as Arthur did at Christmas, he did at Candlemas, and pulled out the sword easily, whereof the barons were sore aggrieved and put it off in delay till the high feast of Easter. And as Arthur sped before, so did he at Easter, yet there were some of the great lords had indignation that Arthur should be king, and put it off in a delay till the feast of Pentecost. Then the Archbishop of Canterbury by Merlin's providence let purvey then of the best knights that they might get, and such knights as Uther Pendragon loved best and most trusted in his days. And such knights were put about Arthur as Sir Baudwin of Britain, Sir Kay, Sir Ulfius, Sir Brastias—all these, with many other, were always about Arthur, day and night, till the feast of Pentecost.

And at the feast of Pentecost all manner of men assayed to pull at the [7] sword that would assay, but none might prevail but Arthur, and pulled it out before all the lords and commons that were there; wherefore all the commons cried at once, 'We will have Arthur unto our king, we will put him no more in delay; for we all see that it is God's will that he shall be our king. And who that holdeth against it, we will slay him.'

And therewith all they kneeled at once, both rich and poor, and cried Arthur mercy because they had delayed him so long. And Arthur forgave them, and took the sword between both his hands and offered it upon the altar where the archbishop was, and so was he made knight of the best man that was there.

And so anon was the coronation made. And there was he sworn unto his lords and the commons for to be a true king, to stand with true justice from thenceforth the days of this life. Also then he made all lords that held of the crown to come in, and to do service as they ought to do.

sped] succeeded

And many complaints were made unto Sir Arthur of great wrongs that were done since the death of King Uther, of many lands that were bereft lords, knights, ladies, and gentlemen, wherefore King Arthur made the lands to be given again unto them that owned them.

When this was done, that the King had established all the countries about London, then he let make Sir Kay seneschal of England; and Sir Baudwin of Britain was made constable; and Sir Ulfius was made chamberlain;* and Sir Brastias was made warden to wait upon the north from Trent forwards, for it was that time the most part the King's enemies. But within few years after, Arthur won all the north, Scotland, and all that were under their obeisance. Also Wales, a part of it, held against Arthur, but he overcame them all, as he did the remnant, through the noble prowess of himself and his knights of the Round Table.

[8]   Then the King removed into Wales, and let cry a great feast that it should be held at Pentecost after the coronation of him at the city of Caerleon. Unto the feast came King Lot of Lothian and of Orkney, with five hundred knights with him; also there came to the feast King Uriens of Gore with four hundred knights with him; also there came to that feast King Nentres of Garlot, with seven hundred knights with him; also there came to the feast the King of Scotland with six hundred knights with him, and he was but a young man; also there came to the feast a king that was called the King with the Hundred Knights, but he and his men were passing well beseen at all points; also there came the King Carados with five hundred knights. And King Arthur was glad of their coming, for he weened that all the kings and knights had come for great love, and to have done him worship at his feast; wherefore the King made great joy, and sent the kings and knights great presents. But the kings would none receive, but rebuked the messengers shamefully, and said they had no joy to receive no gifts of a beardless boy that was come of low blood;* and sent him word they would none of his gifts, but that they were come to give him gifts with hard swords betwixt the neck and the shoulders. And therefore they came thither, so they told to the messengers plainly, for it was great shame to all them to see such a boy to have a rule of so noble a realm as this land was.

With this answer the messengers departed and told to King Arthur this answer. Wherefore, by the advice of his barons, he took him to a

bereft] taken from   beseen°] clothed, equipped

strong tower with five hundred good men with him; and all the kings aforesaid in a manner laid a siege before him, but King Arthur was well victualled.*

And within fifteen days there came Merlin among them into the city of Caerleon. Then all the kings were passing glad of Merlin, and asked him, 'For what cause is that boy Arthur made your king?'

'Sirs,' said Merlin, 'I shall tell you the cause: for he is King Uther Pendragon's son, born in wedlock, begotten on Igraine, the Duke's wife of Tintagel.'

'Then is he a bastard,' they said all.

'Nay,' said Merlin, 'after the death of the duke, more than three hours, was Arthur begotten, and thirteen days after, King Uther wedded Igraine; and therefore I prove him he is no bastard.* And whoever saith nay, he shall be king and overcome all his enemies; and, or he die, he shall be long king of all England, and have under his obedience Wales, Ireland, and Scotland, and more realms than I will now rehearse.'

Some of the kings had marvel of Merlin's words, and deemed well that it should be as he said; and some of them laughed him to scorn, as King Lot; and more others called him a witch.* But then were they accorded with Merlin that King Arthur should come out and speak with the kings, and to come safe and to go safe: such assurance there was made.

So Merlin went unto King Arthur and told him how he had done, and bade him fear not, 'but come out boldly and speak with them, and spare them not, but answer them as their king and chieftain; for ye shall overcome them all, whether they will or nill.'

Then King Arthur came out of his tower, and had under his gown a [9] jesseraunt of double mail; and there went with him the Archbishop of Canterbury, and Sir Baudwin of Britain, and Sir Kay, and Sir Brastias: these were the men of most worship that were with him. And when they were met, there was no meekness, but stout words on both sides; but always King Arthur answered them, and said he would make them to bow and he lived. Wherefore they departed with wrath, and King Arthur bade keep them well, and they bade the King keep him well. So the King returned to the tower again and armed him and all his knights.

whoever saith nay] no matter who denies it   nill] will not   jesseraunt]
mail coat   to bow and he lived] to submit if he survived

'What will ye do?' said Merlin to the kings. 'Ye were better for to stint, for ye shall not here prevail though ye were ten so many.'

'Be we well advised to be afraid of a dream-reader?' said King Lot.

With that Merlin vanished away, and came to King Arthur, and bade him set on them fiercely. And in the meanwhile there were three hundred good men of the best that were with the kings, that went straight unto King Arthur; and that comforted him greatly.

'Sir,' said Merlin to Arthur, 'fight not with the sword that ye had by miracle, till that ye see ye go unto the worse: then draw it out and do your best.'

So forthwith King Arthur set upon them in their lodging. And Sir Baudwin, Sir Kay, and Sir Brastias slew on the right hand and on the left hand that it was marvel; and always King Arthur on horseback laid on with a sword and did marvellous deeds of arms, that many of the kings had great joy of his deeds and hardiness. Then King Lot broke out on the back side, and the King with the Hundred Knights, and King Carados, and set on Arthur fiercely behind him. With that Sir Arthur turned with his knights, and smote behind and before, and ever Sir Arthur was in the foremost press till his horse was slain underneath him; and therewith King Lot smote down King Arthur. With that his four knights received him and set him on horseback. Then he drew his sword Excalibur,* but it was so bright in his enemies' eyes that it gave light like thirty torches. And therewith he put them aback, and slew much people. And then the commons of Caerleon arose with clubs and staves and slew many knights; but all the kings held them together with their knights that were left alive, and so fled and departed. And Merlin came unto Arthur, and counselled him to follow them no further.

[10]   So after the feast and journey, King Arthur drew him unto London, and so by the counsel of Merlin the King let call his barons to council, for Merlin had told the King that the six kings that made war upon him would in all haste be awroke on him and on his lands; wherefore the King asked counsel at them all. They could no counsel give, but said they were big enough.

'Ye say well,' said Arthur; 'I thank you for your good courage, but will ye all that loveth me speak with Merlin? Ye know well that he hath done much for me, and he knoweth many things, and when he is before you, I would that ye prayed him heartily of his best advice.'

stint°] cease   awroke] revenged

All the barons said they would pray him and desire him. So Merlin was sent for, and fair desired of all the barons to give them best counsel.

'I shall say you,' said Merlin, 'I warn you all, your enemies are passing strong for you, and they are good men of arms as be alive, and by this time they have gotten to them four kings more and a mighty duke; and unless that our king have more chivalry with him than he may make within the bounds of his own realm, and he fight with them in battle, he shall be overcome and slain.'

'What were best to do in this cause?' said all the barons.

'I shall tell you', said Merlin, 'my advice: there are two brethren beyond the sea, and they be kings both and marvellous good men of their hands; and the one hight King Ban of Benwick, and the other hight King Bors of Gaul, that is France. And on these two kings warreth a mighty man of men, the King Claudas, and striveth with them for a castle, and great war is betwixt them; but this Claudas is so mighty of goods whereof he getteth good knights, that he putteth these two kings the most part to the worse. Wherefore this is my counsel: that our king and sovereign lord send unto the kings Ban and Bors by two trusty knights with letters well devised, that and they will come and see* King Arthur and his court, and to help him in his wars, that he would be sworn unto them to help them in their wars against King Claudas. Now, what say ye unto this counsel?' said Merlin.

'This is well counselled,' said the King.

[King Ban and King Bors agree to help Arthur, and they meet in battle with the eleven kings.]

By then came into the field King Ban as fierce as a lion, with bands of green and thereupon gold.

'A ha!' said King Lot, 'we must be discomfited, for yonder I see the most valiant knight of the world, and the man of most renown. For such two brethren as is King Ban and King Bors are not living, wherefore we must needs avoid or die. And but if we avoid manly and wisely there is but death.'

So when these two kings, Ban and Bors, came into the battle, they came in so fiercely that the strokes rebounded again from the wood and

[16]

more chivalry . . . may make] more knights than he can gather   with bands . . .
gold] i.e. as his heraldic device   avoid] leave the field

the water; wherefore King Lot wept for pity and dole that he saw so many good knights take their end. But through the great force of King Ban they made both the northern battles that were departed hurtle together for great dread. And the three kings and their knights slew on ever, that it was pity to see and to behold the multitude of the people that fled. But King Lot and the King with the Hundred Knights and King Morganor gathered the people together passing knightly, and did great prowess of arms, and held the battle all the day alike hard.

When the King with the Hundred Knights beheld the great damage that King Ban did, he thrust unto him with his horse, and smote him on high on the helm a great stroke, and astoned him sore. Then King Ban was wood wroth with him, and followed on him fiercely; the other saw that, and cast up his shield and spurred his horse forward. But the stroke of King Ban down fell and carved a cantle off the shield, and the sword slid down by the hauberk behind his back, and cut through the trapper of steel and the horse even in two pieces, that the sword fell to the earth. Then the King of the Hundred Knights voided the horse lightly, and with his sword he broached the horse of King Ban through and through. With that King Ban voided lightly from the dead horse, and smote at that other so eagerly on the helm that he fell to the earth. Also in that ire he felled King Morganor, and there was great slaughter of good knights and much people.

By that time came into the press King Arthur, and found King Ban standing among the dead men and dead horses, fighting on foot as a wood lion, that there came none nigh him as far as he might reach with his sword but he caught a grievous buffet; whereof King Arthur had great pity. And King Arthur was so bloody that by his shield there might no man know him, for all was blood and brains that stuck on his sword and on his shield. And as King Arthur looked beside him he saw a knight that was passingly well horsed; and therewith King Arthur ran to him and smote him on the helm that his sword went unto his teeth, and the knight sank down to the earth dead. And anon King Arthur took the horse by the rein and led him unto King Ban, and said, 'Fair brother, have ye this horse, for ye have great mister thereof, and me repents sore of your great damage.'

'It shall be soon revenged,' said King Ban, 'for, I trust in God, my hurt is none such but some of them may sore repent this.'

'I will well,' said King Arthur, 'for I see your deeds full actual; nevertheless, I might not come to you at that time.'

But when King Ban was mounted on horseback, then there began a new battle which was sore and hard, and passing great slaughter. And so through great force King Arthur, King Ban, and King Bors made their knights a little to withdraw them to a little wood, and so over a little river, and there they rested them; for on the night before they had no great rest in the field. And then the eleven kings put them on a heap all together, as men adread and out of all comfort. But there was no man that might pass them, they held them so hard together both behind and before, that King Arthur had marvel of their deeds of arms and was passing wroth.

'Ah, Sir Arthur,' said King Ban and King Bors, 'blame them not, for they do as good men ought to do. For, by my faith,' said King Ban, 'they are the best fighting men, and knights of most prowess, that ever I saw or heard speak of. And those eleven kings are men of great worship; and if they were belonging to you there were no king under heaven that had such eleven kings, nor of such worship.'

'I may not love them,' said King Arthur, 'for they would destroy me.'

'That know we well,' said King Ban and King Bors, 'for they are your mortal enemies; and that hath been proved beforehand. And this day they have done their part, and that is great pity of their wilfulness.'

Then all the eleven kings drew them together. And then said King Lot, 'Lords, ye must do otherwise than ye do, or else the great loss is behind. For ye may see what people we have lost, and what good men we lose, because we wait always on these foot-men; and ever in saving of one of these foot-men we lose ten horsemen for him. Therefore this is my advice: let us put our foot-men from us, for it is near night. For this noble King Arthur will not tarry on the foot-men, for they may save themselves; the wood is near hand. And when we horsemen be together, look every each of you kings let make such ordinance that none break upon pain of death. And who that seeth any man dress him to flee, lightly that he be slain; for it is better we slay a coward, than

actual] active, vigorous   put them on a heap all together] kept as close together as they could   dress° him] set himself, prepare   lightly that he be slain] let him be killed swiftly through a coward all we be slain. How say ye?' said King Lot, 'Answer me, all ye kings.'

'Ye say well,' said King Nentres. So said the King with the Hundred Knights; the same said King Carados, and King Uriens; so said King Idres and King Brandegoris; so did King Cradelmas, and the Duke of Caudebenet; the same said King Clariance, and so did King Angwissance, and swore they would never fail other for life nor for death. And whoso that fled, all they should be slain.

Then they amended their harness and righted their shields, and took new spears and set them on their thighs, and stood still as it had been a plumb of wood.

[17]   When King Arthur and King Ban and Bors beheld them and all their knights, they praised them much for their noble cheer of chivalry, for the hardiest fighters that ever they heard or saw.*

So there came into the thick of the press Arthur, Ban, and Bors, and slew downright on both hands, that their horses went in blood up to the fetlocks. But ever the eleven kings and the host was ever in the visage of Arthur. Wherefore King Ban and Bors had great marvel, considering the great slaughter that there was; but at the last they were driven aback over a little river.

With that came Merlin on a great black horse, and said unto King Arthur, 'Thou hast never done, hast thou not done enough? Of three score thousand this day hast thou left alive but fifteen thousand, therefore it is time to say "Whoa!" For God is wroth with thee, for thou wilt never have done. For yonder eleven kings at this time will not be overthrown; but and thou tarry on them any longer, thy fortune will turn and they shall increase. And therefore withdraw you unto your lodging and rest you as soon as ye may, and reward your good knights with gold and with silver, for they have well deserved it; there may no riches be too dear for them, for of so few men as ye have, there were never men did more worshipfully in prowess than ye have done today. For ye have matched this day with the best fighters of the world.'

'That is truth,' said King Ban and Bors.

Then Merlin bade them, 'Withdraw where ye list, for these three years I dare undertake they shall not dere you; and by that time ye shall hear new tidings.' Then Merlin said unto Arthur, 'These eleven kings have more on hand than they are aware of. For the Saracens are landed

plumb] block   dere] injure

in their countries, more than forty thousand, and burn and slay, and
have laid siege to the Castle Wandesborough, and make great destruction; therefore dread you not these three years. Also, sir, all the goods
that be gotten at this battle, let it be searched, and when ye have it in
your hands, let it be given friendly unto these two kings, Ban and Bors,
that they may reward their knights withal; and that shall cause
strangers to be of better will to do you service at need. Also ye be able
to reward your own knights at what time soever it liketh you.'

'Ye say well,' said Arthur, 'and as thou hast devised, so shall it be done.'

When it was delivered to these kings, Ban and Bors, they gave the
goods as freely to their knights as it was given to them. Then Merlin
took his leave of King Arthur and of the two kings for to go see his master Bloise, that dwelled in Northumberland; and so he departed and
came to his master, that was passing glad of his coming. And there he
told how Arthur and the two kings had sped at the great battle, and
how it was ended, and told the names of every king and knight of worship that was there. And so Bloise wrote the battle word by word as
Merlin told him, how it began, and by whom; and in like wise how it
was ended, and who had the worst. And all the battles that were done
in Arthur's days, Merlin did his master Bloise write them; also he did
write all the battles that every worthy knight did of Arthur's court.*

So after this Merlin departed from his master and came to King
Arthur, that was in the castle of Bedgraine, that was one of the castles
that standeth in the forest of Sherwood. And Merlin* was so disguised
that King Arthur knew him not, for he was all befurred in black sheep-
skins, and a great pair of boots, and a bow and arrows, in a russet gown,
and brought wild geese in his hand. And it was on the morn after
Candlemas Day. But King Arthur knew him not.

'Sir,' said Merlin unto the King, 'will ye give me a gift?'

'Wherefore,' said King Arthur, 'should I give thee a gift, churl?'

'Sir,' said Merlin, 'ye were better to give me a gift that is not in your
hand than to lose great riches. For here, in the same place where the
great battle was, is great treasure hid in the earth.'

'Who told thee so, churl?'

'Sir, Merlin told me so,' said he.

Then Ulfius and Brastias knew him well enough, and smiled. 'Sir,'
said these two knights, 'it is Merlin that so speaketh unto you.'

Merlin did° his master . . . write them] Merlin had his master . . . write them

Then King Arthur was greatly abashed, and had marvel of Merlin; and so had King Ban and Bors. So they had great disport at him.

Then in the meanwhile there came a damosel that was an earl's daughter—his name was Sanam, and her name was Lionors, a passing fair damosel—and so she came thither for to do homage, as other lords did after that great battle. And King Arthur set his love greatly on her, and so did she upon him; and so the King had ado with her and begot on her a child. And his name was Borre, that was after a good knight, and of the Table Round.

Then there came word that King Roince of North Wales made great war on King Lodegreance of Camelard, for the which King Arthur was wroth, for he loved him well, and hated King Roince, for always he was against him.*

[18] And then King Arthur, King Ban, and King Bors departed with their fellowship, a twenty thousand, and came within six days into the country of Camelard, and there rescued King Lodegreance, and slew there much people of King Roince unto the number of ten thousand, and put them to flight. And then had these three kings great cheer of King Lodegreance, that thanked them of their great goodness, that they would revenge him of his enemies. And there had Arthur the first sight of Queen Guenivere, the king's daughter of the land of Camelard, and ever after he loved her; and after, they were wedded, as it telleth in the book.

So, briefly to make an end, they took their leave to go into their own countries, for King Claudas did great destruction on their lands. Then said Arthur, 'I will go with you.'

'Nay,' said the kings, 'ye shall not at this time, for ye have much to do yet in this land. Therefore we will depart; with the great goods that we have gotten in this land by your gifts, we shall wage good knights and withstand the King Claudas' malice. For by the grace of God, and we have need, we will send to you for succour. And ye have need, send for us, and we will not tarry, by the faith of our bodies.'

'It shall not need', said Merlin, 'these two kings to come again in the way of war. But I know well King Arthur may not be long from you; for within a year or two ye shall have great need, then shall he revenge you of your enemies as ye have done on his. For these eleven kings shall die all in one day by the great might and prowess of arms of two valiant

disport] amusement

knights' (as it telleth after; their names were Balin le Savage and Balan, his brother, that were marvellous knights as any was then living).*

Then after the departing of King Ban and Bors, King Arthur rode [19] unto Caerleon. And thither came unto him King Lot's wife of Orkney, in manner of a message, but she was sent thither to espy the court of King Arthur; and she came richly beseen, with her four sons Gawain, Gaheris, Agravain, and Gareth, with many other knights and ladies, for she was a passing fair lady. Wherefore the King cast great love unto her, and desired to lie by her. And so they were agreed, and he begot upon her Sir Mordred, and she was sister on the mother's side, Igraine, unto Arthur. So there she rested her a month, and at the last she departed.

Then the King dreamed a marvellous dream whereof he was sore adread. But all this time King Arthur knew not King Lot's wife was his sister.

But thus was the dream of Arthur: he thought there was come into his land griffins and serpents, and he thought they burnt and slew all the people in the land; and then he thought he fought with them and they did him great harm and wounded him full sore, but at the last he slew them.

When the King waked, he was passing heavy of his dream. And so to put it out of thought, he made him ready with many knights to ride on hunting; and as soon as he was in the forest the King saw a great hart before him.

'This hart will I chase,' said King Arthur, and so he spurred his horse, and rode after long.

And so by fine force often he was like to have smitten the hart; wherefore as the King had chased the hart so long, his horse lost his breath and fell down dead. Then a yeoman fetched the King another horse. So the King saw the hart imbossed and his horse dead, he set him down by a fountain, and there he fell down in great thought. And as he sat so, him thought he heard a noise of hounds, to the sum of thirty. And with that the King saw coming toward him the strangest beast that ever he saw or heard of. So this beast went to the well and drank, and the noise was in the beast's belly like unto the questing of thirty couple hounds; but all the while the beast drank there was no noise in the beast's belly.* And therewith the beast departed with a

So the King . . . imbossed] when the King saw the hart had taken cover

great noise, whereof the King had great marvel; and so he was in a great thought, and therewith he fell asleep.

Right so there came a knight on foot unto Arthur and said, 'Knight full of thought and sleepy, tell me if thou saw any strange beast pass this way.'

'Such one saw I,' said King Arthur, 'that is passed nigh two miles. What would ye with that beast?' said Arthur.

'Sir, I have followed that beast long and killed my horse, so would God I had another to follow my quest.'

Right so came one with the King's horse; and when the knight saw the horse, he prayed the King to give him the horse: 'for I have followed this quest this twelvemonth, and either I shall achieve him, or bleed of the best blood in my body.' (His name was King Pellinore that that time followed the Questing Beast, and after his death Sir Palomides followed it.)

[20]   'Sir knight,' said the King, 'leave that quest and suffer me to have it, and I will follow it another twelvemonth.'

'Ah, fool,' said the king unto Arthur, 'it is in vain thy desire, for it shall never be achieved but by me, or by my next kin.' And therewith he started unto the King's horse and mounted into the saddle, and said, 'Gramercy, for this horse is my own.'

'Well,' said the King, 'thou mayst take my horse by force, but and I might prove it I would wit whether thou were better worthy to have him or I.'

When the king heard him say so, he said, 'Seek me here when thou wilt, and here nigh this well thou shalt find me,' and so passed on his way.

Then the King sat in a study, and bade his men fetch another horse as fast as they might.

Right so came by him Merlin like a child of fourteen years of age, and saluted the King, and asked him why he was so pensive.

'I may well be pensive,' said the King, 'for I have seen the most marvellous sight that ever I saw.'

'That know I well,' said Merlin, 'as well as thyself, and of all thy thoughts, but thou art a fool to take thought for it: that will not amend thee. Also I know what thou art, and who was thy father, and of whom thou were begotten; for King Uther was thy father, and begot thee on Igraine.'

Gramercy°] thank you, *grand merci*

'That is false,' said King Arthur. 'How shouldst thou know it?—for thou art not so old of years to know my father.'

'Yes,' said Merlin, 'I know it better than ye or any man living.'

'I will not believe thee,' said Arthur, and was wroth with the child.

So departed Merlin, and came again in the likeness of an old man of fourscore years of age, whereof the King was passing glad, for he seemed to be right wise. Then said the old man, 'Why are ye so sad?'

'I may well be sad,' said Arthur, 'for many things; for right now there was a child here, and told me many things that me seemeth he should not know, for he was not of age to know my father.'

'Yes,' said the old man, 'the child told you truth, and more would he have told you and ye would have suffered him. But ye have done a thing late that God is displeased with you, for ye have lain by your sister, and on her ye have begotten a child that shall destroy you and all the knights of your realm.'

'What are ye,' said Arthur, 'that tell me these tidings?'

'Sir, I am Merlin, and I was he in the child's likeness.'

'Ah,' said the King, 'ye are a marvellous man! But I marvel much of thy words that I must die in battle.'

'Marvel not,' said Merlin, 'for it is God's will that your body should be punished for your foul deeds. But I ought ever to be heavy,' said Merlin, 'for I shall die a shameful death, to be put in the earth quick, and ye shall die a worshipful death.'

And as they talked thus, came one with the King's horse, and so the King mounted on his horse and Merlin on another, and so rode unto Caerleon. And anon the King asked Ector and Ulfius how he was begotten; and they told him how King Uther was his father and Queen Igraine his mother.

'So Merlin told me. I will that my mother be sent for, that I might speak with her; and if she say so herself, then will I believe it.'

So in all haste the queen was sent for, and she brought with her Morgan le Fay, her daughter, that was a fair lady as any might be; and the King welcomed Igraine in the best manner. Right so came in Ulfius, [21] and said openly that the King and all might hear that were feasted that day, 'Ye are the falsest lady of the world, and the most treacherous unto the King's person.'

'Beware,' said King Arthur, 'what thou sayest; thou speakest a great word.'

quick] alive

'Sir, I am well aware', said Ulfius, 'what I speak, and here is my glove to prove it upon any man that will say the contrary,* that this Queen Igraine is the causer of your great damage, and of your great war; for, and she would have uttered it in the life of Uther, of the birth of you and how ye were begotten, then had ye never had the mortal wars that ye have had; for the most part of your barons of your realm knew never whose son ye were, nor of whom ye were begotten. And she that bore you of her body should have made it known openly in excusing of her worship and yours, and in like wise to all the realm. Wherefore I prove her false to God and to you and to all your realm; and who will say the contrary I will prove it on his body.'

Then spoke Igraine and said, 'I am a woman and I may not fight; but rather than I should be dishonoured, there would some good man take my quarrel! But thus,' she said, 'Merlin knoweth well, and ye, Sir Ulfius, how King Uther came to me into the castle of Tintagel in the likeness of my lord, that was dead three hours before, and there begot a child that night upon me; and after the thirteenth day King Uther wedded me. And by his commandment, when the child was born it was delivered unto Merlin and fostered by him, and so I saw the child never after, nor wot not what is his name, for I knew him never yet.'

Then Ulfius said unto Merlin, 'Ye are then more to blame than the queen.'

'Sir, well I wot I bore a child by my lord King Uther; but I wot never where he is become.'

Then the King took Merlin by the hand, saying these words, 'Is this my mother?'

'For sooth, sir, yea.'

And therewith came in Sir Ector, and bore witness how he fostered him by King Uther's commandment. And therewith King Arthur took his mother Queen Igraine in his arms and kissed her, and either wept upon other. Then the King let make a feast that lasted eight days.

So on a day there came into the court a squire on horseback leading a knight before him wounded to the death, and told how there was a knight in the forest that had reared up a pavilion by a well, 'that hath slain my master, a good knight—his name was Miles—wherefore I beseech you that my master may be buried; and that some knight may revenge my master's death.'

pavilion°] ornamental tent

Then the noise was great of that knight's death in the court, and every man said his advice. Then came Griflet that was but a squire, and he was but young of age. So he besought the King, for all his service that he had done him, to give him the order of knighthood.

'Thou art but young and tender of age,' said Arthur, 'for to take so high an order upon you.' [22]

'Sir,' said Griflet, 'I beseech you to make me knight.'

'Sir,' said Merlin, 'it were pity to lose Griflet, for he will be a passing good man when he is of age, and he shall abide with you the term of his life. And if he adventure his body with yonder knight at the fountain, it is in great peril if ever he come again, for he is one of the best knights of the world and the strongest man of arms.'

'Well,' said Arthur, 'at thy own desire thou shalt be made knight. Now,' said Arthur unto Griflet, 'sith I have made thee knight thou must give me a gift.'

'What ye will,' said Griflet.

'Thou shalt promise me by thy faith of thy body, when thou hast jousted with that knight at the fountain, whether it fall ye be on horse-back or on foot, that right so ye shall come again unto me without mak-ing any more debate.'

'I will promise you,' said Griflet, 'as your desire is.'

Then took Griflet his horse in great haste, and dressed his shield and took a spear in his hand, and so he rode a great gallop till he came to the fountain. And thereby he saw a rich pavilion, and thereby under a cloth stood a horse well saddled and bridled, and on a tree hung a shield of divers colours and a great spear thereby. Then Griflet smote on the shield with the butt of his spear, that the shield fell down.

With that the knight came out of the pavilion, and said, 'Fair knight, why smote ye down my shield?'

'Sir, for I will joust with you,' said Griflet.

'Sir, it is better ye do not,' said the knight, 'for ye are but young, and late made knight, and your might is naught to mine.'

'As for that,' said Griflet, 'I will joust with you.'

'That is me loath,' said the knight, 'but sithen I must needs, I will dress me thereto. Of whence be ye?' said the knight.

'Sir, I am of King Arthur's court.'

So the two knights ran together that Griflet's spear all to-shivered.

sith°] since   dressed°] set in place   divers°] various   to-shivered]
broke in pieces

And therewith he smote Griflet through the shield and the left side, and broke the spear that the truncheon stuck in his body, and horse and man fell down to the earth.

[23]   When the knight saw him lie so on the ground, he alit, and was passing heavy for he weened he had slain him; and then he unlaced his helm and got him wind. And so with the truncheon set him on his horse and got him wind, and so betook him to God, and said he had a mighty heart; and said, if he might live, he would prove a passing good knight. And so rode forth Sir Griflet unto the court, whereof passing great dole was made for him. But through good leeches he was healed and saved.

Right so came into the court twelve knights that were aged men, which came from the Emperor of Rome. And they asked of Arthur truage for his realm, or else the emperor would destroy him and all his land.

'Well,' said King Arthur, 'ye are messengers, therefore ye may say what ye will, or else ye should die therefor. But this is my answer: I owe the emperor no truage, nor none will I yield him, but on a fair field I shall yield him my truage: that shall be with a sharp spear or else with a sharp sword. And that shall not be long, by my father's soul, Uther.' And therewith the messengers departed passingly wroth, and King Arthur as wroth, for in an evil time came they.

But the King was passingly wroth for the hurt of Sir Griflet. And so he commanded a privy man of his chamber that or it were day his best horse and armour, 'and all that longeth to my person, be without the city or tomorrow day.'

Right so he met with his man and his horse, and so mounted up and dressed his shield and took his spear, and bade his chamberlain tarry there till he came again. And so Arthur rode a soft pace till it was day. And then was he ware of three churls chasing Merlin, and would have slain him. Then the King rode unto them, and bade them, 'Flee, churls!' Then they feared sore when they saw a knight come, and fled.

'Ah, Merlin,' said Arthur, 'here hadst thou been slain for all thy crafts had not I been.'

'Nay,' said Merlin, 'not so, for I could have saved myself and I had willed. But thou art more near thy death than I am, for thou goest to thy deathward and God be not thy friend.'

---

truncheon°] broken part of a spear   betook] commended   leeches°]
doctors   truage] tribute

So as they went thus talking they came to the fountain and the rich pavilion there by it. Then King Arthur was ware where sat a knight armed in a chair.

'Sir knight,' said Arthur, 'for what cause abidest thou here, that there may no knight ride this way but if he joust with thee? I rede thee to leave that custom.'

'This custom,' said the knight, 'have I used and will use maugre who saith nay. And who that is aggrieved with my custom, let him amend it.'

'That shall I amend,' said Arthur.

'And I shall defend thee,' said the knight.

And anon he took his horse and dressed his shield and took a great spear in his hand, and they came together so hard that either smote other in midst the shields, that all to-shivered their spears. Therewith anon Arthur pulled out his sword.

'Nay, not so,' said the knight, 'it is better that we twain run more together with sharp spears.'

'I will well,' said Arthur, 'and I had any more spears here.'

'I have enough,' said the knight. So there came a squire and brought forth two spears; and Arthur chose one and he another. So they spurred their horses and came together with all their might, that either broke their spears to their hands. Then Arthur set hand on his sword.

'Nay,' said the knight, 'ye shall do better, ye are a passing good jouster as ever I met with; and once for the high order of knighthood let us joust again.'

'I assent me,' said Arthur.

And anon there were brought forth two great spears, and anon every knight got a spear, and therewith they ran together that Arthur's spear all to-shivered. But this other knight smote him so hard in midst the shield that horse and man fell to the earth. And therewith Arthur was eager, and pulled out his sword and said, 'I will assay thee, sir knight, on foot; for I have lost the honour on horseback,' said the King.

'Sir, I will be on horseback still to assay thee.'

Then was Arthur wroth, and dressed his shield toward him with his sword drawn. When the knight saw that, he alit; for him thought no worship to have a knight at such avail, he to be on horseback and his adversary on foot, and so he alit and dressed his shield unto Arthur.

rede°] advise   maugre°] despite   defend°] forbid, prevent

And there began a strong battle with many great strokes, and so they hewed with their swords that the cantles flew unto the fields, and much blood they bled both, that all the place there as they fought was overbled with blood; and thus they fought long and rested them. And then they went to the battle again, and so hurtled together like two rams, that either fell to the earth. So at the last they smote together that both their swords met even together. But King Arthur's sword broke in two pieces, wherefore he was heavy.

Then said the knight unto Arthur, 'Thou art in my danger whether me list to save thee or slay thee; and but thou yield thee to me as overcome and recreant,* thou shalt die.'

'As for that,' said King Arthur, 'death is welcome to me when it cometh; but to yield me unto thee, I will not.'

And therewith the King leapt unto King Pellinore, and took him by the middle and overthrew him, and rased off his helm. So when the knight felt that, he was adread, for he was a passing big man of might. And so forthwith he wrothe Arthur under him, and rased off his helm and would have smitten off his head.

[24]   And therewith came Merlin and said, 'Knight, hold thy hand, for and thou slay that knight thou puttest this realm in the greatest damage that ever was realm, for this knight is a man of more worship than thou wotest of.'

'Why, what is he?' said the knight.

'For it is King Arthur,' said Merlin.

Then would he have slain him for dread of his wrath, and so he lifted up his sword. And therewith Merlin cast an enchantment on the knight, that he fell to the earth in a great sleep. Then Merlin took up King Arthur, and rode forth on the knight's horse.

'Alas,' said Arthur, 'what hast thou done, Merlin? Hast thou slain this good knight by thy crafts?—for there liveth not so worshipful a knight as he was. For I had liever than the stint of my land a year that he were alive.'

'Care ye not,' said Merlin, 'for he is wholer than ye; he is but asleep, and will awake within this hour. I told you', said Merlin, 'what a knight he was. Now here had ye been slain had I not been. Also there liveth not a bigger knight than he is one; and after this he shall do you good service. And his name is King Pellinore; and he shall

cantles] pieces   danger] power   me list°] it pleases me   rased°] pulled   wrothe] twisted   liever°] rather   stint] value

have two sons that shall be passing good men as any living— save one, in this world they shall have no fellows of prowess and of good living, and their names shall be Percival and Sir Lamorak of Gales. And he shall tell you the name of your own son begotten of your sister that shall be the destruction of all this realm.'

Right so the King and he departed and went unto a hermitage, and [25] there was a good man and a great leech; so the hermit searched the King's wounds and gave him good salves. And so the King was there three days; and then were his wounds well mended, that he might ride and go, and so departed.

And as they rode, King Arthur said, 'I have no sword.'

'No force,' said Merlin, 'hereby is a sword that shall be yours, and I may.'

So they rode till they came to a lake that was a fair water and broad. And in the midst Arthur was ware of an arm clothed in white samite, that held a fair sword in that hand.

'Lo,' said Merlin, 'yonder is the sword that I spoke of.'

So with that they saw a damosel going upon the lake.

'What damosel is that?' said Arthur.

'That is the Lady of the Lake,' said Merlin. 'And within that lake there is a great rock, and therein is as fair a palace as any on earth, and richly beseen. And this damosel will come to you anon; and then speak ye fair to her that she may give you that sword.'

So anon came this damosel to Arthur and saluted him, and he her again.

'Damosel,' said Arthur, 'what sword is that yonder that the arm holdeth above the water? I would it were mine, for I have no sword.'

'Sir Arthur,' said the damosel, 'that sword is mine. And if ye will give me a gift when I ask it you, ye shall have it.'

'By my faith,' said Arthur, 'I will give you what gift that ye will ask.'

'Well,' said the damosel. 'Go ye into yonder barge and row yourself to the sword, and take it and the scabbard with you; and I will ask my gift when I see my time.'

So King Arthur and Merlin alit and tied their horses unto two trees, and so they went into the barge; and when they came to the sword that the hand held, then King Arthur took it up by the handles and bore it

---

ride and go] ride and walk   No force] no matter   and I may] if I can bring
it about   samite°] rich silk

with him, and the arm and the hand went under the water. And so he came unto the land and rode forth. And King Arthur saw a rich pavilion.

'What signifieth yonder pavilion?'

'Sir, that is the knight's pavilions that ye fought with last, Sir Pellinore; but he is out, he is not at home, for he hath had ado with a knight of yours that hight Eglam, and they had fought together. But at the last Eglam fled, and else he had been dead; and he hath chased him even to Caerleon. And we shall meet with him anon in the highway.'

'That is well said!' said Arthur. 'Now I have a sword, I will wage battle with him and be avenged on him.'

'Sir,' said Merlin, 'not so; for the knight is weary of fighting and chasing, that ye shall have no worship to have ado with him; also, he will not lightly be matched of one knight living. And therefore it is my counsel, let him pass, for he shall do you good service in short time, and his sons after his days. Also ye shall see that day in short space that ye shall be right glad to give him your sister to wed for his good service. Therefore have not ado with him when ye see him.'

'I will do as ye advise me.'

Then King Arthur looked on the sword, and liked it passing well. Then said Merlin, 'Whether like ye better the sword or the scabbard?'

'I like better the sword,' said Arthur.

'Ye are the more unwise, for the scabbard is worth ten of the sword; for while ye have the scabbard upon you, ye shall lose no blood be ye never so sore wounded. Therefore keep well the scabbard always with you.'

So they rode unto Caerleon, and by the way they met with King Pellinore; but Merlin had done such a craft unto him that King Pellinore saw not King Arthur, and so passed by without any words.

'I marvel', said Arthur, 'that the knight would not speak.'

'Sir, he saw you not, for had he seen you, he had not lightly parted.'

So they came unto Caerleon, whereof his knights were passing glad. And when they heard of his adventures, they marvelled that he would jeopard his person so, alone. But all men of worship said it was merry to be under such a chieftain that would put his person in adventure as other poor knights did.

[26] So this meanwhile came a messenger from King Roince of North Wales, and king he was of all Ireland and of the Isles. And this was his message, greeting well King Arthur in this manner of wise, saying

that King Roince had discomfited and overcome eleven kings, and
each of them did him homage. And that was thus to say, they gave
their beards clean flayed off, as much beard as there was; wherefore
the messenger came for King Arthur's beard. For King Roince had
purfiled a mantle with kings' beards, and there lacked one place of the
mantle; wherefore he sent for his beard, or else he would enter into his
lands and burn and slay, and never leave till he have the head and the
beard both.

'Well,' said Arthur, 'thou hast said thy message, the which is the
most orgulous and lewdest message that ever man had sent unto a king.
Also, thou mayest see my beard is full young yet to make of a purfile.
But tell thou thy king thus, that I owe him no homage, nor none of my
elders; but or it be long, he shall do me homage on both his knees, or
else he shall lose his head, by the faith of my body, for this is the most
shamefullest message that ever I heard speak of. I have espied thy king
never yet met with worshipful man. But tell him I will have his head
without he do me homage.' Then this messenger departed.

'Now is there any here that knoweth King Roince?'

Then answered a knight that hight Naram, 'Sir, I know the king
well; he is a passing good man of his body as few be living, and a passing proud man. And sir, doubt ye not, he will make war on you with a
mighty puissance.'

'Well,' said Arthur. 'I shall ordain for him in short time.'

Then King Arthur let send for all the children that were born on May-   [27]
day, begotten of lords and born of ladies; for Merlin told King Arthur
that he that should destroy him and all the land should be born on May-
day. Wherefore he sent for them all, on pain of death; and so there were
found many lords' sons and many knights' sons, and all were sent unto
the King. And so was Mordred sent by King Lot's wife; and all were put
in a ship to the sea, and some were four weeks old, and some less. And
so by fortune the ship drove unto a castle and was all to-riven, and
destroyed the most part save that Mordred was cast up; and a good man
found him and fostered him till he was fourteen years of age, and then
brought him to the court, as it rehearseth afterwards and toward the
end of the *Morte Arthur* .*

purfiled] trimmed   orgulous and lewdest] arrogant and boorish   with-
out] unless   puissance] power   to-riven] smashed to pieces

So many lords and barons of this realm were displeased for their children were so lost, and many put the wite on Merlin more than on Arthur. So what for dread and for love, they held their peace.

But when the messenger came to the King Roince, then was he wood out of measure, and purveyed him for a great host, as it rehearseth after in the book of Balin le Savage that followeth next after: that was the adventure how Balin got the sword.

wite] blame

The Tale of Balin and Balan

So it befell on a time when King Arthur was at London, there came a knight and told the King tidings how the King Roince of North Wales had reared a great number of people, and were entered in the land, and burnt and slew the King's true liege people.

'If this be true,' said Arthur, 'it were great shame unto my estate but that he were mightily withstood.'

'It is truth,' said the knight, 'for I saw the host myself.'

'Well,' said the King, 'I shall ordain to withstand his malice.'

Then the King let make a cry that all the lords, knights, and gentlemen of arms should draw unto the castle called Camelot in those days, and there the King would let make a council-general and a great jousts. So when the King was come thither with all his baronage, and lodged as they seemed best, also there was come a damosel the which was sent from the great Lady l'Isle of Avilion. And when she came before King Arthur, she told from whence she came, and how she was sent on message unto him for these causes. Then she let her mantle fall that was richly furred; and then was she girt with a noble sword, whereof the King had marvel, and said, 'Damosel, for what cause are ye girt with that sword? It beseemeth you not.'

'Now shall I tell you,' said the damosel. 'This sword that I am girt withal doth me great sorrow and encumbrance, for I may not be delivered of this sword but by a knight, and he must be a passing good man of his hands and of his deeds, and without villainy or treachery, and without treason. And if I may find such a knight that hath all these virtues, he may draw out this sword out of the sheath. For I have been at King Roince's, for it was told me, there were passing good knights; and he and all his knights have assayed and none can speed.'

'This is a great marvel,' said Arthur. 'If this be sooth, I will assay myself to draw out the sword, not presuming myself that I am the best knight, but I will begin to draw your sword in giving an example to all

reared] raised   but that he were] if he were not   let make a cry] had it proclaimed   beseemeth you not] does not become you, is not fitting for you   speed] succeed

the barons that they shall assay every one after other when I have assayed.'

Then Arthur took the sword by the sheath and girdle and pulled at it eagerly, but the sword would not out.

'Sir,' said the damosel, 'you need not for to pull half so sore, for he that shall pull it out shall do it with little might.'

'Ye say well,' said Arthur. 'Now assay ye, all my barons.'

'But beware ye be not defiled with shame, treachery, nor guile, for then it will not avail,' said the damosel, 'for he must be a clean knight without villainy, and of gentle strain of father side and of mother side.'

The most part of all the barons of the Round Table that were there at that time assayed all by row, but there might none speed. Wherefore the damosel made great sorrow out of measure, and said, 'Alas! I weened in this court had been the best knights of the world without treachery or treason.'

'By my faith,' said Arthur, 'here are good knights, as I deem, as any be in the world. But their grace is not to help you, wherefore I am sore displeased.'

[2]   Then it befell so that time there was a poor knight with King Arthur, that had been prisoner with him half a year for slaying of a knight which was cousin unto King Arthur. And the name of this knight was called Balin, and by good means of the barons he was delivered out of prison, for he was a good man named of his body, and he was born in Northumberland. And so he went privily into the court, and saw this adventure; whereof it raised his heart, and would have assayed as other knights did, but for he was poor and poorly arrayed he put him not far in press. But in his heart he was fully assured to do as well, if his grace happed him, as any knight that there was. And as the damosel took her leave of Arthur and of all the barons, so departing, this knight Balin called unto her, and said,

'Damosel, I pray of your courtesy, suffer me as well to assay as these other lords; though that I be poorly arrayed, yet in my heart me seemeth I am fully assured as some of these other, and me seemeth in my heart to speed right well.'

This damosel then beheld this poor knight, and saw he was a likely man; but for his poor arrayment she thought he should not be of no worship without villainy or treachery. And then she said unto that

gentle°|noble   put him not far in press] did not push himself forward

knight, 'Sir, it needeth not you to put me to no more pain, for it seemeth not you to speed there as all these other knights have failed.'

'Ah, fair damosel,' said Balin, 'worthiness, and good tatches and also good deeds, is not only in arrayment; but manhood and worship is within a man's person, and many a worshipful knight is not known unto all people. And therefore worship and hardiness is not in arrayment.'

'By God,' said the damosel, 'ye say sooth; therefore ye shall assay to do what ye may.'

Then Balin took the sword by the girdle and sheath, and drew it out easily; and when he looked on the sword it pleased him much. Then had the king and all the barons great marvel that Balin had done that adventure; many knights had great despite at him.

'Certes,' said the damosel, 'this is a passing good knight, and the best that ever I found, and most of worship without treason, treachery, or felony, and many marvels shall he do. Now, gentle and courteous knight, give me the sword again.'

'Nay,' said Balin, 'for this sword will I keep, but it be taken from me with force.'

'Well,' said the damosel, 'ye are not wise to keep the sword from me, for ye shall slay with that sword the best friend that ye have, and the man that ye most love in the world, and that sword shall be your destruction.'

'I shall take the adventure,' said Balin, 'that God will ordain for me. But the sword ye shall not have at this time, by the faith of my body.'

'Ye shall repent it within short time,' said the damosel, 'for I would have the sword more for your advantage than for mine, for I am passing heavy for your sake; for and ye will not leave that sword, it shall be your destruction, and that is great pity.' So with that departed the damosel, and great sorrow she made.

And anon after, Balin sent for his horse and armour, and so would depart from the court, and took his leave of King Arthur.

'Nay,' said the King, 'I suppose ye will not depart so lightly from this fellowship. I suppose that ye are displeased that I have showed you unkindness; but blame me the less, for I was misinformed against you. But I weened ye had not been such a knight as ye are of worship and

---

it seemeth not you] you are not likely   tatches] qualities   arrayment] clothing and outward show

prowess. And if ye will abide in this court among my fellowship, I shall so advance you as ye shall be pleased.'

'God thank your highness,' said Balin, 'your bounty may no man praise half unto the value; but at this time I must needs depart, beseeching you always of your good grace.'

'Truly,' said the King, 'I am right wroth of your departing. But I pray you, fair knight, that ye tarry not long from me; and ye shall be right welcome unto me and to my barons, and I shall amend all miss that I have done against you.'

'God thank your good grace,' said Balin, and therewith made him ready to depart. Then the most part of the knights of the Round Table said that Balin did not this adventure only by might, but by witchcraft.

[3] So the meanwhile that this knight was making him ready to depart, there came into the court the Lady of the Lake. And she came on horseback, richly beseen, and saluted King Arthur, and there asked him a gift that he promised her when she gave him the sword.

'That is sooth,' said Arthur, 'a gift I promised you; but I have forgotten the name of my sword that ye gave me.'

'The name of it,' said the lady, 'is Excalibur, that is as much to say as Cut-steel.'

'Ye say well,' said the King, 'ask what ye will and ye shall have it, and it lie in my power to give it.'

'Well,' said this lady, 'then I ask the head of this knight that hath won the sword, or else the damosel's head that brought it; I take no force though I have both their heads, for he slew my brother, a good knight and a true, and that gentlewoman was causer of my father's death.'

'Truly,' said King Arthur, 'I may not grant you neither of their heads with my worship, therefore ask what ye will else, and I shall fulfil your desire.'

'I will ask no other thing,' said the lady.

So when Balin was ready to depart, he saw the Lady of the Lake, which by her means had slain his mother; and he had sought her three years before. And when it was told him how she had asked his head of King Arthur, he went to her straight and said, 'Evil be ye found; ye would have my head, and therefore ye shall lose yours.' And with his sword lightly he smote off her head before King Arthur.

all miss] whatever amiss   I take no force though] I don't mind if

'Alas, for shame!' said the King. 'Why have ye done so? Ye have shamed me and all my court, for this lady was a lady that I was much beholden to, and hither she came under my safe-conduct. Therefore I shall never forgive you that trespass.'

'Sir,' said Balin, 'me forthinketh of your displeasure, for this same lady was the untruest lady living, and by enchantment and by sorcery she hath been the destroyer of many good knights. And she was causer that my mother was burnt, through her falsehood and treachery.'

'For what cause soever ye had,' said Arthur, 'ye should have forborne in my presence. Therefore, think not the contrary, ye shall repent it, for such another despite had I never in my court; therefore withdraw you out of my court in all the haste that ye may.'

Then Balin took up the head of the lady and bore it with him to his hostelry, and there met with his squire, that was sorry he had displeased King Arthur; and so they rode forth out of town.

'Now,' said Balin, 'we must part; therefore take thou this head and bear it to my friends, and tell them how I have sped, and tell them in Northumberland how my most foe is dead. Also tell them how I am out of prison, and what adventure befell me at the getting of this sword.'

'Alas!' said the squire, 'ye are greatly to blame for to displease King Arthur.'

'As for that,' said Balin, 'I will hie me in all haste that I may to meet with King Roince and destroy him, or else to die therefor. And if it may hap me to win him, then will King Arthur be my good friend.'

'Sir, where shall I meet with you?' said the squire.

'In King Arthur's court,' said Balin. So his squire and he parted at that time.

Then King Arthur and all the court made great dole and had great shame of the Lady of the Lake. Then the King buried her richly.*

And Balin turned his horse and looked towards a fair forest. And then [6] was he ware, by his arms, that there came riding his brother Balan. And when they were met they put off their helms and kissed together, and wept for joy and pity.* Anon the knight Balin told his brother of his adventure of the sword, and of the death of the Lady of the Lake.

'Truly,' said Balin, 'I am right heavy that my lord Arthur is displeased with me, for he is the most worshipful king that reigneth now

me forthinketh°] I regret

in earth, and his love will I get or else I will put my life in adventure, for King Roince lieth at the siege of the Castle Terrabil, and thither will we draw in all goodly haste to prove our worship and prowess upon him.'

'I will well,' said Balan, 'that ye so do, and I will ride with you and put my body in adventure with you, as a brother ought to do.'

[8]   And as they rode together they met with Merlin, disguised so that they knew him not.

'But whitherward ride ye?' said Merlin.

'We had little ado to tell you,' said these two knights. 'But what is thy name?' said Balin.

'At this time', said Merlin, 'I will not tell.'

'It is an evil sign', said the knights, 'that thou art a true man, that thou wilt not tell thy name.'

'As for that,' said Merlin, 'be as it be may. But I can tell you wherefore ye ride this way, for to meet with King Roince; but it will not avail you without ye have my counsel.'

'Ah,' said Balin, 'ye are Merlin; we will be ruled by your counsel.'

'Come on,' said Merlin, 'and ye shall have great worship, and look that ye do knightly, for ye shall have need.'

'As for that,' said Balin, 'dread you not, for we will do what we may.'

[9]   Then there lodged Merlin and these two knights in a wood among the leaves beside the highway, and took off the bridles of their horses and put them to grass, and laid them down to rest till it was nigh midnight. Then Merlin bade them rise and make them ready, 'For here cometh the king nigh hand,' that was stolen away from his host with three score horses of his best knights; and twenty of them rode before the lord to warn the Lady de Vance that the king was coming, for that night King Roince should have lain with her.

'Which is the king?' said Balin.

'Abide,' said Merlin, 'for here in a strait ye shall meet with him.' And therewith he showed Balin and his brother the king. And anon they met with him and smote him down, and wounded him freshly, and laid him to the ground; and there they slew on the right hand and on the left hand more than forty of his men, and the remnant fled. Then went they again to King Roince and would have slain him had he not yielded him unto their grace.

strait] narrow way   freshly] eagerly

Then said he thus, 'Knights full of prowess, slay me not, for by my life ye may win, and by my death little.'

'Ye say sooth,' said the knights, and so laid him on a horse-litter.

So with that Merlin vanished, and came to King Arthur beforehand and told him how his most enemy was taken and discomfited.

'By whom?' said King Arthur.

'By two knights', said Merlin, 'that would fain have your lordship, and tomorrow ye shall know what knights they are.'

So anon after came the Knight with the Two Swords and his brother, and brought with them King Roince of North Wales, and there delivered him to the porters and charged them with him; and so they two returned again in the dawning of the day. Then King Arthur came to King Roince and said, 'Sir king, ye are welcome. By what adventure came ye hither?'

'Sir,' said King Roince, 'I came hither by a hard adventure.'

'Who won you?' said King Arthur.

'Sir,' said he, 'the Knight with the Two Swords and his brother, which are two marvellous knights of prowess.'

'I know them not,' said Arthur, 'but much am I beholden to them.'

'Ah, sir,' said Merlin, 'I shall tell you: it is Balin that achieved the sword, and his brother Balan, a good knight; there liveth not a better of prowess nor of worthiness, and it shall be the greatest dole of him that ever I knew of knight, for he shall not long endure.'

'Alas,' said King Arthur, 'that is great pity; for I am much beholden unto him, and I have evil deserved it again for his kindness.'

'Nay, nay' said Merlin, 'he shall do much more for you, and that shall ye know in haste. But, sir, are ye purveyed?' said Merlin, 'for tomorrow the host of King Nero, King Roince's brother, will set on you or noon with a great host, and therefore make you ready, for I will depart from you.'

Then King Arthur made his host ready in ten battles, and Nero was   [10] ready in the field before the Castle Terrabil with a great host, and he had ten battles, with many more people than King Arthur had. Then Nero had the vanguard with the most part of his people.

win] profit   porters] gate-keepers   evil deserved it again] repaid him badly   purveyed] prepared   battles] battalions

And Merlin came to King Lot of the Isle of Orkney, and held him with a tale of prophecy, till Nero and his people were destroyed.*

So in the meanwhile came one to King Lot, and told him while he tarried there how Nero was destroyed and slain with all his host.

'Alas,' said King Lot, 'I am ashamed, for in my default there is many a worshipful man slain, for and we had been together there is no host under heaven were able to have matched us. But this faitor with his prophecy hath mocked me.'

All that did Merlin, for he knew well that and King Lot had been with his body at the first battle, King Arthur had been slain and all his people distressed. And well Merlin knew the one of the kings should be dead that day, and loath was Merlin that any of them both should be slain; but of the twain, he had liever King Lot of Orkney had been slain than Arthur.

'What is best to do?' said King Lot. 'Whether is me better to treat with King Arthur or to fight?—for the greater part of our people are slain and distressed.'

'Sir,' said a knight, 'set ye on Arthur, for they are weary and for-foughten and we be fresh.'

'As for me,' said King Lot, 'I would that every knight would do his part as I would do mine.'

Then they advanced banners and smote together and bruised their spears; and Arthur's knights, with the help of the Knight with the Two Swords and his brother Balan, put King Lot and his host to the worse. But always King Lot held him in the forefront, and did marvellous deeds of arms; for all his host was borne up by his hands, for he abode all knights. Alas, he might not endure, the which was great pity; so worthy a knight as he was one, that he should be overmatched, that of late time before he had been a knight of King Arthur's, and wedded the sister of him. And for because that King Arthur lay by his wife and begot on her Sir Mordred, therefore King Lot held ever against Arthur.

So there was a knight that was called the Knight with the Strange Beast, and at that time his right name was called Pellinore, which was a good man of prowess as few in those days living; and he struck a mighty stroke at King Lot as he fought with his enemies, and he failed

faitor] impostor   body] troops   Whether . . . to treat] is it better for me to negotiate   forfoughten] exhausted with fighting   borne up by his hands] sustained by his prowess

of his stroke and smote the horse's neck that he foundered to the earth with King Lot, and therewith anon King Pellinore smote him a great stroke through the helm and head unto the brows. Then all the host of Orkney fled for the death of King Lot, and there they were taken and slain, all the host. But King Pellinore bore the wite of the death of King Lot, wherefore Sir Gawain revenged the death of his father the tenth year after he was made knight, and slew King Pellinore with his own hands.

Also there was slain at that battle twelve kings on the side of King Lot with Nero, and were buried in the church of Saint Stephen's in Camelot, and the remnant of knights and others were buried in a great rock.*

'Sir,' said Merlin, 'look ye keep well the scabbard of Excalibur, for ye [11] shall lose no blood while ye have the scabbard upon you, though ye have as many wounds upon you as ye may have.'

So after, for great trust, Arthur betook the scabbard unto Morgan le Fay his sister, and she loved another knight better than her husband King Uriens or King Arthur. And she would have had Arthur her brother slain, and therefore she let make another scabbard for Excalibur like it by enchantment, and gave the scabbard Excalibur to her love; and the knight's name was called Accolon, that after had near slain King Arthur. But after this Merlin told unto King Arthur of the prophecy that there should be a great battle beside Salisbury, and Mordred his own son should be against him.

So within a day or two King Arthur was somewhat sick, and he let [12] pitch his pavilion in a meadow, and there he laid him down on a pallet to sleep, but he might have no rest. Right so he heard a great noise of a horse, and therewith the King looked out at the porch door of the pavilion and saw a knight coming even by him making great dole.

'Abide, fair sir,' said Arthur, 'and tell me wherefore thou makest this sorrow.'

'Ye may little amend me,' said the knight, and so passed forth to the castle of Meliot.

And anon after that came Balin, and when he saw King Arthur he alit off his horse and came to the King on foot, and saluted him.

wite] blame

'By my head,' said Arthur, 'ye be welcome. Sir, right now came rid-ing this way a knight making great moan, and for what cause I cannot tell; wherefore I would desire of you of your courtesy and of your gentle-ness to fetch again that knight either by force or by his good will.'

'I shall do more for your lordship than that,' said Balin, 'or else I will grieve him.'

So Balin rode more than apace and found the knight with a damosel under a forest, and said, 'Sir knight, ye must come with me unto King Arthur, for to tell him of your sorrow.'

'That will I not,' said the knight, 'for it will harm me greatly, and do you no avail.'

'Sir,' said Balin, 'I pray you make you ready, for ye must go with me, or else I must fight with you and bring you by force; and that were me loath to do.'

'Will ye be my warrant,' said the knight, 'and I go with you?'

'Yea,' said Balin, 'or else by the faith of my body I will die therefore.'

And so he made him ready to go with Balin, and left the damosel still. And as they were even before Arthur's pavilion, there came one invisible, and smote the knight that went with Balin throughout the body with a spear.

'Alas,' said the knight, 'I am slain under your conduct with a knight called Garlonde. Therefore take my horse, that is better than yours, and ride to the damosel, and follow the quest that I was in as she will lead you, and revenge my death when ye may.'

'That shall I do,' said Balin, 'and that I make avow to God and knighthood.' And so he departed from King Arthur with great sorrow.

So King Arthur let bury this knight richly, and made mention on his tomb how here was slain Berbeus and by whom the treachery was done, of the knight Garlonde. But ever the damosel bore the trun-cheon of the spear with her that Sir Harleus le Berbeus was slain withal.

[13]   So Balin and the damosel rode into the forest, and there met with a knight that had been hunting. And that knight asked Balin for what cause he made so great sorrow.

'Me list not to tell,' said Balin.

'Now,' said the knight, 'and I were armed as ye be, I would fight with you but if ye told me.'

---

gentleness°] nobility   more than apace] very fast

'That should little need,' said Balin, 'I am not afraid to tell you,' and so told him all the case how it was.

'Ah,' said the knight, 'is this all? Here I assure you by the faith of my body never to depart from you while my life lasteth.'

And so they went to their hostelry and armed them, and so rode forth with Balin. And as they came by a hermitage even by a church-yard, there came Garlonde invisible, and smote this knight, Perin de Mount Beliard, through the body with a glaive.

'Alas,' said the knight, 'I am slain by this traitor knight that rideth invisible.'

'Alas,' said Balin, 'this is not the first despite that he hath done me.'

And there the hermit and Balin buried the knight under a rich stone and a tomb royal; and on the morn they found letters of gold written, how that Sir Gawain shall revenge his father's death on King Pellinore.

And anon after this Balin and the damosel rode forth till they came to a castle, and anon Balin alit and went in. And as soon as he was within, the portcullis was let down at his back, and there fell many men about the damosel and would have slain her. When Balin saw that, he was sore grieved, for he might not help her. But then he went up into a tower, and leapt over the walls into the ditch, and hurt not himself; and anon he pulled out his sword and would have fought with them. And they all said nay, they would not fight with him, for they did nothing but the old custom of this castle; and told him how that their lady was sick and had lain many years, and she might not be whole but if she had blood in a silver dish full, of a clean maid and a king's daughter. 'And therefore the custom of this castle is that there shall no damosel pass this way but she shall bleed of her blood a silver dish full.'

'Well,' said Balin, 'she shall bleed as much as she may bleed, but I will not lose the life of her while my life lasteth.'

And so Balin made her to bleed by her good will, but her blood helped not the lady. And so she and he rested there all that night and had good cheer, and in the morning they passed on their ways. And as it telleth after in the Sangrail, that Sir Percival's sister helped that lady with her blood, whereof she was dead.

[Balin is told that he will find Garlonde at the court of King Pellam, and goes there to seek him.]

glaive] sword   clean] pure

So after this Balin asked a knight and said, 'Is there not a knight in this court which his name is Garlonde?'

'Yes, sir, yonder he goeth, the knight with the black face; for he is the marvellest knight that is now living. And he destroyeth many good knights, for he goeth invisible.'

'Well,' said Balin, 'is that he?' Then Balin advised him long, and thought, 'If I slay him here I shall not escape. And if I leave him now, peradventure I shall never meet with him again at such a steven, and much harm he will do and he live.'

And therewith this Garlonde espied that Balin visaged him, so he came and slapped him on the face with the back of his hand, and said, 'Knight, why beholdest thou me so, for shame? Eat thy meat and do that thou came for.'

'Thou sayest sooth,' said Balin, 'this is not the first spite that thou hast done me. And therefore I will do that I came for,' and rose him up fiercely and cleft his head to the shoulders. 'Now give me your truncheon,' said Balin to his lady, 'that he slew your knight with.' And anon she gave it him, for always she bore the truncheon with her. And therewith Balin smote him through the body and said openly, 'With that truncheon thou slewest a good knight, and now it sticketh in thy body.'*

[15]   So anon all the knights rose from the table for to set on Balin. And King Pellam himself arose up fiercely and said, 'Knight, why hast thou slain my brother? Thou shalt die therefore before thou depart.'

'Well,' said Balin, 'do it yourself.'

'Yes,' said King Pellam, 'there shall no man have ado with thee but I myself, for the love of my brother.'

Then King Pellam caught in his hand a grim weapon and smote eagerly at Balin, but he put his sword betwixt his head and the stroke, and therewith his sword brast asunder. And when Balin was weaponless he ran into a chamber for to seek a weapon, from chamber to chamber, and no weapon could he find; and always King Pellam followed after him. And at the last he entered into a chamber which was marvellously dight and rich, and a bed arrayed with cloth of gold, the richest that might be, and one lying therein. And thereby stood a table of clean gold; and upon the table stood a marvellous spear strangely wrought.

So when Balin saw the spear, he got it in his hand and turned to King

advised] gazed at   steven] appointed moment   brast] broke

Pellam, and felled him and smote him passingly sore with that spear, that King Pellam fell down in a swoon. And therewith the castle broke, roof and walls, and fell down to the earth. And Balin fell down and might not stir hand nor foot; and for the most part of that castle was dead through the dolorous stroke.

Right so lay King Pellam and Balin three days. Then Merlin came thither and took up Balin, and got him a good horse, for his was dead, and bade him void out of that country.

'Sir, I would have my damosel,' said Balin.

'Lo,' said Merlin, 'where she lieth dead.'

And King Pellam lay so many years sore wounded, and might never be whole till that Galahad the haut prince healed him in the quest of the Sangrail. For in that place was part of the blood of Our Lord Jesus Christ, which Joseph of Arimathea brought into this land,* and there himself lay in that rich bed. And that was the spear which Longius smote Our Lord with to the heart.* And King Pellam was nigh of Joseph's kin, and that was the most worshipful man alive in those days, and great pity it was of his hurt, for through that stroke it turned to great dole, tray, and tene.

Then departed Balin from Merlin, for he said, 'Never in this world we part nor meet no more.' So he rode forth through the fair countries and cities, and found the people dead, slain on every side. And all that ever were alive cried and said, 'Ah, Balin, thou hast done and caused great vengeance in these countries! For the dolorous stroke thou gave unto King Pellam, these three countries are destroyed. And doubt not but the vengeance will fall on thee at the last.'

But when Balin was past those countries he was passing fain.*

And within three days he came by a cross, and thereon were letters of [17]*
gold written, that said, 'It is not for no knight alone to ride towards this castle.'

Then saw he an old hoar gentleman coming toward him, that said, 'Balin le Savage, thou passest thy bounds to come this way, therefore turn again and it will avail thee.' And he vanished away anon.

And so he heard a horn blow as it had been the death of a beast. 'That blast', said Balin, 'is blown for me, for I am the prize; and yet am I not dead.'

---

void out of] leave   dole, tray, and tene] grief, pain, and suffering

Anon withal he saw a hundred ladies and many knights, that welcomed him with fair semblant and made him passing good cheer unto his sight, and led him into the castle, and there was dancing and minstrelsy and all manner of joy.

Then the chief lady of the castle said, 'Knight with the Two Swords, ye must have ado and joust with a knight hereby that keepeth an island, for there may no man pass this way, but he must joust or he pass.'

'That is an unhappy custom,' said Balin, 'that a knight may not pass this way but if he joust.'

'Ye shall not have ado but with one knight,' said the lady.

'Well,' said Balin, 'since I shall, thereto I am ready; but travelling men are oft weary, and their horses too. But though my horse be weary, my heart is not weary. I would be fain there my death should be.'

'Sir,' said a knight to Balin, 'me thinketh your shield is not good, I will lend you a bigger, thereof I pray you.'

And so he took the shield that was unknown and left his own, and so rode unto the island, and put him and his horse in a great boat. And when he came on the other side he met with a damosel, and she said, 'O knight Balin, why have ye left your own shield? Alas, ye have put yourself in great danger, for by your shield ye should have been known. It is great pity of you as ever was of knight, for of thy prowess and hardiness thou hast no fellow living.'

'Me repenteth', said Balin, 'that ever I came within this country; but I may not turn now again for shame, and what adventure shall fall to me, be it life or death, I will take the adventure that shall come to me.' And then he looked on his armour, and understood he was well armed, and therewith blessed him and mounted upon his horse.

[18]   Then before him he saw come riding out of a castle a knight, and his horse trapped all red, and himself in the same colour. When this knight in the red beheld Balin, him thought it should be his brother Balin because of his two swords, but because he knew not his shield he deemed it was not he.

And so they aventred their spears and came marvellously fast together, and they smote other in the shields, but their spears and their courses were so big that it bore down horse and man, that they lay both

semblant] outward show   I would be fain there my death should be] I would gladly be where my death is to happen   blessed him] crossed himself aventred] readied for combat

in a swoon. But Balin was bruised sore with the fall of his horse, for he was weary of travel. And Balan was the first that rose on foot and drew his sword, and went towards Balin, and he arose and went against him. But Balan smote Balin first, and he put up his shield and smote him through the shield and tamed his helm. Then Balin smote him again with that unhappy sword,* and well nigh had felled his brother Balan, and so they fought there together till their breaths failed.

Then Balin looked up to the castle and saw the towers stand full of ladies. So they went unto battle again, and wounded each other dolefully, and then they breathed ofttimes; and so went unto battle that all the place where they fought was blood red. And at that time there was none of them both but they had either smitten other seven great wounds, so that the least of them might have been the death of the mightiest giant in this world. Then they went to battle again so marvellously that doubt it was to hear of that battle for the great blood-shedding. And their hauberks unnailed, that naked they were on every side.

At last Balan, the younger brother, withdrew him a little and laid him down.

Then said Balin le Savage, 'What knight art thou? For or now I found never no knight that matched me.'

'My name is', said he, 'Balan, brother unto the good knight Balin.'

'Alas,' said Balin, 'that ever I should see this day,' and therewith he fell backward in a swoon.

Then Balan yede on all four feet and hands, and put off the helm of his brother, and might not know him by the visage, it was so full hewn and bled; but when he awoke he said, 'O Balan, my brother, thou hast slain me and I thee, wherefore all the wide world shall speak of us both.'

'Alas,' said Balan, 'that ever I saw this day, that through mishap I might not know you! For I espied well your two swords, but because ye had another shield I deemed ye had been another knight.'

'Alas,' said Balin, 'all that made an unhappy knight in the castle, for he caused me to leave my own shield to our both's destruction. And if I might live, I would destroy that castle for ill customs.'

'That were well done,' said Balan, 'for I had never grace to depart from them since that I came hither, for here it happed me to slay a

---

tamed] pierced   doubt] fearful thing   yede°] went

knight that kept this island, and since might I never depart; and no more should ye, brother, and ye might have slain me as ye have and escaped yourself with the life.'

Right so came the lady of the tower with four knights and six ladies and six yeomen unto them, and there she heard how they made their moan either to other, and said, 'We came both out of one womb, that is to say one mother's belly, and so shall we lie both in one pit.'

So Balan prayed the lady of her gentleness, for his true service, that she would bury them both in that same place where the battle was done. And she granted them with weeping it should be done richly in the best manner.

'Now, will ye send for a priest, that we may receive our sacrament, and receive the blessed body of Our Lord Jesus Christ?'

'Yea,' said the lady, 'it shall be done.' And so she sent for a priest and gave them their rites.

'Now,' said Balin, 'when we are buried in one tomb, and the mention made over us how two brethren slew each other, there will never good knight nor good man see our tomb but they will pray for our souls.'

And so all the ladies and gentlewomen wept for pity. Then anon Balan died, but Balin died not till the midnight after. And so were they buried both, and the lady let make a mention of Balan how he was there [19] slain by his brother's hands, but she knew not Balin's name.

In the morn came Merlin and let write Balin's name on the tomb with letters of gold, that 'Here lieth Balin le Savage that was the Knight with the Two Swords, and he that smote the dolorous stroke.'* Also Merlin let make by his subtlety that Balin's sword was put into a marble stone standing upright, as great as a mill stone, and it hoved always above the water and did many years. And so by adventure it swam down by the stream unto the city of Camelot, that is in English called Winchester.* And that same day Galahad the haut prince came with King Arthur; and so Galahad achieved the sword that was there in the marble stone hoving upon the water. And on Whitsunday he achieved the sword, as it is rehearsed in the Book of the Sangrail.

Soon after this was done Merlin came to King Arthur and told him of the dolorous stroke that Balin gave King Pellam, and how Balin and Balan fought together the marvellest battle that ever was heard of, and how they were buried both in one tomb.

---

and ye might have slain me] if you had been able to kill me   hoved] floated

'Alas,' said King Arthur, 'this is the greatest pity that ever I heard tell of two knights, for in this world I knew never such two knights.'

Thus endeth the tale of Balin and of Balan, two brethren that were born in Northumberland, that were two passing good knights as ever were in those days.

The Wedding of King Arthur

[III.1] In the beginning of Arthur, after he was chosen king by adventure and by grace, for the most part of the barons knew not he was Uther Pendragon's son but as Merlin made it openly known, but yet many kings and lords held him great war for that cause. But well Arthur overcame them all. The most part the days of his life he was ruled much by the counsel of Merlin. So it fell on a time King Arthur said unto Merlin, 'My barons will let me have no rest, but needs I must take a wife, and I would none take but by thy counsel and advice.'

'It is well done', said Merlin, 'that ye take a wife, for a man of your bounty and noblesse should not be without a wife. Now is there any,' said Merlin, 'that ye love more than another?'

'Yea,' said King Arthur, 'I love Guenivere the king's daughter of Lodegreance, of the land of Camelard, the which holdeth in his house the Table Round that ye told me he had it of my father Uther. And this damosel is the most valiant and fairest that I know living, or yet that ever I could find.'

'Certes,' said Merlin, 'as of her beauty and fairness she is one of the fairest alive. But and ye loved her not so well as ye do, I should find you a damosel of beauty and of goodness that should like you and please you, and your heart were not set. But there as man's heart is set, he will be loath to return.'

'That is truth,' said King Arthur.

But Merlin warned the King covertly that Guenivere was not wholesome for him to take to wife, for he warned him that Lancelot should love her, and she him again; and so he turned his tale to the adventures of the Sangrail. Then Merlin desired of the King for to have men with him that should enquire of Guenivere, and so the King granted him; and so Merlin went forth unto King Lodegreance of Camelard, and told him of the desire of the King that he would have unto his wife Guenivere his daughter.

'That is to me', said King Lodegreance, 'the best tidings that ever I heard, that so worthy a king of prowess and noblesse will wed my daughter. And as for my lands, I would give it him if I wist it might

---

but as Merlin] except as Merlin   noblesse] nobility

please him; but he hath lands enough, he needeth none. But I shall send him a gift shall please him much more, for I shall give him the Table Round, which Uther, his father, gave me. And when it is fully complete, there is a hundred knights and fifty; and as for a hundred good knights, I have myself; but I want fifty, for so many have been slain in my days.'

And so King Lodegreance delivered his daughter Guenivere unto Merlin, and the Table Round with the hundred knights; and so they rode freshly with great royalty, what by water and by land, till that they came nigh unto London.

When King Arthur heard of the coming of Queen Guenivere and the [2] hundred knights with the Table Round, then King Arthur made great joy for her coming, and that rich present, and said openly, 'This fair lady is passingly welcome to me, for I have loved her long, and therefore there is nothing so lief to me; and these knights with the Table Round please me more than right great riches.'

And in all haste the King let ordain for the marriage and the coronation in the most honourable wise that could be devised.

'Now, Merlin,' said King Arthur, 'go thou and espy me in all this land fifty knights which be of most prowess and worship.'

So within short time Merlin had found such knights that should fulfil twenty and eight knights, but no more would he find. Then the bishop of Canterbury was fetched, and he blessed the sieges with great royalty and devotion, and there set the eight and twenty knights in their sieges. And when this was done Merlin said, 'Fair sirs, you must all arise and come to King Arthur for to do him homage; he will the better be in will to maintain you.' And so they arose and did their homage. And when they were gone Merlin found in every siege letters of gold that told the knights' names that had sat there, but two sieges were void.

And so anon came in young Gawain and asked the King a gift.

'Ask,' said the King, 'and I shall grant you.'

'Sir, I ask that ye shall make me knight that same day that ye shall wed dame Guenivere.'

'I will do it with a good will,' said King Arthur, 'and do unto you all the worship that I may, for I must by reason ye are my nephew, my sister's son.'

freshly] gaily   lief] dear   sieges°] seats   the better be in will] be the
more willing

[3]   Forthwith there came a poor man into the court, and brought with him a fair young man of eighteen years of age riding upon a lean mare.* And the poor man asked all men that he met, 'Where shall I find King Arthur?'

'Yonder he is,' said the knights. 'Wilt thou anything with him?'

'Yea,' said the poor man, 'therefore I came hither.'

And as soon as he came before the King, he saluted him and said, 'King Arthur, the flower of all kings, I beseech Jesu save thee! Sir, it was told me that at this time of your marriage ye would give any man the gift that he would ask you, except it were unreasonable.'

'That is truth,' said the King, 'such cries I let make, and that will I hold, so it appair not my realm nor my estate.'

'Ye say well and graciously,' said the poor man. 'Sir, I ask nothing else but that ye will make my son knight.'

'It is a great thing thou askest of me,' said the King. 'What is thy name?' said the King to the poor man.

'Sir, my name is Aries the cowherd.'

'Whether cometh this of thee, or else of thy son?' said the King.

'Nay, sir,' said Aries, 'this desire cometh of my son and not of me. For I shall tell you, I have thirteen sons; and all they will fall to what labour I put them and will be right glad to do labour, but this child will not labour for nothing that my wife and I may do, but always he will be shooting or casting darts, and glad for to see battles and to behold knights. And always day and night he desireth of me to be made knight.'

'What is thy name?' said the King unto the young man.

'Sir, my name is Tor.'

Then the King beheld him fast, and saw he was passingly well-visaged and well made of his years.

'Well,' said King Arthur unto Aries the cowherd, 'go fetch all thy sons before me that I may see them.'

And so the poor man did, and all were shaped much like the poor man. But Tor was not like him neither in shape nor in countenance, for he was much more than any of them.

'Now,' said King Arthur unto the cowherd, 'where is the sword he shall be made knight withal?'

'It is here,' said Tor.

---

such cries I let make] I had such proclamations made   appair] damage

'Take it out of the sheath,' said the King, 'and require me to make you knight.'

Then Tor alit off his mare and pulled out his sword, kneeling, and requiring the King to make him knight, and that he made him knight of the Table Round.

'As for a knight, I will make you,' and therewith smote him in the neck with the sword. 'Be ye a good knight, and so I pray to God ye may be, and if ye be of prowess and worthiness ye shall be of the Table Round. Now, Merlin,' said Arthur, 'whether this Tor shall be a good man?'

'Yea, hardily, sir, he ought to be a good man, for he is come of good kindred as any alive, and of king's blood.'

'How so, sir?' said the King.

'I shall tell you,' said Merlin. 'This poor man, Aries the cowherd, is not his father, he is no sib to him; for King Pellinore is his father.'

'I suppose not,' said the cowherd.

'Well, fetch thy wife before me,' said Merlin, 'and she shall not say nay.'

Anon the wife was fetched forth, which was a fair housewife. And there she answered Merlin full womanly, and there she told the King and Merlin that when she was a maid and went to milk her kine, 'there met with me a stern knight, and half by force he had my maidenhood;* and at that time he begot my son Tor, and he took away from me my greyhound that I had that time with me, and said he would keep the greyhound for my love.'

'Ah,' said the cowherd, 'I weened it had not been thus, but I may believe it well, for he had never no tatches of me.'

Sir Tor said unto Merlin, 'Dishonour not my mother.'

'Sir,' said Merlin, 'it is more for your worship than hurt, for your father is a good knight and a king. And he may right well advance you and your mother both, for ye were begotten or ever she was wedded.'

'That is truth,' said the wife.

'It is the less grief unto me,' said the cowherd.

So on the morn King Pellinore came to the court of King Arthur. [4] And he had great joy of him, and told him of Sir Tor, how he was his son, and how he had made him knight at the request of the cowherd. When King Pellinore beheld Sir Tor, he pleased him much. So the

hardily] indeed   sib] blood relation   tatches] marks

King made Gawain knight; but Sir Tor was the first he made at that feast.

'What is the cause', said King Arthur, 'that there is two places void in the sieges?'

'Sir,' said Merlin, 'there shall no man sit in those places but they that shall be most of worship. But in the Siege Perilous there shall never man sit but one, and if there be any so hardy to do it he shall be destroyed. And he that shall sit therein shall have no fellow.'

And therewith Merlin took King Pellinore by the hand, and in that one hand next the two sieges and the Siege Perilous he said, in open audience, 'This is your place, for best are ye worthy to sit therein of any that here is.'

And thereat had Sir Gawain great envy and told Gaheris his brother, 'Yonder knight is put to great worship, which grieveth me sore, for he slew our father King Lot. Therefore I will slay him,' said Gawain, 'with a sword that was sent me that is passing trenchant.'

'Ye shall not so', said Gaheris, 'at this time, for as now I am but your squire; and when I am made knight I will be avenged on him. And therefore, brother, it is best to suffer till another time that we may have him out of court, for and we did so we shall trouble this high feast.'

'I will well,' said Gawain.

[5]   Then was this feast made ready, and the King was wedded at Camelot unto Dame Guenivere in the church of Saint Stephen's, with great solemnity.

Then as every man was set as his degree asked, Merlin went to all the knights of the Round Table and bade them sit still, 'that none of you remove, for ye shall see a strange and a marvellous adventure.'

Right so as they sat there came running in a white hart into the hall, and a white brachet next him, and thirty couple of black running hounds came after with a great cry; and the hart went about the Round Table, and as he went by the side boards the brachet ever bit him by the buttock and pulled out a piece, wherethrough the hart leapt a great leap and overthrew a knight that sat at the side board. And therewith the knight arose and took up the brachet, and so went forth out of the hall, and took his horse and rode his way with the brachet.

Right so came in a lady on a white palfrey, and cried aloud unto King

void in the sieges] empty among the seats   trenchant] sharp   brachet°]
hunting-dog   side boards] lower tables

Arthur and said, 'Sir, suffer me not to have this despite, for the brachet is mine that the knight hath led away.'

'I may not do therewith,' said the King.

So with this there came a knight riding all armed on a great horse and took the lady away with force with him, and ever she cried and made great dole. So when she was gone the King was glad, for she made such a noise.

'Nay,' said Merlin, 'ye may not leave it so, this adventure, so lightly, for these adventures must be brought to an end, or else it will be disworship to you and to your feast.'

'I will', said the King, 'that all be done by your advice.'

Then he let call Sir Gawain, for he must bring again the white hart.*

Here beginneth the first battle that ever Sir Gawain did after he was made knight

Sir Gawain rode more than apace, and Gaheris his brother rode with him in the stead of a squire to do him service. And they let slip at the hart three couple of greyhounds; and so they chased the hart into a castle, and in the chief place of the castle they slew the hart, and Sir Gawain and Gaheris followed after. Right so there came a knight out of a chamber with a sword drawn in his hand and slew two of the greyhounds even in the sight of Sir Gawain, and the remnant he chased with his sword out of the castle. And when he came again, he said, 'Ah, my white hart, me repents that thou art dead, for my sovereign lady gave thee to me, and evil have I kept thee; and thy death shall be evil bought and I live.' And anon he went into his chamber and armed him, and came out fiercely.

And there met he with Sir Gawain; and he said, 'Why have ye slain my hounds? I would that ye had wrought your anger upon me rather than upon a dumb beast.'

'Thou sayest truth,' said the knight, 'I have avenged me on thy hounds, and so I will on thee or thou go.'

Then Sir Gawain alit on foot and dressed his shield, and struck together mightily, and cleft their shields and stooned their helms and

[6]
[7]

I may not do therewith] I cannot do anything about that   evil bought] purchased for a bitter price   stooned] crushed

broke their hauberks that the blood thirled down to their feet. So at the last Sir Gawain smote so hard that the knight fell to the earth; and then he cried mercy and yielded him, and besought him as he was a gentle knight to save his life.

'Thou shalt die,' said Sir Gawain, 'for slaying of my hounds.'

'I will make amends,' said the knight, 'to my power.'

Bur Sir Gawain would no mercy have, but unlaced his helm to have struck off his head. Right so came his lady out of a chamber and fell over him, and so he smote off her head by misfortune.

'Alas,' said Gaheris, 'that is foul and shamefully done, for that shame shall never from you! Also ye should give mercy unto them that ask mercy, for a knight without mercy is without worship.'

So Sir Gawain was sore astoned of the death of this fair lady that he wist not what he did, and said unto the knight, 'Arise, I will give thee mercy.'

'Nay, nay,' said the knight, 'I take no force of thy mercy now, for thou hast slain with villainy my love and my lady that I loved best of all earthly thing.'

'Me sore repenteth it,' said Sir Gawain, 'for I meant the stroke unto thee. But now thou shalt go unto King Arthur and tell him of thy adventure, and how thou art overcome by the knight that went in the quest of the white hart.'

'I take no force,' said the knight, 'whether I live or die.' But at the last for fear of death he swore to go unto King Arthur.

[8]   Right so Sir Gawain rode forth unto Camelot. And anon as he was come, Merlin did make King Arthur that Sir Gáwain was sworn to tell of his adventure, and how he slew the lady, and how he would give no mercy unto the knight, wherethrough the lady was slain. Then the King and the Queen were greatly displeased with Sir Gawain for the slaying of the lady; and there by ordinance of the Queen there was set an inquest of ladies upon Sir Gawain, and they judged him for ever while he lived to be with all ladies and to fight for their quarrels, and ever that he should be courteous, and never to refuse mercy to him that asketh mercy. Thus was Gawain sworn upon the four Evangelists that he should never be against lady nor gentlewoman, but if he fight for a lady and his adversary fighteth for another.

thirled] flowed   take no force of] care nothing for   did make King Arthur] had King Arthur order

And thus endeth the adventure of Sir Gawain that he did at the marriage of Arthur.*

Then the King established all the knights, and gave them riches and [15] lands; and charged them never to do outrage nor murder, and always to flee treason, and to give mercy unto him that asketh mercy, upon pain of forfeiture of their worship and lordship of King Arthur for evermore; and always to do ladies, damosels, and gentlewomen and widows succour; strengthen them in their rights, and never to enforce them, upon pain of death. Also, that no man take no battles in a wrongful quarrel for no love, nor for no worldly goods. So unto this were all the knights sworn of the Table Round, both old and young.* And every year so were they sworn at the high feast of Pentecost.

Explicit the Wedding of King Arthur

enforce] rape

Of Nenive and Morgan le Fay

[IV.1] Then it befell that Merlin fell in a dotage on the damosel that King Pellinore brought to court, and she was one of the damosels of the Lady of the Lake, that hight Nenive. But Merlin would not let her have no rest, but always he would be with her. And ever she made Merlin good cheer till she had learned of him all manner of thing that she desired; and he was besotted upon her, that he might not be from her.

So on a time he told to King Arthur that he should not endure long, but for all his crafts he should be put into the earth quick. And so he told the King many things that should befall, but always he warned the King to keep well his sword and the scabbard, for he told him how the sword and the scabbard should be stolen by a woman from him, that he most trusted. Also he told King Arthur that he should miss him, 'And yet had ye liever than all your lands have me again.'

'Ah,' said the King, 'since ye know of your evil adventure, purvey for it, and put it away by your crafts, that misadventure.'

'Nay,' said Merlin, 'it will not be.'

He departed from the King; and within a while the damosel of the Lake departed, and Merlin went with her evermore wheresoever she yede, and oftentimes Merlin would have had her privily away by his subtle crafts. Then she made him to swear that he should never do no enchantment upon her if he would have his will, and so he swore. Then she and Merlin went over the sea unto the land of Benwick, there as King Ban was king that had great war against King Claudas.

And there Merlin spoke with King Ban's wife, a fair lady and a good, her name was Elaine; and there he saw young Lancelot. And there the queen made great sorrow for the mortal war that King Claudas made on her lord.

'Take no heaviness,' said Merlin, 'for this same child young Lancelot shall within these twenty years revenge you on King Claudas, that all Christendom shall speak of it; and this same child shall be the most man of worship of the world. And his first name is Galahad, that know I well,' said Merlin, 'and since ye have confirmed him Lancelot.'

quick] alive　　　Take no heaviness] do not grieve

'That is truth,' said the queen, 'his name was first Galahad. Ah, Merlin,' said the queen, 'shall I live to see my son such a man of prowess?'

'Yea, hardily, lady, on my peril ye shall see it, and live many winters after.'

Then soon after the lady and Merlin departed. And by ways he showed her many wonders, and so came into Cornwall. And always he lay about to have her maidenhood, and she was ever passing weary of him and would have been delivered of him, for she was afraid of him for cause he was a devil's son,* and she could not be shift of him by no mean. And so on a time Merlin did show her in a rock where as was a great wonder, and wrought by enchantment, that went under a great stone. So by her subtle working she made Merlin to go under that stone to let her wit of the marvels there, but she wrought so there for him that he came never out for all the craft he could do. And so she departed and left Merlin.

[There follows a brief war against five kings, in which Sir Kay, Sir Gawain, and Sir Griflet particularly distinguish themselves.]

And King Arthur called King Pellinore unto him and said, 'Ye under- [4] stand well that we have lost eight knights of the best of the Table Round, and by your advice we must choose eight knights of the best we may find in this court.'

'Sir,' said Pellinore, 'I shall counsel you after my conceit the best wise. There are in your court full noble knights both of old and young; and by my advice ye shall choose half of the old and half of the young.'

'Which be the old?' said King Arthur.

'Sir, me seemeth King Uriens that hath wedded your sister Morgan le Fay; and the King of the Lake; and Sir Hervis de Revel, a noble knight; and Sir Galagars, the fourth.'

'This is well devised,' said Arthur, 'and right so shall it be. Now, which are the four young knights?'

'Sir, the first is Sir Gawain, your nephew, that is as good a knight of his time as is any in this land. And the second as me seemeth best is Sir Griflet le Fils de Dieu, that is a good knight and full desirous in arms, and who may see him live he shall prove a good knight. And the

shift] rid   conceit] intelligence

third as me seemeth is well worthy to be one of the Table Round, Sir Kay the Seneschal, for many times he hath done full worshipfully; and now at your last battle he did full honourably for to undertake to slay two kings.'

'By my head,' said Arthur, 'ye say sooth: he is best worthy to be a knight of the Round Table of any that is rehearsed yet, and he had done no more prowess his life days.'

[5]   'Now,' said King Pellinore, 'choose you of two knights that I shall rehearse which is most worthy, of Sir Bagdemagus, and Sir Tor, my son. But for because he is my son I may not praise him, but else, and he were not my son, I durst say that of his age there is not in this land a better knight than he is, nor of better conditions, and loath to do any wrong, and loath to take any wrong.'

'By my head,' said Arthur, 'he is a passing good knight as any ye spoke of this day. That wot I well,' said the King, 'for I have seen him proved; but he saith but little, but he doth much more, for I know none in all this court, and he were as well born on his mother's side as he is on your side, that is like him of prowess and of might. And therefore I will have him at this time, and leave Sir Bagdemagus till another time.'

So when they were chosen by the assent of the barons, so were there found in their sieges every knight's name that here are rehearsed, and so were they set in their sieges; whereof Sir Bagdemagus was wonderly wroth that Sir Tor was advanced before him, and therefore suddenly he departed from the court and took his squire with him, and rode long in a forest.*

So, as Sir Bagdemagus rode to see many adventures, so it happed him to come to the rock there as the Lady of the Lake had put Merlin under the stone, and there he heard him make a great dole; wherefore Sir Bagdemagus would have helped him, and went unto the great stone, and it was so heavy that a hundred men might not lift it up. When Merlin wist that he was there, he bade him leave his labour, for all was in vain, for he might never be helped but by her that put him there. And so Bagdemagus departed and did many adventures, and proved after a full good knight, and came again to the court and was made knight of the Round Table.

So on the morn there befell new tidings and many other adventures.

[6]   Then it befell that Arthur and many of his knights rode on hunting into a great forest. And it happed King Arthur and King Uriens and

and he had done] even if he had done

Sir Accolon of Gaul followed a great hart, for they three were well horsed; and so they chased so fast that within a while they three were more than ten miles from their fellowship. And at the last they chased so sore that they slew their horses underneath them, and the horses were so free that they fell down dead. Then were they all three on foot, and ever they saw the hart before them passing weary and imbossed.

'What shall we do?' said King Arthur. 'We are hard bestead.'

'Let us go on foot,' said King Uriens, 'till we may meet with some lodging.'

Then were they ware of the hart that lay on a great water bank, and a brachet biting on his throat, and more other hounds came after. Then King Arthur blew the prize and dight the hart. Then the King looked about the world, and saw before him in a great water a little ship, all apparelled with silk down to the water; and the ship came right unto them and landed on the sands. Then Arthur went to the bank and looked in, and saw no earthly creature therein.

'Sirs,' said the King, 'come thence, and let us see what is in this ship.'

So at the last they went into the ship all three, and found it richly behung with cloth of silk. So by that time it was dark night, there suddenly was about them a hundred torches set upon all the ship-boards, and it gave great light. And therewith there came twelve fair damosels and saluted King Arthur on their knees, and called him by his name, and said he was right welcome, and such cheer as they had he should have of the best. Then the King thanked them fair. Therewith they led the King and his fellows into a fair chamber, and there was a cloth laid richly beseen of all that longed unto a table, and there were they served of all wines and meats that they could think of. But of that the King had great marvel, for he never fared better in his life as for one supper.

And so when they had supped at their leisure, King Arthur was led into a chamber—a richer beseen chamber saw he never none. And so was King Uriens served, and led into such another chamber; and Sir Accolon was led into the third chamber passing richly and well

---

so free] so eager to gallop   imbossed] taken cover   blew the prize and dight] blew his horn for the capture and killed   a cloth laid richly beseen . . . table] a richly decorated cloth laid with everything appropriate for a meal

beseen. And so they were laid in their beds easily, and anon they fell asleep and slept marvellously sore all the night.

And on the morn King Uriens was in Camelot abed in his wife's arms, Morgan le Fay. And when he woke he had great marvel how he came there, for on the even before he was two days' journey from Camelot. And when King Arthur awoke he found himself in a dark prison, hearing about him many complaints of woeful knights.

'What are ye that so complain?' said King Arthur.

[7]   'We be here twenty knights, prisoners, and some of us have lain here eight year, and some more and some less.'

'For what cause?' said Arthur.

'We shall tell you,' said the knights. 'This lord of this castle, his name is Sir Damas; and he is the falsest knight that liveth and full of treason, and a very coward as liveth. And he hath a younger brother, a good knight of prowess; his name is Sir Outlake. And this traitor Damas, the elder brother, will give him no part of his lands, but as Sir Outlake keepeth through prowess of his hands; and so he keepeth from him a full fair manor and a rich, and therein Sir Outlake dwelleth worshipfully, and is well beloved with all people. And this Sir Damas our master is as evil beloved, for he is without mercy, and he is a coward, and great war hath been betwixt them. But Outlake hath ever the better, and ever he proffereth Sir Damas to fight for the livelihood, body for body, but he will not of it; or else to find a knight to fight for him. Unto that Sir Damas hath granted, to find a knight, but he is so evil beloved and hated that there is no knight will fight for him. And when Damas saw this, that there was never a knight would fight for him, he hath daily lain await with many a knight with him, and taken all the knights in this country to see and espy their adventures; he hath taken them by force and brought them to his prison. And so he took us severally as we rode on our adventures; and many good knights have died in this prison for hunger, to the number of eighteen knights. And if any of us all that here is, or hath been, would have fought with his brother Outlake, he would have delivered us. But for because this Damas is so false and so full of treason we would never fight for him to die for it. And we be so meagre for hunger that uneath we may stand on our feet. God deliver you, for His great mercy!'

sore] heavily   but as] except for what   severally] one by one   uneath°]
scarcely

Anon withal there came a damosel unto Arthur, and asked him what cheer.

'I cannot say,' said Arthur.

'Sir,' said she, 'and ye will fight for my lord, ye shall be delivered out of prison, and else ye escape never with the life.'

'Now,' said Arthur, 'that is hard, yet had I liever to fight with a knight than to die in prison. With this,' said Arthur, 'I may be delivered and all these prisoners, I will do the battle.'

'Yes,' said the damosel.

'Then I am ready,' said Arthur, 'and I had horse and armour.'

'Ye shall lack none,' said the damosel.

'Me seemeth, damosel, I should have seen you in the court of Arthur.'

'Nay,' said the damosel, 'I came never there. I am the lord's daughter of this castle.' Yet was she false, for she was one of the damosels of Morgan le Fay.

Anon she went unto Sir Damas, and told him how he would do battle for him; and so he sent for Arthur. And when he came, he was well coloured and well made of his limbs, that all knights that saw him said it were pity that such a knight should die in prison. So Sir Damas and he were agreed that he should fight for him upon this covenant, that all the other knights should be delivered; and unto that was Sir Damas sworn unto Arthur, and also he to do the battle to the uttermost. And with that all the twenty knights were brought out of the dark prison into the hall and delivered, and so they all abode to see the battle.

Now turn we unto Accolon of Gaul, that when he awoke he found himself by a deep well's side, within half a foot, in great peril of death. And there came out of that fountain a pipe of silver, and out of that pipe ran water all on high in a stone of marble. When Sir Accolon saw this, he blessed him and said, 'Jesu save my lord King Arthur and King Uriens, for these damosels in this ship have betrayed us—they were fiends and no women, and if I may escape this misadventure I shall destroy them all that I may find of these false damosels that fare thus with their enchantments.'

And right with that there came a dwarf with a great mouth and a flat nose, and saluted Sir Accolon, and told him how he came from Queen

[8]

With this] on this condition

Morgan le Fay. 'And she greets you well, and biddeth you be of strong heart, for ye shall fight tomorrow with a knight at the hour of prime. And therefore she hath sent thee Excalibur, Arthur's sword, and the scabbard, and she biddeth you as ye love her that ye do that battle to the uttermost, without any mercy, like as ye promised her when ye spoke last together in private. And what damosel that bringeth her the knight's head, which ye shall fight withal, she will make her a queen.'

'Now I understand you,' said Accolon, 'I shall hold that I have promised her now I have the sword. Sir, when saw ye my lady Morgan le Fay?'

'Right late,' said the dwarf.

Then Accolon took him in his arms and said, 'Recommend me unto my lady the queen, and tell her all shall be done that I promised her, and else I will die for it. Now I suppose,' said Accolon, 'she hath made all these crafts and enchantment for this battle.'

'Sir, ye may well believe it,' said the dwarf.

Right so there came a knight and a lady with six squires, and saluted Accolon, and prayed him to arise, and come and rest him at his manor. And so Accolon mounted upon a void horse and went with the knight unto a fair manor by a priory; and there he had passing good cheer.

Then Sir Damas sent unto his brother Outlake, and bade make him ready by tomorrow at the hour of prime, and to be in the field to fight with a good knight, for he had found a knight that was ready to do battle at all points. When this word came to Sir Outlake he was passing heavy, for he was wounded a little before through both his thighs with a glaive, and he made great dole; but as he was, wounded, he would have taken the battle on hand.

So it happed at that time, by the means of Morgan le Fay, Accolon was lodged with Sir Outlake. And when he heard of that battle, and how Outlake was wounded, he said that he would fight for him, because that Morgan le Fay had sent him Excalibur and the sheath for to fight with the knight on the morn. This was the cause Sir Accolon took the battle upon him. Then Sir Outlake was passing glad, and thanked Sir Accolon with all his heart that he would do so much for him. And therewith Sir Outlake sent unto his brother Sir Damas that he had a knight ready that should fight with him in the field by the hour of prime.

void] unoccupied   glaive] sword

So on the morn Sir Arthur was armed and well horsed, and asked Sir Damas, 'When shall we to the field?'

'Sir,' said Sir Damas, 'ye shall hear Mass.'

And so Arthur heard a Mass; and when Mass was done there came a squire and asked Sir Damas if his knight were ready, 'for our knight is ready in the field.'

Then Sir Arthur mounted upon horseback; and there were all the knights and commons of that country, and so by all their advice there were chosen twelve good men of the country for to wait upon the two knights. And right as Arthur was on horseback there came a damosel from Morgan le Fay, and brought unto Sir Arthur a sword like unto Excalibur, and the scabbard, and said unto Arthur, 'She sends here your sword for great love.' And he thanked her, and weened it had been so; but she was false, for the sword and the scabbard was counterfeit, and brittle, and false.

Then they dressed them on two parts of the field, and let their horses run so fast that either smote other in the midst of the shield; and their spears held, that both horse and man went to the earth. And then they started up both, and pulled out their swords. [9]

The meanwhile that they were thus at the battle, came the Damosel of the Lake into the field, that put Merlin under the stone; and she came thither for the love of King Arthur; for she knew how Morgan le Fay had ordained, for Arthur should have been slain that day, and therefore she came to save his life.

And so they went eagerly to the battle, and gave many great strokes. But always Arthur's sword bit not like Accolon's sword; and for the most part, every stroke that Accolon gave, he wounded Sir Arthur sore, that it was marvel he stood, and always his blood fell from him fast. When Arthur beheld the ground so sore be-bled he was dismayed, and then he deemed treason that his sword was changed; for his sword bit not steel as it was wont to do, therefore he dread him sore to be dead, for ever him seemed that the sword in Accolon's hand was Excalibur, for at every stroke that Accolon struck he drew blood on Arthur.*

'Now, knight,' said Accolon unto Arthur, 'keep thee well from me!'

But Arthur answered not again, but gave him such a buffet on the helm that he made him to stoop nigh falling to the earth. Then Sir Accolon withdrew him a little, and came on with Excalibur on high, and smote Sir Arthur such a buffet that he fell nigh to the earth.

Then were they both wroth out of measure, and gave many sore strokes. But always Sir Arthur lost so much blood that it was marvel he stood on his feet, but he was so full of knighthood that he endured the pain. And Sir Accolon lost not a deal of blood; therefore he waxed passing light. And Sir Arthur was passing feeble, and weened verily to have died; but for all that he made countenance as he might well endure, and held Accolon as short as he might. But Accolon was so bold because of Excalibur that he waxed passing hardy. But all men that beheld them said they saw never knight fight so well as Arthur did, considering the blood that he bled. But all that people were sorry that these two brethren would not accord. So always they fought together as fierce knights.

And at the last King Arthur withdrew him a little for to rest him; and Sir Accolon called him to battle and said, 'It is no time for me to suffer thee to rest.' And therewith he came fiercely upon Arthur. But Arthur therewith was wroth for the blood that he had lost, and smote Accolon on high upon the helm so mightily that he made him nigh fall to the earth; and therewith Arthur's sword brast at the cross and fell on the grass among the blood, and the pommel and the sure handles he held in his hand. When King Arthur saw that, he was in great fear to die, but always he held up his shield and lost no ground, nor bated no cheer.

[10]   Then Sir Accolon began with words of treason, and said, 'Knight, thou art overcome and mayst not endure, and also thou art weaponless, and lost thou hast much of thy blood; and I am full loath to slay thee. Therefore yield thee to me recreant.'

'Nay,' said Sir Arthur, 'I may not so. For I promised by the faith of my body to do this battle to the uttermost while my life lasteth; and therefore I had liever to die with honour than to live with shame. And if it were possible for me to die a hundred times, I had liever to die so often than yield me to thee, for though I lack weapon, yet shall I lack no worship. And if thou slay me weaponless, that shall be thy shame.'

'Well,' said Accolon, 'as for that shame I will not spare. Now keep thee from me, for thou art but a dead man.'

And therewith Accolon gave him such a stroke that he fell nigh to the earth, and would have had Arthur to have cried him mercy. But

sure handles] hilt guards   nor bated no cheer] nor looked less fierce

Sir Arthur pressed unto Accolon with his shield, and gave him with the pommel in his hand such a buffet that he reeled three strides aback.

When the Damosel of the Lake beheld Arthur, how full of prowess his body was, and the false treason that was wrought for him to have had him slain, she had great pity that so good a knight and such a man of worship should so be destroyed. And at the next stroke, Sir Accolon struck at him such a stroke that by the damosel's enchantment the sword Excalibur fell out of Accolon's hand to the earth. And therewith Sir Arthur lightly leapt to it and got it in his hand, and forthwith he knew it, that it was his sword Excalibur.

'Ah,' said Arthur, 'thou hast been from me all too long, and much damage hast thou done me;' and therewith he espied the scabbard by his side, and suddenly he started to him and pulled the scabbard from him, and threw it from him as far as he might throw it.

'Ah, sir knight,' said King Arthur, 'this day hast thou done me great damage with this sword. Now are ye come unto your death, for I shall not warrant you but ye shall be as well rewarded with this sword or ever we depart as ye have rewarded me, for much pain have ye made me to endure and much blood have I lost.'

And therewith Sir Arthur rushed on him with all his might and pulled him to the earth, and then rased off his helm and gave him such a buffet on his head that the blood came out at his ears, nose, and mouth.

'Now will I slay thee,' said Arthur.

'Slay me ye may well,' said Sir Accolon, 'and it please you, for ye are the best knight that ever I found, and I see well that God is with you. But for I promised', said Accolon, 'to do this battle to the uttermost and never to be recreant while I lived, therefore shall I never yield me with my mouth, but God do with my body what He will.'

Then Sir Arthur remembered him, and thought he should have seen this knight.

'Now tell me,' said Arthur, 'or I will slay thee, of what country ye be, and of what court.'

'Sir knight,' said Sir Accolon, 'I am of the royal court of King Arthur, and my name is Accolon of Gaul.'

Then was Arthur more dismayed than he was beforehand, for then he remembered him of his sister Morgan le Fay, and of the enchantment of the ship.

'Ah, sir knight, I pray you, who gave you this sword, and by whom ye had it?'

[11]   Then Sir Accolon bethought him, and said, 'Woe worth this sword, for by it I have gotten my death!'

'It may well be,' said the King.

'Now, sir,' said Accolon, 'I will tell you. This sword hath been in my keeping the most part of this twelvemonth; and Morgan le Fay, King Uriens' wife, sent it me yesterday by a dwarf, to the intent to slay King Arthur, her brother—for ye shall understand that King Arthur is the man in the world that she hateth most, because he is most of worship and of prowess of any of her blood. Also she loveth me out of measure as paramour, and I her again; and if she might bring it about to slay Arthur by her crafts, she would slay her husband King Uriens lightly. And then had she devised to have me king in this land, and so to reign, and she to be my queen. But that is now done,' said Accolon, 'for I am sure of my death.'

'Well,' said King Arthur, 'I feel by you ye would have been king of this land; yet it had been great damage to have destroyed your lord,' said Arthur.

'It is truth,' said Accolon, 'but now I have told you the truth; wherefore I pray you tell me of whence ye are, and of what court.'

'Ah, Accolon,' said King Arthur, 'now I let thee wit that I am King Arthur that thou hast done great damage to.'

When Accolon heard that, he cried aloud, 'Fair sweet lord, have mercy on me, for I knew you not.'

'Ah, Sir Accolon,' said King Arthur, 'mercy thou shalt have, because I feel by thy words at this time thou knewest me not. But I feel by thy words that thou hast agreed to the death of my person, and therefore thou art a traitor. But I wite thee the less, for my sister Morgan le Fay by her false crafts made thee to agree to her false lusts. But I shall be sore avenged upon her, that all Christendom shall speak of it. God knoweth I have honoured her and worshipped her more than all my kin, and more have I trusted her than my wife and all my kin after.'

Then King Arthur called the keepers of the field and said, 'Sirs, cometh hither, for here are we two knights that have fought unto great damage unto us both, and likely each of us to have slain other; and had any of us known other, here had been no battle, nor no stroke stricken.'

Then all aloud cried Accolon unto all the knights and men that were there, and said, 'Ah, lords, this knight that I have fought with is the

wite] blame

most man of prowess and of worship in the world, for it is himself King Arthur, our all liege lord, and with mishap and misadventure have I done this battle with the lord and king that I am withheld with.'

Then all the people fell down on their knees and cried King Arthur [12] mercy.

'Mercy shall ye have,' said Arthur. 'Here may ye see what sudden adventures befall often of errant knights, how that I have fought with a knight of my own unto my great damage and his both. But sirs, because I am sore hurt, and he both, and I had great need of a little rest, ye shall understand this shall be the opinion betwixt you two brethren. As to thee, Sir Damas, for whom I have been champion and won the field of this knight, yet will I judge, because ye, Sir Damas, are called an orgulous knight and full of villainy, and not worthy of prowess of your deeds. Therefore will I that ye give unto your brother all the whole manor with the appurtenance, under this form: that Sir Outlake hold the manor of you, and yearly to give you a palfrey to ride upon, for that will become you better to ride on than upon a courser.* Also I charge thee, Sir Damas, upon pain of death, that thou never distress no knights errant that ride on their adventure; and also that thou restore these twenty knights that thou hast kept long prisoners, of all their harms, that they be content. For and any of them come to my court and complain on thee, by my head thou shalt die therefor.

'Also, Sir Outlake, as to you, because ye are named a good knight and full of prowess, and true and gentle in all your deeds, this shall be your charge I will give you: that in all goodly haste ye come unto me and my court. And ye shall be a knight of mine; and if your deeds be thereafter, I shall so prefer you, by the grace of God, that ye shall in short time be in ease as for to live as worshipfully as your brother Damas.'

'God thank your largeness of your great goodness and of your bounty! I shall be from henceforward in all times at your commandment. For,' said Sir Outlake, 'as God would, I was hurt but late with an adventurous knight through both the thighs, and else had I done this battle with you.'

'God would', said Sir Arthur, 'it had been so, for then had not I been hurt as I am. I shall tell you the cause why: for I had not been hurt as I am, had not been my own sword that was stolen from me by treason;

withheld with] retained by   opinion] judgement   orgulous] proud   restore . . . of all their harms] i.e. make satisfactory reparation for their injury
thereafter] corresponding   largeness] generosity

and this battle was ordained aforehand to have slain me, and so it was brought to the purpose by false treason and by enchantment.'

'Alas,' said Sir Outlake, 'that is great pity that ever so noble a man as ye are of your deeds and prowess, that any man or woman might find in their hearts to work any treason against you.'

'I shall reward them,' said Arthur. 'Now tell me,' said Arthur, 'how far am I from Camelot?'

'Sir, ye are two days' journey.'

'I would be at some place of worship,' said Sir Arthur, 'that I might rest me.'

'Sir,' said Outlake, 'hereby is a rich abbey of your elders' foundation, of nuns, but three miles hence.'

So the King took his leave of all the people, and mounted upon horseback, and Sir Accolon with him. And when they were come to the abbey, he let fetch leeches and searched his wounds and Sir Accolon's both. But Sir Accolon died within four days, for he had bled so much blood that he might not live, but King Arthur was well recovered. So when Accolon was dead he let send him in a horse-bier with six knights unto Camelot, and bade, 'Bear him unto my sister Morgan le Fay, and say that I send her him as a present. And tell her I have my sword Excalibur and the scabbard.'

So they departed with the body.

[13] The meanwhile Morgan le Fay had weened King Arthur had been dead. So on a day she espied King Uriens lay asleep on his bed, then she called unto her a maiden of her counsel and said, 'Go fetch me my lord's sword, for I saw never better time to slay him than now.'

'Ah, madam,' said the damosel, 'and ye slay my lord ye can never escape.'

'Care thee not,' said Morgan, 'for now I see my time is best to do it; and therefore hie thee fast and fetch me the sword.'

Then the damosel departed and found Sir Uwain sleeping upon a bed in another chamber; so she went unto Sir Uwain and awaked him and bade him arise, 'and wait on my lady your mother, for she will slay the king your father sleeping on his bed, for I go to fetch his sword.'

'Well,' said Sir Uwain, 'go on your way, and let me deal.'

Anon the damosel brought the queen the sword with quaking hands; and lightly she took the sword and pulled it out, and went

let fetch leeches] had doctors fetched   let me deal] leave everything to me boldly unto the bed's side and awaited how and where she might slay him best. And as she heaved up the sword to smite, Sir Uwain leapt unto his mother and caught her by the hand and said, 'Ah, fiend, what wilt thou do? And thou were not my mother, with this sword I should smite off thy head. Ah', said Sir Uwain, 'men said that Merlin was begotten of a fiend, but I may say an earthly fiend bore me.'

'Ah, fair son Uwain, have mercy upon me! I was tempted with a fiend, wherefore I cry thee mercy. I will never more do so; and save my worship and discover me not.'

'On this covenant,' said Sir Uwain, 'I will forgive you, so ye will never be about to do such deeds.'

'Nay, son, and that I make you assurance.'

Then came tidings unto Morgan le Fay that Accolon was dead, and his body brought unto the church, and how King Arthur had his sword again. But when Queen Morgan wist that Accolon was dead, she was so sorrowful that nigh her heart tobrast; but because she would not it were known out, she kept her countenance, and made no semblant of dole. But well she wist, and she abode till her brother Arthur came thither, there should no gold go for her life. Then she went unto the Queen Guenivere, and asked her leave to ride into her country. [14]

'Ye may abide,' said the Queen, 'till your brother the king come home.'

'I may not, madam,' said Morgan le Fay, 'for I have such hasty tidings.'

'Well,' said the Queen, 'ye may depart when ye will.'

So early on the morn, or it was day, she took her horse and rode all that day and most part of the night, and on the morn by noon she came to the same abbey of nuns where lay King Arthur; and she wist that he was there. And anon she asked where he was; and they answered and said how he was laid him on his bed to sleep, for he had but little rest these three nights.

'Well,' said she, 'I charge you that none of you awake him till I do.'

And then she alit off her horse, and thought for to steal away Excalibur his sword. And she went straight unto his chamber, and no man durst disobey her commandment. And there she found Arthur asleep

awaited] looked   save my worship and discover me not] preserve my good name and don't inform on me   be about] set about   and she abode] if she were to stay [at court]

on his bed, and Excalibur in his right hand naked. When she saw that, she was passing heavy that she might not come by the sword without she had awaked him, and then she wist well she had been dead. So she took the scabbard and went her way on horseback.

When the King awoke and missed his scabbard, he was wroth, and so he asked who had been there; and they said his sister Queen Morgan le Fay had been there, and had put the scabbard under her mantle, 'and is gone.'

'Alas,' said Arthur, 'falsely have ye watched me.'

'Sir,' said they all, 'we durst not disobey your sister's command-ment.'

'Ah,' said the King, 'let fetch me the best horse that may be found, and bid Sir Outlake arm him in all haste and take another good horse and ride with me.'

So anon the King and Outlake were well armed, and rode after this lady. And so they came by a cross and found a cowherd, and they asked the poor man if there came any lady late riding that way.

'Sir,' said this poor man, 'right late came a lady riding this way with forty horses, and to yonder forest she rode.'

And so they followed fast, and within a while Arthur had a sight of Morgan le Fay; then he chased as fast as he might. When she espied him following her, she rode a great pace through the forest till she came to a plain. And when she saw she might not escape, she rode unto a lake thereby, and said, 'Whatsoever come of me, my brother shall not have this scabbard.' And then she let throw the scabbard in the deepest of the water. So it sank, for it was heavy of gold and precious stones.

Then she rode into a valley where many great stones were, and when she saw she must be overtaken, she shaped herself, horse and man, by enchantment unto great marble stones. And anon withal came Sir Arthur and Sir Outlake there as the King might not know his sister and her men, and one knight from another.

'Ah,' said the King, 'here may ye see the vengeance of God, and now am I sorry this misadventure is befallen.'

And then he looked for the scabbard, but it would not be found; so he returned to the abbey where she came from. So when Arthur was gone, they turned all their likeness as she and they were before, and said, 'Sirs, now may we go where we will.'*

had been dead] i.e. he would have killed her

And so she departed into the country of Gore, and there was she [15] richly received, and made her castles and towns strong, for always she dreaded much King Arthur.

When the King had well rested him at the abbey, he rode unto Camelot and found his queen and his barons right glad of his coming. And when they heard of his strange adventures, as it is before rehearsed, then all had marvel of the falsehood of Morgan le Fay; many knights wished her burnt.

'Well,' said the King, 'she is a kind sister! I shall so be avenged on her and I live, that all Christendom shall speak of it.'

So on the morn there came a damosel on message from Morgan le Fay to the King, and she brought with her the richest mantle that ever was seen in the court, for it was set all full of precious stones as one might stand by another, and therein were the richest stones that ever the King saw. And the damosel said, 'Your sister sendeth you this mantle and desireth that ye should take this gift of her; and what thing she hath offended, she will amend it at your own pleasure.'

When the King beheld this mantle it pleased him much; he said but little.

With that came the Damosel of the Lake unto the King and said, [16] 'Sir, I must speak with you in private.'

'Say on,' said the King, 'what ye will.'

'Sir,' said this damosel, 'put not upon you this mantle till ye have seen more; and in no wise let it not come on you nor on no knight of yours till ye command the bringer thereof to put it upon her.'

'Well,' said the King, 'it shall be as you counsel me.'

And then he said unto the damosel that came from his sister, 'Damosel, this mantle that ye have brought me, I will see it upon you.'

'Sir,' she said, 'it will not beseem me to wear a king's garment.'

'By my head,' said Arthur, 'ye shall wear it or it come on my back, or on any man's back that here is.'

And so the King made to put it upon her, and forthwith she fell down dead, and never spoke word after, and burnt to coals. Then was the King wonderly wroth, more than he was beforehand, and said unto King Uriens, 'My sister, your wife, is always about to betray me, and

---

as one might stand by another] set as closely together as possible   beseem me] be proper for me

well I wot either ye, or my nephew, your son, is of counsel with her to have me destroyed. But as for you,' said the King unto King Uriens, 'I deem not greatly that ye be of counsel, for Accolon confessed to me by his own mouth that she would have destroyed you as well as me, therefore I hold you excused. But as for your son, Sir Uwain, I hold him suspect; therefore I charge you, put him out of my court.'

So Sir Uwain was discharged.

And when Sir Gawain wist that, he made him ready to go with him, 'for whoso banisheth my cousin germain shall banish me.'

So they two departed, and rode into a great forest; and so they came unto an abbey of monks, and there were well lodged. But when the King wist that Sir Gawain was departed from the court, there was made great sorrow among all the estates.

'Now,' said Gaheris, Gawain's brother, 'we have lost two good knights for the love of one.'

[Gawain and Uwain decide to go separate ways.*]

[19/20]*   Now Sir Gawain held that way till that he came to a fair manor where dwelled an old knight and a good householder; and there Sir Gawain asked the knight if he knew of any adventures.

'I shall show you tomorrow', said the knight, 'marvellous adventures.'

So on the morn they rode into the forest of adventures till they came to a laund, and thereby they found a cross; and as they stood and hoved, there came by them the fairest knight and the seemliest man that ever they saw, but he made the greatest dole that ever man made. And then he was ware of Sir Gawain, and saluted him, and prayed to God to send him much worship.

'As for that,' said Sir Gawain, 'gramercy; also I pray to God send you honour and worship.'

'Ah,' said the knight, 'I may lay that aside, for sorrow and shame cometh unto me after worship.'

[20/21]   And therewith he passed unto the one side of the laund; and on the other side saw Sir Gawain ten knights that hoved and made them ready with their shields and with their spears against that one knight that

cousin germain] first cousin   all the estates] all ranks   laund] open space,
glade   hoved] lingered

came by Sir Gawain. Then this one knight fewtered a great spear, and one of the ten knights encountered with him; but this woeful knight smote him so hard that he fell over his horse's tail. So this dolorous knight served them all, that at the least way he smote down horse and man; and all he did with one spear. And so when they were all ten on foot, they went to that one knight, and he stood stone still and suffered them to pull him down off his horse, and bound him hand and foot and tied him under the horse's belly, and so led him with them.

'Ah, Jesu!' said Sir Gawain, 'this is a doleful sight, to see the yonder knight so to be treated! And it seemeth by the knight that he suffereth them to bind him so, for he maketh no resistance.'*

'Ah,' said the knight, 'that is the best knight I trow in the world, and the most man of prowess. And it is the greatest pity of him as of any knight living, for he hath been served so as he was this time more than ten times. And his name hight Sir Pelleas; and he loveth a great lady in this country, and her name is Ettard. And so when he loved her there was cried in this country a great jousts three days, and all the knights of this country were there and gentlewomen. And who that proved him the best knight should have a passing good sword and a circlet of gold; and that circlet, the knight should give it to the fairest lady that was at that jousts. And this knight Sir Pelleas was far the best of any that was there, and there were five hundred knights, but there was never man that ever Sir Pelleas met but he struck him down, or else from his horse. And every day of three days he struck down twenty knights, and therefore they gave him the prize. And forthwith he went there as the lady Ettard was, and gave her the circlet, and said openly she was the fairest lady that there was, and that would he prove upon any knight that would say nay.

'And so he chose her for his sovereign lady, and never to love other [21/22] but her. But she was so proud that she had scorn of him, and said that she would never love him though he would die for her; wherefore all ladies and gentlewomen had scorn of her that she was so proud. For there were fairer than she; and there was none that was there, but, and Sir Pelleas would have proffered them love, they would have showed him the same for his noble prowess. And so this knight promised Ettard to follow her into this country, and never to leave her till she loved him. And thus he is here the most part nigh her, and lodged by a

fewtered°] laid in rest ready for combat

priory; and every week she sends knights to fight with him. And when he hath put them to the worse, then will he suffer them wilfully to take him prisoner, because he would have a sight of this lady. And always she doth him great despite, for sometimes she maketh her knights to tie him to his horse's tail, and sometimes bind him under the horse's belly. Thus in the most shamefullest wise that she can think he is brought to her. And all she doth it for to cause him to leave this country, and to leave his loving; but all this cannot make him to leave, for and he would have fought on foot he might have had the better of the ten knights as well on foot as on horseback.'

'Alas,' said Sir Gawain, 'it is great pity of him! And after this night I will seek him tomorrow in this forest, to do him all the help I can.'

So on the morrow Sir Gawain took his leave of his host Sir Carados, and rode into the forest; and at the last he met with Sir Pelleas, making great moan out of measure. So each of them saluted other, and asked him why he made such sorrow. And as it above rehearseth, Sir Pelleas told Sir Gawain.

'But always I suffer her knights to fare so with me as ye saw yesterday, in trust at the last to win her love; for she knoweth well all her knights should not lightly win me and me list to fight with them to the uttermost. Wherefore and I loved her not so sore, I had liever die a hundred times, and I might die so oft, rather than I would suffer that despite; but I trust she will have pity upon me at the last. For love causeth many a good knight to suffer to have his intent, but alas, I am unfortunate.'

And therewith he made so great dole and sorrow that uneath he might hold him on his horse's back.

'Now,' said Sir Gawain, 'leave your mourning, and I shall promise you by the faith of my body to do all that lieth in my power to get you the love of your lady, and thereto I will plight you my troth.'

'Ah,' said Sir Pelleas, 'of what court are ye?'

'Sir, I am of the court of King Arthur and his sister's son, and King Lot of Orkney was my father, and my name is Sir Gawain.'

'And my name is Sir Pelleas, born in the Isles, and of many isles I am lord; and never loved I lady nor damosel till now. And, sir knight, since ye are so nigh cousin unto King Arthur, and are a king's son, therefore betray me not, but help me, for I may never come by her but by some good knight. For she is in a strong castle here fast by, within this four

and me list] if it pleased me   and I might die] if I could die

mile, and over all this country she is lady. And so I may never come to her presence but as I suffer her knights to take me; and but if I did so that I might have a sight of her, I had been dead long or this time, and yet fair word had I never none of her. But when I am brought before her she rebuketh me in the foulest manner; and then they take me, my horse, and harness, and put me out of the gates, and she will not suffer me to eat nor drink. And always I offer me to be her prisoner, but that she will not suffer me; for I would desire no more, what pains that ever I had, so that I might have a sight of her daily.'

'Well,' said Sir Gawain, 'all this shall I amend and ye will do as I shall devise. I will have your armour, and so will I ride unto her castle and tell her that I have slain you, and so shall I come within her to cause her to cherish me. And then shall I do my true part, that ye shall not fail to have the love of her.'

And therewith Sir Gawain plight his troth unto Sir Pelleas to be true [22/23] and faithful unto him; so each one plight their troth to other, and so they changed horses and harness. And Sir Gawain departed and came to the castle, where stood her pavilions without the gate. And as soon as Ettard had espied Sir Gawain she fled in toward the castle. But Sir Gawain spoke on high and bade her abide, for he was not Sir Pelleas: 'I am another knight that have slain Sir Pelleas.'

'Then do off your helm,' said the Lady Ettard, 'that I may see your visage.'

So when she saw that it was not Sir Pelleas, she made him alight and led him into her castle, and asked him faithfully whether he had slain Sir Pelleas; and he said yea. Then he told her his name was Sir Gawain, of the court of King Arthur, and his sister's son, and how he had slain Sir Pelleas.

'Truly,' said she, 'that is great pity, for he was a passing good knight of his body. But of all men alive I hated him most, for I could never be quit of him; and for ye have slain him I shall be your woman, and to do anything that may please you.' So she made Sir Gawain good cheer.

Then Sir Gawain said that that he loved a lady, and by no means she would love him.

'She is to blame,' said Ettard, 'and she will not love you; for ye that be so well born a man and such a man of prowess, there is no lady in this world too good for you.'

but if I did] if I did not act   harness] armour   come within her] get access
to her

'Will ye,' said Sir Gawain, 'promise me to do what that ye may do, by the faith of your body, to get me the love of my lady?'

'Yea, sir, and that I promise you, by my faith.'

'Now,' said Sir Gawain, 'it is yourself that I love so well, therefore hold your promise.'

'I may not choose,' said the Lady Ettard, 'but if I should be forsworn.' And so she granted him to fulfil all his desire.

So it was in the month of May, that she and Sir Gawain went out of the castle and supped in a pavilion; and there was made a bed. And there Sir Gawain and Ettard went to bed together; and in another pavilion she laid her damosels, and in the third pavilion she laid part of her knights, for then she had no dread of Sir Pelleas. And there Sir Gawain lay with her in the pavilion two days and two nights.

And on the third day on the morn early, Sir Pelleas armed him, for he had never slept since Sir Gawain departed from him; for Sir Gawain had promised him by the faith of his body to come to him unto his pavilion by the priory within the space of a day and a night. Then Sir Pelleas mounted upon horseback and came to the pavilions that stood without the castle, and found in the first pavilion three knights in three beds, and three squires lying at their feet. Then went he to the second pavilion and found four gentlewomen lying in four beds. And then he yode to the third pavilion and found Sir Gawain lying in the bed with his Lady Ettard, and either clipping other in arms. And when he saw that, his heart well nigh brast for sorrow, and said, 'Alas, that ever a knight should be found so false!'

And then he took his horse and might not abide no longer for pure sorrow. And when he had ridden nigh half a mile, he turned again and thought for to slay them both. And when he saw them lie so, both sleeping fast, then uneath he might hold him on horseback for sorrow, and said thus to himself: 'Though this knight be never so false, I will never slay him sleeping, for I will never destroy the high order of knighthood;' and therewith he departed again.

And or he had ridden half a mile he returned again and thought then to slay them both, making the greatest sorrow that ever man made. And when he came to the pavilions he tied his horse to a tree, and pulled out his sword naked in his hand, and went to them there as they lay; and yet he thought shame to slay them, and laid the naked

---

either clipping other] embracing each other

sword overthwart both their throats, and so took his horse and rode his way.

And when Sir Pelleas came to his pavilions he told his knights and his squires how he had sped, and said thus unto them: 'For your good and true service ye have done me I shall give you all my goods, for I will go unto my bed and never arise till I be dead. And when that I am dead, I charge you that ye take the heart out of my body and bear it her betwixt two silver dishes, and tell her how I saw her lie with that false knight Sir Gawain.'

Right so Sir Pelleas unarmed himself, and went unto his bed making marvellous dole and sorrow.

Then Sir Gawain and Ettard awoke of their sleep, and found the naked sword overthwart their throats. Then she knew it was the sword of Sir Pelleas.

'Alas,' she said, 'Sir Gawain, ye have betrayed Sir Pelleas and me! But had he been so uncourteous unto you as ye have been to him, ye had been a dead knight. But ye have deceived me, that all ladies and damosels may beware by you and me.'

And therewith Sir Gawain made him ready, and went into the forest.

So it happed the Damosel of the Lake, Nenive, met with a knight of Sir Pelleas', that went on his foot in this forest making great dole, and she asked him the cause. And so the woeful knight told her all how his master and lord was betrayed through a knight and a lady, and how 'he will never arise out of his bed till he be dead.'

'Bring me to him,' said she, 'anon, and I will warrant his life he shall not die for love. And she that hath caused him so to love, she shall be in as evil plight as he is or it be long, too; for it is no joy of such a proud lady that will not have no mercy of such a valiant knight.'

Anon that knight brought her unto him. And when she saw him lie on his bed, she thought she saw never so likely a knight; and therewith she threw an enchantment upon him, and he fell asleep. And then she rode unto the Lady Ettard, and charged that no man should awake him till she came again. So within two hours she brought the Lady Ettard thither, and both ladies found him asleep.

'Lo,' said the Damosel of the Lake, 'ye ought to be ashamed for to murder such a knight.' And therewith she threw such an enchantment

---

or it be long] before long

upon her that she loved him so sore that well nigh she was near out of her mind.

'Ah, Lord Jesu,' said this Lady Ettard, 'how is it befallen unto me that I love now that I have hated most of any man alive?'

'That is the righteous judgement of God,' said the damosel.

And then anon Sir Pelleas awaked and looked upon Ettard; and when he saw her he knew her, and then he hated her more than any woman alive, and said, 'Away, traitress, and come never in my sight.'

And when she heard him say so, she wept and made great sorrow out of mind.

[23/24]   'Sir knight Pelleas,' said the Damosel of the Lake, 'take your horse and come forthwith out of this country, and ye shall love a lady that will love you.'

'I will well,' said Sir Pelleas, 'for this lady Ettard hath done me great despite and shame.' And there he told her the beginning and ending, and how he had never purposed to have risen again till he had been dead. 'And now such grace God hath sent me, that I hate her as much as I have loved her.'

'Thank me therefor,' said the Lady of the Lake.

Anon Sir Pelleas armed him and took his horse, and commanded his men to bring after his pavilions and his stuff where the Lady of the Lake would assign them. So this Lady Ettard died for sorrow, and the Damosel of the Lake rejoiced Sir Pelleas, and loved together during their life.

[28/29]   So against the feast of Pentecost came the Damosel of the Lake and brought with her Sir Pelleas. And at the high feast there was great jousts; of all knights that were at that jousts, Sir Pelleas had the prize, and Sir Marhalt was named next. But Sir Pelleas was so strong that there might but few knights stand him a buffet with a spear. And at that next feast Sir Pelleas and Sir Marhalt were made knights of the Round Table; for there were two sieges void, for two knights were slain that twelvemonth. And great joy had King Arthur of Sir Pelleas and of Sir Marhalt. But Pelleas loved never after Sir Gawain. But as he spared him for the love of the King, oftentimes at jousts and at tournaments Sir Pelleas quit Sir Gawain, for so it rehearseth in the book of French.*

But as] although   quit] requited

Here endeth this tale, as the French book saith, from the marriage of King Uther unto King Arthur that reigned after him and did many battles. And this book endeth there as Sir Lancelot and Sir Tristram came to court. Who that will make any more, let him seek other books of King Arthur or of Sir Lancelot or Sir Tristram; for this was drawn by a knight prisoner, Sir Thomas Malory. That God send him good recovery, amen! *

THE NOBLE TALE BETWIXT KING ARTHUR
AND LUCIUS THE EMPEROR OF ROME

[v.1] It befell when King Arthur had wedded Queen Guenivere and fulfilled the Round Table, and so after his marvellous knights and he had vanquished the most part of his enemies, then soon after came Sir Lancelot du Lake unto the court, and Tristram came that time also. And then so it befell that the Emperor of Rome, Lucius, sent unto Arthur messengers commanding him for to pay his truage that his ancestors have paid before him. When King Arthur wist what they meant, he looked up with his grey eyes, and angered at the messengers passing sore. Then were these messengers afraid, and kneeled still and durst not arise, they were so afraid of his grim countenance.

Then one of the knights messengers spoke aloud and said, 'Crowned king, misdo no messengers, for we be come at his commandment as servitors should.'

Then spoke the conqueror, 'Thou recreant and coward knight, why fearest thou my countenance? There be in this hall, and they were sore aggrieved, thou durst not for a dukedom of land look in their faces.'

'Sir,' said one of the senators, 'so Christ me help, I was so afraid when I looked in thy face that my heart would not serve for to say my message. But sithen it is my will for to say my errand: thee greets well Lucius, the Emperor of Rome, and commands thee, upon pain that will fall, to send him the truage of this realm that thy father Uther Pendragon paid; or else he will bereave thee all thy realms that thou wieldest.'

'Thou sayest well,' said Arthur, 'but for all thy breme words I will not be too over-hasty; and therefore thou and thy fellows shall abide here seven days. And I shall call unto me my council of my most trusty knights and dukes and regent kings and earls and barons and of my most wise doctors; and when we have taken our advisement ye shall have your answer plainly, such as I shall abide by.'

Then the noble King commanded Sir Clegis to look that these men be settled and served with the best, that there be no dainties

truage] tribute   misdo] mistreat   sithen°] since   breme] fierce
wise doctors] learned men

spared upon them, that neither child nor horse faulted nothing—'For they are full royal people; and though they have grieved me and my court, yet we must remember on our worship.' So they were led into chambers, and served as richly of dainties that might be gotten. So the Romans had thereof great marvel.

Then the King unto counsel called his noble knights, and within a tower there they assembled, the most part of the knights of the Round Table. Then the King commanded them of their best counsel.

'Sir,' said Sir Cador of Cornwall, 'as for me, I am not heavy of this message, for we have been many days rested. Now the letters of Lucius the Emperor like me well, for now shall we have war and worship.'

'By Christ, I believe well,' said the King, 'Sir Cador, this message likes thee; but yet they may not be so answered, for their spiteous speech grieveth so my heart that truage to Rome I shall never pay. Therefore counsel me, my knights, for Christ's love of heaven. For this much have I found in the chronicles of this land, that Sir Beline and Sir Brine, of my blood elders, that born were in Britain, they have occupied the empireship eight score winters. And after, Constantine our kinsman conquered it, and dame Helena's son of England was Emperor of Rome;* and he recovered the cross that Christ died upon. And thus was the empire kept by my kind elders, and thus we have evidence enough to the empire of whole Rome.'*

So when the sevennight was at an end, the senators besought the King [2] to have an answer.

'It is well,' said the King. 'Now say ye to your emperor that I shall in all haste make me ready with my keen knights, and by the river of Rome hold my Round Table. And I will bring with me the best people of fifteen realms, and with them ride on the mountains in the mainlands, and mine down the walls of Milan the proud, and sith ride unto Rome with my royallest knights. Now ye have your answer, hie you that ye were hence, and from this place to the port where ye shall pass over; and I shall give you seven days to pass unto Sandwich. Now speed you, I counsel you, and spare not your horses; and look ye go by Watling

neither child nor horse faulted nothing] that nothing should be wanting to either page or horse   like me well] please me well   spiteous] contemptuous kind elders] natural ancestors   evidence enough] a sufficient claim   sith] afterwards   hie you that ye were hence] make haste to be gone

Street* and no way else. And where night falls on you, look ye there abide, be it fell or town, I take no keep; for it longeth not to no aliens for to ride on nights. And may any be found a spear-length out of the way, and that ye be in the water by the sevennight's end, there shall no gold under God pay for your ransom.'

'Sir,' said these senators, 'this is a hard conduct! We beseech you that we may pass safely.'

'Care ye not,' said the King. 'Your conduct is able.'

Thus they passed from Carlisle unto Sandwich-ward, that had but seven days for to pass through the land. And so Sir Cador brought them on their ways. But the senators spared for no horse, but hired them hackneys from town to town; and by the sun was set at the seven days' end they came unto Sandwich—so blithe were they never. And so the same night they took the water, and passed into Flanders, and after that over the great mountain that hight Gotthard, and so after through Lombardy and through Tuscany. And soon after they came to the Emperor Lucius, and there they showed him the letters of King Arthur, and how he was the gastfullest man that ever they looked on. When the Emperor Lucius had read the letters and understood them well of their credence, he fared as a man that were razed of his wit.

'I weened that Arthur would have obeyed you and served you unto your hands, for so he beseemed—or any king christened—for to obey any senator that is sent from my person.'

'Sir,' said the senators, 'let be such words, for that we have escaped alive, we may thank God ever; for we would not pass again to do that message for all your broad lands. And therefore, sirs, trust to our saws, ye shall find him your utter enemy. And seek ye him and ye list, for into these lands will he come, and that shall ye find within this half year; for he thinks to be emperor himself. For he saith ye have occupied the empire with great wrong, for all his true ancestors save his father Uther were emperors of Rome. And of all the sovereigns that we saw ever, he is the royallest king that liveth on earth; for we saw on New Year's Day at his Round Table nine kings, and the fairest fellowship of knights are with him that dures alive, and thereto of wisdom and of fair speech and

take no keep] do not care   and that ye be in the water] unless you are at sea
hard conduct] dangerous safe-conduct   able] sufficient   gastfullest]
most frightening   credence] message   served you unto your hands]
waited on you   beseemed] ought   saws] words   dures] exist

all royalty and riches they fail of none. Therefore, Sir, by my counsel, rear up your liege people and send kings and dukes to look unto your marches, and that the mountains of Almain be mightily kept.'

'By Easter,' said the Emperor, 'I cast me for to pass Almain, and so forth into France, and there bereave him his lands. I shall bring with me many giants of Genoa,* that one of them shall be worth a hundred of knights; and perilous passage shall be surely kept with my good knights.'*

And so Lucius came unto Cologne, and thereby besieges a castle; [3] and won it within a while, and feoffed it with Saracens. And thus Lucius within a while destroyed many fair countries that Arthur had won before of the mighty King Claudas. So this Lucius dispersed abroad his host, sixty miles large, and commanded them to meet with him in Normandy, in the country of Constantine.

'And at Barfleet, there ye me abide; for the Duchy of Britanny, I shall thoroughly destroy it.'*

Now leave we Sir Lucius; and speak we of King Arthur, that commanded all that were under his obedience after the utas of St Hilary that all should be assembled for to hold a parliament at York, within the walls. And there they concluded shortly, to arrest all the ships of this land and within fifteen days to be ready at Sandwich.

'Now, sirs,' said Arthur, 'I purpose me to pass many perilous ways, and to occupy the Empire that my elders before have claimed. Therefore I pray you, counsel me what may be best and most worship.'

The kings and knights gathered them unto counsel, and were condescended for to make two chieftains: that was Sir Baudwin of Britain, an ancient and an honourable knight, for to counsel and comfort Sir Cador's son of Cornwall, that was at that time called Sir Constantine, that after was king after Arthur's days.* And there in the presence of all the lords, the King resigned all the rule unto these two lords and Queen Guenivere.

And Sir Tristram at that time left with King Mark of Cornwall for love of La Belle Isode, wherefore Sir Lancelot was passing wroth.*

---

fail of none] are second to none   Almain] Germany   cast me] intend
feoffed] peopled   Barfleet] Barfleur   utas of St Hilary] i.e. 21 January:
the eighth day after St Hilary's Day   arrest] commandeer   condescended] agreed

Then Queen Guenivere made great sorrow that the King and all the lords should so be departed, and there she fell down in a swoon; and her ladies bore her to her chamber. Then the King commended them to God and left the Queen in Sir Constantine's and Sir Baudwin's hands, and all England to rule as themselves deemed best.

And when the King was on horseback he said, in hearing of all the lords, 'If that I die in this journey, here make I thee, Sir Constantine, my true heir, for thou art next of my kin save Sir Cador thy father; and therefore, if that I die, I will that ye be crowned king.'

Right so he and his knights sought towards Sandwich, where he found before him many galliard knights; for there were the most part of all the Round Table ready on those banks for to sail when the King liked. Then in all haste that might be, they shipped their horses and harness and all manner of ordinance that falleth for the war.*

Here followeth the dream of King Arthur

[4] As the King was in his cog and lay in his cabin, he fell in a slumbering; and dreamed how a dreadful dragon did drown much of his people, and came flying on wing out of the west parts.* And his head, him seemed, was enamelled with azure, and his shoulders shone as the gold, and his womb was like mail of a marvellous hue; and his tail was full of tatters, and his feet were flourished as it were fine sable, and his claws were like clean gold. And a hideous flame of fire there flowed out of his mouth, like as the land and water had flamed all on fire.

Then him seemed there came out of the Orient a grimly bear all black, in a cloud; and his paws were as big as a post. He was all wrinkled with lowering looks, and he was the foulest beast that ever any man saw. He roamed and roared so rudely that marvel it were to tell. Then the dreadful dragon dressed him against him and came in the wind like a falcon, and freshly strikes the bear. And again the grisly bear cuts with his grisly tusks, that his breast was bloody, and the blood railed all over the sea. Then the worm winds away and flies upon high, and came down with such a sough, and touched the bear on the ridge that from the top to the tail was ten foot large. And so he rends the bear and burns

sought] made their way   galliard] high-spirited   falleth] is required
cog] ship   womb] belly   dressed him] prepared for combat   railed]
flowed   worm] serpent   sough] blast of wind   ridge] line of the
spine

him up clean, that all fell in powder, both the flesh and the bones; and so it fluttered abroad on the sea.

Anon the King waked of his dream; and in all haste he sent for a philosopher, and charged him to tell what signified his dream.

'Sir,' said the philosopher, 'the dragon thou dreamest of betokens thy own person, that thus here sails with thy sure knights; and the colour of his wings is thy kingdoms that thou hast with thy knights won; and his tail that was all tattered signified your noble knights of the Round Table. And the bear that the dragon slew above in the clouds betokens some tyrant that torments thy people; or thou art likely to fight with some giant boldly in battle by thyself alone. Therefore of this dreadful dream dread thee but a little, and care not now, sir conqueror, but comfort thyself.'

Then within a while they had a sight of the banks of Normandy, and at the same tide the King arrived at Barfleet and found there many of his great lords, as he had himself commanded at Christmas before.

Then came there a husbandman out of the country and talked unto the King wonderful words, and said, 'Sir, here is a foul giant of Genoa that tormenteth thy people—more than five hundred, and many more of our children, that hath been his sustenance all these seven winters. Yet is the sot never ceased, but in the country of Constantine he hath killed all our knave children. And this night he hath cleight the Duchess of Brittany as she rode by a river with her rich knights, and led her unto yonder mountain to lie by her while her life lasteth. Many folks followed him, more than five hundred barons and bachelors and knights full noble; but ever she shrieked wonderly loud, that we shall never cure the sorrow of that lady. She was thy cousin's wife, Sir Howell the hend, a man that we call nigh of thy blood.* Now, as thou art our righteous king, rue on this lady and on thy liege people, and revenge us as a noble conqueror should.'

'Alas,' said King Arthur, 'this is a great mischief. I had liever than all the realms I wield unto my crown that I had been before that freke a furlong way for to have rescued that lady, and I would have done my pain. Now, fellow,' said Arthur, 'wouldst thou ken me where that carl dwells? I trow I shall treat with him before I further pass.'

[5]

---

the sot never ceased] the glutton never satisfied   knave] boy   cleight]
seized   bachelors] young knights   hend] noble   freke] creature
pain] utmost   ken] tell   carl] churl

'Sir conqueror,' said the good man, 'behold yonder two fires, for there thou shalt find that carl beyond the cold strands. And treasure out of number there mayst thou surely find—more treasure, as I suppose, than is in all France after.'

The King said, 'Good man, peace, and carp to me no more. Thy sooth saws have grieved sore my heart.' Then he turned towards his tents, and carped but little.

Then the King said unto Sir Kay in counsel, and to Sir Bedivere* the bold thus said he: 'Look that ye two after evensong be surely armed, and your best horses, for I will ride on pilgrimage privily, and none but we three. And when my lords are served, we will ride to St Michael's Mount, where marvels are showed.'

Anon Sir Arthur went to his wardrobe and cast on his armour, both his jesseraunt and his basinet with his broad shield. And so he busked him to his steed that on the bent hoved; then he started up aloft and hent the bridle, and stirred him stoutly. And soon he found his two knights full cleanly arrayed; and then they trotted on stilly together over a blithe country full of many merry birds. And when they came to the foreland, Arthur and they alit on foot.

'Now fasten,' said Arthur, 'our horses, that none nigh other; for I will seek this saint by myself alone, and speak with this master man that keeps this mountain.'

Then the King yode up to the crest of the crag, and then he comforted himself with the cold wind. And then he yode forth by two well-streams, and there he found two fires flaming full high; and at the one fire he found a careful widow wringing her hands, sitting on a grave that was new marked. Then Arthur saluted her, and she him again, and asked her why she sat sorrowing.

'Alas,' she said, 'careful knight, thou carps overloud. Yonder is a warlock will destroy us both: I hold thee unhappy! What dost thou on this mountain? Though here were fifty such, ye were too feeble for to match him all at once. Whereto bears thou armour? It may thee little avail, for he needs no other weapon but his bare fist. Here is a duchess dead, the fairest that lived. He hath murdered that mild without any

---

carp] speak   in counsel] privately   jesseraunt and his basinet] mailcoat
and helmet   busked] hastened   on the bent hoved] wandered over the
grass   hent] seized   stilly] quietly   that none nigh] so that none
can get near   careful] sorrowful   carps overloud] speak too loudly
mild] sweet lady

mercy: he forced her by filth of himself, and so after slit her unto the navel.'

'Dame,' said the King, 'I am come from the conqueror Sir Arthur, for to treat with that tyrant for his liege people.'

'Fie on such treaties!' she said then, 'for he sets nought by the King, nor by no man else. But and thou have brought Arthur's wife, Dame Guenivere, he will be more blither of her than thou hadst given him half France. And but if thou have brought her, press him not too nigh. Look what he hath done unto fifteen kings: he hath made him a coat full of precious stones, and the borders thereof is the beards of fifteen kings, and they were of the greatest blood that dured on earth. This present was sent him this last Christmas—they sent him in faith for saving of their people. And for Arthur's wife he lodges him here, for he hath more treasure than ever had Arthur or any of his elders. And now thou shalt find him at supper with six knave children, and there he hath made pickle and powder with many precious wines, and three fair maidens that turns the broach that bide to go to his bed, for they three shall be dead within four hours or the filth is fulfilled that his flesh asks.'

'Well,' said Arthur, 'I will fulfil my message, for all your grim words.'

'Then fare thou to yonder fire that flames so high, and there thou shalt find him surely, for sooth.'

Then he passed forth to the crest of the hill, and saw where he sat at his supper alone, gnawing on a limb of a large man; and there he baked his broad loins by the bright fire, and breeches-less he seemed. And three damsels turned three broaches, and thereon were twelve children but lately born; and they were broached in manner like birds. When the King beheld that sight, his heart was nigh bleeding for sorrow. Then he hailed him with angerful words:

'Now He that all wields, give thee sorrow, thief, where thou sittest! For thou art the foulest freke that ever was formed, and fiendly thou feedest thee, the devil have thy soul! And by what cause, thou carl, hast thou killed these Christian children? Thou hast made many martyrs by murdering in these lands; therefore thou shalt have thy meed, through Michael that owneth this mount. And also, why hast thou

dured] existed   at supper with six knave children] supping on six boys   broach] spit   or the filth is fulfilled . . . flesh asks] before his foul sexual require-ments are satisfied   baked] i.e. warmed   freke] creature   meed] reward

slain this fair duchess? Therefore dress thee, dog's son, for thou shalt die this day through the dint of my hands.'

Then the glutton glared, and grieved full foul. He had teeth like a greyhound; he was the foulest wight that ever man saw, and there was never such one formed on earth, for there was never devil in hell more horribly made, for he was from the head to the foot five fathom long and large. And therewith sturdily he started up on his legs, and caught a club in his hand all of clean iron. Then he swapped at the King with that kid weapon; he crushed down with the club the coronet down to the cold earth. The King covered himself with his shield and reached a box even-informed in the midst of his forehead, that the slipped blade reached unto the brain. Yet he shaped at Sir Arthur, but the King shunted a little and reached him a dint high upon the haunch, and there he swapped his genitals asunder. Then he roared and brayed, and yet angerly he struck, and failed of Sir Arthur and hit the earth, that he cut into the swarf a large sword-length and more. Then the King started up unto him and reached him a buffet and cut his belly asunder, that out went the gore that the grass and the ground was become all foul. Then he cast away the club and caught the King in his arms, and handled the King so hard that he crushed his ribs. Then the baleful maidens wrung their hands, and kneeled on the ground and called to Christ. With that the warlock writhed Arthur under, and so they weltered and tumbled over the crags and bushes, and either clenched other full fast in their arms. And other whiles King Arthur was above and other whiles under; and so they never left till they fell there as the flood marked. But ever in the weltering, Arthur hit him with a short dagger up to the hilts, and in his falling there brast of the giant's ribs three even at once; and by fortune they fell there as the two knights abode with their horses.

When Sir Kay saw the King and the giant so clenched together, 'Alas,' said Sir Kay, 'we are forfeit for ever! Yonder is our overlord, overfallen with a fiend.'

'It is not so,' said the King, 'but help me, Sir Kay, for this corsaint* have I clegged out of the yonder cloughs.'

dress thee] prepare yourself for combat   wight] creature   five fathom] i.e. thirty feet (ten metres)   clean] solid   swapped] struck   kid] notorious   reached a box even-informed] aimed a well-directed blow   slipped] moving   shaped] aimed a blow   shunted] dodged   swarf] earth   baleful] wretched   forfeit] lost   overfallen with] overwhelmed by   this corsaint . . . cloughs] I have seized this saint's body from the ravines up there

'In faith,' said Sir Bedivere, 'this is a foul carl,' and caught the corsaint out of the King's arms; and there he said, 'I have much wonder,
and Michael be of such making, that ever God would suffer him to
abide in Heaven! And if saints be such that serve Jesu, I will never seek
for none, by the faith of my body.'

The King then laughed at Bedivere's words and said, 'This saint
have I sought nigh unto my great danger. But strike off his head and
set it on a truncheon of a spear, and give it to thy servant that is
swift-horsed and bear it unto Sir Howell that is in hard bonds; and
bid him be merry, for his enemy is destroyed. And after, in Barfleet,
let brace it on a barbican, that all the commons of this country may
behold it.'*

Then the King and they started upon their horses; and so they rode
from thence there as they came from. And anon the clamour was huge
about all the country; and then they went with one voice before the
King, and thanked God and him that their enemy was destroyed.

'All thank ye God,' said Arthur, 'and no man else.'*

Then he commanded his cousin, Sir Howell, to make a church on
that same crag in the worship of St Michael.

[Arthur and his forces leave Barfleet and engage in various skir-
mishes with the Emperor's supporters, culminating in a great
battle against Lucius himself in which Lancelot, Gawain, Kay,
Cador, and many others notably distinguish themselves, Arthur
himself kills Lucius in hand-to-hand combat, and a hundred
thousand of their enemies are killed.]

Then the King rode straight there as the Emperor lay, and gart lift [8]
him up lordly with barons full bold. And the Sultan of Syria and the
King of Ethiopia, and two knights full noble of Egypt and of India,
with seventeen other kings were taken up also, and also sixty senators
of Rome that were honoured full noble men, and all the elders. The
King let embalm all these with many good gums, and sithen let lap
them in sixtyfold of sendal large, and then let lap them in lead that

let brace it on a barbican] have it set over a gate of the city   gart lift him up
lordly] caused him to be carried like a lord   let lap them in sixtyfold of sendal
large] had them wrapped sixty times round in broad silk

for chafing or changing they should never savour; and sithen let close them in chests full cleanly arrayed, and their banners above on their bodies and their shields turned upwards, that every man might know of what country they were.

So on the morn they found in the heath three senators of Rome. When they were brought to the King, he said these words:

'Now to save your lives I take no great force, with that ye will move on my message unto great Rome and present these corpses unto the proud Potentate, and after them my letters and my whole intent. And tell them in haste they shall see me, and I trow they will beware how they bourde with me and my knights.'

Then the Emperor himself was dressed in a chariot, and every two knights in a chariot sued after other, and the senators came after by couples in accord.

'Now say ye to the Potentate and all the lords after, that I send them the tribute that I owe to Rome; for this is the true tribute that I and mine elders have lost these ten score winters. And say them as me seems I have sent them the whole sum; and if they think it not enough, I shall amend it when that I come.'

So on the morrow these senators raked unto Rome; and within eighteen days they came to the Potentate and told him how they had brought the tax and the truage of ten score winters, both of England, Ireland, and of all the East lands. 'For King Arthur commands you, neither tribute nor tax ye never none ask, upon pain of your heads, but if your title be the truer than ever any of your elders owned. And for these causes we have fought in France, and there us is foul happed; for all is chopped to the death, both the better and the worse. Therefore I rede you, store you with stuff, for war is at hand.'*

[9] Now turn we to Arthur and his noble knights, that entered straight into Luxemburg; and so through Flanders and then to Lorraine he laught up all the lordships, and sithen he drew him into Almain and unto Lombardy the rich, and set laws in that land that endured long after; and so into Tuscany, and there destroyed the tyrants. And there

---

for chafing or changing] because of abrasion of the silk or corruption of the corpses   I take no great force . . . my message] I have little concern, unless you bear my message   bourde] jest   sued] followed   raked] went   us is foul happed] evil has befallen us   laught up] seized

were captains full keen that kept Arthur's coming, and at strait passages slew much of his people. And there they victualled and garnished many good towns.*

But soon after, on a Saturday, sought unto King Arthur all the senators [12] that were alive, and of the cunningest cardinals that dwelled in the court, and prayed him of peace and proffered him full large; and besought him as a sovereign, most governor under God, for to give them licence for six weeks large that they might be assembled all, and then in the city of Syon that is called Rome to crown him there kindly with chrismed hands, with sceptre for sooth as an emperor should.

'I assent me,' said the King, 'as ye have devised, and comely by Christmas to be crowned; hereafter to reign in my estate and to keep my Round Table, with the rents of Rome to rule as me likes; and then, as I am advised, to get me over the salt sea with good men of arms, to deem for His death that for us all on the Rood died.'*

When the senators had this answer, unto Rome they turned and made ready for his crowning in the most noble wise; and at the day assigned, as the romance tells,* he was crowned Emperor by the Pope's hands, with all the royalty in the world to wield for ever. There they sojourned that season till after the time and established all the lands from Rome unto France, and gave lands and rents unto knights that had them well deserved: there was none that complained on his part, rich nor poor.

Then he commanded Sir Lancelot and Sir Bors to take keep unto their fathers' lands that King Ban and King Bors wielded, and their fathers: 'Look that ye take seisin in all your broad lands and cause your liege men to know you as for their kind lord; and suffer never your sovereignty to be alledged with your subjects, nor the sovereignty of your person and lands. Also, the mighty King Claudas I give you for to part betwixt you even,* for to maintain your kindred that be noble knights, so that ye and they to the Round Table make your repair.'

Sir Lancelot and Sir Bors de Ganis thanked the King fair, and said their hearts and service should ever be his own.* Thus the King gave

---

kept] resisted   strait passages] narrow ways   cunningest] most learned
proffered him full large] made generous offers   kindly with chrismed hands]
fittingly, with hands anointed with holy oil   deem for] acknowledge
Rood] Cross   seisin] possession   alledged with] reduced by

many lands; there was none that would ask that might complain of his part, for of riches and wealth they had all at their will.

Then the knights and lords that longed to the King called a council upon a fair morn, and said, 'Sir King, we beseech thee for to hear us all. We are under your lordship well stuffed, blessed be God, of many things, and also we have wives wedded. We will beseech your good grace to release us to sport with our wives, for, worshipped be Christ, this journey is well overcome.'

'Ye say well,' said the King, 'for enough is as good as a feast; for to tempt God overmuch, I hold it not wisdom. And therefore make you all ready, and return we into England.'

Then there was trussing of harness with carriage full noble. And the King took his leave of the Holy Father the Pope, and patriarchs and cardinals and senators full rich, and left good governance in that noble city and all the countries of Rome for to ward and to keep on pain of death, that in no wise his commandment be broken. Thus he passeth through the countries of all parts; and so King Arthur passed over the sea unto Sandwich haven.

When Queen Guenivere heard of his coming, she met with him at London, and so did all other queens and noble ladies. For there was never a solemner meeting in one city together, for all manner of riches they brought with them at the full.

Here endeth the tale of the noble King Arthur that was emperor himself through the dignity of his hands; and here followeth after many noble tales of Sir Lancelot du Lake.

Explicit the noble tale betwixt King Arthur and Lucius the Emperor of Rome.

stuffed] provided   trussing of harness with carriage] packing up and transport
of war-gear

A NOBLE TALE OF
SIR LANCELOT DU LAKE

Soon after that King Arthur was come from Rome into England, then [VI.1] all the knights of the Table Round resorted unto the King and made many jousts and tournaments. And some there were, that were but knights, increased in arms and worship that passed all other of their fellows in prowess and noble deeds, and that was well proved on many. But in especial it was proved on Sir Lancelot du Lake, for in all tournaments, jousts, and deeds of arms, both for life and death, he passed all other knights; and at no time was he overcome but if it were by treason or enchantment. So this Sir Lancelot increased so marvellously in worship and honour: therefore he is the first knight that the French book maketh mention of after King Arthur came from Rome. Wherefore Queen Guenivere had him in great favour above all other knights, and so he loved the Queen again above all other ladies days of his life, and for her he did many deeds of arms, and saved her from the fire through his noble chivalry.

Thus Sir Lancelot rested him long with play and game; and then he thought to prove himself in strange adventures, and bade his nephew, Sir Lionel, for to make him ready, 'for we must go seek adventures.' So they mounted on their horses, armed at all rights, and rode into a deep forest and so into a plain.

So the weather was hot about noon, and Sir Lancelot had great lust to sleep. Then Sir Lionel espied a great apple tree that stood by a hedge, and said, 'Sir, yonder is a fair shadow; there may we rest us and our horses.'

'It is truth,' said Sir Lancelot, 'for these seven years I was not so sleepy as I am now.'

So there they alit and tied their horses unto sundry trees, and Sir Lancelot laid him down under this apple tree, and his helmet under his head. And Sir Lionel waked while he slept.

So Sir Lancelot slept passing fast; and in the meanwhile came there three knights riding, as fast fleeing as they might ride, and there followed them three but one knight. And when Sir Lionel saw him, he thought he saw never so great a knight, nor so well-faring a man and

well apparelled unto all rights. So within a while this strong knight had
overtaken one of the three knights, and there he smote him to the cold
earth that he lay still. And then he rode unto the second knight, and
smote him so that man and horse fell down; and so straight unto the
third knight, and smote him behind his horse's arse a spear-length.
And then he alit down and reined his horse on the bridle, and bound all
three knights fast with the reins of their own bridles.

When Sir Lionel had seen him do thus, he thought to assay him, and
made him ready, and privily he took his horse, and thought not for to
awake Sir Lancelot; and so mounted upon his horse and overtook the
strong knight. He bade him turn, and so he turned and smote Sir
Lionel so hard that horse and man he bore to the earth; and so he alit
down and bound him fast and threw him overthwart his own horse as
he had served the other three, and so rode with them till he came to his
own castle. Then he unarmed them and beat them with thorns all
naked, and after put them in deep prison where were many more
knights that made great dole.

[2] So when Sir Ector de Maris wist that Sir Lancelot was passed out of
the court to seek adventures, he was wroth with himself and made him
ready to seek Sir Lancelot. And as he had ridden long in a great forest,
he met with a man was like a forester.

'Fair fellow,' said Sir Ector, 'dost thou know this country, or any
adventures that be nigh hand?'

'Sir,' said the forester, 'this country know I well. And hereby within
this mile is a strong manor, and well dyked; and by that manor, on the
left hand there is a fair ford for horses to drink of, and over that ford
there grows a fair tree, and thereon hangeth many fair shields that
good knights sometime wielded, and at the body of the tree hangs a
basin of copper and latten. And strike upon that basin with the butt of
thy spear three times, and soon after thou shalt hear new tidings; and
else hast thou the fairest grace that ever had knight this many years that
passed through this forest.'

'Gramercy,' said Sir Ector, and departed and came unto this tree,
and saw many fair shields. And among them all he saw his brother's
shield, Sir Lionel, and many more that he knew that were of his fellows
of the Round Table, the which grieved his heart, and promised to

dyked] moated   latten] brass

revenge his brother. Then anon Sir Ector beat on the basin as he were
wood, and then he gave his horse drink at the ford. And there came a
knight behind him and bade him come out of the water and make him
ready. Sir Ector turned him shortly, and in fewter cast his spear, and
smote the other knight a great buffet that his horse turned twice about.

'That was well done,' said the strong knight, 'and knightly thou hast
struck me!' And therewith he rushed his horse on Sir Ector and caught
him under his right arm and bore him clean out of the saddle; and so
rode with him away into his castle and threw him down in the middle
of the floor.

Then this said Tarquin said unto Sir Ector, 'For thou hast done this
day more unto me than any knight did these twelve years, now will I
grant thee thy life so thou wilt be sworn to be my true prisoner.'

'Nay,' said Sir Ector, 'that will I never promise thee, but that I will
do my advantage.'

'That me repents,' said Sir Tarquin. Then he gan unarm him, and
beat him with thorns all naked, and sithen put him down into a deep
dungeon; and there he knew many of his fellows. But when Sir Ector
saw Sir Lionel, then made he great sorrow.

'Alas, brother,' said Sir Ector, 'how may this be, and where is my
brother, Sir Lancelot?'

'Fair brother, I left him asleep when that I from him yode, under an
apple tree; and what is become of him I cannot tell you.'

'Alas,' said the prisoners, 'but if Sir Lancelot help us we shall never
be delivered, for we know now no knight that is able to match with our
master Tarquin.'

Now leave we these knights prisoners, and speak we of Sir Lancelot du   [3]
Lake that lieth under the apple tree sleeping about the noon. So there
came by him four queens of great estate; and, for the heat should not
nigh them, there rode four knights about them and bore a cloth of
green silk on four spears betwixt them and the sun. And the queens
rode on four white mules. Thus as they rode they heard a great horse
beside them grimly neigh. Then they looked and were ware of a sleeping knight lay all armed under an apple tree. And anon as they looked
on his face, they knew well it was Sir Lancelot, and began to strive for
that knight; and each of them said they would have him to her love.

in fewter cast] lowered for combat   do my advantage] seek my own good
but if Sir Lancelot] unless Sir Lancelot

'We shall not strive,' said Morgan le Fay, that was King Arthur's sister. 'I shall put an enchantment upon him that he shall not awake of all
these seven hours, and then I will lead him away unto my castle. And
when he is surely within my hold, I shall take the enchantment from
him, and then let him choose which of us he will have unto paramour.'

So this enchantment was cast upon Sir Lancelot, and then they laid
him upon his shield and bore him so on horseback betwixt two knights,
and brought him unto the Castle Chariot; and there they laid him in a
chamber cold, and at night they sent unto him a fair damosel with his
supper ready dight—by that, the enchantment was past. And when
she came she saluted him, and asked him what cheer.

'I cannot say, fair damosel,' said Sir Lancelot, 'for I wot not how I
came into this castle but it be by enchantment.'

'Sir,' said she, 'ye must make good cheer, and if ye be such a knight
as is said ye be, I shall tell you more to-morrow by prime of the day.'

'Gramercy, fair damosel,' said Sir Lancelot, 'of your good will.'

And so she departed; and there he lay all that night without any
comfort. And on the morn early came these four queens passingly well
beseen, and all they bidding him good morrow, and he them again.

'Sir knight,' the four queens said, 'thou must understand thou art
our prisoner. And we know thee well that thou art Sir Lancelot du
Lake, King Ban's son; and because that we understand your worthiness, that thou art the noblest knight living, and also we know well
there can no lady have thy love but one, and that is Queen Guenivere,
and now thou shalt lose her love for ever, and she thine. For it behoveth
thee now to choose one of us four: for I am Queen Morgan le Fay,
queen of the land of Gore; and here is the Queen of Northgales, and
the Queen of Eastland, and the Queen of the Out Isles. Now choose
one of us which that thou wilt have to thy paramour, or else to die in
this prison.'

'This is a hard case,' said Sir Lancelot, 'that either I must die or to
choose one of you. Yet had I liever die in this prison with worship, than
to have one of you to my paramour maugre my head. And therefore ye
be answered, I will none of you, for ye be false enchanters. And as for
my lady, Dame Guenivere, were I at my liberty as I was, I would prove
it on yours that she is the truest lady unto her lord living.'

dight] prepared   well beseen] beautifully adorned   maugre° my head]
against my will

'Well,' said the queens, 'is this your answer, that ye will refuse us?'

'Yea, on my life,' said Sir Lancelot, 'refused ye be of me.' So they departed and left him there alone that made great sorrow.

So after that noon came the damosel unto him with his dinner, and [4] asked him what cheer.

'Truly, damosel,' said Sir Lancclot, 'never so ill.'

'Sir,' she said, 'that me repents; but and ye will be ruled by me, I shall help you out of this distress, and ye shall have no shame nor villainy, so that ye hold me a promise.'

'Fair damosel, I grant you; but sore I am afraid of these queens' crafts, for they have destroyed many a good knight.'

'Sir,' said she, 'that is sooth; and for the renown and bounty that they hear of you they will have your love. And, sir, they say your name is Sir Lancelot du Lake, the flower of knights; and they be passing wroth with you that ye have refused them. But sir, and ye would promise me to help my father on Tuesday next coming, that hath made a tournament betwixt him and the King of Northgales, for the last Tuesday past my father lost the field through three knights of Arthur's court—and if ye will be there on Tuesday next coming and help my father, tomorrow by prime by the grace of God I shall deliver you clean.'

'Now, fair damosel,' said Sir Lancelot, 'tell me your father's name, and then shall I give you an answer.'

'Sir knight,' she said, 'my father's name is King Bagdemagus, that was foul rebuked at the last tournament.'

'I know your father well,' said Sir Lancelot, 'for a noble king and a good knight; and by the faith of my body, your father shall have my service, and you both, at that day.'

'Sir,' she said, 'gramercy, and tomorrow look ye be ready betimes, and I shall deliver you and take you your armour, your horse, shield, and spear. And hereby within these ten miles is an abbey of white monks;* and there I pray you to abide me, and thither shall I bring my father unto you.'

'And all this shall be done,' said Sir Lancelot, 'as I am true knight.'

And so she departed, and came on the morn early and found him ready. Then she brought him out of twelve locks, and took him his armour and his own horse; and lightly he saddled him, and took his spear in his hand and so rode forth, and said, 'Damosel, I shall not fail, by the grace of God.'

And so he rode into a great forest all that day and never could find no highway, and so the night fell on him; and then was he ware in a slade of a pavilion of red sendal.

'By my faith,' said Sir Lancelot, 'in that pavilion will I lodge all this night.' And so he there alit down and tied his horse to the pavilion, and there he unarmed him. And there he found a bed, and laid him therein and fell asleep sadly.

[5]   Then within an hour there came that knight that owned the pavil-ion; he weened that his leman had lain in that bed, and so laid him down by Sir Lancelot and took him in his arms and began to kiss him. And when Sir Lancelot felt a rough beard kissing him, he started out of the bed lightly, and the other knight after him; and either of them got their swords in their hands, and out at the pavilion door went the knight of the pavilion. And Sir Lancelot followed him; and there by a little slade Sir Lancelot wounded him sore, nigh unto the death. And then he yielded him unto Sir Lancelot, and so he granted him, so that he would tell him why he came into the bed.

'Sir,' said the knight, 'the pavilion is my own; and as this night, I had assigned my lady to have slept with her, and now I am likely to die of this wound.'

'That me repenteth,' said Lancelot, 'of your hurt, but I was adread of treason, for I was late beguiled. And therefore come on your way into your pavilion and take your rest, and as I suppose I shall staunch your blood.'

And so they went both into the pavilion, and anon Sir Lancelot staunched his blood. Therewith came the knight's lady, that was a passing fair lady; and when she espied that her lord Belleus was sore wounded, she cried out on Sir Lancelot, and made great dole out of measure.

'Peace, my lady and my love,' said Belleus, 'for this knight is a good man, and a knight of adventures.' And there he told her all the case how he was wounded. 'And when that I yielded me unto him, he left me goodly, and hath staunched my blood.'

'Sir,' said the lady, 'I require thee, tell me what knight thou art, and what is your name.'

'Fair lady,' he said, 'my name is Sir Lancelot du Lake.'

'So me thought ever by your speech,' said the lady, 'for I have seen

slade| valley; dell   sendal] silk   sadly] soundly   leman] mistress

you often or this, and I know you better than ye ween. But now would ye promise me of your courtesy, for the harms that ye have done to me and to my lord Sir Belleus, that when ye come unto King Arthur's court for to cause him to be made knight of the Round Table? For he is a passing good man of arms, and a mighty lord of lands of many out isles.'

'Fair lady,' said Sir Lancelot, 'let him come unto the court the next high feast, and look ye come with him, and I shall do my power; and he prove him doughty of his hands, he shall have his desire.'

So within a while the night passed, and the day shone.

Then Sir Lancelot armed him and took his horse, and so he was taught to the abbey. And soon as he came thither, the daughter of King [6] Bagdemagus heard a great horse trot on the pavement; and she then arose and yode to a window, and there she saw Sir Lancelot. And anon she made men fast to take his horse from him and let lead him into a stable, and himself unto a chamber, and unarmed him. And this lady sent him a long gown, and came herself and made him good cheer; and she said he was the knight in the world that was most welcome unto her.

Then in all haste she sent for her father Bagdemagus, that was within twelve miles of that abbey; and before eve he came with a fair fellowship of knights with him. And when the king was alit off his horse, he yode straight unto Sir Lancelot's chamber, and there he found his daughter. And then the king took him in his arms, and either made other good cheer.

Then Sir Lancelot made his complaint unto the king how he was betrayed, and how he was brother unto Sir Lionel, which was departed from him he wist not where, and how his daughter had delivered him out of prison. 'Therefore while that I live I shall do her service and all her kindred.'

'Then am I sure of your help', said the king, 'on Tuesday next coming?'

'Yea, sir,' said Sir Lancelot, 'I shall not fail you, for so have I promised my lady your daughter. But, sir, what knights be those of my lord King Arthur's that were with the King of Northgales?'

'Sir, it was Sir Mador de la Porte, and Sir Mordred, and Sir Gahalantine that all forfared my knights, for against them three I nor none of mine might bear no strength.'

and he prove him doughty of his hands] if he proves himself a powerful fighter
taught] directed   forfared] destroyed

'Sir,' said Sir Lancelot, 'as I hear say, that the tournament shall be here within these three miles of this abbey. But sir, ye shall send unto me three knights of yours such as ye trust, and look that the three knights have all white shields, and no picture on their shields, and ye shall send me another of the same suit; and we four will come out of a little wood in midst of both parties, and we shall fall on the front of our enemies and grieve them that we may. And thus shall I not be known what manner a knight I am.'

So they took their rest that night, and this was on the Sunday; and so the king departed, and sent unto Sir Lancelot three knights with four white shields. And on the Tuesday they lodged them in a little leaved wood beside where the tournament should be. And there were scaffolds and towers, that lords and ladies might behold and give the prize.

Then came into the field the King of Northgales with nine score helms; and then the three knights of King Arthur's stood by themselves. Then came into the field King Bagdemagus with four score helms. And then they fewtered their spears, and came together with a great dash, and there were slain of knights at the first encounter twelve knights of King Badgemagus' party, and six of the King of Northgales' side and party; and King Bagdemagus' party were far set aside and aback.

[7]   With that came in Sir Lancelot, and he thrust in with his spear in the thickest of the press; and there he smote down with one spear five knights, and of four of them he broke their backs. And in that throng he smote down the King of Northgales, and broke his thigh in that fall. All this doing of Sir Lancelot saw the three knights of Arthur's.

'Yonder is a shrewd guest,' said Sir Mador de la Porte, 'therefore have here once at him.'

So they encountered, and Sir Lancelot bore him down horse and man, that his shoulder went out of joint.

'Now it befalleth me,' said Mordred, 'to stir me, for Sir Mador hath a sore fall.'

And then Sir Lancelot was ware of him, and got a spear in his hand and met with him. And Sir Mordred broke his spear upon him, and Sir Lancelot gave him such a buffet that the arson of the saddle broke, and so he drove over the horse's tail that his helm smote into the earth a foot and more, that nigh his neck was broken; and there he lay long in a swoon.

scaffolds] platforms   arson] saddle-bow

Then came in Sir Gahalantine with a great spear, and Sir Lancelot against him in all that they might drive, that both their spears to-brast even to their hands; and then they flung out with their swords and gave many sore strokes. Then was Sir Lancelot wroth out of measure, and then he smote Sir Gahalantine on the helm that his nose, ears, and mouth brast out on blood, and therewith his head hung low; and with that his horse ran away with him, and he fell down to the earth.

Anon therewith Sir Lancelot got a spear in his hand, and or ever that spear broke he bore down to the earth sixteen knights, some horse and man, and some the man and not the horse; and there was none that he hit surely but that he bore no arms that day. And then he got a spear and smote down twelve knights, and the most part of them never throve after. And then the knights of the King of Northgales' party would joust no more; and there the gree was given to King Bagdemagus.

So either party departed unto his own, and Sir Lancelot rode forth with King Bagdemagus unto his castle; and there he had passing good cheer both with the king and with his daughter, and they proffered him great gifts. And on the morn he took his leave, and told the king that he would seek his brother Sir Lionel that went from him when he slept. So he took his horse, and betaught them all to God. And there he said unto the king's daughter, 'If that ye have need any time of my service, I pray you let me have knowledge, and I shall not fail you as I am true knight.'

And so Sir Lancelot departed, and by adventure he came into the same forest where he was taking his sleep before. And in the midst of a highway he met a damosel riding on a white palfrey, and there either saluted other.

'Fair damosel,' said Sir Lancelot, 'know ye in this country any adventures near hand?'

'Sir knight,' said the damosel, 'here are adventures nigh, and thou durst prove them.'

'Why should I not prove?' said Sir Lancelot. 'For for that cause came I hither.'

'Well,' said she, 'thou seemest well to be a good knight; and if thou dare meet with a good knight, I shall bring thee where is the best knight and the mightiest that ever thou found, so thou wilt tell me thy name and what knight thou art.'

to–brast] shattered   gree] prize   betaught] commended

'Damosel, as for to tell you my name, I take no great force: truly, my name is Sir Lancelot du Lake.'

'Sir, thou seemest well; here is adventures fast by that falleth for thee. For hereby dwelleth a knight that will not be overmatched for no man I know but ye do overmatch him, and his name is Sir Tarquin. And, as I understand, he hath in his prison, of Arthur's court, good knights three score and four, that he hath won with his own hands. But when ye have done that journey, ye shall promise me as ye are a true knight for to go and help me and other damosels that are distressed daily with a false knight.'

'All your intent, damosel, and desire I will fulfil, so ye will bring me unto this knight.'

'Now, fair knight, come on your way.'

And so she brought him unto the ford and the tree where hung the basin. So Sir Lancelot let his horse drink, and sithen he beat on the basin with the butt of his spear till the bottom fell out; and long did he so, but he saw no man. Then he rode endlong the gates of that manor nigh half an hour. And then was he ware of a great knight that drove a horse before him, and overthwart the horse lay an armed knight bound. And ever as they came near and near, Sir Lancelot thought he should know him. Then was he ware that it was Sir Gaheris, Gawain's brother, a knight of the Table Round.

'Now, fair damosel,' said Sir Lancelot, 'I see yonder a knight fast bound that is a fellow of mine, and brother he is unto Sir Gawain. And at the first beginning I promise you, by the leave of God, for to rescue that knight. But if his master sit the better in his saddle, I shall deliver all the prisoners that he hath out of danger, for I am sure he hath two brethren of mine prisoners with him.'

But by that time that either had seen other, they gripped their spears unto them.

'Now, fair knight,' said Sir Lancelot, 'put that wounded knight off that horse and let him rest awhile, and let us two prove our strengths; for as it is informed me, thou dost and hast done me great despite and shame unto knights of the Round Table; and therefore now defend thee.'

I take no great force] I do not greatly mind   falleth for thee] belong to you   will not be overmatched . . . overmatch him] who will not be overcome by any man I know of unless you overcome him   journey] day's work   endlong] to and fro before   But if] unless

'And thou be of the Round Table,' said Tarquin, 'I defy thee and all thy fellowship.'

'That is overmuch said', Sir Lancelot said, 'of thee at this time.'

And then they put their spears in their rests, and came together with [8] their horses as fast as they might run; and either smote other in midst of their shields that both their horses' backs brast under them, and the knights were both astoned. And as soon as they might, they avoided their horses, and took their shields before them and drew out their swords, and came together eagerly; and either gave other many strong strokes, for there might neither shields nor harness hold their strokes. And so within a while they had both many grim wounds, and bled passing grievously. Thus they fared two hours and more, tracing and razing each other where they might hit any bare place. Then at the last they were breathless both, and stood leaning on their swords.

'Now, fellow,' said Sir Tarquin, 'hold thy hand a while, and tell me what I shall ask of thee.'

'Say on,' said Sir Lancelot.

Then Sir Tarquin said, 'Thou art the biggest man that ever I met withal, and the best breathed, and as like one knight that I hate above all other knights; so be it that thou be not he, I will lightly accord with thee. And for thy love I will deliver all the prisoners that I have, that is three score and four, so thou would tell me thy name. And thou and I will be fellows together, and never to fail thee while that I live.'

'Ye say well,' said Sir Lancelot, 'but sithen it is so that I may have thy friendship, what knight is that that thou hatest above all thing?'

'Faithfully,' said Sir Tarquin, 'his name is Sir Lancelot du Lake; for he slew my brother, Sir Carados, at the Dolorous Tower, that was one of the best knights alive. And therefore him I except of all knights, for may I him once meet, the one shall make an end, I make my avow. And for Sir Lancelot's sake I have slain a hundred good knights, and as many I have maimed all utterly that they might never after help themselves; and many have died in prison. And yet have I three score and four, and all shall be delivered so thou wilt tell me thy name, so be it that thou be not Sir Lancelot.'

'Now see I well,' said Sir Lancelot, 'that such a man I might be, I might have peace; and such a man I might be, that there should be mortal war betwixt us. And now, sir knight, at thy request I will that thou wit

avoided° their horses] dismounted   tracing and razing] pursuing and slashing

and know that I am Lancelot du Lake, King Ban's son of Benwick, and very knight of the Table Round. And now I defy thee, and do thy best.'

'Ah,' said Sir Tarquin, 'thou art to me most welcome of any knight, for we shall never depart till the one of us be dead.'

Then they hurtled together as two wild bulls, rushing and lashing with their shields and swords, that sometimes they fell both on their noses. Thus they fought still two hours and more and never would have rest; and Sir Tarquin gave Sir Lancelot many wounds, that all the ground there as they fought was all besparkled with blood.

Then at the last Sir Tarquin waxed faint, and gave somewhat aback, and bore his shield low for weariness. That espied Sir Lancelot, and leapt upon him fiercely and got him by the beaver of his helmet, and plucked him down on his knees; and anon he rased off his helm and smote his neck in sunder. And when Sir Lancelot had done this, he yode unto the damosel and said, 'Damosel, I am ready to go with you where ye will have me, but I have no horse.'

'Fair sir,' said this wounded knight, 'take my horse; and then let me go into this manor, and deliver all these prisoners.' So he took Sir Gaheris' horse, and prayed him not to be grieved.

'Nay, fair lord, I will that ye have him at your commandment, for ye have both saved me and my horse. And this day I say ye are the best knight in the world, for ye have slain this day in my sight the mightiest man and the best knight except you that ever I saw. But, fair sir,' said Gaheris, 'I pray you tell me your name.'

'Sir, my name is Sir Lancelot du Lake, that ought to help you of right for King Arthur's sake, and in especial for my lord Sir Gawain's sake, your own brother. And when that ye come within yonder manor, I am sure ye shall find there many knights of the Round Table, for I have seen many of their shields that I know hanging on yonder tree. There is Sir Kay's shield, and Sir Galihud's shield, and Sir Brian de Listenoise's shield, and Sir Aliduke's shield, with many more that I am not now advised of; and Sir Marhalt's, and also my two brethren's shields, Sir Ector de Maris and Sir Lionel. Wherefore I pray you greet them all from me, and say that I bid them to take such stuff there as they find, that in any wise my two brethren go unto the court and abide me there till that I come. For by the feast of Pentecost I cast me to be there; for as at this time I must ride with this damosel for to save my promise.'

beaver] lower face-guard

And so they departed from Gaheris; and Gaheris yode into the manor, and there he found a yeoman porter keeping many keys. Then Sir Gaheris threw the porter unto the ground and took the keys from him, and hastily he opened the prison door, and there he let all the prisoners out, and every man loosed other of their bonds. And when they saw Sir Gaheris, all they thanked him, for they weened that he had slain Sir Tarquin because that he was wounded.

'Not so, sirs,' said Sir Gaheris, 'it was Sir Lancelot that slew him worshipfully with his own hands. And he greets you all well, and prayeth you to haste you to the court; and as unto you, Sir Lionel and Sir Ector de Maris, he prayeth you to abide him at the court of King Arthur.'

'That shall we not do,' said his brethren, 'we will find him and we may live.'

'So shall I', said Sir Kay, 'find him or I come to the court, as I am true knight.'

Then they sought the house there as the armour was, and then they armed them; and every knight found his own horse and all that longed unto him.

So forthwith there came a forester with four horses laden with fat venison. And anon Sir Kay said, 'Here is good meat for us for one meal, for we had not many a day no good repast.' And so that venison was roasted, seethed, and baked; and so after supper some abode there all night. But Sir Lionel and Sir Ector de Maris and Sir Kay rode after Sir Lancelot to find him if they might.

Now turn we to Sir Lancelot, that rode with the damosel in a fair highway. [10]

'Sir,' said the damosel, 'here by this way haunts a knight that distresses all ladies and gentlewomen, and at the least he robbeth them or lieth by them.'

'What,' said Sir Lancelot, 'is he a thief and a knight and a ravisher of women? He doth shame unto the order of knighthood, and contrary unto his oath; it is pity that he liveth. But, fair damosel, ye shall ride on before, yourself, and I will keep myself in covert; and if that he trouble you or distress you, I shall be your rescue and learn him to be ruled as a knight.'

seethed] boiled

So this maid rode on by the way a soft ambling pace. And within a while came out a knight on horseback out of the wood, and his page with him; and there he put the damosel from her horse, and then she cried. With that came Sir Lancelot as fast as he might till he came to the knight, saying, 'Ah, false knight and traitor unto knighthood, who did learn thee to distress ladies, damosels, and gentlewomen?'

When the knight saw Sir Lancelot thus rebuking him he answered not, but drew his sword and rode unto Sir Lancelot. And Sir Lancelot threw his spear from him, and drew his sword, and struck him such a buffet on the helmet that he cleft his head and neck unto the throat.

'Now hast thou thy payment that long thou hast deserved.'

'That is truth,' said the damosel. 'For like as Tarquin watched to distress good knights, so did this knight attend to destroy and distress ladies, damosels, and gentlewomen. And his name was Sir Peris de Forest Savage.'

'Now, damosel,' said Sir Lancelot, 'will ye any more service of me?'

'Nay, sir,' she said, 'at this time, but almighty Jesu preserve you wheresoever ye ride or go, for the most courteous knight thou art and meekest unto all ladies and gentlewomen that now liveth. But one thing, sir knight, me thinks ye lack, ye that are a knight wifeless, that ye will not love some maiden or gentlewoman. For I could never hear say that ever ye loved any of no manner of degree, and that is great pity. But it is noised that ye love Queen Guenivere, and that she hath ordained by enchantment that ye shall never love no other but her, nor no other damosel nor lady shall rejoice you; wherefore there be many in this land of high estate and low that make great sorrow.'

'Fair damosel,' said Sir Lancelot, 'I may not warn people to speak of me what it pleaseth them; but for to be a wedded man, I think it not; for then I must couch with her, and leave arms and tournaments, battles and adventures. And as for to say to take my pleasance with paramours, that will I refuse, in principal for dread of God. For knights that be adventurous should not be adulterers nor lecherous, for then they be not happy nor fortunate unto the wars; for either they shall be overcome with a simpler knight than they be themselves, or else they shall slay by unhap and their cursedness better men than they be themselves. And so who that useth paramours shall be unhappy, and all thing unhappy that is about them.'

warn] forbid   in principal] above all   unhappy] unfortunate, doomed

And so Sir Lancelot and she parted. And then he rode in a deep forest two days and more, and had strait lodging. So on the third day he rode on a long bridge, and there started upon him suddenly a passing foul churl; and he smote his horse on the nose that he turned about, and asked him why he rode over that bridge without licence.

'Why should I not ride this way?' said Sir Lancelot. 'I may not ride beside.'

'Thou shalt not choose,' said the churl, and lashed at him with a great club shod with iron. Then Sir Lancelot drew his sword and put the stroke aback, and cleft his head unto the paps. And at the end of the bridge was a fair village, and all the people, men and women, cried on Sir Lancelot and said, 'Sir knight, a worse deed didst thou never for thyself, for thou hast slain the chief porter of our castle.'

Sir Lancelot let them say what they would, and straight he rode into the castle. And when he came into the castle he alit, and tied his horse to a ring on the wall; and there he saw a fair green court, and thither he addressed him, for there him thought was a fair place to fight in. So he looked about him, and saw much people in doors and windows that said, 'Fair knight, thou art unhappy to come here.'

Anon withal came there upon him two great giants, well armed [11] all save their heads, with two horrible clubs in their hands. Sir Lancelot put his shield before him and put the stroke away of that one giant, and with his sword he cleft his head asunder. When his fellow saw that, he ran away as he were wood, and Sir Lancelot after him with all his might, and smote him on the shoulder and cleft him to the navel.

Then Sir Lancelot went into the hall, and there came before him three score of ladies and damosels, and all kneeled unto him and thanked God and him of his deliverance.

'For,' they said, 'the most part of us have been here these seven years prisoners, and we have worked all manner of silk works for our meat, and we are all great gentlewomen born. And blessed be the time, knight, that ever thou were born; for thou hast done the most worship that ever did knight in this world, that will we bear record. And we all pray you to tell us your name, that we may tell our friends who delivered us out of prison.'

'Fair damosels,' he said, 'my name is Sir Lancelot du Lake.'

had strait lodging] was poorly lodged   meat] food

'Ah, sir,' said they all, 'well mayest thou be he, for else, save yourself, as we deemed, there might never knight have the better of these giants; for many fair knights have assayed, and here have ended. And many times have we here wished after you, and these two giants dreaded never knight but you.'

'Now may ye say', said Sir Lancelot, 'unto your friends, and greet them all from me. And if that I come in any of your marches, show me such cheer as ye have cause. And what treasure that there is in this castle, I give it you for a reward for your grievances. And the lord that is owner of this castle, I would he received it as is his right.'

'Fair sir,' they said, 'the name of this castle is called Tintagel, and a duke owned it sometime that had wedded fair Igraine. And so after that she was wedded to Uther Pendragon, and he begot on her Arthur.'

'Well,' said Sir Lancelot, 'I understand to whom this castle belongeth.'

And so he departed from them and betaught them unto God; and then he mounted upon his horse, and rode into many strange countries and through many waters and valleys, and evil was he lodged. And at the last by fortune him happened against night to come to a fair curtilage, and therein he found an old gentlewoman that lodged him with good will; and there he had good cheer for him and his horse. And when time was, his host brought him into a garret over the gate to his bed. There Sir Lancelot unarmed him and set his harness by him, and went to bed; and anon he fell asleep.

So after, there came one on horseback, and knocked at the gate in great haste. When Sir Lancelot heard this, he arose up and looked out at the window, and saw by the moonlight three knights come riding after that one man, and all three lashing on him at once with swords; and that one knight turned on them knightly again and defended him.

'Truly,' said Sir Lancelot, 'yonder one knight shall I help, for it were shame for me to see three knights on one. And if he be there slain, I am partner of his death.'

And therewith he took his harness, and went out at a window by a sheet down to the four knights. And then Sir Lancelot said on high, 'Turn you knights unto me, and leave this fighting with that knight.'

marches] territorial borders　　　betaught] commended　　　him happened against night] he chanced at nightfall　　　curtilage] house with a courtyard partner of] jointly responsible for

And then they three left Sir Kay and turned unto Sir Lancelot, and assailed him on every hand. Then Sir Kay dressed him for to have helped Sir Lancelot.

'Nay, sir,' said he, 'I will none of your help; therefore as ye will have my help, let me alone with them.'

Sir Kay, for the pleasure of that knight, suffered him for to do his will, and so stood aside. Then anon within seven strokes, Sir Lancelot had stricken them to the earth. And then they all three cried, 'Sir knight, we yield us unto you as man of might matchless.'

'As to that, I will not take your yielding unto me, but so that ye will yield you unto this knight: and on that covenant I will save your lives, and else not.'

'Fair knight, that were us loath, for as for that knight, we chased him hither, and had overcome him had not ye been. Therefore to yield us unto him it were no reason.'

'Well, as to that, advise you well, for ye may choose whether ye will die or live; for and ye be yielded, it shall be unto Sir Kay.'

'Now, fair knight,' they said, 'in saving of our lives we will do as thou commandest us.'

'Then shall ye,' said Sir Lancelot, 'on Whitsunday next coming, go unto the court of King Arthur; and there shall ye yield you unto Queen Guenivere and put you all three in her grace and mercy, and say that Sir Kay sent you thither to be her prisoners.'

'Sir,' they said, 'it shall be done by the faith of our bodies, and we be men living.' And there they swore every knight upon his sword, and so Sir Lancelot suffered them so to depart.

And then Sir Lancelot knocked at the gate with the pommel of his sword; and with that came his host, and in they entered, he and Sir Kay.

'Sir,' said his host, 'I weened ye had been in your bed.'

'So I was; but I arose and leapt out at my window for to help an old fellow of mine.'

So when they came nigh the light, Sir Kay knew well it was Sir Lancelot; and therewith he kneeled down and thanked him of all his kindness, that he had helped him twice from the death.

'Sir,' he said, 'I have nothing done but that me ought for to do, and ye are welcome; and here shall ye repose you and take your rest.'

and we be men living] if we survive

When Sir Kay was unarmed, he asked after meat. Anon there was meat fetched for him, and he ate strongly. And when he had supped, they went to their beds and were lodged together in one bed.*

So on the morn Sir Lancelot arose early, and left Sir Kay sleeping. And Sir Lancelot took Sir Kay's armour and his shield, and armed him; and so he went to the stable and saddled his horse, and took his leave of his host and departed. Then soon after arose Sir Kay and missed Sir Lancelot; and then he espied that he had his armour and his horse.

'Now by my faith, I know well that he will grieve some of the court of King Arthur; for on him knights will be bold, and deem that it is I, and that will beguile them. And because of his armour and shield I am sure I shall ride in peace.'

And then soon Sir Kay departed and thanked his host.*

[13]   So Sir Lancelot rode into a deep forest, and there in a slade he saw four knights hoving under an oak, and they were of Arthur's court: one was Sir Sagramore le Desirous, and Sir Ector de Maris, and Sir Gawain, and Sir Uwain. And anon as these four knights had espied Sir Lancelot, they weened by his arms it had been Sir Kay.

'Now by my faith,' said Sir Sagramore, 'I will prove Sir Kay's might,' and got his spear in his hand and came towards Sir Lancelot. Then Sir Lancelot was ware of his coming and knew him well, and fewtered his spear against him and smote Sir Sagramore so sore that horse and man went both to the earth.

'Lo, my fellows,' said Sir Ector, 'yonder may ye see what a buffet he hath given. Methinketh that knight is much bigger than ever was Sir Kay. Now shall ye see what I may do to him.'

So Sir Ector got his spear in his hand and galloped toward Sir Lancelot, and Sir Lancelot smote him even through the shield and his shoulder, that man and horse went to the earth; and ever his spear held.

'By my faith,' said Sir Uwain, 'yonder is a strong knight, and I am sure he hath slain Sir Kay; and I see by his great strength it will be hard to match him.'

And therewith Sir Uwain got his spear and rode toward Sir Lancelot; and Sir Lancelot knew him well, and let his horse run on the plain and gave him such a buffet that he was astoned, and long he wist not where he was.

'Now see I well,' said Sir Gawain, 'I must encounter with that knight,' and dressed his shield and got a good spear in his hand and let run at Sir Lancelot with all his might; and either knight smote other in midst of the shield. But Sir Gawain's spear brast, and Sir Lancelot charged so sore upon him that his horse reversed upside down; and much sorrow had Sir Gawain to avoid his horse.

And so Sir Lancelot passed on apace and smiled, and said, 'God give him joy that made this spear, for there came never a better in my hand.'

Then the four knights went each one to other and comforted each other and said, 'What say ye by this guest,' said Sir Gawain, 'that with one spear hath felled us all four?'

'We commend him to the devil,' they said all, 'for he is a man of great might.'

'Ye may say it well,' said Sir Gawain, 'that he is a man of might, for I dare lay my head it is Sir Lancelot: I know him well by his riding.'

'Let him go,' said Sir Uwain, 'for when we come to the court we shall wit.'

Then had they much sorrow to get their horses again.

Now leave we there, and speak we of Sir Lancelot, that rode a great while in a deep forest. And as he rode he saw a black brachet, seeking in manner as it had been in the feute of a hurt deer, and therewith he rode after the brachet; and he saw lie on the ground a large feute of blood.   [14]

And then Sir Lancelot rode faster, and ever the brachet looked behind her. And so she went through a great marsh, and ever Sir Lancelot followed. And then was he ware of an old manor; and thither ran the brachet, and so over a bridge. So Sir Lancelot rode over that bridge that was old and feeble; and when he came in the midst of a great hall, there he saw lie dead a knight that was a seemly man, and that brachet licked his wounds. And therewith came out a lady weep-ing and wringing her hands, and said, 'Knight, too much sorrow hast thou brought me.'

'Why say ye so?' said Sir Lancelot, 'I did never this knight no harm, for hither by the feute of blood this brachet brought me; and therefore, fair lady, be not displeased with me, for I am full sore grieved for your grievance.'

guest] stranger   feute] track

'Truly, sir,' she said, 'I trow it be not ye that hath slain my husband, for he that did that deed is sore wounded and is never likely to be whole, that shall I ensure him.'

'What was your husband's name?' said Sir Lancelot.

'Sir, his name was called Sir Gilbert the Bastard, one of the best knights of the world, and he that hath slain him I know not his name.'

'Now God send you better comfort,' said Sir Lancelot.

And so he departed and went into the forest again, and there he met with a damosel the which knew him well. And she said aloud, 'Well be ye found, my lord; and now I require you of your knighthood, help my brother that is sore wounded and never stinteth bleeding; for this day he fought with Sir Gilbert the Bastard and slew him in plain battle, and there was my brother sore wounded. And there is a lady, a sorceress, that dwelleth in a castle here beside, and this day she told me my brother's wounds should never be whole till I could find a knight that would go into the Chapel Perilous, and there he should find a sword and a bloody cloth that the wounded knight was lapped in; and a piece of that cloth and that sword should heal my brother, with that his wounds were searched with the sword and the cloth.'

'This is a marvellous thing,' said Sir Lancelot. 'But what is your brother's name?'

'Sir,' she said, 'Sir Meliot de Logris.'

'That me repents,' said Sir Lancelot, 'for he is a fellow of the Table Round, and to his help I will do my power.'

Then she said, 'Sir, follow ye even this highway, and it will bring you to the Chapel Perilous; and here I shall abide till God send you again. And if you speed not, I know no knight living that may achieve that adventure.'

[15]   Right so Sir Lancelot departed, and when he came to the Chapel Perilous he alit down and tied his horse unto a little gate. And as soon as he was within the churchyard, he saw on the front of the chapel many fair rich shields turned upside down,* and many of those shields Sir Lancelot had seen knights bear beforehand. With that he saw by him there stand thirty great knights, more by a yard than any man that ever he had seen; and all they grinned and gnashed at Sir Lancelot. And when he saw their countenance he dreaded him sore, and so put his shield before him, and took his sword in his hand ready unto battle;

---

searched] probed, cleaned out   more by a yard] three feet (a metre) taller and they were all armed all in black harness, ready with their shields and their swords ready drawn.

And as Sir Lancelot would have gone through them, they scattered on every side of him and gave him the way; and therewith he waxed bold and entered into the chapel. And there he saw no light but a dim lamp burning, and then was he ware of a corpse hilled with a cloth of silk. Then Sir Lancelot stooped down and cut a piece away of that cloth, and then it fared under him as the ground had quaked a little; therewith he feared. And then he saw a fair sword lie by the dead knight, and that he got in his hand and hied him out of the chapel. Anon as ever he was in the chapel yard all the knights spake to him with grim voices, and said, 'Knight Sir Lancelot, lay that sword from thee or thou shalt die.'

'Whether that I live or die,' said Sir Lancelot, 'with no great words get ye it again, therefore fight for it and ye list.'

Then right so he passed throughout them. And beyond the chapel yard there met him a fair damosel, and said, 'Sir Lancelot, leave that sword behind thee, or thou will die for it.'

'I leave it not,' said Sir Lancelot, 'for no threatening.'

'No,' said she, 'and thou didst leave that sword, Queen Guenivere should thou never see.'

'Then were I a fool and I would leave this sword.'

'Now, gentle knight,' said the damosel, 'I require thee to kiss me but once.'

'Nay,' said Sir Lancelot, 'that God me forbid.'

'Well, sir,' said she, 'and thou hadst kissed me, thy life days had been done; and now, alas,' she said, 'I have lost all my labour, for I ordained this chapel for thy sake, and for Sir Gawain. And once I had him with me, and at that time he fought with this knight that lieth dead in yonder chapel, Sir Gilbert the Bastard, and at that time he smote the left hand off Sir Gilbert. And, Sir Lancelot, now I tell thee, I have loved thee these seven years; but there may no woman have thy love but Queen Guenivere. And sithen I might not rejoice thee nor thy body alive, I had kept no more joy in this world but to have thy body dead. Then would I have embalmed it and cered it, and so to have kept it my life days, and daily I should have clipped thee and kissed thee, despite of Queen Guenivere.'

hilled] wrapped   Anon as ever] as soon as   cered] wrapped in waxed cloth
clipped] embraced

'Ye say well,' said Sir Lancelot. 'Jesu preserve me from your subtle crafts.'

And therewith he took his horse and so departed from her. And as the book saith, when Sir Lancelot was departed she took such sorrow that she died within a fortnight. And her name was called Hallewes the sorceress, Lady of the Castle Nigramous.

And anon Sir Lancelot met with the damosel, Sir Meliot's sister; and when she saw him she clapped her hands and wept for joy. And then they rode into a castle thereby where lay Sir Meliot. And anon as Sir Lancelot saw him he knew him, but he was passing pale as the earth for bleeding.

When Sir Meliot saw Sir Lancelot he kneeled upon his knees and cried on high, 'Ah, lord Sir Lancelot, help me anon!'

Then Sir Lancelot leapt unto him and touched his wounds with Sir Gilbert's sword, and then he wiped his wounds with a part of the bloody cloth that Sir Gilbert was wrapped in; and anon a wholer man in his life was he never. And then there was great joy between them, and they made Sir Lancelot all the cheer that they might.

And so on the morn Sir Lancelot took his leave, and bade Sir Meliot hie him 'to the court of my lord Arthur, for it draweth nigh to the feast of Pentecost. And there by the grace of God ye shall find me.' And therewith they departed.

[16]   And so Sir Lancelot rode through many strange countries, over moors and valleys, till by fortune he came to a fair castle; and as he passed beyond the castle him thought he heard bells ring. And then was he ware of a falcon came over his head flying toward a high elm, and long lunes about her feet; and as she flew unto the elm to take her perch, the lunes overcast about a bough. And when she would have taken her flight she hung by the legs fast; and Sir Lancelot saw how she hung, and beheld the fair Périgord falcon,* and he was sorry for her.

The meanwhile came a lady out of a castle and cried on high, 'Ah, Lancelot, Lancelot, as thou art flower of all knights, help me to get me my hawk, for and my hawk be lost my lord will destroy me; for I kept the hawk and she slipped from me. And if my lord my husband wit it, he is so hasty that he will slay me.'

'What is your lord's name?' said Sir Lancelot.

---

lunes] leashes for a hawk's feet

'Sir,' she said, 'his name is Sir Phelot, a knight that longeth unto the King of Northgales.'

'Well, fair lady, since that ye know my name and require me of knighthood to help, I will do what I may to get your hawk. And yet, God knoweth, I am an evil climber, and the tree is passing high, and few boughs to help me withal.'

And therewith Sir Lancelot alit and tied his horse to the same tree, and prayed the lady to unarm him. And so when he was unarmed, he put off all his clothes unto his shirt and his breeches, and with might and great force he climbed up to the falcon and tied the lunes to a great rotten bough, and threw the hawk down with the bough; and anon the lady got the hawk in her hand. And therewith came out Sir Phelot out of the groves suddenly, that was her husband, all armed and with his naked sword in his hand, and said, 'Ah, knight, Sir Lancelot, now I have found thee as I would,' he standing at the bole of the tree to slay him.

'Ah, lady,' said Sir Lancelot, 'why have ye betrayed me?'

'She hath done', said Sir Phelot, 'but as I commanded her, and therefore there is no other boot but thine hour is come that thou must die.'

'That were shame unto thee,' said Sir Lancelot, 'thou an armed knight to slay a naked man by treason.'

'Thou gettest no other grace,' said Sir Phelot, 'and therefore help thyself and thou can.'

'Truly,' said Sir Lancelot, 'that shall be thy shame! But since thou wilt do no other, take my harness with thee, and hang my sword there upon a bough that I may get it, and then do thy best to slay me and thou can.'

'Nay,' said Sir Phelot, 'for I know thee better than thou weenest; therefore thou gettest no weapon and I may keep thee therefrom.'

'Alas,' said Sir Lancelot, 'that ever a knight should die weaponless!' And therewith he waited above him and under him, and over him above his head he saw a rough spike, a big bough leafless, and therewith he broke it off by the body. And then he came lower and awaited how his own horse stood, and suddenly he leapt on the further side of the horse fromward the knight. And then Sir Phelot lashed at him eagerly to have slain him; but Sir Lancelot put away the stroke with the rough

boot°] remedy   waited] looked   awaited] noted spike and therewith took him on the head, that he fell in a swoon to the ground. So then Sir Lancelot took his sword out of his hand, and struck his neck in two pieces.

'Alas,' then cried the lady, 'why hast thou slain my husband?'

'I am not causer,' said Sir Lancelot. 'But with falsehood ye would have had me slain with treason, and now it is fallen on you both.'

And then she swooned as though she would die. And therewith Sir Lancelot got all his armour as well as he might, and put it upon him for dread of more receit, for he dreaded him that the knight's castle was so nigh him. And as soon as he might he took his horse and departed, and thanked God that he had escaped that hard adventure.*

[18] Now Sir Lancelot du Lake came home two days before the feast of Pentecost; and the King and all the court were passing fain. And when Gawain, Sir Uwain, Sir Sagramore, and Sir Ector de Maris saw Sir Lancelot in Kay's armour, then they wist well that it was he that smote them down all with one spear. Then there was laughing and smiling among them. And ever now and now came all the knights home that were prisoners with Sir Tarquin, and they all honoured Sir Lancelot.

When Sir Gaheris heard them speak, he said, 'I saw all the battle from the beginning to the ending.' And there he told King Arthur all how it was, and how Sir Tarquin was the strongest knight that ever he saw except Sir Lancelot; and there were many knights bore him record, three score. Then Sir Kay told the King how Sir Lancelot had rescued him when he should have been slain, and how 'he made the three knights yield them to me, and not to him.' And there they were all three, and bore record. 'And by Jesu,' said Sir Kay, 'Sir Lancelot took my harness and left me his; and I rode in God's peace, and no man would have ado with me.'

And then Sir Meliot de Logris came home, and told the King how Sir Lancelot had saved him from the death.

And all his deeds were known, how the queens, sorceresses four, had him in prison, and how he was delivered by the king Bagdemagus' daughter. Also there was told all the great arms that Sir Lancelot did betwixt the two kings, that is for to say the King of Northgales and King Bagdemagus. All the truth Sir Gahalantine did tell, and Sir Mador de la Porte and Sir Mordred, for they were at that same

took] hit   more receit] receiving more injury

tournament. Then came in the lady that knew Sir Lancelot when that he wounded Sir Belleus at the pavilion; and there, at the request of Sir Lancelot, Sir Belleus was made knight of the Round Table.

And so at that time Sir Lancelot had the greatest name of any knight of the world, and most he was honoured of high and low.

Explicit a noble tale of Sir Lancelot du Lake. Here followeth Sir Gareth's tale of Orkney, that was called Beaumains by Sir Kay.

THE TALE OF SIR GARETH OF ORKNEY

[VII.1] In Arthur's days, when he held the Round Table most plenour, it fortuned the King commanded that the high feast of Pentecost should be held at a city and a castle, in those days that was called Kinkenadon, upon the sands that marched nigh Wales. So ever the King had a custom that at the feast of Pentecost in especial before other feasts in the year, he would not go that day to meat until he had heard or seen of a great marvel. And for that custom all manner of strange adventures came before Arthur as at that feast before all other feasts.

And so Sir Gawain, a little before the noon of the day of Pentecost, espied at a window three men upon horseback and a dwarf upon foot; and so the three men alit, and the dwarf kept their horses, and one of the three men was higher than the other two by a foot and a half.

Then Sir Gawain went unto the King and said, 'Sir, go to your meat, for here at hand come strange adventures.'

So the King went unto his meat with many other kings; and there were all the knights of the Round Table, unless that any were prisoners or slain at encounters. Then at the high feast evermore they should be fulfilled the whole number of a hundred and fifty, for then was the Round Table fully accomplished.

Right so came into the hall two men well beseen and richly, and upon their shoulders there leaned the goodliest young man and the fairest that ever they all saw; and he was large and long and broad in the shoulders, well visaged, and the largest and the fairest hands that ever man saw.* But he fared as he might not go nor bear himself but if he leaned upon their shoulders. Anon as the King saw him there was made peace and room, and right so they yode with him unto the high dais, without saying of any words.

Then this young much man pulled him aback and easily stretched upright, saying, 'The most noble king, King Arthur, God you bless and all your fair fellowship, and in especial the fellowship of the Table Round. And for this cause I come hither, to pray you and require you to give me three gifts; and they shall not be unreasonably asked, but

---

most plenour] i.e. with the full number of knights   marched nigh] bordered
might not go] could not walk

that ye may worshipfully grant them me, and to you no great hurt nor loss. And the first gift I will ask now, and the other two gifts I will ask this day twelvemonth, wheresoever ye hold your high feast.'

'Now ask ye,' said King Arthur, 'and ye shall have your asking.'

'Now, sir, this is my petition at this feast: that ye will give me meat and drink sufficiently for this twelvemonth, and at that day I will ask my other two gifts.'

'My fair son,' said King Arthur, 'ask better, I counsel thee, for this is but a simple asking; for my heart giveth me to thee greatly, that thou art come of men of worship. And greatly my conceit faileth me but thou shalt prove a man of right great worship.'

'Sir,' he said, 'thereof be as be may, for I have asked that I will ask at this time.'

'Well,' said the King, 'ye shall have meat and drink enough; I never forbade it my friend nor my foe. But what is thy name, I would wit?'

'Sir, I cannot tell you.'

'That is marvel,' said the King, 'that thou knowest not thy name, and thou art one of the goodliest young men that ever I saw.'

Then the King betook him to Sir Kay the steward, and charged him that he had of all manner of meats and drinks of the best, and also that he had all manner of finding as though he were a lord's son.

'That shall little need', said Sir Kay, 'to do such cost upon him; for I undertake he is a villein born, and never will make man. For and he had been come of gentle men he would have asked horse and armour, but as he is, so he asketh. And sithen he hath no name, I shall give him a name which shall be called Beaumains, that is to say Fair-hands. And into the kitchen I shall bring him; and there he shall have fat broths every day, that he shall be as fat at the twelvemonth's end as a pork hog.'

Right so the two men departed and left him with Sir Kay, that scorned him and mocked him. Thereat was Sir Gawain wroth, and in especial Sir Lancelot bade Sir Kay leave his mocking, 'for I dare lay my head he shall prove a man of great worship.' [2]

'Let be,' said Sir Kay, 'it may not be by reason, for he desireth ever meat and drink and broth; upon pain of my life he was fostered up in some abbey, and, howsoever it was, they failed meat and drink, and so hither he is come for his sustenance.'*

conceit] opinion   betook] entrusted   finding] provision

And so Sir Kay bade get him a place and sit down to meat. So Beaumains went to the hall door and set him down among boys and lads, and there he ate sadly. And then Sir Lancelot after meat bade him come to his chamber, and there he should have meat and drink enough. And so did Sir Gawain; but he refused them all, for he would do no other but as Sir Kay commanded him, for no proffer. But as touching Sir Gawain, he had reason to proffer him lodging, meat, and drink, for that proffer came of his blood, for he was nearer kin to him than he wist of; but that Sir Lancelot did was of his great gentleness and courtesy.

So thus he was put into the kitchen, and lay nightly as the kitchen boys did. And so he endured all that twelvemonth, and never displeased man nor child, but always he was meek and mild. But ever when he saw any jousting of knights, that would he see and he might. And ever Sir Lancelot would give him gold to spend and clothes, and so did Sir Gawain. And where there were any masteries doing, thereat would he be, and there might none cast bar nor stone to him by two yards. Then would Sir Kay say, 'How liketh you my boy of the kitchen?'

So this passed on till the feast of Whitsuntide. And at that time the King held it at Caerleon in the most royalest wise that might be, like as he did yearly. But the King would no meat eat upon Whitsunday until he heard of some adventures. Then came there a squire unto the King and said, 'Sir, ye may go to your meat, for here cometh a damosel with some strange adventures.' Then was the King glad and set him down. Right so there came a damosel unto the hall and saluted the King, and prayed him of succour.

'For whom?' said the King. 'What is the adventure?'

'Sir,' she said, 'I have a lady of great worship to my sister, and she is besieged with a tyrant, that she may not out of her castle; and because here are called the noblest knights of the world, I come to you for succour.'

'What is your lady called, and where dwelleth she? and who is he and what is his name that hath besieged her?'

'Sir King,' she said, 'as for my lady's name, that shall not ye know for me as at this time, but I let you wit she is a lady of great worship and of

---

ate sadly] ate his fill   for no proffer] not for any invitation   and he might]
if he could   masteries] contests of strength or skill   cast . . . to him] throw
. . . as far as he did

great lands. And as for that tyrant that besiegeth her and destroyeth her lands, he is called the Red Knight of the Red Launds.'

'I know him not,' said the King.

'Sir,' said Sir Gawain, 'I know him well, for he is one of the most perilous knights of the world; men say that he hath seven men's strength, and from him I escaped once full hard with my life.'

'Fair damosel,' said the King, 'there be knights here would do their power for to rescue your lady; but because you will not tell her name, nor where she dwelleth, therefore none of my knights that here be now shall go with you by my will.'

'Then must I seek further,' said the damosel.

So with these words came Beaumains before the King while the [3] damosel was there, and thus he said: 'Sir king, God thank you, I have been this twelvemonth in your kitchen and have had my full sustenance; and now I will ask my other two gifts that be behind.'

'Ask on now, upon my peril,' said the King.

'Sir, this shall be my first gift of the two gifts: that ye will grant me to have this adventure of this damosel, for it belongeth unto me.'

'Thou shalt have it,' said the King, 'I grant it thee.'

'Then, sir, this is that other gift that ye shall grant me: that Sir Lancelot du Lake shall make me knight, for of him I will be made knight and else of none. And when I am passed, I pray you let him ride after me and make me knight when I require him.'

'All this shall be done,' said the King.

'Fie on thee,' said the damosel, 'shall I have none but one that is your kitchen knave?' Then was she waxed angry, and anon she took her horse.

And with that there came one to Beaumains and told him his horse and armour was come for him; and a dwarf had brought him all thing that him needed in the richest wise. Threat the court had much marvel from whence came all that gear. So when he was armed there was none but few so goodly a man as he was; and right so he came into the hall and took his leave of King Arthur and Sir Gawain, and of Sir Lancelot, and prayed him to hie after him. And so he departed and rode after the damosel.

But there went many after to behold how well he was horsed and [4] trapped in cloth of gold, but he had neither spear nor shield.

Then Sir Kay said all openly in the hall, 'I will ride after my boy of the kitchen, to wit whether he will know me for his better.'

'Yet', said Sir Lancelot and Sir Gawain, 'abide at home.'

So Sir Kay made him ready and took his horse and his spear, and rode after him. And right as Beaumains overtook the damosel, right so came Sir Kay and said, 'Beaumains, what, sir, know ye not me?'

Then he turned his horse and knew it was Sir Kay, that had done all the despite to him, as ye have heard before. Then said Beaumains, 'Yea, I know you well for an ungentle knight of the court, and therefore beware of me.'

Therewith Sir Kay put his spear in the rest and ran straight upon him. And Beaumains came as fast upon him with his sword, and with a foin° thrust him through the side that Sir Kay fell down as he had been dead. Then Beaumains alit down and took Sir Kay's shield and his spear, and started upon his own horse and rode his way.

All that saw Sir Lancelot, and so did the damosel. And then Beaumains bade his dwarf start upon Sir Kay's horse, and so he did. By that Sir Lancelot was come, and anon he proffered Sir Lancelot to joust; and either made them ready, and came together so fiercely that either bore other down to the earth, and sore were they bruised. Then Sir Lancelot arose and helped him from his horse; and then Beaumains threw his shield from him, and proffered to fight with Sir Lancelot on foot. So they rushed together like two boars, tracing and traversing and foining the mountenance° of an hour. And Sir Lancelot felt him so big that he marvelled of his strength, for he fought more like a giant than a knight; and his fighting was so passing durable° and passing perilous, for Sir Lancelot had so much ado with him that he dreaded himself to be shamed, and said, 'Beaumains, fight not so sore! Your quarrel and mine is not so great but we may soon leave off.'

'Truly that is truth,' said Beaumains, 'but it doth me good to feel your might; and yet, my lord, I showed not the° utterance°.'

[5]   'In God's name,' said Sir Lancelot, 'for I promise you by the faith of my body, I had as much to do as I might have to save myself from you unshamed; and therefore have ye no doubt° of no earthly knight.'

'Hope ye so that I may any while stand a proved knight?'

'Do as ye have done to me,' said Sir Lancelot, 'and I shall be your warrant.'

---

foin°] thrust   mountenance] extent   durable] well-sustained   the utterance] my utmost   doubt] fear   Hope ye so . . . a proved knight?] Do you believe I could withstand a tested knight for long?

'Then I pray you,' said Beaumains, 'give me the order of knight-hood.'

'Sir, then must ye tell me your name of right, and of what kin ye be born.'

'Sir, so that ye will not discover me, I shall tell you my name.'

'Nay, sir,' said Sir Lancelot, 'and that I promise you by the faith of my body, until it be openly known.'

Then he said, 'My name is Gareth, and brother unto Sir Gawain of father's side and mother's side.'

'Ah, sir, I am more gladder of you than I was; for ever me thought ye should be of great blood, and that ye came not to the court neither for meat nor for drink.'

Then Sir Lancelot gave him the order of knighthood. And then Sir Gareth prayed him for to depart, and so he to follow the lady. So Sir Lancelot departed from him and came to Sir Kay, and made him to be borne home upon his shield, and so he was healed hardly with the life. And all men scorned Sir Kay; and in especial Sir Gawain and Sir Lancelot said that it was not his part to rebuke no young man, 'for full little know ye of what birth he is come of, and for what cause he came to the court.'

And so we leave off Sir Kay, and turn we unto Beaumains: when that he had overtaken the damosel, anon she said, 'What dost thou here? Thou stinkest all of the kitchen, thy clothes be bawdy of the grease and tallow. What, weenest thou', said the lady, 'that I will allow thee for yonder knight that thou killed? Nay truly, for thou slewest him unhappily and cowardly; therefore turn again, thou bawdy kitchen knave! I know thee well, for Sir Kay named thee Beaumains. What art thou but a lusk and a turner of broaches and a ladle-washer?'

'Damosel,' said Sir Beaumains, 'say to me what ye will, yet will I not go from you whatsoever ye say; for I have undertaken to King Arthur for to achieve your adventure, and so shall I finish it to the end, or else I shall die therefore.'

'Fie on thee, kitchen knave, wilt thou finish my adventure? Thou shalt anon be met with, that thou wouldst not for all the broth that ever thou supped once to look him in the face.'

'As for that, I shall assay,' said Beaumains.

bawdy] filthy   allow thee] give you credit   unhappily] by mischance
a lusk and a turner of broaches] layabout and spit-turner   assay] make the
attempt

So right thus as they rode in the wood, there came a man fleeing all that ever he might.

'Whither wilt thou?' said Beaumains.

'Ah, lord,' he said, 'help me, for here by in a slade are six thieves that have taken my lord and bound him sore, and I am afraid lest that they will slay him.'

'Bring me thither,' said Beaumains.

And so they rode together until they came there as was the knight bound; and straight he rode unto them, and struck one to the death and then another, and at the third stroke he slew the third. And then the other three fled, and he rode after them and overtook them; and then they three turned again and assailed Sir Beaumains hard, but at the last he slew them, and returned and unbound the knight. And the knight thanked him, and prayed him to ride with him to his castle there a little beside, and he should worshipfully reward him for his good deeds.

'Sir,' said Beaumains, 'I will no reward have. Sir, this day I was made knight of noble Sir Lancelot, and therefore I will no reward have but God reward me. And also I must follow this damosel.'

So when he came nigh to her she bade him ride outer, 'For thou smellest all of the kitchen. What, weenest thou that I have joy of thee for all this deed? For that thou hast done is but mishap; but thou shalt see soon a sight that shall make thee to turn again, and that lightly.'

Then the same knight rode after the damosel and prayed her to lodge with him all that night. And because it was near night, the damosel rode with him to his castle, and there they had great cheer; and at supper the knight set Sir Beaumains before the damosel.

'Fie, fie,' then said she. 'Sir knight, ye are uncourteous to set a kitchen page before me; him seemeth better to stick a swine than to sit before a damosel of high parage.'

Then the knight was ashamed at her words, and took him up and set him at a side board, and set himself before him.* So all that night they had good cheer and merry rest.

[6]   And on the morn the damosel took her leave and thanked the knight, and so departed and rode on her way until they came to a great forest; and there was a great river and but one passage, and there were ready two knights on the further side to let the passage.

---

slade] valley   but God reward me] unless God rewards me   ride outer]
ride further off   parage] lineage   let the passage] bar the passage

'What say you?' said the damosel. 'Will ye match yonder two knights, or else turn again?'

'Nay,' said Sir Beaumains, 'I will not turn again and they were six more.'

And therewith he rushed unto the water, and in midst of the water either broke their spears upon other to their hands; and then they drew their swords, and smote eagerly at other. And at the last Sir Beaumains smote the other upon the helm that his head astoned, and therewith he fell down in the water, and there was he drowned. And then he spurred his horse upon the land, and therewith the other knight fell upon him and broke his spear; and so they drew their swords and fought long together. But at the last Sir Beaumains cleaved his helm and his head down to the shoulders; and so he rode unto the damosel and bade her ride forth on her way.

'Alas,' she said, 'that ever such a kitchen page should have the fortune to destroy such two knights. Yet thou weenest thou hast done doughtily, that is not so; for the first knight's horse stumbled, and there he was drowned in the water, and never it was by thy force nor by thy might. And the last knight, by mishap thou camest behind him, and by misfortune thou slewest him.'

'Damosel,' said Beaumains, 'ye may say what ye will; but whomsoever I have ado withal, I trust to God to serve him or I and he depart. And therefore I reck not what ye say, so that I may win your lady.'

'Fie, fie, foul kitchen knave, thou shalt see knights that shall abate thy boast.'

'Fair damosel, give me goodly language, and then my care is past; for what knights soever they be, I care not, nor I doubt them not.'

'Also,' said she, 'I say it for thy avail, for yet mayest thou turn again with thy worship; for and thou follow, thou art but slain, for I see all that ever thou dost is by misadventure, and not by prowess of thy hands.'

'Well, damosel, ye may say what ye will, but wheresoever ye go I will follow you.'

So this Beaumains rode with that lady till evensong, and ever she chid him and would not rest. So at the last they came to a black laund, and there was a black hawthorn; and thereon hung a banner, and on the other side there hung a black shield, and by it stood a black spear great

reck | care   doubt | fear   laund | clearing, plain

and long, and a great black horse covered with silk, and a black stone
[7] fast by. Also there sat a knight all armed in black harness, and his name
was called the Knight of the Black Launds. Then the damosel, when
she saw that knight, she bade him flee down that valley, for his horse
was not saddled.

'Gramercy,' said Beaumains, 'for always ye would have me a coward.'

So when the black knight saw her, he said, 'Damosel, have ye
brought this knight from the court of King Arthur to be your champion?'

'Nay, fair knight, this is but a kitchen knave that was fed in King
Arthur's kitchen for alms.'

Then said the knight, 'Why cometh he in such array? For it is shame
that he beareth you company.'

'Sir, I cannot be delivered of him, for with me he rideth maugre my
head. God would,' said she, 'that ye would put him from me, or to slay
him and ye may, for he is an unhappy knave, and unhappily he hath
done this day through mishap; for I saw him slay two knights at the
passage of the water, and other deeds he did before right marvellous
and through unhappiness.'

'That marvels me,' said the black knight, 'that any man of worship
will have ado with him.'

'Sir, they know him not,' said the damosel. 'And for because he
rideth with me, they ween that he be some man of worship born.'

'That may be,' said the black knight. 'Howbeit as ye say that he is no
man of worship born, he is a full likely person, and full like to be a
strong man. But this much shall I grant you,' said the knight, 'I shall
put him down on foot, and his horse and his harness he shall leave with
me; for it were shame to me to do him any more harm.'

When Sir Beaumains heard him say thus, he said, 'Sir knight, thou
art full large of my horse and harness; I let thee wit it cost thee nought,
and whether thou like well or evil, this laund will I pass maugre thy
head, and horse nor harness gettest thou none of mine but if thou win
them with thy hands. Therefore let see what thou canst do.'

'Sayest thou that?' said the black knight. 'Now yield thy lady from
thee, for it beseemed never a kitchen knave to ride with such a lady.'

'Thou liest,' said Beaumains, 'I am a gentleman born, and of more
high lineage than thou, and that will I prove on thy body.'

unhappiness] mischance   full large of] very generous with

Then in great wrath they departed their horses and came together as it had been thunder, and the black knight's spear broke; and Beaumains thrust him through both sides, and therewith his spear broke, and the truncheon was left still in his side. But nevertheless the black knight drew his sword, and smote many eager strokes of great might, and hurt Beaumains full sore. But at the last the black knight, within an hour and a half, he fell down off his horse in a swoon and there died.

And when Sir Beaumains saw him so well horsed and armed, then he alit down and armed him in his armour, and so took his horse and rode after the damosel.

When she saw him come nigh, she said, 'Away, kitchen knave, out of the wind, for the smell of thy bawdy clothes grieveth me. Alas,' she said, 'that ever such a knave should by mishap slay so good a knight as thou hast done—but all is thine unhappiness. But hereby is one that shall pay thee all thy payment, and therefore yet I rede thee flee.'

'It may happen me', said Beaumains, 'to be beaten or slain, but I warn you, fair damosel, I will not flee away neither leave your company, for all that ye can say; for ever ye say that they will slay me or beat me, but howsoever it happeneth, I escape and they lie on the ground. And therefore it were as good for you to hold you still thus all day rebuking me, for away will I not till I see the uttermost of this journey, or else I will be slain, or thoroughly beaten; therefore ride on your way, for follow you I will whatsoever happen me.'

Thus as they rode together, they saw a knight come driving by them all [8] in green, both his horse and his harness. And when he came nigh the damosel, he asked her, 'Is that my brother the black knight that ye have brought with you?'

'Nay, nay,' she said, 'this unhappy kitchen knave hath slain thy brother through unhappiness.'

'Alas,' said the green knight, 'that is great pity, that so noble a knight as he was should so unhappily be slain, and namely of a knave's hand, as ye say that he is. Ah, traitor,' said the green knight, 'thou shalt die for slaying of my brother; he was a full noble knight!' (And his name was Sir Perard.)

'I defy thee,' said Sir Beaumains, 'for I let thee wit I slew him knightly and not shamefully.'

driving] riding fast   namely] especially

Therewith the green knight rode unto a horn that was green, and it hung upon a thorn; and there he blew three deadly motes, and anon there came two damosels and armed him lightly. And then he took a great horse, and a green shield and a green spear; and then they ran together with all their mights, and brake their spears unto their hands. And then they drew their swords and gave many sad strokes, and either of them wounded other full ill. And at the last, at an overthwart stroke Sir Beaumains with his horse struck the green knight's horse upon the side, that he fell to the earth. And then the green knight voided his horse deliverly and dressed him on foot. That saw Beaumains, and therewith he alit; and they rushed together like two mighty kemps a long while, and sore they bled both.

With that came the damosel and said, 'My lord the green knight, why for shame stand ye so long fighting with that kitchen knave? Alas, it is shame that ever ye were made knight, to see such a lad to match you as the weed groweth over the corn.'

Therewith the green knight was ashamed, and therewith he gave a great stroke of might and cleft his shield through. When Beaumains saw his shield cloven asunder, he was a little ashamed of that stroke and of her language. And then he gave him such a buffet upon the helm that he fell on his knees, and so suddenly Beaumains pulled him on the ground grovelling; and then the green knight cried him mercy and yielded him unto Beaumains, and prayed him not to slay him.

'All is in vain,' said Beaumains, 'for thou shalt die but if this damosel that came with me pray me to save thy life.' And therewith he unlaced his helm like as he would slay him.

'Fie upon thee, false kitchen page! I will never pray thee to save his life, for I will not be so much in thy danger.'

'Then shall he die,' said Beaumains.

'Not so hardy, thou bawdy knave,' said the damosel, 'that thou slay him.'

'Alas,' said the green knight, 'suffer me not to die for a fair word speaking. Fair knight,' said the green knight, 'save my life, and I will forgive thee the death of my brother, and for ever to become thy man, and thirty knights that hold of me for ever shall do you service.'

'In the devil's name,' said the damosel, 'that such a bawdy kitchen knave should have thirty knights' service, and thine!'

motes] blasts   overthwart] crosswise   deliverly°] agilely   kemps] champions   danger] power

'Sir knight,' said Beaumains, 'all this availeth thee not but if my damosel speak to me for thy life.' And therewith he made a semblant to slay him.

'Let be,' said the damosel, 'thou bawdy kitchen knave! Slay him not, for and thou do thou shalt repent it.'

'Damosel,' said Beaumains, 'your charge is to me a pleasure, and at your commandment his life shall be saved, and else not.' Then he said, 'Sir knight with the green arms, I release thee quit at this damosel's request; for I will not make her wroth, for I will fulfil all that she chargeth me.' And then the green knight kneeled down and did him homage with his sword.

Then said the damosel, 'Me repents of this green knight's damage and of your brother's death, the black knight; for of your help I had great mister, for I dread me sore to pass this forest.'

'Nay, dread you not,' said the green knight, 'for ye all shall lodge with me this night, and tomorrow I shall help you through this forest.'

So they took their horses and rode to his manor that was fast by. And [9] ever this damosel rebuked Beaumains and would not suffer him to sit at her table, but as the green knight took him and sat with him at a side table.

'Damosel, marvel methinketh,' said the green knight, 'why ye rebuke this noble knight as ye do, for I warn you he is a full noble man, and I know no knight that is able to match him. Therefore ye do great wrong so to rebuke him, for he shall do you right good service. For whatsoever he maketh himself, he shall prove at the end that he is come of full noble blood and of king's lineage.'

'Fie, fie,' said the damosel, 'it is shame for you to say him such worship.'

'Truly,' said the green knight, 'it were shame to me to say him any disworship, for he hath proved himself a better knight than I am. And many is the noble knight that I have met with in my days; and never or this time found I no knight his match.'

And so that night they yode unto rest, and all night the green knight commanded thirty knights privily to watch Beaumains for to keep him from all treason.

And so on the morn they all arose, and heard their Mass and broke their fast. And then they took their horses and rode their way, and the

mister] need

green knight conveyed them through the forest. Then the green knight said, 'My lord Sir Beaumains, my body and these thirty knights shall be always at your summons, both early and late, at your calling, and whither that ever ye will send us.'

'Ye say well,' said Sir Beaumains. 'When that I call upon you, ye must yield you unto King Arthur, and all your knights, if that I so command you.'

'We shall be ready at all times,' said the green knight.

'Fie, fie upon thee, in the devil's name,' said the damosel, 'that any good knight should be obedient unto a kitchen knave!'

So then parted the green knight and the damosel.

And then she said unto Beaumains, 'Why followest thou me, kitchen knave? Cast away thy shield and thy spear, and flee away; yet I counsel thee betimes or thou shalt say right soon "alas!" For and thou were as wight as Sir Lancelot, Sir Tristram, or the good knight Sir Lamorak,* thou shalt not pass a pass here that is called the Pass Perilous.'

'Damosel,' said Beaumains, 'who is afraid, let him flee; for it were shame to turn again sith I have ridden so long with you.'

'Well,' said she, 'ye shall soon, whether ye will or will not.'

[10]   So within a while they saw a white tower as any snow, well machicolated all about and double dyked; and over the tower gate there hung fifty shields of divers colours. And under that tower there was a fair meadow, and therein were many knights and squires to behold, scaffolds and pavilions; for there upon the morn should be a great tournament. And the lord of the tower was within his castle, and looked out at a window and saw a damosel, a dwarf, and a knight armed at all points.

'So God me help,' said the lord, 'with that knight will I joust, for I see that he is a knight errant.'

And so he armed him and horsed him hastily. When he was on horseback with his shield and his spear, it was all red, both his horse and his harness and all that to him belonged. And when that he came nigh him he weened it had been his brother the black knight; and then loud he cried and said, 'Brother, what do ye here in these marches?'

'Nay, nay,' said the damosel, 'it is not he; for this is but a kitchen knave that was brought up for alms in King Arthur's court.'

wight] strong   scaffolds] platforms for spectators

'Nevertheless,' said the red knight, 'I will speak with him or he depart.'

'Ah,' said this damosel, 'this knave hath slain your brother, and Sir Kay named him Beaumains; and this horse and this harness was thy brother's, the black knight. Also I saw thy brother the green knight overcome of his hands. But now may ye be revenged on him, for I may never be quit of him.'

With this every knight departed in sunder and came together all that they might drive; and either of their horses fell to the earth. Then they avoided their horses, and put their shields before them and drew their swords, and either gave other sad strokes, now here, now there, tracing, traversing, and foining, razing and hurling like two boars, the space of two hours. Then she cried on high to the red knight,

'Alas, thou noble red knight, think what worship hath evermore followed thee! Let never a kitchen knave endure thee so long as he doth.'

Then the red knight waxed wroth and doubled his strokes, and hurt Beaumains wonderly sore, that the blood ran down to the ground, that it was wonder to see that strong battle; yet at the last Sir Beaumains struck him to the earth. And as he would have slain the red knight, he cried, 'Mercy, noble knight! Slay me not, and I shall yield me to thee with fifty knights with me that be at my commandment, and forgive thee all the despite that thou hast done to me, and the death of my brother the black knight and the winning of my brother the green knight.'

'All this availeth not,' said Beaumains, 'but if my damosel pray me to save thy life.' And therewith he made semblant to strike off his head.

'Let be, thou Beaumains, and slay him not, for he is a noble knight; and not so hardy, upon thy head, but that thou save him.'

Then Beaumains bade the red knight to stand up, 'and thank this damosel now of thy life.' Then the red knight prayed him to see his castle and to repose them all that night. So the damosel granted him, and there they had good cheer. But always this damosel said many foul words unto Beaumains, whereof the red knight had great marvel. And all that night the red knight made three score knights to watch Beaumains, that he should have no shame nor villainy. And upon the morn they heard Mass and dined; and the red knight came before Beaumains

---

every knight] both knights   not so hardy, upon thy head] don't be so bold, as
you value your life

with his three score knights, and there he proffered him his homage and fealty at all times, he and his knights to do him service.

'I thank you,' said Beaumains, 'but this ye shall grant me: when I call upon you, to come before my lord King Arthur, and yield you unto him to be his knights.'

'Sir,' said the red knight, 'I will be ready, and my fellowship, at your summons.'

So Sir Beaumains departed and the damosel; and ever she rode chiding him in the foulest manner wise that she could.

[11] 'Damosel,' said Beaumains, 'ye are uncourteous so to rebuke me as ye do, for me seemeth I have done you good service; and ever ye threaten me I shall be beaten with knights that we meet, but ever for all your boast they all lie in the dust or in the mire. And therefore I pray you, rebuke me no more; and when ye see me beaten or yielded as recreant, then may you bid me go from you shamefully. But first, I let you wit I will not depart from you, for then I were worse than a fool and I would depart from you all the while that I win worship.'

'Well,' said she, 'right soon shall meet thee a knight that shall pay thee all thy wages, for he is the most man of worship of the world except King Arthur.'

'I will well,' said Beaumains. 'The more he is of worship, the more shall be my worship to have ado with him.'

Then anon they were ware where was before them a city rich and fair, and betwixt them and the city, a mile and more, there was a fair meadow that seemed new mown, and therein were many pavilions fair to behold.

'Lo,' said the damosel, 'yonder is a lord that owneth yonder city, and his custom is when the weather is fair to lie in this meadow to joust and to tourney. And ever there is about him five hundred knights and gentlemen of arms, and there is all manner of games that any gentleman can devise.'

'That goodly lord', said Beaumains, 'would I fain see.'

'Thou shalt see him time enough,' said the damosel. And so as she rode near she espied the pavilion where the lord was.

'Lo,' said she, 'seest thou yonder pavilion that is all of the colour of inde, and all manner of thing that there is about?'—men and women,

inde] indigo (of India)

and horses trapped, shields and spears, were all of the colour of inde. 'And his name is Sir Persant of Inde, the most lordliest knight that ever thou looked on.'

'It may well be,' said Sir Beaumains, 'but be he never so stout a knight, in this field I shall abide till that I see him under his shield.'

'Ah, fool,' said she, 'thou were better to flee betimes.'

'Why?' said Beaumains, 'and he be such a knight as ye make him, he will not set upon me with all his men; for and there come no more but one at once, I shall him not fail whilst my life may last.'

'Fie, fie,' said the damosel, 'that ever such a stinking kitchen knave should blow such a boast!'

'Damosel,' he said, 'ye are to blame so to rebuke me, for I had liever do five battles than so to be rebuked. Let him come, and then let him do his worst.'

'Sir,' she said, 'I marvel what thou art and of what kin thou art come; for boldly thou speakest, and boldly thou hast done, that have I seen. Therefore I pray thee, save thyself and thou may, for thy horse and thou have had great travail, and I dread that we dwell over long from the siege; for it is hence but seven mile, and all perilous passages we are passed save all only this passage, and here I dread me sore lest ye shall catch some hurt—therefore I would ye were hence, that ye were not bruised nor hurt with this strong knight. But I let you wit this Sir Persant of Inde is nothing of might nor strength unto the knight that lieth at the siege about my lady.'*

'As for that,' said Sir Beaumains, 'be as be may; for sithen I am come so nigh this knight I will prove his might or I depart from him, and else I shall be shamed and I now withdraw from him. And therefore, damosel, have ye no doubt, by the grace of God I shall so deal with this knight that within two hours after noon I shall deliver him, and then shall we come to the siege by daylight.'

'Ah, Jesu, marvel have I,' said the damosel, 'what manner a man ye be, for it may never be other but that ye be come of gentle blood; for so foul and shamefully did never woman revile a knight as I have done you, and ever courteously ye have suffered me, and that came never but of gentle blood.'

'Damosel,' said Beaumains, 'a knight may little do that may not suffer a gentlewoman, for whatsoever ye said unto me I took no heed to your words; for the more ye said the more ye angered me, and my wrath I wreaked upon them that I had ado withal. The missaying that

ye missaid me in my battle furthered me much, and caused me to think
to show and prove myself at the end what I was; for peradventure
though it list me to be fed in King Arthur's court, I might have had
meat in other places, but I did it for to prove my friends, and that shall
be known another day whether that I be a gentleman born or none. For
I let you wit, fair damosel, I have done you gentleman's service; and
peradventure better service yet will I do or I depart from you.'

'Alas,' she said, 'fair Beaumains, forgive me all that I have missaid or
done against you.'

'With all my will,' said he, 'I forgive it you, for ye did nothing but as
ye should do, for all your evil words pleased me. Damosel,' said Beaumains, 'since it liketh you to say thus fair unto me, wit ye well it gladdeth my heart greatly, and now me seemeth there is no knight living
but I am able enough for him.'

[12]   With this Sir Persant of Inde had espied them as they hoved in the
field, and knightly he sent unto them whether he came in war or in
peace.*

'Say to thy lord I take no force, but whether as him list.'

So the messenger went again unto Sir Persant and told him all his
answer.

'Well, then will I have ado with him to the utterance.' And so he purveyed him and rode against him.

When Beaumains saw him, he made him ready, and met with all
their mights together as fast as their horses might run, and either brast
their spears in three pieces, and their horses down to the earth. And
deliverly they avoided their horses and put their shields before them,
and drew their swords and gave many great strokes, that sometimes
they hurled so together that they fell grovelling on the ground. Thus
they fought two hours and more, that their shields and hauberks were
all forhewn, and in many places were they wounded. So at the last
Sir Beaumains smote him through the cost of the body, and then he
retrayed him here and there, and knightly maintained his battle long
time. And at the last, though him loath were, Beaumains smote
Sir Persant above upon the helm, that he fell grovelling to the earth;
and then he leapt upon him overthwart and unlaced his helm to have
slain him. Then Sir Persant yielded him and asked him mercy. With
that came the damosel and prayed him to save his life.

peradventure though it list me] maybe although it pleased me   hoved] lingered
cost] side   retrayed him] drew back

'I will well,' he said, 'for it were pity this noble knight should die.'

'Gramercy,' said Sir Persant, 'for now I wot well it was ye that slew my brother the black knight at the black thorn; he was a full noble knight, his name was Sir Perard. Also, I am sure that ye are he that won my other brother the green knight, his name is Sir Pertolepe. Also ye won my brother the red knight, Sir Perimones. And now, sir, ye have won me. This shall I do for to please you: ye shall have homage and fealty of me and of a hundred knights to be always at your command-ment, to go and ride where ye will command us.'

And so they went unto Sir Persant's pavilion and drank wine and ate spices. And afterward Sir Persant made him to rest upon a bed until supper time, and after supper to bed again. So when Sir Beaumains was abed, Sir Persant had a daughter, a fair lady of eighteen year of age, and there he called her unto him, and charged her and commanded her upon his blessing to go unto the knight's bed and lie down by his side, 'and make him no strange cheer, but good cheer, and take him in your arms and kiss him; and look that this be done, I charge you, as ye will have my love and my good will.'

So Sir Persant's daughter did as her father bade her; and so she yode unto Sir Beaumains' bed, and privily she despoiled her and laid her down by him. And then he awoke and saw her, and asked her what she was.

'Sir,' she said, 'I am Sir Persant's daughter, that by the command-ment of my father I am come hither.'

'Be ye a pucelle or a wife?'

'Sir,' she said 'I am a clean maiden.'

'God defend me,' said he then, 'that ever I should defile you to do Sir Persant such a shame.* Therefore I pray you, fair damosel, arise out of this bed or else I will.'

'Sir,' she said, 'I came not hither by my own will, but as I was com-manded.'

'Alas,' said Sir Beaumains, 'I were a shameful knight and I would do your father any disworship.'

But so he kissed her, and so she departed and came unto Sir Persant her father, and told him all how she had sped.

'Truly,' said Sir Persant, 'whatsoever he be, he is come of full noble blood.'

despoiled her] undressed   pucelle] virgin

And so we leave them there till on the morn.

[13]   And so on the morn the damosel and Sir Beaumains heard Mass and broke their fast, and so took their leave.

'Fair damosel,' said Sir Persant, 'whitherward are ye away leading this knight?'

'Sir,' she said, 'this knight is going to the Castle Dangerous there as my sister is besieged.'

'Aha,' said Sir Persant, 'that is the Knight of the Red Launds, which is the most perilous knight that I know now living, and a man that is without mercy; and men say that he hath seven men's strength. God save you, Sir Beaumains, from that knight, for he doth great wrong to that lady, and that is great pity, for she is one of the fairest ladies of the world, and me seemeth that your damosel is her sister: is not your name Lyonet?'

'Sir, so I hight; and my lady my sister hight Dame Lyonesse.'

'Now shall I tell you,' said Sir Persant. 'This Red Knight of the Red Launds hath lain long at that siege, well-nigh this two years, and many times he might have had her and he had would; but he prolongeth the time to this intent, for to have Sir Lancelot du Lake to do battle with him, or with Sir Tristram, or Sir Lamorak de Gales, or Sir Gawain, and this is his tarrying so long at the siege. Now my lord,' said Sir Persant of Inde, 'be ye strong and of good heart, for ye shall have ado with a good knight.'

'Let me deal,' said Sir Beaumains.

'Sir,' said this damosel Lyonet, 'I require you that ye will make this gentleman knight or ever he fight with the Red Knight.'

'I will with all my heart,' said Sir Persant, 'and it please him to take the order of knighthood of so simple a man as I am.'

'Sir,' said Beaumains, 'I thank you; for I am better sped, for certainly the noble knight Sir Lancelot made me knight.'

'Ah,' said Sir Persant, 'of a more renowned man might ye not be made knight; for of all knights he may be called chief of knighthood; and so all the world saith, that betwixt three knights is departed clearly knighthood, that is Sir Lancelot du Lake, Sir Tristram de Lionesse, and Sir Lamorak de Gales: these bear now the renown. Yet there be many other noble knights, as Sir Palomides the Saracen and Sir Safer his brother; also Sir Bleoberis and Sir Blamor de Ganis, his brother;

and he had would] if he had wished

also Sir Bors de Ganis and Sir Ector de Maris and Sir Percival de Gales—these and many more be noble knights, but there be none that bear the name but these three above said. Therefore God speed you well,' said Sir Persant, 'for and ye may match that Red Knight, ye shall be called the fourth of the world.'

'Sir,' said Beaumains, 'I would fain be of good fame and of knight-hood. And I let you wit, I am come of good men, for I dare say my father was a nobleman. And so that ye will keep it in close, and this damosel, I will tell you of what kin I am come of.'

'We will not discover you,' said they both, 'till ye command us, by the faith we owe to Jesu.'

'Truly then,' said he, 'my name is Sir Gareth of Orkney, and King Lot was my father, and my mother is King Arthur's sister, her name is Dame Morgause. And Sir Gawain is my brother, and Sir Agravain and Sir Gaheris, and I am youngest of them all. And yet wot not King Arthur nor Sir Gawain what I am.'

So the book saith that the lady that was besieged had word of her sis- [14] ter's coming by the dwarf, and a knight with her, and how he had passed all the perilous passages.

'What manner a man is he?' said the lady.

'He is a noble knight truly, madam,' said the dwarf, 'and but a young man; but he is as likely a man as ever ye saw any.'

'What is he, and of what kin', said the lady, 'is he come, and of whom was he made knight?'

'Madam,' said the dwarf, he was 'king's son of Orkney, but his name I will not tell you as at this time; but wit ye well, of Sir Lancelot was he made knight, for of none other would he be made knight. And Sir Kay named him Beaumains.'

'How escaped he', said the lady, 'from the brethren of Sir Persant?'

'Madam,' he said, 'as a noble knight should. First, he slew two brethren at a passage of a water.'

'Ah!' said she, 'they were two good knights, but they were murder-ers. That one hight Sir Garrard le Breuse, and that other hight Sir Arnold le Breuse.'

'Then, madam, he encountered the black knight, and slew him in plain battle; and so he took his horse and his armour, and fought with the green knight and won him in plain battle. And in like wise he served the red knight, and after in the same wise he served the blue knight and won him in plain battle.'

'Then,' said the lady, 'he hath overcome Sir Persant of Inde, that is one of the noblest knights of the world.'

'Truly, madam,' said the dwarf, 'he hath won all the four brethren and slain the black knight, and yet he did more before: he overthrew Sir Kay and left him nigh dead upon the ground. Also he did a great battle with Sir Lancelot, and there they departed on even hands; and then Sir Lancelot made him knight.'

'Dwarf,' said the lady, 'I am glad of these tidings. Therefore go thou unto a hermitage of mine hereby, and bear with thee of my wine in two flagons of silver, they are of two gallons; and also two cast of bread with the fat venison baked and dainty fowls; and a cup of gold here I deliver thee, that is rich of precious stones. And bear all this to my hermitage, and put it in the hermit's hands; and sithen go thou to my sister and greet her well, and commend me unto that gentle knight, and pray him to eat and drink and make him strong. And say him I thank him of his courtesy and goodness, that he would take upon him such labour for me that never did him bounty nor courtesy. Also pray him that he be of good heart and courage himself, for he shall meet with a full noble knight, but he is neither of courtesy, bounty, nor gentleness, for he attendeth unto nothing but to murder; and that is the cause I cannot praise him nor love him.'

So this dwarf departed, and came to Sir Persant, where he found the damosel Lyonet and Sir Beaumains, and there he told them all as ye have heard. And then they took their leave; but Sir Persant took an ambling hackney and conveyed them on their ways, and then betook he them unto God. And so within a little while they came to the hermitage, and there they drank the wine, and ate the venison and the fowls baked.

And so when they had repasted them well, the dwarf returned again with his vessel unto the castle. And there met with him the Red Knight of the Red Launds, and asked him from whence he came, and where he had been.

'Sir,' said the dwarf, 'I have been with my lady's sister of the castle and she hath been at King Arthur's court, and brought a knight with her.'

'Then I account her travail but lorn; for though she had brought with her Sir Lancelot, Sir Tristram, and Sir Lamorak or Sir Gawain, I would think myself good enough for them all.'

cast] batches   betook] commended   I account her travail but lorn] I reckon her effort wasted

'It may well be,' said the dwarf, 'but this knight hath passed all the perilous passages, and slain the black knight and other two more, and won the green knight, the red knight, and the blue knight.'

'Then is he one of these four that I have before rehearsed.'

'He is none of these,' said the dwarf, 'but he is a king's son.'

'What is his name?' said the Red Knight of the Red Launds.

'That will I not tell you; but Sir Kay in scorn named him Beaumains.'

'I care not,' said the knight, 'whatsoever he be, for I shall soon deliver him; and if I overmatch him he shall have a shameful death, as many others have had.'

'That were pity,' said the dwarf, 'and it is pity that ye make such shameful war upon noble knights.'

Now leave we the knight and the dwarf and speak we of Beaumains, [15] that all night lay in the hermitage; and upon the morn he and the damosel Lyonet heard their Mass and broke their fast, and then they took their horses and rode throughout a fair forest. And then they came to a plain, and saw where were many pavilions and tents, and a fair castle, and there was much smoke and great noise. And when they came near the siege, Sir Beaumains espied on great trees, as he rode, how there hung full goodly armed knights by the neck, and their shields about their necks with their swords, and gilt spurs upon their heels. And so there hung nigh forty knights shamefully with full rich arms. Then Sir Beaumains abated his countenance and said, 'What meaneth this?'

'Fair sir,' said the damosel, 'abate not your cheer for all this sight, for ye must courage yourself, or else ye be all shent. For all these knights came hither to this siege to rescue my sister Dame Lyonesse; and when the Red Knight of the Red Launds had overcome them, he put them to this shameful death without mercy and pity, and in the same wise he will serve you but if ye quit you the better.'

'Now Jesu defend me', said Beaumains, 'from such villainous death and shondship of harms; for rather than I should so be fared withal, I will rather be slain in plain battle.'

'So were ye better,' said the damosel, 'for trust not, in him is no courtesy, but all goeth to the death or shameful murder. And that is

---

deliver] dispose of   shent] destroyed   shondship of harms] disgraceful injury   fared withal] treated

pity,' said the damosel, 'for he is a full likely man and a noble knight of prowess, and a lord of great lands and of great possessions.'

'Truly,' said Sir Beaumains, 'he may well be a good knight, but he useth shameful customs. And it is marvel that he endureth so long, that none of the noble knights of my lord Arthur's have not dealt with him.'

And then they rode unto the dykes, and saw them double-dyked with full warlike walls; and there were lodged many great lords nigh the walls, and there was great noise of minstrelsy. And the sea beat upon that one side of the walls, where were many ships and mariners' noise with 'hale and ho'.* And also there was fast by a sycamore tree, and thereon hung a horn, the greatest that ever they saw, of an elephant's bone;* 'and this Knight of the Red Launds hath hung it up there to this intent, that if there come any errant knight, he must blow that horn, and then will he make him ready and come to him to do battle. But, sir, I pray you,' said the damosel, 'blow ye not the horn till it be high noon; for now it is about prime, and now increaseth his might, that as men say he hath seven men's strength.'

'Ah, fie, for shame, fair damosel, say ye never so more to me! For and he were as good a knight as ever was any, I shall never fail him in his most might, for either I will win worship worshipfully, or die knightly in the field.'

And therewith he spurred his horse straight to the sycamore tree, and so blew the horn eagerly that all the siege and the castle rang thereof. And then there leapt out many knights out of their tents and pavilions; and they within the castle looked over the walls and out at windows.

Then the Red Knight of the Red Launds armed him hastily, and two barons set on his spurs on his heels, and all was blood-red, his armour, spear, and shield; and an earl buckled his helm on his head, and then they brought him a red spear and a red steed; and so he rode into a little vale under the castle, that all that were in the castle and at the siege might behold the battle.

[16]   'Sir,' said the damosel Lyonet unto Sir Beaumains, 'look ye be glad and light, for yonder is your deadly enemy; and at yonder window is my lady, my sister Dame Lyonesse.'

'Where?' said Beaumains.

'Yonder,' said the damosel, and pointed with her finger.

'That is truth,' said Beaumains. 'She beseemeth afar the fairest lady that ever I looked upon; and truly,' he said, 'I ask no better quarrel than now for to do battle, for truly she shall be my lady, and for her will I fight;' and ever he looked up to the window with glad countenance. And this lady Dame Lyonesse made curtsey to him down to the earth, holding up both her hands.

With that the Red Knight called unto Beaumains and said, 'Sir knight, leave thy beholding and look on me, I counsel thee; for I warn thee well, she is my lady, and for her I have done many strong battles.'

'If thou so have done,' said Beaumains, 'me seemeth it was but waste labour, for she loveth none of thy fellowship; and thou to love that loveth not thee is but great folly. For and I understood that she were not right glad of my coming, I would be advised or I did battle for her. But I understand by the sieging of this castle, she may forbear thy fellowship. And therefore wit thou well, thou Red Knight, I love her and will rescue her, or else to die therefor.'

'Sayest thou that?' said the Red Knight. 'Me seemeth thou oughtest of reason to be ware by yonder knights that thou sawest hang on yonder trees.'

'Fie, for shame,' said Beaumains, 'that ever thou shouldest say so, or do so evil, for in that thou shamest thyself and all knighthood; and thou mayest be sure there will no lady love thee that knoweth thee and thy wicked customs. And now thou weenest that the sight of those hanged knights should fear me. Nay truly, not so; that shameful sight causeth me to have courage and hardiness against thee much more than I would have against thee and thou were a well-ruled knight.'

'Make thee ready,' said the Red Knight, 'and talk no more with me.'

Then they put their spears in the rest and came together with all the might that they had both, and either smote other in the midst of their shields that the paytrels, surcingles, and cruppers brast, and fell to the earth both, and the reins of their bridles in their hands. And so they lay a great while sore astoned, that all that were in the castle and in the siege weened their necks had been broken. Then many a stranger and other said the strange knight was a big man, and a noble jouster, 'for or now we saw never no knight match the Red Knight of the Red Launds'. Thus they said both within and without.

Then lightly and deliverly they avoided their horses and put their shields before them and drew their swords, and ran together like two

may forbear thy fellowship] can do without your company   be ware] take warning   paytrels, surcingles, and cruppers] fastenings of the horses' harness

fierce lions; and either gave other such two buffets upon their helms that they reeled backward both two strides. And then they recovered both, and hewed great pieces off other's harness and their shields, that a great part fell in the fields.

[17] And then thus they fought till it was past noon, and never would stint, till at the last they lacked wind both; and then they stood wagging, staggering, panting, blowing, and bleeding, that all that beheld them for the most part wept for pity. So when they had rested them a while they yode to battle again, tracing, traversing, foining, and razing as two boars. And at some time they took their bere as it had been two rams and hurled together, that sometime they fell grovelling to the earth; and at some time they were so amated that either took other's sword instead of his own. And thus they endured till evensong, that there was none that beheld them might know which was like to win the battle. And their armour was so forhewen that men might see their naked sides; and in other places they were naked, but ever the naked places they did defend. And the Red Knight was a wily knight in fighting, and that taught Beaumains to be wise; but he bought it full sore or he did espy his fighting.

And thus by assent of them both they granted either other to rest; and so they set them down upon two molehills there besides the fighting place, and either of them unlaced their helms and took the cold wind; for either of their pages was fast by them, to come when they called them to unlace their harness and to set them on again at their commandment. And then Sir Beaumains, when his helm was off, he looked up to the window. And there he saw the fair lady Dame Lyonesse, and she made him such countenance that his heart waxed light and jolly; and therewith he bade the Red Knight of the Red Launds make him ready, 'and let us do our battle to the utterance.'

'I will well,' said the knight.

And then they laced on their helms, and avoided their pages, and yede together and fought freshly. But the Red Knight of the Red Launds awaited him at an overthwart and smote him that his sword fell out of his hand; and yet he gave him another buffet upon the helm that

wagging] shaking   took their bere] got extra impetus   amated] confused
bought it . . . fighting] paid bitterly before he worked out his methods of fighting
avoided] dismissed   awaited him at an overthwart] watched for a chance to
strike crosswise

he fell grovelling to the earth, and the Red Knight fell over him for to hold him down.

Then cried the maiden Lyonet on high and said, 'Ah, Sir Beaumains, where is thy courage become? Alas, my lady my sister beholdeth thee, and she shrieks and weeps so that it maketh my heart heavy.'

When Sir Beaumains heard her say so, he abraided up with a great might and got him upon his feet, and lightly he leapt to his sword and gripped it in his hand, and doubled his pace unto the Red Knight, and there they fought a new battle together. But Sir Beaumains then doubled his strokes, and smote so thick that his sword fell out of his hand; and then he smote him on the helm that he fell to the earth. And Sir Beaumains fell upon him and unlaced his helm to have slain him; and then he yielded him and asked mercy, and said with a loud voice, 'Ah, noble knight, I yield me to thy mercy.'

Then Sir Beaumains bethought him on his knights that he had made to be hanged shamefully; and then he said, 'I may not with my worship to save thy life, for the shameful deaths that thou hast caused many full good knights to die.'

'Sir,' said the Red Knight, 'hold your hand, and ye shall know the causes why I put them to so shameful a death.'

'Say on,' said Sir Beaumains.

'Sir, I loved once a lady fair, and she had her brother slain; and she said it was Sir Lancelot du Lake, or else Sir Gawain; and she prayed me as I loved her heartily, that I would make her a promise by the faith of my knighthood for to labour in arms daily until that I had met with one of them; and all that I might overcome, I should put them to villainous death. And so I assured her to do all the villainy unto Arthur's knights, and that I should take vengeance upon all these knights. And, sir, now I will tell thee that every day my strength increaseth till noon until I have seven men's strength.'

Then came there many earls and barons and noble knights, and [18] prayed that knight to save his life, 'and take him to your prisoner.' And all they fell upon their knees and prayed him of mercy that he would save his life.

'And, sir,' they all said, 'it were fairer to take homage and fealty of him and let him hold his lands of you than for to slay him, for by his death ye shall have no advantage; and his misdeeds that be done may

---

abraided] sprang

not be undone. And therefore make ye amends for all parties, and we all will become your men and do you homage and fealty.'

'Fair lords,' said Beaumains, 'wit you well I am full loath to slay this knight; nevertheless he hath done passing ill and shamefully. But insomuch as all that he did was at a lady's request, I blame him the less; and so for your sake I will release him, that he shall have his life, upon this covenant: that he go into this castle and yield him to the lady. And if she will forgive and acquit him, I will well; with this, he make her amends of all the trespass he hath done against her and her lands. And also, when that is done, that he go unto the court of King Arthur, and that he ask Sir Lancelot mercy, and Sir Gawain, for the evil will he hath had against them.'

'Sir,' said the Red Knight, 'all this will I do as ye command me, and siker assurance and borrows ye shall have.'

So then when the assurance was made, he made his homage and fealty, and all those earls and barons with him. And then the maiden Lyonet came to Sir Beaumains and unarmed him and searched his wounds, and staunched the blood, and in like wise she did to the Red Knight of the Red Launds; and there they sojourned ten days in their tents. And ever the Red Knight made all his lords and servants to do all the pleasure that they might unto Sir Beaumains that they might do.

And so within a while the Red Knight yode unto the castle and put him in her grace; and so she received him upon sufficient surety, so that all her hurts were well restored of all that she could complain. And then he departed unto the court of King Arthur, and there openly the Red Knight put himself in the mercy of Sir Lancelot and of Sir Gawain. And there he told openly how he was overcome and by whom, and also he told all the battles from the beginning to the ending.

'Jesu mercy,' said King Arthur and Sir Gawain, 'we marvel much of what blood he is come, for he is a noble knight.'

'Have ye no marvel,' said Sir Lancelot, 'for ye shall right well know that he is come of full noble blood; and as for his might and hardiness, there be but full few now living that is so mighty as he is, and of so noble prowess.'

'It seemeth by you,' said King Arthur, 'that ye know his name, and from whence he came.'

siker assurance and borrows] safe promises and pledges

'I suppose I do so,' said Lancelot, 'or else I would not have given him the high order of knighthood; but he gave me such charge at that time that I should never discover him until he require me, or else it be known openly by some other.'

Now turn we unto Sir Beaumains, that desired Dame Lyonet that he might see her lady. [19]

'Sir,' she said, 'I would ye saw her fain.'

Then Sir Beaumains all armed took his horse and his spear, and rode straight unto the castle. And when he came to the gate he found there men armed, and pulled up the drawbridge and drew the portcullis. Then he marvelled why they would not suffer him to enter. And then he looked up to the window; and there he saw fair Dame Lyonesse, that said on high,

'Go thy way, Sir Beaumains, for as yet thou shalt not have wholly my love, unto the time that thou be called one of the number of the worthy knights. And therefore go and labour in worship this twelvemonth, and then ye shall hear new tidings.'

'Alas, fair lady,' said Sir Beaumains, 'I have not deserved that ye should show me this strangeness. And I had weened I should have had right good cheer with you, and unto my power I have deserved thanks; and well I am sure I have bought your love with part of the best blood within my body.'

'Fair courteous knight,' said Dame Lyonesse, 'be not displeased, neither be not over-hasty; for wit you well your great travail nor your good love shall not be lost, for I consider your great labour and your hardiness, your bounty and your goodness, as me ought to do. And therefore go on your way, and look that ye be of good comfort, for all shall be for your worship and for the best; and pardie, a twelvemonth will soon be done. And trust me, fair knight, I shall be true to you and never betray you, but to my death I shall love you and none other.' And therewith she turned from the window.

And Sir Beaumains rode awayward from the castle making great dole. And so he rode now here, now there, he wist not whither, till it was dark night. And then it happened him to come to a poor man's house, and there he was harboured all that night. But Sir Beaumains had no rest, but wallowed and writhed for the love of the lady of that castle.

pardie] by God

And so upon the morn he took his horse and rode until evening, and then he came to a broad water. And there he alit to sleep, and laid his head upon his shield and betook his horse to the dwarf, and commanded the dwarf to watch all night.

Now turn we to the lady of the same castle, that thought much upon Beaumains. And then she called unto her Sir Gringamore, her brother, and prayed him, in all manner, as he loved her heartily, that he would ride after Sir Beaumains.

'And ever have ye wait upon him till ye may find him sleeping, for I am sure in his heaviness he will alight down in some place and lay him down to sleep. And therefore have ye your wait upon him in privy manner, and take his dwarf and come your way with him as fast as ye may; for my sister Lyonet telleth me that he can tell of what kindred he is come of. And in the meanwhile I and my sister will ride unto your castle to await when ye bring with you the dwarf; and then will I have him in examination myself, for till that I know what is his right name and of what kindred he is come, shall I never be merry at my heart.'

'Sister,' said Sir Gringamore, 'all this shall be done after your intent.'

And so he rode all that other day and the night till he had lodged him. And when he saw Sir Beaumains fast asleep, he came stilly stalking behind the dwarf and plucked him fast under his arm, and so he rode away with him unto his own castle. And this Sir Gringamore was all in black, his armour and his horse and all that to him longeth. But ever as he rode with the dwarf toward the castle, he cried unto his lord and prayed him of help. And therewith awoke Sir Beaumains, and up he leapt lightly and saw where the black knight rode his way with the dwarf, and so he rode out of his sight.

[20] Then Sir Beaumains put on his helm and buckled on his shield, and took his horse, and rode after him all that ever he might through moors and fells and great sloughs, that many times his horse and he plunged over their heads in deep mires; for he knew not the way, but took the gainest way in that woodness, that many times he was like to perish. And at the last him happened to come to a fair green way, and there he met with a poor man of the country and asked him whether he met not with a knight upon a black horse and all black harness, and a little dwarf sitting behind him with heavy cheer.

'Sir,' said the poor man, 'here by me came Sir Gringamore the

wait] watch   stilly] silently   gainest] quickest   woodness] anger

knight with such a dwarf; and therefore I rede you not to follow him, for he is one of the periloust knights of the world, and his castle is here nearhand but two mile. Therefore, we advise you, ride not after Sir Gringamore, but if ye owe him good will.'

So leave we Sir Beaumains riding toward the castle, and speak we of Sir Gringamore and the dwarf. Anon as the dwarf was come to the castle, Dame Lyonesse and Dame Lyonet her sister asked the dwarf where was his master born, and of what lineage was he come. 'And but if thou tell me,' said Dame Lyonesse, 'thou shalt never escape this castle, but ever here to be prisoner.'

'As for that,' said the dwarf, 'I fear not greatly to tell his name and of what kin he is come of. Wit you well he is a king's son and a queen's; and his father hight King Lot of Orkney and his mother is sister to King Arthur, and he is brother to Sir Gawain, and his name is Sir Gareth of Orkney. And now I have told you his right name, I pray you, fair lady, let me go to my lord again, for he will never out of this country till he have me again. And if he be angry he will do harm or that he be stinted, and work you wrack in this country.'

'As for that, be as be may.'

'Nay,' said Sir Gringamore, 'as for that threating, we will go to dinner.'

And so they washed and went to meat, and made them merry and well at ease; because the Lady Lyonesse of the Castle Perilous was there, they made the greater joy.

'Truly, madam,' said Lyonet unto her sister, 'well may he be a king's son, for he hath many good tatches; for he is courteous and mild, and the most suffering man that ever I met withal. For I dare say there was never gentlewoman reviled man in so foul a manner as I have rebuked him; and at all times he gave me goodly and meek answers again.'

And as they sat thus talking, there came Sir Gareth in at the gate with his sword drawn in his hand, and cried aloud that all the castle might hear, 'Thou traitor knight, Sir Gringamore, deliver me my dwarf again, or by the faith that I owe to God and to the high order of knighthood, I shall do thee all the harm that may lie in my power.'

Then Sir Gringamore looked out at a window and said, 'Sir Gareth of Orkney, leave thy boasting words, for thou gettest not thy dwarf again.'

wrack] injury   tatches] qualities   suffering] patient

'Then, coward knight,' said Gareth, 'bring him with thee, and come and do battle with me, and win him and take him.'

'So will I do,' said Sir Gringamore, 'and me list, but for all thy great words thou gettest him not.'

'Ah, fair brother,' said Dame Lyonesse, 'I would he had his dwarf again, for I would he were not wroth; for now he hath told me all my desire, I keep no more of the dwarf. And also, brother, he hath done much for me, and delivered me from the Red Knight of the Red Launds. And therefore, brother, I owe him my service before all knights living; and wit you well that I love him before all other knights living, and full fain I would speak with him. But in no wise I would not that he wist what I were, but as I were another strange lady.'

'Well, sister,' said Sir Gringamore, 'sithen that I know now your will, I will obey me now unto him.'

And so therewith he went down and said, 'Sir Gareth, I cry you mercy, and all that I have misdone I will amend it at your will. And therefore I pray you that ye would alight, and take such cheer as I can make you in this castle.'

'Shall I have my dwarf?' said Sir Gareth.

'Yea, sir, and all the pleasure that I can make you; for as soon as your dwarf told me what ye were and of what kind ye are come, and what noble deeds ye have done in these marches, then I repented me of my deeds.'

Then Sir Gareth alit, and there came his dwarf and took his horse.

'Ah, my fellow,'* said Sir Gareth, 'I have had much adventures for thy sake!'

[21]   And so Sir Gringamore took him by the hand and led him into the hall where his own wife was. And then came forth Dame Lyonesse arrayed like a princess; and there she made him passing good cheer, and he her again, and they had goodly language and lovely counten-ance. And Sir Gareth thought many times, 'Jesu, would that the lady of this Castle Perilous were so fair as she is.'

And there was all manner of games and plays, of dancing and singing. And evermore Sir Gareth beheld that lady; and the more he looked on her, the more he burned in love, that he passed himself far in his reason. And forth towards night they yode unto supper; and Sir Gareth might not eat, for his love was so hot that he wist not where he was.

keep no more of] no longer mind about   passed himself far in] lost

All these looks espied Sir Gringamore; and then after supper he called his sister Dame Lyonesse unto a chamber, and said, 'Fair sister, I have well espied your countenance betwixt you and this knight, and I will, sister, that ye wit he is a full noble knight; and if ye can make him to abide here I will do him all the pleasure that I can, for and ye were better than ye are, ye were well bewared upon him.'

'Fair brother,' said Dame Lyonesse, 'I understand well that the knight is a good knight, and come he is out of a noble house. Notwithstanding, I will assay him better, howbeit I am most beholden to him of any earthly man; for he hath had great labour for my love, and passed many dangerous passages.'

Right so Sir Gringamore went unto Sir Gareth and said, 'Sir, make ye good cheer, for ye shall have no other cause; for this lady, my sister, is yours at all times, her worship saved, for wit you well she loveth you as well as ye do her, and better if better may be.'

'And I wist that,' said Sir Gareth, 'there lived not a gladder man than I would be.'

'Upon my worship,' said Sir Gringamore, 'trust unto my promise. And as long as it liketh you ye shall sojourn with me, and this lady shall be with us daily and nightly to make you all the cheer that she can.'

'I will well,' said Sir Gareth, 'for I have promised to be nigh this country this twelvemonth. And well I am sure King Arthur and other noble knights will find me where that I am within this twelvemonth, for I shall be sought and found if that I be alive.'

And then Sir Gareth went unto the lady Dame Lyonesse and kissed her many times, and either made great joy of other; and there she promised him her love certainly to love him and none other days of her life. Then this lady Dame Lyonesse by the assent of her brother told Sir Gareth all the truth what she was, and how she was the same lady that he did battle for, and how she was lady of the Castle Perilous; and there she told him how she caused her brother to take away his dwarf, 'for this cause, to know the certainty what was your name, and of what [22] kin ye were come.'

And then she let fetch before him her sister Lyonet, that had ridden with him many a wildsome way. Then was Sir Gareth more gladder than he was before. And then they troth-plight, other to love and never to fail while their life lasteth. And so they burnt both in hot love that

bewared] bestowed   no other cause] no reason to do otherwise

they were accorded to abate their lusts secretly. And there Dame Lyonesse counselled Sir Gareth to sleep in no other place but in the hall, and there she promised him to come to his bed a little before midnight.

This counsel was not so privily kept but it was understood; for they were but young both, and tender of age, and had not used such crafts before. Wherefore the damosel Lyonet was a little displeased, and she thought her sister Dame Lyonesse was a little over-hasty, that she might not abide the time of her marriage; and for saving of her worship she thought to abate their hot lusts. And she let ordain by her subtle crafts that they had not their intents either with other as in their delights, until they were married.

And so it passed on at after-supper was made a clean avoidance, that every lord and lady should go unto his rest. But Sir Gareth said plainly he would go no further than the hall, for in such places, he said, was convenient for an errant knight to take his rest in. And so there was ordained great couches and thereon feather beds, and there laid him down to sleep. And within a while came Dame Lyonesse, wrapped in a mantle furred with ermine, and laid her down by the side of Sir Gareth; and therewith he began to clip her and to kiss her.

And therewith he looked before him and saw an armed knight with many lights about him; and this knight had a long giserne in his hand, and made a grim countenance to smite him. When Sir Gareth saw him come in that wise, he leapt out of his bed, and got in his hand a sword and leapt toward that knight. And when the knight saw Sir Gareth come so fiercely upon him, he smote him with a foin through the thick of the thigh, that the wound was a shaftmon broad and had cut a-two many veins and sinews. And therewith Sir Gareth smote him upon the helm such a buffet that he fell grovelling; and then he leapt over him and unlaced his helm, and smote off his head from the body. And then he bled so fast that he might not stand, but so he laid him down upon his bed, and there he swooned and lay as he had been dead.

Then Dame Lyonesse cried aloud, that Sir Gringamore heard it and came down. And when he saw Sir Gareth so shamefully wounded he was sore displeased, and said, 'I am shamed that this noble knight is

---

not so privily . . . understood] this secret was not kept so closely that it didn't get out made a clean avoidance] i.e. the hall was cleared   clip] embrace   giserne] battle-axe   shaftmon] hand's breadth

thus dishonoured. Sister,' said Sir Gringamore, 'how may this be, that this noble knight is thus wounded?'

'Brother,' she said, 'I can not tell you, for it was not done by me, nor by my assent; for he is my lord, and I am his, and he must be my husband. Therefore, brother, I will that ye wit I shame not to be with him, nor to do him all the pleasure that I can.'

'Sister,' said Gringamore, 'and I will that ye wit it, and Gareth both, that it was never done by me, nor by my assent this unhappy deed was never done.'

And there they staunched his bleeding as well as they might, and great sorrow made Sir Gringamore and Dame Lyonesse. And forthwith came Dame Lyonet, and took up the head in the sight of them all, and anointed it with an ointment there as it was smitten off; and in the same wise she did to the other part there as the head stuck. And then she set it together, and it stuck as fast as ever it did; and the knight arose lightly up, and the damosel Lyonet put him in her chamber. All this saw Sir Gringamore and Dame Lyonesse, and so did Sir Gareth; and well he espied that it was Dame Lyonet, that rode with him through the perilous passages.

'Ah well, damosel,' said Sir Gareth, 'I weened ye would not have done as ye have done.'

'My lord Sir Gareth,' said Lyonet, 'all that I have done I will avow it, and all shall be for your worship and us all.'

And so within a while Sir Gareth was nigh whole, and waxed light and jocund, and sang and danced, that again Sir Gareth and Dame Lyonesse were so hot in burning love that they made their covenants at the tenth night after, that she should come to his bed. And because he was wounded before, he laid his armour and his sword nigh his bed's side.

And right as she promised she came; and she was not so soon in his [23] bed but she espied an armed knight coming toward the bed, and anon she warned Sir Gareth. And lightly through the good help of Dame Lyonesse he was armed; and they hurled together with great ire and malice all about the hall. And there was great light as it had been the number of twenty torches both before and behind. So Sir Gareth strained him, so that his old wound brast again on bleeding; but he was hot and courageous and took no keep, but with his great force he struck

avow] acknowledge   keep] notice

down the knight, and voided his helm and struck off his head. Then he
hewed the head upon a hundred pieces, and when he had done so he
took up all those pieces and threw them out at a window into the
ditches of the castle. And by this done, he was so faint that uneath he
might stand for bleeding; and by then he was almost unarmed, he
fell in a deadly swoon on the floor. Then Dame Lyonesse cried, that
Sir Gringamore heard her; and when he came and found Sir Gareth in
that plight he made great sorrow, and there he awaked Sir Gareth, and
gave him a drink that relieved him wonderly well. But the sorrow that
Dame Lyonesse made there may no tongue tell, for she so fared with
herself as she would have died.

Right so came this damosel Lyonet before them all, and she had
fetched all the gobbets of the head that Sir Gareth had thrown out at
the window, and there she anointed it as she did before, and put them
to the body in the sight of them all.

'Well, damosel Lyonet,' said Sir Gareth, 'I have not deserved all this
despite that ye do unto me.'

'Sir knight,' she said, 'I have nothing done but I will avow it, and all
that I have done shall be to your worship, and to us all.'

Then was Sir Gareth staunched of his bleeding; but the leeches said
there was no man that bore the life should heal him thoroughly of his
wound but if they healed them that caused the stroke by enchantment.

So leave we Sir Gareth there with Sir Gringamore and his sisters, and
turn we unto King Arthur, that at the next feast of Pentecost there
came the green knight and fifty knights with him, and yielded them all
unto King Arthur. Then there came the red knight his brother, and
yielded him to King Arthur with three score knights with him. Also
there came the blue knight his brother with a hundred knights, and
yielded them to King Arthur; and the green knight's name was Sir
Pertolepe, and the red knight's name was Sir Perimones, and the blue
knight's name was Sir Persant of Inde. These three brethren told King
Arthur how they were overcome by a knight that a damosel had with
her, and called him Sir Beaumains.

'Jesu,' said the King, 'I marvel what knight he is, and of what lineage
he is come. Here he was with me a twelvemonth, and poorly and

but if . . . enchantment] unless those who brought about the enchanted blow healed
his wounds

shamefully he was fostered; and Sir Kay in scorn named him Beaumains.'

So right as the King stood so talking with these three brethren, there came Sir Lancelot du Lake and told the King that there was come a goodly lord with five hundred knights with him. Then the King was at Caerleon, for there was the feast held; and thither came to him this lord and saluted the King with goodly manner.

'What would ye,' said King Arthur, 'and what is your errand?'

'Sir,' he said, 'I am called the Red Knight of the Red Launds, but my name is Sir Ironside. And sir, wit you well, hither I am sent to you from a knight that is called Sir Beaumains, for he won me in plain battle hand for hand, and so did never knight but he that ever had the better of me these twenty winters. And I am commanded to yield me to you at your will.'

'Ye are welcome,' said the King, 'for ye have been long a great foe of ours, to me and to my court, and now I trust to God I shall so entreat you that ye shall be my friend.'

'Sir, both I and these five hundred knights shall always be at your summons to do you such service as may lie in our powers.'

'Gramercy,' said King Arthur, 'I am much beholden unto that knight that hath so put his body in devoir to worship me and my court. And as to thee, Sir Ironside, that is called the Red Knight of the Red Launds, thou art called a perilous knight; and if thou wilt hold of me I shall worship thee and make thee knight of the Table Round—but then thou must be no man-murderer.'

'Sir, as to that, I have made my promise unto Sir Beaumains never more to use such customs, for all the shameful customs that I used I did it at the request of a lady that I loved. And therefore I must go unto Sir Lancelot and unto Sir Gawain, and ask them forgiveness of the evil will I had unto them; for all those that I put to death was all only for their love of Sir Lancelot and of Sir Gawain.'

'They be here', said the King, 'before thee: now may ye say to them what ye will.'

And then he kneeled down unto Sir Lancelot and to Sir Gawain, and prayed them of forgiveness of his enmity that he had against them. Then goodly they said all at once, 'God forgive you, and we do. And we pray you that ye will tell us where we may find Sir Beaumains.' [24]

---

put his body in devoir] jeopardized himself out of duty

'Fair lord,' said Sir Ironside, 'I cannot tell you, for it is full hard to find him; for such young knights as he is, when they be in their adventures be never abiding in no place.'

But to say the worship that the Red Knight of the Red Launds and Sir Persant and his brethren said by him, it was marvel to hear.

'Well, my fair lords,' said King Arthur, 'wit you well I shall do you honour for the love of Sir Beaumains, and as soon as ever I may meet with him I shall make you all upon a day knights of the Table Round. And as to thee, Sir Persant of Inde, thou hast been ever called a full noble knight, and so have evermore thy three brethren been called. But I marvel,' said the King, 'that I hear not of the black knight your brother: he was a full noble knight.'

'Sir,' said Pertolepe the green knight, 'Sir Beaumains slew him in an encounter with his spear: his name was Sir Perard.'

'That was great pity,' said the King, and so said many knights; for these four brethren were full well known in King Arthur's court for noble knights, for long time they had held war against the knights of the Round Table.

Then Pertolepe the green knight told the King that at a passage of the water of Mortaise there encountered Sir Beaumains with two brethren that ever for the most part kept that passage, and they were two deadly knights. And there he slew the eldest brother in the water, and smote him upon the head such a buffet that he fell down in the water, and there he was drowned; and his name was Sir Garrard le Breuse. And after he slew the other brother upon the land; his name was Sir Arnold le Breuse.

[25/6]*   So then the King went to meat and were served in the best manner. And as they sat at the meat there came in the Queen of Orkney with ladies and knights a great number. And then Sir Gawain, Sir Agravain, and Sir Gaheris arose and went to their mother and saluted her upon their knees and asked her blessing, for of fifteen years before they had not seen her. Then she spake upon high to her brother King Arthur, 'Where have ye done my young son Sir Gareth? For he was here amongst you a twelvemonth, and ye made a kitchen knave of him, the which is shame to you all. Alas, where have ye done mine own dear son that was my joy and bliss?'

'Ah, dear mother,' said Sir Gawain, 'I knew him not.'

'Nor I,' said the King. 'That now me repents! But thanked be God he is proved a worshipful knight as any that is now living of his years; and I shall never be glad till that I may find him.'

'Ah, brother,' said the queen unto King Arthur, 'ye did yourself great shame when ye amongst you kept my son in the kitchen and fed him like a hog.'

'Fair sister,' said King Arthur, 'ye shall right well wit that I knew him not, neither no more did Sir Gawain nor his brethren. But sith it is so,' said the King, 'that he thus is gone from us all, we must shape a remedy to find him. Also, sister, me seemeth ye might have done me to wit of his coming, and then if I had not done well to him ye might have blamed me; for when he came to this court, he came leaning upon two men's shoulders, as though he might not have gone. And then he asked me three gifts; and one he asked that same day, and that was that I would give him meat enough that twelvemonth. And the other two gifts he asked that day twelvemonth, and that was that he might have the adventure of the damosel Lyonet; and the third, that Sir Lancelot should make him knight when he desired him. And so I granted him all his desire. And many in this court marvelled that he desired his sustenance for a twelvemonth, and thereby we deemed, many of us, that he was not come out of a noble house.'

'Sir,' said the Queen of Orkney unto King Arthur her brother, 'wit you well that I sent him unto you right well armed and horsed and worshipfully beseen of his body, and gold and silver plenty to spend.'

'It may be so,' said the King, 'but thereof saw we none, save that same day that he departed from us, knights told me that there came a dwarf hither suddenly, and brought him armour and a good horse full well and richly beseen; and thereat all we had marvel from whence that riches came. Then we deemed all that he was come of men of worship.'

'Brother,' said the queen, 'all that ye say we believe it, for ever sithen he was grown he was marvellously witted, and ever he was faithful and true of his promise. But I marvel,' said she, 'that Sir Kay did mock and scorn him, and gave him to name Beaumains; yet Sir Kay', said the queen, 'named him more righteously than he weened; for I dare say he is as fair a handed man, and he be alive, as any living.'

'Sister,' said Arthur, 'let this language now be still, and by the grace of God he shall be found and he be within these seven realms. And let all this pass, and be merry, for he is proved a man of worship, and that is my joy.'

---

done me to wit] let me know   might not have gone] could not walk

[26/7]   Then said Sir Gawain and his brethren unto King Arthur, 'Sir, and ye will give us leave, we will go seek our brother.'

'Nay,' said Sir Lancelot, 'that shall not need.' And so said Sir Baudwin of Britain: 'for as by our advice, the King shall send unto Dame Lyonesse a messenger and pray her that she will come to the court in all haste that she may, and doubt ye not she will come; and then she may give you the best counsel where ye shall find Sir Gareth.'

'This is well said of you,' said the King.

So then goodly letters were made, and the messenger sent forth, that went night and day till he came to the Castle Perilous. And then the lady Dame Lyonesse was sent for, there as she was with Sir Gringamore her brother and Sir Gareth. And when she understood this messenger, she bade him ride on his way unto King Arthur, and she would come after in all the most goodly haste. Then she came unto Sir Gringamore and to Sir Gareth, and told them all how King Athur had sent for her.

'That is because of me,' said Sir Gareth.

'Now advise ye me,' said Dame Lyonesse, 'what I shall say, and in what manner I shall rule me.'

'My lady and my love,' said Sir Gareth, 'I pray you in no wise be ye knowing where I am. But well I wot my mother is there and all my brethren, and they will take upon them to seek me; I will that they do. But this, madam, I will ye say and advise the King when he questions with you of me: then may ye say this is your advice, that and it like his good grace, ye will do make a cry against the Assumption of Our Lady,* that what knight that proveth him best, he shall wield you and all your land. And if so be that he be a wedded man that wins the degree, he shall have a coronal of gold set with stones of virtue to the value of a thousand pounds, and a white gerfalcon.'

So Dame Lyonesse departed. And to brief this tale: when she came to King Arthur she was nobly received, and there she was sore questioned of the King, and of the Queen of Orkney. And she answered, where Sir Gareth was she could not tell. But this much she said unto King Arthur: 'Sir, by your advice I will let cry a tournament that shall be done before my castle at the Assumption of Our Lady, and the cry shall be this: that you, my lord Arthur, shall be there, and your knights, and I will purvey that my knights shall be against yours; and then I am sure I shall hear of Sir Gareth.'

do make a cry] have it proclaimed

'This is well advised,' said King Arthur.

And so she departed; and the King and she made great provision to the tournament.

When Dame Lyonesse was come to the Isle of Avilion—that was the same isle there as her brother Sir Gringamore dwelled—then she told them all how she had done, and what promise she had made to King Arthur.

'Alas,' said Sir Gareth, 'I have been so sore wounded with unhappiness sithen I came into this castle that I shall not be able to do at that tournament like a knight; for I was never thoroughly whole since I was hurt.'

'Be ye of good cheer,' said the damosel Lyonet, 'for I undertake within these fifteen days to make you as whole and as lusty as ever ye were.'

And then she laid an ointment and salve to him as it pleased her, that he was never so fresh nor so lusty as he was then.

Then said the damosel Lyonet, 'Send you unto Sir Persant of Inde, and summon him that he be ready there with his whole summons of knights like as he made his promise. Also, that ye send unto Ironside that is Knight of the Red Launds, and charge him that he be there with you with his whole sum of knights, and then shall ye be able to match with King Arthur and his knights.'

So this was done, and all the knights were sent for unto the Castle Perilous.

[The tournament is announced, and many knights prepare to come.]

Now let us speak of the great array that was made within the castle and about the castle; for this lady Dame Lyonesse ordained great array upon her part for her noble knights, for all manner of lodging and victual that came by land and by water, that there lacked nothing for her party nor for the other party; but there was plenty to be had for gold and silver for King Arthur and all his knights. And then there came the harbingers from King Arthur for to harbour him and his kings, dukes, earls, barons, and knights.

[27/8]

with unhappiness] through misfortune   harbingers] emissaries sent ahead to
prepare lodging

Then Sir Gareth prayed Dame Lyonesse and the Red Knight of the Red Launds, and Sir Persant and his brethren and Sir Gringamore, that in no wise there should none of them tell his name, and make no more of him than of the least knight that there was, 'for,' he said, 'I will not be known of neither more nor less, neither at the beginning nor at the ending.'

Then Dame Lyonesse said unto Sir Gareth, 'Sir, I would leave with you a ring of mine; but I would pray you, as ye love me heartily, let me have it again when the tournament is done, for that ring increaseth my beauty much more than it is of myself. And the virtue of my ring is this: that that is green it will turn to red, and that that is red will turn in likeness to green, and that that is blue will turn to white, and that that is white will in likeness to blue, and so it will do of all manner of colours; also who that beareth this ring shall lose no blood. And for great love I will give you this ring.'

'Gramercy,' said Sir Gareth, 'mine own lady, for this ring is passing meet for me; for it will turn all manner of likeness that I am in, and that shall cause me that I shall not be known.'

Then Sir Gringamore gave Sir Gareth a bay courser that was a passing good horse; also he gave him good armour and sure, and a noble sword that sometime Sir Gringamore's father won upon a heathen tyrant. And so thus every knight made him ready to that tournament.

And King Arthur was come two days before the Assumption of Our Lady. And there was all manner of royalty, of all manner of minstrelsy that might be found. Also there came Queen Guenivere and the Queen of Orkney, Sir Gareth's mother.

And upon the Assumption Day, when Mass and matins was done, there were heralds with trumpets commanded to blow to the field. And so there came out Sir Epinogris, the king's son of Northumberland, from the castle, and there encountered with him Sir Sagramore le Desirous, and either of them broke their spears to their hands. And then came in Sir Palomides out of the castle, and there encountered with him Sir Gawain, and either of them smote other so hard that both good knights and their horses fell to the earth. And then the knights of either party rescued other.*

And then came in the Red Knight of the Red Launds and Sir Gareth from the castle, and there encountered with them Sir Bors de Ganis and Sir Bleoberis. And there the Red Knight and Sir Bors smote other so hard that their spears brast and their horses fell grovelling to the earth. Then Sir Blamor broke another spear upon Sir Gareth, but of that stroke Sir Blamor fell to the earth.

That saw Sir Galihodin, and bade Sir Gareth keep him; and Sir Gareth smote him anon to the earth. Then Sir Galihud got a spear to avenge his brother, and in the same wise Sir Gareth served him. And in the same manner Sir Gareth served Sir Dinadan and his brother, Sir La Cote Mal Taillé, and Sir Sagramore le Desirous, and Sir Dodinas le Savage. All these knights he bore down with one spear.

When King Angwish of Ireland saw Sir Gareth fare so, he marvelled what knight he was; for at one time he seemed green, and another time at his again coming he seemed blue. And thus at every course that he rode to and fro he changed white to red and black, that there might neither king nor knight have ready cognizance of him.

'So God me help,' said King Arthur, 'that same knight with the many colours is a good knight.' Wherefore the King called unto him Sir Lancelot and prayed him to encounter with that knight.

'Sir,' said Sir Lancelot, 'I may well find in my heart for to forbear him as at this time, for he hath had travail enough this day. And when a good knight doth so well upon some day, it is no good knight's part to let him of his worship, and namely when he seeth a good knight hath done so great labour. For peradventure,' said Sir Lancelot, 'his quarrel is here this day, and peradventure he is best beloved with this lady of all that be here; for I see well he paineth him and enforceth him to do great deeds. And therefore,' said Sir Lancelot, 'as for me, this day he shall have the honour; though it lay in my power to put him from it, yet would I not.'

Then when this was done there was drawing of swords, and then   [29/30]
there began a sore tournament. And there did Sir Lamorak marvellous deeds of arms; and betwixt Sir Lamorak and Sir Ironside, that was the Red Knight of the Red Launds, there was a strong battle. Then came in Sir Lancelot, and he smote Sir Tarquin and he him; and then came in Sir Carados his brother, and both at once they assailed him, and he as the most noblest knight of the world worshipfully fought with them both and held them hot, that all men wondered of the noblesse of Sir Lancelot.

And then came in Sir Gareth, and knew that it was Sir Lancelot that fought with those perilous knights, and parted them in sunder; and no

let him of his worship] deprive him of his honour

stroke would he smite Sir Lancelot. That espied Sir Lancelot, and deemed it should be the good knight Sir Gareth. And then Sir Gareth rode here and there, and smote on the right hand and on the left hand, that all folks might well espy where that he rode. And by fortune he met with his brother Sir Gawain, and there he put him to the worse, for he put off his helm; and so he served five or six knights of the Round Table, that all men said he put him in most pain, and best he did his devoir. For when Sir Tristram beheld him how he first jousted and after fought so well with a sword, then he rode unto Sir Ironside and to Sir Persant of Inde, and asked them by their faith, 'What manner a knight yonder knight is that seemeth in so many divers colours? Truly, me seemeth', said Sir Tristram, 'that he putteth himself in great pain, for he never ceaseth.'

'Wot ye not what he is?' said Ironside.

'No,' said Sir Tristram.

'Then shall ye know that this is he that loveth the lady of the castle, and she him again; and this is he that won me when I besieged the lady of this castle; and this is he that won Sir Persant of Inde and his three brethren.'

'What is his name,' said Sir Tristram, 'and of what blood is he come?'

'Sir, he was called in the court of King Arthur Beaumains; but his right name is Sir Gareth of Orkney, brother unto Sir Gawain.'

'By my head,' said Sir Tristram, 'he is a good knight, and a big man of arms; and if he be young he shall prove a full noble knight.'

'Sir, he is but a child,' he said, 'and of Sir Lancelot he was made knight.'

'Therefore is he much the better,' said Sir Tristram.

And then Sir Tristram, Sir Ironside, Sir Persant, and his brethren rode together for to help Sir Gareth; and then there were many sad strokes.

· And then Sir Gareth rode out on the one side to amend his helm. Then said his dwarf, 'Take me your ring, that ye lose it not while that ye drink.' And so when he had drunk, he got on his helm and eagerly took his horse and rode into the field, and left his ring with his dwarf; and the dwarf was glad the ring was from him, for then he wist well he should be known.

devoir] duty   Take] Give

And when Sir Gareth was in the field, all folks saw him well and plainly that he was in yellow colours. And there he rased off helms and pulled down knights, that King Arthur had marvel what knight he was, for the King saw by his horse that it was the same knight, 'but before he was in so many colours, and now he is but in one colour, and that is yellow. Now go,' said King Arthur unto divers heralds, and bade them ride about him, 'and espy if ye can see what manner of knight he is; for I have spered of many knights this day that is upon his party, and all say they know him not.' [30/1]

But at the last a herald rode nigh Sir Gareth as he could; and there he saw written about his helm in gold, saying, 'This helm is Sir Gareth's of Orkney.' Then the herald cried as he were wood, and many heralds with him: 'This is Sir Gareth of Orkney in the yellow arms!' Thereby all the kings and knights of King Arthur's party beheld and awaited, and then they pressed all to behold him, and ever the heralds cried and said, 'This is Sir Gareth, King Lot's son of Orkney!'

And when Sir Gareth espied that he was discovered, then he doubled his strokes and smote down there Sir Sagramore, and his brother Sir Gawain.

'Ah, brother,' said Sir Gawain, 'I weened ye would not have smitten me so.'*

When he heard him say so he thrang here and there, and so with great pain he got out of the press, and there he met with his dwarf.

'Ah, boy,' said Sir Gareth, 'thou hast beguiled me foul this day of my ring. Give it me fast, that I may hide my body withal.' And so he took it him, and then they all wist not where he was become.

And Sir Gawain had in manner espied where Sir Gareth rode, and then he rode after with all his might. That espied Sir Gareth and rode wightly into the forest; for all that Sir Gawain could do, he wist not where he was become. And when Sir Gareth wist that Sir Gawain was passed, he asked the dwarf of best counsel.

'Sir,' said the dwarf, 'me seemeth it were best, now that ye are escaped from spying, that ye send my lady Dame Lyonesse of the castle her ring.'

'It is well advised,' said Sir Gareth. 'Now have it here and bear it her, and say that I recommend me unto her good grace; and say her I will

---

spered] enquired   thrang] forced his way   took] gave   wightly] vigorously

come when I may, and pray her to be true and faithful to me as I will be to her.'

'Sir,' said the dwarf, 'it shall be done as ye command.' And so he rode his way, and did his errand unto the lady.

Then said she, 'Where is my knight, Sir Gareth?'

'Madam, he bade me say that he would not be long from you.'

And so lightly the dwarf came again unto Sir Gareth, that would full fain have had a lodging, for he had need to be reposed. And then fell there a thunder and a rain, as heaven and earth should go together. And Sir Gareth was not a little weary, for of all that day he had but little rest, neither his horse nor he.

[Gareth proceeds to have various adventures in the forest.]

[33/4] And as Sir Gareth stood he saw an armed knight on horseback coming toward him. Then Sir Gareth mounted upon horseback, and so without any words they ran together as thunder. And there that knight hurt Sir Gareth under the side with his spear; and then they alit and drew their swords and gave great strokes, that the blood trailed down to the ground, and so they fought two hours. So at the last there came the damosel Lyonet, that some men call the Damosel Savage, and she came riding upon an ambling mule; and there she cried all on high, 'Sir Gawain, leave thy fighting with thy brother Sir Gareth!'

And when he heard her say so, he threw away his shield and his sword, and ran to Sir Gareth and took him in his arms, and sithen kneeled down and asked him mercy.

'What are ye,' said Sir Gareth, 'that right now were so strong and so mighty, and now so suddenly is yielded to me?'

'Ah, Sir Gareth, I am your brother Sir Gawain, that for your sake have had great labour and travail.'

Then Sir Gareth unlaced his helm, and kneeled down to him and asked him mercy. Then they arose both, and embraced either other in their arms, and wept a great while or they might speak; and either of them gave other the prize of the battle, and there were many kind words between them.

'Alas, my fair brother,' said Sir Gawain, 'I ought of right to worship you and ye were not my brother; for ye have worshipped King Arthur

and ye were not my brother] even if . . .   worshipped] brought honour to

and all his court, for ye have sent more worshipful knights this twelvemonth than five the best of the Round Table have done, except Sir Lancelot.'

Then came the lady Savage that was the lady Lyonet that rode with Sir Gareth so long; and there she did staunch Sir Gareth's wounds and Sir Gawain's.

'Now what will ye do?' said the damosel Savage. 'Me seemeth that it were best that King Arthur had witting of you both, for your horses are so bruised that they may not bear.'

'Now, fair damosel,' said Sir Gawain, 'I pray you ride unto my lord, my uncle King Arthur, and tell him what adventure is betid me here, and I suppose he will not tarry long.'

Then she took her mule and lightly she rode to King Arthur, that was but two mile thence. And when she had told her tidings to the King, the King bade, 'Get me a palfrey.' And when he was on horseback he bade the lords and ladies come after and they would; and there was saddling and bridling of queens' and princes' horses, and well was he that soonest might be ready.

So when the King came there, he saw Sir Gawain and Sir Gareth sit upon a little hillside. Then the King avoided his horse, and when he came nigh to Sir Gareth he would have spoken and might not; and therewith he sank down in a swoon for gladness. And so they started unto their uncle, and required him of his good grace to be of good comfort. Wit you well the King made great joy, and many a piteous complaint he made to Sir Gareth, and ever he wept as he had been a child.

So with this came his mother, the Queen of Orkney, Dame Morgause; and when she saw Sir Gareth readily in the visage she might not weep, but suddenly fell down in a swoon, and lay there a great while like as she had been dead. And then Sir Gareth recomforted her in such wise that she recovered and made good cheer.

Then the King commanded that all manner of knights that were under his obeisance should make their lodging right there for the love of his two nephews. And so it was done, and all manner of purveyance purveyed, that there lacked nothing that might be gotten for gold nor silver, neither of wild nor tame. And then by the means of the damosel Savage Sir Gawain and Sir Gareth were healed of their wounds; and there they sojourned eight days.

---

is betid] has befallen   wild nor tame] meat obtained by hunting or farming

Then said King Arthur unto the damosel Savage, 'I marvel that your sister, Dame Lyonesse, cometh not hither to me, and in especial that she cometh not to visit her knight, my nephew Sir Gareth, that hath had so much travail for her love.'

'My lord,' said the damosel Lyonet, 'ye must of your good grace hold her excused, for she knoweth not that my lord Sir Gareth is here.'

'Go ye then for her,' said King Arthur, 'that we may be appointed what is best to do, according to the pleasure of my nephew.'

'Sir,' said the damosel, 'it shall be done.'

And so she rode unto her sister; and as lightly as she might make her ready she came on the morn with her brother Sir Gringamore, and with her forty knights. And so when she was come she had all the cheer that might be done, both of the King, and of many other knights and [34/5] also queens. And among all these ladies she was named the fairest, and peerless. Then when Sir Gareth met with her, there was many a goodly look and goodly words, that all men of worship had joy to behold them.

Then came King Arthur and many other kings, and Dame Gueni-vere and Queen Morgause his mother. And there the King asked his nephew Sir Gareth whether he would have this lady as paramour, or else to have her to his wife.

'My lord, wit you well that I love her above all ladies living.'

'Now, fair lady,' said King Arthur, 'what say ye?'

'My most noble king,' said Dame Lyonesse, 'wit you well that my lord Sir Gareth is to me more liever to have and wield as my husband than any king or prince that is christened; and if I may not have him, I promise you I will never have none. For, my lord Arthur,' said Dame Lyonesse, 'wit you well he is my first love, and he shall be the last; and if ye will suffer him to have his will and free choice I dare say he will have me.'

'That is truth,' said Sir Gareth; 'and I have not you and wield you as my wife, there shall never lady nor gentlewoman rejoice me.'

'What, nephew,' said the King, 'is the wind in that door? For wit you well, I would not for the stint of my crown to be causer to withdraw your hearts; and wit you well, ye cannot love so well but I shall rather increase it than decrease it. And also ye shall have my love and my lord-ship in the uttermost wise that may lie in my power.' And in the same wise said Sir Gareth's mother.

liever] desirable   stint] value

So anon there was made a provision for the day of marriage; and by the King's advice it was provided that it should be at Michaelmas following, at Kinkenadon by the seaside, for there is a plenteous country. And so it was cried in all the places through the realm. And then Sir Gareth sent his summons to all those knights and ladies that he had won in battle before, that they should be at his day of marriage at Kinkenadon by the seaside.

And then Dame Lyonesse and the damosel Lyonet, with Sir Gringamore, rode to their castle; and a goodly and a rich ring she gave to Sir Gareth, and he gave her another. And King Arthur gave her a rich bee of gold; and so she departed. And King Arthur and his fellowship rode toward Kinkenadon; and Sir Gareth brought his lady on the way, and so came to the King again and rode with him.

Lord, the great cheer that Sir Lancelot made of Sir Gareth, and he of him! For there was no knight that Sir Gareth loved so well as he did Sir Lancelot; and ever for the most part he would be in Sir Lancelot's company. For after Sir Gareth had espied Sir Gawain's conditions, he withdrew himself from his brother Sir Gawain's fellowship, for he was ever vengeable, and where he hated he would be avenged with murder; and that hated Sir Gareth.*

So it drew fast to Michaelmas, that thither came the lady Dame [35/6] Lyonesse, the lady of the Castle Perilous, and her sister the damosel Lyonet, with Sir Gringamore her brother with them, for he had the conduct of these ladies; and there they were lodged at the device of King Arthur. And upon Michaelmas Day the Bishop of Canterbury made the wedding between Sir Gareth and Dame Lyonesse with great solemnity. And King Arthur made Sir Gaheris to wed the damosel Savage, Dame Lyonet; and Sir Agravain King Arthur made to wed Dame Lyonesse's niece, a fair lady—her name was Dame Laurel.

And so when this solemnity was done, then came in the green knight, Sir Pertolepe, with thirty knights, and there he did homage and fealty to Sir Gareth, and these knights to hold their lands of him for evermore. Also Sir Pertolepe said, 'I pray you that at this feast I may be your chamberlain.'

'With good will,' said Sir Gareth, 'sith it like you to take so simple an office.'

bee] ring

Then came in the red knight with three score knights with him, and did to Sir Gareth homage and fealty, and all those knights to hold of him for evermore. And then Sir Perimones prayed Sir Gareth to grant him to be his chief butler at the high feast.

'I will well', said Sir Gareth, 'that ye have this office, and it were better.'

Then came in Sir Persant of Inde with a hundred knights with him, and there he did homage and fealty, and all his knights should do him service and hold their lands of him for ever; and there he prayed Sir Gareth to make him his sewer-chief at that high feast.

'I will well', said Sir Gareth, 'that ye have it, and it were better.'*

Then came the Red Knight of the Red Launds that hight Sir Ironside, and he brought with him three hundred knights; and there he did homage and fealty, and all those knights to hold their lands of him for ever. And then he asked of Sir Gareth to be his carver.

'I will well,' said Sir Gareth, 'and it please you.'

So then the kings, queens, princes, earls, barons, and many bold knights went to meat; and well may ye wit that there were all manner of plenty and all manner of revels and game, with all manner of minstrelsy that was used those days. Also there was great jousts three days; but the King would not suffer Sir Gareth to joust, because of his new bride, for, as the French book saith, that Dame Lyonesse desired of the King that none that were wedded should joust at that feast.*

But when these jousts were done, Sir Lamorak and Sir Tristram departed suddenly and would not be known, for the which King Arthur and all the court was sore displeased.

And so they held the court forty days with great solemnity. And this Sir Gareth was a noble knight, that wedded Dame Lyonesse of the Castle Perilous. And also Sir Gaheris wedded her sister, Dame Lyonet, that was called the damosel Savage. And Sir Agravain wedded Dame Laurel, a fair lady with great and mighty lands with great riches given with them, that royally they might live till their lives' end.

And I pray you all that readeth this tale to pray for him that this wrote, that God send him good deliverance soon and hastily. Amen.

Here endeth the tale of Sir Gareth of Orkney.

and it were better] i.e. and would do even if it were better   sewer-chief] chief server

THE BOOK OF
SIR TRISTRAM DE LYONESSE

Here beginneth the first book of Sir Tristram de Lyonesse, and who was his father and mother; and how he was born and fostered, and how he was made knight of King Mark of Cornwall.

There was a king that hight Meliodas, and he was lord of the country [VIII.1] of Lyonesse; and this Meliodas was a likely knight as any was that time living. And by fortune he wedded King Mark's sister of Cornwall, and she was called Elizabeth, that was called both good and fair.*

So when this King Meliodas had been with his wife, within a while she waxed great with child. And she was a full meek lady, and well she loved her lord, and he her again; so there was great joy betwixt them.

So there was a lady in that country that had loved King Meliodas long, and by no mean she never could get his love. Therefore she let ordain upon a day, as King Meliodas rode an-hunting (for he was a great chaser of deer), and there by enchantment she made him chase a hart by himself alone till that he came to an old castle, and there anon he was taken prisoner by the lady that loved him.

When Elizabeth, King Meliodas' wife, missed her lord, she was nigh out of her wit; and also, as great with child as she was, she took a gentlewoman with her, and ran into the forest suddenly to seek her lord. And when she was far in the forest she might no further, but right there she began to travail fast of her child; and she had many grimly throes, but her gentlewoman helped her all that she might. And so by miracle of Our Lady of Heaven she was delivered with great pains; but she had taken such cold for the default of help that the deep draughts of death took her, that needs she must die and depart out of this world, there was no other boot.

When this Queen Elizabeth saw that she might not escape, she made great dole, and said unto her gentlewoman, 'When ye see my lord, King Meliodas, recommend me unto him, and tell him what pains I endure here for his love, and how I must die here for his sake for default of good help; and let him wit that I am full sorry to depart out of this world from him, therefore pray him to be friend to my soul. Now let me see my little child, for whom I have had all this sorrow.' And when she saw him she said thus: 'Ah, my little son, thou hast murdered thy mother! And therefore, I suppose, thou that art a murderer so young, thou art full likely to be a manly man in thine age. And because I shall die of the birth of thee, I charge my gentlewoman that she pray my lord, the King Meliodas, that when he is christened let call him Tristram, that is as much to say as a sorrowful birth.'

And therewith the queen gave up the ghost and died. Then the gentlewoman laid her under an umber of a great tree, and then she lapped the child as well as she might from cold.

Right so there came the barons of King Meliodas following after the queen; and when they saw that she was dead, and understood none [2] other but that the king was destroyed, then certain of them would have slain the child, because they would have been lords of that country of Lyonesse. But then through the fair speech of the gentlewoman and by the means that she made, the most part of the barons would not assent thereto. But then they let carry home the dead queen, and much sorrow was made for her.

Then this meanwhile Merlin had delivered King Meliodas out of prison, on the morn after his queen was dead; and so when the king was come home, the most part of the barons made great joy. But the sorrow that the king made for his queen there might no tongue tell. So then the king let inter her richly, and after he let christen his child as his wife had commanded before her death. And then he let call him Tristram, the sorrowful-born child.

Then King Meliodas endured after that seven years without a wife, and all this time Tristram was fostered well. Then it befell that the King Meliodas wedded King Howell of Brittany's daughter, and anon she had children by King Meliodas. Then was she heavy and wroth that her children should not rejoice the country of Lyonesse, wherefore this queen ordained for to poison young Tristram. So at the last she let poison be put in a piece of silver in the chamber where Tristram and her children were together, unto that intent that when Tristram were thirsty he should drink that drink. And so it fell upon a day, the queen's son, as he was in that chamber, espied the piece with poison, and he weened it had been good drink; and because the child was thirsty he took the piece with poison and drank freely, and therewith the child suddenly brast and was dead.

umber] shade   rejoice] enjoy [possession of]   piece] vessel

So when the queen of Meliodas wist of the death of her son, wit ye well that she was heavy. But yet the king understood nothing of her treason. Notwithstanding, the queen would not leave by this, but eft she let ordain more poison and put it in a piece. And by fortune King Meliodas her husband found the piece with wine wherein was the poison, and as he that was thirsty took the piece for to drink. And as he would have drunk thereof, the queen espied him and ran unto him, and pulled the piece from him suddenly. The king marvelled of her why she did so, and remembered him suddenly how her son was slain with poison. And then he took her by the hand, and said, 'Thou false traitress, thou shalt tell me what manner of drink this is, or else I shall slay thee.'

And therewith he pulled out his sword, and swore a great oath that he should slay her but if she told him the truth.

'Ah, mercy, my lord,' said she, 'and I shall tell you all.' And then she told him why she would have slain Tristram, because her children should rejoice his land.

'Well,' said the king, 'and therefore ye shall have the law.'

And so she was damned by the assent of the barons to be burnt; and then was there made a great fire, and right as she was at the fire to take her execution, this same young Tristram kneeled before his father King Meliodas and besought him to give him a done.

'I will well,' said the king.

Then said young Tristram, 'Give me the life of your queen, my stepmother.'

'That is unrightfully asked,' said the King Meliodas. 'For thou ought of right to hate her, for she would have slain thee with poison; and for thy sake most is my cause that she should be dead.'

'Sir,' said Tristram, 'as for that, I beseech you of your mercy that ye will forgive her; and as for my part, God forgive her, and I do. And it liked so much your highness to grant me my boon, for God's love I require you hold your promise.'

'Sithen it is so,' said the king, 'I will that ye have her life,' and said, 'I give her you, and go ye to the fire and take her, and do with her what ye will.'

So thus Sir Tristram* went to the fire, and by the commandment of the king delivered her from the death. But after that King Meliodas

eft] again   damned] condemned   done] gift   And it liked] Since it
pleased

would never have ado with her as at bed and at board. But by the means of young Tristram, he made the king and her accorded. But then the king would not suffer young Tristram to abide but little in his court.

[3]   And then he let ordain a gentleman that was well learned and taught, and his name was Gouvernail; and then he sent young Tristram with Gouvernail into France to learn the language and nurture and deeds of arms, and there was Tristram more than seven years. So when he had learned what he might in those countries, then he came home to his father King Meliodas again.

And so Tristram learned to be a harper passing all other, that there was none such called in no country; and so he applied him for to learn in harping and on instruments of music in his youth. And after, as he grew in might and strength, he laboured in hunting and in hawking, never gentleman more that ever we heard read of. And as the book saith, he began good measures of blowing of beasts of venery, and beasts of chase, and all manner of vermins, and all the terms we have yet of hawking and hunting. And therefore the book of venery, of hawking and hunting, is called the book of Sir Tristram.*

Wherefore, as me seemeth, all gentlemen that beareth old arms ought of right to honour Sir Tristram for the goodly terms that gentlemen have and use, and shall do unto the day of doom, that thereby in a manner all men of worship may dissever a gentleman from a yeoman, and a yeoman from a villein. For he that gentle is will draw him to gentle tatches, and to follow the noble customs of gentlemen.

Thus Tristram endured in Lyonesse until that he was strong and big, unto the age of eighteen years. And then King Meliodas had great joy of young Tristram, and so had the queen his wife; for ever after in her life, because Sir Tristram saved her from the fire, she did never hate him more after, but ever loved him and gave him many great gifts. For every estate loved him, where that he went.

[4]   Then it befell that King Angwish of Ireland sent unto King Mark of Cornwall for his truage, that Cornwall had paid many winters; and all that time King Mark was behind of the truage for seven years. And King Mark and his barons gave unto the messengers of Ireland these

---

measures of blowing] i.e. the different blasts on a hunting-horn   beareth old arms] of ancient lineage   dissever] distinguish   villein] peasant tatches] virtues   truage] tribute

words and answer, that they would none pay; and bade the messengers go unto their king Angwish, 'and tell him we will pay him no truage, but tell your lord, and he will always have truage of us of Cornwall, bid him send a trusty knight of his land that will fight for his right, and we shall find another for to defend us.'

So the messengers departed into Ireland. And when King Angwish understood the answer of the messengers, he was wroth; and then he called unto him Sir Marhalt, the good knight, that was nobly proved and a knight of the Round Table; and this Marhalt was brother unto the Queen of Ireland.

Then the king said thus: 'Fair brother, Sir Marhalt, I pray you go unto Cornwall for my sake, to do battle for our truage that we of right ought to have. And whatsoever ye spend, ye shall have sufficiently more than ye shall need.'

'Sir,' said Marhalt, 'wit ye well that I shall not be loath to do battle in the right of you and your land with the best knight of the Table Round, for I know them, for the most part, what be their deeds; and for to advance my deeds and to increase my worship, I will right gladly go unto this journey.'

So in all haste there was made purveyance for Sir Marhalt, and he had all thing that him needed; and so he departed out of Ireland, and arrived up in Cornwall even by the castle of Tintagel. And when King Mark understood that he was there arrived to fight for Ireland, then made King Mark great sorrow when he understood that the good knight Sir Marhalt was come, for they knew no knight that durst have ado with him; for at that time Sir Marhalt was called one of the famousest knights of the world.

And thus Sir Marhalt abode in the sea, and every day he sent unto King Mark for to pay the truage that was behind seven years, or else to find a knight to fight with him for the truage. This manner of message Sir Marhalt sent unto King Mark.

Then they of Cornwall let make cries that what knight would fight for to save the truage of Comwall, he should be rewarded to fare the better, term of his life. Then some of the barons said to King Mark, and counselled him to send to the court of King Arthur for to seek Sir Lancelot du Lake, that was that time named for the marvellest knight of the world. Then there were other barons that said that it was labour in vain, because Sir Marhalt was a knight of the Round Table, therefore any of them would be loath to have ado with other, but if it were so that any knight at his own request would fight disguised and unknown. So the king and all his barons assented that it was no boot to seek after no knight of the Round Table.

This meanwhile came the language and the noise unto King Meliodas, how that Sir Marhalt abode fast by Tintagel, and how King Mark could find no manner of knight to fight for him. So when young Tristram heard of this he was wroth and sore ashamed that there durst no knight in Cornwall have ado with Sir Marhalt of Ireland. Therewith Tristram went unto his father, King Meliodas, and asked him counsel what was best to do for to recover Cornwall from bondage. 'For as me seemeth,' said Tristram, 'it were shame that Sir Marhalt, the queen's brother of Ireland, should go away unless that he were fought withal.'

'As for that,' said King Meliodas, 'wit you well, son Tristram, that Sir Marhalt is called one of the best knights of the world; and therefore I know no knight in this country is able to match him.'

'Alas,' said Sir Tristram, 'that I were not made knight! And if Sir Marhalt should thus depart into Ireland, God let me never have worship. And sir,' said Tristram, 'I pray you give me leave to ride to King Mark; and so ye will be not displeased, of King Mark will I be made knight.'

'I will well', said King Meliodas, 'that ye be ruled as your courage will rule you.'

Then Sir Tristram thanked his father, and then he made him ready to ride into Cornwall.

So in the meanwhile there came letters of love from King Faramon of France's daughter unto Sir Tristram, that were piteous letters; but in no wise Tristram had no joy of her letters nor regard unto her. Also she sent him a little brachet that was passing fair. But when the king's daughter understood that Tristram would not love her, as the book saith, she died.* And then the same squire that brought the letters and the brachet came again unto Sir Tristram, as after ye shall hear in the tale following.

So after this young Tristram rode unto his eme King Mark of Cornwall. And when he came there he heard say that there would no knight fight with Sir Marhalt.

'Sir,' said Tristram, 'if ye will give me the order of knighthood, I will do battle with Sir Marhalt.'

[5]

eme] uncle

'What are ye,' said the king, 'and from whence be ye come?'

'Sir,' said Tristram, 'I come from King Meliodas that wedded your sister; and a gentleman wit you well I am.'

So King Mark beheld Tristram and saw that he was but a young man of age, but he was passingly well made and big.

'Fair sir,' said the king, 'what is your name, and where were ye born?'

'Sir, my name is Tristram, and in the country of Lyonesse was I born.'

'Ye say well,' said the king, 'and if ye will do this battle I shall make you knight.'

'Therefore came I to you,' said Sir Tristram, 'and for no other cause.'

But then King Mark made him knight. And therewith, anon as he had made him knight, he sent unto Sir Marhalt that he had found a young knight ready for to take the battle to the utterance.

'It may well be so,' said Sir Marhalt. 'But tell King Mark I will not fight with no knight but he be of blood royal, that is to say either king's son or queen's son, born of princes or of princesses.'

When King Mark understood that, he sent for Sir Tristram de Lyonesse and told him what was the answer of Sir Marhalt. Then said Sir Tristram, 'Sithen that he sayeth so, let him wit that I am come of father side and mother side of as noble blood as he is. For sir, now shall ye know that I am King Meliodas' son, born of your own sister, Dame Elizabeth, that died in the forest in the birth of me.'

'Ah, Jesu!' said King Mark, 'ye are welcome, fair nephew, to me.'

Then in all the haste the king horsed Sir Tristram, and armed him in the best manner that might be gotten for gold or silver. And then King Mark sent unto Sir Marhalt, and did him to wit that a better man born than he was himself should fight with him: 'and his name is Sir Tristram de Lyonesse, begotten of King Meliodas and born of King Mark's sister.'

Then was Sir Marhalt glad and blithe that he should fight with such a gentleman. And so by the assent of King Mark they let ordain that they should fight within an island nigh Sir Marhalt's ships. And so was Sir Tristram put into a vessel, both his horse and he, and all that to him longed both for his body and for his horse, that he lacked nothing. And

to the utterance] to the death   did him to wit] informed him

when King Mark and his barons of Cornwall beheld how young Sir Tristram departed with such a carriage to fight for the right of Cornwall, there was neither man nor woman of worship but they wept to see and understand so young a knight to jeopard himself for their right.

[6]   So to shorten this tale, when Sir Tristram arrived within the island he looked to the further side, and there he saw at an anchor six other ships nigh to the land; and under the shadow of the ships upon the land there hoved the noble knight Sir Marhalt of Ireland. Then Sir Tristram commanded to have his horse upon the land. And then Gouvernail, his servant, dressed his harness at all manner of rights; and then Sir Tristram mounted upon his horse, and when he was in his saddle well apparelled and his shield dressed upon his shoulder, so Sir Tristram asked Gouvernail, 'Where is this knight that I shall have ado withal?'

'Sir,' said Gouvernail, 'see ye him not? I weened that ye had seen him, for yonder he hoveth under the umber of his ships, on horseback with his spear in his hand and his shield upon his shoulder.'

'That is truth,' said Sir Tristram, 'now I see him.'*

Then he commanded Gouvernail to go to his vessel again; 'and commend me unto mine eme King Mark, and pray him, if that I be slain in this battle, for to inter my body as him seemeth best. And as for me, let him wit I will never be yielded for cowardice; and if I be slain and flee not, then they have lost no truage for me. And if so be that I flee or yield me as recreant, bid mine eme bury me never in Christian burials. And upon thy life,' said Sir Tristram unto Gouvernail, 'that thou come not nigh this island till that thou see me overcome or slain, or else that I win yonder knight.'

So either departed from other sore weeping.

[7]   And then Sir Marhalt avised Sir Tristram, and said thus: 'Young knight, Sir Tristram, what dost thou here? Me sore repents of thy courage, for wit thou well I have been assayed with many noble knights, and the best knights of this land have been assayed of my hands; and also the best knights of the world, I have matched them. And therefore by my counsel return again unto thy vessel.'

'Ah, fair knight and well-proved,' said Sir Tristram, 'thou shalt well wit I may not forsake thee in this quarrel, for I am for thy sake made

umber] shadow   avised] looked at

knight. And thou shalt well wit that I am a king's son born, and begotten upon a queen; and such promise I have made at my uncle's request
and my own seeking, that I shall fight with thee unto the uttermost and
deliver Cornwall from the old truage. And also wit thou well,
Sir Marhalt, that this is the greatest cause that thou couragest me to
have ado with thee, for thou art called one of the most renowned
knights of the world; and because of that noise and fame that thou hast
thou givest me courage to have ado with thee, for never yet was I
proved with good knight. And sithen I took the order of knighthood
this day, I am right well pleased and to me most worship that I may
have ado with such a knight as thou art. And now wit thou well,
Sir Marhalt, that I cast me to get worship on thy body; and if that I be
not proved, I trust to God to be worshipfully proved upon thy body,
and to deliver the country of Cornwall for ever from all manner of
truage from Ireland for ever.'

When Sir Marhalt had heard him say what he would, he said thus
again: 'Fair knight, sithen it is so that thou castest to win worship of
me, I let thee wit, worship may thou none lose by me if thou may stand
me three strokes. For I let thee wit, for my noble deeds proved and seen
King Arthur made me knight of the Table Round.'

Then they began to fewter their spears, and they met so fiercely
together that they smote each other down, both horse and man. But
Sir Marhalt smote Sir Tristram a great wound in the side with his
spear; and then they avoided their horses and pulled out their swords
and threw their shields before them, and then they lashed together as
men that were wild and courageous. And when they had stricken
together long, that their arms failed, then they left their strokes, and
foined at breasts and visors; and when they saw that that it might not
prevail them, then they hurtled together like rams to bear either other
down. Thus they fought still together more than half a day, and either
of them were wounded passing sore, that the blood ran down from
them upon the ground.

By then Sir Tristram waxed more fiercer than he did, and
Sir Marhalt feebled, and Sir Tristram ever more well-winded and
bigger; and with a mighty stroke he smote Sir Marhalt upon the helm
such a buffet that it went through his helm and through the coif of steel
and through the brain-pan, and the sword stuck so fast in the helm and
in his brain-pan that Sir Tristram pulled three times at his sword or
ever he might pull it out from his head. And there Sir Marhalt fell

down on his knees, and the edge of the sword left in his brain-pan. And suddenly Sir Marhalt rose grovelling and threw his sword and his shield from him, and so he ran to his ships and fled his way; and Sir Tristram had ever his shield and his sword.

And when Sir Tristram saw Sir Marhalt withdraw him, he said, 'Ah, sir knight of the Round Table, why withdrawest thou thee? Thou dost thyself and thy kin great shame, for I am but a young knight; or now I was never proved. And rather than I should withdraw me from thee, I had rather be hewn in piecemeal.'

Sir Marhalt answered no word, but yede his way sore groaning.

'Well, sir knight,' said Sir Tristram, 'I promise thee thy sword and thy shield shall be mine; and thy shield shall I wear in all places where I ride on my adventures, and in the sight of King Arthur and all the Round Table.'

[8]   So Sir Marhalt and his fellowship departed into Ireland. And as soon as he came to the king his brother, they searched his wounds; and when his head was searched, a piece of Sir Tristram's sword was therein found, and might never be had out of his head for no leechcraft. And so he died of Sir Tristram's sword; and that piece of the sword the queen, his sister, kept it for ever with her, for she thought to be revenged and she might.

Now turn we again unto Sir Tristram, that was sore wounded and sore for-bled, that he might not within a little while stand when he had taken cold, and uneath stir him of his limbs. And then he set him down softly upon a little hill, and bled fast. Then anon came Gouvernail, his man, with his vessel. And the king and the most part of his barons came with procession against Sir Tristram; and when he was come unto the land, King Mark took him in his arms, and he and Sir Dinas the Seneschal led Sir Tristram into the castle of Tintagel, and then was he searched in the best manner, and laid in his bed. And when King Mark saw his wounds he wept heartily, and so did all his lords.

'So God me help,' said King Mark, 'I would not for all my lands that my nephew died.'

So Sir Tristram lay there a month and more, and ever he was like to die of the stroke that Sir Marhalt smote him first with the spear; for as

---

leechcraft] medical skill   was he searched] his wounds were cleaned

the French book saith, the spearhead was envenomed, that Sir Tris-tram might not be whole. Then was King Mark and all his barons pass-ing heavy, for they deemed none other but that Sir Tristram should not recover. Then the king let send after all manner of leeches and sur-geons, both unto men and women, and there was none that would behote him the life.

Then came there a lady that was a witty lady; and she said plainly unto King Mark and to Sir Tristram and to all his barons, that he should never be whole but if that Sir Tristram went into the same country that the venom came from, and in that country should he be helped or else never—thus said the lady unto the king. So when the king understood it, he let purvey for Sir Tristram a fair vessel and well victualled, and therein was put Sir Tristram, and Gouvernail with him; and Sir Tristram took his harp with him. And so he was put into the sea to sail into Ireland.

And so by good fortune he arrived up in Ireland even fast by a castle where the king and the queen was. And at his arrival he sat and harped in his bed a merry lay—such one heard they never none in Ireland before that time. And when it was told the king and the queen of such a sick knight that was such a harper, anon the king sent for him and let search his wounds, and then he asked him his name. Then he answered and said, 'I am of the country of Lyonesse; and my name is Tramtrist, that was thus wounded in a battle as I fought for a lady's right.'

'So God me help,' said King Angwish, 'ye shall have all the help in this land that ye may have here. But in Cornwall but late I had a great loss as ever had king, for there I lost the best knight of the world; his name was Sir Marhalt, a full noble knight, and knight of the Table Round.' And there he told Sir Tramtrist wherefore Sir Marhalt was slain. So Sir Tramtrist made semblant as he had been sorry, and better he knew how it was than the king.

Then the king for great favour made Tramtrist to be put in his [9] daughter's ward and keeping, because she was a noble surgeon. And when she had searched him, she found in the bottom of his wound that therein was poison, and so she healed him in a while; and therefore Sir Tramtrist cast great love to La Belle Isode, for she was at that time the fairest lady and maiden of the world. And there Tramtrist learned her to harp, and she began to have a great fancy unto him.

behote] promise   witty] clever   learned] taught

And at that time Sir Palomides the Saracen was in that country, and well cherished with the king and the queen. And every day Sir Palomides drew unto La Belle Isode and proffered her many gifts, for he loved her passingly well. All that espied Tramtrist, and full well knew he Palomides for a noble knight and a mighty man. And wit you well, Sir Tramtrist had great despite at Sir Palomides, for La Belle Isode told Tramtrist that Palomides was in will to be christened for her sake. Thus was there great envy betwixt Tramtrist and Sir Palomides.

Then it befell that King Angwish let cry a great jousts and a great tournament for a lady that was called the Lady of the Launds, and she was nigh cousin unto the king; and what man won her, four days after should wed her and have all her lands. This cry was made in England, Wales, and Scotland, and also in France and in Brittany.

So it befell upon a day, La Belle Isode came unto Sir Tramtrist and told him of this tournament. He answered and said, 'Fair lady, I am but a feeble knight, and but late I had been dead had not your good ladyship* been. Now, fair lady, what would ye that I should do in this matter? Well ye wot, my lady, that I may not joust.'

'Ah, Tramtrist,' said La Belle Isode, 'why will ye not have ado at that tournament? For well I wot that Sir Palomides will be there, and to do what he may. And therefore, Sir Tramtrist, I pray you for to be there, for else Sir Palomides is like to win the degree.'

'Madam, as for that, it may be so, for he is a proved knight, and I am but a young knight and late made; and the first battle that ever I did, it mishapped me to be sore wounded as ye see. But and I wist that ye would be my better lady, at that tournament will I be, on this covenant: so that ye will keep my counsel and let no creature have knowledge that I shall joust, but yourself and such as ye will to keep your counsel, my poor person shall jeopard there for your sake, that peradventure Sir Palomides shall know when that I come.'

'Thereto,' said La Belle Isode, 'do your best; and as I can, I shall purvey horse and armour for you at my device.'

'As ye will, so be it,' said Sir Tramtrist. 'I will be at your commandment.'

So at the day of jousts there came Sir Palomides with a black shield, and he overthrew many knights, that all people had marvel; for he put to the worse Sir Gawain, Gaheris, Agravain, Bagdemagus, Kay,

degree] first place

Dodinas le Savage, Sagramore le Desirous, Gumret le Petit, and Griflet le Fils de Dieu—all these the first day Sir Palomides struck down
to the earth. And then all manner of knights were adread of Sir Palomides, and many called him the Knight with the Black Shield. So that
day Sir Palomides had great worship.

Then came King Angwish unto Tramtrist, and asked him why he
would not joust.

'Sir,' he said, 'I was but late hurt, and as yet I dare not adventure.'

Then there came the same squire that was sent from the king's
daughter of France unto Sir Tramtrist, and when he had espied
Sir Tristram he fell flat to his feet; and that espied La Belle Isode, what
courtesy the squire made to Tramtrist. And therewith suddenly
Sir Tristram ran unto the squire (his name was called Hebes le
Renowne) and prayed him heartily in no wise to tell his name.

'Sir,' said Hebes, 'I will not discover your name but if ye command
me.'

Then Sir Tristram asked him what he did in these countries.   [10]

'Sir,' he said, 'I came hither with Sir Gawain for to be made knight;
and if it please you, of your hands that I may be made knight.'

'Well, await on me tomorrow secretly, and in the field I shall make
you knight.'

Then had La Belle Isode great suspicion unto Tramtrist that he was
some man of worship proved; and therewith she comforted herself,
and cast more love unto him, for well she deemed he was some man of
worship.

And so on the morn Sir Palomides made him ready to come into the
field as he did the first day, and there he smote down the King with the
Hundred Knights, and the King of Scots. Then had La Belle Isode
ordained and well arrayed Sir Tramtrist with white horse and white
arms, and right so she let put him out at a privy postern; and he came
so into the field as it had been a bright angel. And anon Sir Palomides
espied him, and therewith he fewtered his spear unto Sir Tristram,
and he again unto him; and there Sir Tristram smote down Sir Palomides unto the earth. And then there was a great noise of people: some
said Sir Palomides had a fall, some said, 'The Knight with the Black
Shield hath a fall!' And wit you well La Belle Isode was passing glad.
And then Sir Gawain and his fellows nine had marvel who it might be

discover] reveal

that had smitten down Sir Palomides. Then would there none joust with Tramtrist, but all that there were forsook him, most and least.

Then Sir Tristram made Hebes a knight, and caused him to put himself forth, and he did right well that day. So after that, Sir Hebes held him with Sir Tristram.

And when Sir Palomides had received his fall, wit ye well that he was sore ashamed, and as privily as he might he withdrew him out of the field. All that espied Sir Tramtrist, and lightly he rode after Sir Palomides and overtook him and bade him turn, for better he would assay him or ever he departed. Then Sir Palomides turned him, and either lashed at other with their swords; but at the first stroke, Sir Tristram smote down Sir Palomides, and gave him such a stroke upon the head that he fell to the earth. So then Sir Tristram bade him yield him and do his command-ment, or else he would slay him. When Sir Palomides beheld his coun-tenance, he dreaded his buffets so, that he granted all his askings.

'Well,' said Sir Tramtrist, 'this shall be your charge. First, upon pain of your life, that ye forsake my lady La Belle Isode, and in no man-ner of wise that ye draw no more to her. Also, this twelvemonth and a day that ye bear no arms nor no harness of war. Now promise me this, or here shalt thou die.'

'Alas,' said Palomides, 'for ever I am shamed.'

Then he swore as Sir Tristram had commanded him. So for despite and anger Sir Palomides cut off his harness and threw them away. And so Sir Tristram turned again to the castle where was La Belle Isode; and by the way he met with a damosel that asked after Sir Lancelot, that won the Dolorous Gard.* And this damosel asked Sir Tristram what he was, for it was told her that it was he that smote down Sir Palomides, by whom the ten knights of Arthur's were smitten down. Then the damosel prayed Sir Tristram to tell her what he was, and whether that he were Sir Lancelot du Lake, for she deemed that there was no knight in the world that might do such deeds of arms but if it were Sir Lancelot.

'Wit you well that I am not Sir Lancelot, fair damosel, for I was never of such prowess. But in God is all; He may make me as good a knight as that good knight Sir Lancelot is.'

'Now, gentle knight, put up thy visor.' And when she beheld his visage, she thought she saw never a better man's visage, nor a better-faring knight.

better-faring] more handsome

So when the damosel knew certainly that he was not Sir Lancelot, then she took her leave and departed from him. And then Sir Tristram rode privily unto the postern where kept him La Belle Isode; and there she made him great cheer, and thanked God of his good speed.

So anon within a while the king and the queen and all the court understood that it was Sir Tramtrist that smote down Sir Palomides; and then was he much made of, more than he was before.

Thus was Sir Tramtrist long there well cherished with the king and [11] with the queen, and namely with La Belle Isode. So upon a day the queen and La Belle Isode made a bain for Sir Tramtrist.* And when he was in his bain the queen and Isode her daughter roamed up and down in the chamber the while Gouvernail and Hebes attended upon Tramtrist. The queen beheld his sword as it lay upon his bed, and then at unhap the queen drew out his sword and beheld it a long while. And both they thought it a passing fair sword; but within a foot and a half of the point there was a great piece thereof out broken of the edge. And when the queen had espied that gap in the sword, she remembered her of a piece of a sword that was found in the brain-pan of Sir Marhalt, that was her brother.

'Alas,' then said she unto her daughter La Belle Isode, 'this is the same traitor knight that slew my brother, thine eme.'

When Isode heard her say so she was passing sore abashed, for passing well she loved Tramtrist, and full well she knew the cruelness of her mother the queen.

So anon therewith the queen went unto her own chamber and sought her coffer, and there she took out the piece of the sword that was pulled out of Sir Marhalt's brain-pan after that he was dead. And then she ran with that piece of iron to the sword, and when she put that piece of steel and iron unto the sword, it was as meet as it might be when it was new broken. And then the queen gripped that sword in her hand fiercely, and with all her might she ran straight upon Tramtrist where he sat in his bain. And there she had rived him through, had not Sir Hebes been: he got her in his arms and pulled the sword from her, and else she had thrust him through. So when she was let of her evil will she ran to the king her husband and said, 'Ah, my lord!' On her knees kneeling, she said, 'Here have ye in your house that traitor

kept] awaited   namely] especially   bain] bath   at unhap] by misfortune   eme] uncle   meet] well-fitting   let of] prevented from

knight that slew my brother and your servant, the noble knight Sir Marhalt.'

'Who is that,' said the king, 'and where is he?'

'Sir,' she said, 'it is Sir Tramtrist, the same knight that my daughter healed.'

'Alas,' said the king, 'therefore I am right heavy, for he is a full noble knight as ever I saw in field. But I charge you,' said the king, 'that ye have not ado with that knight, but let me deal with him.'

Then the king went into the chamber unto Sir Tramtrist; and then was he gone unto his own chamber, and the king found him all ready armed to mount upon his horse. So when the king saw him all ready armed to go unto horseback, the king said, 'Nay, Tramtrist, it will not avail to compare against me; but thus much I shall do for my worship and for thy love. In so much as thou art within my court, it were no worship to slay thee; therefore upon this condition I will give thee leave for to depart from this court in safety, so thou wilt tell me who was thy father and what is thy name, and also if thou slew Sir Marhalt, my brother.'

[12] 'Sir,' said Tramtrist, 'now I shall tell you all the truth. My father's name is Sir Meliodas, King of Lyonesse, and my mother hight Eliza–beth, that was sister unto King Mark of Cornwall; and my mother died of me in the forest, and because thereof she commanded or she died that when I was christened they should christen me Tristram. And because I would not be known in this country, I turned my name and let call me Tramtrist. And for the truage of Cornwall I fought for my eme's sake and for the right of Cornwall that ye had been possessed many years. And wit you well,' said Sir Tristram unto the king, 'I did the battle for the love of my uncle King Mark, and for the love of the country of Cornwall, and for to increase my honour; for that same day that I fought with Sir Marhalt I was made knight, and never or then did I no battle with no knight. And from me he went alive, and left his shield and his sword behind him.'

'So God me help,' said the king, 'I may not say but ye did as a knight should do, and it was your part to do for your quarrel, and to increase your worship as a knight should do. Howbeit I may not maintain you in this country with my worship but that I should displease many of my barons and my wife and my kin.'

compare] contend

'Sir,' said Sir Tristram, 'I thank you of your good lordship that I
have had within here with you, and the great goodness my lady your
daughter hath showed me. And therefore,' said Sir Tristram, 'it may so
be that ye shall win more by my life than by my death; for in the parts
of England it may happen I may do you service at some season, that ye
shall be glad that ever ye showed me your good lordship. With more I
promise you as I am true knight, that in all places I shall be my lady
your daughter's servant and knight in all right and in wrong, and I shall
never fail her to do as much as a knight may do. Also I beseech your
good grace that I may take my leave at my lady your daughter, and at all
the barons and knights.'

'I will well,' said the king.

Then Sir Tristram went unto La Belle Isode and took his leave of
her. And then he told what he was, and how a lady told him that he
should never be whole 'until I came into this country where the poison
was made wherethrough I was near my death, had not your ladyship
been.'

'Ah, gentle knight,' said La Belle Isode, 'full woe I am of thy departing, for I saw never man that I owed so good will to.' And therewith she
wept heartily.

'Madam,' said Sir Tristram, 'ye shall understand that my name is
Sir Tristram de Lyonesse, begotten of a king and born of a queen. And
I promise you faithfully, I shall be all the days of my life your knight.'

'Gramercy,' said La Belle Isode, 'and I promise you thereagainst, I
shall not be married this seven years but by your assent; and whom that
ye will, I shall be married to him and he will have me, if ye will consent
thereto.' And then Sir Tristram gave her a ring, and she gave him
another.

And therewith he departed and came into the court among all the
barons, and there he took his leave at most and least. And openly he
said among them all, 'Fair lords, now it is so that I must depart. If there
be any man here that I have offended unto, or that any man be with me
grieved, let him complain him here before me or that ever I depart, and
I shall amend it unto my power. And if there be any man that will proffer me wrong, or say me wrong or shame me behind my back, say it
now or else never; and here is my body to make it good, body against
body.'

thereagainst] in return

And all they stood still: there was not one that would say one word. Yet were there some knights that were of the queen's blood, and of Sir Marhalt's blood, but they would not meddle with him.

[13] So Sir Tristram departed and took the sea, and with good wind he arrived up at Tintagel in Cornwall. And when King Mark was whole in his prosperity there came tidings that Sir Tristram was arrived, and whole of his wounds. Thereof was King Mark passing glad, and so were all the barons. And when he saw his time he rode unto his father King Meliodas, and there he had all the cheer that the king and the queen could make him. And then largely King Meliodas and his queen parted of their lands and goods to Sir Tristram.

Then by the licence of his father he returned again unto the court of King Mark. And there he lived long in great joy long time, until at the last there befell a jealousy and an unkindness betwixt King Mark and Sir Tristram, for they loved both one lady; and she was an earl's wife that hight Sir Segwarides. And this lady loved Sir Tristram passingly well, and he loved her again; for she was a passing fair lady, and that espied Sir Tristram well. Then King Mark understood that and was jealous, for King Mark loved her passingly well.

So it befell upon a day, this lady sent a dwarf unto Sir Tristram and bade him as he loved her that he would be with her the next night following. 'Also she charged you that ye come not to her but if ye be well armed'—for her lord was called a good knight.

Sir Tristram answered to the dwarf and said, 'Recommend me unto my lady and tell her I will not fail, but I shall be with her the term that she hath set me.' And therewith the dwarf departed.

And King Mark espied that the dwarf was with Sir Tristram upon message from Segwarides' wife; then King Mark sent for the dwarf, and when he was come he made the dwarf by force to tell him all why and wherefore that he came on message to Sir Tristram, and then he told him.

'Well,' said King Mark, 'go where thou wilt, and upon pain of death that thou say no word that thou spake with me.' So the dwarf departed.

And that same night that the steven was set betwixt Segwarides' wife and Sir Tristram, so King Mark armed and made him ready, and took two knights of his counsel with him. And so he rode before for to

steven] assignation   of his counsel] in his confidence

abide by the ways for to await upon Sir Tristram. And as Sir Tristram came riding upon his way with his spear in his hand, King Mark came hurtling upon him, and his two knights, suddenly, and all three smote him with their spears; and King Mark hurt Sir Tristram on the breast right sore. And then Sir Tristram fewtered his spear, and smote King Mark so sore that he rushed him to the earth and bruised him that he lay still in a swoon; and long it was or he might wield himself. And then he ran to the one knight, and after to the other, and smote them to the cold earth, that they lay still.

And therewith Sir Tristram rode forth sore wounded to the lady, and found her abiding him at a postern. And there she welcomed him fair, and either halsed other in arms; and so she let put up his horse in the best wise, and then she unarmed him. And so they supped lightly, and went to bed with great joy and pleasance. And so in his raging he took no keep of his green wound that King Mark had given him; and so Sir Tristram be-bled both the over sheet and the nether sheet, and the pillows and the head sheet. And within a while there came one before, that warned her that her lord Sir Segwarides was near hand, within a bow draught. So she made Sir Tristram to arise, and he armed him and took his horse and so departed. So by then was Sir Segwarides her lord come; and when he found his bed troubled and broken, he went near and looked by candlelight and he saw that there had lain a wounded knight.

'Ah, false traitress,' he said, 'why hast thou betrayed me?' And therewith he swung out a sword and said, 'But if thou tell me all, now shalt thou die!'

'Ah, my lord, mercy!' said the lady, and held up her hands, 'and slay me not, and I shall tell you all who hath been here.'

'Then anon,' said Segwarides, 'say and tell me the truth.'

Anon for dread she said, 'Here was Sir Tristram with me, and by the way as he came to me-ward, he was sore wounded.'

'Ah, false traitress, where is he become?'

'Sir,' she said, 'he is armed, and departed on horseback not yet hence half a mile.'

'Ye say well,' said Segwarides.

Then he armed him lightly and got his horse, and rode after Sir Tristram the straight way unto Tintagel. And within a while he

halsed] embraced   raging] passion   green] fresh   bow draught]
bowshot   But if] Unless

overtook Sir Tristram, and then he bade him, 'Turn, false traitor knight!'

And therewith Sir Segwarides smote Sir Tristram with a spear, that it all tobrast; and then he swung out his sword and smote fast at Sir Tristram.

'Sir knight,' said Sir Tristram, 'I counsel you, smite no more, howbeit for the wrongs that I have done you I will forbear you as long as I may.'

'Nay,' said Segwarides, 'that shall not be, for either thou shalt die or else I.'

Then Sir Tristram drew out his sword and hurled his horse unto him freshly, and through the waist of the body he smote Sir Segwarides that he fell to the earth in swoon; and so Sir Tristram departed and left him there. And so he rode unto Tintagel and took his lodging secretly, for he would not be known that he was hurt. Also Sir Segwarides' men rode after their master, and brought him home on his shield; and there he lay long or he were whole, but at the last he recovered.

Also King Mark would not be known of that he had done unto Sir Tristram when he met that night; and as for Sir Tristram, he knew not that King Mark had met with him. And so the king came askance to Sir Tristram to comfort him as he lay sick in his bed. But as long as King Mark lived he loved never after Sir Tristram. So after that, though there were fair speech, love was there none.*

askance] hypocritically

So when this was done King Mark cast all the ways that he might to [19]
destroy Sir Tristram; and then imagined in himself to send Sir Tristram into Ireland for La Belle Isode. For Sir Tristram had so praised
her for her beauty and her goodness that King Mark said that he would
wed her; whereupon he prayed Sir Tristram to take his way into
Ireland for him on message—and all this was done to the intent to slay
Sir Tristram. Notwithstanding, he would not refuse the message for
no danger nor peril that might fall, for the pleasure of his uncle. So he
made him ready to go in the most goodliest wise that might be devised;
for he took with him the most goodliest knights that he might find in
the court, and they were arrayed after the guise that was used in that
time in the most goodliest manner.

So Sir Tristram departed and took the sea with all his fellowship.
And anon as he was in the sea a tempest took them, and drove them
into the coast of England; and there they arrived fast by Camelot, and
full fain they were to take the land. And when they were landed
Sir Tristram set up his pavilion upon the land of Camelot, and there he
let hang his shield upon the pavilion.

And that same day came two knights of King Arthur's: that one was
Sir Ector de Maris, and that other was Sir Morganor. And these two
touched the shield, and bade him come out of the pavilion for to joust
and he would.

'Anon ye shall be answered,' said Sir Tristram, 'and ye will tarry a
little while.'

So he made him ready, and first he smote down Sir Ector and then
Sir Morganor, all with one spear, and sore bruised them. And when
they lay upon the earth they asked Sir Tristram what he was, and of
what country he was knight.

'Fair lords,' said Sir Tristram, 'wit you well that I am of Cornwall.'

'Alas,' said Sir Ector, 'now am I ashamed that ever any Cornish
knight should overcome me.' And then for despite Sir Ector put off his
armour from him and went on foot, and would not ride.

Then it befell that Sir Bleoberis and Sir Blamor de Ganis, that were [20]
brethren, they had summoned King Angwish of Ireland for to come to
King Arthur's court upon pain of forfeiture of King Arthur's good
grace; and if the King of Ireland came not in to the day assigned and
set, the king should lose his lands. So by King Arthur it was happened
that day that neither he nor Sir Lancelot might not be there where the
judgement should be given, for King Arthur was with Sir Lancelot at

Joyous Gard. And so King Arthur assigned King Carados and the
King of Scots to be there that day as judges.

So when these kings were at Camelot, King Angwish of Ireland was
come to know his accusers. Then was Sir Blamor de Ganis there that
appealed the King of Ireland of treason, that he had slain a cousin of
theirs in his court in Ireland by treason. Then the king was sore
abashed of his accusation for why he was at the summons of King
Arthur, and or that he came at Camelot he wist not wherefore he was
sent for. So when the king heard him say his will, he understood well
there was none other remedy but to answer him knightly; for the custom was such in those days, that and any man were appealed of any treason or of murder he should fight body for body, or else to find another
knight for him. And all manner of murders in those days were called
treason. So when King Angwish understood his accusing he was passing heavy, for he knew Sir Blamor de Ganis that he was a noble knight
and of noble knights come. So the King of Ireland was but simply purveyed of his answer; therefore the judges gave him respite by the third
day to give his answer. So the king departed unto his lodging.*

[21]   Then when Sir Tristram was in his pavilion, Gouvernail, his man,
came and told him how that King Angwish of Ireland was come
thither, and he was in great distress; and there he told him how he was
summoned and appealed of murder.

'So God me help,' said Sir Tristram, 'this is the best tidings that ever
came to me these seven years, for now shall the King of Ireland have
need of my help; for I dare say there is no knight in this country that is
not in Arthur's court dare do battle with Sir Blamor de Ganis. And for
to win the love of the King of Ireland I will take the battle upon me; and
therefore, Gouvernail, bear me this word, I charge thee, to the king.'

Then Gouvernail went unto King Angwish of Ireland and saluted
him full fair. So the king welcomed him and asked what he would.

'Sir,' he said, 'here is a knight near hand that desireth to speak with
you, for he bade me say that he would do you service.'

'What knight is he?' said the king.

'Sir, it is Sir Tristram de Lyonesse, that for the good grace ye
showed him in your lands he will reward you in these countries.'

'Come on, fellow,' said the king, 'with me anon, and bring me unto
Sir Tristram.'

appealed] accused   simply purveyed] ill-equipped

So the king took a little hackney and but few fellowship with him, till that he came unto Sir Tristram's pavilion. And when Sir Tristram saw the king he ran unto him and would have held his stirrup; but the king leapt from his horse lightly, and either halsed other in their arms.

'My gracious lord,' said Sir Tristram, 'gramercy of your great goodnesses that ye showed unto me in your marches and lands. And at that time I promised you to do you service and ever it lay in my power.'

'Ah, gentle knight,' said the king unto Sir Tristram, 'now have I great need of you—never had I so great need of no knight's help.'

'How so, my good lord?' said Sir Tristram.

'I shall tell you,' said the king. 'I am summoned and appealed from my country for the death of a knight that was kin unto the good knight Sir Lancelot; wherefore Sir Blamor de Ganis and Sir Bleoberis his brother hath appealed me to fight with him or for to find a knight in my stead. And well I wot,' said the king, 'these that are come of King Ban's blood, as Sir Lancelot and these others, are passing good hard knights, and hard men for to win in battle as any that I know now living.'

'Sir,' said Sir Tristram, 'for the good lordship ye showed unto me in Ireland, and for my lady your daughter's sake, La Belle Isode, I will take the battle for you upon this condition, that ye shall grant me two things: one is that ye shall swear unto me that ye are in the right, and that ye were never consenting to the knight's death. Sir, then,' said Sir Tristram, 'when I have done this battle, if God give me grace to speed, that ye shall give me a reward, what thing reasonable that I will ask you.'

'So God me help,' said the king, 'ye shall have whatsoever ye will.'

'Ye say well,' said Sir Tristram. 'Now make your answer that your champion is ready, for I shall die in your quarrel rather than to be recreant.' [22]

'I have no doubt of you,' said the king, 'that and ye should have ado with Sir Lancelot de Lake.'

'As for Sir Lancelot, he is called the noblest of the world of knights, and wit you well that the knights of his blood are noble men, and dread shame; therefore upon my head it is no shame to call him a good knight.'

'Sir, it is noised', said the king, 'that Sir Blamor is the hardier knight.'

halsed] embraced   that and ye should have ado] even if you had to fight

'As for that, let him be. He shall not be refused and he were the best knight that beareth shield or spear.'

So King Angwish departed unto King Carados and the kings that were that time as judges, and told them how that he had found his champion ready. Then by the commandment of the kings Sir Blamor de Ganis and Sir Tristram de Lyonesse were sent for to hear their charge. And when they were come before the judges there were many kings and knights that beheld Sir Tristram, and much speech they had of him because he slew Sir Marhalt the good knight, and because he forjousted Sir Palomides the good knight. So when they had taken their charge they withdrew them to make them ready to do battle.

Then said Sir Bleoberis to his brother Sir Blamor, 'Fair dear brother,' said he, 'remember of what kin we be come of, and what a man is Sir Lancelot du Lake, neither further nor nearer but brothers' children; and there was never none of our kin that ever was shamed in battle. But rather, brother, suffer death than to be shamed.'

'Brother,' said Sir Blamor, 'have ye no doubt of me, for I shall never shame none of my blood. How be I am sure that yonder knight is called a passing good knight as of his time as any in the world, yet shall I never yield me nor say the loath word. Well may he happen to smite me down with his great might of chivalry, but rather shall he slay me than I shall yield me recreant.'

'God speed you well,' said Sir Bleoberis, 'for ye shall find him the mightiest knight that ever ye had ado withal.'

'God me speed!' said Sir Blamor. And therewith he took his horse at the one end of the lists, and Sir Tristram at the other end of the lists, and so they fewtered their spears and came together as it had been thunder. And there Sir Tristram through great might smote down Sir Blamor and his horse to the earth. Then anon Sir Blamor avoided his horse and pulled out his sword and took his shield before him, and bade Sir Tristram alight, 'For though my horse hath failed, I trust to God the earth will not fail me.'

And then Sir Tristram alit and dressed him unto battle; and there they lashed together strongly, razing, foining, and dashing many sad strokes, that the kings and knights had great wonder that they might

---

forjousted] overthrew   loath word] i.e. of yielding   razing, foining, and dashing many sad strokes] slashing, thrusting, and striking many grievous strokes

stand, for ever they fought like wood men. There was never seen of two knights that fought more fiercely, for Sir Blamor was so hasty he would have no rest, that all men wondered that they had breath to stand on their feet, that all the place was bloody that they fought in. And at the last Sir Tristram smote Sir Blamor such a buffet upon the helm that he there sank down upon his side, and Sir Tristram stood still and beheld him.

So when Sir Blamor might speak, he said thus: 'Sir Tristram de [23] Lyonesse, I require thee, as thou art a noble knight and the best knight that ever I found, that thou wilt slay me out, for I would not live to be made lord of all the earth, for I have liever die here with worship than live here with shame. And needs, Sir Tristram, thou must slay me, or else thou shalt never win the field, for I will never say the loath word. And therefore if thou dare slay me, slay me, I require thee.'

When Sir Tristram heard him say so knightly, in his heart he wist not what to do with him, remembering him of both parts, of what blood he was come of, and for Sir Lancelot's sake he would be loath to slay him; and in the other part, in no wise he might not choose but that he must make him say the loath word, or else to slay him.

Then Sir Tristram started aback and went to the kings that were judges; and there he kneeled down before them, and besought them of their worships, and for King Arthur's love and for Sir Lancelot's sake, that they would take this matter in their hands.

'For, my fair lords,' said Sir Tristram, 'it were shame and pity that this noble knight that yonder lieth should be slain; for ye hear well, shamed will he not be, and I pray to God that he never be slain nor shamed for me. And as for the king whom I fight for, I shall require him, as I am his true champion and true knight in this field, that he will have mercy upon this knight.'

'So God me help,' said King Angwish, 'I will for your sake, Sir Tristram, be ruled as ye will have me, for I will heartily pray the kings that be here judges to take it in their hands.'

Then the kings that were judges called Sir Bleoberis to them and asked his advice.

'My lords,' said Sir Bleoberis, 'though my brother be beaten and have the worse in his body through might of arms, he hath not beaten his heart, and thank God he is not shamed this day. And rather than he be shamed, I require you,' said Sir Bleoberis, 'let Sir Tristram slay him out.'

'It shall not be so,' said the kings. 'For his part, his adversary, both the king and the champion, have pity on Sir Blamor's knighthood.'

'My lords,' said Sir Bleoberis, 'I will right as ye will.'

Then the kings called the King of Ireland, and found him goodly and treatable. And then, by all their advices, Sir Tristram and Sir Bleoberis took up Sir Blamor, and the two brethren were made accorded with King Angwish, and kissed together and made friends for ever. And then Sir Blamor and Sir Tristram kissed together, and there they made their oaths that they would never none of them two brethren fight with Sir Tristram, and Sir Tristram made the same oath. And for that gentle battle all the blood of Sir Lancelot loved Sir Tristram for ever.

Then King Angwish and Sir Tristram took their leave; and so he sailed into Ireland with great noblesse and joy. So when they were in Ireland the king let make it known throughout all the land how and in what manner Sir Tristram had done for him. Then the queen and all that there were made the most of him that they might. But the joy that La Belle Isode made of Sir Tristram there might no tongue tell, for of all men earthly she loved him most.

[24]   Then upon a day King Angwish asked Sir Tristram why he asked not his boon. Then said Sir Tristram, 'Now it is time. Sir, this is all that I will desire, that ye will give La Belle Isode, your daughter, not for myself, but for my uncle King Mark shall have her to wife, for so have I promised him.'

'Alas,' said the king, 'I had liever than all the land that I have that ye would have wedded her yourself.'

'Sir, and I did so, I were shamed for ever in this world and false of my promise. Therefore,' said Sir Tristram, 'I require you, hold your promise that ye promised me; for this is my desire, that ye will give me La Belle Isode to go with me into Cornwall for to be wedded unto King Mark, my uncle.'

'As for that,' King Angwish said, 'ye shall have her with you to do with her what it please you; that is for to say, if that ye list to wed her yourself, that is me lievest, and if ye will give her unto King Mark your uncle, that is in your choice.'

So to make short conclusion, La Belle Isode was made ready to go with Sir Tristram, and Dame Brangwain went with her for her chief

---

treatable] co-operative   that is me lievest] that is what I would most like

gentlewoman, with many other. Then the queen, Isode's mother, gave Dame Brangwain unto her to be her gentlewoman. And also she and Gouvernail had a drink of the queen, and she charged them that where King Mark should wed, that same day they should give him that drink, that King Mark should drink to La Belle Isode. 'And then,' said the queen, 'either shall love other days of their life.' So this drink was given unto Dame Brangwain and unto Gouvernail.

So Sir Tristram took the sea; and when he and La Belle Isode were in their cabin, it happed so they were thirsty; and then they saw a little flacket of gold stand by them, and it seemed by the colour and the taste that it was noble wine. So Sir Tristram took the flacket in his hand and said, 'Madam Isode, here is a draught of good wine that Dame Brangwain your maiden and Gouvernail my servant have kept for themselves.'

Then they laughed and made good cheer, and either drank to other freely, and they thought never drink that ever they drank so sweet nor so good to them. But by that drink was in their bodies, they loved either other so well that never their love departed, for weal nor for woe. And thus it happed first the love betwixt Sir Tristram and La Belle Isode, the which love never departed days of their life.*

And in the meanwhile word came to Sir Tristram that King Carados,   [28] the mighty king that was made like a giant, fought with Sir Gawain and gave him such strokes that he swooned in his saddle; and after that he took him by the collar and pulled him out of the saddle, and bound him fast to the saddle-bow, and so rode his way with him toward his castle. And as he rode, Sir Lancelot by fortune met with King Carados, and anon he knew Sir Gawain that lay bound before him.

'Ah', said Sir Lancelot unto Sir Gawain, 'how standeth it with you?'

'Never so hard,' said Sir Gawain, 'unless that ye help me, for so God me help, without ye rescue me I know no knight that may, but you or Sir Tristram.' Wherefore Sir Lancelot was heavy at Sir Gawain's words.

And then Sir Lancelot bade Sir Carados, 'Lay down that knight and fight with me.'

'Thou art but a fool,' said Sir Carados, 'for I will serve thee in the same wise.'

---

flacket] flask   by that drink] by the time that that drink

'As for that,' said Sir Lancelot, 'spare me not, for I warn thee I will not spare thee.'

And then he bound Sir Gawain hand and foot, and so threw him to the ground. And then he got his spear in his hand of his squire, and departed from Sir Lancelot to fetch his course; and so either met with other and brake their spears to their hands. And then they pulled out their swords and hurtled together on horseback more than an hour, and at last Sir Lancelot smote Sir Carados such a buffet on the helm that it pierced his brain-pan. So then Sir Lancelot took Sir Carados by the collar and pulled him under his horse's feet, and then he alit and pulled off his helm and struck off his head. Then Sir Lancelot unbound Sir Gawain.

So this same tale was told to Sir Tristram, and said, 'Now may ye hear the noblesse that followeth Sir Lancelot.'

'Alas,' said Sir Tristram, 'and I had not this message in hand with this fair lady, truly I would never stint or that I had found Sir Lancelot.'

Then Sir Tristram and La Belle Isode came into Cornwall, and there all the barons met them.

message] business

And anon they were richly wedded with great noblesse. But ever, as the [29]
French book saith, Sir Tristram and La Belle Isode loved ever together.
Then was there great jousts and great tourneying, and many lords and
ladies were at that feast, and Sir Tristram was most praised of all other.

So thus dured the feast long; and after that feast was done, within a
little while after, by the assent of two ladies that were with the queen,
they ordained for hate and envy for to destroy Dame Brangwain, that
was maiden and lady unto La Belle Isode.* And she was sent into the
forest for to fetch herbs; and there she was bound hand and foot to a
tree, and so she was bound three days. And by fortune Sir Palomides
found Dame Brangwain, and there he delivered her from the death,
and brought her to a nunnery therebeside for to be recovered.

When Isode the queen missed her maiden, wit you well she was
right heavy as ever any queen might be, for of all earthly women she
loved her best, and most cause why, she came with her out of her country. And so upon a day Queen Isode walked into the forest to put away
her thoughts, and there she went herself unto a well and made great
moan. And suddenly there came Sir Palomides unto her and heard all
her complaint, and said, 'Madam Isode, and ye will grant me my boon,
I shall bring again to you Dame Brangwain safe and sound.'

Then the queen was so glad of his proffer that suddenly unadvised
she granted all his asking.

'Well, madam,' said Sir Palomides, 'I trust to your promise, and if ye
will abide half an hour here I shall bring her to you.'

'Sir, I shall abide you,' said the queen.

Then Sir Palomides rode forth his way to that nunnery, and lightly
he came again with Dame Brangwain; but by her good will she would
not have come to the queen, for cause she stood in adventure of her life.
Notwithstanding, half against her will, she came with Sir Palomides
unto the queen. And when the queen saw her she was passing glad.

'Now, madam,' said Sir Palomides, 'remember upon your promise,
for I have fulfilled my promise.'

'Sir Palomides,' said the queen, 'I wot not what is your desire, but I
will that ye wit, howbeit that I proffered you largely, I thought no evil,
neither, I warn you, no evil will I do.'

'Madam,' said Sir Palomides, 'as at this time ye shall not know my
desire.'

---

most cause why] in particular because   unadvised] without thinking

'But before my lord my husband, there shall ye know that ye shall have your desire that I promised you.'*

And then the queen rode home unto the king, and Sir Palomides rode with her. And when Sir Palomides came before the king, he said, 'Sir king, I require thee as thou art righteous king, that ye will judge me the right.'

'Tell me your cause,' said the king, 'and ye shall have right.'

[30] 'Sir,' said Sir Palomides, 'I promised your queen, my lady Dame Isode, to bring again Dame Brangwain that she had lost, upon this covenant, that she should grant me a boon that I would ask; and without grudging or advisement, she granted me.'

'What say ye, my lady?' said the king.

'It is as he saith, so God me help, to say the sooth,' said the queen. 'I promised him his asking for love and joy I had to see her.'

'Well, madam!' said the king. 'And if she were hasty to grant what boon he would ask, I would well that she performed her promise.'*

Then said Sir Palomides, 'I will that ye wit that I will have your queen to lead her and to govern her where as me list.'

Therewith the king stood still, and bethought him of Sir Tristram, and deemed that he would rescue her. And then hastily the king answered and said, 'Take her to thee, and the adventures withal that will fall of it, for as I suppose thou wilt not enjoy her no while.'

'As for that,' said Sir Palomides, 'I dare right well abide the adventure.'

And so, to make short tale, Sir Palomides took her by the hand and said, 'Madam, grudge not to go with me, for I desire nothing but your own promise.'

'As for that,' said the queen, 'wit thou well, I fear not greatly to go with thee, howbeit thou hast me at advantage upon my promise; for I doubt not I shall be worshipfully rescued from thee.'

'As for that,' said Sir Palomides, 'be as it be may.'

So Queen Isode was set behind Sir Palomides, and rode his way. And anon the king sent unto Sir Tristram, but in no wise he would not be found, for he was in the forest an-hunting; for that was always his custom, but if he used arms, to chase and to hunt in the forest.

'Alas,' said the king, 'now am I shamed forever, that by my own assent my lady and my queen shall be devoured.'

devoured] destroyed

Then came there forth a knight that hight Lambegus, and he was a knight of Sir Tristram's.

'My lord,' said the knight, 'sith that ye have such trust in my lord Sir Tristram, wit you well for his sake I will ride after your queen and rescue her, or else shall I be beaten.'

'Grantmercy,' said the king. 'And I live, Sir Lambegus, I shall deserve it.'

And then Sir Lambegus armed him and rode after them as fast as he might; and then within a while he overtook them. And then Sir Palomides left the queen and said, 'What art thou?' said Sir Palomides, 'art thou Sir Tristram?'

'Nay,' he said, 'I am his servant, and my name is Sir Lambegus.'

'That me repents,' said Sir Palomides, 'I had liever thou had been Sir Tristram.'

'I believe you well,' said Sir Lambegus, 'but when thou meetest with Sir Tristram, thou shalt have both thy hands full.'

And then they hurtled together and all tobrast their spears; and then they pulled out their swords and hewed on their helms and hauberks. At the last Sir Palomides gave Sir Lambegus such a wound that he fell down like a dead man to the earth. Then he looked after La Belle Isode; and then she was gone, he wist not where. Wit you well that Sir Palomides was never so heavy!

So the queen ran into the forest, and there she found a well; and therein she had thought to have drowned herself. And as good fortune would, there came a knight to her that had a castle there beside, and his name was Sir Adtherp. And when he found the queen in that mischief, he rescued her and brought her to his castle. And when he wist what she was, he armed him and took his horse, and said he would be avenged upon Sir Palomides; and so he rode unto the time he met with him. And there Sir Palomides wounded him sore, and by force he made him to tell the cause why he did battle with him; and he told him how he led the queen La Belle Isode into his own castle.

'Now bring me there,' said Sir Palomides, 'or thou shalt of my hands die.'

'Sir,' said Sir Adtherp, 'I am so sore wounded I may not follow; but ride you this way, and it shall bring you to my castle, and therein is the queen.'

Grantmercy°] gramercy, thank you   deserve] reward

Sir Palomides rode till that he came to the castle; and at a window La Belle Isode saw Sir Palomides. Then she made the gates to be shut strongly. And when he saw he might not enter into the castle, he put off his horse's bridle and his saddle, and so put his horse to pasture; and set himself down at the gate like a man that was out of his wit, that recked not of himself.

[31]　　Now turn we unto Sir Tristram, that when he was come home and wist that La Belle Isode was gone with Sir Palomides, wit you well he was wroth out of measure.

'Alas,' said Sir Tristram, 'I am this day shamed.' Then he called Gouvernail, his man, and said, 'Haste thee that I were armed and on horseback, for well I wot Sir Lambegus hath no might nor strength to withstand Sir Palomides. Alas I had not been in his stead!'

So anon he was armed and horsed and rode after into the forest; and within a while he found his knight Sir Lambegus almost to death wounded. And Sir Tristram bare him to a forester, and charged him to keep him well. And then he rode forth and found Sir Adtherp sore wounded. And he told all, and how 'the queen had drowned herself had I not been, and how for her sake I took upon me to do battle with Sir Palomides.'

'Where is my lady?' said Sir Tristram.

'Sir,' said the knight, 'she is sure enough within my castle, and she can hold her within it.'

'Grantmercy,' said Sir Tristram, 'of thy great goodness.'

And so he rode till that he came nigh his castle. And then Sir Palomides sat at the gate and saw where Sir Tristram came; and he sat as had slept, and his horse pastured before him.

'Now go thou, Gouvernail,' said Sir Tristram, 'and bid him awake and make him ready.'

So Gouvernail rode unto him and said, 'Sir Palomides, arise and take thy harness!'

But he was in such a study that he heard not what he said. So Gouvernail came again to Sir Tristram, and told him he slept, or else he was mad.

'Go thou again,' said Sir Tristram, 'and bid him arise, and tell him I am here, his mortal foe.'

So Gouvernail rode again, and put upon him with the butt of his

recked not of] did not care about

spear, and said, 'Sir Palomides, make thee ready, for wit thou well Sir Tristram hoveth yonder, and sendeth thee word he is thy mortal foe.'

And therewith Sir Palomides arose stilly without any words, and got his horse anon and saddled him and bridled him; and lightly he leapt upon him, and got his spear in his hand. And either fewtered their spears and hurled fast together, and anon Sir Tristram smote down Sir Palomides over his horse's tail. Then lightly Sir Palomides put his shield before him and drew his sword; and there began strong battle on both parts, for both they fought for the love of one lady. And ever she lay on the walls and beheld them, how they fought out of measure, and either were wounded passing sore, but Sir Palomides was much sorer wounded. For they fought thus, tracing and traversing, more than two hours, that well nigh for dole and sorrow La Belle Isode swooned, and said,

'Alas, that one I loved and yet do, and the other I love not, that they should fight! And yet it were great pity that I should see Sir Palomides slain, for well I know by that the end be done Sir Palomides is but a dead man because that he is not christened, and I would be loath that he should die a Saracen.*'

And therewith she came down and besought them for her love to fight no more.

'Ah, madam,' said Sir Tristram, 'what mean you? Will ye have me shamed? For well ye know that I will be ruled by you.'

'Ah, my own lord,' said La Belle Isode, 'full well ye wot I would not your dishonour, but I would that ye would for my sake spare this unhappy Saracen Sir Palomides.'

'Madam,' said Sir Tristram, 'I will leave for your sake.'

Then said she to Sir Palomides, 'This shall be thy charge: thou shalt go out of this country while I am queen thereof.'

'Madam, I will obey your commandment,' said Sir Palomides, 'which is sore against my will.'

'Then take thy way,' said La Belle Isode, 'unto the court of King Arthur; and there recommend me unto Queen Guenivere, and tell her that I send her word that there be within this land but four lovers, and that is Sir Lancelot and Dame Guenivere, and Sir Tristram and Queen Isode.'

stilly] silently

[32]   And so Sir Palomides departed with great heaviness. And Sir Tristram took the queen and brought her again unto King Mark; and then
was there made great joy of her homecoming. Then who was cherished
but Sir Tristram! Then Sir Tristram let fetch home Sir Lambegus his
knight from the forester's house; and it was long or he was whole, but
so at the last he recovered.

     And thus they lived with joy and play a long while. But ever
Sir Andret, that was nigh cousin unto Sir Tristram, lay in wait betwixt
Sir Tristram and La Belle Isode for to take him and devour him.*

[33]   And then the king and the queen went an-hunting, and Sir Tristram.
So the king and the queen made their pavilions and their tents in that
forest beside a river; and there was daily jousting and hunting, for there
was ever ready thirty knights to joust unto all that came at that time.
And there by fortune came Sir Lamorak de Gales and Sir Driant; and
there Sir Driant jousted well, but at the last he had a fall. Then
Sir Lamorak proffered, and when he began he fared so with the thirty
knights that there was not one of them but he gave a fall, and some of
them were sore hurt.

     'I marvel,' said King Mark, 'what knight he is that doth such deeds
of arms.'

     'Sir,' said Sir Tristram, 'I know him well for a noble knight as few
now be living, and his name is Sir Lamorak de Gales.'

     'It were shame', said the king, 'that he should go thus away unless
that he were manhandled.'

     'Sir,' said Sir Tristram, 'me seemeth it were no worship for a noble-
man to have ado with him, and for this cause: for at this time he hath
done overmuch for any mean knight living. And as me seemeth,' said
Sir Tristram, 'it were shame to tempt him any more, for his horse is
weary and himself both; for the deeds of arms that he hath done this
day, well considered, it were enough for Sir Lancelot du Lake.'

     'As for that,' said King Mark, 'I require you, as ye love me and my
lady the queen La Belle Isode, take your arms and joust with Sir Lamorak de Gales.'

     'Sir,' said Sir Tristram, 'ye bid me do a thing that is against knight-
hood; and well I can think that I shall give him a fall, for it is no

---

devour] destroy   unless that he were manhandled] without being given rough
treatment   mean] ordinary

mastery, for my horse and I be fresh, and so is not his horse and he. And wit you well that he will take it for great unkindness, for ever one good knight is loath to take another at advantage. But because I will not displease, as ye require me, so must I do, and obey your commandment.'

And so Sir Tristram armed him and took his horse and put him forth. And there Sir Lamorak met him mightily; and what with the might of his own spear and of Sir Tristram's spear, Sir Lamorak's horse fell to the earth, and he sitting in the saddle. So as soon as he might, he avoided the saddle and his horse, and put his shield before him and drew his sword. And then he bade Sir Tristram, 'Alight, thou knight, and thou darest!'

'Nay, sir,' said Sir Tristram, 'I will no more have ado with you, for I have done thee overmuch unto my dishonour and to thy worship.'

'As for that,' said Sir Lamorak, 'I can thee no thank. Since thou hast forjousted me on horseback, I require thee and beseech thee, and thou be Sir Tristram de Lyonesse, fight with me on foot.'

'I will not,' said Sir Tristram. 'And wit you well, my name is Sir Tristram de Lyonesse, and well I know that ye be Sir Lamorak de Gales. And this have I done to you against my will, but I was required thereto; but to say that I will do at your request as at this time, I will not have no more ado with you at this time, for me shameth of that I have done.'

'As for the shame,' said Sir Lamorak, 'on thy part or on mine, bear thou it and thou will; for though a mare's son hath failed me now, yet a queen's son shall not fail thee. And therefore, and thou be such a knight as men call thee, I require thee alight and fight with me.'

'Sir Lamorak,' said Sir Tristram, 'I understand your heart is great; and cause why ye have, to say the sooth, for it would grieve me and any good knight should keep him fresh and then to strike down a weary knight!—for that knight nor horse was never formed that always may endure. And therefore,' said Sir Tristram, 'I will not have ado with you, for me forthinks of that I have done.'

'As for that,' said Sir Lamorak, 'I shall requite you and ever I see my time.'

So he departed from him with Sir Driant; and by the way they met [34] with a knight that was sent from Dame Morgan le Fay unto King Arthur. And this knight had a fair horn harnessed with gold, and the horn had such a virtue that there might no lady nor gentlewoman drink of that horn but if she were true to her husband; and if she were false she should spill all the drink, and if she were true to her lord she might drink thereof peaceably. And because of the Queen Guenivere and in the despite of Sir Lancelot, this horn was sent unto King Arthur. And so by force Sir Lamorak made that knight to tell all the cause why he bore the horn; and so he told him all whole.

'Now shalt thou bear this horn', said Sir Lamorak, 'to King Mark, or choose to die! For in the despite of Sir Tristram thou shalt bear it him, that horn, and say that I sent it him for to assay his lady; and if she be true he shall prove her.'

So this knight went his way unto King Mark and brought him that rich horn, and said that Sir Lamorak sent it him; and so he told him the virtue of that horn. Then the king made his queen to drink thereof, and a hundred ladies with her; and there were but four ladies of all those that drank cleanly.

'Alas,' said King Mark, 'this is a great despite!', and swore a great oath that she should be burned and the other ladies also.

Then the barons gathered them together and said plainly they would not have those ladies burned for a horn made by sorcery, that came 'from the false sorceress and witch most that is now living'. For that horn did never good, but caused strife and debate; and always in her days she was an enemy to all true lovers. So there were many knights that made there a vow that and ever they met with Morgan le Fay, that they would show her short courtesy. Also Sir Tristram was passing wroth that Sir Lamorak sent that horn unto King Mark, for well he knew that it was done in the despite of him; and therefore he thought to requite Sir Lamorak. —

Then Sir Tristram used daily and nightly to go to Queen Isode ever when he might; and ever Sir Andret, his cousin, watched him night by night for to take him with La Belle Isode. And so upon a night Sir Andret espied his hour and the time when Sir Tristram went to his lady. Then Sir Andret got unto him twelve knights, and at midnight he set upon Sir Tristram secretly and suddenly; and there Sir Tristram was taken naked abed with La Belle Isode, and so was he bound hand and foot and kept till day.

And then by the assent of King Mark and of Sir Andret and of some of the barons, Sir Tristram was led unto a chapel that stood upon the sea rocks, there for to take his judgement. And so he was led bound with forty knights.

And when Sir Tristram saw that there was no other boot but needs he must die, then said he, 'Fair lords, remember what I have done for the country of Cornwall, and what jeopardy I have been in for the weal of you all! For when I fought with Sir Marhalt the good knight, I was promised to be better rewarded, when ye all refused to take the battle. Therefore, as ye be good gentle knights, see me not thus shamefully to die; for it is shame to all knighthood thus to see me die. For I dare say,' said Sir Tristram, 'that I met never with no knight but I was as good as he, or better.'

'Fie upon thee,' said Sir Andret, 'false traitor thou art, with thine advantage! For all thy boast, thou shalt die this day.'

'Ah, Andret, Andret,' said Sir Tristram, 'thou shouldst be my kinsman, and now art to me full unfriendly. But and there were no more but thou and I, thou wouldst not put me to death.'

'No?' said Sir Andret, and therewith he drew his sword and would have slain him.

So when Sir Tristram saw him make that countenance, he looked upon both his hands that were fast bound unto two knights, and suddenly he pulled them both unto him and unwrast his hands, and leaped unto his cousin Sir Andret and writhed his sword out of his hands. And then he smote Sir Andret that he fell down to the earth; and so he fought that he killed ten knights. So then Sir Tristram got the chapel and kept it mightily.

Then the cry was great, and people drew fast unto Sir Andret, more than a hundred. So when Sir Tristram saw the people draw unto him, he remembered he was naked, and sparred fast the chapel door and broke the bars of a window, and so he leapt out and fell upon the crags in the sea. And so at that time Sir Andret nor none of his fellows might not get him. But when they were departed, Gouvernail and Sir Lambegus and Sir Sentrail de Lushon, that were Sir Tristram's men, sought sore after their master when they heard he was escaped. And so on the rocks they found him, and with towels pulled him up. And then Sir Tristram asked where was La Belle Isode.

'Sir,' said Gouvernail, 'she is put in a lazar-cote.'

[35]

unwrast] wrenched free   naked] unarmed   towels] i.e. a rope made of
cloths tied together   lazar-cote] house for lepers

'Alas,' said Sir Tristram, 'that is a full ungodly place for such a fair lady, and if I may she shall not be long there.'

And so he took his men and went there as was La Belle Isode, and fetched her away, and brought her into a fair forest to a fair manor; and so he abode there with her.

So now this good knight bade his men depart, for at that time he might not help them. And so they departed, all save Gouvernail. And so upon a day Sir Tristram yode into the forest for to disport him, and there he fell asleep. And so happened there came to Sir Tristram a man that he had slain his brother. And so when this man had found him, he shot him through the shoulder, and anon Sir Tristram started up and killed that man.

And in the meantime it was told unto King Mark how Sir Tristram and La Belle Isode were in that same manor. And thither he came with many knights to slay Sir Tristram; and when he came there he found him gone. And anon he took La Belle Isode home with him and kept her strait, that by no means she might never write nor send. And when Sir Tristram came toward the manor, he found the track of many horses, and looked about in the place and knew that his lady was gone. And then Sir Tristram took great sorrow, and endured with great sorrow and pain long time, for the arrow that he was hurt withal was envenomed.

So by the means of La Belle Isode, she bade a lady that was cousin unto Dame Brangwain, and she came unto Sir Tristram and told him that he might not be whole by no means, 'for thy lady Isode may not help thee. Therefore she biddeth you, haste you into Brittany unto King Howell, and there shall ye find his daughter that is called Isode les Blanches Mains, and there shall ye find that she shall help you.'

Then Sir Tristram and Gouvernail got them shipping, and so sailed into Brittany. And when King Howell knew that it was Sir Tristram, he was full glad of him.

'Sir,' said Sir Tristram, 'I am come unto this country to have help of your daughter.'

And so she healed him.

[36] There was an earl that hight Gripe; and this earl made great war upon the king, and put him to the worse and besieged him. And on a time

Isode les Blanches Mains] Isode of the White Hands

Sir Kehydius that was son to the King Howell, as he issued out he was sore wounded nigh to the death.

Then Gouvernail went to the king and said, 'Sir, I counsel you to desire my lord Sir Tristram as in your need to help you.'

'I will do by your counsel,' said the king. And so he yode unto Sir Tristram and prayed him as in his wars to help him, 'for my son Sir Keyhidius may not go unto the field.'

'Sir,' said Sir Tristram, 'I will go to the field and do what I may.'

So Sir Tristram issued out of the town with such fellowship as he might make, and did such deeds that all Brittany spoke of him. And then at the last by great force he slew the Earl Gripe with his own hands, and more than a hundred knights he slew that day. And then Sir Tristram was received into the city worshipfully with procession.

Then King Howell embraced him in his arms and said, 'Sir Tristram, all my kingdom I will resign to you.'

'God defend!' said Sir Tristram, 'for I am beholden thereto for your daughter's sake to do for you more than that.'

So by the great means of the king and his son, there grew great love betwixt Isode and Sir Tristram; for that lady was both good and fair and a woman of noble blood and fame, and for because that Sir Tristram had such cheer and riches and all other pleasance that he had almost forsaken La Belle Isode.

And so upon a time Sir Tristram agreed to wed this Isode les Blanches Mäins;* and so at the last they were wedded, and solemnly held their marriage. And so when they were abed both, Sir Tristram remembered him of his old lady La Belle Isode, and then he took such a thought suddenly that he was all dismayed. And other cheer made he none but with clipping and kissing; as for fleshly lusts, Sir Tristram had never ado with her—such mention maketh the French book. Also it maketh mention that the lady weened there had been no pleasure but kissing and clipping.

And in the meantime there was a knight in Brittany, his name was Sir Suppinabiles, and he came over the sea into England. And so he came into the court of King Arthur, and there he met with Sir Lancelot du Lake and told him of the marriage of Sir Tristram.

Then said Sir Lancelot, 'Fie upon him, untrue knight to his lady! That so noble a knight as Sir Tristram is should be found to his first

clipping] embracing

lady and love untrue, that is the queen of Cornwall! But say ye to him thus,' said Sir Lancelot, 'that of all knights in the world I have loved him, and all was for his noble deeds. And let him wit that the love between him and me is done for ever, and that I give him warning, from this day forth I will be his mortal enemy.'

[37]   So departed Sir Suppinabiles unto Brittany again, and there he found Sir Tristram and told him that he had been in King Arthur's court.

Then Sir Tristram said, 'Heard ye anything of me?'

'So God me help,' said Sir Suppinabiles, 'there I heard Sir Lancelot speak of you great shame, and that ye are a false knight to your lady. And he bade me do you to wit that he will be your mortal foe in every place where he may meet with you.'

'That me repenteth,' said Sir Tristram, 'for of all knights I loved most to be in his fellowship.'

Then Sir Tristram was ashamed and made great moan, that ever any knights should defame him for the sake of his lady.

And so in this mean while La Belle Isode made a letter unto Queen Guenivere, complaining her of the untruth of Sir Tristram, how he had wedded the king's daughter of Brittany. So Queen Guenivere sent her another letter and bade her be of good comfort, for she should have joy after sorrow; for Sir Tristram was so noble a knight called, that by crafts of sorcery ladies would make such noble men to wed them. But the end Queen Guinevere said should be thus: 'that he shall hate her and love you better than ever he did.'*

do you to wit] inform you

Now turn we unto Sir Tristram de Lyonesse that was in Brittany, that [IX.10]
when La Belle Isode understood that he was wedded, she sent to him
by her maiden, Dame Brangwain, piteous letters as could be thought
and made; and her conclusion was thus, that if it pleased Sir Tristram,
to come to her court and bring with him Isode les Blanches Mains, and
they should be kept as well as herself.

Then Sir Tristram called unto him Sir Kehydius, and asked him
whether he would go with him into Cornwall secretly: he answered
him and said that he was ready at all times. And then he let ordain privily a little vessel, and therein they sailed, Sir Tristram, Sir Kehydius,
and Dame Brangwain and Gouvernail, Sir Tristram's squire. So when
they were in the sea a contrarious wind blew them unto the coasts of
North Wales, nigh the Forest Perilous.

Then said Sir Tristram, 'Here shall ye abide me these ten days, and
Gouvernail my squire with you. And if so be I come not again by that
day, take the next way into Cornwall; for in this forest are many strange
adventures, as I have heard say, and some of them I cast to prove or that
I depart. And when I may I shall hie me after you.'

Then Sir Tristram and Sir Kehydius took their horses and departed
from their fellowship; and so they rode within that forest a mile and
more. And at the last Sir Tristram saw before them a likely knight sitting armed by a well, and a strong mighty horse stood passing nigh him
tied to an oak, and a man hoving and riding by him leading a horse
loaded with spears. And this knight that sat at the well seemed by his
countenance to be passing heavy.

Then Sir Tristram rode near him and said, 'Fair knight, why sit you
so drooping? Ye seem to be a knight errant by your arms and harness,
and therefore dress you to joust with one of us, or with both.'

Therewithal that knight made no words, but took his shield and
buckled it about his neck, and lightly he took his horse and leapt upon
him; and then he took a great spear of his squire, and departed his way
a furlong.

Then Sir Kehydius asked leave of Sir Tristram to joust first.

'Sir, do your best,' said Sir Tristram.

So they met together, and there Sir Kehydius had a fall, and was sore
wounded on high above the paps.

I cast to prove or that I depart] I intend to undertake before I leave   hoving]
passing

Then Sir Tristram said, 'Knight, that is well jousted! Now make you ready unto me.'

'Sir, I am ready,' said the knight.

And anon he took a great spear and encountered with Sir Tristram; and there by fortune and by great force that knight smote down Sir Tristram from his horse, and had a great fall. Then Sir Tristram was sore ashamed, and lightly he avoided his horse, and put his shield before his shoulder, and drew his sword. And then Sir Tristram required that knight of his knighthood to alight upon foot and fight with him.

'I will well,' said the knight.

And so he alit upon foot and avoided his horse, and cast his shield upon his shoulder and drew out his sword; and there they fought a long battle together nigh two hours.

Then Sir Tristram said, 'Fair knight, hold thy hand a little while, and tell me of whence thou art and what is thy name.'

'As for that,' said the knight, 'I will be advised; but and ye will tell me your name, peradventure I will tell you mine.'

[11]   'Now, fair knight,' he said, 'my name is Sir Tristram de Lyonesse.'

'Sir, and my name is Sir Lamorak de Gales.'

'Ah, Sir Lamorak,' said Sir Tristram, 'well be we met! And bethink thee now of the despite thou didst me of the sending of the horn unto King Mark's court, to the intent to have slain or dishonoured my lady, queen La Belle Isode. And therefore wit thou well,' said Sir Tristram, 'the one of us two shall die or we depart.'

So Sir Tristram would make no longer delays, but lashed at Sir Lamorak; and thus they fought long till either were weary of other.

Then Sir Tristram said unto Sir Lamorak, 'In all my life met I never with such a knight that was so big and so well-breathed. Therefore,' said Sir Tristram, 'it were pity that any of us both should here be mischieved.'

'Sir,' said Sir Lamorak, 'for your renown and your name I will that ye have the worship, and therefore I will yield me unto you.' And therewith he took the point of his sword to yield him.

'Nay,' said Sir Tristram, 'ye shall not do so, for well I know your proffers are more of your gentleness than for any fear or dread ye have of me.' And therewithal Sir Tristram proffered him his sword and said, 'Sir Lamorak, as an overcome knight I yield me to you as a man of most noble prowess that I ever met.'

'Nay,' said Sir Lamorak, 'I will do you gentleness, I require you! Let us be sworn together that never none of us shall after this day have ado with other.'

And therewith Sir Tristram and Sir Lamorak swore that never none of them should fight against other, for weal nor for woe.

And this meanwhile there came Sir Palomides, the good knight, fol-   [12]
lowing the Questing Beast, that had in shape like a serpent's head, and a body like a leopard, buttocked like a lion and footed like a hart; and in his body there was such a noise as it had been twenty couple of hounds questing, and such noise that beast made wheresoever he went. And this beast evermore Sir Palomides followed, for it was called his quest. And right so as he followed this beast it came by Sir Tristram, and soon after came Sir Palomides. And to brief this matter, he smote down Sir Tristram and Sir Lamorak both with one spear, and so he departed after the Beast Glatissant, that was called the Questing Beast; where-fore these two knights were passing wroth that Sir Palomides would not fight with them on foot.

Here men may understand that be men of worship, that man was never formed that all times might attain, but some time he was put to the worse by malfortune; and at some time the weaker knight put the bigger knight to a rebuke.

Then Sir Tristram and Sir Lamorak got Sir Kehydius upon a shield betwixt them both. And so they rode with him to the ship where they   [16/17]*
left Dame Brangwain and Gouvernail, and so they sailed into Corn-wall all whole together.

And by assent and by information of Dame Brangwain, when they were landed they rode unto Sir Dinas the Seneschal, a trusty friend of Sir Tristram's. And so Sir Dinas and Dame Brangwain rode to the court of King Mark, and told the queen La Belle Isode that Sir Tristram was nigh her in the country. Then for very pure joy La Belle Isode swooned; and when she might speak, she said, 'Gentle seneschal, help that I might speak with him, or my heart will brast.'

Then Sir Dinas and Dame Brangwain brought Sir Tristram and Sir Kehydius privily unto the court, unto her chamber where as La Belle Isode assigned them. And to tell the joys that were betwixt La Belle Isode and Sir Tristram, there is no maker can make it, nor no heart can think it, nor no pen can write it, nor no mouth can speak it.

Glatissant] baying   no maker can make it] no poet can describe it

And as the French book maketh mention, at the first time that ever Sir Kehydius saw La Belle Isode he was so enamoured upon her that for very pure love he might never withdraw it; and at the last, as ye shall hear or the book be ended, Sir Kehydius died for the love of Isode. And then privily he wrote unto her letters and ballads of the most goodliest that were used in those days. And when La Belle Isode understood his letters she had pity of his complaint, and unadvised she wrote another letter to comfort him withal.

And Sir Tristram was all this while in a turret at the commandment of La Belle Isode, and when she might she yode and came to Sir Tristram.

So on a day King Mark played at the chess under a chamber window; and at that time Sir Tristram and Sir Kehydius were within the chamber over King Mark. And as it mishapped, Sir Tristram found the letter that Sir Kehydius sent unto La Belle Isode; also he had found the letter that she wrote unto Sir Kehydius, and at the same time La Belle Isode was in the same chamber.

Then Sir Tristram came unto La Belle Isode and said, 'Madam, here is a letter that was sent unto you, and here is the letter that ye sent unto him that sent you that letter. Alas, madam, the good love that I have loved you, and many lands and great riches have I forsaken for your love; and now ye are a traitress unto me, which doth me great pain. But as for thee, Sir Kehydius, I brought thee out of Brittany into this country, and thy father, King Howell, I won his lands. Howbeit I wedded thy sister Isode les Blanches Mains for the goodness she did unto me, and yet, as I am a true knight, she is a clean maiden for me. But wit thou well, Sir Kehydius, for this falsehood and treason thou hast done unto me, I will revenge it upon thee.' And therewith Sir Tristram drew out his sword and said, 'Sir Kehydius, keep thee!' And then La Belle Isode swooned to the earth.

And when Sir Kehydius saw Sir Tristam come upon him, he saw no other boot but leapt out at a bay-window even over the head where sat King Mark playing at the chess. And when the king saw one come hurling over his head, he said, 'Fellow, what art thou, and what is the cause thou leap out at that window?'

'My lord king,' said Kehydius, 'it fortuned me that I was asleep in the window above your head, and as I slept I slumbered, and so I fell down.'

[17/18] Thus Sir Kehydius excused him, and Sir Tristram dread him lest he were discovered unto the king that he was there; wherefore he drew him to the strength of the tower, and armed him in such armour as he had for to fight with them that would withstand him.

And so when Sir Tristram saw there was no resistance against him he sent Gouvernail for his horse and his spear, and knightly he rode forth out of the castle openly, that was called the castle of Tintagel. And even at the gate he met with Sir Gingalin, Sir Gawain's son;* and anon Sir Gingalin put his spear in the rest, and ran upon Sir Tristram and broke his spear. And Sir Tristram at that time had but a sword, and gave him such a buffet upon the helm that he fell down from his saddle, and his sword slid down and carved asunder his horse's neck. And so Sir Tristram rode his way into the forest.

And all this doing saw King Mark. And then he sent a squire unto the hurt knight and commanded him to come to him, and so he did. And when King Mark wist that it was Sir Gingalin, he welcomed him and gave him another horse, and so he asked him what knight it was that encountered with him.

'Sir,' said Sir Gingalin, 'I wot not what knight it was, but well I wot he sigheth and maketh great dole.'

Then Sir Tristram within a while met with a knight of his own (his name was Sir Fergus), and when he had met with him he made such sorrow that he fell down off his horse in a swoon; and in such sorrow he was in three days and three nights. Then at the last Sir Tristram sent unto the court by Sir Fergus, for to spere what tidings. And so as he rode by the way he met with a damosel that came from Sir Palomides to know and seek how Sir Tristram did. Then Sir Fergus told her how he was almost out of his mind.

'Alas,' said the damosel, 'where shall I find him?'

In such a place, said Sir Fergus.

Then Sir Fergus found Queen Isode sick in her bed, making the greatest dole that ever any earthly woman made.

And when the damosel found Sir Tristram, she made great dole because she might not amend him, for the more she made of him the more was his pain. And at the last Sir Tristram took his horse and rode away from her; and then was it three days or that she could find him, and then she brought him meat and drink, but he would none. And then another time Sir Tristram escaped away from the damosel, and it happened him to ride by the same castle where Sir Palomides and

to spere what tidings] to find out what was going on

Sir Tristram did battle when La Belle Isode parted them. And there by fortune the damosel met with Sir Tristram again, making the greatest dole that ever earthly creature made; and she yode to the lady of that castle and told of the misadventure of Sir Tristram.

'Alas,' said the lady of that castle, 'where is my lord Sir Tristram?'

'Right here by your castle,' said the damosel.

'In good time', said the lady, 'is he so nigh me: he shall have meat and drink of the best. And a harp I have of his whereupon he taught me, for of goodly harping he beareth the prize of the world.'

So this lady and damosel brought him meat and drink, but he ate little thereof. Then upon a night he put his horse from him and unlaced his armour, and so he yode unto the wilderness, and brast down the trees and boughs. And otherwhile,when he found the harp that the lady sent him, then would he harp and play thereupon and weep together. And sometime when he was in the wood the lady wist not where he was; then would she set her down and play upon the harp. And anon Sir Tristram would come to the harp and hearken thereto, and sometime he would harp himself.

Thus he there endured a quarter of a year. And so at the last he ran his way, and she wist not where he was become; and then was he naked and waxed lean and poor of flesh. And so he fell in the fellowship of herdmen and shepherds, and daily they would give him some of their meat and drink. And when he did any shrewd deed they would beat him with rods; and so they clipped him with shears and made him like a fool.*

[19/20]   Then Sir Andret, that was cousin unto Sir Tristram, made a lady that was his paramour to say and to noise it that she was with Sir Tristram or ever he died. And this tale she brought unto King Mark's court, that she buried him by a well, and that or he died he besought King Mark to make his cousin Sir Andret king of the country of Lyonesse, of the which Sir Tristram was lord of. And all this did Sir Andret because he would have had Sir Tristram's lands.

And when King Mark heard tell that Sir Tristram was dead he wept and made great dole. But when Queen Isode heard of these tidings she made such sorrow that she was nigh out of her mind. And so upon a day she thought to slay herself, and never to live after the death of Sir Tristram. And so upon a day La Belle Isode got a sword privily and

shrewd] troublesome

bore it into her garden, and there she pitched the sword through a plum tree up to the hilts, so that it stuck fast, and it stood breast high. And as she would have run upon the sword and to have slain herself, all this espied King Mark, how she kneeled down and said, 'Sweet Lord Jesu, have mercy upon me, for I may not live after the death of Sir Tristram de Lyonesse! For he was my first love, and shall be the last.'

And with these words came King Mark and took her in his arms. And then he took up the sword, and bore her away with him into a tower; and there he made her to be kept, and watched her surely. And after that she lay long sick, nigh at the point of death.

So this meanwhile ran Sir Tristram naked in the forest, and so he came to a hermitage, and there he laid him down and slept; and in the meanwhile the hermit laid meat down by him. Thus was he kept there ten days; and at the last he departed and came to the herdmen again.

And there was a giant in that country that hight Tauleas, and for fear of Sir Tristram more than seven years he durst never much go at large, but for the most part he kept him in a sure castle of his own. And so this Tauleas heard tell that Sir Tristram was dead, by the noise of the court of King Mark. Then this giant Tauleas yode daily at his large. And so he happed upon a day he came to the herdmen wandering and lingering, and there he set him down to rest among them. And in the meanwhile there came a knight of Cornwall that led a lady with him, and his name was Sir Dinant; and when the giant saw him he went from the herdmen and hid him under a tree. And so the knight came to that well, and there he alit to repose him; and as soon as he was from his horse, this giant Tauleas came betwixt this knight and his horse and leapt upon him. And so forthwith he rode unto Sir Dinant and took him by the collar and pulled him before him upon his horse, and would have stricken off his head.

Then the herdmen said unto Sir Tristram, 'Help yonder knight!'

'Help ye him,' said Sir Tristram.

'We dare not,' said the herdmen.

Then Sir Tristram was ware of the sword of the knight there as it lay, and so thither he ran and took up the sword and smote to Sir Tauleas and so struck off his head, and so he yode his way to the herdmen.

Then Sir Dinant took up the giant's head and bore it with him unto [20/1] King Mark, and told him what adventure betided him in the forest, and how a naked man rescued him from the grimly giant Sir Tauleas.

at his large] wherever he pleased

'Where had ye this adventure?' said King Mark.

'Forsooth,' said Sir Dinant, 'at the fair fountain in the forest where many adventurous knights meet, and there is the mad man.'

'Well,' said King Mark, 'I will see that wood man.'

So within a day or two King Mark commanded his knights and his hunters to be ready, and said that he would hunt on the morn. And so upon the morn he went into that forest; and when the king came to that well he found there lying a fair naked man, and a sword by him. Then King Mark blew and straked, and therewith his knights came to him; and then he commanded his knights to take the naked man with fairness, 'and bring him to my castle'. And so they did safely and fair, and cast mantles upon Sir Tristram, and so led him unto Tintagel. And there they bathed him and washed him and gave him hot suppings, till they had brought him well to his remembrance. But all this while there was no creature that knew Sir Tristram, nor what manner man he was.

So it befell upon a day that the queen, La Belle Isode, heard of such a man that ran naked in the forest, and how the king had brought him home to the court. Then La Belle Isode called unto her Dame Brangwain and said, 'Come on with me, for we will go see this man that my lord brought from the forest the last day.'

So they passed forth and spered where was the sick man; and then a squire told the queen that he was in the garden taking his rest to repose him against the sun. So when the queen looked upon Sir Tristram she was not remembered of him; but ever she said unto Dame Brangwain, 'Me seems I should have seen this man here before in many places.'

But as soon as Sir Tristram saw her he knew her well enough; and then he turned away his visage and wept.

Then the queen had always a little brachet that Sir Tristram gave her the first time that ever she came into Cornwall, and never would that brachet depart from her but if Sir Tristram were nigh there as was La Belle Isode; and this brachet was first sent from the king's daughter of France unto Sir Tristram for great love. And anon this little brachet felt a savour of Sir Tristram, she leapt upon him and licked his leres and his ears; and then she whined and quested, and she smelled at his feet and at his hands and on all the parts of his body that she might come to.

'Ah, my lady,' said Dame Brangwain, 'alas, I see it is mine own lord, Sir Tristram.'

---

blew and straked] blew the call for the end of the hunt   leres] cheeks

And thereupon La Belle Isode fell down in a swoon, and so lay a great while. And when she might speak she said, 'Ah, my lord Sir Tristram, blessed be God ye have your life! And now I am sure ye shall be discovered by this little brachet, for she will never leave you. And also I am sure, as soon as my lord King Mark do know you he will banish you out of the country of Cornwall, or else he will destroy you. And therefore, for God's sake, my own lord, grant King Mark his will. And then draw you unto the court of King Arthur, for there are ye beloved; and ever when I may I shall send unto you. And when ye list ye may come to me; and at all times early and late I will be at your commandment, to live as poor a life as ever did queen or lady.'

'Ah, madam,' said Sir Tristram, 'go from me, for much anger and danger have I escaped for your love.'

Then the queen departed, but the brachet would not from him; and therewith came King Mark, and the brachet set upon him and bayed at them all. And therewith Sir Andret spake and said, 'Sir, this is Sir Tristram, I see well by that brachet.' [21/2]

'Nay,' said the king, 'I cannot suppose that.'

Then the king asked him upon his faith what he was, and what was his name.

'So God me help,' said he, 'my name is Sir Tristram de Lyonesse. Now do by me what ye list.'

'Ah,' said King Mark, 'me repents of your recovering.'

And so he let call his barons to give judgement unto Sir Tristram to the death. Then many of his barons would not assent thereto, and in especial Sir Dinas the Seneschal and Sir Fergus. And so by the advice of them all Sir Tristram was banished out of the country for ten years, and thereupon he took his oath upon a book before the king and his barons. And so he was made to depart out of the country of Cornwall; and there were many barons brought him unto his ship, that some were of his friends and some were of his foes.

And in the meanwhile there came a knight of King Arthur's, and his name was Sir Dinadan; and his coming was for to seek after Sir Tristram. Then they showed him where he was, armed at all points, going to the ship.

'Now, fair knight,' said Sir Dinadan, 'or ye pass this court, that ye will joust with me!'

'With a good will,' said Sir Tristram, 'and these lords will give me leave.'

Then the barons granted thereto; and so they ran together, and there Sir Tristram gave Sir Dinadan a fall. And then he prayed Sir Tristram of his gentleness to give him leave to go in his fellowship.

'Ye shall be right welcome,' said he.

And then Sir Tristram and Sir Dinadan took their horses and rode to their ships together.

And when Sir Tristram was in the sea, he said, 'Greet well King Mark and all mine enemies, and say to them I will come again when I may. And say him, well am I rewarded for the fighting with Sir Marhalt, and delivered all his country from servage. And well am I rewarded for the fetching and costs of Queen Isode out of Ireland, and the danger that I was in first and last.* And well am I rewarded when I fought with Sir Blamor de Ganis for King Angwish, father unto La Belle Isode. And well am I rewarded when I smote down the good knight Sir Lamorak de Gales at King Mark's request. And well I am rewarded for the slaying of Tauleas, the mighty giant. And many other deeds have I done for him; and now have I my warison. And tell King Mark that many noble knights of the Round Table have spared the barons of this country for my sake. And also I am not well rewarded when I fought with the good knight Sir Palomides and rescued Queen Isode from him; and at that time King Mark said afore all his barons I should have been better rewarded.'

And forthwith he took the sea.

[22/3] And at the next landing, fast by the sea, there met with Sir Tristram and with Sir Dinadan, Sir Ector de Maris and Sir Bors de Ganis; and there Sir Ector jousted with Sir Dinadan, and he smote him and his horse down. And then Sir Tristram would have jousted with Sir Bors, and Sir Bors said that he would not joust with no Cornish knights, for they are not called men of worship. And all this was done upon a bridge. And with this came Sir Bleoberis and Sir Driant, and Sir Bleoberis proffered to joust with Sir Tristram, and there Sir Tristram smote down Sir Bleoberis.

Then said Sir Bors de Ganis, 'I wist never Cornish knight of so great valour nor so valiant as that knight that beareth the trappings embroidered with crowns.'

And then Sir Tristram and Sir Dinadan departed from them into a forest, and there met them a damosel that came for the love of

warison] reward

Sir Lancelot to seek after some noble knights of King Arthur's court for to rescue Sir Lancelot. For he was ordained for by the treason of Queen Morgan le Fay to have slain him, and for that cause she ordained thirty knights to lie in wait for Sir Lancelot; and this damosel knew this treason, and for this cause she came for to seek noble knights to help Sir Lancelot. For that night, or the day after, Sir Lancelot should come where these thirty knights were. And so this damosel met with Sir Bors and Sir Ector and with Sir Driant, and there she told them all four of the treason of Morgan le Fay; and then they promised her that they would be nigh her when Sir Lancelot should meet with the thirty knights. 'And if so be they set upon him, we will do rescues as we can.'

So the damosel departed, and by adventure she met with Sir Tristram and with Sir Dinadan, and there the damosel told them all the treason that was ordained for Sir Lancelot.

'Now, fair damosel,' said Sir Tristram, 'bring me to that same place where they should meet with Sir Lancelot.'

Then said Sir Dinadan, 'What will ye do? It is not for us to fight with thirty knights, and wit you well I will not thereof! As to match one knight, two or three is enough and they be men; but for to match fifteen knights, that I will never undertake.'

'Fie, for shame,' said Sir Tristram, 'do but your part.'

'Nay,' said Sir Dinadan, 'I will not thereof but if ye will lend me your shield, for ye bear a shield of Cornwall; and for the cowardice that is named to the knights of Cornwall, by your shields ye be ever forborne.'

'Nay,' said Sir Tristram, 'I will not depart from my shield for her sake that gave it me. But one thing,' said Sir Tristram, 'I promise thee, Sir Dinadan: but if thou wilt promise me to abide with me, right here I shall slay thee, for I desire no more of thee but answer one knight. And if thy heart will not serve thee, stand by and look upon.'

'Sir,' said Sir Dinadan, 'I will promise you to look upon, and to do what I may to save myself; but I would I had not met with you!'

So then anon these thirty knights came fast by these four knights, and they were ware of them, and either of other; and so these thirty knights let for this cause, that they would not wrath them if case be that they had ado with Sir Lancelot. And the four knights let them pass to this intent, that they would see and behold what they would do with

answer] take on   let] held off

Sir Lancelot. And so the thirty knights passed on and came by Sir Tristram and by Sir Dinadan; and then Sir Tristram cried on high, 'Lo, here is a knight against you for the love of Sir Lancelot!'

And there he slew two with a spear and ten with his sword; and then came in Sir Dinadan, and he did passing well. And so of the thirty knights there yode but ten away, and they fled.

And all this battle saw Sir Bors de Ganis and his three fellows, and then they saw well it was the same knight that jousted with them at the bridge. Then they took their horses and rode unto Sir Tristram, and praised him and thanked him of his good deeds; and they all desired Sir Tristram to go with them to their lodging, and he said he would not go to no lodging. Then they four knights prayed him to tell his name.

'Fair lords,' said Sir Tristram, 'as at this time I will not tell you my name.'

[23/4]   Then Sir Tristram and Sir Dinadan rode forth their way till they came to shepherds and to herdmen, and there they asked them if they knew any lodging there nearhand.

'Sir,' said the herdmen, 'hereby is good harbour in a castle; but there is such a custom that there shall no knight harbour there but if he joust with two knights, and if he be but one knight he must joust with two knights. And as ye be, soon shall ye be matched.'

'There is shrewd harbour,' said Sir Dinadan. 'Lodge where ye will, for I will not lodge there.'

'Fie, for shame,' said Sir Tristram, 'are ye not a knight of the Table Round?—wherefore ye may not with your worship refuse your lodging.'

'Not so,' said the herdmen, 'for and ye be beaten and have the worse, ye shall not be lodged there, and if ye beat them ye shall well be harboured.'

'Ah,' said Sir Dinadan, 'I understand they are two good knights.'

Then Sir Dinadan would not lodge there in no manner, but as Sir Tristram required him of his knighthood; and so they rode thither. And to make short tale, Sir Tristram and Sir Dinadan smote them down both, and so they entered into the castle and had good cheer as they could think or devise. And when they were unarmed, and thought to be merry and in good rest, there came in at the gates Sir Palomides and Sir Gaheris, requiring to have the custom of the castle.

shrewd harbour] a wretched place to stay

'What array is this?' said Sir Dinadan, 'I would fain have my rest.'

'That may not be,' said Sir Tristram. 'Now must we needs defend the custom of this castle, insomuch as we have the better of these lords of this castle. And therefore,' said Sir Tristram, 'needs must ye make you ready.'

'In the devil's name', said Sir Dinadan, 'came I into your company!'

And so they made them ready, and Sir Gaheris encountered with Sir Tristram, and Sir Gaheris had a fall; and Sir Palomides encountered with Sir Dinadan, and Sir Dinadan had a fall; then was it fall for fall. So then must they fight on foot; and that would not Sir Dinadan, for he was sore bruised of that fall that Sir Palomides gave him. Then Sir Tristram laced on Sir Dinadan's helm, and prayed him to help him.

'I will not,' said Sir Dinadan, 'for I am sore wounded of the thirty knights that we had ado withal. But ye fare,' said Sir Dinadan, 'as a man were out of his mind that would cast himself away. And I may curse the time that ever I saw you, for in all the world are not two such knights that are so wood as is Sir Lancelot and ye, Sir Tristram; for once I fell in the fellowship of Sir Lancelot as I have done now with you, and he set me so a work that a quarter of a year I kept my bed. Jesu defend me', said Sir Dinadan, 'from such two knights, and specially from your fellowship.'

'Then,' said Sir Tristram, 'I will fight with them both.' And anon Sir Tristram bade them come forth both, 'for I will fight with you.'

Then Sir Palomides and Sir Gaheris dressed and smote at them both. Then Sir Dinadan smote at Sir Gaheris a stroke or two, and turned from him.

'Nay,' said Sir Palomides, 'it is too much shame for us two knights to fight with one.' And then he did bid Sir Gaheris, 'Stand aside with that knight that hath no list to fight.'

Then they rode together and fought long, and at the last Sir Tristram doubled his strokes and drove Sir Palomides aback more than three strides. And then by one assent Sir Gaheris and Sir Dinadan went betwixt them and departed them in sunder. And then by the assent of Sir Tristram they would have lodged together; but Sir Dinadan would not lodge in that castle, and then he cursed the time that ever he came in their fellowship, and so he took his horse and his harness and departed. Then Sir Tristram prayed the lords of that castle to lend him a man to bring him to a lodging; and so they did, and overtook Sir Dinadan, and rode to their lodging two mile thence with a good man in a priory, and there they were well at ease.

And that same night Sir Bors and Sir Bleoberis and Sir Ector and Sir Driant abode still in the same place there as Sir Tristram fought with the thirty knights. And there they met with Sir Lancelot the same night, and had made promise to lodge with Sir Colgrevance the same [24/5] night. But anon as Sir Lancelot heard of the shield of Cornwall, he wist well it was Sir Tristram that had fought with his enemies; and then Sir Lancelot praised Sir Tristram, and called him the man of most worship in the world.*

And on the next day following, Sir Tristram met with pursuivants, and they told him that there was made a great cry of tournament between King Carados of Scotland and the King of Northgales, and either should joust against other before the Castle of Maidens. And these pursuivants sought all the country after good knights, and in especial King Carados let make great seeking for Sir Lancelot, and the King of Northgales let seek specially for Sir Tristram de Lyonesse. And at that time Sir Tristram thought to be at that jousts.

[Sir Tristram appears at the tournament with a black shield, and over the course of three days overthrows all his opponents including Sir Palomides.]

[33/4] Then Sir Lancelot got a great spear in his hand, and cried, 'Knight with the Black Shield, make ye ready to joust with me!'

When Sir Tristram heard him say so, he got his spear in his hand; and either abased their heads down low and came together as thunder, that Sir Tristram's spear broke in pieces. And Sir Lancelot by malfortune struck Sir Tristram on the side a deep wound nigh to the death; but yet Sir Tristram avoided not his saddle, and so the spear broke therewithal. And yet Sir Tristram got out his sword, and he rushed to Sir Lancelot and gave him three great strokes upon the helm, that the fire sprang out, and Sir Launcelot abased his head low toward his saddle-bow. And so therewith Tristram departed from the field, for he felt him so wounded that he weened he should have died; and Sir Dinadan espied him and followed him into the forest. Then Sir Lancelot abode and did marvellous deeds.

So when Sir Tristram was departed by the forest's side, he alit, and unlaced his harness and freshed his wound. Then weened Sir Dinadan that he should have died, and wept.

pursuivants] heralds   abode] i.e. stayed in the lists

'Nay, nay,' said Sir Tristram, 'never dread you, Sir Dinadan, for I am heart-whole, and of this wound I shall soon be whole, by the mercy of God.'

And anon Sir Dinadan was ware where came Palomides riding straight upon them. Then Sir Tristram was ware that Sir Palomides came to have destroyed him; and so Sir Dinadan gave him warning, and said, 'Sir Tristram, my lord, ye are so sore wounded that ye may not have ado with him, therefore I will ride against him and do to him what I may; and if I be slain, ye may pray for my soul. And so in the meanwhile ye may withdraw you and go into the castle or into the forest, that he shall not meet with you.'

Sir Tristram smiled and said, 'I thank you, Sir Dinadan; but ye shall understand that I am able to handle him.'

And anon hastily he armed him and took his horse, and a great spear in his hand, and said to Sir Dinadan adieu, and rode toward Sir Palomides a soft pace. When Sir Palomides saw him, he alit and made a countenance to amend his horse, but he did it for this cause, for he abode Sir Gaheris that came after him. And when he was come he rode toward Sir Tristram.

Then Sir Tristram sent unto Sir Palomides and required him to joust with him; and if he smote down Sir Palomides he would do no more to him, and if Sir Palomides smote down Sir Tristram, he bade him do his utterance. And so they were accorded and met together; and Sir Tristram smote down Sir Palomides, that he had a villainous fall and lay still as he had been dead. And then Sir Tristram ran upon Sir Gaheris, and he would not have jousted; but whether he would or not, Sir Tristram smote him over his horse's croup, that he lay still.* And Sir Tristram and Sir Dinadan rode to an old knight's place to lodge them; and this old knight had five sons at the tournament, that prayed God heartily for their coming home.

And so forthwith came Sir Gaheris and told King Arthur how [34/5] Sir Tristram had smitten down Sir Palomides, and it was at his own request.

'Alas,' said King Arthur, 'that was great dishonour to Sir Palomides, inasmuch as Sir Tristram was so sore wounded. And may we all, kings and knights and men of worship, say that Sir Tristram may be called a

---

made a countenance to amend his horse] pretended to check his horse's harness
do his utterance] i.e. kill him

noble knight, and one of the best knights that ever I saw days of my life. For I will that ye all, kings and knights, know,' said King Arthur, 'that I never saw knight do so marvellously as he hath done these three days; for he was the first that began and longest that held on, save this last day. And though he were hurt, it was a manly adventure of two noble knights. And when two noble men encounter, needs must the one have the worse, like as God will suffer at that time.'

'As for me,' said Sir Lancelot, 'for all the lands that ever my father left, I would not have hurt Sir Tristram and I had known him at that time that I hurt him, for I saw not his shield. For and I had seen his black shield, I would not have meddled with him for many causes,' said Sir Lancelot, 'for but late he did as much for me as ever did knight, and that is well known that he had ado with thirty knights, and no help save only Sir Dinadan. And one thing shall I promise you,' said Sir Lancelot, 'Sir Palomides shall repent it as in his unknightly dealing, so for to follow that noble knight that I by misfortune hurt him thus.'

So Sir Lancelot said all the worship that might be spoken by Sir Tristram. Then King Arthur made a great feast to all that would come. And thus we let pass King Arthur.

And a little we will turn unto Sir Palomides, that after he had a fall of Sir Tristram, he was nigh-hand raged out of his wit for despite of Sir Tristram, and so he followed him by adventure. And as he came by a river, in his woodness he would have made his horse to have leapt over the water; and the horse failed footing and fell in the river, wherefore Sir Palomides was adread lest he should have been drowned. And then he avoided his horse and swam to the land, and let his horse go down

[35/6] by adventure. And when he came to the land he took off his harness, and sat roaring and crying as a man out of his mind.

Right so came a damosel even by Sir Palomides, and he and she had language together which pleased neither of them. And so this damosel rode her ways till she came to that old knight's place, and there she told that old knight how she met with the woodest knight by adventure that ever she met withal.

'What bore he in his shield?' said Sir Tristram.

'Sir, it was indented with white and black,' said the damosel.

'Ah,' said Sir Tristram, 'that was Palomides, the good knight. For well I know him,' said Sir Tristram, 'for one of the best knights living in this realm.'

Then that old knight took a little hackney, and rode for Sir Palomides, and brought him unto his own manor. And full well knew Sir Tristram him, but he said but little. For at that time Sir Tristram was walking upon his feet and well amended of his hurts; and always when Sir Palomides saw Sir Tristram he would behold him full marvellously, and ever him seemed that he had seen him. Then would he say unto Sir Dinadan, 'And ever I meet with Sir Tristram, he shall not escape my hands.'

'I marvel,' said Sir Dinadan, 'that ye do boast behind Sir Tristram so, for it is but late that he was in your hands and ye in his hands: why would ye not hold him when ye had him? For I saw myself twice or thrice that ye got but little worship of Sir Tristram.'

Then was Sir Palomides ashamed.*

So there came a damosel that told Sir Darras that three of his sons were [36/7] slain at that tournament, and two grievously wounded so that they were never like to help themselves; and all this was done by a noble knight that bore a black shield, and that was he that bore the prize. Then came one and told Sir Darras that the same knight was within his court that bore the black shield. Then Sir Darras yode unto Sir Tristram's chamber, and there he found his shield and showed it to the damosel.

'Ah, sir,' said the damosel, 'this same is he that slew your three sons.'

Then without any tarrying Sir Darras put Sir Tristram, Sir Palomides, and Sir Dinadan within a strong prison, and there Sir Tristram was like to have died of great sickness; and every day Sir Palomides would reprove Sir Tristram of old hate betwixt them, and ever Sir Tristram spake fair and said little. But when Sir Palomides saw that Sir Tristram was fallen in sickness, then was he heavy for him, and comforted him in all the best wise he could.

So Sir Tristram endured there great pain, for sickness had undertaken him, and that is the greatest pain a prisoner may have; for all the while a prisoner may have his health of body he may endure under the mercy of God and in hope of good deliverance. But when sickness toucheth a prisoner's body, then may a prisoner say all wealth is him bereft, and then hath he cause to wail and to weep.* Right so did Sir Tristram when sickness had undertaken him, for then he took such sorrow that he had almost slain himself.

would reprove Sir Tristram of old hate betwixt them] would say how he blamed Sir Tristram for the long-standing hatred between them

[39/40]   And every day Sir Palomides brawled and said language against Sir Tristram.

Then said Sir Dinadan, 'I marvel of thee, Sir Palomides, whether and thou hadst Sir Tristram here, I trow thou wouldst do no harm; for and a wolf and a sheep were together in a prison, the sheep would suffer the wolf to be in peace.* And wit thou well,' said Sir Dinadan, 'this same is Sir Tristram, at a word, and now mayst thou do thy best with him, and let see ye now skift it with your hands.'

Then was Sir Palomides abashed and said little.

Then said Sir Tristram to Sir Palomides, 'I have heard much of your maugre against me, but I will not meddle with you as at this time by my will, because the lord of this place that hath us in governance, and I dread him not more than I do thee, soon it should be skift.'

And so they peaced themselves.*

Then soon after this Sir Tristram fell sick, that he weened to have died. Then Sir Dinadan wept, and so did Sir Palomides, among them both making great sorrow. So a damosel came in to them and found them mourning. Then she went unto Sir Darras, and told him how the mighty knight that bore the black shield was likely to die.

'That shall not be,' said Sir Darras, 'for God defend, when knights come to me for succour, that I should suffer them to die within my prison. Therefore,' said Sir Darras to the damosel, 'go fetch me that sick knight and his fellows before me.'

And when Sir Darras saw Sir Tristram brought before him, he said, 'Sir knight, me repenteth of your sickness, for ye are called a full noble knight, and so it seemeth by you. And wit you well, it shall never be said that I, Sir Darras, shall destroy such a noble knight as ye are in prison, howbeit that ye have slain three of my sons, wherefore I was greatly aggrieved. But now shalt thou go, and thy fellows, and take your horse and your armour, for they have been fair and clean kept. And ye shall go where it liketh you upon this covenant, that ye, knight, will promise me to be good friend to my sons two that be now alive, and also that ye tell me thy name.'

'Sir, my name is Sir Tristram de Lyonesse, and in Cornwall was I born, and nephew I am unto King Mark. And as for the death of your

---

skift] settle   maugre] ill will   and I dread . . . should be skift] if I did not fear him more than you, it would soon be settled

three sons, I might not do withal; for and they had been the next kin that I have, I might have done none otherwise. And if I had slain them by treason or treachery, I had been worthy to have died.'

'All this I consider,' said Sir Darras, 'that all that ye did was by force of knighthood, and that was the cause I would not put you to death. But sith ye be Sir Tristram, the good knight, I pray you heartily to be my good friend, and my sons'.'

'Sir,' said Sir Tristram, 'I promise you by the faith of my body, ever while I live I will do you service, for ye have done to us but as a natural knight ought to do.'

Then Sir Tristram reposed him there a while till that he was amended of his sickness; and when he was big and strong they took their leave. And every knight took their horses and harness, and so departed and rode together till they came to a crossway.

'Now, fellows,' said Sir Tristram, 'here will we depart in sunder.'*

---

might not do withal] could not avoid it

[X.1] Then Sir Tristram departed, and in every place he asked after Sir Lancelot, but in no place he could hear of him whether he were dead or alive; wherefore Sir Tristram made great dole and sorrow.

So Sir Tristram rode by a forest, and then was he ware of a fair tower by a marsh on the one side, and on that other side was a fair meadow, and there he saw ten knights fighting together. And ever the nearer he came, he saw how there was but one knight did battle against nine knights, and that one knight did so marvellously that Sir Tristram had great wonder that ever one knight might do so great deeds of arms. And then within a little while he had slain half their horses and unhorsed them, and their horses ran into the fields and forests. Then Sir Tristram had so great pity of that one knight that endured so great pain, and ever him thought it should be Sir Palomides by his shield. So he rode unto the knights and cried unto them and bade them cease of that battle, for they did themselves great shame, so many knights to fight with one.

Then answered the master of those knights—his name was called Sir Breunis sans Pité, that was at that time the most mischievoust knight living—and said thus: 'Sir knight, what have ye ado with us to meddle? And therefore, and ye be wise, depart on your way as ye came, for this knight shall not escape us.'

'That were great pity,' said Sir Tristram, 'that so good a knight as he is should be slain so cowardly; and therefore I make you ware, I will succour him with all my puissance.'

[2] So Sir Tristram alit off his horse because they were on foot, that they should not slay his horse. And then Sir Tristram dressed his shield, with his sword in his hand, and he smote on the right hand and on the left hand passing sore, that well nigh every stroke he struck down a knight. And when they espied his strokes they fled, both Sir Breunis sans Pité and his fellowship, unto the tower, and Sir Tristram followed fast after with his sword in his hand; but they escaped into the tower and shut Sir Tristram without the gate. And when Sir Tristram saw that, he returned back unto Sir Palomides, and found him sitting under a tree sore wounded.

'Ah, fair knight,' said Sir Tristram, 'well be ye found.'

'Gramercy,' said Sir Palomides, 'of your great goodness, for ye have rescued me of my life and saved me from my death.'

puissance] might

'What is your name?' said Sir Tristram.

'Sir, my name is Sir Palomides.'

'Ah, Jesu,' said Sir Tristram, 'thou hast a fair grace of me this day that I should rescue thee, and thou art the man in the world that I most hate! But now make thee ready, for I shall do battle with thee.'

'What is your name?' said Sir Palomides.

'My name is Sir Tristram, your mortal enemy.'

'It may be so,' said Sir Palomides, 'but ye have done over much for me this day that I should fight with you; for inasmuch as ye have saved my life it will be no worship for you to have ado with me, for ye are fresh and I am sore wounded. And therefore, and ye will needs have ado with me, assign me a day, and then I shall meet with you without fail.'

'Ye say well,' said Sir Tristram. 'Now I assign you to meet me in the meadow by the river of Camelot, where Merlin set the perron.'*

So they were agreed. Then Sir Tristram asked Sir Palomides why the nine knights did battle with him.

'For this cause,' said Sir Palomides. 'As I rode upon my adventures in a forest here beside, I espied where lay a dead knight, and a lady weeping beside him. And when I saw her making such dole, I asked her who slew her lord. "Sir," she said, "the falsest knight of the world, and most he is of villainy, and his name is Sir Breunis sans Pité." Then for pity I made the damosel to leap on her palfrey, and I promised her to be her warrant, and to help her to inter her lord. And suddenly, as I came riding by this tower, there came out Sir Breunis sans Pité, and suddenly he struck me from my horse; and or ever I might recover my horse, this Sir Breunis slew the damosel. And so I took my horse again, and I was sore ashamed; and so began this melée betwixt us, and this is the cause wherefore we did this battle.'

'Well,' said Sir Tristram, 'now I understand the manner of your battle. But in any wise, that ye have remembrance of your promise that ye have made with me, to do battle this day fortnight.'

'I shall not fail you,' said Sir Palomides.

[Sir Tristram meets various knights as he rides.]

Then Sir Tristram rode straight to Camelot, to the perron that Merlin had made before. So when Sir Tristram came to the tomb of stone he looked about him after Sir Palomides. Then was he ware where came a seemly knight riding against him all in white, and the shield covered. [5]

When he came nigh Sir Tristram, he said on high, 'Ye be welcome, sir knight, and well and truly have ye held your promise.'

And then they dressed their shields and spears, and came together with all their mights of their horses. And they met so fiercely that both the horses and knights fell to the earth, and as fast as they might avoid their horses and put their shields before them; and they struck together with bright swords, as men that were of might, and either wounded other wonderly sore, that the blood ran out upon the grass. And thus they fought the space of four hours, that never one would speak to other. And of their harness they had hewn off many pieces.

'Ah, lord Jesu,' said Gouvernail, 'I marvel greatly of the great strokes my master hath given to your master.'

'By my head,' said Sir Lancelot's servant, 'your master hath not given him so many but your master hath received so many, or more.'

'Ah, Jesu,' said Gouvernail, 'it is too much for Sir Palomides to suffer, or Sir Lancelot; and yet pity it were that either of these good knights should destroy other's blood.'

So they stood and wept both, and made great dole when they saw the bright swords over-covered with blood of their bodies.

Then at the last Sir Lancelot spake and said, 'Knight, thou fightest wonder well as ever I saw knight! Therefore, and it please you, tell me your name.'

'Sir,' said Sir Tristram, 'that is me loath, to tell any man my name.'

'Truly,' said Sir Lancelot, 'and I were required, I was never loath to tell my name.'

'It is well said,' said Sir Tristram. 'Then I require you to tell me your name.'

'Fair knight, my name is Sir Lancelot du Lake.'

'Alas,' said Sir Tristram, 'what have I done? For ye are the man in the world that I love best.'

'Now, fair knight,' said Sir Lancelot, 'tell me your name.'

'Truly, sir, I hight Sir Tristram de Lyonesse.'

'Ah, Jesu,' said Sir Lancelot, 'what adventure is befallen me!'

And therewith Sir Lancelot kneeled down and yielded him up his sword. And therewith Sir Tristram kneeled down and yielded him up his sword; and so either gave other the degree. And then they both forthwith went to the stone and set them down upon it, and took off

degree] recognition of victory

their helms to cool them, and either kissed other a hundred times. And then anon after they took their horses and rode to Camelot; and there they met with Sir Gawain and with Sir Gaheris, that had made promise to Arthur never to come again to the court till they had brought Sir Tristram with them.

'Return again,' said Sir Lancelot, 'for your quest is done, for I have met with Sir Tristram: lo, here is his own person!' [6]

Then was Sir Gawain glad, and said to Sir Tristram, 'Ye are welcome, for now have ye eased me greatly of my great labour. For what cause', said Sir Gawain, 'came ye into this country?'

'Fair sir,' said Sir Tristram, 'I came into this country because of Sir Palomides; for he and I had assigned at this day to have done battle together at the perron, and I marvel I hear not of him. And thus by adventure my lord Sir Lancelot and I met together.'

So with this came King Arthur; and when he wist that Sir Tristram was there, he yode unto him and took him by the hand and said, 'Sir Tristram, ye are as welcome as any knight that ever came unto this court.'

And when the King heard how Sir Lancelot and he had fought, and either had wounded other wonderly sore, then the King made great dole.*

Then King Arthur took Sir Tristram by the hand and went to the Table Round. Then came Queen Guenivere and many ladies with her, and all those ladies said at one voice, 'Welcome, Sir Tristram!' 'Welcome,' said the damosels.

'Welcome,' said King Arthur, 'for one of the best knights and the gentlest of the world, and the man of most worship. For of all manner of hunting thou bearest the prize, and of all measures of blowing thou art the beginning; of all the terms of hunting and hawking ye are the beginner; of all instruments of music ye are the best. Therefore, gentle knight,' said King Arthur, 'ye are welcome to this court.* And also, I pray you,' said Arthur, 'grant me a done.'

'Sir, it shall be at your commandment,' said Sir Tristram.

'Well,' said King Arthur, 'I will desire that ye shall abide in my court.'

'Sir,' said Sir Tristram, 'thereto me is loath, for I have to do in many countries.'

done] gift

'Not so,' said King Arthur. 'Ye have promised me; ye may not say nay.'

'Sir,' said Sir Tristram, 'I will as ye will.'

Then went King Arthur unto the sieges about the Round Table, and looked on every siege which were void that lacked knights. And then the King saw in the siege of Sir Marhalt letters that said, 'This is the siege of the noble knight Sir Tristram.' And then King Arthur made Sir Tristram a knight of the Round Table, with as great noblesse and feast as might be thought.

So leave we Sir Tristram and turn we unto King Mark.*

So when Sir Tristram was departed out of Cornwall into England, [7]
King Mark heard of the great prowess that Sir Tristram did there,
with the which he grieved. So he sent on his part men to espy what
deeds he did; and the queen sent privily on her part spies to know
what deeds he had done, for full great love was between them. So
when the messengers were come home they told the truth as they
heard, and how he passed all other knights but if it were Sir Lancelot.
Then King Mark was right heavy of those tidings, and as glad was La
Belle Isode.

Then great despite King Mark had at him; and so he took with him
two knights and two squires, and disguised himself, and took his way
into England, to the intent to slay Sir Tristram. And one of those
knights hight Sir Bersules, and the other knight was called Amant. So
as they rode, King Mark asked a knight that he met, where he should
find King Arthur.

'Sir,' he said, 'at Camelot.'

Also he asked that knight after Sir Tristram, whether he heard of
him in the court of King Arthur.

'Wit you well,' said that knight, 'ye shall find Sir Tristram there for
a man of worship most that is now living; for through his prowess he
won the tournament of the Castle of Maidens that standeth by the
Roche Dure. And sithen he hath won with his hands thirty knights
that were men of great honour; and the last battle that ever he did he
fought with Sir Lancelot, and that was a marvellous battle. And by love
not by force Sir Lancelot brought Sir Tristram to the court. And of
him King Arthur made passing great joy and so made him knight of
the Table Round, and his seat is in the same place where Sir Marhalt
the good knight's seat was.'

Then was King Mark passing sorry when he heard of the honour of
Sir Tristram; and so they departed. Then said King Mark unto his two
knights, 'Now will I tell you my counsel, for ye are the men that I most
trust alive. And I will that ye wit my coming hither is to this intent, for
to destroy Sir Tristram by some wiles or by treason; and it shall be hard
and ever he escape our hands.'

'Alas,' said Sir Bersules, 'my lord, what mean you? For and ye be set
in such a way, ye are disposed shamefully; for Sir Tristram is the knight
of most worship that we know living, and therefore I warn you plainly

it shall be hard and ever he escape our hands] he shall escape us only with difficulty

I will not consent to the death of him—and therefore I will yield him my service, and forsake you.'

When King Mark heard him say so, suddenly he drew his sword and said, 'Ah, traitor!' and smote Sir Bersules on the head, that the sword went to his teeth. When Sir Amant, his fellow, saw him do that villainous deed, and his squire also, they said to the king it was foully done, and mischievously: 'Wherefore we will do you no more service; and wit you well, we will appeal you of treason before King Arthur.'

Then was King Mark wonderly wroth and would have slain Amant; but he and the two squires held them together, and set nought by his malice. So when King Mark saw he might not be revenged on them, he said thus unto the knight Amant, 'Wit thou well, and thou impeach me of treason I shall thereof defend me before King Arthur; but I require thee that thou tell not my name, that I am King Mark, whatsoever come of me.'

'As for that,' said Sir Amant, 'I will not discover your name.'

And so they departed, and Amant and his fellows took the body of Bersules and buried it.

[King Mark encounters Sir Lamorak lamenting for the love of Queen Morgause, and then Sir Dinadan; he proves himself a notable coward in their company. He also overhears Sir Palomides lamenting for the love of La Belle Isode.]

[14] And so King Mark rode as fast as he might unto Camelot; and the same day he found there Sir Amant, the knight, ready, that before King Arthur had appealed him of treason; and so, lightly the King commanded them to do battle. And by misadventure King Mark smote Sir Amant through the body, and yet was Sir Amant in the righteous quarrel. And right so he took his horse and departed from the court for dread of Sir Dinadan, that he would tell Sir Tristram and Sir Palomides what he was.

Then was there damosels that La Belle Isode had sent to Sir Tris-
[15] tram, that knew Sir Amant well. Then by the licence of King Arthur they went to him and spoke with him, for while the truncheon of the spear stuck in his body he spoke.*

'Ah, fair damosels,' said Amant, 'recommend me unto La Belle

appeal] accuse   impeach] accuse

Isode, and tell her that I am slain for the love of her and of Sir Tristram.' And there he told the damosels how cowardly King Mark had slain him, and Sir Bersules, his fellow. 'And for that deed I appealed him of treason, and here am I slain in a righteous quarrel; and all was because Sir Bersules and I would not consent by treason to slay the noble knight Sir Tristram.'

Then the two maidens cried aloud that all the court might hear, and said, 'Ah, sweet Jesu that knowest all hidden things, why sufferest Thou so false a traitor to vanquish and slay a true knight that fought in a righteous quarrel?'

Then anon it was sprung to the King and the Queen and to all the lords that it was King Mark that had slain Sir Amant, and Sir Bersules beforehand, wherefore they did there that battle. Then was King Arthur wroth out of measure, and so was all other knights. But when Sir Tristram wist all, he wept for sorrow for the loss of Sir Bersules and of Sir Amant. When Sir Lancelot espied Sir Tristram weep, he went hastily to King Arthur, and said, 'Sir, I pray you, give me leave to return again yonder false king and knight.'

'I pray you,' said King Arthur, 'fetch him again; but I would not ye slew him, for my worship.'

Then Sir Lancelot armed him in all haste, and mounted upon a great horse, and took a spear in his hand and rode after King Mark. And from thence three miles English,* Sir Lancelot overtook him and bade him turn him: 'Recreant king and knight! for whether thou wilt or not, thou shalt go with me to King Arthur's court.'

Then King Mark returned and looked upon Sir Lancelot, and said, 'Fair sir, what is your name?'

'Wit you well, my name is Sir Lancelot, and therefore defend thee.'

And when King Mark knew that it was Sir Lancelot and came so fast upon him with a spear, he cried then aloud and said, 'I yield me to thee, Sir Lancelot, honourable knight.'

But Sir Lancelot would not hear him, but came fast upon him. King Mark saw that, and made no defence, but tumbled down out of his saddle to the earth as a sack, and there he lay still and cried, 'Sir Lancelot, have mercy upon me.'

'Arise, recreant king and knight!'

'Sir, I will not fight,' said King Mark, 'but whither that ye will I will go with you.'

return again] bring back

'Alas,' said Sir Lancelot, 'that I might not give thee one buffet for the love of Sir Tristram and of La Belle Isode, and for the two knights that thou hast slain traitorly.'

And so he mounted upon his horse and brought him to King Arthur; and there King Mark alit in that same place, and threw his helm from him upon the earth, and his sword, and fell flat to the earth at King Arthur's feet, and put him in his grace and mercy.

'So God me help,' said King Arthur, 'ye are welcome in a manner, and in a manner ye are not welcome. In this manner ye are welcome, that ye come hither maugre your head, as I suppose.'

'That is truth,' said King Mark, 'and else I had not been here now, for my lord Sir Lancelot brought me hither by fine force, and to him am I yielded to as recreant.'

'Well,' said King Arthur, 'ye ought to do me service, homage, and fealty; and never would ye do me none, but ever ye have been against me, and a destroyer of my knights. Now how will ye acquit you?'

'Sir,' said King Mark, 'right as your lordship will require me, unto my power, I will make a large amends.' For he was a fair speaker, and false thereunder.

Then for great pleasure of Sir Tristram, to make them two accorded, the King withheld King Mark as at that time, and made a broken love day between them.*

[Sir Dinadan meets Sir Palomides, who reveals that he was in prison at the time when he should have encountered Sir Tristram for their promised combat.]

[21] So within three days after, the King let make a jousting at a priory, and there made them ready many knights of the Round Table. And Sir Gawain and his brethren made them ready to joust; but Sir Lancelot, Sir Tristram, nor Sir Dinadan would not joust, but suffered Sir Gawain, for the love of King Arthur, with his brethren to win the degree if they might. So on the morn they apparelled them to joust, Sir Gawain and his four brethren; they did great deeds of arms, and Sir Ector de Maris did marvellously well. But Sir Gawain passed all that fellowship, wherefore King Arthur and all the knights gave Sir Gawain the honour at the beginning.

---

fine] pure   withheld] kept with him   degree] prize

Right so was King Arthur ware of a knight and two squires that came out of a forest side, with a covered shield of leather. Then he came in stiffly and hurtled here and there, and anon with one spear he had smitten down two knights of the Round Table. And so with his hurtling he lost the covering of his shield; then was the King and all others ware that he bore a red shield.

'Ah, Jesu,' said King Arthur, 'see where rideth a strong knight, he with the red shield.'

And there was a noise and a great cry, 'Beware the knight with the red shield!'

So within a little while he had overthrown three brethren of Sir Gawain's.

'So God me help,' said King Arthur, 'me seemeth yonder is the best jouster that ever I saw.'

So he looked about and saw him encounter with Sir Gawain, and he smote him down with so great force that he made his horse to avoid his saddle.

'How now?' said the King to Sir Gawain, 'methinketh ye have a fall; well were me and I knew what knight he were with the red shield.'

'I know him well enough,' said Sir Dinadan, 'but as at this time ye shall not know his name.'

'By my head,' said Sir Tristram, 'he jousteth better than Sir Palomides, and if ye list to know, his name is Sir Lamorak de Gales.'

And as they stood thus, they saw Sir Gawain and he encountered together again; and there he smote Sir Gawain from his horse and bruised him sore. And in the sight of King Arthur he smote down twenty knights, beside Sir Gawain; and so clearly was the prize given him as a knight peerless. Then slyly and marvellously Sir Lamorak withdrew him from all the fellowship into the forest's side. All this espied King Arthur, for his eye went never from him. Then the King, Sir Lancelot, and Sir Tristram and Sir Dinadan took their hackneys, and rode straight after the good knight Sir Lamorak de Gales, and there found him. And thus said the King, 'Ah, fair knight, well be ye found.'

When he saw the King, he put off his helm and saluted him; and when he saw Sir Tristram he alit down off his horse and ran to take him

---

stiffly] boldly   avoid] part company with   slyly and marvellously] so as to attract remarkably little notice

by the stirrup. But Sir Tristram would not suffer him, but he alit or that he came, and either took other in arms and made great joy of other.

Then the King was glad, and so was all the fellowship of the Round Table, except Sir Gawain and his brethren. And when they wist that it was Sir Lamorak, they had great despite of him, and were wonderly wroth with him that he had put him to such a dishonour that day.

Then he called to him privily in council all his brethren, and to them said thus: 'Fair brethren, here may ye see, whom that we hate King Arthur loveth, and whom that we love he hateth. And wit you well, my fair brethren, that this Sir Lamorak will never love us, because we slew his father, King Pellinore, for we deemed that he slew our father, King Lot of Orkney. And for the death of King Pellinore, Sir Lamorak did us a shame to our mother; therefore I will be revenged.'

'Sir,' said Sir Gawain's brethren, 'let see devise how ye will be revenged, and ye shall find us ready.'

'Well,' said Sir Gawain, 'hold ye still, and we shall espy our time.'

[22] Now pass we on our matter, and leave we Sir Gawain; and speak we of King Arthur, that on a day said unto King Mark, 'Sir, I pray you give me a gift that I shall ask you.'

'Sir,' said King Mark, 'I will give you what gift I may give you.'

'Sir, gramercy,' said King Arthur. 'This will I ask you: that ye be good lord* unto Sir Tristram, for he is a man of great honour; and that ye will take him with you into Cornwall and let him see his friends, and there cherish him for my sake.'

'Sir,' said King Mark, 'I promise you by my faith and by the faith that I owe unto God and to you, I shall worship him for your sake all that I can or may.'

'Sir,' said King Arthur, 'and I will forgive you all the evil will that ever I owed you, and ye swear that upon a book before me.'

'With a good will,' said King Mark; and so he there swore upon a book before him and all his knights, and therewith King Mark and Sir Tristram took each other by the hands hard knit together. But for all this King Mark thought falsely, as it proved after; for he put Sir Tristram in prison, and cowardly would have slain him.

Then soon after, King Mark took his leave to ride into Cornwall; and Sir Tristram made him ready to ride with him, whereof the

let see devise] consider

most part of the Round Table were wroth and heavy, and in especial
Sir Lancelot and Sir Lamorak and Sir Dinadan were wroth out of measure. For well they wist King Mark would slay or destroy Sir Tristram.

'Alas,' said Sir Dinadan, 'that my lord Sir Tristram shall depart!'

And Sir Tristram took such a sorrow that he was amazed.

'Alas,' said Sir Lancelot unto King Arthur, 'what have ye done? for
ye shall lose the man of most worship that ever came into your court.'

'Sir, it was his own desire,' said King Arthur, 'and therefore I might
not do withal; for I have done all that I can and made them at accord.'

'Accord?' said Sir Lancelot, 'now fie on that accord! For ye shall hear
that he shall slay Sir Tristram or put him in prison, for he is the most
coward and the villainest king and knight that is now living.'

And therewith Sir Lancelot departed, and came to King Mark and
said to him thus: 'Sir king, wit you well the good knight Sir Tristram
shall go with thee. Beware, I rede thee, of treason, for and thou mischief that knight by any manner of falsehood or treason, by the faith I
owe to God and to the order of knighthood, I shall slay thee with mine
own hands.'

'Sir Lancelot, overmuch have ye said unto me, and I have sworn and
said over-largely before King Arthur in hearing of all his knights, and
overmuch shame it were to me to break my promise.'

'Ye say well,' said Sir Lancelot, 'but ye are called so false and full of
felony that no man may believe you. Pardieu, it is known well for what
cause ye came into this country, and for none other cause but to slay
Sir Tristram.'*

So with great dole King Mark and Sir Tristram rode together; for it
was by Sir Tristram's will and his means to go with King Mark, and all
was for the intent to see La Belle Isode, for without the sight of her
Sir Tristram might not endure.

amazed] beside himself　　　　do withal] act otherwise

[23] Now turn we again unto Sir Lamorak, and speak we of his brethren: Sir Tor, which was King Pellinore's first son and begotten of Aries' wife the cowherd, for he was a bastard; and Sir Agloval was his first son begotten in wedlock; Sir Lamorak, Dornar, Percival, these were his sons too in wedlock.

So when King Mark and Sir Tristram were departed from the court there was made great dole and sorrow for the departing of Sir Tristram. Then the King and his knights made no manner of joys eight days after. And at the eight days' end there came to the court a knight with a young squire with him; and when this knight was unarmed, he went to the King and required him to make the young squire a knight.

'Of what lineage is he come?' said King Arthur.

'Sir,' said the knight, 'he is the son of King Pellinore, that did you some time good service, and he is brother unto Sir Lamorak de Gales, the good knight.'

'Well,' said the King, 'for what cause desire ye that of me, that I should make him knight?'

'Wit you well, my lord the king, that this young squire is brother to me as well as to Sir Lamorak, and my name is Agloval.'

'Sir Agloval,' said Arthur, 'for the love of Sir Lamorak and for his father's love, he shall be made knight tomorrow. Now tell me,' said Arthur, 'what is his name?'

'Sir,' said the knight, 'his name is Percival de Gales.'

So on the morn the King made him knight in Camelot; but the King and all the knights thought it would be long or that he proved a good knight. Then at the dinner, when the King was set at the table, and every knight after he was of prowess, the King commanded him to be set among mean knights; and so was Sir Percival set as the King commanded.

Then was there a maiden in the Queen's court that was come of high blood, and she was dumb and never spoke word. Right so she came straight into the hall, and went unto Sir Percival, and took him by the hand and said aloud, that the King and all the knights might hear it, 'Arise, Sir Percival, the noble knight and God's knight, and go with me.'

And so he did; and there she brought him to the right side of the Siege Perilous, and said, 'Fair knight, take here thy siege, for that siege appertaineth to thee and to none other.'

after he was] according as he was

Right so she departed and asked a priest; and as she was confessed and houselled, then she died. Then the King and all the court made great joy of Sir Percival.

Now turn we unto Sir Lamorak, that much was there praised. Then by [24] the mean of Sir Gawain and his brethren, they sent for their mother there besides, fast by a castle beside Camelot; and all was to that intent to slay Sir Lamorak. The Queen of Orkney was there but a while, but Sir Lamorak wist of her being, and was full fain; and for to make an end of this matter, he sent unto her, and there betwixt them was a night assigned that Sir Lamorak should come to her. Thereof Sir Gaheris was ware, and rode before the same night, and waited upon Sir Lamorak. And then he saw where he came riding all armed, and where he alit and tied his horse to a privy postern, and so he went into a parlour and unarmed him. And then he went unto the queen's bed, and she made of him passing great joy, and he of her again, for either loved other passing sore.

So when Sir Gaheris saw his time, he came to their bedside all armed, with his sword naked, and suddenly he got his mother by the hair and struck off her head. When Sir Lamorak saw the blood dash upon him all hot, which was the blood that he loved passing well, wit you well he was sore abashed and dismayed of that dolorous sight. And therewith Sir Lamorak leapt out of the bed in his shirt as a knight dismayed, saying thus, 'Ah, Sir Gaheris, knight of the Table Round, foul and evil have ye done, and to you great shame. Alas, why have ye slain your mother that bore you? For with more right ye should have slain me.'

'The offence hast thou done,' said Gaheris, 'notwithstanding a man is born to offer his service; but yet shouldst thou beware with whom thou meddlest, for thou hast put my brethren and me to a shame. And thy father slew our father; and thou to lie by our mother is too much shame for us to suffer. And as for thy father, King Pellinore, my brother Sir Gawain and I slew him.'

'Ye did the more wrong,' said Sir Lamorak, 'for my father slew not your father: it was Balin le Savage. And as yet, my father's death is not revenged.'*

'Leave those words,' said Sir Gaheris, 'for and thou speak villainously I will slay thee!—but because thou art naked I am ashamed to

houselled] given the Eucharist   privy postern] secluded gate   service] homage in love

slay thee. But wit thou well, in what place I may get thee I will slay thee.
And now is my mother quit of thee, for she shall never shame her children. And therefore hie thee and withdraw thee and take thine
armour, that thou were gone.'

So Sir Lamorak saw there was no other boot, but fast armed him,
and took his horse and rode his way making great sorrow. But for
shame and sorrow he would not ride to King Arthur's court, but rode
another way. But when it was known that Sir Gaheris had slain his
mother, the King was passing wroth and commanded him to go out of
his court. Wit you well Sir Gawain was wroth that Sir Gaheris had
slain his mother and let Sir Lamorak escape. And for this matter was
the King passing wroth, and many other knights.

'Sir,' said Sir Lancelot, 'here is a great mischief befallen by felony
and by forecast, that your sister is thus shamefully slain. And I dare say
it was wrought by treason; and I dare say also that ye shall lose that
good knight, Sir Lamorak. And I wot well, and Sir Tristram wist it, he
would never come within your court.'

'God defend,' said King Arthur, 'that I should lose Sir Lamorak!'

'Yes,' said Sir Lancelot, 'for Sir Gawain and his brethren will slay
him by one mean or by another.'

'That shall I let,' said King Arthur.

[25] Now leave we of Sir Lamorak, and speak we of Sir Gawain's brethren
Sir Agravain and Sir Mordred. As they rode on their adventures they
met with a knight flying sore wounded, and they asked him what
tidings.

'Fair knights,' said he, 'here cometh a knight after me that will slay
me.'

So with that came Sir Dinadan fast riding to them by adventure, but
he would promise them no help. But Sir Agravain and Sir Mordred
promised him to rescue him, and therewith came that knight straight
unto them, and anon he proffered to joust. That saw Sir Mordred and
rode to him and struck him, but he smote Sir Mordred over his horse's
tail. That saw Sir Agravain; and right so as he served Sir Mordred, so
he served Sir Agravain, and said, 'Wit you well, sirs both, that I am
Sir Breunis sans Pité that hath done this to you.' And yet he rode over
Sir Agravain five or six times.

forecast] malice aforethought   let] prevent

When Sir Dinadan saw this, he must needs joust with him for shame, and so Sir Dinadan and he encountered together. But with pure strength Sir Dinadan smote him over his horse's tail; then he took his horse and fled, for he was on foot one of the valiant knights in Arthur's days, and a great destroyer of all good knights. Then rode Sir Dinadan unto Sir Mordred and unto Sir Agravain.

'Sir knight, well have ye done, and well have ye revenged us, wherefore we pray you tell us your name.'

'Fair sirs, ye ought to know my name, which is called Sir Dinadan.'

When they understood that it was Sir Dinadan they were more wroth than they were before, for they hated him out of measure because of Sir Lamorak. For Sir Dinadan had such a custom that he loved all good knights that were valiant, and he hated all those that were destroyers of good knights. And there was none that hated Sir Dinadan but those that ever were called murderers.

Then spake the hurt knight that Breunis sans Pité had chased—his name was Dalan—and said, 'If thou be Sir Dinadan, thou slew my father.'

'It might well be so,' said Dinadan, 'but then it was in my defence and at his request.'

'By my head,' said Dalan, 'thou shalt die therefore.' And therewith he dressed his spear and his shield; and to make short tale, Sir Dinadan smote him down off his horse, that his neck was nigh broken, and in the same wise he smote Sir Mordred and Sir Agravain. And after, in the quest of the Sangrail, cowardly and feloniously they slew Sir Dinadan, which was great damage*, for he was a great bourder and a passing good knight.*

Now turn we again unto King Arthur. There came a knight out of [26] Cornwall—his name was Sir Fergus, a fellow of the Round Table— and there he told the King and Sir Lancelot good tidings of Sir Tristram, and there was brought goodly letters, and how he left him in the castle of Tintagel. Then came a damosel that brought goodly letters unto King Arthur and unto Sir Lancelot, and there she had passing good cheer of the King and of the Queen and of Sir Lancelot, and so they wrote goodly letters again. But Sir Lancelot bade ever Sir Tristram beware of King Mark, for ever he called him in his letters King

bourder] joker   wrote goodly letters again] wrote letters back

Fox, as who saith, he fareth always with wiles and treason. Whereof Sir Tristram in his heart thanked Sir Lancelot.

Then the damosel went unto La Belle Isode, and bore her letters from the King and from Sir Lancelot, whereof she was in great joy.

'Fair damosel,' said Isode, 'how fareth my lord Arthur, and Queen Guenivere, and the noble knight Sir Lancelot?'

She answered, and to make short tale, 'Much the better that ye and Sir Tristram be in joy.'

'God reward them,' said La Belle Isode, 'for Sir Tristram hath suffered great pain for me, and I for him.'

So the damosel departed and brought the letters to King Mark. And when he had read them and understood them, he was wroth with Sir Tristram, for he deemed that he had sent the damosel to King Arthur. For King Arthur and Sir Lancelot in a manner threatened King Mark in his letters, and as King Mark read these letters he deemed treason by Sir Tristram.

'Damosel,' said King Mark, 'will ye ride again and bear letters from me unto King Arthur?'

'Sir,' she said, 'I will be at your commandment to ride when ye will.'

'Ye say well,' said the king. 'Come ye again tomorrow and fetch your letters.'

Then she departed and came to La Belle Isode and to Sir Tristram, and told them how she should ride again with letters to King Arthur.

'Then we pray you,' said they, 'that when ye have received your letters, that ye would come by us, that we may see the privity of your letters.'

'All that I may do, madam, ye wot well I must do for Sir Tristram, for I have been long his own maiden.'

So on the morn the damosel went unto King Mark to have received his letters and to depart.

'Damosel, I am not advised,' said King Mark, 'as at this time to send my letters.'

But so privily and secretly he sent letters unto King Arthur and unto Queen Guenivere and unto Sir Lancelot. So the varlet departed, and found the King and Queen in Wales, at Caerleon. And as the King and the Queen were at Mass the varlet came with the letters; and when Mass was done, the King and the Queen opened the letters privily.

advised] prepared

And to begin, the king's letters spoke wonderly short unto King Arthur, and bade him entermete with himself and with his wife, and of his knights, for he was able to rule his wife and his knights.

When King Arthur understood the letter, he mused of many things, [27] and thought on his sister's words, Queen Morgan le Fay, that she had said betwixt Queen Guenivere and Sir Lancelot; and in this thought he studied a great while. Then he bethought him again how his own sister was his enemy, and that she hated the Queen and Sir Lancelot to the death, and so he put that all out of his thought. Then King Arthur read the letter again, and the latter clause said that King Mark took Sir Tristram for his mortal enemy; wherefore he put King Arthur out of doubt he would be revenged of Sir Tristram. Then was King Arthur wroth with King Mark.

And when Queen Guenivere read her letter and understood it, she was wroth out of measure, for the letter spoke shame by her and by Sir Lancelot; and so privily she sent the letter unto Sir Lancelot. And when he wist the intent of the letter he was so wroth that he laid him down on his bed to sleep, whereof Sir Dinadan was ware, for it was his manner to be privy with all good knights. And as Sir Lancelot slept, he stole the letter out of his hand and read it word by word; and then he made great sorrow for anger. And Sir Lancelot so wakened, and went to a window and read the letter again, which made him angry.

'Sir,' said Sir Dinadan, 'wherefore be ye angry? I pray you, discover your heart to me; for pardieu, ye know well that I would you but well, for I am a poor knight and a servitor unto you and to all good knights. For though I be not of worship myself, I love all those that be of worship.'

'It is truth,' said Sir Lancelot, 'ye are a trusty knight, and for great trust I will show you my counsel.'

And when Sir Dinadan understood it well, he said, 'Sir, this is my counsel: set you right nought by these threatenings, for King Mark is so villainous a knight that by fair speech shall never man get aught of him. But ye shall see what I shall do: I will make a lay for him, and when it is made I shall make a harper to sing it before him.'

And so anon he went and made it, and taught it to a harper that hight Eliot; and when he could it he taught it to many harpers. And so by the will of King Arthur and of Sir Lancelot, the harpers went into Wales

entermete with] look to   could it] knew it by heart

and into Cornwall to sing the lay that Sir Dinadan made of King Mark, which was the worst lay that ever harper sang with harp or with any other instrument.*

[31]　　Then came Eliot the harper with the lay that Sir Dinadan had made, and secretly brought it unto Sir Tristram, and told him the lay that Sir Dinadan had made by King Mark. And when Sir Tristram heard it, he said, 'O lord Jesu, that Sir Dinadan can make wonderly well, and ill where he should make evil!*'

'Sir,' said Eliot, 'dare I sing this song before King Mark?'

'Yea, on my peril,' said Sir Tristram, 'for I shall be thy warrant.'

So at the meat, in came Eliot the harper among other minstrels, and began to harp. And because he was a curious harper, men heard him sing the same lay that Sir Dinadan made, which spoke the most villainy by King Mark and of his treason that ever man heard. And when the harper had sung his song to the end, King Mark was wonderly wroth, and said, 'Harper, how durst thou be so bold, on thy head, to sing this song before me?'

'Sir,' said Eliot, 'wit thou well I am a minstrel, and I must do as I am commanded of those lords that I bear the arms of.* And sir, wit you well that Sir Dinadan, a knight of the Table Round, made this song, and made me to sing it before you.'

'Thou sayest well,' said King Mark, 'and because thou art a minstrel thou shalt go quit. But I charge thee, hie thee fast out of my sight.'

So Eliot the harper departed, and went to Sir Tristram and told him how he had sped. Then Sir Tristram let make letters as goodly as he could to Camelot and to Sir Dinadan, and so he let conduct the harper out of the country. But King Mark was wonderly wroth, for he deemed that the lay that was sung before him was made by Sir Tristram's counsel; wherefore he thought to slay him and all his well-willers in that country.*

[Sir Galahalt the Haut Prince holds a seven-day tournament at Surluse, at which Sir Dinadan, among others, does many feats of arms.]

[49]　Then by all the assent they gave Sir Lancelot the prize; the next was Sir Lamorak de Gales, and the third was Sir Palomides, the fourth was

---

be thy warrant] guarantee your safety　　　curious] skilled　　　go quit] get away with it

King Bagdemagus. So these four knights had the prize, and there was great joy and great noblesse in all the court.

And on the morn Queen Guenivere and Sir Lancelot departed unto King Arthur, but in no wise Sir Lamorak would not go with them.

'Sir, I shall undertake,' said Sir Lancelot, 'that and ye will go with us, King Arthur shall charge Sir Gawain and his brethren never to do you hurt.'

'As for that,' said Sir Lamorak, 'I will not trust to Sir Gawain nor none of his brethren. And wit you well, Sir Lancelot, and it were not for my lord King Arthur's sake, I should match Sir Gawain and his brethren well enough. But for to say that I shall trust them, that shall I never. And I pray you recommend me unto King Arthur and all my lords of the Round Table. And in what place that ever I come, I shall do you service to my power.'

Then Sir Lamorak departed from Sir Lancelot and all the fellowship, and either of them wept at their departing.

[50] Now turn we from this matter and speak of Sir Tristram, of whom this book is principally of; and leave we the King and the Queen and Sir Lancelot and Sir Lamorak; and here beginneth the treason of King Mark, that he ordained against Sir Tristram.

And there was cried by the coasts of Cornwall a great tournament and jousts, and all was done by Sir Galahalt the Haut Prince and King Bagdemagus, to the intent to slay Sir Lancelot, or else utterly to destroy him and shame him, because Sir Lancelot had evermore the higher degree. Therefore this prince and this king made this jousts against Sir Lancelot, and thus their counsel was discovered unto King Mark, whereof he was glad. Then King Mark bethought him that he would have Sir Tristram unto the tournament disguised that no man should know him, to that intent that the Haut Prince should ween that Sir Tristram were Sir Lancelot.

And so at that jousts came in Sir Tristram; and at that time Sir Lancelot was not there. But when they saw a knight disguised do such deeds of arms, they weened it had been Sir Lancelot, and in especial King Mark said it was Sir Lancelot plainly. Then they set upon him, both King Bagdemagus and the Haut Prince; and their knights said that it was wonder that ever Sir Tristram might endure that pain. Nothwithstanding for all the pain that they did him, he won the degree at that tournament, and there he hurt many knights and bruised them wonderly sore.

So when the jousts was all done they knew well that he was Sir Tristram de Lyonesse; and all they that were on King Mark's party were glad that Sir Tristram was hurt, and all the remnant were sorry of his hurt. For Sir Tristram was not so hated as was Sir Lancelot, not within the realm of England.

Then came King Mark unto Sir Tristram and said, 'Fair nephew, I am heavy of your hurts.'

'Gramercy, my lord,' said Sir Tristram.

Then King Mark made him to be put in a horse litter in great tokening of love, and said, 'Fair cousin, I shall be your leech myself.'

And so he rode forth with Sir Tristram, and brought him into a castle by daylight. And then King Mark made Sir Tristram to eat, and after that he gave him a drink; and anon as he had drunk he fell asleep. And when it was night he made him to be carried to another castle, and there he put him in a strong prison, and a man and a woman to give him his meat and his drink. So there he was a great while.

Then was Sir Tristram missed, and no creature wist where he was become.*

When Queen Isode understood that Sir Tristram was in prison, she [51] made great sorrow as ever made lady or gentlewoman. Then Sir Tristram sent a letter unto La Belle Isode and prayed her to be his good lady, and said, if it pleased her to make a vessel ready for her and him, he would go with her unto the realm of Logris, that is this land.*

When La Belle Isode understood Sir Tristram and his intent, she sent him another and bade him be of good comfort, for she would do make the vessel ready and all manner of thing to purpose. Then La Belle Isode sent unto Sir Dinas and to Sir Sadok, and prayed them in any wise to take King Mark and put him in prison unto the time that she and Sir Tristram were departed unto the realm of Logris. When Sir Dinas the Seneschal understood the treason of King Mark, he promised her to do her commandment, and sent her word again that King Mark should be put in prison; and so as they devised it was done. And then Sir Tristram was delivered out of prison; and anon in all haste Queen Isode and Sir Tristram went and took their counsel, and so they took with them what them list best, and so they departed.

Then La Belle Isode and Sir Tristram took their vessel, and came by [52] water into this land; and so they were not four days in this land but there was made a cry of a jousts and tournament that King Arthur let make. When Sir Tristram heard tell of that tournament he disguised himself, and La Belle Isode, and rode unto that tournament. And when he came there he saw many knights joust and tourney; and so Sir Tristram dressed him to the range, and to make short conclusion, he overthrew fourteen knights of the Round Table. When Sir Lancelot saw these knights thus overthrown, he dressed him to Sir Tristram; and that saw La Belle Isode, how Sir Lancelot was come into the field. Then she sent unto Sir Lancelot a ring to let him wit it was Sir Tristram de Lyonesse. When Sir Lancelot understood that he was Sir Tristram, he was full glad, and would not joust. And then Sir Lancelot espied whither Sir Tristram yode, and after him he rode;

range] lists

and then either made great joy of other. And so Sir Lancelot brought Sir Tristram and Isode unto Joyous Gard, that was his own castle, and he had won it with his own hands; and there Sir Lancelot put them in, to wield it for their own. And wit you well, that castle was garnished and furnished for a king and a queen royal there to have sojourned. And Sir Lancelot charged all his people to honour them and love them as they would do himself.

So Sir Lancelot departed unto King Arthur; and then he told Queen Guenivere how he that jousted so well at the last tournament was Sir Tristram. And there he told her how he had with him La Belle Isode maugre King Mark, and so Queen Guenivere told all this to King Arthur. And when King Arthur wist that Sir Tristram was escaped and come from King Mark and had brought La Belle Isode with him, then was he passing glad. So because of Sir Tristram King Arthur let make a cry, that on May Day should be a jousts before the Castle of Lonazep; and that castle was fast by Joyous Gard.

And thus King Arthur devised, that all the knights of this land, of Cornwall, and of North Wales, should joust against all these countries: Ireland and Scotland and the remnant of Wales, and the country of Gore, and Surluse, and of Listinoise, and they of Northumberland, and all those that held lands of King Arthur's on this half the sea. So when this cry was made many knights were glad and many were sad.

'Sir,' said Sir Lancelot unto Arthur, 'by this cry that ye have made ye will put us that be about you in great jeopardy, for there be many knights that hath envy to us; therefore when we shall meet at the day of jousts there will be hard shift for us.'

'As for that,' said King Arthur, 'I care not; there shall we prove who shall be best of his hands.'

So when Sir Lancelot understood wherefore King Arthur made this jousting, then he made such purveyance that La Belle Isode should behold the jousts in a secret place that was honest for her estate.

Now turn we unto Sir Tristram and to La Belle Isode, how they made joy together daily with all manner of mirths that they could devise. And every day Sir Tristram would go ride an-hunting, for he was called that time the chief chaser of the world, and the noblest blower of a horn of all manner of measures; for as books report, of

let make a cry] had it proclaimed   shift] dealing

Sir Tristram came all the good terms of venery and of hunting, and all the sizes and measures of all blowing with a horn; and of him we had first all the terms of hawking, and which were beasts of chase and beasts of venery, and which were vermin; and all the blasts that longed to all manner of game*—that all manner gentlemen have cause to the world's end to praise Sir Tristram, and to pray for his soul. Amen, said Sir Thomas Malory.

So on a day La Belle Isode said unto Sir Tristram, 'I marvel me [53] much that ye remember not yourself, how ye be here in a strange country, and here be many perilous knights, and well ye wot that King Mark is full of treason; and that ye will ride thus to chase and to hunt unarmed, ye might be soon destroyed.'

'My fair lady and my love, *merci*. I will no more do so.'

So then Sir Tristram rode daily an-hunting armed, and his men bearing his shield and his spear.*

Now as Sir Tristram rode an-hunting he met with Sir Dinadan, that [55] was come into the country to seek Sir Tristram. And anon Sir Dinadan told Sir Tristram his name, but Sir Tristram would not tell his name, wherefore Sir Dinadan was wroth.

'For such a foolish knight as ye are,' said Sir Dinadan, 'I saw but late this day lying by a well, and he fared as he slept; and there he lay like a fool grinning, and would not speak, and his shield lay by him, and his horse also stood by him. And well I wot he was a lover.'

'Ah, fair sir,' said Sir Tristram, 'are not ye a lover?'

'Marry, fie on that craft!' said Sir Dinadan.

'Sir, that is evil said,' said Sir Tristram, 'for a knight may never be of prowess but if he be a lover.'

'Ye say well,' said Sir Dinadan. 'Now I pray you tell me your name, sith ye be such a lover; or else I shall do battle with you.'

'As for that,' said Sir Tristram, 'it is no reason to fight with me but if I tell you my name. And as for my name, ye shall not wit as at this time for me.'

'Fie, for shame, are ye a knight and dare not tell your name to me? Therefore, sir, I will fight with you.'

'As for that,' said Sir Tristram, 'I will be advised, for I will not do battle but if me list. And if I do battle with you,' said Sir Tristram, 'ye are not able to withstand me.'

'Fie on thee, coward,' said Sir Dinadan.

'Nay,' said Sir Tristram, 'I will not joust as at this time, but take your horse and let us go hence.'

'God defend me', said Sir Dinadan, 'from thy fellowship, for I never sped well since I met with thee.'

'Well,' said Sir Tristram, 'peradventure I could tell you tidings of Sir Tristram.'

'God save me', said Sir Dinadan, 'from thy fellowship, for Sir Tristram were mickle the worse and he were in thy company.' And they departed.

'Sir,' said Sir Tristram, 'yet it may happen that I may meet with you in other places.'

So rode Sir Tristram unto Joyous Gard, and there he heard in that town great noise and cry.

'What is this noise?' said Sir Tristram.

'Sir,' said they, 'here is a knight of this castle that hath been long among us, and right now he is slain with two knights, and for none other cause but that our knight said that Sir Lancelot was better knight than Sir Gawain.'

'That was a simple cause,' said Sir Tristram, 'for to slay a good knight for saying well by his master.'

'That is little remedy to us,' said the men of the town. 'For and Sir Lancelot had been here, soon we should have been revenged upon those false knights.'

When Sir Tristram heard them say so, he sent for his shield and for his spear; and lightly so within a while he had overtaken them, and bade them turn and amend that they had misdone.

'What amends wouldst thou have?' said the one knight.

And therewith they took their course, and either met other so hard that Sir Tristram smote down that knight over his horse's tail. Then the other knight dressed him to Sir Tristram, and in the same wise he served the other knight. And then they got off their horses as well as they might, and dressed their shields and swords to do battle to the utterance.

'Now, knights,' said Sir Tristram, 'will ye tell me of whence ye be, and what are your names? For such men ye might be ye should hard escape my hands, and also ye might be such men and of such a country that for all your evil deeds ye might pass quit.'

mickle] much   simple] trivial

'Wit thou well, sir knight,' said they, 'we fear not much to tell thee our names, for my name is Sir Agravain, and my name is Sir Gaheris, brethren unto the good knight Sir Gawain, and we be nephews unto King Arthur.'

'Well,' said Sir Tristram, 'for King Arthur's sake I shall let you pass as at this time. But it is shame,' said Sir Tristram, 'that Sir Gawain and ye be come of so great blood, that ye four brethren are so named as ye be, for ye be called the greatest destroyers and murderers of good knights that is now in this realm of England. And as I have heard say, Sir Gawain and ye, his brethren, among you slew a better knight than ever any of you was, which was called the noble knight Sir Lamorak de Gales. And it had pleased God,' said Sir Tristram, 'I would I had been by him at his death day.'

'Then shouldst thou have gone the same way,' said Sir Gaheris.

'Now, fair knights, then must there have been many more good knights than ye of your blood.'

And therewith Sir Tristram departed from them toward Joyous Gard. And when he was departed they took their horses, and the one said to the other, 'We will overtake him and be revenged upon him in the despite of Sir Lamorak.'

So when they had overtaken Sir Tristram, Sir Agravain bade him, [56] 'Turn, traitor knight.'

'Ye say well,' said Sir Tristram; and therewith he pulled out his sword and smote Sir Agravain such a buffet upon the helm that he tumbled down off his horse in a swoon, and he had a grievous wound. And then he turned to Sir Gaheris, and Sir Tristram smote his sword and his helm together with such a might that Sir Gaheris fell out of his saddle.

And so Sir Tristram rode unto Joyous Gard, and there he alit and unarmed him. So Sir Tristram told La Belle Isode of all this adventure, as ye have heard before. And when she heard him tell of Sir Dinadan, 'Sir,' she said, 'is not that he that made the song by King Mark?'

'That same is he,' said Sir Tristram, 'for he is the best bourder and japer that I know, and a noble knight of his hands, and the best fellow that I know; and all good knights loveth his fellowship.'

'Alas, sir,' said she, 'why brought ye him not with you hither?'

'Have ye no care,' said Sir Tristram, 'for he rideth to seek me in this country; and therefore he will not away till he have met with me.' And there Sir Tristram told La Belle Isode how Sir Dinadan held against all lovers.

Right so came in a varlet and told Sir Tristram how there was come an errant knight into the town, with such colours upon his shield.

'By my faith, that is Sir Dinadan,' said Sir Tristram. 'Therefore, madam, wit ye what ye shall do: send ye for him, and I will not be seen, and ye shall hear the merriest knight that ever ye spake withal, and the maddest talker. And I pray you heartily that ye make him good cheer.'

So anon La Belle Isode sent unto the town, and prayed Sir Dinadan that he would come into the castle and repose him there with a lady.

'With a good will,' said Sir Dinadan; and so he mounted upon his horse and rode into the castle, and there he alit, and was unarmed and brought into the hall.

And anon La Belle Isode came unto him, and either saluted other. Then she asked him of whence that he was.

'Madam,' said Sir Dinadan, 'I am of the court of King Arthur, and a knight of the Table Round, and my name is Sir Dinadan.'

'What do ye in this country?' said La Belle Isode.

'For sooth, madam, I seek after Sir Tristram, the good knight, for it was told me that he was in this country.'

'It may well be,' said La Belle Isode, 'but I am not ware of him.'

'Madam,' said Sir Dinadan, 'I marvel at Sir Tristram and more other such lovers. What aileth them to be so mad and so besotted upon women?'

'Why,' said La Belle Isode, 'are ye a knight and are no lover? For sooth, it is great shame to you; wherefore ye may not be called a good knight by reason but if ye make a quarrel for a lady.'

'God defend me,' said Sir Dinadan, 'for the joy of love is too short, and the sorrow thereof is duras over long.'

'Ah,' said La Belle Isode, 'say ye nevermore so, for here fast by was the good knight Sir Bleoberis de Ganis, that fought with four knights at once for a damosel, and he won her before the King of Northumberland—and that was worshipfully done,' said La Belle Isode.

'For sooth, it was so,' said Sir Dinadan, 'for I know him well for a good knight and a noble, and come he is of noble blood; and all be noble knights of the blood of Sir Lancelot du Lake.'

'Now I pray you, for my love,' said La Belle Isode, 'will ye fight for me with three knights that do me great wrong? And insomuch as ye be a knight of King Arthur's, I require you to do battle for me.'

duras] affliction

'Then,' Sir Dinadan said, 'I shall say you ye be as fair a lady as ever I saw any, and much fairer than is my lady Queen Guenivere; but wit you well, at one word, I will not fight for you with three knights—Jesu me defend!'

Then Isode laughed, and had good game at him. So he had all the cheer that she might make him, and there he lay all that night. And on the morn early Sir Tristram armed him, and La Belle Isode gave him a good helm. And then he promised her that he would meet with Sir Dinadan, and so they two would ride together unto Lonazep, where the tournament should be. 'And there shall I make ready for you where ye shall see all the sight.'

So departed Sir Tristram with two squires that bore his shield and his spears that were great and long. So after that Sir Dinadan departed, and rode his way a great shake until he had overtaken Sir Tristram; and when Sir Dinadan had overtaken him he knew him anon, and hated the fellowship of him of all other knights. [57]

'Ah,' said Sir Dinadan, 'art thou that coward knight that I met with yesterday? Well, keep thee, for thou shalt joust with me maugre thy head.'

'Well,' said Sir Tristram, 'and I am passing loath to joust.'

And so they let their horses run, and Sir Tristram missed of him on purpose, and Sir Dinadan brake his spear all to shivers; and therewith Sir Dinadan dressed him to draw out his sword.

'Not so, sir,' said Sir Tristram, 'why are ye so wroth? I am not disposed to fight at this time.'

'Fie on thee, coward,' said Sir Dinadan, 'thou shamest all knights.'

'As for that,' said Sir Tristram, 'I care not, for I will wait upon you and be under your protection, for cause ye are so good a knight that ye may save me.'

'God* deliver me of thee!' said Sir Dinadan. 'For thou art as goodly a man of arms and of thy person as ever I saw, and also the most coward that ever I saw. What wilt thou do with great spears and such weapons as thou carriest with thee?'

'Sir, I shall give them', said Sir Tristram, 'to some good knight when I come to the tournament; and if I see that you do best, sir, I shall give them to you.'

So thus as they rode talking they saw where came an errant knight before them, that dressed him to joust.

'Lo,' said Sir Tristram, 'yonder is one that will joust: now dress you to him.'

'Ah, shame betide thee,' said Sir Dinadan.

'Nay, not so,' said Sir Tristram, 'for that knight seemeth a shrew.'

'Then shall I,' said Sir Dinadan.

And so they dressed their shields and their spears, and there they met together so hard that the other knight smote down Sir Dinadan from his horse.

'Lo,' said Sir Tristram, 'it had been better ye had left.'

'Fie on thee, coward,' said Sir Dinadan.

And then he started up and got his sword in his hand, and proffered to do battle on foot.

'Whether in love or in wrath?' said the other knight.

'Sir, let us do battle in love,' said Sir Dinadan.

'What is your name?' said that knight, 'I pray you tell me.'

'Sir, wit you well my name is Sir Dinadan.'

'Ah, Sir Dinadan,' said that knight, 'and my name is Sir Gareth, youngest brother unto Sir Gawain.'

Then either made of other great cheer, for this Sir Gareth was the best knight of all the brethren, and he proved a good knight. Then they took their horses, and there they spoke of Sir Tristram, how such a coward he was; and every word Sir Tristram heard, and laughed them to scorn. Then were they ware where came a knight before them well horsed and well armed, and he made him ready to joust.

'Now, fair knights,' said Sir Tristram, 'look betwixt you who shall joust with yonder knight, for I warn you I will not have ado with him.'

'Then shall I,' said Sir Gareth.

And so they encountered together, and there that knight smote down Sir Gareth over his horse's croup.

'How now?' said Sir Tristram unto Sir Dinadan. 'Now dress you and revenge the good knight Sir Gareth.'

'That shall I not,' said Sir Dinadan, 'for he hath struck down a much bigger knight than I am.'

'Ah, Sir Dinadan,' said Sir Tristram, 'now I see and feel that your heart faileth you, and therefore now shall ye see what I shall do.' And

shrew] menace

then Sir Tristram hurtled unto that knight, and smote him quite from his horse.

And when Sir Dinadan saw that, he marvelled greatly; and then he deemed that it was Sir Tristram. And anon this knight that was on foot pulled out his sword to do battle.

'Sir, what is your name?' said Sir Tristram.

'Wit you well,' said that knight, 'my name is Sir Palomides.'

'Ah, sir knight, which knight hate ye most in the world?' said Sir Tristram.

'For sooth,' said he, 'I hate Sir Tristram most, to the death, for and I may meet with him the one of us shall die.'

'Ye say well,' said Sir Tristram. 'And now, wit you well that my name is Sir Tristram de Lyonesse; and now do your worst.'

When Sir Palomides heard him say so he was astonished. And then he said thus: 'I pray you, Sir Tristram, forgive me all my evil will! And if I live, I shall do you service before all knights that be living; and there as I have owed you evil will, me sore repents. I wot not what aileth me, for me seemeth that ye are a good knight; and that any other knight that nameth himself a good knight should hate you, me sore marvelleth. And therefore I require you, Sir Tristram, take no displeasure at my unkind words.'

'Sir Palomides,' said Sir Tristram, 'ye say well, and well I wot ye are a good knight, for I have seen you proved; and many great enterprises ye have done, and well achieved them. Therefore,' said Sir Tristram, 'and ye have any evil will to me, now may ye right it, for I am ready at your hand.'

'Not so, my lord Sir Tristram, for I will do you knightly service in all thing as ye will command me.'

'Sir, right so I will take you,' said Sir Tristram.

And so they rode forth on their ways talking of many things.

Then said Sir Dinadan, 'Ah, my lord Sir Tristram, foul have ye mocked me, for God knoweth I came into this country for your sake, and by the advice of my lord Sir Lancelot; and yet would he not tell me the certainty of you where I should find you.'

'Truly,' said Sir Tristram, 'and Sir Lancelot wist best where I was, for I abide in his own castle.'

And thus they rode until they were ware of the coast of Lonazep; [58] and then were they ware of four hundred tents and pavilions, and marvellous great ordinance.

coast] border   ordinance] martial preparations

'So God me help,' said Sir Tristram, 'yonder I see the greatest ordinance that ever I saw.'

'Sir,' said Palomides, 'me seemeth that there was as great ordinance at the Castle of Maidens upon the rock, where ye won the prize, for I saw myself where ye for-jousted thirty knights.'

'Sir,' said Sir Dinadan, 'and in Surluse, at the tournament that Sir Galahalt of the Long Isles made, which there dured seven days; for there was as great a gathering as is here, for there were many nations.'

'Sir, who was the best there?' said Sir Tristram.

'Sir, it was Sir Lancelot du Lake and the noble knight, Sir Lamorak de Gales.'

'By my faith,' said Sir Tristram, 'and Sir Lancelot were there, I doubt not', said Sir Tristram, 'but he won the worship, so he had not been overmatched with many knights. And of the death of Sir Lamorak,' said Sir Tristram, 'it was over-great pity, for I dare say he was the cleanest-mighted man and the best-winded of his age that was alive; for I knew him that he was one of the best knights that ever I met withal, but if it were Sir Lancelot.'

'Alas,' said Sir Dinadan and Sir Tristram, 'that full woe is us for his death! And if they were not the cousins of my lord King Arthur that slew him, they should die for it, all that were consenting to his death.'

'And for such things,' said Sir Tristram, 'I fear to draw unto the court of King Arthur; sir, I will that ye wit it,' said Sir Tristram unto Sir Gareth.

'As for that, I blame you not,' said Sir Gareth, 'for well I understand the vengeance of my brethren, Sir Gawain, Sir Agravain, Sir Gaheris, and Sir Mordred. But as for me,' said Sir Gareth, 'I meddle not of their matters, and therefore there is none of them that loveth me. And for cause that I understand they be murderers of good knights, I left their company; and would God would I had been beside Sir Gawain when that most noble knight Sir Lamorak was slain.'

'Now as Jesu be my help,' said Sir Tristram, 'it is passingly well said of you, for I had liever', said Sir Tristram, 'than all the gold betwixt this and Rome I had been there.'

'Iwis,' said Sir Palomides, 'so would I, and yet had I never the degree at no jousts nor tournament and that noble knight Sir Lamorak had

cleanest-mighted man and the best-winded] strongest and fittest　　　Iwis] indeed
degree] prize

been there, but either on horseback or else on foot he put me ever to the worse. And that day that Sir Lamorak was slain he did the most deeds of arms that ever I saw knight do in my life. And when he was given the degree by my lord King Arthur, Sir Gawain and his three brethren, Sir Agravain, Sir Gaheris, and Sir Mordred, set upon Sir Lamorak in a privy place, and there they slew his horse. And so they fought with him on foot more than three hours, both before him and behind him; and so Sir Mordred gave him his death's wound behind him at his back, and all to-hewed him; for one of his squires told me that saw it.'

'Now fie upon treason,' said Sir Tristram, 'for it slayeth my heart to hear this tale.'

'And so it doth mine,' said Sir Gareth, 'brethren as they be mine.'

'Now speak we of other deeds,' said Sir Palomides, 'and let him be, for his life ye may not get again.'

'That is the more pity,' said Sir Dinadan, 'for Sir Gawain and his brethren, except you, Sir Gareth, hateth all good knights of the Round Table for the most part; for well I wot, privily they hate my lord Sir Lancelot and all his kin, and great privy despite they have at him; and that is my lord Sir Lancelot well ware of, and that causeth him the more to have the good knights of his kin about him.'*

[65] 'Well,' said Sir Tristram, 'we must forward as tomorrow.' And then he devised how it should be; and there Sir Tristram devised to send his two pavilions to set them fast by the well of Lonazep, 'and therein shall be the queen, La Belle Isode.'

'Ye say well,' said Sir Dinadan.

But when Sir Palomides heard of that, his heart was ravished out of measure; notwithstanding, he said but little. So when they came to Joyous Gard, Sir Palomides would not have gone into the castle, but as Sir Tristram led him by the hand into Joyous Gard. And when Sir Palomides saw La Belle Isode, he was so ravished that he might uneath speak. So they went unto meat; but Sir Palomides might not eat. And there was all the cheer that might be had.

And so on the morn they were apparelled for to ride toward Lonazep.*

[68] 'Now, sirs, upon what party is it best,' said Sir Tristram, 'to be with tomorrow?'

'Sir,' said Sir Palomides, 'ye shall have my advice to be against King Arthur as tomorrow, for on his party will be Sir Lancelot and many good knights of his blood with him; and the more men of worship that they be, the more worship shall we win.'

'That is full knightly spoken,' said Sir Tristram, 'and so shall it be, right as ye counsel me.'

'In the name of God,' said they all.

So that night they were reposed with the best. And in the morn when it was day, they were arrayed all in green trappings, both shields and spears, and La Belle Isode in the same colour, and her three damsels. And right so these four knights came into the field, endlong and thorough, and so they led La Belle Isode thither as she should stand and behold all the jousts in a bay window; but always she was wimpled, that no man might see her visage. And then these four knights rode straight unto the party of the King of Scots.

When King Arthur had seen them do all this, he asked Sir Lancelot what were these knights and this queen.

'Sir,' said Sir Lancelot, 'I cannot tell you for no certain; but if Sir Tristram be in this country, or Sir Palomides, sir, wit you well it be they, and there is Queen La Belle Isode.'

---

endlong and thorough] riding its whole length

[The tournament gets under way*]

And this meanwhile Sir Tristram rode through the thickest press, and [69] smote down knights on the right hand and on the left hand, and rased off helms, and so passed forth unto his pavilions, and left Sir Palomides on foot. And then Sir Tristram changed his horse and disguised himself all in red, horse and harness.

And when Queen Isode saw Sir Tristram unhorsed and she wist not [70] where he was become, then she wept heartily. But Sir Tristram when he was ready came dashing lightly into the field, and then La Belle Isode espied him. And so he did great deeds of arms with one spear that was great, for Sir Tristram smote down five knights or ever he stinted.

So when La Belle Isode espied Sir Tristram again upon his horse's back she was passing glad, and then she laughed and made good cheer. And as it happened, Sir Palomides looked up toward her; she was in the window, and Sir Palomides espied how she laughed. And therewith he took such a rejoicing that he smote down, what with his spear and with his sword, all that ever he met; for through the sight of her he was so enamoured in her love that he seemed at that time, that and both Sir Tristram and Sir Lancelot had been both against him they should have won no worship of him. And in his heart, as the book saith, Sir Palomides wished that with his worship he might have ado with Sir Tristram before all men, because of La Belle Isode.

Then Sir Palomides began to double his strength, and he did so marvellously that all men had wonder; and ever he cast his eye unto La Belle Isode. And when he saw her make such cheer he fared like a lion, that there might no man withstand him. And then Sir Tristram beheld him how he stirred about, and said unto Sir Dinadan, 'So God me help, Sir Palomides is passing well enduring! But such deeds saw I him never do, nor never erst heard I tell that ever he did so much in one day.'

'Sir, it is his day,' said Sir Dinadan, and he would say no more unto Sir Tristram; but to himself he said thus, 'And Sir Tristram knew for whose love he doth all these deeds of arms, soon would he abate his courage.'

'Alas,' said Sir Tristram, 'that Sir Palomides is not christened.' So said King Arthur, and so said all those that beheld them. Then all people gave him the prize as for the best knight that day, and he passed Sir Lancelot or else Sir Tristram.

'Well,' said Sir Dinadan to himself, 'all this worship that Sir Palomides hath here this day, he may thank the Queen Isode; for had she been away this day, had not Sir Palomides gotten the prize.'

[71] And then the King let blow to lodging; and because Sir Palomides began first, and never he went nor rode out of the field to repose him, but ever he was doing on horseback or on foot, and longest enduring, King Arthur and all the kings gave Sir Palomides the honour and the degree as for that day.

Then Sir Tristram commanded Sir Dinadan to fetch the queen, La Belle Isode, and bring her to his two pavilions by the well; and so Sir Dinadan did as he was commanded. But when Sir Palomides understood and wist that Sir Tristram was he that was in the red armour and on the red horse, wit you well that he was glad, and so was Sir Gareth and Sir Dinadan, for all they weened that Sir Tristram had been taken prisoner.

And then every knight drew to his inn. And then King Arthur and every king spoke of those knights; but of all men they gave Sir Palomides the prize, and all knights that knew Sir Palomides had wonder of his deeds.

'Sir,' said Sir Lancelot unto King Arthur, 'as for Sir Palomides, and he be the green knight, I dare say as for this day he is best worthy to have the degree, for he reposed him never, nor never changed his weeds, and he began first and longest held on. And yet well I wot,' said Sir Lancelot, 'that there was a better knight than he, and that ye shall prove or we depart from them, on my life.'

Thus they talked on either party; and so Sir Dinadan railed with Sir Tristram and said, 'What the devil is upon thee this day? For Sir Palomides' strength feebled never this day, but ever he doubled.

[72] And Sir Tristram fared all this day as he had been asleep, and therefore I call him a coward.'

And so Sir Tristram was in manner wroth with Sir Dinadan. But all this language Sir Dinadan said because he would anger Sir Tristram, for to cause him to wake his spirits; for well knew Sir Dinadan that, and Sir Tristram were thoroughly wroth, Sir Palomides should win no worship upon the morrow. And for this intent Sir Dinadan said all this railing and language against Sir Tristram.

[73] So on the morn Sir Tristram was ready, and La Belle Isode with

weeds] clothing

Sir Palomides and Sir Gareth. And so they rode all in green full freshly beseen unto the forest. And Sir Tristram left Sir Dinadan sleeping in his bed.*

Then Sir Tristram sent Queen Isode unto her lodging into the priory, there to behold all the tournament.

Then there was a cry unto all knights made, that when they heard the [74] horn blow they should make jousts as they did the first day. And then came in Sir Tristram de Lyonesse and smote down Sir Uwain and Sir Lucanor, and Sir Palomides smote down other two knights; and then came Sir Gareth and smote down other two good knights.

Then said King Arthur unto Sir Lancelot, 'Ah, see yonder three knights do passingly well, and namely the first that jousted.'

'Sir,' said Sir Lancelot, 'that knight began not yet, but ye shall see him do marvellously.'

And then came into the place the knights of Orkney, and then they began to do many deeds of arms. When Sir Tristram saw them so begin, he said to Sir Palomides, 'How feel ye yourself? May ye do this day as ye did yesterday?'

'Nay,' said Sir Palomides, 'I feel myself so weary and so sore bruised of the deeds of yesterday, that I may not endure as I did.'

'That me repenteth,' said Sir Tristram, 'for I shall lack you this day.'

'But help yourself,' said Sir Palomides, 'and trust not to me, for I may not do as I did.' And all these words said Palomides but to beguile Sir Tristram.

Then said Sir Tristram unto Sir Gareth, 'Then must I trust upon you; wherefore I pray you be not far from me to rescue me and need be.'

'Sir, I shall not fail you,' said Sir Gareth, 'in all that I may do.'

Then Sir Palomides rode by himself; and then in despite of Sir Tristram he put himself in the thickest press amongst them of Orkney. And there he did so marvellous deeds of arms that all men had wonder of him, for there might none stand him a stroke. When Sir Tristram saw Sir Palomides do such deeds, he marvelled and said to himself, 'Me thinketh he is weary of my company.'

So Sir Tristram beheld him a great while and did but little else, for the noise and cry was so great that Sir Tristram marvelled from whence came the strength that Sir Palomides had there.

namely] especially

'Sir,' said Sir Gareth unto Sir Tristram, 'remember ye not of the words that Sir Dinadan said to you yesterday, when he called you coward? Pardieu, sir, he said it for none ill, for ye are the man in the world that he loveth best, and all that he said was for your worship. And therefore,' said Sir Gareth, 'let me know this day what ye be! And wonder ye not so upon Sir Palomides, for he forceth himself to win all the honour from you.'

'I may well believe it,' said Sir Tristram. 'And sithen I understand his evil will and his envy, ye shall see, if that I enforce myself, that the noise shall be left that is now upon him.'

Then Sir Tristram rode into the thickest of the press, and then he did so marvellously well and did so great deeds of arms that all men said that Sir Tristram did double so much deeds of arms as did Sir Palomides beforehand. And then the noise went clean from Sir Palomides, and all the people cried upon Sir Tristram and said, 'Ah, Jesu, ah, see how Sir Tristram smiteth with his spear so many knights to the earth! And see,' said they all, 'how many knights he smiteth down with his sword, and how many knights he raseth off their helms and their shields!'

And so he beat all of Orkney before him.

'How now?' said Sir Lancelot unto King Arthur, 'I told you that this day there would a knight play his pageant, for yonder rideth a knight: ye may see he doth all knightly, for he hath strength and wind enough.'

'So God me help,' said King Arthur to Sir Lancelot, 'ye say sooth, for I saw never a better knight, for he passeth far Sir Palomides.'

'Sir, wit you well,' said Sir Lancelot, 'it must be so of right, for it is himself that noble knight Sir Tristram.'

'I may right well believe it,' said King Arthur.

But when Sir Palomides heard the noise and the cry was turned from him, he rode out on one side and beheld Sir Tristram. And when he saw him do so marvellously well, he wept passingly sore for despite, for he wist well then he should no worship win that day; for well knew Sir Palomides, when Sir Tristram would put forth his strength and his manhood, that he should get but little worship that day.

[75]   Then came King Arthur, and the King of Northgales, and Sir Lancelot du Lake; and Sir Bleoberis and Sir Bors de Ganis and Sir Ector de Maris, these three knights came into the field with

forceth] strains

Sir Lancelot. And so they four did so great deeds of arms that all the noise began upon Sir Lancelot. And so they beat the King of Northgales and the King of Scots far aback, and made them to void the field. But Sir Tristram and Sir Gareth abode still in the field and endured all that ever there came, that all men had wonder that ever any knight endured so many great strokes. But ever Sir Lancelot and his three kinsmen forbore Sir Tristram and Sir Gareth.

Then said King Arthur, 'Is that Sir Palomides that endureth so well?' 'Nay,' said Sir Lancelot, 'wit you well it is the good knight Sir Tristram, for yonder ye may see Sir Palomides beholdeth and hoveth, and doth little or nought. And sir, ye shall understand that Sir Tristram weeneth this day to beat us all out of the field. And as for me,' said Sir Lancelot, 'I shall not meet him, meet him whoso will. But sir,' said Lancelot, 'ye may see how Sir Palomides hoveth yonder as though he were in a dream; and wit you well he is full heavy that Sir Tristram doth such deeds of arms.'

'Then is he but a fool,' said King Arthur, 'for never was Sir Palomides such a knight, nor never shall be of such prowess. And if he have any envy at Sir Tristram,' said King Arthur, 'and cometh in with him upon his side, he is a false knight.'

And as the King and Sir Lancelot thus spoke, Sir Tristram rode privily out of the press, that no man espied him but La Belle Isode and Sir Palomides; for they two would not leave off their eyesight of him. And when Sir Tristram came to his pavilions he found Sir Dinadan in his bed asleep.

'Awake,' said Sir Tristram, 'for ye ought to be ashamed so to sleep when knights have ado in the field.'

Then Sir Dinadan arose lightly and said, 'Sir, what will ye do?'

'Make you ready', said Sir Tristram, 'to ride with me into the field.'

So when Sir Dinadan was armed he looked upon Sir Tristram's helm and on his shield, and when he saw so many strokes upon his helm and upon his shield he said, 'In good time was I thus asleep; for had I been with you I must needs for shame have followed you, more for shame than for any prowess that is in me! For I see well now by thy strokes that I should have been truly beaten, as I was yesterday.'

'Leave your japes,' said Sir Tristram, 'and come off, that we were in the field again.'

hoveth] waits

'What,' said Sir Dinadan, 'is your heart up now? Yesterday ye fared as ye had dreamed.'

So then Sir Tristram was arrayed all in black harness.

'Ah, Jesu,' said Sir Dinadan, 'what aileth you this day? Me seemeth that ye be more wilder than ye were yesterday.'

Then smiled Sir Tristram and said to Sir Dinadan, 'Await well upon me if ye see me overmatched, and look that ever ye be behind me, and I shall make you ready way, by God's grace.'

So they took their horses. And all this espied Sir Palomides, both the going and the coming; and so did La Belle Isode, for she knew Sir Tristram passing well.

[76] Then Sir Palomides saw that Sir Tristram was disguised, and thought to shame him. And so he rode unto a knight that was sore wounded, that sat under a thorn a good way from the field.

'Sir knight,' said Sir Palomides, 'I pray you to lend me your armour and your shield, for mine is over-well known in this field, and that hath done me great damage. And ye shall have my armour and my shield that is as sure as yours.'

'I will well,' said the knight, 'that ye have my armour and my shield; if they may do you any avail, I am well pleased.'

So Sir Palomides armed him hastily in that knight's armour and his shield that shone like any crystal or silver, and so he came riding into the field. And then there was neither Sir Tristram nor none of his party nor of King Arthur's that knew Sir Palomides. And as soon as he was come into the field Sir Tristram smote down three knights, even in the sight of Sir Palomides. And then he rode against Sir Tristram, and either met other with great spears, that they all to-brast to their hands, and then they dashed together with swords eagerly. Then Sir Tristram had marvel what knight he was that did battle so mightily with him.

Then was Sir Tristram wroth, for he felt him passing strong, and he deemed that he could not have ado with the remnant of the knights because of the strength of Sir Palomides. So they lashed together and gave many sad strokes together, and many knights marvelled what knight he was that so encountered with the black knight, Sir Tristram. And full well knew La Belle Isode that it was Sir Palomides that fought with Sir Tristram, for she espied all in her window where that she stood, how Sir Palomides changed his harness with the wounded knight; and then she began to weep so heartily for the despite of Sir Palomides that wellnigh she swooned.

Then came in Sir Lancelot with the knights of Orkney; and when the other party had espied Sir Lancelot, they cried and said, 'Return, for here cometh Sir Lancelot.'

So there came in a knight unto Sir Lancelot and said, 'Sir, ye must needs fight with yonder knight in the black harness' (which was Sir Tristram), 'for he hath almost overcome that good knight that fighteth with him with the silver shield' (which was Sir Palomides).

Then Sir Lancelot rode betwixt them, and Sir Lancelot said unto Sir Palomides, 'Sir knight, let me have this battle, for ye have need to be reposed.'

Sir Palomides knew well Sir Lancelot, and so did Sir Tristram. But because Sir Lancelot was far hardier knight and bigger than Sir Palomides, he was right glad to suffer Sir Lancelot to fight with Sir Tristram; for well wist he that Sir Lancelot knew not Sir Tristram, and there he hoped that Sir Lancelot should beat or shame Sir Tristram, and thereof Sir Palomides was full fain. And so Sir Lancelot lashed at Sir Tristram many sad strokes; but Sir Lancelot knew not Sir Tristram, but Sir Tristram knew well Sir Lancelot. And thus they fought long together, which made La Belle Isode wellnigh out of her mind for sorrow.

Then Sir Dinadan told Sir Gareth how that knight in the black harness was their lord Sir Tristram; 'and that other is Sir Lancelot that fighteth with him, that must needs have the better of him, for Sir Tristram hath had overmuch travail this day.'

'Then let us smite him down,' said Sir Gareth.

'So it is best that we do,' said Sir Dinadan, 'rather than Sir Tristram should be shamed, for yonder hoveth the strange knight with the silver shield to fall upon Sir Tristram if need be.'

And so forthwith Sir Gareth rushed upon Sir Lancelot and gave him a great stroke upon the helm, that he was astonied. And then came in Sir Dinadan with his spear, and he smote Sir Lancelot such a buffet that horse and man yode to the earth and had a great fall.

'Now fie, for shame,' said Sir Tristram unto Sir Gareth and Sir Dinadan, 'why did ye so, to smite down so good a knight as he is, and namely when I had ado with him? Ah, Jesu, ye do yourself great shame, and him no disworship, for I held him reasonably hot though ye had not helped me.'

I held him reasonably hot] I was giving him a hard enough time

Then came Sir Palomides which was disguised, and smote down Sir Dinadan from his horse. Then Sir Lancelot, because Sir Dinadan had smitten him down beforehand, therefore he assailed Sir Dinadan passing sore, and Sir Dinadan defended him mightily. But well understood Sir Tristram that Sir Dinadan might not endure against Sir Lancelot, wherefore Sir Tristram was sorry.

Then came Sir Palomides fresh upon Sir Tristram; and when Sir Tristram saw Sir Palomides come so freshly, he thought to deliver him at once, because that he would help Sir Dinadan that stood in peril with Sir Lancelot. Then Sir Tristram hurtled unto Sir Palomides and gave him a great buffet, and then Sir Tristram got Sir Palomides and pulled him down underneath his horse's feet. And then Sir Tristram lightly leapt up and left Sir Palomides, and went betwixt Sir Lancelot and Sir Dinadan, and then they began to do battle together.

And right so Sir Dinadan got Sir Tristram's horse, and said on high that Sir Lancelot might hear, 'My lord Sir Tristram, take your horse.'

And when Sir Lancelot heard him name Sir Tristram, 'Ah, Jesu, what have I done?' said Sir Lancelot, 'for now am I dishonoured;' and said, 'Ah, my lord Sir Tristram, why were ye now disguised? Ye have put yourself this day in great peril. But I pray you to pardon me, for and I had known you we had not done this battle.'

'Sir,' said Sir Tristram, 'this is not the first kindness and goodness that ye have showed unto me.'

And anon they were horsed both again. So all the people on the one side gave Sir Lancelot the honour and the degree, and all the people on the other side gave Sir Tristram the honour and the degree. But Sir Lancelot said nay thereto: 'For I am not worthy to have this honour, for I will report me to all knights that Sir Tristram hath been longer in the field than I, and he hath smitten down many more knights this day than I have done. And therefore I will give Sir Tristram my voice and my name, and so I pray all my lords and fellows so to do.'

Then there was the whole voice of kings, dukes and earls, barons and knights, that 'Sir Tristram de Lyonesse this day is proved the best knight.'

[77]   Then they blew unto lodging, and Queen Isode was led unto her pavilions. But wit you well she was wroth out of measure with

---

deliver] deal with   my voice and my name] my vote and support

Sir Palomides, for she saw all his treason from the beginning to the ending. And all this while neither Sir Tristram, Sir Gareth, nor Sir Dinadan knew not of the treason of Sir Palomides. But afterward ye shall hear how there befell the greatest debate betwixt Sir Tristram and Sir Palomides that might be.

So when the tournament was done, Sir Tristram, Sir Gareth, and Sir Dinadan rode with La Belle Isode to his pavilions; and ever Sir Palomides rode with them in their company, disguised as he was. But when Sir Tristram had espied him that he was the same knight with the shield of silver that held him so hot that day, then said Sir Tristram, 'Sir knight, wit thou well here is none that hath need of your fellowship, and therefore I pray you depart from us.'

Then Sir Palomides answered again as though he had not known Sir Tristram, 'Wit you well, sir knight, that from this fellowship will I not depart, for one of the best knights of the world commanded me to be in this company, and till he discharge me of my service I will not be discharged.'

So by his language Sir Tristram knew that it was Sir Palomides, and said, 'Ah, sir, are ye such a knight? Ye have been named wrong, for ye have been called ever a gentle knight, and as this day ye have showed me great ungentleness, for ye had almost brought me to my death. But, as for you, I suppose I should have done well enough, but Sir Lancelot with you was overmuch; for I know no knight living but Sir Lancelot is too over-good for him, and he will do his uttermost.'

'Alas,' said Sir Palomides, 'are ye my lord Sir Tristram?'

'Yea, sir, and that know you well enough.'

'By my knighthood,' said Sir Palomides, 'until now I knew you not; for I weened that ye had been the King of Ireland, for well I wot that ye bore his arms.'

'I bore his arms,' said Sir Tristram, 'and that will I abide by, for I won them once in a field of a full noble knight whose name was Sir Marhalt; and with great pain I won that knight, for there was no other recover. But Sir Marhalt died through false leeches; and yet was he never yielded to me.'

'Sir,' said Palomides, 'I weened that ye had been turned upon Sir Lancelot's party, and that caused me to turn.'

'Ye say well,' said Sir Tristram, 'and so I take you, and forgive you.'

recover] way out   false leeches] medical malpractice

So then they rode to their pavilions; and when they were alit they unarmed them and washed their faces and their hands, and so yode unto meat, and were set at their table. But when La Belle Isode saw Sir Palomides, she changed then her colour for wrath—she might not speak. Anon Sir Tristram espied her countenance and said, 'Madam, for what cause make ye us such cheer? We have been sore travailed all this day.'

'Mine own lord,' said La Belle Isode, 'for God's sake be ye not displeased with me, for I may no otherwise do. I saw this day how ye were betrayed and nigh brought unto your death—truly, sir, I saw every deal, how and in what wise. And therefore, sir, how should I suffer in your presence such a felon and traitor as is Sir Palomides? For I saw him with mine eyes how he beheld you when ye went out of the field, for ever he hoved still upon his horse till that he saw you come again-ward, and then forthwith I saw him ride to the hurt knight and changed his harness with him; and then straight I saw him how he sought you all the field. And anon as he had found you he encountered with you, and wilfully Sir Palomides did battle with you. And as for him, sir, I was not greatly afraid, but I dread sore Sir Lancelot, which knew you not.'

'Madam,' said Sir Palomides, 'ye may say what ye will, I may not contrary you; but by my knighthood I knew not my lord Sir Tristram.'

'No force,' said Sir Tristram unto Sir Palomides, 'I will take your excuse, but well I wot ye spared me but little. But no force: all is pardoned as on my part.'

Then La Belle Isode held down her head and said no more at that time.

[78] And therewith two knights armed came into the pavilion, and there they alit both, and came in armed at all pieces.

'Fair knights,' said Sir Tristram, 'ye are to blame to come thus armed at all pieces upon me while we are at our meat. And if ye would anything with us when we were in the field, there might ye have eased your hearts.'

'Not so, sir,' said the one of those knights. 'We come not for that intent. But wit you well, Sir Tristram, we be come as your friends; and I am come hither for to see you, and this knight is come for to see your queen Isode.'

No force] no matter

Then said Sir Tristram, 'I require you, do off your helms, that I may see you.'

'Sir, that will we do at your desire,' said the knights.

And when their helms were off, Sir Tristram thought that he should know them. Then spake Sir Dinadan privily unto Sir Tristram, 'That is my lord King Arthur, and that other that spake to you first is my lord Sir Lancelot.'*

'Ah, madam, I pray you arise,' said Sir Tristram, 'for here is my lord, King Arthur.'

Then the King and the queen kissed, and Sir Lancelot and Sir Tristram embraced either other in arms, and then there was joy without measure. And at the request of La Belle Isode, King Arthur and Sir Lancelot were unarmed, and then there was merry talking.

'Madam,' said King Arthur, 'it is many a day ago sithen I desired first to see you, for ye have been praised so fair a lady! And now I dare say ye are the fairest that ever I saw, and Sir Tristram is as fair and as good a knight as any that I know. And therefore me seemeth ye are well beset together.'

'Sir, God thank you,' said Sir Tristram and La Belle Isode. 'Of your goodness and of your largesse ye are peerless.'

And thus they talked of many things and of all the whole jousts.

'But for what cause,' said King Arthur, 'were ye, Sir Tristram, against us? And ye are a knight of the Table Round, and of right ye should have been with us.'

'Sir,' said Sir Tristram, 'here is Sir Dinadan, and Sir Gareth your own nephew, caused me to be against you.'

'My lord Arthur,' said Sir Gareth, 'I may bear well, for my back is broad enough; but for sooth, it was Sir Tristram's own deeds.'

'By God, that may I repent,' said Sir Dinadan, 'for this unhappy Sir Tristram brought us to this tournament, and many great buffets he hath caused us to have.'

Then the King and Sir Lancelot laughed that uneath they might sit.

'But what knight was that,' said King Arthur, 'that held you so short?'

'Sir,' said Sir Tristram, 'here he sitteth at this table.'

'What,' said King Arthur, 'was it Sir Palomides?'

'Sir, wit you well that it was he,' said La Belle Isode.

beset] suited   largesse] generosity

'So God me help,' said King Arthur, 'that was unknightly done of you as of so good a knight, for I have heard many people call you a courteous knight.'

'Sir,' said Palomides, 'I knew not Sir Tristram, for he was so disguised.'

'So God help me,' said Sir Lancelot, 'it may well be, for I knew him not myself.'

'Sir, as for that,' said Sir Tristram, 'I have pardoned him, and I would be right loath to leave his fellowship, for I love right well his company.'

And so they left off and talked of other things; and in the evening King Arthur and Sir Lancelot departed unto their lodging.

But wit you well Sir Palomides had great envy heartily, for all that night he had never rest in his bed, but wailed and wept out of measure. So on the morn Sir Tristram, Sir Gareth, and Sir Dinadan arose early and went unto Sir Palomides' chamber, and there they found him fast asleep, for he had all night watched. And it was seen upon his cheeks that he had wept full sore.

'Say ye nothing,' said Sir Tristram, 'for I am sure he hath taken anger and sorrow for the rebuke that I gave him, and La Belle Isode.'

[After the tournament is concluded, Sir Palomides rides off alone, and meets with his brother Sir Safer.]

[84] So on the morn Sir Safer and Sir Palomides rode all that day until after noon. And at the last they heard a great weeping and a great noise down in a manor.

'Sir,' said Sir Safer, 'let us wit what noise this is.'

'I will well,' said Sir Palomides.

And so they rode till that they came to a fair gate of a manor, and there sat an old man saying his prayers and beads. Then Sir Palomides and Sir Safer alit and left their horses, and went within the gates, and there they saw full goodly men weeping.

'Now, fair sirs,' said Sir Palomides, 'wherefore weep ye and make this sorrow?'

And anon one of those knights of the castle beheld Sir Palomides and knew him, and then he went to his fellows and said, 'Fair fellows, wit you well all, we have within this castle the same knight that slew our lord at Lonazep, for I know him well for Sir Palomides.'

Then they went unto harness, all that might bear harness, some on horseback and some upon foot, to the number of three score. And when they were ready they came freshly upon Sir Palomides and upon Sir Safer with a great noise, and said thus, 'Keep thee, Sir Palomides, for thou art known! And by right thou must be dead, for thou hast slain our lord. And therefore wit thou well we may do thee none other favour but slay thee, and therefore defend thee.'

Then Sir Palomides and Sir Safer, the one set his back to the other, and gave many sad strokes, and also took many great strokes. And thus they fought with twenty knights and forty gentlemen and yeomen nigh two hours. But at the last though they were never so loath, Sir Palomides and Sir Safer were taken and yielded, and put in a strong prison. And within three days twelve knights passed upon them, and they found Sir Palomides guilty, and Sir Safer not guilty, of their lord's death. And when Sir Safer should be delivered there was great dole betwixt his brother and him, and many piteous complaints that was made at their departition; there is no maker can rehearse the tenth part.

'Now, fair brother, let be your dolour,' said Sir Palomides, 'and your sorrow, for and I be ordained to die a shameful death, welcome be it! But and I had wist of this death that I am deemed unto, I should never have been yielded.'

So departed Sir Safer, his brother, with the greatest sorrow that ever made knight. And on the morrow they of the castle ordained twelve knights for to ride with Sir Palomides unto the father of the same knight that Sir Palomides slew; and so they bound his legs under an old steed's belly, and then they rode with Sir Palomides unto a castle by the seaside, that hight Pelownes, and there Sir Palomides should have his justice— thus was their ordinance. And so they rode with Sir Palomides fast by the castle of Joyous Gard. And as they passed by that castle there came riding one of that castle by them that knew Sir Palomides; and when that knight saw him led bound upon a crooked courser, then the knight asked Sir Palomides for what cause he was so led.

'Ah, my fair fellow and knight,' said Sir Palomides, 'I ride now toward my death for the slaying of a knight at the tournament of Lonazep; and if I had not departed from my lord Sir Tristram as I ought to have done, now might I have been sure to have had my life

passed] passed judgement   maker] poet   deemed] sentenced

saved. But I pray you, sir knight, recommend me unto my lord Sir Tristram, and unto my lady Queen Isode, and say to them, if ever I trespassed to them, I ask them forgiveness. And also I beseech you recommend me unto my lord King Arthur, and to all the fellowship of the Round Table, unto my power.'

Then that knight wept for pity, and therewith he rode unto Joyous Gard as fast as his horse might run; and lightly that knight descended down off his horse and went unto Sir Tristram, and there he told him all as ye have heard. And ever the knight wept as he were wood.

[85]   When Sir Tristram knew how Sir Palomides went to his death, he was heavy to hear thereof, and said, 'Howbeit that I am wroth with him, yet I will not suffer him to die so shameful a death, for he is a full noble knight.'

And anon Sir Tristram asked his arms; and when he was armed he took his horse and two squires with him, and rode a great pace through a forest after Sir Palomides, the next way unto the Castle of Pelownes where Sir Palomides was judged to his death. And as the twelve knights led him before them, there was the noble knight Sir Lancelot which was alit by a well, and had tied his horse to a tree, and had taken off his helm to drink of that well. And when he saw such a rout which seemed knights, Sir Lancelot put on his helm and suffered them to pass by him. And anon was he ware of Sir Palomides, bound and led shamefully toward his death.

'Ah, Jesu,' said Sir Lancelot, 'what misadventure is befallen him that he is thus led toward his death? Yet, pardieu,' said Sir Lancelot, 'it were shame to me to suffer this noble knight thus to die and I might help him; and therefore I will help him whatsoever come of it, or else I shall die for his sake.'

And then Sir Lancelot mounted on his horse and got his spear in his hand, and rode after the twelve knights which led Sir Palomides.

'Fair knights,' said Sir Lancelot, 'whither lead ye that knight? For it beseemeth him full evil to ride bound.'

Then these twelve knights turned suddenly their horses and said to Sir Lancelot, 'Sir knight, we counsel thee not to meddle of this knight, for he hath deserved death, and unto death he is judged.'

'That me repenteth,' said Sir Lancelot, 'that I may not borrow him

a rout which seemed knights] a company that appeared to be knights   borrow]
ransom

with fairness, for he is over good a knight to die such a shameful death. And therefore, fair knights,' said Sir Lancelot, 'then keep you as well as ye can, for I will rescue that knight or else die for it.'

Then they began to dress their spears, and Sir Lancelot smote the foremost down, horse and man, and so he served three more with one spear; and then that spear brast, and therewith Sir Lancelot drew his sword, and then he smote on the right hand and on the left hand. And so within a while he left none of those knights but he had laid them to the earth, and the most part of them were sore wounded. And then Sir Lancelot took the best horse, and loosed Sir Palomides and set him upon that horse; and so they returned again unto Joyous Gard. And then was Sir Palomides ware of Sir Tristram, how he came riding. And when Sir Lancelot saw him he knew him well, but Sir Tristram knew not him because he had on his shoulder a golden shield. So Sir Lancelot made him ready to joust with Sir Tristram, because he should not ween that he were Sir Lancelot.

Then Sir Palomides cried aloud to Sir Tristram and said, 'Ah, my lord, I require you, joust not with this knight, for he hath saved me from my death.'

When Sir Tristram heard him say so he came a soft trotting pace toward him. And then Sir Palomides said, 'My lord Sir Tristram, much am I beholden unto you of your great goodness, that would proffer your noble body to rescue me undeserved, for I have greatly offended you. Notwithstanding,' said Sir Palomides, 'here met we with this noble knight that worshipfully and manly rescued me from twelve knights, and smote them down all and sore wounded them.'

'Fair knight,' said Sir Tristram unto Sir Lancelot, 'of whence be [86] ye?'

'I am a knight errant,' said Sir Lancelot, 'that rideth to seek many deeds.'

'Sir, what is your name?' said Sir Tristram.

'Sir, at this time I will not tell you.' Then Sir Lancelot said unto Sir Tristram and to Sir Palomides, 'Now are ye met together either with other, and now I will depart from you.'

'Not so,' said Sir Tristram, 'I pray you and require you of knighthood to ride with me unto my castle.'

'Wit you well,' said Sir Lancelot, 'I may not ride with you, for I have many deeds to do in other places, that at this time I may not abide with you.'

'Ah, mercy Jesu,' said Sir Tristram, 'I require you as ye be a true knight to the order of knighthood, play you with me this night.'

Then Sir Tristram had a grant of Sir Lancelot; howbeit, though he had not desired him, he would have ridden with them or soon have come after him, for Sir Lancelot came for no other cause into that country but for to see Sir Tristram.

And when they were come within Joyous Gard they alit, and their horses were led into a stable. And then they unarmed them; for Sir Lancelot, as soon as his helm was off, Sir Tristram and Sir Palomides knew him. Then Sir Tristram took Sir Lancelot in his arms, and so did La Belle Isode; and Sir Palomides kneeled down upon his knees and thanked Sir Lancelot. And when he saw Sir Palomides kneel, he lightly took him up and said thus: 'Wit thou well, Sir Palomides, that I, and any knight of worship in this land, must of very right succour and rescue so noble a knight as ye are proved and renowned, throughout all this realm endlong and overthwart.'

Then was there great joy among them. And the oftener that Sir Palomides saw La Belle Isode, the heavier he waxed day by day. Then Sir Lancelot within three or four days departed, and with him rode Sir Ector de Maris and Sir Dinadan; and Sir Palomides was left there with Sir Tristram a two months and more. But ever Sir Palomides faded and mourned, that all men had marvel wherefore he faded so away. So upon a day, in the dawning, Sir Palomides went into the forest by himself alone; and there he found a well, and then he looked into the well, and in the water he saw his own visage, how he was discoloured and defaded, nothing like as he was.

'Lord Jesu, what may this mean?' said Sir Palomides; and thus he said to himself: 'Ah, Palomides, Palomides, why art thou thus defaded, and ever was wont to be called one of the fairest knights of the world? Forsooth, I will no more live this life, for I love that I may never get nor recover.'

And therewith he laid him down by the well, and so began to make a rhyme of La Belle Isode. And in the meanwhile Sir Tristram was ridden into the same forest to chase a hart of grease; but Sir Tristram would not ride an-hunting never more unarmed, because of Sir Breunis sans Pité. And so Sir Tristram rode into the forest up and down, and as he rode he heard one sing marvellously loud, and that was

play] pass the time had a grant] received the consent defaded] pale
hart of grease] fat deer

Sir Palomides which lay by the well. And then Sir Tristram rode softly thither, for he deemed there was some knight errant which was at the well. And when Sir Tristram came nigh he descended down from his horse and tied his horse fast to a tree; and so he came near on foot, and soon after he was ware where lay Sir Palomides by the well and sang loud and merrily. And ever the complaints were of La Belle Isode, which was marvellously well said, and piteously and full dolefully. And all the whole song Sir Tristram heard word by word; and when he had heard all Sir Palomides' complaint, he was wroth out of measure, and thought for to slay him there as he lay.

Then Sir Tristram remembered himself that Sir Palomides was unarmed, and of so noble a name that Sir Palomides had, and also the noble name that himself had, then he made a restraint of his anger. And so he went unto Sir Palomides a soft pace and said, 'Sir Palomides, I have heard your complaint, and of your treason that ye have owed me long, and wit you well, therefore ye shall die. And if it were not for shame of knighthood thou shouldst not escape my hands, for now I know well thou hast awaited me with treason. And therefore,' said Sir Tristram, 'tell me how thou wilt acquit thee.'

'Sir, I shall acquit me thus: as for Queen La Belle Isode, thou shalt wit that I love her above all other ladies in this world; and well I wot it shall befall by me as for her love as befell the noble knight Sir Kehydius, that died for the love of La Belle Isode. And now, Sir Tristram, I will that ye wit that I have loved La Belle Isode many a long day, and she hath been the causer of my worship; and else I had been the most simplest knight in the world, for by her, and because of her, I have won the worship that I have. For when I remembered me of Queen Isode I won the worship wheresoever I came, for the most part, and yet I had never reward nor bounty of her days of my life, and yet I have been her knight long guerdonless. And therefore, Sir Tristram, as for any death I dread not, for I had as lief die as live. And if I were armed as ye are, I should lightly do battle with thee.'

'Sir, well have ye uttered your treason,' said Sir Tristram.

'Sir, I have done to you no treason,' said Sir Palomides, 'for love is free for all men, and though I have loved your lady, she is my lady as well as yours. Howbeit that I have wrong if any wrong be, for ye rejoice her and have your desire of her; and so had I never, nor never am like

guerdonless] without reward   rejoice] enjoy

to have, and yet shall I love her to the uttermost days of my life as well as ye.'

[87] Then said Sir Tristram, 'I will fight with you to the uttermost.'

'I grant,' said Sir Palomides, 'for in a better quarrel keep I never to fight. For and I die of your hands, of a better knight's hands might I never be slain. And sithen I understand that I shall never rejoice La Belle Isode, I have as good will to die as to live.'

'Then set ye a day,' said Sir Tristram, 'that we shall do battle.'

'Sir, this day fifteen days,' said Sir Palomides, 'I will meet with you hereby, in the meadow under Joyous Gard.'

'Now fie, for shame,' said Sir Tristram, 'will ye set so long a day? Let us fight tomorrow.'

'Not so,' said Sir Palomides, 'for I am meagre, and have been long sick for the love of La Belle Isode; and therefore I will repose me till I have my strength again.'

So then Sir Tristram and Sir Palomides promised faithfully to meet at the well that day fifteen days.*

Right so departed Sir Tristram and Sir Palomides.

And so in the meanwhile Sir Tristram chased and hunted at all manner of venery; and about three days before the battle that should be, as Sir Tristram chased a hart, there was an archer shot at the hart, and by misfortune he smote Sir Tristram in the thick of the thigh, and the same arrow slew Sir Tristram's horse under him. When Sir Tristram was so hurt he was passing heavy, and wit ye well he bled passing sore; and then he took another horse and rode unto Joyous Gard with great heaviness, more for the promise that he had made with Sir Palomides to do battle with him within three days after.

[88] And so when the fifteenth day was come, Sir Palomides came to the well with four knights with him of King Arthur's court and three sergeants-of-arms. And for this intent Sir Palomides brought those knights with him and the sergeants-of-arms, for they should bear record of the battle betwixt Sir Tristram and him. And one sergeant brought in his helm, and the other his spear, and the third his sword. So Sir Palomides came into the field, and there he abode nigh two hours; and then he sent a squire unto Sir Tristram and desired him to come into the field to hold his promise.

When the squire was come unto Joyous Gard, anon as Sir Tristram

keep] care

heard of his coming he let command that the squire should come to his presence there as he lay in his bed.

'My lord Sir Tristram,' said Sir Palomides' squire, 'wit you well, my lord Sir Palomides abideth you in the field, and he would wit whether ye would do battle or not.'

'Ah, my fair brother,' said Sir Tristram, 'wit you well that I am right heavy for these tidings. But tell your lord Sir Palomides, and I were well at ease I would not lie here, neither he should have no need to send for me and I might either ride or go. And for thou shalt see that I am no liar'—Sir Tristram showed him his thigh, and the deepness of the wound was six inches deep. 'And now thou hast seen my hurt, tell thy lord that this is no feigned matter, and tell him that I had liever than all the gold that King Arthur hath that I were whole. And let him wit that as for me, as soon as I may ride I shall seek him endlong and overthwart this land, and that I promise you as I am a true knight. And if ever I may meet him, tell your lord Sir Palomides, he shall have of me his fill of battle.'

And so the squire departed. And when Sir Palomides knew that Sir Tristram was hurt, then he said thus: 'Truly, I am glad of his hurt, and for this cause: for now I am sure I shall have no shame. For I wot well, and we had meddled, I should have had hard handling of him; and by likelihood I must needs have had the worse, for he is the hardest knight in battle that now is living except Sir Lancelot.' And then departed Sir Palomides where as fortune led him.

And within a month Sir Tristram was whole of his hurt; and then he took his horse and rode from country to country, and all strange adventures he achieved wheresoever he rode. And always he enquired for Sir Palomides, but of all that quarter of summer Sir Tristram could never meet with Sir Palomides.*

But thus as Sir Tristram sought and enquired after Sir Palomides, Sir Tristram achieved many great battles, wherethrough all the noise and bruit fell to Sir Tristram, and the name ceased of Sir Lancelot. And therefore Sir Lancelot's brethren and his kinsmen would have slain Sir Tristram because of his fame. But when Sir Lancelot wist how his kinsmen were set, he said to them openly, 'Wit you well that and any of you all be so hardy to await my lord Sir Tristram with any hurt, shame, or villainy, as I am true knight I shall slay the best of you all with

---

ride or go] ride or walk   bruit] fame

mine own hands. Alas, fie for shame, should ye for his noble deeds await to slay him! Jesu defend', said Sir Lancelot, 'that ever any noble knight as Sir Tristram is should be destroyed with treason.'

So of this noise and fame sprang into Cornwall and unto them of Lyonesse, whereof they were passing glad and made great joy. And then they of Lyonesse sent letters unto Sir Tristram of recommendation,* and many great gifts to maintain Sir Tristram's estate. And ever between, Sir Tristram resorted unto Joyous Gard where as La Belle Isode was, that loved him ever.

Of Sir Galahad, Sir Lancelot's son,
how he was begotten*

Now leave we Sir Tristram de Lyonesse, and speak we of Sir Lancelot du Lake, and of Sir Galahad, Sir Lancelot's son, how he was begotten, and in what manner, as the book of French maketh mention.

Before the time that Sir Galahad was begotten or born, there came in a hermit unto King Arthur upon Whitsunday, as the knights sat at the Table Round. And when the hermit saw the Siege Perilous, he asked the King and all the knights why that siege was void. Then King Arthur for all the knights answered and said, 'There shall never none sit in that siege but one, but if he be destroyed.'

Then said the hermit, 'Sir, wot ye what he is?'

'Nay,' said King Arthur and all the knights, 'we know not who he is yet that shall sit there.'

'Then wot I,' said the hermit. 'For he that shall sit there is yet unborn and unbegotten, and this same year he shall be begotten that shall sit in that Siege Perilous, and he shall win the Sangrail.'

When this hermit had made this mention, he departed from the court of King Arthur.

And so after this feast Sir Lancelot rode on his adventure, till on a time by adventure he passed over the Pont de Corbin; and there he saw the fairest tower that ever he saw, and thereunder was a fair little town full of people. And all the people, men and women, cried at once, 'Welcome, Sir Lancelot, the flower of knighthood, for by thee we shall be helped out of danger.'

'What mean ye,' said Sir Lancelot, 'that ye cry thus upon me?'

'Ah, fair knight,' said they all, 'here is within this tower a dolorous lady that hath been there in pains many winters and days, for ever she boileth in scalding water. And but late,' said all the people, 'Sir Gawain was here and he might not help her, and so he left her in pain still.'

'Peradventure so may I,' said Sir Lancelot, 'leave her in pain as well as Sir Gawain.'

but if he be] without his being

'Nay,' said the people, 'we know well that it is ye, Sir Lancelot, that shall deliver her.'

'Well,' said Lancelot, 'then tell me what I shall do.'

And so anon they brought Sir Lancelot into the tower; and when he came to the chamber there as this lady was, the doors of iron unlocked and unbolted. And so Sir Lancelot went into the chamber that was as hot as any stew; and there Sir Lancelot took the fairest lady by the hand that ever he saw, and she was as naked as a needle. And by enchantment Queen Morgan le Fay and the Queen of Northgales had put her there in that pains, because she was called the fairest lady of that country; and there she had been five years, and never might she be delivered out of her pains unto the time the best knight of the world had taken her by the hand.

Then the people brought her clothes; and when she was arrayed, Sir Lancelot thought she was the fairest lady that ever he saw, but if it were Queen Guenivere.

Then this lady said to Sir Lancelot, 'Sir, if it please you, will ye go with me hereby into a chapel, that we may give loving to God?'

'Madam,' said Sir Lancelot, 'cometh on with me, and I will go with you.'

So when they came there they gave thankings to God, all the people both learned and lewd, and said, 'Sir knight, since ye have delivered this lady, ye must deliver us also from a serpent, which is here in a tomb.'

Then Sir Lancelot took his shield and said, 'Sirs, bring me thither, and what that I may do to the pleasure of God and of you I shall do.'

So when Sir Lancelot came thither he saw written upon the tomb with letters of gold that said thus: 'Here shall come a leopard of kings' blood, and he shall slay this serpent; and this leopard shall engender a lion in this foreign country, which lion shall pass all other knights.'

So when Sir Lancelot had lifted up the tomb, there came out a horrible and a fiendly dragon spitting wild fire out of his mouth. Then Sir Lancelot drew his sword and fought with that dragon long, and at the last with great pain Sir Lancelot slew that dragon.

And therewith came King Pelles, the good and noble king, and saluted Sir Lancelot, and he him again.

---

stew] heated bathhouse   loving] praise   lewd] uneducated

'Now, fair knight,' said the king, 'what is your name? I require you of your knighthood, tell ye me.'

'Sir,' said Sir Lancelot, 'wit you well my name is Sir Lancelot du [2] Lake.'

'And my name is King Pelles, king of the foreign country, and cousin nigh unto Joseph of Arimathea.'

And then either of them made much of other, and so they went into the castle to take their repast. And anon there came in a dove at a window, and in her mouth there seemed a little censer of gold; and therewith there was such a savour as all the spicery of the world had been there. And forthwith there was upon the table all manner of meats and drinks that they could think upon.

So there came in a damosel passing fair and young, and she bore a vessel of gold betwixt her hands; and thereto the king kneeled devoutly and said his prayers, and so did all that were there.

'Ah, Jesu,' said Sir Lancelot, 'what may this mean?'

'Sir,' said the king, 'this is the richest thing that any man hath living, and when this thing goeth abroad, the Round Table shall be broken for a season. And wit you well,' said the king, 'this is the Holy Sangrail that ye have here seen.'

So the king and Sir Lancelot led their life the most part of that day together. And fain would King Pelles have found the means that Sir Lancelot should have lain by his daughter, fair Elaine, and for this intent: the king knew well that Sir Lancelot should beget a pucel* upon his daughter, which should be called Sir Galahad, the good knight, by whom all the foreign country should be brought out of danger; and by him the Holy Grail should be achieved.

Then came forth a lady that hight Dame Brusen, and she said unto the king, 'Sir, wit you well Sir Lancelot loveth no lady in the world but all only Queen Guenivere; and therefore work ye by my counsel, and I shall make him to lie with your daughter, and he shall not wit but that he lieth by Queen Guenivere.'

'Ah, fair lady,' said the king, 'hope ye that ye may bring this matter about?'

'Sir,' said she, 'upon pain of my life let me deal.' For this Dame Brusen was one of the greatest enchanters that was that time in the world. And so anon by Dame Brusen's wit she made one to come to

pucel] i.e. boy (see note)

Sir Lancelot that he knew well, and this man brought a ring from Queen Guenivere like as it had come from her. And when Sir Lancelot saw that token, wit you well he was never so fain.

'Where is my lady?' said Sir Lancelot.

'In the castle of Case,' said the messenger, 'but five miles hence.'

Then thought Sir Lancelot to be there the same night. And then this Dame Brusen, by the commandment of King Pelles, let send Elaine to this castle with five and twenty knights. Then Sir Lancelot against night rode unto the castle, and there anon he was received worshipfully with such people to his seeming as were about Queen Guenivere secret.

So when Sir Lancelot was alit, he asked where the queen was; so Dame Brusen said she was in her bed. And then the people were avoided, and Sir Lancelot was led into her chamber. And then Dame Brusen brought Sir Lancelot a cup of wine, and anon as he had drunk that wine he was so besotted and mad that he might make no delay; but without any let he went to bed, and so he weened that maiden Elaine had been Queen Guenivere. And wit you well that Sir Lancelot was glad, and so was that lady Elaine that she had got Sir Lancelot in her arms; for well she knew that that same night should be begotten Sir Galahad upon her, that should prove the best knight of the world. And so they lay together until undern of the morn; and all the windows and holes of that chamber were stopped that no manner of day might be seen. And anon Sir Lancelot remembered him, and arose up and went [3] to the window; and anon as he had unshut the window the enchantment was passed. Then he knew himself, that he had done amiss.

'Alas,' he said, 'that I have loved* so long, for now I am shamed!'

And anon he got his sword in his hand and said, 'Thou traitress, what art thou that I have lain by all this night? Thou shalt die right here of my hands.'

Then this fair lady Elaine skipped out of her bed all naked and said, 'Fair courteous knight Sir Lancelot,'—kneeling before him—'ye are come of kings' blood, and therefore I require you have mercy upon me, and as thou art renowned the most noble knight of the world, slay me not; for I have in my womb begotten of thee that shall be the most noblest knight of the world.'

as were about Queen Guenivere secret] i.e. her confidential servants   let] delay
undern°] about 9 a.m.

'Ah, false traitress, why hast thou betrayed me? Tell me anon', said Sir Lancelot, 'what thou art.'

'Sir,' she said, 'I am Elaine, the daughter of King Pelles.'

'Well,' said Sir Lancelot, 'I will forgive you.' And therewith he took her up in his arms and kissed her, for she was a fair lady, and thereto lusty and young, and wise as any was that time living.

'So God me help,' said Sir Lancelot, 'I may not wite you; but her that made this enchantment upon me and between you and me, and I may find her, that same lady Dame Brusen shall lose her head for her witchcrafts, for there was never knight deceived as I am this night.'

Then she said, 'My lord Sir Lancelot, I beseech you see me as soon as ye may, for I have obeyed me unto the prophecy that my father told me. And by his commandment to fulfil this prophecy I have given thee the greatest riches and the fairest flower that ever I had, and that is my maidenhood that I shall never have again; and therefore, gentle knight, owe me your good will.'*

And so Sir Lancelot arrayed him and armed him, and took his leave mildly at that lady young Elaine. And so he departed, and rode to the castle of Corbin, where her father was.

And as fast as her time came she was delivered of a fair child, and they christened him Galahad; and wit you well, that child was well kept and well nourished. And he was so named Galahad because Sir Lancelot was so named at the fountain stone; and after that, the Lady of the Lake confirmed him Sir Lancelot du Lake.*

And so the noise sprang in King Arthur's court that Sir Lancelot [6] had begotten a child upon Elaine, the daughter of King Pelles; wherefore Queen Guenivere was wroth, and she gave many rebukes to Sir Lancelot, and called him false knight. And then Sir Lancelot told the Queen all, and how he was made to lie by her 'in the likeness of you, my lady the queen'. And so the Queen held Sir Lancelot excused.

And as the book saith, King Arthur had been in France, and had warred upon the mighty king Claudas and had won much of his lands.* And when the King was come again he let cry a great feast, that all lords and ladies of all England should be there but if it were such as were rebellious against him.

wite] blame

[7]   And when Dame Elaine, the daughter of King Pelles, heard of this feast she yode to her father and required him that he would give her leave to ride to that feast.

The king answered and said, 'I will that ye go thither, but in any wise as ye love me and will have my blessing, look that ye be well beseen in the richest wise, and look that ye spare not for no cost. Ask, and ye shall have all that needeth unto you.'

Then by the advice of Dame Brusen, her maiden, all thing was apparelled unto the purpose, that there was never no lady richlier beseen. So she rode with twenty knights and ten ladies and gentle-women, to the number of a hundred horses; and when she came to Camelot, King Arthur and Queen Guenivere said with all the knights that Dame Elaine was the best beseen lady that ever was seen in that court.

And anon as King Arthur wist that she was come he met her and saluted her, and so did the most part of all the knights of the Round Table, both Sir Tristram, Sir Bleoberis, and Sir Gawain, and many more that I will not rehearse. But when Sir Lancelot saw her he was so ashamed, because he drew his sword to her on the morn after that he had lain by her, that he would not salute her nor speak with her; and yet Sir Lancelot thought she was the fairest woman that ever he saw in his life days. But when Dame Elaine saw Sir Lancelot would not speak unto her, she was so heavy she weened her heart would have to-brast; for wit you well, out of measure she loved him. And then Dame Elaine said unto her woman, Dame Brusen, 'The unkindness of Sir Lancelot near slayeth my heart.'

'Ah, peace, madam,' said Dame Brusen, 'I shall undertake that this night he shall lie with you, and ye will hold you still.'

'That were me liever', said Dame Elaine, 'than all the gold that is above earth.'

'Let me deal,' said Dame Brusen.

So when Dame Elaine was brought unto the Queen, either made other good cheer as by countenance, but nothing with their hearts. But all men and women spoke of the beauty of Dame Elaine. And then it was ordained that Dame Elaine should sleep in a chamber nigh by the Queen, and all under one roof; and so it was done as the King* commanded. Then the Queen sent for Sir Lancelot and bade him come to

hold you still] stay calm

her chamber that night, 'Or else,' said the Queen, 'I am sure that ye will go to your lady's bed, Dame Elaine, by whom ye begot Galahad.'

'Ah, madam,' said Sir Lancelot, 'never say ye so, for that I did was against my will.'

'Then,' said the Queen, 'look that ye come to me when I send for you.'

'Madam' said Sir Lancelot, 'I shall not fail you, but I shall be ready at your commandment.'

So this bargain was not so soon done and made between them but Dame Brusen knew it by her crafts, and told it unto her lady Dame Elaine.

'Alas,' said she, 'how shall I do?'

'Let me deal,' said Dame Brusen, 'for I shall bring him by the hand even to your bed, and he shall ween that I am Queen Guenivere's messenger.'

'Then well were me,' said Dame Elaine, 'for all the world I love not so much as I do Sir Lancelot.'

So when time came that all folks were to bed, Dame Brusen came to Sir Lancelot's bedside and said, 'Sir Lancelot du Lake, sleep ye? My lady Queen Guenivere lieth and awaiteth upon you.'   [8]

'Ah, my fair lady,' said Sir Lancelot, 'I am ready to go with you whither ye will have me.'

So Lancelot threw upon him a long gown, and so he took his sword in his hand; and then Dame Brusen took him by his finger and led him to her lady's bed, Dame Elaine, and then she departed and left them there in bed together. And wit you well this lady was glad, and so was Sir Lancelot, for he weened that he had had another in his arms.

Now leave we them kissing and clipping, as was a kindly thing; and now speak we of Queen Guenivere, that sent one of her women that she most trusted unto Sir Lancelot's bed. And when she came there, she found the bed cold, and he was not therein; and so she came to the Queen and told her all.

'Alas,' said the Queen, 'where is that false knight become?'

So the Queen was nigh out of her wit, and then she writhed and weltered as a mad woman, and might not sleep four or five hours.

Then Sir Lancelot had a condition, that he used of custom to clatter in his sleep and to speak often of his lady Queen Guenivere. So

---

kindly] natural, loving   clatter] chatter

Sir Lancelot had waked as long as it had pleased him, and so by course of kind he slept and Dame Elaine both. And in his sleep he talked and clattered as a jay* of the love that had been betwixt Queen Guenivere and him; and so he talked so loud that the Queen heard him there as she lay in her chamber, and when she heard him so clatter she was wroth out of measure. And then she coughed so loud that Sir Lancelot awaked, and anon he knew her hemming, and then he knew well that he lay by the lady Elaine; and therewith he leapt out of his bed as he had been a wood man, in his shirt. And anon the Queen met him in the floor, and thus she said: 'Ah, thou false traitor knight, look thou never abide in my court, and lightly that thou void my chamber! And not so hardy, thou false traitor knight, that evermore thou come in my sight.'

'Alas,' said Sir Lancelot; and therewith he took such a heartly sorrow at her words that he fell down to the floor in a swoon. And therewith Queen Guenivere departed; and when Sir Lancelot awoke out of his swoon, he leapt out at a bay window into a garden, and there with thorns he was all to-scratched of his visage and his body. And so he ran forth he knew not whither, and was as wild as ever was man; and so he ran two years, and never man had grace to know him.

[9] Now turn we unto Queen Guenivere and to the fair lady Elaine, that when Dame Elaine heard the Queen so rebuke Sir Lancelot, and how also he swooned and how he leapt out of the bay window—then she said unto Queen Guenivere, 'Madam, ye are greatly to blame for Sir Lancelot, for now have ye lost him, for I saw and heard by his countenance that he is mad for ever. And therefore alas, madam, ye have done great sin and yourself great dishonour, for ye have a lord royal of your own, and therefore it were your part for to love him; for there is no queen in this world that hath such another king as ye have. And if ye were not, I might have got the love of my lord Sir Lancelot; and a great cause I have to love him, for he had my maidenhood, and by him I have borne a fair son whose name is Sir Galahad; and he shall be in his time the best knight of the world.'*

'Well, Dame Elaine,' said the Queen, 'as soon as it is daylight I charge you to avoid my court. And for the love ye owe unto Sir Lancelot, discover not his counsel, for and ye do, it will be his death.'

---

hemming] clearing the throat wood] mad if ye were not] if you did not exist

'As for that,' said Dame Elaine, 'I dare undertake he is marred for ever, and that have you made. For neither ye nor I are likely to rejoice him, for he made the most piteous groans when he leapt out at yonder bay window that ever I heard man make. Alas,' said fair Elaine, and 'Alas,' said the Queen, 'for now I wot well that we have lost him for ever.'

So on the morn Dame Elaine took her leave to depart and would no longer abide. Then King Arthur brought her on her way with more than a hundred knights throughout a forest; and by the way she told Sir Bors de Ganis all how it betided that same night, and how Sir Lancelot leapt out at a window araged out of his wit.

'Alas,' then said Sir Bors, 'where is my lord Sir Lancelot become?'

'Sir,' said Dame Elaine, 'I wot not where.'

'Now alas,' said Sir Bors, 'betwixt you both ye have destroyed a good knight.'

'As for me, sir' said Dame Elaine, 'I said never nor did thing that should in any wise displease him. But with the rebuke, sir, that Queen Guenivere gave him I saw him swoon to the earth; and when he awoke he took his sword in his hand, naked save his shirt, and leapt out at a window with the grisliest groan that ever I heard man make.'

'Now farewell, Dame Elaine,' said Sir Bors, 'and hold my lord King Arthur with a tale as long as ye can, for I will turn again unto Queen Guenivere and give her a hete. And I require you, as ever ye will have my service, make good watch and espy if ever it may happen you to see my lord Sir Lancelot.'

'Truly,' said Dame Elaine, 'I shall do all that I may do, for I would lose my life for him rather than he should be hurt.'

'Madam,' said Dame Brusen, 'let Sir Bors depart and hie him as fast as he may to seek Sir Lancelot, for I warn you he is clean out of his mind; and yet he shall be well helped, and but by miracle.'

Then wept Dame Elaine, and so did Sir Bors de Ganis, and anon they departed. And Sir Bors rode straight unto Queen Guenivere; and when she saw Sir Bors she wept as she were wood.

'Now fie on your weeping,' said Sir Bors de Ganis, 'for ye weep never but when there is no boot. Alas,' said Sir Bors, 'that ever Sir Lancelot or any of his blood ever saw you, for now have ye lost the best knight of our

---

araged] frenzied   hete] rebuke   and but by miracle] even if only by miracle

blood, and he that was all our leader and our succour. And I dare say and make it good that all kings, christened nor heathen, may not find such a knight, for to speak of his nobleness and courtesy, with his beauty and his gentleness. Alas,' said Sir Bors, 'what shall we do that be of his blood?'*

'Alas,' said Sir Ector de Maris, and 'Alas,' said Sir Lionel.

[10]   And when the Queen heard them say so she fell to the earth in a dead swoon. And then Sir Bors took her up, and dawed her; and when she was awaked she kneeled before those three knights and held up both hands and besought them to seek him, 'and spare not for no goods but that he be found, for I wot well that he is out of his mind.'

And Sir Bors, Sir Ector, and Sir Lionel departed from the Queen, for they might not abide no longer for sorrow. And then the Queen sent them treasure enough for their expense, and so they took their horses and their armour and departed. And then they rode from country to country, in forests and in wildernesses and in wastes; and ever they laid watch both at forests and at all manner of men as they rode, to hearken and to spere after him, as he that was a naked man, in his shirt, with a sword in his hand. And thus they rode nigh a quarter of a year, endlong and overthwart, and never could hear word of him; and wit you well, these three knights were passing sorry. And so at the last Sir Bors and his fellows met with a knight that hight Sir Melion de Tartare.

'Now, fair knight,' said Sir Bors, 'whither be ye away?'—for they knew each other aforetime.

'Sir,' said Sir Melion, 'I am in the way to the court of King Arthur.'

'Then we pray you,' said Sir Bors, 'that ye will tell my lord Arthur and my lady Queen Guenivere, and all the fellowship of the Round Table, that we cannot in no wise hear tell where Sir Lancelot is become.'

Then Sir Melion departed from them, and said that he would tell the King and the Queen and all the fellowship of the Round Table as they had desired him.

And when Sir Melion came to the court he told the King and the Queen and all the fellowship as they had desired him, how Sir Bors had said of Sir Lancelot. Then Sir Gawain, Sir Uwain, Sir Sagramore le Desirous, Sir Agloval, and Sir Percival de Gales took upon them by the great desire of the King, and in especial by the Queen, to seek all

make it good] prove it in combat   dawed] revived   spere] enquire

England, Wales, and Scotland to find Sir Lancelot, and with them rode eighteen knights more to bear them fellowship; and wit you well, they lacked no manner of spending. And so were they three and twenty knights.

Now turn we unto Sir Lancelot, and speak we of his care and woe, and what pain he there endured; for cold, hunger, and thirst he had plenty.

And thus as these noble knights rode together, they by assent departed, and then they rode by two and by three, and by four and by five, and ever they assigned where they should meet.*

And now will we turn unto Sir Percival that rode long; and in a forest [13] he met a knight with a broken shield and a broken helm, and as soon as either saw other they made them ready to joust. And so they hurtled together with all their might, and they met together so hard that Sir Percival was smitten to the earth; and then Sir Percival arose deliverly, and cast his shield on his shoulder and drew his sword, and bade the other knight alight and do battle unto the uttermost.

'Well, sir, will ye more yet?' said that knight; and therewith he alit, and put his horse from him. And then they came together an easy pace and lashed together with noble swords, and sometimes they struck and sometimes they foined, that either gave other many sad strokes and wounds. And thus they fought nearhand half a day and never rested but little, and there was none of them both that had less wounds but he had fifteen; and they bled so much that it was marvel they stood on their feet. But this knight that fought with Sir Percival was a proved knight and a wise fighting knight, and Sir Percival was young and strong, not knowing in fighting as the other was.

Then Sir Percival spoke first, and said, 'Sir knight, hold thy hand a while, for we have fought over long for a simple matter and quarrel. And therefore I require thee, tell me thy name, for I was never or this time thus matched.'

'So God me help,' said that knight, 'and never or this time was there never knight that wounded me so sore as thou hast done, and yet have I fought in many battles. And now shalt thou wit that I am a knight of the Table Round, and my name is Sir Ector de Maris, brother unto the good knight Sir Lancelot du Lake.'

knowing] experienced

'Alas,' said Sir Percival, 'and my name is Sir Percival de Gales, which hath made my quest to seek Sir Lancelot; and now I am sure that I shall never finish my quest, for ye have slain me with your hands.'

'It is not so,' said Sir Ector, 'for I am slain by your hands, and may not live. And therefore I require you,' said Sir Ector unto Sir Percival, 'ride ye here fast by to a priory and bring me a priest that I may receive my Saviour, for I may not live. And when ye come to the court of King Arthur, tell not my brother Sir Lancelot how that ye slew me, for then he will be your mortal enemy. But ye may say that I was slain in my quest as I sought him.'

'Alas,' said Sir Percival, 'ye say that thing that never will be, for I am so faint for bleeding that I may uneath stand. How should I then take my horse?'

Then they made both great dole out of measure.

'This will not avail,' said Sir Percival, and then he kneeled down and made his prayer devoutly unto Almighty Jesu; for he was one of the best knights of the world at that time, in whom the very faith stood most in. Right so there came by the holy vessel, the Sangrail, with all manner of sweetness and savour; but they could not see readily who bore the vessel. But Sir Percival had a glimmering of the vessel and of the maiden that bore it, for he was a perfect maiden. And forthwith they were as whole of hide and limb as ever they were in their life. Then they gave thankings to God with great mildness.

'Ah, Jesu,' said Sir Percival, 'what may this mean, that we be thus healed, and right now we were at the point of dying?'

'I wot full well,' said Sir Ector, 'what it is. It is a holy vessel that is borne by a maiden, and therein is a part of the holy blood of Our Lord Jesu Christ. But it may not be seen,' said Sir Ector, 'but if it be by a perfect man.'

'So God me help,' said Sir Percival, 'I saw a damosel, as me thought, all in white, with a vessel in both her hands, and forthwith I was whole.'

So then they took their horses and their harness, and mended it as well as they might that was broken; and so they mounted up and rode talking together. And there Sir Ector de Maris told Sir Percival how he had sought his brother Sir Lancelot long, and never could hear witting of him; 'In many hard adventures have I been in this quest.'

And so either told other of their great adventures.

witting] knowledge

Of Sir Lancelot, that suffered and
endured many sharp showers*

And now leave we off a while of Sir Ector and of Sir Percival, and speak [XII.1] we of Sir Lancelot that suffered and endured many sharp showers, that ever ran wild wood from place to place, and lived by fruit and such as he might get, and drank water two years; and other clothing had he but little but in his shirt and his breeches.

And thus as Sir Lancelot wandered here and there, he came into a fair meadow where he found a pavilion; and thereby upon a tree there hung a white shield, and two swords hung thereby, and two spears leaned thereby to a tree. And when Sir Lancelot saw the swords, anon he leapt to the one sword and clutched that sword in his hand and drew it out; and then he lashed at the shield that all the meadow rang of the dints, that he gave such a noise as ten knights had fought together. Then came forth a dwarf and leapt unto Sir Lancelot, and would have had the sword out of his hand. And then Sir Lancelot took him by the both shoulders and threw him unto the ground, that he fell upon his neck and had nigh broken it; and therewith the dwarf cried help.

Then there came forth a likely knight, and well apparelled in scarlet furred with minever; and anon as he saw Sir Lancelot, he deemed that he should be out of his wit. And then he said with fair speech, 'Good man, lay down that sword, for as me seemeth thou hadst more need of a sleep and of warm clothes than to wield that sword.'

'As for that,' said Sir Lancelot, 'come not too nigh, for and thou do, wit thou well I will slay thee.'

And when the knight of the pavilion saw that, he started backward into his pavilion. And then the dwarf armed him lightly; and so the knight thought by force and might to have taken the sword from Sir Lancelot. And so he came stepping upon him; and when Sir Lancelot saw him come so armed with his sword in his hand, then Sir Lancelot flew to him with such a might and smote him upon the helm such a buffet, that the stroke troubled his brain, and therewith the sword broke in three. And the knight fell to the earth and seemed as he had been dead,

showers] troubles   wild wood] mad as a wild man   minever] fur trimming the blood bursting out of his mouth, nose, and ears. And then Sir Lancelot ran into the pavilion, and rushed even into the warm bed, and there was a lady that lay in that bed. And anon she got her smock and ran out of the pavilion; and when she saw her lord lie at the ground like to be dead, then she cried and wept as she had been mad. And so with her noise the knight awaked out of his swoon, and looked up weakly with his eyes; and then he asked where was that mad man which had given him such a buffet, 'For such a one had I never of man's hand.'

'Sir,' said the dwarf, 'it is not your worship to hurt him, for he is a man out of his wit; and doubt ye not he hath been a man of great worship, and for some heartly sorrow that he hath taken he is fallen mad. And me seemeth,' said the dwarf, 'that he resembleth much unto Sir Lancelot, for him I saw at the tournament of Lonazep.'

'Jesu defend,' said that knight, 'that ever that noble knight Sir Lancelot should be in such a plight! But whatsoever he be,' said that knight, 'no harm will I do him.'

And this knight's name was Sir Bliant, the which said unto the dwarf, 'Go thou fast on horseback unto my brother, Sir Selivant, which is in the Castle Blank, and tell him of my adventure, and bid him bring with him a horse litter; and then will we bear this knight unto my castle.'

[2]   So the dwarf rode fast, and he came again and brought Sir Selivant with him, and six men with a horse litter; and so they took up the feather bed with Sir Lancelot, and so carried all away with them unto the Castle Blank, and he never awaked till he was within the castle. And then they bound his hands and his feet, and gave him good meats and good drinks, and brought him again to his strength and his fairness; but in his wit they could not bring him, nor to know himself. And thus was Sir Lancelot there more than a year and a half, honestly arrayed and fair faren withal.

Then upon a day this lord of that castle, Sir Bliant, took his arms, on horseback with a spear to seek adventures. And as he rode in a forest there met him two knights adventurous: the one was Sir Breunis sans Pité, and his brother, Sir Bartelot. And these two ran both at once on Sir Bliant and broke their spears upon his body. And then they drew out their swords and made great battle, and fought long together. But

Castle Blank] i.e. the White Castle   fair faren] well treated

at the last Sir Bliant was sore wounded and felt himself faint, and anon
he fled on horseback toward his castle. And as they came hurling under
the castle, there was Sir Lancelot at a window and saw how two knights
laid upon Sir Bliant with their swords. And when Sir Lancelot saw
that, yet as wood as he was, he was sorry for his lord Sir Bliant. And
then in a brade Sir Lancelot broke his chains off his legs and off his
arms, and in the breaking he hurt his hands sore; and so Sir Lancelot
ran out at a postern, and there he met with those two knights that
chased Sir Bliant. And there he pulled down Sir Bartelot with his bare
hands from his horse, and therewith he wrothe out the sword out of his
hand; and so he leapt unto Sir Breunis, and gave him such a buffet
upon the head that he tumbled backward over his horse's croup. And
when Sir Bartelot saw his brother have such a buffet, he got a spear in
his hand and would have run Sir Lancelot through; and that saw
Sir Bliant, and struck off the hand of Sir Bartelot. And then Sir Breunis
and Sir Bartelot got their horses and fled away as fast as they might.

So when Sir Selivant came and saw what Sir Lancelot had done for
his brother, then he thanked God, and so did his brother, that ever they
did him any good. But when Sir Bliant saw that Sir Lancelot was hurt
with the breaking of his irons, then was he heavy that ever he bound
him.

'I pray you, brother Sir Selivant, bind him no more, for he is happy
and gracious.'

Then they made great joy of Sir Lancelot; and so he abode thereafter a half year and more.

And so on a morn, Sir Lancelot was ware where came a great boar
with many hounds after him. But the boar was so big there might no
hounds tarry him; and the hunters came after, blowing their horns,
both upon horseback and some upon foot. And then Sir Lancelot was
ware where one alit and tied his horse to a tree and leaned his spear
against the tree. So there came Sir Lancelot and found the horse, and   [3]
a good sword tied to the saddle bow; and anon Sir Lancelot leapt into
the saddle and got that spear in his hand, and then he rode fast after the
boar. And anon he was ware where he set his arse to a rock fast by a
hermitage. And then Sir Lancelot ran at the boar with his spear and all
to-shivered his spear; and therewith the boar turned him lightly, and
rove out the lungs and the heart of the horse, that Sir Lancelot fell to

brade] great pull   wrothe] twisted   happy] blessed the earth. And or ever he might get from his horse, the boar smote him on the brawn of the thigh up unto the hough bone. And then Sir Lancelot was wroth, and up he got upon his feet, and took his sword and smote off the boar's head at one stroke. And therewith came out the hermit, and saw him have such a wound; anon he bemoaned him, and would have had him home unto his hermitage. But when Sir Lancelot heard him speak, he was so wroth with his wound that he ran upon the hermit to have slain him. Then the hermit ran away; and when Sir Lancelot might not overget him, he threw his sword after him, for he might no further for bleeding. Then the hermit turned again and asked Sir Lancelot how he was hurt.

'Ah, my fellow,' said Sir Lancelot, 'this boar hath bitten me sore.'

'Then come ye with me,' said the hermit, 'and I shall heal you.'

'Go thy way,' said Sir Lancelot, 'and deal not with me.'

Then the hermit ran his way, and there he met with a goodly knight.

'Sir,' said the hermit, 'here is fast by my place the goodliest man that ever I saw, and he is sore wounded with a boar, and yet he hath slain the boar. But well I wot,' said the good man, 'and he be not helped, he shall die of that wound, and that were great pity.'

Then that knight at the desire of the hermit got a cart, and therein he put the boar and Sir Lancelot; for he was so feeble that they might right easily deal with him. And so Sir Lancelot was brought unto the hermitage, and there the hermit healed him of his wound. But the hermit might not find him his sustenance, and so he impaired and waxed feeble both of body and of his wit; for default of sustenance he waxed more wooder than he was aforetime.

And then upon a day Sir Lancelot ran his way into the forest; and by adventure he came to the city of Corbin, where Dame Elaine was, that bore Galahad, Sir Lancelot's son. And so when he was entered into the town he ran through the town to the castle; and then all the young men of that city ran after Sir Lancelot, and there they threw turfs at him and gave him many sad strokes. And ever as Sir Lancelot might reach any of them, he threw them so that they would never come in his hands no more, for of some he broke the legs and arms, and so he fled into the castle; and then came out knights and squires and rescued Sir Lancelot. When they beheld him and looked upon his person, they

overget] overtake   might not find him his sustenance] could not provide him
with enough food

thought they saw never so goodly a man, and when they saw so many wounds upon him, they deemed that he had been a man of worship. And then they ordained him clothes to his body, and straw and litter under the gate of the castle to lie in; and so every day they would throw him meat and set him drink. But there was but few that would bring him meat to his hands.

So it befell that King Pelles had a nephew whose name was Castor; [4] and so he desired of the king to be made knight, and at his own request the king made him knight at the feast of Candlemas. And when Sir Castor was made knight, that same day he gave many gowns. And then Sir Castor sent for the fool, which was Sir Lancelot; and when he was come before Sir Castor, he gave Sir Lancelot a robe of scarlet and all that longed unto him. And when Sir Lancelot was so arrayed like a knight, he was the seemliest man in all the court, and none so well made.

So when he saw his time he went into the garden, and there he laid him down by a well and slept. And so at after noon Dame Elaine and her maidens came into the garden to sport them; and as they roamed up and down one of Dame Elaine's maidens espied where lay a goodly man by the well sleeping.

'Peace,' said Dame Elaine, 'and say no word, but show me that man where he lieth.'

So anon she brought Dame Elaine where he lay. And when that she beheld him, anon she fell in remembrance of him and knew him verily for Sir Lancelot; and therewith she fell on weeping so heartily that she sank even to the earth. And when she had thus wept a great while, then she arose and called her maidens and said she was sick. And so she yode out of the garden as straight to her father as she could, and there she took him by herself apart; and then she said, 'Ah, my dear father, now have I need of your help, and but if that ye help me now, farewell my good days for ever.'

'What is that, daughter?' said King Pelles.

'In your garden I was to sport me, and there by the well I found Sir Lancelot du Lake sleeping.'

'I may not believe it,' said King Pelles.

'Truly, sir, he is there,' she said, 'and me seemeth he should be yet distract out of his wit.'

'Then hold you still,' said the king, 'and let me deal.'

Then the king called unto him such as he most trusted, a four persons, and Dame Elaine, his daughter, and Dame Brusen, her servant.

And when they came to the well and beheld Sir Lancelot, anon Dame Brusen said to the king, 'We must be wise how we deal with him, for this knight is out of his mind; and if we awake him rudely, what he will do we all know not. And therefore abide ye a while, and I shall throw an enchantment upon him that he shall not awake of an hour.' And so she did. And then the king commanded that all people should avoid, that none should be in that way there as the king would come.

And so when this was done, these four men and these ladies laid hand on Sir Lancelot, and so they bore him into a tower and so into a chamber where was the holy vessel of the Sangrail, and before that holy vessel was Sir Lancelot laid. And there came an holy man and unhilled that vessel, and so by miracle and by virtue of that holy vessel Sir Lancelot was healed and recovered. And as soon as he was awaked he groaned and sighed, and complained him sore of his woodness and

[5] strokes that he had had. And as soon as Sir Lancelot saw King Pelles and Dame Elaine, he waxed ashamed and said thus, 'Ah, Lord Jesu, how I came hither? For God's sake, my fair lord, let me wit how that I came hither.'

'Sir,' said Dame Elaine, 'into this country ye came like a mazed man, clean out of your wit. And here have ye been kept as a fool; and no creature here knew what ye were, until by fortune a maiden of mine brought me unto you where as ye lay sleeping by a well. And anon as I verily beheld you, then I told my father; and so were ye brought before this holy vessel, and by the virtue of it thus were ye healed.'

'Ah, Jesu, mercy,' said Sir Lancelot. 'If this be sooth, how many be there that knoweth of my woodness?'

'So God me help,' said Dame Elaine, 'no more but my father, and I, and Dame Brusen.'

'Now for Christ's love,' said Sir Lancelot, 'keep it counsel, and let no man know it in the world; for I am sore ashamed that I have been misfortuned, for I am banished the country of England.'

And so Sir Lancelot lay more than a fortnight or ever that he might stir for soreness. And then upon a day he said unto Dame Elaine these words: 'Fair lady Elaine, for your sake I have had much care and anguish—it needeth not to rehearse it, ye know how. Notwithstanding I know well I have done foully to you when that I drew my sword to you to have slain you upon the morn after when that I had lain with you,

unhilled] uncovered   mazed] deranged   counsel] secret and all was for the cause that ye and Dame Brusen made me for to lie by you maugre my head; and as ye say, Sir Galahad your son was begotten.'

'That is truth,' said Dame Elaine.

'Then will ye for my sake,' said Sir Lancelot, 'go unto your father and get me a place of him wherein I may dwell? For in the court of King Arthur may I never come.'

'Sir,' said Dame Elaine, 'I will live and die with you, only for your sake; and if my life might not avail you and my death might avail you, wit you well I would die for your sake. And I will to my father, and I am right sure there is nothing that I can desire of him but I shall have it. And where ye be, my lord Sir Lancelot, doubt ye not but I will be with you, with all the service that I may do.'

So forthwith she went to her father and said, 'Sir, my lord Sir Lancelot desireth to be here by you in some castle of yours.'

'Well, daughter,' said the king, 'sithen it is his desire to abide in these marches he shall be in the castle of Bliant, and there shall ye be with him, and twenty of the fairest young ladies that be in this country, and they shall be all of the greatest blood in this country, and ye shall have twenty knights with you; for, daughter, I will that ye wit we all be honoured by the blood of Sir Lancelot.'

Then went Dame Elaine unto Sir Lancelot, and told him all how her father had devised. [6]

Then came a knight which was called Sir Castor, that was nephew unto King Pelles, and he came unto Sir Lancelot and asked him what was his name.

'Sir,' said Sir Lancelot, 'my name is "Le Chevaler Malfait"—that is to say, "the knight that hath trespassed".'

'Sir,' said Sir Castor, 'it may well be so. But ever me seemeth your name should be Sir Lancelot du Lake, for or now I have seen you.'

'Sir,' said Sir Lancelot, 'ye are not gentle; for I put a case that my name were Sir Lancelot and that it list me not to discover my name, what should it grieve you here to keep my counsel, and ye not hurt thereby? But wit you well, and ever it lie in my power, I shall grieve you and ever I meet with you in my way.'

Then Sir Castor kneeled down and besought Sir Lancelot of mercy, 'for I shall never utter what ye be while that ye are in these parts.' Then Sir Lancelot pardoned him.

And so King Pelles with twenty knights and Dame Elaine with her twenty ladies rode unto the castle of Bliant, that stood in an island beclosed environ with a fair water deep and large. And when they were there Sir Lancelot let call it the Joyous Isle; and there was he called none otherwise but Le Chevaler Malfait, 'the knight that hath trespassed'.

Then Sir Lancelot let make him a shield all of sable, and a queen crowned in the midst of silver, and a knight clean armed kneeling before her. And every day once, for any mirths that all the ladies might make him, he would once every day look toward the realm of Logris, where King Arthur and Queen Guenivere was; and then would he fall upon a weeping as his heart should to-brast.

So it befell that time Sir Lancelot heard of a jousting fast by, within three leagues. Then he called unto him a dwarf, and he bade him go unto that jousting: 'And or ever the knights depart, look that thou make there a cry in hearing of all knights, that there is one knight in Joyous Isle, which is the castle of Bliant, and say that his name is Le Chevaler Malfait, that will joust against knights all that will come. And who that putteth that knight to the worse, he shall have a fair maiden and a gerfalcon.'

[7]   So when this cry was cried, unto Joyous Isle drew the number of five hundred knights. And wit you well, there was never seen in King Arthur's days one knight that did so much deeds of arms as Sir Lancelot did three days together; for as the book maketh truly mention, he had the better of all the five hundred knights, and there was not one slain of them. And after that Sir Lancelot made them all a great feast.

And in the meanwhile came Sir Percival de Gales and Sir Ector de Maris under that castle which was called the Joyous Isle. And as they beheld that gay castle they would have gone to that castle, but they might not for the broad water, and bridge could they find none. Then were they ware on the other side where stood a lady with a sparrowhawk on her hand, and Sir Percival called unto her and asked that lady who was in that castle.

'Fair knights,' she said, 'here within this castle is the fairest lady in this land, and her name is Dame Elaine. Also we have in this castle one of the fairest knights and the mightiest man that is I dare say living, and he calleth himself Le Chevaler Malfait.'

'How came he into these marches?' said Sir Percival.

'Truly,' said the damosel, 'he came into this country like a mad man, with dogs and boys chasing him through the city of Corbin, and by the

beclosed environ] enclosed around

holy vessel of the Sangrail he was brought into his wit again. But he will not do battle with no knight but by undern or noon. And if ye list to come into the castle,' said the lady, 'ye must ride unto the further side of the castle, and there shall ye find a vessel that will bear you and your horse.'

Then they departed, and came unto the vessel. And then Sir Percival alit, and said unto Sir Ector de Maris, 'Ye shall abide me here until that I wit what manner a knight he is; for it were shame unto us, inasmuch as he is but one knight, and we should both do battle with him.'

'Do as ye list,' said Sir Ector, 'and here I shall abide you until that I hear of you.'

Then passed Sir Percival the water, and when he came to the castle gate he said unto the porter, 'Go thou to the good knight of this castle, and tell him here is come an errant knight to joust with him.'

Then the porter yode in and came again, and bade him ride 'into the common place there as the jousting shall be, where lords and ladies may behold you'.

And so anon as Sir Lancelot had a warning he was soon ready, and there Sir Percival and Sir Lancelot were come both. They encountered with such a might, and their spears were so rude, that both the horses and the knights fell to the ground. Then they avoided their horses and flung out their noble swords, and hewed away many cantles of their shields, and so hurtled together like two boars, and either wounded other passing sore. And so at the last Sir Percival spoke first, when they had fought there long, more than two hours.

'Now, fair knight,' said Sir Percival, 'I require you of your knighthood to tell me your name, for I met never with such another knight.'

'Sir, as for my name,' said Sir Lancelot, 'I will not hide it from you, but my name is Le Chevaler Malfait. Now tell me your name,' said Sir Lancelot, 'I require you.'

'Truly,' said Sir Percival, 'my name is Sir Percival de Gales, that was brother unto the good knight Sir Lamorak de Gales; and King Pellinore was our father, and Sir Agloval is my brother.'

'Alas,' said Sir Lancelot, 'what have I done to fight with you, which are a knight of the Table Round?—and some time I was your fellow.'

And therewith Sir Lancelot kneeled down upon his knees, and [8] threw away his shield and his sword from him. When Sir Percival saw

rude] strong   cantles] pieces

him do so, he marvelled what he meant, and then he said thus: 'Sir knight, whatsoever ye be, I require you upon the high order of knighthood to tell me your true name.'

Then he answered and said, 'So God me help, my name is Sir Lancelot du Lake, King Ban's son of Benwick.'

'Alas,' then said Sir Percival, 'what have I now done? For I was sent by the Queen for to seek you, and so I have sought you nigh these two years; and yonder is Sir Ector de Maris, your brother, which abideth me on the yonder side of the water. And therefore, for God's sake,' said Sir Percival, 'forgive me my offences that I have here done.'

'Sir, it is soon forgiven,' said Sir Lancelot.

Then Sir Percival sent for Sir Ector de Maris, and when Sir Lancelot had a sight of him, he ran unto him and took him in his arms; and then Sir Ector kneeled down, and either wept upon other, that all men had pity to behold them.

Then came forth Dame Elaine; and she made them great cheer as might be made. And there she told Sir Ector and Sir Percival how and in what manner Sir Lancelot came into that country, and how he was healed. And there it was known how long Sir Lancelot was with Sir Bliant and with Sir Selivant, and how he first met with them, and departed from them because he was hurt with a boar; and how the hermit healed him of his great wound, and how that he came to the city of Corbin.*

[9]   So it befell on a day that Sir Ector and Sir Percival came unto Sir Lancelot and asked of him what he would do, and whether he would go with them unto King Arthur.

'Nay,' said Sir Lancelot, 'that may I not do by no means, for I was so vengeably defended the court that I cast me never to come there more.'

'Sir,' said Sir Ector, 'I am your brother, and ye are the man in the world that I love most; and if I understood that it were your disworship, ye may understand I would never counsel you thereto. But King Arthur and all his knights, and in especial Queen Guenivere, maketh such dole and sorrow for you that it is marvel to hear and see. And ye must remember the great worship and renown that ye be of, how that ye have been more spoken of than any other knight that is now living; for there is none that beareth the name now but ye and Sir Tristram. And therefore, brother,' said Sir Ector, 'make you ready to ride to the

defended] forbidden   cast me] intend

court with us. And I dare say and make it good,' said Sir Ector, 'it hath cost my lady the queen twenty thousand pound the seeking of you.'*

'Well, brother,' said Sir Lancelot, 'I will do after your counsel, and ride with you.'

So then they took their horses and made ready, and anon they took their leave at King Pelles and at Dame Elaine. And when Sir Lancelot should depart, Dame Elaine made great sorrow.

'My lord, Sir Lancelot,' said Dame Elaine, 'this same feast of Pentecost shall your son and mine, Galahad, be made knight, for he is fully now fifteen winters old.'

'Madam, do as ye list,' said Sir Lancelot, 'and God give him grace to prove a good knight.'

'As for that,' said Dame Elaine, 'I doubt not he shall prove the best man of his kin, except one.'*

'Then shall he be a good man enough,' said Sir Lancelot.

So anon they departed, and within fifteen days' journey they came [10] unto Camelot, that is in English called Winchester. And when Sir Lancelot was come among them, the King and all the knights made great joy of his homecoming. And there Sir Percival and Sir Ector de Maris began and told the whole adventures: how Sir Lancelot had been out of his mind in the time of his absence, and how he called himself Le Chevaler Malfait, the knight that had trespassed; and in three days within Joyous Isle Sir Lancelot smote down five hundred knights. And ever as Sir Ector and Sir Percival told these tales of Sir Lancelot, Queen Guenivere wept as she should have died. Then the Queen made him great cheer.

'Ah, Jesu,' said King Arthur, 'I marvel for what cause ye, Sir Lancelot, went out of your mind. For I and many other deem it was for the love of fair Elaine, the daughter of King Pelles, by whom ye are noised that ye have begotten a child, and his name is Galahad; and men say that he shall do many marvellous things.'

'My lord,' said Sir Lancelot, 'if I did any folly, I have that I sought.'

And therewith the King spoke no more. But all Sir Lancelot's kin knew for whom he went out of his mind.

And then there was made great feasts, and great joy was there among them; and all lords and ladies made great joy when they heard how Sir Lancelot was come again unto the court.

that I sought] what I asked for

[11] Now will we leave off this matter, and speak we of Sir Tristram, and of Sir Palomides that was the Saracen unchristened.

When Sir Tristram was come home unto Joyous Gard from his adventures (and all this while that Sir Lancelot was thus missed, two years and more, Sir Tristram bore the bruit and renown through all the realm of Logris, and many strange adventures befell him, and full well and worshipfully he brought them to an end), so when he was come home La Belle Isode told him of the great feast that should be at Pentecost next following. And there she told him how Sir Lancelot had been missed two years, and all that while he had been out of his mind, and how he was helped by the holy vessel of the Sangrail.

'Alas,' said Sir Tristram. 'That caused some debate betwixt him and Queen Guenivere.'

'Sir,' said Dame Isode, 'I know it all, for Queen Guenivere sent me a letter all how it was done, for because I should require you to seek him. And now, blessed be God,' said La Belle Isode, 'he is whole and sound and come again to the court.'

'Ah, Jesu, thereof am I fain,' said Sir Tristram. 'And now shall ye and I make us ready, for both ye and I will be at that feast.'

'Sir,' said Dame Isode, 'and it please you, I will not be there, for through me ye be marked of many good knights, and that causeth you to have much more labour for my sake than needeth you to have.'

'Then will I not be there,' said Sir Tristram, 'but if ye be there.'

'God defend,' said La Belle Isode, 'for then shall I be spoken of shame among all queens and ladies of estate; for ye that are called one of the noblest knights of the world, and a knight of the Round Table, how may ye be missed at that feast? For what shall be said of you among all knights? "Ah, see how Sir Tristram hunteth, and hawketh, and cowereth within a castle with his lady, and forsaketh us. Alas," shall some say, "it is pity that ever he was made knight, or ever he should have the

bruit] fame

love of a lady." Also, what shall queens and ladies say of me? It is pity that I have my life, that I would hold so noble a knight as ye are from his worship.'*

'So God me help,' said Sir Tristram unto La Belle Isode, 'it is passingly well said of you, and nobly counselled! And now I well understand that ye love me, and like as ye have counselled me I will do a part thereafter; but there shall no man nor child ride with me, but myself alone. And so I will ride on Tuesday next coming, and no more harness of war but my spear and my sword.'

And so when the day came Sir Tristram took his leave at La Belle [12] Isode, and she sent with him four knights, and within half a mile he sent them again. And within a mile way after, Sir Tristram saw before him where Sir Palomides had struck down a knight, and almost wounded him to the death. Then Sir Tristram repented him that he was not armed, and therewith he hoved still. And anon as Sir Palomides saw Sir Tristram he cried on high, 'Sir Tristram, now be we met, for or we depart we shall redress all our old sores!'

'As for that,' said Sir Tristram, 'there was never yet no Christian man that ever might make his boast that ever I fled from him. And wit ye well, Sir Palomides, thou that art a Saracen shall never make thy boast that ever Sir Tristram de Lyonesse shall flee from thee.'

And therewith Sir Tristram made his horse to run, and with all his might he came straight upon Sir Palomides and brast his spear upon him in a hundred pieces; and forthwith Sir Tristram drew his sword, and then he turned his horse and struck together six strokes upon his helm. And then Sir Palomides stood still and beheld Sir Tristram, and marvelled greatly at his woodness and of his folly.

And then Sir Palomides said unto himself, 'And this Sir Tristram were armed, it were hard to cease him from his battle; and if I turn again and slay him, I am shamed wheresoever I go.'

Then Sir Tristram spoke and said, 'Thou coward knight, what casteth thou to do? and why wilt thou not do battle with me? For have thou no doubt I shall endure thee and all thy malice.'

'Ah, Sir Tristram,' said Palomides, 'full well thou wotest I may not have ado with thee for shame, for thou art here naked and I am armed; and if that I slay thee, dishonour shall be mine. And well thou wotest,' said Sir Palomides unto Sir Tristram, 'I know thy strength and thy hardiness to endure against a good knight.'

'That is truth,' said Sir Tristram. 'I understand thy valiantness.'

'Ye say well,' said Sir Palomides. 'Now, I require you, tell me a question that I shall say unto you.'

'Then tell me what it is,' said Sir Tristram, 'and I shall answer you of the truth, as God me help.'

'Sir, I put a case,' said Sir Palomides, 'that ye were armed at all rights as well as I am, and I naked as ye be, what would ye do to me now, by your true knighthood?'

'Ah,' said Sir Tristram, 'now I understand thee well, Sir Palomides, for now must I say my own judgement; and as God me bless, that I shall say shall not be said for no fear that I have of thee, Sir Palomides. But this is all: wit thou well, Sir Palomides, as at this time thou shouldst depart from me, for I would not have ado with thee.'

'No more will I,' said Sir Palomides, 'and therefore ride forth on thy way.'

'As for that,' said Sir Tristram, 'I may choose either to ride or to abide. But Sir Palomides,' said Sir Tristram, 'I marvel greatly of one thing, that thou that art so good a knight, that thou wilt not be christened—and thy brother, Sir Safer, hath been christened many a day.'

[13]   'As for that,' said Sir Palomides, 'I may not yet be christened for a vow that I have made many years ago, howbeit in my heart and in my soul I have had many a day a good belief in Jesu Christ and his mild mother Mary. But I have but one battle to do, and were that once done I would be baptized.'

'By my head,' said Sir Tristram, 'as for one battle, thou shalt not seek it long! For God defend,' said Sir Tristram, 'that through my default thou shouldst longer live thus a Saracen. For yonder is a knight that ye have hurt and smitten down: now help me then that I were armed in his armour, and I shall soon fulfil thy vows.'

'As ye will,' said Palomides, 'so shall it be.'

So they rode both unto that knight that sat upon a bank, and then Sir Tristram saluted him, and he weakly saluted him again.

'Sir knight,' said Sir Tristram, 'I require you tell me your right name.'

'Sir,' he said, 'my right name is Sir Galleron of Galway, and a knight of the Table Round.'

'So God me help,' said Sir Tristram, 'I am right heavy of your hurts. But this is all, I must pray you to lend me your whole armour, for ye see I am unarmed, and I must do battle with this knight.'

'Sir, ye shall have it with a good will, but ye must beware, for I warn you that knight is a hardy knight as ever I met withal. But, sir,' said Sir Galleron, 'I pray you tell me your name, and what is that knight's name that hath beaten me.'

'Sir, as for my name, wit you well it is Sir Tristram de Lyonesse; and as for him, his name is Sir Palomides, brother unto the good knight Sir Safer, and yet is Sir Palomides unchristened.'

'Alas,' said Sir Galleron, 'that is great pity that so good a knight and so noble a man of arms should be unchristened.'

'So God me help,' said Sir Tristram, 'either he shall slay me or I him, but that he shall be christened or ever we depart in sunder.'

'My lord Sir Tristram,' said Sir Galleron, 'your renown and worship is well known through many realms, and God save you this day from senship and shame!'

Then Sir Tristram unarmed Sir Galleron, the which was a noble knight, and had done many deeds of arms; and he was a large knight of flesh and bone. And when he was unarmed he stood on his feet, for he was sore bruised in the back with a spear; yet as well as Sir Galleron might, he armed Sir Tristram. And then Sir Tristram mounted upon his horse, and in his hand he got Sir Galleron's spear. And therewith Sir Palomides was ready, and so they came hurtling together, and either smote other in midst of their shields; and therewith Sir Palomides' spear broke, and Sir Tristram smote down Sir Palomides, horse and man, to the earth. And then Sir Palomides as soon as he might avoided his horse, and dressed his shield and pulled out his sword. That saw Sir Tristram, and therewith he alit and tied his horse to a tree. And then they came together eagerly as two wild boars, and so [14] they lashed together, tracing and traversing as noble men that often had been well proved in battle. But ever Sir Palomides dreaded passing sore the might of Sir Tristram, and therefore he suffered him to breathe him, and thus they fought more than two hours; but oftentimes Sir Tristram smote such strokes at Sir Palomides that he made him to kneel. And Sir Palomides brake and cut many pieces of Sir Tristram's shield, and then Sir Palomides wounded Sir Tristram passing sore, for he was a well-fighting man.

Then Sir Tristram waxed wood wroth out of measure and rushed upon Sir Palomides with such a might that Sir Palomides fell grovelling to the earth, and therewith he leapt up lightly upon his feet.

senship] disgrace

And then Sir Tristram wounded sore Sir Palomides through the shoulder; and ever Sir Tristram fought still alike hard, and Sir Palomides failed him not but gave him many sad strokes again. And at the last Sir Tristram doubled his strokes upon him; and by fortune Sir Tristram smote Sir Palomides' sword out of his hand, and if Sir Palomides had stooped for his sword he had been slain. And then Sir Palomides stood still and beheld his sword with a sorrowful heart.

'How now,' said Sir Tristram, 'for now I have thee at advantage,' said Sir Tristram, 'as thou hadst me this day; but it shall never be said in no court nor among no good knights that Sir Tristram shall slay any knight that is weaponless. And therefore take thou thy sword, and let us make an end of this battle.'

'As for to do this battle,' said Sir Palomides, 'I dare right well end it; but I have no great lust to fight no more, and for this cause,' said Sir Palomides: 'my offence to you is not so great but that we may be friends, for all that I have offended is and was for the love of La Belle Isode. And as for her, I dare say she is peerless of all other ladies, and also I proffered her never no manner of dishonour; and by her I have gotten the most part of my worship. And sithen I offended never as to her own person, and as for the offence that I have done, it was against your own person, and for that offence ye have given me this day many sad strokes, and some I have given you again; and now I dare say I felt never man of your might, nor so well-breathed, but if it were Sir Lancelot du Lake. Wherefore I require you, my lord, forgive me all that I have offended unto you. And this same day, have me to the next church, and first let me be clean confessed, and after that see yourself that I be truly baptized. And then will we all ride together unto the court of King Arthur, that we may be there at the next high feast following.'

'Then take your horse,' said Sir Tristram, 'and as ye say, so it shall be. And all thy evil will, God forgive it you, and I do. And hereby within this mile is the suffragan of Carlisle, which shall give you the sacrament of baptism.'

And anon they took their horses, and Sir Galleron rode with them; and when they came to the suffragan, Sir Tristram told him their desire. Then the suffragan let fill a great vessel with water, and when he had hallowed it he then confessed clean Sir Palomides. And Sir Tristram and Sir Galleron were his two godfathers.

suffragan] bishop

And then soon after they departed and rode toward Camelot, where that King Arthur and Queen Guenivere was, and the most part of all the knights of the Round Table were there also. And so the King and all the court were right glad that Sir Palomides was christened.

And that same feast, in came Sir Galahad that was son unto Sir Lancelot du Lake, and sat in the Siege Perilous. And so therewith they departed and dissevered, all the knights of the Round Table. And then Sir Tristram returned unto Joyous Gard, and Sir Palomides followed after the Questing Beast.

Here endeth the second book of Sir Tristram de Lyonesse, which was drawn out of French by Sir Thomas Malory, knight, as Jesu be his help: amen. But here is no rehearsal of the third book.* But here followeth the noble tale of the Sangrail, which is called the holy vessel, and the signification of the blessed blood of Our Lord Jesu Christ, which was brought into this land by Joseph of Arimathea. Therefore on all sinful souls, blessed Lord, and on thy knight have mercy. Amen.

THE NOBLE TALE OF THE SANGRAIL

[XIII.1] At the vigil of Pentecost, when all the fellowship of the Round Table were come unto Camelot and there heard their service,* so at the last the tables were set ready to the meat. Right so entered into the hall a full fair gentlewoman on horseback, that had ridden full fast, for her horse was all besweat. Then she there alit, and came before the King and saluted him; and he said, 'Damosel, God you bless.'

'Sir,' said she, 'for God's sake, tell me where is Sir Lancelot.'

'He is yonder: ye may see him,' said the King.

Then she went unto Sir Lancelot and said, 'Sir Lancelot, I salute you on King Pelles' behalf, and I also require you to come on with me hereby into a forest.'

Then Sir Lancelot asked her with whom she dwelled.

'I dwell', she said, 'with King Pelles.'

'What will ye with me?' said Sir Lancelot.

'Ye shall know', she said, 'when ye come thither.'

'Well,' said he, 'I will gladly go with you.'

So Sir Lancelot bade his squire saddle his horse and bring his arms in haste; so he did his commandment. Then came the Queen unto Sir Lancelot, and said, 'Will ye leave us now alone at this high feast?'

'Madam,' said the gentlewoman, 'wit you well, he shall be with you tomorrow by dinner time.'

'If I wist', said the Queen, 'that he should not be here with us tomorrow, he should not go with you by my good will.'

Right so departed Sir Lancelot, and rode until that he came into a forest and into a great valley where they saw an abbey of nuns; and there was a squire ready and opened the gates, and so they entered and descended off their horses. And anon there came a fair fellowship about Sir Lancelot, and welcomed him, and then they led him unto the abbess's chamber and unarmed him. And right so he was ware upon a bed lying two of his cousins, Sir Bors and Sir Lionel, and anon he waked them; and when they saw him they made great joy.

'Sir,' said Sir Bors unto Sir Lancelot, 'what adventure hath brought you hither?—for we weened to have found you tomorrow at Camelot.'

'So God me help,' said Sir Lancelot, 'a gentlewoman brought me hither, but I know not the cause.'

So in the meanwhile that they thus talked together, there came in twelve nuns that brought with them Galahad, the which was passing fair and well made, that uneath in the world men might not find his match; and all those ladies wept.

'Sir,' said they all, 'we bring you here this child the which we have nourished; and we pray you to make him knight, for of a more worthier man's hand may he not receive the order of knighthood.'

Sir Lancelot beheld this young squire and saw him seemly and demure as a dove, with all manner of good features, that he weened of his age never to have seen so fair a form of a man. Then said Sir Lancelot, 'Cometh this desire of himself?'

He and all they said yes.

'Then shall he', said Sir Lancelot, 'receive the order of knighthood at the reverence of the high feast.'

So that night Sir Lancelot had passing good cheer; and on the morn at the hour of prime, at Galahad's desire he made him knight and said, 'God make you a good man, for of beauty faileth you none as any that is now living. Now, fair sir,' said Sir Lancelot, 'will ye come with me [2] unto the court of King Arthur?'

'Nay,' said he, 'I will not go with you at this time.'

Then he departed from them and took his two cousins with him; and so they came unto Camelot by the hour of undern on Whitsunday. So by that time the King and the Queen were gone to the minster to hear their service. Then the King and the Queen were passing glad of Sir Bors and Sir Lionel, and so was all the fellowship.

So when the King and all the knights were come from service, the barons espied in the sieges of the Round Table all about, written with golden letters, 'Here ought to sit he', and 'He ought to sit here'. And thus they went so long till that they came to the Siege Perilous, where they found letters newly written of gold which said: 'Four hundred winters and four and fifty accomplished after the Passion of Our Lord Jesu Christ ought this siege to be fulfilled.'

Then all they said, 'This is a marvellous thing, and an adventurous.'

'In the name of God!' said Sir Lancelot; and then accounted the term of the writing from the birth of Our Lord until that day. 'It seemeth me', said Sir Lancelot, 'that this siege ought to be fulfilled this same day, for this is the feast of Pentecost after the four hundred and four and fiftieth year. And if it would please all parties, I would none of these letters were seen this day, till that he be come that ought to achieve this adventure.'

Then made they to ordain a cloth of silk for to cover these letters in the Siege Perilous. Then the King bade haste unto dinner.

'Sir,' said Sir Kay, the Steward, 'if ye go now unto your meat ye shall break your old custom of your court, for ye have not used on this day to sit at your meat or that ye have seen some adventure.'*

'Ye say sooth,' said the King, 'but I had so great joy of Sir Lancelot and of his cousins, which be come to the court whole and sound, that I bethought me not of no old custom.'

So as they stood speaking, in came a squire that said unto the King, 'Sir, I bring unto you marvellous tidings.'

'What be they?' said the King.

'Sir, there is here beneath at the river a great stone which I saw float above the water, and therein I saw sticking a sword.'

Then the King said, 'I will see that marvel.'

So all the knights went with him, and when they came unto the river they found there a stone floating, as it were of red marble, and therein stuck a fair rich sword, and the pommel thereof was of precious stones wrought with letters of gold subtly. Then the barons read the letters, which said in this wise: 'Never shall man take me hence but only he by whose side I ought to hang; and he shall be the best knight of the world.'

So when the King had seen the letters, he said unto Sir Lancelot, 'Fair sir, this sword ought to be yours, for I am sure ye be the best knight of the world.'

Then Sir Lancelot answered full soberly, 'Sir, it is not my sword; also I have no hardiness to set my hand thereto, for it belongeth not to hang by my side. Also, who that assayeth to take it and faileth of that sword, he shall receive a wound by that sword that he shall not be whole long after. And I will that ye wit that this same day shall the adventure of the Sangrail begin, that is called the holy vessel.'

[3]   'Now, fair nephew,' said the King unto Sir Gawain, 'assay ye, for my love.'

'Sir,' he said, 'save your good grace, I shall not do that.'

'Sir,' said the King, 'assay to take the sword for my love and at my commandment.'

'Sir, your commandment I will obey.'

And therewith he took the sword by the handles, but he might not stir it.

'I thank you,' said the King.

'My lord Sir Gawain,' said Sir Lancelot, 'now wit you well, this sword shall touch you so sore that ye would not ye had set your hand thereto for the best castle of this realm.'

'Sir,' he said, 'I might not withsay my uncle's will.'

But when the King heard this he repented it much, and said unto Sir Percival, 'Sir, will ye assay, for my love?'

And he assayed gladly, for to bear Sir Gawain fellowship; and therewith he set his hand on the sword and drew at it strongly, but he might not move it. Then were there no more that durst be so hardy to set their hands thereto.

'Now may ye go to your dinner,' said Sir Kay unto the King, 'for a marvellous adventure have ye seen.'

So the King and all they went unto the court, and every knight knew his own place and set him therein; and young men that were good knights served them. So when they were served, and all sieges fulfilled save only the Siege Perilous, anon there befell a marvellous adventure, that all the doors and windows of the palace shut by themselves; not for that the hall was not greatly darkened, and therewith they abashed, both one and other.

Then King Arthur spoke first and said, 'By God, fair fellows and lords, we have seen this day marvels, but or night I suppose we shall see greater marvels.'

In the meanwhile came in a good old man and an ancient, clothed all in white, and there was no knight knew from whence he came. And with him he brought a young knight, and both on foot, in red arms, without sword or shield, save a scabbard hanging by his side. And these words he said: 'Peace be with you, fair lords.'

Then the old man said unto King Arthur, 'Sir, I bring you here a young knight the which is of kings' lineage, and of the kindred of Joseph of Arimathea, whereby the marvels of this court and of strange realms shall be fully accomplished.'

The King was right glad of his words, and said unto the good man, [4] 'Sir, ye be right welcome, and the young knight with you.'

Then the old man made the young man to unarm him; and he was in a coat of red sendal, and bore a mantle upon his shoulder that was

sendal] silk

furred with ermine, and put that upon him. And the old knight said unto the young knight, 'Sir, sueth me.'

And anon he led him to the Siege Perilous, where beside sat Sir Lancelot; and the good man lifted up the cloth and found there letters that said thus: 'This is the siege of Galahad, the haut prince.'

'Sir,' said the old knight, 'wit you well that place is yours.'

And then he set him down surely in that siege; and then he said to the old man, 'Now may ye, sir, go your way, for well have ye done in that that ye were commanded. And recommend me unto my grandsire King Pelles, and unto my lord King Pecheur,* and say them on my behalf, I shall come and see them as soon as ever I may.'

So the good man departed; and there met him twenty noble squires, and so took their horses and went their way.

Then all the knights of the Table Round marvelled greatly of Sir Galahad, that he durst sit there and was so tender of age, and wist not from whence he came but all only by God. All they said, 'This is he by whom the Sangrail shall be achieved, for there sat never none but he there but he were mischieved.'

Then Sir Lancelot beheld his son and had great joy of him. Then Sir Bors told his fellows, 'Upon pain of my life, this young knight shall come to great worship.'

So this noise was great in all the court, that it came unto the Queen; and she had marvel what knight it might be that durst adventure him to sit in that Siege Perilous. Then some said he resembled much unto Sir Lancelot.

'I may well suppose', said the Queen, 'that Sir Lancelot begot him on King Pelles' daughter, which made him to lie by her by enchantment, and his name is Galahad. I would fain see him,' said the Queen, 'for he must needs be a noble man, for so his father is that him begot, I report me unto all the Table Round.'

So when the meat was done, that the King and all were risen, the King yode to the Siege Perilous and lifted up the cloth, and found there the name of Galahad. And then he showed it unto Sir Gawain, and said, 'Fair nephew, now have we among us Sir Galahad, the good knight that shall worship us all. And upon pain of my life he shall

---

sueth] follow   haut] high   for there sat . . . he were mischieved] no one but he ever sat there without coming to harm   worship] bring honour to

achieve the Sangrail, right as Sir Lancelot had done us to understand.'
Then came King Arthur unto Sir Galahad and said, 'Sir, ye be right
welcome, for ye shall move many good knights to the quest of the Sangrail, and ye shall achieve that many other knights might never bring
to an end.' Then the King took him by the hand, and went down from
the palace to show Galahad the adventures of the stone.

Then the Queen heard thereof and came after with many ladies, and   [5]
they showed her the stone where it hoved on the water.

'Sir,' said the King unto Sir Galahad, 'here is a great marvel as ever
I saw, and right good knights have assayed and failed.'

'Sir,' said Galahad, 'it is no marvel, for this adventure is not theirs
but mine; and for the surety of this sword, I brought none with me, but
here by my side hangeth the scabbard.' And anon he laid his hand on
the sword and lightly drew it out of the stone, and put it in the sheath,
and said unto the King, 'Now it goeth better than it did beforehand.'

'Sir,' said the King, 'a shield God may send you.'

'Now have I the sword that sometime was the good knight's, Balin's
le Savage, and he was a passing good knight of his hands; and with this
sword he slew his brother Balan, and that was great pity, for he was a
good knight. And either slew other through a dolorous stroke that
Balin gave unto King Pellam, the which is not yet whole, nor naught
shall be till that I heal him.'

So therewith the King had espied come riding down the river a lady
on a white palfrey a great pace toward them. Then she saluted the King
and the Queen, and asked if that Sir Lancelot were there; and then he
answered himself and said, 'I am here, my fair lady.'

Then she said all with weeping cheer, 'Ah, Sir Lancelot, how your
great doing is changed sithen this day in the morn!'

'Damosel, why say ye so?'

'Sir, I say you sooth,' said the damosel, 'for ye were this day in the
morn the best knight of the world; but who should say so now, he
should be a liar, for there is now one better than ye be. And well it is
proved by the adventure of the sword whereto ye durst not set to your
hand—and that is the change of your name, and leaving. Wherefore I
make unto you a remembrance, that ye shall not ween from henceforth
that ye be the best knight of the world.'

hoved] floated   that is the change of your name, and leaving] i.e. that shows you
have lost the title of best knight of the world

'As touching unto that,' said Lancelot, 'I know well I was never none of the best.'

'Yes,' said the damosel, 'that were ye, and are yet, of any sinful man of the world. And, sir king, Nacien the hermit sendeth thee word that thee shall befall the greatest worship that ever befell king in Britain, and I say you wherefore: for this day the Sangrail appeared in thy house and fed thee and all thy fellowship of the Round Table.'

So she departed and went the same way that she came.

[6]   'Now,' said the King, 'I am sure at this quest of the Sangrail shall all ye of the Table Round depart, and never shall I see you again whole together. Therefore I will see you all whole together in the meadow of Camelot to joust and to tourney, that after your death men may speak of it that such good knights were here such a day whole together.'

As unto that counsel and at the King's request they accorded all, and took on the harness that longed unto jousting. But all this moving of the King was for this intent, for to see Galahad proved; for the King deemed he should not lightly come again unto the court after this departing.

So were they assembled in the meadow, both more and less. Then Sir Galahad, by the prayer of the King and the Queen, did on a noble jesseraunt upon him, and also he did on his helm, but shield would he take none for no prayer of the King. So then Sir Gawain and other knights prayed him to take a spear; right so he did.

So the Queen was in a tower with all her ladies for to behold that tournament. Then Sir Galahad dressed him in midst of the meadow and began to break spears marvellously, that all men had wonder of him; for he there surmounted all other knights, for within a while he had defouled many good knights of the Table Round save only twain, that was Sir Lancelot and Sir Percival.

[7]   Then the King at the Queen's desire made him to alight and to unlace his helm, that the Queen might see him in the visage. When she avised him she said, 'I dare well say soothly that Sir Lancelot begot him, for never two men resembled more in likeness. Therefore it is no marvel though he be of great prowess.'

So a lady that stood by the Queen said, 'Madam, for God's sake, ought he of right to be so good a knight?'

jesseraunt] coat of mail   avised] looked in the face

'Yea, forsooth,' said the Queen, 'for he is of all parts come of the best knights of the world and of the highest lineage; for Sir Lancelot is come but of the eighth degree from Our Lord Jesu Christ, and this Sir Galahad is the ninth degree from Our Lord Jesu Christ. Therefore I dare say they be the greatest gentlemen of the world.'

And then the King and all the estates went home unto Camelot, and so went unto evensong to the great monastery; and so after upon that to supper, and every knight sat in his own place as they were beforehand. Then anon they heard cracking and crying of thunder, that them thought the palace should all to-drive. So in the midst of the blast entered a sunbeam more clearer by seven times than ever they saw day, and all they were lighted of the grace of the Holy Ghost. Then began every knight to behold other, and either saw other, by their seeming, fairer than ever they were before. Not for that there was no knight might speak one word a great while, and so they looked every man on other as they had been dumb.

Then entered into the hall the Holy Grail covered with white samite, but there was none that might see it, nor whom that bore it. And there was all the hall fulfilled with good odours, and every knight had such meats and drinks as he best loved in this world.* And when the Holy Grail had been borne through the hall, then the holy vessel departed suddenly, that they wist not where it became. Then had they all breath to speak; and then the King yielded thankings to God of His good grace that he had sent them.

'Certes,' said the King, 'we ought to thank Our Lord Jesu Christ greatly for that he hath showed us this day, at the reverence of this high feast of Pentecost.'

'Now,' said Sir Gawain, 'we have been served this day of what meats and drinks we thought on; but one thing beguiled us, that we might not see the Holy Grail, it was so preciously covered. Wherefore I will make here a vow, that tomorrow, without longer abiding, I shall labour in the quest of the Sangrail, and that I shall hold me out a twelvemonth and a day, or more if need be, and never shall I return unto the court again till I have seen it more openly than it hath been showed here. And if I may not speed I shall return again, as he that may not be against the will of God.'

So when they of the Table Round heard Sir Gawain say so, they arose up the most part and made such vows as Sir Gawain had made.

estates] people of rank   to-drive] shatter

Anon as King Arthur heard this he was greatly displeased, for he wist well he might not gainsay their vows.

'Alas,' said King Arthur unto Sir Gawain, 'ye have nigh slain me for the vow that ye have made, for through you ye have bereft me the fairest and the truest of knighthood that ever was seen together in any realm of the world. For when they depart from hence, I am sure they all shall never meet more together in this world, for they shall die many in the quest. And so it forthinketh me not a little, for I have loved them as well as my life. Wherefore it shall grieve me right sore, the departition of this fellowship; for I have had an old custom to have them in my

[8] fellowship.' And therewith the tears fell in his eyes; and then he said, 'Sir Gawain, ye have set me in great sorrow, for I have great doubt that my true fellowship shall never meet here more again.'

'Ah, sir,' said Sir Lancelot, 'comfort yourself; for it shall be unto us a great honour, and much more than if we died in other places, for of death we be sure.'

'Ah, Lancelot,' said the King, 'the great love that I have had unto you all the days of my life maketh me to say such doleful words; for there was never Christian king that ever had so many worthy men at his table as I have had this day at the Table Round, and that is my great sorrow.'

When the Queen, ladies, and gentlewomen knew of these tidings, they had such sorrow and heaviness that there might no tongue tell, for those knights had held them in honour and charity. But above all other Queen Guenivere made great sorrow.

'I marvel', said she, 'that my lord will suffer them to depart from him.'

Thus was all the court troubled for the love of the departing of these knights. And many of those ladies that loved knights would have gone with their loves; and so had they done, had not an old knight come among them in religious clothing, and spoke all on high and said: 'Fair lords, which have sworn in the quest of the Sangrail, thus Nacien the hermit sendeth you word, that none in this quest lead lady nor gentlewoman with him, for it is not to do in so high a service as they labour in. For I warn you plain, he that is not clean of his sins, he shall not see the mysteries of Our Lord Jesu Christ.' And for this cause they left these ladies and gentlewomen.

So after this the Queen came unto Sir Galahad and asked him of whence he was, and of what country. Then he told her of whence he was; and son unto Sir Lancelot, as to that, he said neither yea or nay.

'So God me help,' said the Queen, 'of your father ye need not shame you, for he is the goodliest knight, and of the best men of the world come, and of the strain of all parts of kings; wherefore ye ought of right to be of your deeds a passing good man. And certain,' she said, 'ye resemble him much.'

Then Sir Galahad was a little ashamed and said, 'Madam, sithen ye know in certain, wherefore do ye ask it me? For he that is my father shall be known openly and all betimes.'

And then they went to rest them. And in honour of the highness of knighthood, Sir Galahad was led into King Arthur's chamber, and there rested in his own bed. And as soon as it was day the King arose, for he had no rest of all that night for sorrow. Then he went unto Sir Gawain and unto Sir Lancelot that were arisen for to hear Mass; and then the King again said, 'Ah, Gawain, Gawain, ye have betrayed me! For never shall my court be amended by you, but ye will never be so sorry for me as I am for you,' and therewith the tears began to run down by his visage. And therewith the King said, 'Ah, courteous knight, Sir Lancelot, I require you that ye counsel me, for I would that this quest were at an end and it might be.'

'Sir,' said Sir Lancelot, 'ye saw yesterday, so many worthy knights there were sworn that they may not leave it in no manner of wise.'

'That wot I well,' said the King, 'but it shall so heavy me at their departing that I wot well there shall no manner of joy remedy me.'

And then the King and the Queen went unto the minster. So anon Sir Lancelot and Sir Gawain commanded their men to bring their arms; and when they all were armed save their shields and their helms, then they came to their fellowship, which were all ready in the same wise, for to go to the monastery for to hear their Mass and service. Then after service the King would wit how many had undertaken the quest of the Holy Grail. Then found they by tally a hundred and fifty, and all those were knights of the Round Table. And then they put on their helms and departed, and recommended them all wholly unto the King and the Queen; and there was weeping and great sorrow. Then the Queen departed into her chamber and held her there, that no man should perceive her great sorrows.

---

of the strain of all parts of kings] of a royal line by all his ancestors   all betimes]
soon enough   and it might be] if it could be brought about

When Sir Lancelot missed the Queen he went to her chamber, and when she saw him she cried aloud and said, 'Ah, Sir Lancelot, Lancelot, ye have betrayed me and put me to the death, for to leave thus my lord.'

'Ah, madam, I pray you be not displeased, for I shall come again as soon as I may with my worship.'

'Alas,' said she, 'that ever I saw you! But He that suffered death upon the cross for all mankind, He be unto you good conduct and safety, and all the whole fellowship.'

Right so departed Sir Lancelot, and found his fellowship that abode his coming. And then they took their horses and rode through the street of Camelot, and there was weeping of rich and poor; and the King turned away and might not speak for weeping.

So within a while they rode all together till that they came to a city and a castle that hight Vagon, and so they entered into the castle; and the lord thereof was an old man and good of his living, and set open the gates and made them all the cheer that he might. And so on the morn they were all accorded that they should depart each from other. And on the morn they departed with weeping cheer, and then every knight took the way that him liked best.

Of Sir Galahad*

Now rideth Galahad yet without shield, and so rode four days without
any adventure. And at the fourth day after evensong he came to a white
abbey,* and there was he received with great reverence and led unto a
chamber, and there was he unarmed. And then was he ware of two
knights of the Table Round, one was Sir Bagdemagus, and Sir Uwain.
And when they saw him they went to Sir Galahad and made of him
great solace, and so they went unto supper.

'Sirs,' said Sir Galahad, 'what adventure brought you hither?'

'Sir,' they said, 'it is told us that in this place is a shield, that no man
may bear it about his neck but he be mischieved or dead within three
days, or maimed for ever.'

'But, sir,' said King Bagdemagus, 'I shall bear it tomorrow for to
assay this adventure.'

'In the name of God,' said Sir Galahad.

'Sir,' said Bagdemagus, 'and I may not achieve the adventure of this
shield ye shall take it upon you, for I am sure ye shall not fail.'

'Sir, I right well agree me thereto, for I have no shield.'

So on the morn they arose and heard Mass; then King Bagdemagus
asked where the adventurous shield was. Anon a monk led him behind
an altar where the shield hung, as white as any snow, but in the midst
was a red cross.

'Sirs,' said the monk, 'this shield ought not to be hung about the
neck of no knight but he be the worthiest knight of the world: therefore
I counsel you, knights, to be well advised.'

'Well,' said Sir Bagdemagus, 'I wot well I am not the best knight, but
I shall assay to bear it'; and so bore it out of the monastery. Then he said
unto Sir Galahad, 'And it please you to abide here still, till that ye wit
how that I speed.'

'Sir, I shall abide you,' said Sir Galahad.

Then King Bagdemagus took with him a good squire, to bring tidings unto Sir Galahad how he sped. Then they rode two miles and
came to a fair valley before a hermitage; and then they saw a knight
come from that part in white armour, horse and all, and he came as fast
as his horse might run, and his spear in his rest. Then Sir Bagdemagus

dressed his spear against him and broke it upon the white knight; but the other struck him so hard that he brast the mails and thrust him through the right shoulder, for the shield covered him not as at that time. And so he bore him from his horse; and therewith he alit and took his white shield from him, saying, 'Knight, thou hast done thyself great folly, for this shield ought not to be borne but by him that shall have no peer that liveth.' And then he came to Bagdemagus' squire and bade him, 'Bear this shield to the good knight Sir Galahad that thou left in the abbey, and greet him well by me.'

'Sir,' said the squire, 'what is your name?'

'Take thou no heed of my name,' said the knight, 'for it is not for thee to know, nor no earthly man.'

'Now, fair sir,' said the squire, 'at the reverence of Jesu Christ, tell me by what cause this shield may not be borne but if the bearer thereof be mischieved.'

'Now since thou hast conjured me so,' said the knight, 'this shield behoveth unto no man but unto Sir Galahad.'

Then the squire went unto Bagdemagus and asked him whether he were sore wounded or no.

'Yea, forsooth,' said he, 'I shall escape hard from the death.'

Then he fetched his horse, and led him with great pain till they came unto the abbey. Then was he taken down softly and unarmed, and laid in his bed and looked there to his wounds. And as the book telleth, he lay there long, and escaped hard with the life.

[10] 'Sir Galahad,' said the squire, 'that knight that wounded Bagdemagus sendeth you greeting, and bade that ye should bear this shield, wherethrough great adventures should befall.'

'Now blessed be good fortune,' said Sir Galahad.

And then he asked his arms, and mounted upon his horse's back and hung the white shield about his neck, and commended them unto God. So Sir Uwain said he would bear him fellowship if it pleased him.

'Sir,' said Sir Galahad, 'that may ye not, for I must go alone.' And so departed Sir Uwain.

Then within a while came Sir Galahad there as the white knight abode him by the hermitage, and each saluted other courteously.

'Sir,' said Sir Galahad, 'by this shield be many marvels fallen?'

'Sir,' said the knight, 'it befell after the passion of Our Lord Jesu

escape hard] hardly escape

Christ two and thirty years, that Joseph of Arimathea, that gentle knight the which took down Our Lord off the holy Cross, at that time he departed from Jerusalem with a great party of his kindred with him. And so he laboured till they came to a city which hight Sarras; and that same hour that Joseph came to Sarras, there was a king that hight Evelake that had great war against the Saracens. Then Joseph, the son of Joseph of Arimathea, went to King Evelake and told him he should be discomfited and slain but he left his belief of the old law and believed upon the new law, and anon he showed him the right belief of the Holy Trinity, to the which he agreed unto with all his heart. And there this shield was made for King Evelake, in the name of Him that died on the Cross.

'So soon after, Joseph would depart, and King Evelake would needs go with him whether he would or not. And so by fortune they came into this land, that at that time was called Great Britain; and there they found a great felon paynim, that put Joseph into prison. And so by fortune tidings came unto a worthy man that hight Mordrains,* and he assembled all his people for the great renown he had heard of Joseph; and so he came into the land of Great Britain and disinherited this felon paynim and confounded him, and therewith delivered Joseph out of prison. And after that all the people turned to the Christian faith.

'So not long after, Joseph was laid in his deadly bed; and when King [11] Evelake saw that, he had much sorrow, and said, "For thy love I left my country, and sith ye shall depart from me out of this world, leave me some token of yours that I may think on you."

'Joseph said, "That will I do full gladly; now bring me your shield that I took you." Then Joseph bled sore at the nose, so that he might not by no mean be staunched; and there upon that shield he made a cross of his own blood, and said, "Now may ye see a remembrance that I love you, for ye shall never see this shield but ye shall think on me. And never shall man bear this shield about his neck but he shall repent it, unto the time that Galahad, the good knight, bear it, and, last of my lineage, have it about his neck, that shall do many marvellous deeds." '*

And then the white knight vanished away.*

And so Sir Galahad took his horse and departed, and rode many jour- [14] neys forward and backward; and departed from a place that hight

paynim] pagan   deadly bed] deathbed   took] gave

Abblasour, and had heard no Mass. Then Sir Galahad came to a mountain where he found a chapel passing old, and found therein nobody, for all was desolate; and there he kneeled before the altar, and besought God of good counsel. And so as he prayed he heard a voice that said, 'Go thou now, thou adventurous knight, to the Castle of Maidens, and there do thou away the wicked customs.'

[15]   When Sir Galahad heard this he thanked God, and took his horse; and he had not ridden but a while but he saw in a valley before him a strong castle with deep ditches, and there ran beside it a fair river that hight Severn. And there he met with a man of great age, and either saluted other, and Sir Galahad asked him the castle's name.

'Fair sir,' said he, 'it is the Castle of Maidens, that is a cursed castle, and all they that be conversant therein; for all pity is out thereof, and all hardiness and mischief is therein. Therefore I counsel you, sir knight, to turn again.'

'Sir,' Sir Galahad said, 'wit you well that I shall not turn again.'

Then looked Sir Galahad on his arms that nothing failed him, and then he put his shield before him. And anon there met him seven fair maidens, the which said unto him, 'Sir knight, ye ride here in great folly, for ye have the water to pass over.'

'Why should I not pass the water?' said Sir Galahad.

So rode he away from them and met with a squire that said, 'Knight, those knights in the castle defy you, and defend you ye go no further till that they wit what ye would.'

'Fair sir,' said Sir Galahad, 'I come for to destroy the wicked custom of this castle.'

'Sir, and ye will abide by that ye shall have enough to do.'

'Go ye now,' said Sir Galahad, 'and haste my needs.'

Then the squire entered into the castle; and anon after there came out of the castle seven knights, and all were brethren. And when they saw Sir Galahad they cried, 'Knight, keep thee, for we assure you nothing but death.'

'Why,' said Sir Galahad, 'will ye all have ado with me at once?'

'Yea,' said they, 'thereto mayst thou trust.'

Then Galahad put forth his spear and smote the foremost to the earth, that nearhand he broke his neck. And therewith the other six smote him on his shield great strokes, that their spears broke. Then

conversant] conducting their lives   defend] forbid

Sir Galahad drew out his sword, and set upon them so hard that it was marvel, and so through great force he made them to forsake the field. And Sir Galahad chased them till they entered into the castle, and so passed through the castle at another gate.

And anon there met Sir Galahad an old man clothed in religious clothing, and said, 'Sir, have here the keys of this castle.'

Then Sir Galahad opened the gates, and saw so much people in the streets that he might not number them; and all they said, 'Sir, ye be welcome, for long have we abided here our deliverance.'

Then came to him a gentlewoman and said, 'Sir, these knights be fled, but they will come again this night, and here to begin again their evil custom.'

'What will ye that I do?' said Sir Galahad.

'Sir,' said the gentlewoman, 'that ye send after all the knights hither that hold their lands of this castle, and make them all to swear for to use the customs that were used here of old time.'

'I will well,' said Sir Galahad.

And there she brought him a horn of ivory, bound with gold richly, and said, 'Sir, blow this horn, which will be heard two miles about.'

When Sir Galahad had blown the horn he set him down upon a bed. Then came a priest to Galahad, and said, 'Sir, it is past seven years ago that these seven brethren came into this castle, and harboured with the lord of this castle, that hight the Duke Lianour, and he was lord of all this country. And when they had espied the duke's daughter, that was a full fair woman, then by their false covin they made a bate betwixt themselves; and the duke of his goodness would have parted them, and there they slew him and his eldest son. And then they took the maiden and the treasure of the castle, and so by great force they held all the knights of this country under great servage and truage. So on a day the duke's daughter said to them, "Ye have done great wrong to slay my father and my brother, and thus to hold our lands. Not for that," she said, "ye shall not hold this castle many years, for by one knight ye shall all be overcome." Thus she prophesied seven years ago. "Well," said the seven knights, "sithen ye say so, there shall never lady nor knight pass this castle but they shall abide maugre their heads, or die therefore, till that knight be come by whom we shall lose this castle." And

---

covin] conspiracy   bate] quarrel   servage and truage] servitude and exactions

therefore it is called the Maidens' Castle, for they have devoured many maidens.'

'Now,' said Sir Galahad, 'is she here for whom this castle was lost?'

'Nay, sir,' said the priest, 'she was dead within three nights after that she was thus forced; and sithen have they kept her younger sister, which endureth great pain, with more other ladies.'

By this were the knights of the country come, and then he made them to do homage and fealty to the duke's daughter, and set them in great ease of heart. And in the morn there came one and told Sir Galahad how that Sir Gawain, Sir Gareth, and Sir Uwain had slain the seven brethren.

'I suppose well,' said Sir Galahad, and took his armour and his horse, and commended them unto God.

Here leaveth the tale of Sir Galahad, and speaketh of Sir Gawain.

devoured] destroyed   suppose well] can well believe it

Of Sir Gawain

Now saith the tale, after Sir Gawain departed, he rode many journeys [16] both toward and forward; and at the last he came to the abbey where Sir Galahad had the white shield, and there Sir Gawain learned the way to sue after Sir Galahad.

'Certes,' said Sir Gawain, 'I am not happy that I took not the way that he went, for and I may meet with him I will not depart from him lightly; for all marvellous adventures Sir Galahad achieveth.'

'Sir,' said one of the monks, 'he will not of your fellowship.'

'Why so?' said Sir Gawain.

'Sir,' said he, 'for ye be wicked and sinful, and he is full blessed.'

So right as they thus talked there came in riding Sir Gareth, and then they made great joy either of other. And on the morn they heard Mass, and so departed. And by the way they met with Sir Uwain le Avoutres; and there Sir Uwain told Sir Gawain how he had met with no adventures sith he departed from the court.

'Nor yet we,' said Sir Gawain.

And so either promised other of those three knights not to part while they were in that quest but if sudden fortune caused it. So they departed and rode by fortune till that they came by the Castle of Maidens; and there the seven brethren espied the three knights, and said, 'Sithen we be flemed by one knight from this castle, we shall destroy all the knights of King Arthur's that we may overcome, for the love of Sir Galahad.'

And therewith the seven knights set upon them three knights; and by fortune Sir Gawain slew one of the brethren, and each one of his fellows overthrew another, and so slew all the remnant. And then they took the way under the castle, and there they lost the way that Sir Galahad rode. And there each of them departed from other.

And Sir Gawain rode till he came to a hermitage, and there he found the good man saying his evensong of Our Lady; and there Sir Gawain asked harbour for charity, and the good man granted him gladly. Then the good man asked him what he was.

toward and forward] one way and another   sue] follow   flemed] put to flight

'Sir,' he said, 'I am a knight of King Arthur's that am in the quest of the Sangrail, and my name is Sir Gawain.'

'Sir,' said the good man, 'I would wit how it standeth betwixt God and you.'

'Sir,' said Sir Gawain, 'I will with a good will show you my life if it please you.'* There he told the hermit how 'a monk of an abbey called me wicked knight'.

'He might well say it,' said the hermit, 'for when ye were first made knight ye should have taken you to knightly deeds and virtuous living; and ye have done the contrary, for ye have lived mischievously many winters. And Sir Galahad is a maid and sinned never, and that is the cause he shall achieve where he goeth what ye nor none such shall never attain, nor none in your fellowship, for ye have used the most untruest life that ever I heard knight live. For certes, had ye not been so wicked as ye are, never had the seven brethren been slain by you and your two fellows; for Sir Galahad himself alone beat them all seven the day before, but his living is such that he shall slay no man lightly.

'Also I may say you that the Castle of Maidens betokeneth the good souls that were in prison before the Incarnation of Our Lord Jesu Christ.* And the seven knights betoken the seven deadly sins that reigned that time in the world. And I may liken the good knight Galahad unto the son of the High Father, that alit within a maiden, and bought all the souls out of thrall: so did Sir Galahad deliver all the maidens out of the woeful castle. Now, Sir Gawain,' said the good man, 'thou must do penance for thy sin.'

'Sir, what penance shall I do?'

'Such as I will give thee,' said the good man.

'Nay,' said Sir Gawain, 'I may do no penance; for we knights adventurous many times suffer great woe and pain.'

'Well,' said the good man, and then he held his peace.

And on the morn, then Sir Gawain departed from the hermit and betaught him unto God. And by adventure he met with Sir Agloval and Sir Griflet, two knights of the Round Table; and so they three rode four days without finding of any adventure. And at the fifth day they parted, and each held as befell them by adventure.

Here leaveth the tale of Sir Gawain and his fellows.

betaught] commended

Of Sir Lancelot

So when Sir Galahad was departed from the Castle of Maidens he rode [17]
till he came to a waste forest, and there he met with Sir Lancelot and
Sir Percival; but they knew him not, for he was new disguised. Right so
his father, Sir Lancelot, dressed his spear and broke it upon Sir Galahad, and Sir Galahad smote him so again that he bore down horse and
man. And then he drew his sword and dressed him unto Sir Percival,
and smote him so on the helm that it rove to the coif of steel; and had
not the sword swerved Sir Percival had been slain. And with the stroke
he fell out of his saddle.

So this jousts was done before the hermitage where a recluse
dwelled. And when she saw Sir Galahad ride, she said, 'God be with
thee, best knight of the world! Ah, certes,' said she all aloud, that
Sir Lancelot and Percival might hear, 'and yonder two knights had
known thee as well as I do, they would not have encountered with thee.'

When Sir Galahad heard her say so, he was adread to be known, and
therewith he smote his horse with his spurs and rode a great pace from
them. Then perceived they both that he was Sir Galahad, and up they
got on their horses and rode fast after him; but within a while he was
out of their sight. And then they turned again with heavy cheer, and
said, 'Let us spere some tidings', said Percival, 'at yonder recluse.'

'Do as ye list,' said Sir Lancelot.

When Sir Percival came to the recluse she knew him well enough,
and Sir Lancelot both. But Sir Lancelot rode overthwart and endlong
a wild forest, and held no path but as wild adventure led him. And at
the last he came to a stony cross which departed two ways in waste
land; and by the cross was a stone that was of marble, but it was so dark
that Sir Lancelot might not wit what it was. Then Sir Lancelot looked
beside him and saw an old chapel, and there he weened to have found
people; and anon Sir Lancelot fastened his horse to a tree, and there he
did off his shield and hung it upon a tree. And then he went to the
chapel door, and found it waste and broken. And within he found a fair
altar, full richly arrayed with cloth of clean silk, and there stood a clean

new disguised] i.e. carrying an unfamiliar shield   rove to the coif of steel] cut
through to the inner steel cap   spere] ask

fair candlestick which bore six great candles therein, and the candle-stick was of silver. And when Sir Lancelot saw this light he had great will for to enter into the chapel, but he could find no place where he might enter. Then was he passing heavy and dismayed, and returned again and came to his horse, and did off his saddle and bridle and let him pasture him; and unlaced his helm and ungirt his sword, and laid him down to sleep upon his shield before the cross.

[18]   And so he fell asleep; and half waking and half sleeping, he saw coming by him two palfreys all fair and white, which bore a litter, and therein lying a sick knight; and when he was nigh the cross he there abode still. All this Sir Lancelot saw and beheld it, for he slept not verily; and he heard him say, 'Ah, sweet Lord, when shall this sorrow leave me, and when shall the holy vessel come by me wherethrough I shall be healed? For I have endured thus long for little trespass.'

A full great while thus complained the knight, and always Sir Lancelot heard it. So with that Sir Lancelot saw the candlestick with the six tapers come before the cross, and he saw nobody that brought it. Also there came a table of silver, and the holy vessel of the Sangrail, which Sir Lancelot had seen beforetime in King Pecheur's house.* And therewith the sick knight sat him up and held up both his hands, and said, 'Fair sweet Lord, which is here within this holy vessel, take heed unto me that I may be whole of this malady.'

And therewith on his hands and on his knees he went so nigh that he touched the holy vessel and kissed it, and anon he was whole. And then he said, 'Lord God, I thank Thee, for I am healed of this sickness.'

So when the holy vessel had been there a great while, it went unto the chapel with the chandelier and the light, so that Sir Lancelot wist not where it was become. For he was overtaken with sin, that he had no power to rise against the holy vessel; wherefore after that many men said him shame, but he took repentance after that.

Then the sick knight dressed him up and kissed the cross. Anon his squire brought him his arms, and asked his lord how he did.

'Certes,' said he, 'I thank God, right well: through the holy vessel I am healed. But I have marvel of this sleeping knight, that he had no power to awake when this holy vessel was brought hither.'

I have endured thus long for little trespass] I have suffered long on account of only a small sin   rise against] stand up in honour of

'I dare well say,' said the squire, 'that he dwelleth in some deadly sin whereof he was never confessed.'

'By my faith,' said the knight, 'whatsoever he be, he is unhappy; for as I deem he is of the fellowship of the Round Table which is entered in the quest of the Sangrail.'

'Sir,' said the squire, 'here I have brought you all your arms save your helm and your sword; and therefore, by my assent, now may ye take this knight's helm and his sword.'

And so he did; and when he was clean armed he took there Sir Lancelot's horse, for he was better than his, and so departed they from the cross.

Then anon Sir Lancelot woke and sat him up, and bethought him [19] what he had seen there, and whether it were dreams or not. Right so heard he a voice that said, 'Sir Lancelot, more harder than is the stone, and more bitter than is the wood, and more naked and barer than is the leaf of the fig tree! Therefore go thou from hence, and withdraw thee from these holy places.'

And when Sir Lancelot heard this, he was passing heavy and wist not what to do; and so departed sore weeping, and cursed the time that he was born, for then he deemed never to have worship more. For those words went to his heart, till that he knew wherefore he was called so.

Then Sir Lancelot went to the cross and found his helm, his sword, and his horse away. And then he called himself a very wretch and most unhappy of all knights; and there he said, 'My sin and my wickedness have brought me unto great dishonour. For when I sought worldly adventures for worldly desires, I ever achieved them and had the better in every place, and never was I discomfited in no quarrel, were it right, were it wrong. And now I take upon me the adventures to seek of holy things, now I see and understand that my old sin hindereth me and shameth me, that I had no power to stir nor speak when the holy blood appeared before me.'

So thus he sorrowed till it was day, and heard the fowls sing; then somewhat he was comforted. But when Sir Lancelot missed his horse and his harness, then he wist well God was displeased with him. And so he departed from the cross on foot into a fair forest; and so by prime he came to a high hill, and found a hermitage and a hermit therein which was going unto Mass. And then Lancelot kneeled down and cried on Our Lord mercy for his wicked works. So when Mass was done, Sir Lancelot called him, and prayed him for saint charity for to hear his life.

'With a good will,' said the good man, and asked him whether he was of King Arthur's, and of the fellowship of the Table Round.

'Yea, forsooth; and my name is Sir Lancelot du Lake, that hath been right well said of. And now my good fortune is changed, for I am the most wretch of the world.'

The hermit beheld him, and had marvel why he was so abashed.

'Sir,' said the hermit, 'ye ought to thank God more than any knight living, for He hath caused you to have more worldly worship than any knight that is now living. And for your presumption to take upon you in deadly sin for to be in His presence where His flesh and His blood was, which caused you ye might not see it with your worldly eyes: for He will not appear where such sinners be, but if it be unto their great hurt or unto their shame. And there is no knight now living that ought to yield God so great thanks as ye, for He hath given you beauty, bounty, seemliness, and great strength over all other knights. And therefore ye are the more beholden unto God than any other man, to love Him and dread Him, for your strength and your manhood will little avail you and God be against you.'

[20]   Then Sir Lancelot wept with heavy heart and said, 'Now I know well ye say me sooth.'

'Sir,' said the good man, 'hide no old sin from me.'

'Truly,' said Sir Lancelot, 'that were me full loath to discover; for this fourteen years I never discovered one thing that I have used, and that may I now wite my shame and my disadventure.'

And then he told there the good man all his life, and how he had loved a queen* unmeasurably and out of measure long. 'And all my great deeds of arms that I have done, for the most part was for the queen's sake, and for her sake would I do battle were it right or wrong; and never did I battle all only for God's sake, but for to win worship and to cause me the better to be beloved, and little or nought I thanked never God of it.' Then Sir Lancelot said, 'Sir, I pray you counsel me.'

'Sir, I will counsel you,' said the hermit. 'Ye shall assure me by your knighthood that ye shall no more come in that queen's fellowship as much as ye may forbear.'

discover] reveal   wite] blame for

And then Sir Lancelot promised him that he would not, by the faith of his body.

'Sir, look that your heart and your mouth accord,' said the good man, 'and I shall assure you ye shall have the more worship than ever ye had.'

'Holy father,' said Sir Lancelot, 'I marvel of the voice that said to me marvellous words, as ye have heard beforehand.'

'Have ye no marvel', said the good man, 'thereof, for it seemeth well God loveth you. For men may understand, a stone is hard of kind, and namely one more than another; and that is to understand by thee, Sir Lancelot, for thou wilt not leave thy sin for no goodness that God hath sent thee. Therefore thou art more harder than any stone, and wouldst never be made nesh neither by water nor by fire: and that is the heat of the Holy Ghost may not enter in thee. Now take heed: in all the world men shall not find one knight to whom Our Lord hath given so much of grace as He hath lent thee, for He hath given thee fairness with seemliness; also He hath given thee wit, and discretion to know good from ill. He hath also given prowess and hardiness, and given thee to work so largely that thou hast had the better all thy days of thy life wheresoever thou came. And now Our Lord would suffer thee no longer but that thou shalt know Him whether thou wilt or not. And why the voice called thee bitterer than the wood: for wheresoever much sin dwelleth, there may be but little sweetness, wherefore thou art likened to an old rotten tree.

'Now have I showed thee why thou art harder than the stone and bitterer than the tree, now shall I show thee why thou art more naked and barer than the fig tree. It befell that Our Lord on Palm Sunday preached in Jerusalem, and there He found in the people that all hardness was harboured in them, and there He found in all the town not one that would harbour him. And then He went out of the town, and found in midst the way a fig tree which was right fair and well garnished of leaves, but fruit had it none. Then Our Lord cursed the tree that bore no fruit; that betokeneth the fig tree unto Jerusalem, that had leaves and no fruit.* So thou, Sir Lancelot, when the Holy Grail was brought before thee, He found in thee no fruit, nor good thought nor good will, and defouled with lechery.'

---

made nesh neither by water nor by fire] softened by water or fire, i.e. baptism or grace given thee to work so largely] so generously endowed you with capacity for action

'Certes,' said Sir Lancelot, 'all that ye have said is true. And from henceforward I cast me, by the grace of God, never to be so wicked as I have been, but as to pursue knighthood and to do feats of arms.'

Then this good man enjoined Sir Lancelot such penance as he might do and to pursue knighthood, and so assoiled him, and prayed him to abide with him all that day.

'I will well,' said Sir Lancelot, 'for I have neither helm, horse, nor sword.'

'As for that,' said the good man, 'I shall help you or tomorrow at even of a horse, and all that longeth unto you.'

And then Sir Lancelot repented him greatly of his misdeeds.

Here leaveth the tale of Sir Lancelot and beginneth of Sir Percival de Gales.

assoiled] absolved   help you or tomorrow at even of a horse] provide you with a horse before tomorrow evening

Of Sir Percival de Gales

Now saith the tale that when Sir Lancelot was ridden after Sir Galahad, the which had all these adventures above said, Sir Percival turned
again unto the recluse, where he deemed to have tidings of that knight
that Sir Lancelot followed. And so he kneeled at her window, and the
recluse opened it and asked Sir Percival what he would.

'Madam,' he said, 'I am a knight of King Arthur's court, and my
name is Sir Percival de Gales.'

When the recluse heard his name she had great joy of him, for
mickle she loved him passing any other knight, for she ought so to do,
for she was his aunt. And then she commanded the gates to be open,
and there he had great cheer, as great as she might make him, or lay in
her power. So on the morn Sir Percival went to the recluse and asked
her if she knew that knight with the white shield.

'Sir,' said she, 'why will ye wit?'

'Truly, madam,' said Sir Percival, 'I shall never be well at ease till
that I know of that knight's fellowship, and that I may fight with him;
for I may not leave him so lightly, for I have the shame as yet.'

'Ah, Sir Percival,' said she, 'would ye fight with him? I see well ye
have great will to be slain, as your father was through outrageousness
slain.'

'Madam, it seemeth by your words that ye know me.'

'Yea,' said she, 'I well ought to know you, for I am your aunt,
although I be in a poor place. For some men called me some time the
Queen of the Waste Lands, and I was called the queen of most riches in
the world. And it pleased me never so much my riches as doth my
poverty.'

Then Percival wept for very pity when that he knew it was his aunt.

'Ah, fair nephew,' said she, 'when heard you tidings of your
mother?'

'Truly,' said he, 'I heard none of her, but I dream of her much in my
sleep; and therefore I wot not whether she be dead or alive.'

'Certes, fair nephew, your mother is dead, for after your departing
from her she took such a sorrow that anon as she was confessed, she
died.'*

'Now God have mercy on her soul,' said Sir Percival. 'It sore for-thinketh me; but all we must change the life. Now, fair aunt, what is that knight? I deem it be he that bore the red arms on Whitsunday.'

'Wit you well,' said she, 'that this is he, for otherwise ought he not to do but to go in red arms. And that same knight hath no peer, for he worketh all by miracle, and he shall never be overcome of no earthly man's hand.'*

[2]   'Now, madam,' said Sir Percival, 'so much have I heard of you, that by my good will I will never have ado with Sir Galahad but by way of goodness; and for God's love, fair aunt, can ye teach me where I might find him? For much I would love the fellowship of him.'

'Fair nephew,' said she, 'ye must ride straight unto the Castle of Car-bonek, where the Maimed King is lying, for there shall ye hear true tidings of him.'

[3]   Then departed Sir Percival from his aunt, either making great sor-row. And so he rode till after evensong, and then he heard a clock smite;* and anon he was ware of a house closed well with walls and deep ditches, and there he knocked at the gate and anon he was let in, and he was led unto a chamber and soon unarmed. And there he had right good cheer all that night, and on the morn he heard his Mass. And in the monastery he found a priest ready at the altar, and on the right side he saw a pew closed with iron; and behind the altar he saw a rich bed and a fair, as of cloth of silk and gold. Then Sir Percival espied that therein was a man or a woman, for the visage was covered. Then he left off his looking and heard his service. And when it came to the sacring, he that lay within the perclose dressed him up, and uncovered his head; and then him beseemed a passing old man, and he had a crown of gold upon his head, and his shoulders were naked and unhilled unto his navel. And then Sir Percival espied his body was full of great wounds, both on the shoulders, arms, and visage. And ever he held up his hands against Our Lord's body, and cried, 'Fair sweet Lord Jesu Christ, forget not me.'

And so he lay not down, but was always in his prayers and orisons; and him seemed to be of the age of three hundred winters. And when the Mass was done the priest took Our Lord's body and bore it unto the

It sore forthinketh me] I regret it bitterly   sacring] consecration (of the Eucharist)   perclose] enclosure   dressed] sat   unhilled] uncovered

sick king. And when he had used it, he did off his crown, and commanded the crown to be set on the altar. Then Sir Percival asked one of the brethren what he was.

'Sir,' said the good man, 'ye have heard much of Joseph of Arimathea, how he was sent into this land for to teach and preach the holy Christian faith; and therefore he suffered many persecutions, the which the enemies of Christ did unto him. And in the city of Sarras he converted a king whose name was Evelake; and so the king came with Joseph into this land, and ever he was busy to be there as the Sangrail was. And on a time he nighed it so nigh that Our Lord was displeased with him, but ever he followed it more and more, till God struck him almost blind. Then this king cried mercy, and said, "Fair Lord, let me never die till the good knight of my blood of the ninth degree be come, that I may see him openly that he shall achieve the Sangrail, and that I might kiss him." When the king thus had made his prayers he heard a [4] voice that said, "Heard be thy prayers, for thou shalt not die till he hath kissed thee. And when that knight shall come, the clearness of your eyes shall come again, and thou shalt see openly, and thy wounds shall be healed; and erst shall they never close."

'And thus befell of King Evelake, and this same king hath lived four hundred years this holy life, and men say the knight is in this court that shall heal him. Sir,' said the good man, 'I pray you tell me what knight that ye be, and if ye be of the Round Table.'

'Yes, forsooth; and my name is Sir Percival de Gales.'

And when the good man understood his name he made great joy of him.

And then Sir Percival departed and rode till the hour of noon. And he met in a valley about twenty men of arms, which bore in a bier a knight deadly slain. And when they saw Sir Percival they asked him of whence he was; and he said, of the court of King Arthur. Then they cried at once, 'Slay him!'

Then Sir Percival smote the first to the earth and his horse upon him. And then seven of the knights smote upon his shield at once, and the remnant slew his horse, that he fell to the earth, and had slain him or taken him, had not the good knight Sir Galahad with the red arms come there by adventure into those parts. And when he saw all those knights upon one knight, he said, 'Save me that knight's life!'

---

used it] i.e. taken the sacrament   erst] before that

And then he dressed him toward the twenty men of arms as fast as his horse might drive, with his spear in his rest, and smote the foremost horse and man to the earth. And when his spear was broken he set his hand to his sword, and smote on the right hand and on the left hand that it was marvel to see. And at every stroke he smote down one or put him to a rebuke, so that they would fight no more, but fled to a thick forest, and Sir Galahad followed them. And when Sir Percival saw him chase them so, he made great sorrow that his horse was away. And then he wist well it was Sir Galahad, and cried aloud and said, 'Fair knight, abide and suffer me to do you thankings, for much have ye done for me.'

But ever Sir Galahad rode fast, that at the last he passed out of his sight. And as fast as Sir Percival might he went after him on foot, crying.*

[5] So in this sorrow there he abode all that day till it was night; and then he was faint, and laid him down and slept till it was midnight. And then he awoke and saw before him a woman which said unto him right fiercely, 'Sir Percival, what dost thou here?'

'I do neither good nor great ill.'

'If thou wilt assure me', said she, 'that thou wilt fulfil my will when I summon thee, I shall lend thee mine own horse which shall bear thee whither thou wilt.'

Sir Percival was glad of her proffer, and assured her to fulfil all her desire.

'Then abide me here, and I shall go fetch you a horse.'

And so she came soon again and brought a horse with her that was inly black. When Sir Percival beheld that horse, he marvelled that he was so great and so well apparelled; and not for that he was so hardy he leapt upon him and took no heed of himself. And anon as he was upon him he thrust to him with his spurs, and so rode by a forest; and the moon shone clear. And within an hour and less he bore him four days' journey thence, until he came to a rough water which roared, and that horse would have borne him into it.

[6] And when Sir Percival came nigh the brim, he saw the water so bois-terous he doubted to pass over it; and then he made a sign of the cross in his forehead.* When the fiend felt him so charged he shook off

inly] entirely   doubted] feared

Sir Percival, and he went into the water crying and making great sorrow, and it seemed unto him that the water burnt. Then Sir Percival perceived it was a fiend, the which would have brought him unto perdition. Then he commended himself unto God, and prayed Our Lord to keep him from all such temptations. And so he prayed all that night till on the morn that it was day; and anon he saw he was in a wild mountain which was closed with the sea nigh all about, that he might see no land about him which might relieve him, but wild beasts.

And then he went down into a valley, and there he saw a serpent bring a young lion by the neck, and so he came by Sir Percival. So with that came a great lion crying and roaring after the serpent. And as fast as Sir Percival saw this he hied him thither; but the lion had overtaken the serpent and began battle with him. And then Sir Percival thought to help the lion, for he was the more natural beast of the two; and therewith he drew his sword and set his shield before him, and there he gave the serpent such a buffet that he had a deadly wound. When the lion saw that, he made no semblant to fight with him, but made him all the cheer that a beast might make a man.

When Sir Percival perceived it, he cast down his shield, which was broken, and then he did off his helm for to gather wind, for he was greatly chafed with the serpent; and the lion went always about him fawning as a spaniel. And then he stroked him on the neck and on the shoulders, and thanked God of the fellowship of that beast.

And about noon the lion took his little whelp and trussed him and bore him there he came from. Then was Sir Percival alone. And as the tale telleth, he was at that time one of the men of the world which most believed in Our Lord Jesu Christ, for in those days there were but few folks at that time that believed perfectly; for in those days the son spared not the father no more than a stranger. And so Sir Percival comforted himself in Our Lord Jesu, and besought Him that no temptation should bring him out of God's service, but to endure as his true champion.

Thus when Sir Percival had prayed, he saw the lion come toward him and couched down at his feet; and so all that night the lion and he slept together. And when Sir Percival slept he dreamed a marvellous

made him all the cheer that a beast might make a man] showed him all the goodwill that an animal could show to a man   chafed] heated   trussed] bundled

dream: that two ladies met with him, and that one sat upon a lion, and that other sat upon a serpent, and that one of them was young, and the other was old; and the youngest, him thought, said, 'Sir Percival, my lord saluteth thee, and sendeth thee word thou array thee and make thee ready, for tomorrow thou must fight with the strongest champion of the world. And if thou be overcome, thou shalt not be quit for losing of any of thy members, but thou shalt be shamed for ever to the world's end.' And then he asked her what was her lord; and she said, the greatest lord of the world. And so she departed suddenly that he wist not where.

[7]   Then came forth the other lady that rode upon the serpent; and she said, 'Sir Percival, I complain unto you of that ye have done unto me, and I have not offended unto you.'

'Certes, madam,' he said, 'unto you nor no lady I never offended.'

'Yes,' said she, 'I shall say you why. I have nourished in this place a great while a serpent which pleased me much, and yesterday ye slew him as he got his prey. Say me for what cause ye slew him, for the lion was not yours.'

'Madam, I know well the lion was not mine. But for the lion is more of gentler nature than the serpent, therefore I slew him; and me seemeth I did not amiss against you, madam,' said he. 'What would ye that I did?'

'I would,' said she, 'for the amends of my beast that ye become my man.'

And then he answered and said, 'That will I not grant you.'

'No,' said she, 'truly ye were never my servant since ye received the homage of Our Lord Jesu Christ. Therefore I you assure that in what place I may find you without keeping I shall take you as he that sometime was my man.'

And so she departed from Sir Percival and left him sleeping, which was sore travailed of his vision. And on the morn he arose and blessed him, and he was passing feeble.

Then was Sir Percival ware in the sea where came a ship sailing toward him; and Sir Percival went unto the ship and found it covered within and without with white samite. And at the helm stood an old man clothed in a surplice, in likeness of a priest.

---

thou shalt not be quit for losing of any of thy members] you shall not get away with losing any of your limbs   without keeping] unguarded   travailed of] troubled by

'Sir,' said Sir Percival, 'ye be welcome.'

'God keep you,' said the good man. ' And of whence be ye?'

'Sir, I am a knight of King Arthur's court and a knight of the Round Table, which am in the quest of the Sangrail; and here I am in great duress, and never like to escape out of this wilderness.'

'Doubt ye not,' said the good man. 'And ye be so true a knight as the order of chivalry requireth, and of heart as ye ought to be, ye should not doubt that no enemy should slay you.'

'What are ye?' said Sir Percival.

'Sir, I am of a strange country, and hither I come to comfort you.'

'Sir,' said Sir Percival, 'what signifieth my dream that I dreamed this night?' And there he told him all together.

'She which rode upon the lion, it betokeneth the New Law of Holy Church, that is to understand, faith, good hope, belief, and baptism. For she seemed younger than that other it is great reason, for she was born in the resurrection and the passion of Our Lord Jesu Christ. And for great love she came to thee to warn thee of thy great battle that shall befall thee.'

'With whom', said Sir Percival, 'shall I fight?'

'With the most doubtful champion of the world; for as the lady said, but if thou quit thee well thou shalt not be quit by losing of one member, but thou shalt be shamed to the world's end. And she that rode on the serpent signifieth the Old Law, and that serpent betokeneth a fiend. And why she blamed thee that thou slewest her servant, it betokeneth nothing but the serpent ye slew; that betokeneth the devil that thou rodest on to the rock, and when thou madest a sign of the cross, there thou slewest him and put away his power.* And when she asked thee amends and to become her man, then thou saidst nay, that was to make thee to believe on her and leave thy baptism.'

So he commanded Sir Percival to depart; and so he leapt over the board, and the ship and all went away he wist not whither. Then he went up into the rock and found the lion which always bore him fellowship, and he stroked him upon the back and had great joy of him.

By that Sir Percival had abided there till midday, he saw a ship come [8] sailing in the sea as all the wind of the world had driven it; and so it landed under that rock. And when Sir Percival saw this he hied him thither, and found the ship covered with silk more blacker than any

doubtful] fearsome   baptism] i.e. Christian faith

bear. And therein was a gentlewoman of great beauty, and she was clothed richly, there might be none better. And when she saw Sir Percival she asked him who brought him into this wilderness, 'where ye be never like to pass hence, for ye shall die here for hunger and mischief.'

'Damosel,' said Sir Percival, 'I serve the best man of the world, and in His service He will not suffer me to die; for who that knocketh shall enter, and who that asketh shall have, and who that seeketh Him, He hideth Him not unto his words.'*

But then she said, 'Sir Percival, wot ye what I am?'

'Who taught you my name now?' said Sir Percival.

'I know you better than ye ween: I came but late out of the waste forests where I found the red knight with the white shield.'

'Ah, fair damosel,' said he, 'that knight would I fain meet with.'

'Sir knight,' said she, 'and ye will assure me by the faith that ye owe unto knighthood that ye shall do my will what time I summon you, I shall bring you unto that knight.'

'Yes,' he said, 'I shall promise you to fulfil your desire.'

'Well,' said she, 'now shall I tell you. I saw him in the waste forest chasing two knights unto the water which is called Mortaise, and they drove into that water for dread of death. And the two knights passed over, and the red knight passed after, and there his horse was drowned, and he through great strength escaped unto the land.'

Thus she told him, and Sir Percival was passing glad thereof. Then she asked him if he had eaten any meat late.

'Nay, madam, truly I ate no meat nigh these three days; but late here I spake with a good man that fed me with his good words and refreshed me greatly.'

'Ah, sir knight, that same man', said she, 'is an enchanter and a multiplier of words. For and ye believe him ye shall be plainly shamed, and die in this rock for pure hunger and be eaten with wild beasts. And ye be a young man and a goodly knight, and I shall help you and ye will.'

'What are ye,' said Sir Percival, 'that proffereth me thus so great kindness?'

'I am,' said she, 'a gentlewoman that am disinherited, which was the richest woman of the world.'

'Damosel,' said Sir Percival, 'who hath disinherited you? For I have great pity of you.'

'Sir,' said she, 'I dwelled with the greatest man of the world, and he made me so fair and clear that there was none like me; and of that great beauty I had a little pride more than I ought to have had.* Also I said a word that pleased him not. And then he would not suffer me to be no longer in his company, and so he drove me from my heritage and disinherited me for ever; and he had never pity of me nor of none of my council, nor of my court. And sithen, sir knight, it hath befallen me to be so overthrown, and all mine, yet have I benome him some of his men and made them to become my men; for they ask never nothing of me but I give them that and much more. Thus I and my servants were against him night and day. Therefore I know now no good knight nor no good man, but I get them on my side and I may. And for that I know that ye are a good knight, I beseech you to help me, and for ye be a fellow of the Round Table, wherefore ye ought not to fail no gentlewoman which is disinherited and she besought you of help.'

Then Sir Percival promised her all the help that he might, and then [9] she thanked him. And at that time the weather was hot. Then she called unto her a gentlewoman and bade her bring forth a pavilion; and so she did, and pitched it upon the gravel.

'Sir,' said she, 'now may ye rest you in this heat of this day.'

Then he thanked her, and she put off his helm and his shield, and there he slept a great while. And so he awoke and asked her if she had any meat, and she said, 'Yea, ye shall have enough.'

And anon there was laid a table, and so much meat was set thereon that he had marvel, for there was all manner of meats that he could think on. Also he drank there the strongest wine that ever he drank, him thought, and therewith he was chafed a little more than he ought to be. With that he beheld that gentlewoman, and him thought she was the fairest creature that ever he saw. And then Sir Percival proffered her love, and prayed her that she would be his. Then she refused him in a manner when he required her, for cause he should be the more ardent on her; and ever he ceased not to pray her of love.

And when she saw him well enchafed, then she said, 'Sir Percival, wit you well I shall not fulfil your will but if ye swear from henceforth ye shall be my true servant, and to do nothing but that I shall command you. Will ye assure me this as ye be a true knight?'

'Yea,' said he, 'fair lady, by the faith of my body.'

'Well,' said she, 'now shall ye do with me what ye will; and now wit ye well ye are the knight in the world that I have most desire to.'

benome] taken away from   chafed] heated

And then two squires were commanded to make a bed in midst of the pavilion, and anon she was unclothed and laid therein. And then Sir Percival laid him down by her naked; and by adventure and grace he saw his sword lie on the earth naked, where in the pommel was a red cross and the sign of the crucifix therein, and bethought him on his knighthood and his promise made unto the good man beforehand; and then he made a sign of the cross in his forehead, and therewith the pavilion turned upside down, and then it changed unto a smoke and a black cloud. And then he dreaded sore and cried aloud, 'Fair sweet Lord Jesu Christ, let me not be shamed, which was nigh lost had not Thy good grace been.'

[10]

And then he looked unto her ship and saw her enter therein, which said, 'Sir Percival, ye have betrayed me!' And so she went with the wind roaring and yelling, that it seemed all the water burnt after her.

Then Sir Percival made great sorrow and drew his sword unto him, and said, 'Sithen my flesh will be my master, I shall punish it.' And therewith he rove himself through the thigh that the blood started about him,* and said, 'Ah, good Lord, take this in recompense of that I have misdone against Thee, Lord.'

So then he clothed him and armed him, and called himself, 'Wretch of all wretches, how nigh I was lost, and to have lost that I should never have gotten again, that was my virginity, for that may never be recovered after it is once lost.' And then he stopped his bleeding wounds with a piece of his shirt.

Thus as he made his moan he saw the same ship come from the orient that the good man was in the day before. And this noble knight was sore ashamed of himself, and therewith he fell in a swoon; and when he awoke he went unto him weakly, and there he saluted the good man.

And then he asked Sir Percival, 'How hast thou done sith I departed?'

'Sir,' said he, 'here was a gentlewoman, and led me into deadly sin.' And there he told him all together.

'Knew ye not that maid?' said the good man.

'Sir,' said he, 'nay, but well I wot the fiend sent her hither to shame me.'

'Ah, good knight,' said he, 'thou art a fool, for that gentlewoman was the master fiend of hell, which hath pousté over all other devils.

pousté] power

And that was the old lady that thou saw in thy vision riding on the serpent.'

Then he told Sir Percival how Our Lord Jesu Christ beat him out of heaven for his sin, which was the most brightest angel of heaven, and therefore he lost his heritage. 'And that was the champion that thou fought withal, which had overcome thee had not the grace of God been. Now, Sir Percival, beware, and take this for an example.'

And then the good man vanished. Then Sir Percival took his arms and entered into the ship, and so he departed from thence.

So leaveth this tale, and turneth unto Sir Lancelot.

Of Sir Lancelot

[xv.1] When the hermit had kept Sir Lancelot three days, then the hermit got him a horse, a helm, and a sword; and then he departed and rode until the hour of noon. And then he saw a little house, and when he came near he saw a little chapel. And there beside he saw an old man which was clothed all in white full richly; and then Sir Lancelot said, 'Sir, God save you.'*

'Sir,' said the good man, 'be ye not Sir Lancelot du Lake?'

'Yea, sir,' said he.

'Sir, what seek you in this country?'

'I go, sir, to seek the adventures of the Sangrail.'

'Well,' said he, 'seek ye it ye may well, but though it were here ye shall have no power to see it, no more than a blind man that should see a bright sword. And that is long on your sin, and else ye were more abler than any man living.'

And then Sir Lancelot began to weep.

Then said the good man, 'Were ye confessed since ye entered into the quest of the Sangrail?'

'Yea, sir,' said Sir Lancelot. 'Father, what shall I do?'

'Now,' said the good man, 'I require you take this hair and put it next thy skin, and it shall avail thee greatly.'

'Sir, then will I do it,' said Sir Lancelot.

'Also, sir, I charge thee that thou eat no flesh as long as ye be in the quest of the Sangrail, neither ye shall drink no wine, and that ye hear Mass daily and ye may come thereto.'

So he took the hair and put it upon him, and so departed at evensong and so rode into a forest; and there he met with a gentlewoman riding upon a white palfrey, and then she asked him, 'Sir knight, whither ride ye?'

'Certes, damosel,' said Sir Lancelot, 'I wot not whither I ride but as fortune leadeth me.'

'Ah, Sir Lancelot,' said she, 'I wot what adventure ye seek, for ye were beforetime nearer than ye be now, and yet shall ye see it more openly than ever ye did, and that shall ye understand in short time.'

long on] due to   hair] hair shirt

Then Sir Lancelot asked her where he might be harboured that night.

'Ye shall none find this day nor night, but tomorrow ye shall find harbour good, and ease of that ye be in doubt of.'

And then he commended her unto God, and so he rode till that he came to a cross, and took that for his host as for that night.

And so he put his horse to pasture, and did off his helm and his shield, [3] and made his prayers unto the cross that he never fall in deadly sin again; and so he laid him down to sleep. And anon as he was asleep, it befell him there a vision, that there came a man before him all becompassed with stars, and that man had a crown of gold on his head; and that man led in his fellowship seven kings and two knights, and all these worshipped the cross, kneeling upon their knees, holding up their hands toward the heaven. And all they said, 'Fair sweet Father of Heaven, come and visit us, and yield unto each of us as we have deserved.'

Then looked Sir Lancelot up to the heaven, and him seemed the clouds did open, and an old man came down with a company of angels and alit among them, and gave unto each his blessing and called them his servants and his good and true knights. And when this old man had said thus he came to one of the knights and said, 'I have lost all that I have set in thee, for thou hast ruled thee against me as a warrior and used wrong wars with vainglory for the pleasure of the world more than to please me, therefore thou shalt be confounded without thou yield me my treasure.'

All this vision saw Sir Lancelot at the cross. And on the morn he took his horse and rode till midday; and there by adventure he met with the same knight that took his horse, helm, and his sword when he slept when the Sangrail appeared afore the cross. So when Sir Lancelot saw him he saluted him not fair, but cried on high, 'Knight, keep thee, for thou didst me great unkindness.'

And then they put before them their spears, and Sir Lancelot came so fiercely that he smote him and his horse down to the earth, that he had nigh broken his neck. Then Sir Lancelot took the knight's horse that was his own beforehand, and descended from the horse he sat upon and mounted upon his horse, and tied the knight's own horse to a tree, that he might find that horse when that he was arisen. Then Sir Lancelot rode till night; and by adventure he met a hermit, and each of them saluted other. And there he rested with that good man all night, and gave his horse such as he might get.

Then said the good man unto Sir Lancelot, 'Of whence be ye?'

'Sir,' said he, 'I am of Arthur's court, and my name is Sir Lancelot du Lake, that am in the quest of the Sangrail. And therefore, sir, I pray you counsel me of a vision that I saw this night.' And so he told him all.

[4]   'Lo, Sir Lancelot,' said the good man, 'there might thou understand the high lineage that thou art come of, that thy vision betokeneth.'

[The hermit describes Lancelot's genealogy from the time of Joseph of Arimathea.]

And then Sir Lancelot and he went to supper, and so laid them to rest; and his hair pricked fast and grieved him sore, but he took it meekly and suffered the pain. And so on the morn he heard his Mass and took [5] his arms, and so took his leave and mounted upon his horse, and rode into a forest and held no highway. And as he looked before him he saw a fair plain, and beside that a fair castle, and before the castle were many pavilions of silk and of divers hue. And him seemed that he saw there five hundred knights riding on horseback, and there were two parties: they that were of the castle were all on black horses and their trappings black, and they that were without were all on white horses and trappings. So there began a great tournament, and each hurtled with other that it marvelled Sir Lancelot greatly. And at the last him thought they of the castle were put to the worse. Then thought Sir Lancelot for to help there the weaker party in increasing of his chivalry.

And so Sir Lancelot thrust in among the party of the castle, and smote down a knight, horse and man, to the earth; and then he rushed here and there and did many marvellous deeds of arms. And then he drew out his sword and struck many knights to the earth, that all that saw him marvelled that ever one knight might do so great deeds of arms.

But always the white knights held them nigh about Sir Lancelot for to tire him and wind him; and at the last Sir Lancelot was so weary of his great deeds that he might not lift up his arms for to give one stroke, that he weened never to have borne arms. And then they all took and led him away into a forest, and there made him to alight to rest him.

he weened never to have borne arms] he thought he would never be able to wield a weapon again

And then all the fellowship of the castle were overcome for the default of him.

Then they said all unto Sir Lancelot, 'Blessed be God that ye be now of our fellowship, for we shall hold you in our prison.' And so they left him with few words.

And then Sir Lancelot made great sorrow, 'For never or now was I never at tournament nor at jousts but I had the best. And now I am shamed, and am sure that I am more sinfuller than ever I was.'

Thus he rode sorrowing half a day, out of despair, till that he came into a deep valley. And when Sir Lancelot saw he might not ride up unto the mountain, he there alit under an apple tree, and there he left his helm and his shield and put his horse unto pasture; and then he laid him down to sleep. And then him thought there came an old man before him, which said, 'Ah, Lancelot, of evil wicked faith and poor belief, wherefore is thy will turned so lightly toward deadly sin?' And when he had said thus he vanished away, and Sir Lancelot wist not where he became.

Then he took his horse, and armed him; and as he rode by the high-way he saw a chapel where was a recluse, which had a window that she might see up to the altar.* And all aloud she called Sir Lancelot, for that he seemed a knight errant. And then he came, and she asked him what he was, and of what place, and where about he went to seek. And [6] then he told her all together word by word, and the truth how it befell him at the tournament; and after that he told her his vision that he had that night in his sleep.

'Ah, Lancelot,' said she, 'as long as ye were knight of earthly knight-hood ye were the most marvellous man of the world, and most adven-turous. Now,' said the lady, 'sithen ye be set among the knights of heavenly adventures, if adventure fall contrary have ye no marvel, for that tournament yesterday was but a tokening of Our Lord. And not for that there was no enchantment, for they at the tournament were earthly knights. Of these earthly knights which were clothed all in black, the covering betokeneth the sins whereof they be not confessed. And they with the covering of white betokeneth virginity, and they that hath chosen chastity; and thus was the quest begun in them. Then thou beheld the sinners and the good men, and when thou sawest the sinners overcome, thou inclined to that party for bobaunce and pride

bobaunce] boastfulness

of the world, and all that must be left in that quest. For in this quest thou shalt have many fellows, and thy betters. But anon thou turned to the sinners; and that caused thy misadventure, that thou should know good from vainglory of the world—it is not worth a pear. And for great pride thou madest great sorrow that thou hadst not overcome all the white knights, therefore God was wroth with you, for in this quest God loveth no such deeds; and that made the vision to say to thee that thou were of evil faith and of poor belief, the which will make thee to fall into the deep pit of hell if thou keep thee not better. Now have I warned thee of thy vainglory and of thy pride, that thou hast many times erred against thy Maker. Beware of everlasting pain, for of all earthly knights I have most pity of thee, for I know well thou hast not thy peer of any earthly sinful man.'

And so she commanded Sir Lancelot to dinner. And after dinner he took his horse and commended her to God, and so rode into a deep valley; and there he saw a river that hight Mortaise,* and through the water he must needs pass, the which was hideous. And then in the name of God he took it with good heart. And when he came over he saw an armed knight, horse and man all black as a bear. Without any word he smote Sir Lancelot's horse to the death; and so he passed on, and wist not where he was become. And then he took his helm and his shield, and thanked God of his adventure.

Here leaveth the tale of Sir Lancelot, and speaketh of Sir Gawain.

Of Sir Gawain and Sir Ector

When Sir Gawain was departed from his fellowship he rode long without any adventure, for he found not the tenth part of adventures as they were wont to have; for Sir Gawain rode from Whitsuntide till Michaelmas and found never adventure that pleased him. So on a day it befell that Gawain met with Sir Ector de Maris, and either made great joy of other; and so they told each other and complained them greatly that they could find no adventure.

'Truly,' said Sir Gawain, 'I am nigh weary of this quest, and loath I am to follow further in strange countries.'

'One thing marvelleth me much,' said Sir Ector. 'I have met with twenty knights that be fellows of mine, and all they complain as I do.'

'I have marvel', said Sir Gawain, 'where that Sir Lancelot, your brother, is.'

'Truly,' said Sir Ector, 'I cannot hear of him, nor of Sir Galahad, Sir Percival, and Sir Bors.'

'Let them be,' said Sir Gawain, 'for they four have no peers. And if one thing were not, Sir Lancelot had no fellow of an earthly man; but he is as we be, but if he take the more pain upon him.* But and these four be met together they will be loath that any man meet with them; for and they fail of the Sangrail, it is in waste of all the remnant to recover it.'

Thus Sir Ector and Sir Gawain rode more than eight days; and on a Saturday they found an ancient chapel which was wasted, that there seemed no man nor woman thither repaired. And there they alit and set their spears at the door; and so they entered into the chapel and there made their orisons a great while. And then they sat them down in the sieges of the chapel; and as they spoke of one thing and of other, for heaviness they fell asleep, and there befell them both marvellous adventures.

Sir Gawain him seemed he came into a meadow full of herbs and flowers, and there he saw a rack of bulls, a hundred and fifty, that were proud and black, save three of them were all white, and one had a black

in waste of all the remnant] wasted time for all the rest of us   sieges] seats
rack] a number sufficient for a feeding-rack

spot. And the other two were so fair and so white that they might be no whiter; and these three bulls which were so fair were tied with two strong cords. And the remnant of the bulls said among them, 'Go we hence to seek better pasture.' And so some went, and some came again, but they were so meagre that they might not stand upright. And of the bulls that were so white, that one came again, and no more. But when this white bull was come again and among these others, there rose up a great cry for lack of viand* that failed them; and so they departed, one here and another there. This vision befell Gawain that night.

[2] But to Sir Ector de Maris befell another vision, the contrary. For it seemed him that his brother Sir Lancelot and he alit out of a chair and leapt upon two horses, and the one said to the other, 'Go we to seek that we shall not find.' And him thought that a man beat Sir Lancelot, and despoiled him, and clothed him in another array which was all full of knots, and set him upon an ass.* And in the meanwhile he trowed that himself, Sir Ector, rode till that he came to a rich man's house where there was a wedding. And there he saw a king which said, 'Sir knight, here is no place for you.' And then he turned again unto the chair that he came from.

And so within a while both Sir Gawain and Sir Ector awoke, and either told other of their vision, which marvelled them greatly.

'Truly,' said Ector, 'I shall never be merry till I hear tidings of my brother Sir Lancelot.'

So as they sat thus talking they saw a hand showing unto the elbow, and was covered with red samite, and upon that a bridle not right rich, that held within the fist a great candle which burned right clear; and so passed before them and entered into the chapel, and then vanished away they wist not whither. And anon came down a voice which said, 'Knights of full evil faith and of poor belief, these two things have failed you, and therefore ye may not come to the adventures of the Sangrail.'

Then first spoke Sir Gawain and said, 'Sir Ector, have ye heard these words?'

'Yea, truly,' said Sir Ector, 'I heard all. Now go we,' said Sir Ector, 'unto some hermit that will tell us of our vision, for it seemeth me we labour all in waste.'

And so they departed and rode into a valley; and there they met with a squire which rode on a hackney, and anon they saluted him fair.

trowed] believed

'Sir,' said Sir Gawain, 'can thou teach us to any hermit?'

'Sir, here is one in a little mountain; but it is so rough there may no horse go thither, and therefore ye must go on foot, and there ye shall find a poor house. And therein is Nacien the hermit, which is the holiest man in this country.'

And so they departed either from other. And then in a valley they met with a knight all armed, which proffered them to fight and joust as soon as he saw them.

'In the name of God,' said Sir Gawain, 'for sithen I departed from Camelot there was none that proffered me to joust but once, and now.'

'Sir,' said Sir Ector, 'let me joust with him.'

'Nay, ye shall not; but if I be beaten, it shall not then forthink me if ye go to him.'

And then either embraced other to joust; and so they came together as fast as they might run, that they brast their shields and mails, and the one more than the other. But Sir Gawain was wounded in the left side, and this other knight was smitten through the breast that the spear came out on the other side. And so they fell both out of their saddles, and in the falling they broke both their spears. And anon Sir Gawain arose and set his hand to his sword, and cast his shield before him. But all for naught was it, for the knight had no power to arise against him.

Then said Sir Gawain, 'Ye must yield you as an overcome man, or else I must slay you.'

'Ah, sir knight,' he said, 'I am but dead! Therefore for God's sake and of your gentleness, lead me here unto an abbey that I may receive my Creator.'

'Sir,' said Sir Gawain, 'I know no house of religion here nigh.'

'Sir, set me on a horse before you, and I shall teach you.'

So Sir Gawain set him up in the saddle, and he leapt up behind him to sustain him; and so they came to the abbey, and there were well received. And anon he was unarmed, and received his Creator. Then he prayed Sir Gawain to draw out the truncheon of the spear out of his body. Then Sir Gawain asked him what he was.

'Sir,' he said, 'I am of King Arthur's court, and was a fellow of the Round Table, and we were sworn together; and now Sir Gawain, thou

---

it shall not then forthink me] I shall not mind   my Creator] i.e. the last rites hast slain me. And my name is Sir Uwain le Avoutres, that sometime was son unto King Uriens; and I was in the quest of the Sangrail. And now God forgive thee, for it shall be ever rehearsed that the one sworn brother hath slain the other.'

[3]   'Alas,' said Gawain, 'that ever this misadventure befell me.'

'No force,' said Sir Uwain, 'sithen I shall die this death, of a much more worshipfuller man's hand might I not die. But when ye come to the court, recommend me unto my lord Arthur and to all them that be left alive. And for old brotherhood think on me.'

Then began Sir Gawain to weep, and also Sir Ector. And then Sir Uwain bade him draw out the truncheon of the spear; and then Sir Gawain drew it out, and anon departed the soul from the body. Then Sir Gawain and Sir Ector buried him as them ought to bury a king's son, and made it written upon his tomb what was his name and by whom he was slain.

Then departed Sir Gawain and Sir Ector as heavy as they might for their misadventure, and so rode till they came to the rough mountain, and there they tied their horses and went on foot to the hermitage. And when they were come up they saw a poor house, and beside the chapel a little curtilage where Nacien the hermit gathered worts to his meat, as he which had tasted no other meat of a great while. And when he saw the errant knights he came to them and saluted them, and they him again.

'Fair lords,' said he, 'what adventure brought you hither?'

Then said Sir Gawain, 'To speak with you for to be confessed.'

'Sir,' said the hermit, 'I am ready.'

Then they told him so much that he wist well what they were; and then he thought to counsel them if he might.

Then began Sir Gawain and told him of his vision that he had in the chapel; and Ector told him all as it is before rehearsed.

'Sir,' said the hermit unto Sir Gawain, 'by the fair meadow and the rack therein ought to be understood the Round Table, and by the meadow ought to be understood humility and patience: those be the things which be always green and quick. At the rack ate a hundred and fifty bulls; but they ate not in the meadow, for if they had, their hearts should have been set in humility and patience; and the bulls were proud and black save only three. And by the bulls is understood the

No force] No matter   curtilage] enclosed yard   worts to his meat] green
plants for his food   quick] living

fellowship of the Round Table, which for their sin and their wickedness be black: blackness is as much to say without good virtues or works. And the three bulls which were white save only one had been spotted, the two white betoken Sir Galahad and Sir Percival, for they be maidens and clean without spot; and the third that had a spot signifieth Sir Bors de Ganis, which trespassed but once in his virginity, but sithen he keepeth himself so well in chastity that all is forgiven him and his misdeeds. And why those three were tied by the necks, they be three knights in virginity and chastity, and there is no pride smitten in them.

'And the black bulls which said, "Go we hence," they were those which at Pentecost at the high feast took upon them the quest of the Sangrail without confession: they might not enter in the meadow of humility and patience. And therefore they turned into waste countries, that signifieth death, for there shall die many of them. For each of them shall slay other for sin, and they that shall escape shall be so meagre that it shall be marvel to see them. And of the three bulls without spot, the one shall come again, and the other two never.'

Then spake Nacien unto Sir Ector, 'Sooth it is that Lancelot and ye [4] came down off one chair: the chair betokeneth mastership and lordship which ye two came down from. But ye two knights,' said the hermit, 'ye go to seek that ye shall not find, that is the Sangrail; for it is the secret things of Our Lord Jesu Christ. But what is to mean that Sir Lancelot fell down off his horse: he hath left pride and taken to humility, for he hath cried mercy loud for his sin and sore repented him, and Our Lord hath clothed him in his clothing which is full of knots, that is the hair that he weareth daily. And the ass that he rode upon is a beast of humility, for God would not ride upon no steed, nor upon no palfrey, in an example that an ass betokeneth meekness;* that thou saw Sir Lancelot ride in thy sleep.

'Now will I tell you what betokeneth the hand with the candle and the bridle: that is to understand the Holy Ghost where charity is ever. And the bridle signifieth abstinence, for when she is bridled in a Christian man's heart she holdeth him so short that he falleth not in deadly sin. And the candle which showeth clearness and light signifieth the right way of Jesu Christ. And when they went he said, "Knights of poor faith and of wicked belief, these three things failed, charity, abstinence, and truth: therefore ye may not attain this adventure of the Sangrail." '

'Sir,' said Sir Gawain, 'it seemeth me by your words that for our sins [5] it will not avail us to travel in this quest.'

'Truly,' said the good man, 'there be a hundred such as ye be shall never prevail but to have shame.'

And when they had heard these words they commended him unto God. Then the good man called Sir Gawain and said, 'It is long time passed sith that ye were made knight, and never since served thou thy Maker; and now thou art so old a tree that in thee is neither leaf nor grass nor fruit. Wherefore bethink thee that thou yield to Our Lord the bare rind, sith the fiend hath the leaves and the fruit.'

'Sir,' said Sir Gawain, 'and I had leisure I would speak with you; but my fellow Sir Ector is gone, and abideth me yonder beneath the hill.'

'Well,' said the good man, 'thou were better to be counselled.'

Then departed Sir Gawain and came to Sir Ector, and so took their horses and rode till that they came to a forester's house, which harboured them right well. And on the morn they departed from their host, and rode long or they could find any adventure.

Now turneth this tale unto Sir Bors de Ganis.

rind] bark

Of Sir Bors de Ganis

When Sir Bors was departed from Camelot he met with a religious [6] man riding on an ass, and anon Sir Bors saluted him. And anon the good man knew that he was one of the knights errant that was in the quest of the Sangrail.

'What are ye?' said the good man.

'Sir,' said he, 'I am a knight that fain would be counselled, that is entered into the quest of the Sangrail; for he shall have much earthly worship that may bring it to an end.'

'Certes,' said the good man, 'that is sooth without fail, for he shall be the best knight of the world and the fairest of the fellowship. But wit you well there shall none attain it but by cleanness, that is pure confession.'

So rode they together till that they came unto a little hermitage, and there he prayed Sir Bors to dwell all that night. And so he put off his armour, and prayed him that he might be confessed; and so they went into the chapel, and there he was clean confessed. And so they ate bread and drank water together.

'Now,' said the good man, 'I pray thee that thou eat none other till that thou sit at the table where the Sangrail shall be.'

'Sir,' said he, 'I agree me thereto; but how know ye that I shall sit there?'

'Yes,' said the good man, 'that know I well, but there shall be but few of your fellows with you.'

'All is welcome,' said Sir Bors, 'that God sendeth me.'

'Also,' said the good man, 'instead of a shirt, and in sign of chastisement, ye shall wear a garment; therefore I pray you do off all your clothes and your shirt.'

And so he did; and then he took him a scarlet coat, so that should be his instead of his shirt till he had fulfilled the quest of the Sangrail.* And this good man found him in so marvellous a life and so stable that he felt he was never greatly corrupt in fleshly lusts, but in one time that he begat Helian le Blanc.

Then he armed him and took his leave, and so departed. And so a little from thence he looked up into a tree, and there he saw a passing great bird upon that old tree, and it was passing dry, without leaf; so he sat above, and had birds which were dead for hunger. So at the last he smote himself with his beak, which was great and sharp, and so the great bird bled so fast that that he died among his birds; and the young birds took life by the blood of the great bird. When Sir Bors saw this he wist well it was a great tokening; for when he saw the great bird arose not, then he took his horse and yode his way. And so by adventure by evensong time, he came to a strong tower and a high, [7] and there was he harboured gladly. And when he was unarmed they led him into a high tower where was a lady, young, lusty, and fair; and she received him with great joy and made him to sit down by her. And anon he was set to supper with flesh and many dainties. But when Sir Bors saw that, he bethought him on his penance, and bade a squire to bring him water. And so he brought him, and he made sops therein and ate them.

'Ah,' said the lady, 'I trow ye like not your meat.'

'Yes, truly,' said Sir Bors, 'God thank you, madam, but I may eat no other meat today.'

Then she spoke no more as at that time, for she was loath to displease him. Then after supper they spoke of one thing and of other.

So with that there came a squire and said, 'Madam, ye must purvey you tomorrow for a champion, for else your sister will have this castle and also your lands, except ye can find a knight that will fight tomorrow in your quarrel against Sir Pridam le Noir.'

Then she made great sorrow and said, 'Ah, Lord God, wherefore granted Ye me to hold my land whereof I should now be disinherited without reason and right?'

And when Sir Bors had heard her say thus, he said, 'I shall comfort you.'

'Sir,' said she, 'I shall tell you. There was here a king that hight Aniause, which held all this land in his keeping. So it mishapped he loved a gentlewoman a great deal elder than I; and so he took her all this land in her keeping and all his men to govern, and she brought up many evil customs whereby she put to death a great part of his kinsmen. And when he saw that, he commanded her out of this land, and betook it me, and all this land in my domains. But anon as that worthy king was dead, this other lady began to war upon me, and hath destroyed many

betook] entrusted

of my men and turned them against me, that I have wellnigh no man left me; and I have nought else but this high tower that she left me. And yet she hath promised me to have this tower, without I can find a knight to fight with her champion.'

'Now tell me,' said Sir Bors, 'what is that Pridam le Noir?'

'Sir, he is the most doubted man of this land.'

'Then may ye send her word that ye have found a knight that shall fight with that Pridam le Noir in God's quarrel and yours.'

So that lady was then glad, and sent her word that she was provided. And so that night Sir Bors had passing good cheer; but in no bed he would come, but laid him on the floor, nor never would do otherwise till that he had met with the quest of the Sangrail.

And anon as he was asleep him befell a vision, that there came two birds, the one white as a swan, and the other was marvellous black; but he was not so great as was the other, but in the likeness of a raven. Then the white bird came to him and said, 'And thou wouldst give me meat and serve me, I should give thee all the riches of the world, and I shall make thee as fair and as white as I am.' So the white bird departed; and then came the black bird to him and said, 'And thou serve me tomorrow and have me in no despite though I be black, for wit thou well that more availeth my blackness than the other's whiteness.' And then he departed.

Then he had another vision: that he came to a great place which seemed a chapel, and there he found a chair set, on the left side of which was a worm-eaten and feeble tree beside it; and on the right hand were two flowers like a lily, and the one would have benome the others their whiteness. But a good man parted them, that they touched not one another;* and then out of each flower came out many flowers, and fruit great plenty. Then him thought the good man said, 'Should not he do great folly that would let these two flowers perish for to succour the rotten tree, that it fell not to the earth?'

'Sir,' said he, 'it seemeth me that this wood might not avail.'

'Now keep thee,' said the good man, 'that thou never see such adventure befall thee.'

---

without] unless   doubted] feared   more availeth my blackness] my blackness is of greater use   the one would have benome the others] [the tree] would have taken away from [the flowers]   might not avail] is good for nothing

Then he awoke and made a sign of the cross in midst of the forehead, and so he arose and clothed him. And anon there came the lady of the place, and she saluted him and he her again, and so went to a chapel and heard their service. And anon there came a company of knights that the lady had sent for to lead Sir Bors unto the battle. Then asked he his arms; and when he was armed, she prayed him to take a little morsel to dine.

'Nay, madam,' said he, 'that shall I not do till I have done my battle, by the grace of God.'

And so he leapt upon his horse and departed, and all the knights and men with him.

And as soon as these two ladies met together, she which Sir Bors should fight for, she complained her and said, 'Madam, ye have done great wrong to bereave me of my lands that King Aniause gave me, and full loath I am there should be any battle.'

'Ye shall not choose,' said the other, 'or else let your knight withdraw him.'

Then there was the cry made, which party had the better of the two knights, that his lady should rejoice all the lands.

Then departed the one knight here and the other there; then they came together with such raundom that they pierced their shields and their habergeons and their spears flew in pieces, and they sore wounded. Then hurtled they together so that they beat each other to the earth, and their horses between their legs; and anon they arose and set hands to their swords, and smote each one other upon their heads that they made great wounds and deep, that the blood went out of their bodies. For there found Sir Bors greater defence in that knight more than he weened; for this Sir Pridam was a passing good knight and wounded Sir Bors full evil, and he him again, but ever Sir Pridam held the stour alike hard. That perceived Sir Bors, and suffered him till he was nigh attaint; and then he ran upon him more and more, and the other went back for dread of death. So in his withdrawing he fell upright; and Sir Bors drew his helm so strongly that he rent it from his head and gave him many sad strokes with the flat of his sword upon the visage, and bade him yield him or he should slay him.

---

rejoice] enjoy   raundom] violence   held the stour] maintained the
onslaught   attaint] exhausted   upright] on his back   sad] heavy

Then he cried him mercy and said, 'Fair knight, for God's love slay me not, and I shall ensure thee never to war against thy lady, but be always toward her.' So Sir Bors gave him his life, and anon the old lady fled with all her knights.

Then called Sir Bors all those that held lands of his lady, and said he [9] should destroy them but if they did such service unto her as longed to their lands. So they did her homage, and they that would not were chased out of their lands, that it befell that the young lady came to her estate again by the mighty prowess of Sir Bors de Ganis.

So when all the country was well set in peace, then Sir Bors took his leave and departed; and she thanked him greatly, and would have given him great gifts, but he refused it.

Then he rode all that day till night, and so he came to a harbour to a lady which knew him well enough and made of him great joy. So on the morn, as soon as the day appeared, Sir Bors departed from thence, and so rode into a forest unto the hour of midday; and there befell him a marvellous adventure. So he met at the departing of the two ways two knights that led Sir Lionel, his brother, all naked, bound upon a strong hackney, and his hands bound before his breast. And each of them held in their hands thorns wherewith they went beating him so sore that the blood trailed down more than in a hundred places of his body, so that he was all bloody before and behind; but he said never a word, as he which was great of heart suffered all that they did to him as though he had felt no anguish. And anon Sir Bors dressed him to rescue him that was his brother.

And so he looked upon the other side of him, and saw a knight which brought a fair gentlewoman and would have set her in the thick of the forest for to have been the more surer out of the way from them that sought her. And she which was nothing assured cried with a high voice, 'Saint Mary, succour your maid.'

And anon as she saw Sir Bors she deemed him a knight of the Round Table; then she conjured him by the faith that he owed 'unto Him in whose service thou art entered, for King Arthur's sake which I suppose made thee knight, that thou help me and suffer me not to be shamed of this knight.'

---

toward her] on her side   for to have been the more surer] in order to be more safely   nothing assured] far from safety

When Sir Bors heard her say thus, he had so much sorrow that he wist not what to do. 'For if I let my brother be in adventure he must be slain, and that would I not for all the earth. And if I help not the maid she is shamed, and she shall lose her virginity which she shall never get again.' Then lifted he up his eyes and said weeping, 'Fair sweet Lord Jesu Christ whose creature I am, keep me Sir Lionel my brother that these knights slay him not; and for pity of You and for mild Mary's sake, I shall succour this maid.'*

[10]   Then dressed he him unto the knight which had the gentlewoman, and then he cried, 'Sir knight, let your hand off your maiden, or ye be but dead.'

And then he set down the maiden, and was armed at all pieces save he lacked his spear. Then he dressed his shield and drew his sword; and Sir Bors smote him so hard that it went through his shield and habergeon on the left shoulder, and through great strength he beat him down to the earth. And at the pulling out of Sir Bors' spear he there swooned.

Then came Sir Bors to the maid and said, 'How seemeth it you? Of this knight ye be delivered at this time.'

'Now sir,' said she, 'I pray you lead me there as this knight had me.'

'So shall I do gladly;' and took the horse of the wounded knight and set the gentlewoman upon him, and so brought her as she desired.

'Sir knight,' said she, 'ye have better sped than ye weened, for and I had lost my maidenhood, five hundred men should have died therefor.'

'What knight was he that had you in the forest?'

'By my faith, he is my cousin. So wot I never with what engine the fiend enchafed him, for yesterday he took me from my father privily; for I nor none of my father's men mistrusted him not. And if he had had my maidenhood he had died for the sin of his body, and shamed and dishonoured for ever.'

Thus as she stood talking with him there came twelve knights seeking after her, and anon she told them all how Sir Bors had delivered her. Then they made great joy and besought him to come to her father, a great lord, and he should be right welcome.

'Truly,' said Sir Bors, 'that may not be at this time, for I have a great

adventure] jeopardy   there as this knight had me] to where this knight captured me   with what engine the fiend enchafed him] by what tricks the devil aroused him

adventure to do in this country.' So he commended them to God and departed.

Then Sir Bors rode after Sir Lionel his brother, by the trace of their horses. Thus he rode seeking a great while; and anon he overtook a man clothed in a religious weed, and rode on a strong black horse blacker than a berry, and said, 'Sir knight, what seek you?'

'Sir,' said he, 'I seek my brother, that I saw erewhile beaten with two knights.'

'Ah, Sir Bors, discomfort you not, nor fall not into no wanhope for I shall tell you tidings, such as they be, for truly he is dead.'

Then showed he him a new-slain body lying in a bush, and it seemed him well that it was the body of Sir Lionel his brother; and then he made such sorrow that he fell to the earth in a swoon, and so lay a great while there. And when he came to himself he said, 'Fair brother, sith the company of you and me is departed shall I never have joy in my heart. And now He which I have taken unto my master, He be my help!' And when he had said thus he took his body lightly in his arms and put it upon the arson of his saddle. And then he said to the man, 'Can ye show me any chapel nigh where that I may bury this body?'

'Come on,' said he, 'here is one fast by.'

And so long they rode till they saw a fair tower, and before it there seemed an old feeble chapel. And then they alit both, and put him in the tomb of marble.

'Now leave we him here,' said the good man, 'and go we to our har-   [11]
bour, till tomorrow we come here again to do him service.'

'Sir,' said Sir Bors, 'be ye a priest?'

'Yea, forsooth,' said he.

'Then I pray you tell me a dream that befell me the last night.'

'Say on,' said he.

So he began so much to tell him of the great bird in the forest, and after told him of his birds one white and another black, and of the rotten tree and of the white flowers.

'Sir, I shall tell you a part now, and the other deal tomorrow. The white fowl betokeneth a gentlewoman fair and rich, which loved thee paramours and hath loved thee long. And if that thou warn her love she

weed] habit   nor fall not . . . tell you tidings] don't fall into despair on account of the news I tell you   arson] saddle-bow   feeble] falling into ruin deal] part   loved thee paramours] desired you sexually   warn] refuse

shall die anon; and if thou have no pity on her, that signifieth the great bird which shall make thee to warn her. Now for no fear that thou hast, nor for no dread that thou hast of God, thou shalt not warn her; for thou wouldst not do it for to be held chaste, for to conquer the love of the vainglory of the world.* For that shall befall thee now and thou warn her, that Sir Lancelot, the good knight, thy cousin, shall die. And then shall men say that thou art a manslayer, both of thy brother Sir Lionel and of thy cousin Sir Lancelot—which thou might have rescued easily, but thou went to rescue a maid which pertaineth nothing to thee. Now look thou whether it had been greater harm, of thy brother's death, or else to have suffered her to have lost her maidenhood.' Then said he, 'Now hast thou heard the tokens of thy dream?'

'Yea,' said Sir Bors.

'Then is it by thy fault if Sir Lancelot thy cousin die.'

'Sir,' said Sir Bors, 'that were me loath, for there is nothing in the world but I had liever do it than to see my lord Sir Lancelot die by my fault.'

'Choose ye now the one or the other.'

Then he led him into the high tower, and there he found knights and ladies that said he was welcome; and so they unarmed him, and when he was in his doublet they brought him a mantle furred with ermine and put it about him. So they made him such cheer that he had forgotten his sorrow; and anon came out of a chamber unto him the fairest lady that ever he saw, and more richer beseen than ever was Queen Guenivere or any other estate.

'Lo,' said they, 'Sir Bors, here is the lady unto whom we owe all our service; and I trow she be the richest lady and the fairest of the world, which loveth you best above all other knights, for she will have no knight but you.'

And when he understood that language he was abashed. Not for that she saluted him, and he her; and then they sat down together and spoke of many things, in so much that she besought him to be her love, for she had loved him above all earthly men, and she should make him richer than ever was man of his age.

When Sir Bors understood her words he was right evil at ease, but in no wise would he break his chastity, and so he wist not how to answer her.

look thou whether it] consider which   tokens] symbolism   age] time

'Alas, Sir Bors,' said she, 'will ye not do my will?'

'Madam,' said he, 'there is no lady in this world whose will I would fulfil as of this thing. She ought not desire it, for my brother lieth dead which was slain right late.'

'Ah, Sir Bors,' said she, 'I have loved you long for the great beauty I have seen in you and the great hardiness that I have heard of you, that needs ye must lie by me tonight; therefore I pray you grant me.'

'Truly,' said he, 'I shall do it in no manner wise.'

Then anon she made him such sorrow as though she would have died.

'Well, Sir Bors,' said she, 'unto this have ye brought me, nigh to mine end.' And therewith she took him by the hand and bade him behold her. 'And ye shall see how I shall die for your love.'

And he said then, 'I shall it never see.'

Then she departed and went up into a high battlement, and led with her twelve gentlewomen; and when they were above, one of the gentlewomen cried, 'Ah, Sir Bors, gentle knight, have mercy on us all, and suffer my lady to have her will; and if ye do not we must suffer death with our lady, for to fall down off this high tower. And if ye suffer us thus to die for so little a thing, all ladies and gentlewomen will say you dishonour.'

Then looked he upward and saw they seemed all ladies of great estate, and richly and well beseen. Then had he of them great pity; not for that he was not uncounselled in himself that he had liever they all had lost their souls than he his soul.* And with that they fell all at once unto the earth; and when he saw that, he was all abashed and had thereof great marvel. And with that he blessed his body and his visage.

And anon he heard a great noise and a great cry, as all the fiends of hell had been about him; and therewith he saw neither tower, lady, nor gentlewoman, nor no chapel where he brought his brother to. Then held he up both his hands to the heaven and said, 'Fair sweet lord, Father and God in Heaven, I am grievously escaped!' And then he took his arms and his horse and set him on his way.

And anon he heard a clock smite on his right hand; and thither he came to an abbey which was closed with high walls, and there was he let in. And anon they supposed that he was one of the knights of the Round Table that was in the quest of the Sangrail, so they led him into a chamber and unarmed him.

'Sirs,' said Sir Bors, 'if there be any holy man in this house, I pray you let me speak with him.'

Then one of them led him unto the abbot, which was in a chapel. And then Sir Bors saluted him and he him again.

'Sir,' said Sir Bors, 'I am a knight errant;' and told him the adventures which he had seen.

'Sir knight,' said the abbot, 'I wot not what ye be, for I weened that a knight of your age might not have been so strong in the grace of Our Lord Jesu Christ. Not for that, ye shall go unto your rest, for I will not counsel you this day: it is too late. And tomorrow I shall counsel you as I can.'

[13]   And that night was Sir Bors served richly, and on the morn early he heard Mass. And then the abbot came to him and bade him good morrow, and Sir Bors to him again; and then he told him he was fellow of the quest of the Sangrail, and how he had charge of the holy man to eat bread and water.

'Then Our Lord showed him unto you in the likeness of a fowl, that suffered great anguish for us when He was put upon the cross and bled His heart blood for mankind: there was the token and the likeness of the Sangrail that appeared before you, for the blood that the great fowl bled raised the chicks from death to life.* And by the bare tree betokeneth the world, which is naked and needy, without fruit but if it come of Our Lord.

'Also the lady for whom ye fought: and King Aniause, which was lord thereto, betokeneth Jesu Christ which is king of the world. And that ye fought with the champion for the lady, thus it betokeneth: when ye took the battle for the lady, by her shall ye understand the law of Jesu Christ and Holy Church; and by the other lady ye shall understand the Old Law and the fiend, which all day warreth against Holy Church. Therefore ye did your battle with right, for ye be Jesu Christ's knight, therefore ye ought to be defenders of Holy Church. And by the black bird might ye understand Holy Church, which sayeth "I am black,"* but he is fair. And by the white bird may men understand the fiend; and I shall tell you how the swan is white without and black within: it is hypocrisy, which is without yellow or pale, and seemeth, without, the servants of Jesu Christ, but they be within so horrible of filth and sin, and beguile the world so evil.

'Also when the fiend appeared to you in likeness of a man of religion and blamed thee that thou left thy brother for a lady, and he led thee where thou seemed thy brother was slain—but he is yet alive; and all

was for to put thee in error, and to bring thee into wanhope and lechery, for he knew thou were tender hearted, and all was for thou
shouldst not find the adventure of the Sangrail. And the third
fowl betokeneth the strong battle against the fair ladies, which were all
devils.

'Also the dry tree and the white lilies: the sere tree betokeneth thy
brother Sir Lionel, which is dry without virtue, and therefore men
ought to call him the rotten tree and the worm-eaten tree, for he is a
murderer and doth contrary to the order of knighthood. And the two
white flowers signify two maidens: the one is a knight which ye
wounded the other day, and the other is the gentlewoman which ye rescued; and why the one flower drew nigh the other, that was the knight
which would have defouled her and himself both. And Sir Bors, ye had
been a great fool and in great peril for to have seen the two flowers perish for to succour the rotten tree, for and they had sinned together they
had been damned; and for ye rescued them both, men might call you a
very knight and the servant of Jesu Christ.'

Then went Sir Bors from thence and commended the abbot to God. [14]
And then he rode all that day, and harboured with an old lady; and on
the morn he rode to a castle in a valley, and there he met with a yeoman
going a great pace toward a forest.

'Say me,' said Sir Bors, 'canst thou tell me of any adventure?'

'Sir,' said he, 'here shall be under this castle a great and a marvellous
tournament.'

'Of what folks shall it be?' said Sir Bors.

'The Earl of Plains shall be on the one party, and the Lady's nephew
of Hervin on the other party.'

Then Sir Bors thought to be there to assay if he might meet with his
brother Sir Lionel, or any other of his fellowship which were in the
quest of the Sangrail. Then he turned to a hermitage that was in the
entry of the forest; and when he was come thither he found there
Sir Lionel his brother, which sat all unarmed at the entry of the chapel
door for to abide there harbour till on the morn that the tournament
should be. And when Sir Bors saw him he had great joy of him, that no
man could tell of greater joy. And then he alit off his horse and said,
'Fair sweet brother, when came ye hither?'

wanhope] despair   sere] withered   very] true   abide there harbour]
keep lodging there

And as Sir Lionel saw him he said, 'Ah, Sir Bors, ye may not make no avaunt, but as for you I might have been slain. When ye saw two knights lead me away beating me, ye left me to succour a gentlewoman, and suffered me in peril of death; for never erst did no brother to another so great an untruth. And for that misdeed I ensure you now but death, for well have ye deserved it. Therefore keep you from me from henceforward, and that shall ye find as soon as I am armed.'

When Sir Bors understood his brother's wrath, he kneeled down before him to the earth and cried him mercy, holding up both his hands, and prayed him to forgive him his evil will.

'Nay, nay,' said Sir Lionel, 'that shall never be and I may have the higher hand, that I make my vow to God: thou shalt have death, for it were pity ye lived any longer.'

Right so he went in and took his harness, and lighted upon his horse and came before him and said, 'Sir Bors, keep thee from me, for I shall do to thee as I would do to a felon or a traitor; for ye be the untruest knight that ever came out of so worthy a house as was King Bors' de Ganis, which was our father. Therefore start upon thy horse, and so shalt thou be most at thy advantage. And but if thou wilt, I will run upon thee there as thou art on foot, and so the shame shall be mine and the harm yours; but of that shame reck I nought.'

When Sir Bors saw that he must fight with his brother or else to die, he wist not what to do; so his heart counselled him not thereto, inasmuch as Sir Lionel was his elder brother, wherefore he ought to bear him reverence. Yet kneeled he down again before Sir Lionel's horse's feet and said, 'Fair sweet brother, have mercy upon me and slay me not, and have in remembrance the great love which ought to be between us two.'

So whatsoever Sir Bors said to Sir Lionel he recked not, for the fiend had brought him in such a will that he should slay him. So when Sir Lionel saw he would do none other, nor would not rise to give him battle, he rushed over him so that he smote Sir Bors with his horse's feet upward to the earth, and hurt him so sore that he swooned for distress which he felt in himself to have died without confession. So when Sir Lionel saw this, he alit off his horse to have smitten off his head; and so he took him by the helm and would have rent it from his head.

---

avaunt] boast   erst] before   and I may have the higher hand] if I can get the upper hand   but if thou wilt] if you will not

Therewith came the hermit running unto him, which was a good man and of great age, and well had heard all the words. He leapt between them, and so fell down upon Sir Bors, and said unto Sir Lionel, [15] 'Ah gentle knight, have mercy upon me and upon thy brother! For if thou slay him thou shalt be dead of that sin; and that were great sorrow, for he is one of the worthiest knights of the world and of best conditions.'

'So God me help, sir priest, but if ye flee from him I shall slay you, and he shall never the sooner be quit.'

'Certes,' said the good man, 'I had liever ye slay me than him, for as for my death shall not be great harm, not half so much as will be for his.'

'Well,' said Sir Lionel, 'I am agreed,' and set his hand to his sword and smote him so hard that his head yode off backward. And not for that he recovered him not of his evil will, but took his brother by the helm and unlaced it to have smitten off his head, and had slain him had not a fellow of his of the Round Table come, whose name was called Sir Colgrevance, that came thither as Our Lord's will would; and when he saw the good man slain he marvelled much what it might be. And then he beheld Sir Lionel that would have slain his brother, Sir Bors, which he loved right well. Then started he down and took Sir Lionel by the shoulders and drew him strongly aback from Sir Bors, and said to Sir Lionel, 'Will ye slay your brother, one the worthiest knight of the world? That should no good man suffer.'

'Why so?' said Sir Lionel, 'will ye let me thereof? For if ye entermete thereof, I shall slay you too, and him thereafter.'

'Why,' said Sir Colgrevance, 'is this sooth that ye will slay him?'

'Yea, slay him will I, whoso say the contrary, for he hath done so much against me that he hath well deserved it;' and so ran upon him, and would have smitten off the head.

And so Sir Colgrevance ran betwixt them, and said, 'And ye be so hardy to do so more, we two shall meddle together.'

So when Sir Lionel understood his words, he took his shield before him, and asked him what that he was.

'Sir, my name is Sir Colgrevance, one of his fellows.'

Then Sir Lionel defied him, and so he started upon him and gave him a great stroke through the helm. Then he drew his sword, for he

he shall never the sooner be quit] he still won't escape   let] prevent
entermete] interfere   meddle] fight

was a passing good knight, and defended him right manfully. And so long dured there the battle that Sir Bors sat up all anguishly and beheld Sir Colgrevance, the good knight that fought with his brother for his quarrel. Thereof he was full heavy, and thought if Sir Colgrevance slew his brother he should never have joy; also, and if his brother slew Sir Colgrevance, 'the same shame should ever be mine.'

Then would he have risen to have parted them, but he had not so much might to stand on foot. And so he abode so long that Sir Colgrevance was overthrown, for this Sir Lionel was of great chivalry and passing hardy; for he had pierced the hauberk and the helm so sore that he abode but death, for he had lost much blood that it was marvel that he might stand upright. Then beheld he Sir Bors which sat dressing upward himself, and said, 'Ah, Sir Bors, why come ye not to rescue me out of peril of death, wherein I have put me to succour you which were right now nigh death?'

'Certes,' said Sir Lionel, 'that shall not avail you, for none of you shall be other's warrant, but ye shall die both of my hand.'

When Sir Bors heard that he said so much, he arose and put on his helm. And then he perceived first the hermit priest which was slain; then made he a marvellous sorrow upon him.

[16]   Then Sir Colgrevance cried often upon Sir Bors and said, 'Why will ye let me die here for your sake? No force, sir, if it please you that I shall die, the death shall please me the better; for to save a worthier man might I never receive the death.'

With that word Sir Lionel smote off the helm from his head. And when Sir Colgrevance saw that he might not escape, then he said, 'Fair sweet Jesu Christ, that I have misdone, have mercy upon my soul. For such sorrow that my heart suffereth for goodness and for alms-deed that I would have done here, be to me alliegement of penance unto my soul's health.'

And so at these words Sir Lionel smote him so sore that he bore him dead to the earth. And when he had slain Sir Colgrevance he ran upon his brother as a fiendly man, and gave him such a stroke that he made him stoop. And he that was full of humility prayed him for God's love to leave his battle, 'For if it befell, fair brother, that I slay you or ye me, we both shall die for that sin.'

dressing] raising   No force] no matter   alliegement] alleviation

'So God me help, I shall never have other mercy and I may have the better hand.'

'Well,' said Sir Bors, and drew his sword, all weeping, and said, 'Fair brother, God knoweth my intent; for ye have done full evil this day to slay a holy priest which never trespassed. Also ye have slain a gentle knight, and one of our fellows. And well ye wot that I am not afraid of you greatly, but I dread the wrath of God; and this is an unkindly war, therefore God show His miracle upon us both. And God have mercy upon me, though I defend my life against my brother.'

And so with that Sir Bors lifted up his hand and would have smitten [17] his brother. And with that he heard a voice which said, 'Flee, Sir Bors, and touch him not, or else thou shalt slay him.'

Right so alit a cloud betwixt them in likeness of a fair and a marvellous flame, that both their two shields burnt. Then were they sore afraid and fell both to the earth, and lay there a great while in a swoon. And when they came to themselves, Sir Bors saw that his brother had no harm; then he held up both his hands, for he dreaded lest God had taken vengeance upon him. So with that he heard a voice that said, 'Sir Bors, go hence, and bear thy fellowship no longer with thy brother; but take thy way anon right to the sea, for Sir Percival abideth thee there.'

Then he said to his brother, 'For God's love, fair sweet brother, forgive me my trespass.'

Then he answered and said, 'God forgive you, and I do gladly.'

So Sir Bors departed from him and rode the next way to the sea.

And at the last by fortune he came to an abbey which was nigh the sea, and that night he rested him there. And as he slept, there came a voice and bade him go to the sea. Then he started up and made a sign of the cross, and took him to his harness and made ready his horse; and at a broken wall he rode out, and by fortune he came to the sea. And upon the sea strand he found a ship that was covered all with white samite. Then he alit and betook him to Jesu Christ. And as soon as he was entered, the ship departed into the sea, and to his seeming it went fleeing; but it was soon dark, that he might know no man. Then he laid him down and slept till it was day.

And when he was waked, he saw in the midst of the ship a knight lie all armed save his helm. And anon he was ware it was Sir Percival de

unkindly] unnatural   betook] entrusted

Gales, and then he made of him right great joy; but Sir Percival was abashed of him and asked him what he was.

'Ah, fair sir,' said Sir Bors, 'know ye me not?'

'Certes,' said he, 'I marvel how ye came hither, but if Our Lord brought you hither Himself.'

Then Sir Bors smiled and did off his helm; and anon Sir Percival knew him, and either made great joy of other that it was marvel to hear. Then Sir Bors told him how he came into the ship, and by whose admonishment. And either told other of their temptations, as ye have heard beforehand.

So went they driving in the sea, one while backward, another while forward, and each man comforted other, and ever they were in their prayers.

Then said Sir Percival, 'We lack nothing but Sir Galahad, the good knight.'

Now turneth the tale unto Sir Galahad.

Of Sir Galahad

Now saith the tale, when Sir Galahad had rescued Sir Percival from the twenty knights, he rode then into a waste forest wherein he did many journeys and found many adventures which he brought all to an end, whereof the tale maketh here no mention.

Then he took his way to the sea. And on a day, as it befell, as he passed by a castle there was a wonder tournament; but they without had done so much that they within were put to the worse, and yet were they within good knights enough. So when Sir Galahad saw those within were at so great mischief that men slew them at the entry of the castle, then he thought to help them, and put a spear forth and smote the first that he flew to the earth, and the spear yode in pieces. Then he drew his sword and smote there as they were thickest; and so he did wonderful deeds of arms, that all they marvelled.

And so it happened that Sir Gawain and Sir Ector de Maris were with the knights without. But then they espied the white shield with the red cross, and anon the one said to the other, 'Yonder is the good knight Sir Galahad, the haut prince. Now forsooth me thinketh he shall be a great fool that shall meet with him to fight.'

But at the last by adventure he came by Sir Gawain, and he smote him so sore that he cleft his helm and the coif of iron unto the head, that Sir Gawain fell to the earth; but the stroke was so great that it slanted down and cut the horse's shoulder in two. So when Sir Ector saw Sir Gawain down, he drew him aside, and thought it no wisdom for to abide him; and also for natural love, because he was his uncle.

Thus through his hardiness he beat aback all the knights without; and then they within came out and chased them all about. But when Sir Galahad saw there would none turn again, he stole away privily, and no man wist where he was become.

'Now by my head,' said Sir Gawain unto Sir Ector, 'now are the wonders true that were said of Sir Lancelot, that the sword which stuck in the stone should give me such a buffet that I would not have it for the best castle in the world; and soothly now it is proved true, for never ere had I such a stroke of man's hand.'

'Sir,' said Sir Ector, 'me seemeth your quest is done; and mine is not done.'

'Well,' said he, 'I shall seek no further.'

Then was Sir Gawain borne into the castle, and unarmed him and laid him in a rich bed, and a leech was found to heal him. And Sir Ector would not depart from him till he was nigh whole.

And so this good knight Sir Galahad rode so fast that he came that night to the Castle of Carbonek. And so it befell him that he was benighted, and came unto a hermitage. So the good man was fain when he saw he was a knight errant.

So when they were at rest, there befell a gentlewoman came and knocked at the door and called Sir Galahad; and so the good man came to the door to wit what she would.

Then she called the hermit, Sir Ulfin, and said, 'I am a gentlewoman that would fain speak with the knight which is with you.'

Then the good man awaked Sir Galahad and bade him arise, 'and speak with a gentlewoman that seemeth she hath great need of you.'

Then Sir Galahad went and asked her what she would.

'Sir Galahad,' said she, 'I will that ye arm you, and light upon this horse and sue me, for I shall show you within these three days the highest adventure that ever any knight saw.'

So anon Sir Galahad armed him and took his horse, and commended the hermit to God; and so he bade the gentlewoman to ride, and he would follow there as she liked.

[2]   So she rode as fast as her palfrey might bear her till that she came to the sea, which was called Collibie. And by night they came unto a castle in a valley, enclosed with a running water, which had strong walls and high; and so she entered into the castle with Sir Galahad, and there had he great cheer, for the lady of that castle was the damosel's lady. So was he unarmed.

Then said the damosel, 'Madam, shall we abide here all this day?'

'Nay,' said she, 'but till he hath dined and slept a little.'

And so he ate and slept a while; and this maid then called him and armed him by torchlight. And when the maiden was horsed and he both, the lady took Sir Galahad a fair shield and rich, and so they departed from the castle and rode till they came to the sea. And there

sue] follow

they found the ship that Sir Bors and Sir Percival were in, which said on the shipboard, 'Sir Galahad, ye be welcome, for we have abided you long.'

And when he heard them he asked them what they were.

'Sir,' said she, 'leave your horse here, and I shall leave mine also;' and took their saddles and their bridles with them, and made a cross on them, and so entered into the ship. And the two knights received them both with great joy, and each knew other. And so the wind arose and drove them through the sea into a marvellous place; and within a while it dawned. Then did Sir Galahad off his helm and his sword, and asked of his fellows from whence came that fair ship.

'Truly,' said they, 'ye wot as well as we, but it come of God's grace.'

And then they told each to other of all their hard adventures, and of their great temptations.

'Truly,' said Galahad, 'ye are much bound to God, for ye have escaped right great adventures. Certes, had not this gentlewoman been, I had not come hither at this time; for as for you two, I weened never to have found you in these strange countries.'

'Ah, Sir Galahad,' said Sir Bors, 'if Sir Lancelot your father were here then were we well at ease, for then me seemed we failed nothing.'

'That may not be,' said Galahad, 'but if it pleased Our Lord.'

By then the ship had run from the land of Logris many miles. So by adventure it arrived up betwixt two rocks passing great and marvellous; but there they might not land, for there was a swallow of the sea, save there was another ship, and upon it they might go without danger.

'Now go we thither,' said the gentlewoman, 'and there shall we see adventures, for so is Our Lord's will.'

And when they came thither they found the ship rich enough, but they found neither man nor woman therein. But they found in the end of the ship two fair letters written, which said a dreadful word and a marvellous:

'Thou man which shalt enter into this ship, beware that thou be in steadfast belief, for I am Faith. And therefore beware how thou enterest but if thou be steadfast, for and thou fail thereof I shall not help thee.'

And then said the gentlewoman, 'Sir Percival,' said she, 'wot ye what I am?'

on the shipboard] from on board the ship   swallow] whirlpool

'Certes,' said he, 'nay; unto my witting I saw you never erst.'

'Wit you well,' said she, 'I am thy sister, which was daughter unto King Pellinore, and therefore wit you well ye are the man that I most love. And if ye be not in perfect belief of Jesu Christ, enter not in no manner of wise; for then should ye perish in the ship, for he is so perfect he will suffer no sinner within him.'

So when Sir Percival understood she was his very sister he was inwardly glad, and said, 'Fair sister, I shall enter in, for if I be a miscreature or an untrue knight there shall I perish.'

[3]   So in the meanwhile Sir Galahad blessed him, and entered therein; and so next the gentlewoman, and then Sir Bors, and then Sir Percival. And when they were in, it was so marvellous fair and rich, and amidst the ship was a fair bed; and anon Sir Galahad went thereto, and found thereon a crown of silk. And at the feet was a sword, rich and fair, and it was drawn out of the sheath a foot and more. And the sword was of divers fashions; and the pommel was of stone, and there was in it all manner of colours that any man might find, and each of the colours had divers virtues. And the scales of the haft were of two ribs of two divers beasts: the one was a serpent which is conversant in Caledonia and is called the serpent of the fiend; and the bone of him is of such virtue that there is no hand that handleth him shall never be weary nor hurt. And the other bone is of a fish which is not right great and haunteth the flood of Euphrates, and that fish is called Ertanax; and the bones be of such manner of kind that who that handleth them shall have so much will that he shall never be weary, and he shall not think on joy nor sorrow that he hath had, but only that thing that he beholdeth before him. And as for this sword, there shall never man grip him—that is to say, the handles—but one; and he shall pass all other.

'In the name of God,' said Sir Percival, 'I shall assay to handle it.' So he set his hand to the sword, but he might not grip it. 'By my faith,' said he, 'now have I failed.'

Then Sir Bors set to his hand, and failed.

Then Sir Galahad beheld the sword, and saw letters like blood that said, 'Let see who dare draw me out of my sheath but if he be more hardier than any other; for who that draweth me out, wit you well he shall never be shamed of his body, nor wounded to the death.'

inwardly] thoroughly   blessed him] crossed himself   virtues] powers
scales of the haft] cross-pieces of the shaft   conversant in Caledonia] inhabits
Scotland

'Par fay,' said Sir Galahad, 'I would draw this sword out of the sheath, but the offending is so great that I shall not set my hand thereto.'

'Now, sirs,' said the gentlewoman, 'the drawing of this sword is warned to all save only to you.'*

And then beheld they the scabbard; it seemed to be of a serpent's [4] skin, and thereon were letters of gold and silver. And the girdle was but poorly to come to, and not able to sustain such a rich sword. And the letters said, 'He which shall wield me ought to be more hardy than any other, if he bear me as truly as me ought to be borne. For the body of him which I ought to hang by, he shall not be shamed in no place while he is girt with the girdle. Nor never none be so hardy to do away this girdle: for it ought not to be done away but by the hands of a maid, and that she be a king's daughter and a queen's. And she must be a maid all the days of her life, both in will and in work, and if she break her virginity she shall die the most villainous death that ever did any woman.'

'Sir,' said she, 'there was a king that hight Pelles, which men called [5] the Maimed King;* and while he might ride he supported much Christendom and Holy Church. So upon a day he hunted in a wood of his which lasted unto the sea; so at the last he lost his hounds and his knights save only one. And so he and his knight went till that they came toward Ireland, and there he found the ship. And when he saw the letters and understood them, yet he entered, for he was right perfect of life; but his knight had no hardiness to enter. And there found he this sword, and drew it out as much as ye may see. So therewith entered a spear wherewith he was smitten him through both thighs; and never since might he be healed, nor nought shall before we come to him. Thus,' said she, 'was King Pelles, your grandsire, maimed for his hardiness.'

'In the name of God, damosel,' said Sir Galahad.

So they went toward the bed to behold all about it; and above the bed there hung two swords. Also there were spindles which were white as snow, and others that were red as blood, and others above green as any emerald: of these three colours were these spindles, and of natural colour within, and without any painting.

'These spindles,' said the damosel, 'were when sinful Eve came to gather fruit, for which she and Adam were put out of paradise, she took with her the bough which the apple hung on. Then perceived she that the branch was fresh and green, and she remembered her of the loss which came of the tree. Then she thought to keep the branch as long as she might; and for she had no coffer to keep it in, she put it in the earth. So by the will of Our Lord the branch grew to a great tree within a little while, and was as white as any snow, branches, boughs, and leaves: that was a token that a maiden planted it. But after that, Our Lord came to Adam and bade him know his wife fleshly as nature required.* So lay Adam with his wife under the same tree; and anon the tree which was white fell to green as any grass, and all that came out of it. And in the same time that they meddled together, Abel was begotten. Thus was the tree long of green colour.

'And so it befell many days after, under the same tree Cain slew Abel, whereof befell great marvel. For as Abel had received death under the green tree, it lost the green colour and became red; and that was in tokening of blood. And anon all the plants died thereof, but the tree grew and waxed marvellously fair, and it was the fairest tree and the most delectable that any man might behold and see; and so did the plants that grew out of it before that Abel was slain under it.

'And so long endured the tree till that Solomon, King David's son, reigned and held the land after his father. So this Solomon was wise, and knew all the virtues of stones and trees; also he knew the course of the stars and of many other divers things. So this Solomon had an evil wife, wherethrough he weened that there had been no good woman born, and therefore he despised them in his books.* So there answered a voice that said to him thus: "Solomon, if heaviness come to a man by a woman, ne reck thou never; for yet shall there come a woman whereof there shall come greater joy to a man a hundred times than this heaviness giveth sorrow, and that woman shall be born of thy lineage."* So when Solomon heard these words he held himself but a fool. That proof had he by old books, the truth; also the Holy Ghost showed him the coming of the glorious Virgin Mary. Then asked he the voice if it should be of the yard of his lineage.

' "Nay," said the voice, "but there shall come a man which shall be a maid, and last of your blood; and he shall be as good a knight as Duke [6] Joshua, thy brother-in-law.* Now have I certified thee of that thou standest in doubt."

---

fell to] turned   ne reck thou never] do not be concerned   yard] branch
certified . . . standest in doubt] explained what puzzled you

'Then was Solomon glad that there should come any such of his lineage, but ever he marvelled and studied who that should be, and what his name might be. So his wife perceived that he studied, and thought she would know at some season; and so she waited her time, and came to him and asked him. And there he told her altogether how the voice had told him.

' "Well," said she, "I shall let make a ship of the best wood and most durable that any man may find."

'So Solomon sent for carpenters, of all the land the best. And when they had made the ship the lady said to Solomon, "Sir, since it is so that this knight ought to pass all knights of chivalry which have been before him and shall come after him, moreover I shall learn you," said she, "ye shall go into Our Lord's temple, where is King David's sword, your father, which is the marvelloust and the sharpest that ever was taken in any knight's hands. Therefore take ye that, and take off the pommel, and thereto make ye a pommel of precious stones; let it be so subtly made that no man perceive it but that they be all one. And after make there a hilt so marvellously that no man may know it; and after that make a marvellous sheath. And when ye have made all this, I shall let make a girdle thereto, such one as shall please me."

'So all this King Solomon did let make as she devised, both the ship and all the remnant. And when the ship was ready in the sea to sail, the lady let make a great bed and marvellous rich, and set her upon the bed's head covered with silk, and laid the sword at the feet. And the girdles were of hemp, and therewith the king was right angry.

' "Sir, wit you well that I have none so high a thing which were worthy to sustain so high a sword. And a maid shall bring other knights thereto; but I wot not when it shall be, nor what time."

'And there she let make a covering to the ship of cloth of silk that should never rot for no manner of weather. Then this lady went and made a carpenter to come to the tree which Abel was slain under.

' "Now," said she, "carve me out of this tree as much wood as will make me a spindle."

' "Ah, madam," said he, "this is the tree the which our first mother planted."

---

learn] instruct   so subtly . . . be all one] made so skilfully that no one can tell it is not all in one piece

' "Do it," said she, "or else I shall destroy thee."

'Anon as he began to work there came out drops of blood; and then would he have left, but she would not suffer him. And so he took as much wood as might make a spindle; and so she made him to take as much of the green tree, and so of the white tree. And when these three spindles were shaped, she made them to be fastened upon the selar of the bed. So when Solomon saw this, he said to his wife, "Ye have done marvellously, for though all the world were here right now, they could not devise wherefore all this was made, but Our Lord Himself; and thou that hast done it wot not what it shall betoken."

' "Now let it be," said she, "for ye shall hear tidings peradventure sooner than ye ween."

'Now here is a wonderful tale of King Solomon and of his wife.*

[7]   'That night lay Solomon before the ship with little fellowship; and when he was asleep, him thought there came from heaven a great company of angels and alit into the ship, and took water which was brought by an angel in a vessel of silver and besprent all the ship. And after he came to the sword and drew letters on the hilt; and after went to the ship's board, and wrote there other letters which said, "Thou man that wilt enter within me, beware that thou be full in the faith, for I ne am but Faith and Belief."

'When Solomon espied those letters he was so abashed that he durst not enter, and so he drew him aback; and the ship was anon shoved in the sea. He went so fast that he had lost the sight of him within a little while. And then a voice said, "Solomon, the last knight of thy kindred shall rest in this bed."

'Then went Solomon and awaked his wife, and told her the adventures of this ship.'

Now saith the tale that a great while the three fellows beheld the bed and the three spindles; then they were at a certainty that they were of natural colours without any painting. Then they lifted up a cloth which was above the ground, and there found a rich purse by seeming. And Sir Percival took it and found therein a writ, and so he read it; and it devised the manner of the spindles and of the ship, whence it came, and by whom it was made.

---

selar] canopy   besprent] sprinkled   I ne am but] I am nothing other than
a rich purse by seeming] what appeared to be a rich purse

'Now,' said Sir Galahad, 'where shall we find the gentlewoman that shall make new girdles to the sword?'

'Fair sirs,' said Percival's sister, 'dismay you not, for by the leave of God I shall let make a girdle to the sword, such one as should belong thereto.'

And then she opened a box and took out girdles which were seemly wrought with golden threads, and upon that were set full precious stones and a rich buckle of gold.

'Lo, lords,' she said, 'here is a girdle that ought to be set about the sword. And wit you well, the greatest part of this girdle was made of my hair, which some time I loved well while that I was a woman of the world. But as soon as I wist that this adventure was ordained me, I clipped off my hair and made this girdle.'

'In the name of God, ye be well found,' said Sir Bors, 'for certes ye have put us out of great pain wherein we should have entered had not your tidings been.'

Then went the gentlewoman and set it on the girdle of the sword.

'Now,' said the fellowship, 'what is the name of the sword, and what shall we call it?'

'Truly,' said she, 'the name of the sword is the Sword with the Strange Girdles; and the sheath, Mover of Blood; for no man that hath blood in him shall never see the one part of the sheath which was made of the tree of life.'

Then they said, 'Sir Galahad, in the name of Jesu Christ, we pray you to gird you with this sword which hath been desired so much in the realm of Logris.'

'Now let me begin', said Galahad, 'to grip this sword for to give you courage; but wit you well it longeth no more to me than it doth to you.'

And then he gripped about it with his fingers a great deal; and then she girt him about the middle with the sword.

'Now reck I not though I die, for now I hold me one of the best blessed maidens of the world, which hath made the worthiest knight of the world.'

'Damosel,' said Sir Galahad, 'ye have done so much that I shall be your knight all the days of my life.'

Then they went from that ship, and went to the other. And anon the wind drove them into the sea a great pace, but they had no victual.

great pain wherein we should have entered] the great difficulty we would have found ourselves in

So it befell that they came on the morn to a castle that men call Carteloise, that was in the marches of Scotland. And when they had passed the port, the gentlewoman said, 'Lords, here be men arrived that, and they wist that ye were of King Arthur's court, ye should be assailed anon.'

'Well, damosel, dismay you not,' said Sir Galahad, 'for He that cast us out of the rock shall deliver us from them.'

[8]   So it befell as they talked thus together, there came a squire by them and asked what they were.

'Sir, we are of King Arthur's house.'

'Is that sooth?' said he. 'Now by my head,' said he, 'ye be evil arrayed;' and then turned again unto the chief fortress, and within a while they heard a horn blow. Then a gentlewoman came to them and asked them of whence they were; anon they told her.

'Now, fair lords,' she said, 'for God's love turn again if ye may, for ye be come to your death.'

'Nay, for sooth,' they said, 'we will not turn again, for He should help us into whose service we were entered in.'

So as they stood talking there came ten knights well armed, and bade them yield or else die.

'That yielding', said they, 'shall be noyous unto you.'

And therewith they let their horses run, and Sir Percival smote the first that he bore him to the earth, and took his horse and bestrode him. And the same wise did Sir Galahad, and also Sir Bors served another so; for they had no horses in that country, for they left their horses when they took their ship. And so when they were horsed then began they to set upon them; and they of the castle fled into strong fortresses, and these three knights after them into the castle, and so alit on foot and with their swords slew them down, and got into the hall. Then when they beheld the great multitude of people that they had slain, they held themselves great sinners.

'Certes,' said Sir Bors, 'I ween, and God had loved them, that we should not have had power to have slain them thus. But they have done so much against Our Lord that He would not suffer them to reign no longer.'

'Say ye not so,' said Galahad, 'for if they misdid against God, the vengeance is not ours, but to Him which hath power thereof.'*

---

arrayed] circumstanced   noyous] grievous

So came there out of a chamber a good man which was a priest, and bore God's body in a cup; and when he saw them which lay dead in the hall he was abashed. Anon Sir Galahad did off his helm and kneeled down, and so did his two fellows.

'Sir,' said they, 'have ye no dread of us, for we be of King Arthur's court.'

Then asked the good man how they were slain so suddenly, and they told him.

'Truly,' said the good man, 'and ye might live as long as the world might endure, might ye not have done so great an alms-deed as this.'

'Sir,' said Sir Galahad, 'I repent me greatly inasmuch as they were christened.'

'Nay, repent you not,' said he, 'for they were not christened. And I shall tell you how that I know of this castle. Here was a lord earl, whose name was Hernox, not but one year; and he had three sons, good knights of arms, and a daughter, the fairest gentlewoman that men knew. So those three knights loved their sister so sore that they burned in love; and so they lay by her maugre her head. And for she cried to her father they slew her, and took their father and put him in prison and wounded him nigh to the death; but a cousin of hers rescued him. And then did they great untruth, for they slew clerks and priests and made beat down chapels, that Our Lord's service might not be said. And this same day her father sent unto me for to be confessed and houseled. But such shame had never man as I had this same day with the three brethren; but the old earl made me to suffer, for he said they should not long endure, for three servants of Our Lord should destroy them. And now it is brought to an end, and by this may you wit that Our Lord is not displeased with your deeds.'

'Certes,' said Sir Galahad, 'and it had not pleased Our Lord, never should we have slain so many men in so little a while.'

And they brought the Earl Hernox out of prison into the midst of the hall, the which knew well Sir Galahad, and yet saw he him never before but by revelation of Our Lord. Then he began to weep right tenderly, and said, 'Long have I abided your coming! But for God's love, hold me in your arms, that my soul may depart out of my body in so good a man's arms as ye be.'* [9]

God's body in a cup] i.e. the Eucharist in a chalice   not but one year] just a year ago   made beat down chapels] caused chapels to be destroyed   houseled] given the Eucharist   suffer] bear patiently

'Full gladly,' said Sir Galahad.

And then one said on high, that all folk heard, 'Sir Galahad, well hast thou been avenged on God's enemies. Now behoveth thee to go to the Maimed King as soon as thou mayst, for he shall receive by thee health which he hath abided so long.'

And therewith the soul departed from the body; and Sir Galahad made him to be buried as he ought to be.*

And then they dwelled there all that day; and upon the morn, when they had heard Mass, they departed and commended the good man to God. And so they came to a castle and passed by; so there came a knight [10] armed after them and said, 'Lords, this gentlewoman that ye lead with you, is she a maid?'

'Yea, sir,' said she, 'a maid I am.'

Then he took her by the bridle and said, 'By the Holy Cross, ye shall not escape me before ye have yielded the custom of this castle.'

'Let her go,' said Sir Percival. 'Ye be not wise, for a maid in what place she cometh is free.'

So in the meanwhile there came out ten or twelve knights armed out of the castle, and with them came gentlewomen the which held a dish of silver. And then they said, 'This gentlewoman must yield us the custom of this castle.'

'Why,' said Sir Galahad, 'what is the custom of this castle?'

'Sir,' said a knight, 'what maid passeth hereby should fill this dish full of blood of her right arm.'

'Blame have he,' said Galahad, 'that brought up such customs! And so God save me, ye may be sure that of this, gentlewomen, shall ye fail while that I have health.'

'So God me help,' said Sir Percival, 'I had liever be slain.'

'And I also,' said Sir Bors.

'By my faith,' said the knight, 'then shall ye die, for ye may not endure against us though ye were the best knights of the world.'

Then let they run each horse to other, and these three knights beat the ten knights, and then set their hands to their swords and beat them down. Then there came out of the castle sixty knights armed.

'Now, fair lords,' said these three knights, 'have mercy on yourselves and have not ado with us.'

'Nay, fair lords,' said the knights of the castle, 'we counsel you to withdraw you, for ye be the best knights of the world; and therefore do no more, for ye have done enough. We will let you go with this harm, but we must needs have the custom.'

'Certes,' said Sir Galahad, 'for nought speak ye.'

'Well,' said they, 'will ye die?'

'Sir, we be not yet come thereto,' said Sir Galahad.

Then began they to meddle together; and Sir Galahad, with the strange girdles, drew his sword and smote on the right hand and on the left hand, and slew whom that ever abode him, and did so marvellously that they had marvel of him, and his two fellows helped him passingly well. And so they held their journey each alike hard till it was nigh night—then must they needs part.

So there came a good knight and said to these three knights, 'If ye will come in tonight and take such harbour as here is, ye shall be right welcome; and we shall assure you by the faith of our bodies and as we be true knights, to leave you in such state tomorrow as here we find you, without any falsehood. And as soon as ye know of the custom, we dare say we will accord.'

'Therefore for God's love,' said the gentlewoman, 'go we thither, and spare not for me.'

'Well, go we,' said Sir Galahad; and so they entered into the castle, and when they were alit they made great joy of them. So within a while the three knights asked the custom of the castle and wherefore it was used.

'Sir, what it is we will say you the sooth. There is in this castle a [11] gentlewoman, which both we and this castle is hers, and many other. So it befell many years ago, there happened on her a malady; and when she had lain a great while she fell into a mesel, and no leech could remedy her. But at the last an old man said and she might have a dish full of blood of a maid, and a clean virgin in will and in work, and a king's daughter, that blood should be her health, for to anoint her withal. And for this thing was this custom made.'

'Now,' said Sir Percival's sister, 'fair knights, I see well that this gentlewoman is but dead without help, and therefore let me bleed.'

'Certes,' said Sir Galahad, 'and ye bleed so much ye must die.'

'Truly,' said she, 'and I die for the health of her I shall get me great worship and soul's health, and worship to my lineage; and better is one harm than twain. And therefore there shall no more battle be, but tomorrow I shall yield you your custom of this castle.'

---

meddle] fight   journey] day's work   mesel] leprosy

And then there was made great joy over there was made before, for else had there been mortal war upon the morn; notwithstanding she would none other, whether they would or would not. So that night were these three fellows eased with the best; and on the morn they heard Mass, and Sir Percival's sister bade them bring forth the sick lady. So she was brought forth, which was full evil at ease.

Then said she, 'Who shall let me blood?'

So one came forth and let her blood, and she bled so much that the dish was full. Then she lifted up her hand and blessed her, and said to this lady, 'Madam, I am come to my death for to heal you, therefore for God's love pray for me.'

And with that she fell in a swoon. Then Sir Galahad and his two fellows started up to her and lifted her up and staunched her blood, but she had bled so much that she might not live.

So when she was awaked, she said, 'Fair brother Sir Percival, I die for the healing of this lady. And when I am dead, I require you that ye bury me not in this country, but as soon as I am dead put me in a boat at the next haven, and let me go as adventure will lead me.* And as soon as ye three come to the city of Sarras, there to achieve the Holy Grail, ye shall find me under a tower arrived; and there bury me in the spiritual palace. For I shall tell you for truth, there shall Sir Galahad be buried, and ye both, in the same place.'

When Sir Percival understood these words, he granted her all weepingly. And then said a voice unto them, 'Lords, tomorrow at the hour of prime ye three shall depart each from other, till the adventure bring you unto the Maimed King.'

Then asked she her Saviour; and as soon as she had received Him the soul departed from the body. So the same day was the lady healed, when she was anointed with her blood.

Then Sir Percival made a letter of all that she had helped them as in strange adventures, and put it in her right hand; and so laid her in a barge, and covered it with black silk. And so the wind arose and drove the barge from the land, and all manner of knights beheld it till it was out of their sight. Then they drew all to the castle, and forthwith there fell a sudden tempest of thunder and lightning and rain, as all the earth would have broken. So half the castle turned upside down. So it passed evensong or the tempest were ceased.

---

evil at ease] in great pain   Saviour] i.e. the Eucharist

Then they saw before them a knight armed and wounded hard in the body and in the head, which said, 'Ah, good Lord, succour me, for now it is need.'

So after this knight there came another knight and a dwarf, which cried to them afar, 'Stand, ye may not escape!'

Then the wounded knight held up his hands, and prayed God that he might not die in such tribulation.

'Truly,' said Sir Galahad, 'I shall succour him, for His sake that he calleth on.'

'Sir,' said Sir Bors, 'I shall do it, for it is not for you, for he is but one knight.'

'Sir,' said he, 'I grant you.'

So Sir Bors took his sword and commended him to God, and rode after to rescue the wounded knight.

Now turn we to Sir Galahad and to Sir Percival.

Now turneth the tale unto Sir Galahad and Sir Percival, that were in a [12] chapel all night in their prayers for to save them Sir Bors. So on the morrow they dressed them in their harness toward the castle, to wit what was fallen of them therein. And when they came there, they found neither man nor woman that he was not dead by the vengeance of Our Lord. So with that they heard a voice that said, 'This vengeance is for blood-shedding of maidens.'

Also they found at the end of the castle a churchyard, and therein they might see sixty fair tombs; and that place was fair, and so delectable that it seemed them there had been no tempest. And there lay the bodies of all the good maidens which were martyred for the sick lady. Also they found there names of each lady, and of what blood they were come of; and all were of kings' blood, and eleven of them were kings' daughters.

Then they departed and went into a forest.

'Now,' said Sir Percival unto Sir Galahad, 'we must part; and therefore pray we Our Lord that we may meet together in short time.'

Then they did off their helms and kissed together, and sore wept at their departing.

Now turneth this tale unto Sir Lancelot.

[13] Now saith the tale, that when Sir Lancelot was come to the water of Mortaise, as it is rehearsed before, he was in great peril. And so he laid him down and slept, and took the adventure that God would send him.

So when he was asleep there came a vision unto him, that said, 'Sir Lancelot, arise up and take thine armour, and enter into the first ship that thou shalt find.'

And when he heard these words he started up and saw great clearness about him; and then he lifted up his hand and blessed him. And so he took his arms and made him ready; and at the last he came by a strand, and found a ship without sail or oar. And as soon as he was within the ship, there he had the most sweetness that ever he felt, and he was fulfilled with all things that he thought on or desired. Then he said, 'Sweet Father, Jesu Christ, I wot not what joy I am in, for this joy passeth all earthly joys that ever I was in.'

And so in this joy he laid him down to the shipboard, and slept till day. And when he awoke he found there a fair bed, and therein lying a gentlewoman dead, which was Sir Percival's sister. And as Sir Lancelot avised her, he espied in her right hand a writ which he read, that told him all the adventures ye have heard before, and of what lineage she was come.

So with this gentlewoman Sir Lancelot was a month and more. If ye would ask how he lived, He that fed the children of Israel with manna in the desert, so was he fed;* for every day when he had said his prayers he was sustained with the grace of the Holy Ghost.

And so on a night he went to play him by the water's side, for he was somewhat weary of the ship. And then he listened and heard a horse come, and one riding upon him; and when he came nigh, him seemed a knight. And so he let him pass and went there as the ship was; and there he alit, and took the saddle and the bridle and put the horse from him, and so went into the ship. And then Sir Lancelot dressed him unto the ship and said, 'Sir, ye be welcome.'

And he answered and saluted him again, and said, 'Sir, what is your name? For much my heart giveth unto you.'

avised her] looked at her face   dressed him] made his way

The Tale of the Sangrail

'Truly,' said he, 'my name is Sir Lancelot du Lake.'

'Sir,' said he, 'then be ye welcome, for ye were the beginner of me in this world.'

'Ah, sir, are ye Sir Galahad?'

'Yea, forsooth.'

And so he kneeled down and asked him his blessing, and after took off his helm and kissed him. And there was great joy betwixt them, for no tongue can tell what joy either made of other. And there each of them told other the adventures that had befallen them sith that they departed from the court.

And anon as Sir Galahad saw the gentlewoman dead in the bed, he knew her well, and said great worship of her, that she was one of the best maidens living, and it was great pity of her death. But when Sir Lancelot heard how the marvellous sword was gotten, and who made it, and all the marvels rehearsed before, then he prayed Sir Galahad that he would show him the sword; and so he brought it forth, and kissed the pommel and the hilts and the scabbard.

'Truly,' said Sir Lancelot, 'never erst knew I of so high adventures done, and so marvellous strange.'*

So dwelled Sir Lancelot and Sir Galahad within that ship half a year, and served God daily and nightly with all their power. And often they arrived in isles far from folk, where there repaired none but wild beasts, and there they found many strange adventures and perilous which they brought to an end; but for those adventures were with wild beasts, and not in the quest of the Sangrail, therefore the tale maketh here no mention thereof, for it would be too long to tell of all those adventures that befell them.

So after, on a Monday, it befell that they arrived in the edge of a for- [14] est before a cross; and then saw they a knight armed all in white, and was richly horsed, and led in his right hand a white horse. And so he came to the ship and saluted the two knights in the high Lord's behalf, and said unto Sir Galahad, 'Sir, ye have been long enough with your father. Therefore come out of the ship, and take this horse and go where the adventures shall lead you in the quest of the Sangrail.'

Then he went to his father and kissed him sweetly, and said, 'Fair sweet father, I wot not when I shall see you more till I see the body of Jesu Christ.'

'Now for God's love,' said Sir Lancelot, 'pray to the Father that He hold me still in His service.'

And so he took his horse; and there they heard a voice that said, 'Each of you think for to do well, for nevermore shall one see the other of you before the dreadful day of doom.'

'Now, my son, Sir Galahad, sith we shall depart and neither of us see other more, I pray to that High Father, conserve me and you both.'

'Sir,' said Sir Galahad, 'no prayer availeth so much as yours.'

And therewith Sir Galahad entered into the forest; and the wind arose, and drove Sir Lancelot more than a month through the sea, where he slept but little, but prayed to God that he might see some tidings of the Sangrail.

So it befell on a night, at midnight, he arrived before a castle on the back side, which was rich and fair, and there was a postern opened toward the sea, and was open without any keeping, save two lions kept the entry; and the moon shone right clear. Anon Sir Lancelot heard a voice that said, 'Lancelot, go out of this ship and enter into the castle, where thou shalt see a great part of thy desire.'

Then he ran to his arms, and so armed him, and so went to the gate and saw the lions; then set he hand to his sword and drew it. So there came a dwarf suddenly, and smote him on the arm so sore that the sword fell out of his hand. Then heard he a voice say, 'O man of evil faith and poor belief, wherefore trustest thou more on thy harness than in thy Maker? For He might more avail thee than thine armour in that service that thou art set in.'

Then said Sir Lancelot, 'Fair Father Jesu Christ, I thank thee of Thy great mercy that Thou reprovest me of my misdeed! Now see I that Thou holdest me for one of Thy servants.'

Then took he his sword again and put it up in his sheath, and made a cross in his forehead, and came to the lions; and they made semblant to do him harm. Notwithstanding he passed by them without hurt, and entered into the castle to the chief fortress. And there were they all at rest.

Then Sir Lancelot entered so armed, for he found no gate nor door but it was open. And at the last he found a chamber whereof the door was shut, and he set his hand thereto to have opened it, but he might [15] not. Then he enforced him mickle to undo the door.

Then he listened and heard a voice which sang so sweetly that it seemed no earthly thing; and him thought the voice said, 'Joy and honour be to the Father of Heaven.'

___

enforced him mickle] exerted himself greatly

Then Lancelot kneeled down before the chamber door, for well wist he that there was the Sangrail within that chamber. Then said he, 'Fair sweet Father, Jesu Christ, if ever I did thing that pleased Thee, Lord, for Thy pity have me not in despite for my sins done beforetime, and that Thou show me something of that I seek.'

And with that he saw the chamber door open, and there came out a great clearness, that the house was as bright as all the torches of the world had been there. So came he to the chamber door, and would have entered. And anon a voice said unto him, 'Sir Lancelot, flee, and enter not, for thou ought not to do it; and if thou enter thou shalt forthink it.' Then he withdrew him aback right heavy.

Then looked he up into the midst of the chamber, and saw a table of silver, and the holy vessel covered with red samite, and many angels about it, whereof one held a candle of wax burning, and the other held a cross and the ornaments of an altar. And before the holy vessel he saw a good man clothed as a priest; and it seemed that he was at the sacring of the Mass. And it seemed to Sir Lancelot that above the priest's hands were three men, whereof the two put the youngest by likeness between the priest's hands; and so he lifted them up right high, and it seemed to show so to the people.* And then Sir Lancelot marvelled not a little, for him thought the priest was so greatly charged of the figure that him seemed that he should fall to the earth. And when he saw none about him that would help him, then came he to the door a great pace, and said, 'Fair Father Jesu Christ, take it not for no sin though I help the good man which hath great need of help.'

Right so entered he into the chamber, and came toward the table of silver; and when he came nigh it, he felt a breath that him thought it was intermeddled with fire, which smote him so sore in the visage that him thought it burnt his visage; and therewith he fell to the earth and had no power to arise, as he that had lost the power of his body and his hearing and sight. Then felt he many hands which took him up and bore him out of the chamber door, and left him there seeming dead to all people.

So upon the morrow when it was fair day, they within were risen, and found Sir Lancelot lying before the chamber door. All they marvelled how that he came in; and so they looked upon him, and felt his pulse to wit whether there were any life in him. And so they found life

sacring] consecration of the Eucharist

in him, but he might not stand nor stir no member that he had. And so they took him by every part of the body and bore him into a chamber and laid him in a rich bed far from folk, and so he lay four days. Then one said he was alive, and another said nay, he was dead.

'In the name of God,' said an old man, 'I do you verily to wit he is not dead, but he is as full of life as the strongest of us all. Therefore I rede you all that he be well kept till God send life in him again.'

[16] So in such manner they kept Sir Lancelot four and twenty days and all so many nights, that ever he lay still as a dead man; and at the twenty-fifth day befell him after midday that he opened his eyes. And when he saw folk he made great sorrow, and said, 'Why have ye awaked me?—for I was more at ease than I am now. Ah, Jesu Christ, who might be so blessed that might see openly Thy great marvels of secretness there where no sinner may be?'

'What have ye seen?' said they about him.

'I have seen,' said he, 'so great marvels that no tongue may tell, and more than any heart can think; and had not my sin been beforetime, else I had seen much more.'

Then they told him how he had lain there four and twenty days and nights. Then him thought it was punishment for the four and twenty years that he had been a sinner, wherefore Our Lord put him in penance the four and twenty days and nights. Then looked Lancelot before him, and saw the hair which he had borne nigh a year; for that he forthought him right much that he had broken his promise unto the hermit, which he had vowed to do.

Then they asked how it stood with him.

'For sooth,' said he, 'I am whole of body, thanked be Our Lord; therefore, for God's love tell me where I am.' Then said they all that he was in the Castle of Carbonek.

Therewith came a gentlewoman and brought him a shirt of small linen cloth; but he changed not there, but took the hair to him again.

'Sir,' said they, 'the quest of the Sangrail is achieved now right in you, and never shall ye see of the Sangrail more than ye have seen.'

'Now I thank God,' said Sir Lancelot, 'for His great mercy of that I have seen, for it sufficeth me. For as I suppose no man in this world hath lived better than I have done to achieve that I have done.'

And therewith he took the hair and clothed him in it, and above that

hair] hair shirt   small] fine

he put a linen shirt, and after that a robe of scarlet, fresh and new. And when he was so arrayed they marvelled all, for they knew him well that he was Sir Lancelot, the good knight. And then they said all, 'Ah, my lord Sir Lancelot, ye be he!'

And he said, 'Yea, truly I am he.'

Then came word to the King Pelles that the knight that had lain so long dead was the noble knight Sir Lancelot. Then was the king right glad, and went to see him; and when Sir Lancelot saw him come he dressed him against him, and then made the king great joy of him. And there the king told him tidings how his fair daughter was dead. Then Sir Lancelot was right heavy, and said, 'Me forthinketh of the death of your daughter, for she was a full fair lady, fresh and young, and well I wot she bore the best knight that is now on earth, or that ever was since God was born.'

So the king held him there four days, and on the morrow he took his leave at King Pelles and at all the fellowship, and thanked them of the great labour.

Right so as they sat at their dinner in the chief hall, it befell that the Sangrail had fulfilled the tables with all meats that any heart might think. And as they sat they saw all the doors of the palace and windows shut without man's hand; so they were all abashed. So a knight which was all armed came to the chief door and knocked, and cried, 'Undo!' But they would not; and ever he cried, 'Undo!' So it annoyed them so much that the king himself arose and came to a window there where the knight called. Then he said, 'Sir knight, ye shall not enter at this time while the Sangrail is here, and therefore go into another fortress. For ye be none of the knights of the Quest, but one of them which have served the fiend, and hast left the service of Our Lord.'

Then he was passing wroth at the king's words.

'Sir knight,' said the king, 'since ye would so fain enter, tell me of what country ye be.'

'Sir,' he said, 'I am of the realm of Logris, and my name is Sir Ector de Maris, brother unto my lord Sir Lancelot.'

'In the name of God,' said the king, 'me forthinks of that I have said, for your brother is herein.'

When Sir Ector de Maris understood that his brother was there, for he was the man in the world that he most dreaded and loved, then he

---

dressed him against him] rose to greet him   since God was born] i.e. since the
Nativity

said, 'Ah, good Lord, now doubleth my sorrow and shame! Full truly said the good man of the hill unto Gawain and to me of our dreams.' Then went he out of the court as fast as his horse might, and so throughout the castle.

[17]   Then King Pelles came to Sir Lancelot and told him tidings of his brother; anon he was sorry therefor, that he wist not what to do. So Sir Lancelot departed and took his arms, and said he would go see the realm of Logris which he had not seen afore in a year; and therewith commended the king to God, and so rode through many realms.

And at the last he came to a white abbey, and there they made him that night great cheer. And on the morn he arose and heard Mass; and before an altar he found a rich tomb, which was newly made. And then he took heed and saw the sides written with gold which said, 'Here lieth King Bagdemagus of Gore, which King Arthur's nephew slew'—and named him, Sir Gawain. Then was he not a little sorry, for Sir Lancelot loved him much more than any other (and had it been any other than Sir Gawain, he should not escape from the death); and said to himself, 'Ah, Lord God, this is a great hurt unto King Arthur's court, the loss of such a man.'

And then he departed and came to the abbey where Sir Galahad did the adventure of the tombs and won the white shield with the red cross. And there had he great cheer all that night, and on the morn he turned to Camelot, where he found King Arthur and the Queen. But many of the knights of the Round Table were slain and destroyed, more than half. And so three of them were come home, Sir Ector, Gawain, and Lionel, and many other that needeth not now to rehearse. And all the court was passing glad of Sir Lancelot, and the King asked him many tidings of his son Sir Galahad.

And there Sir Lancelot told the King of his adventures that befell him since he departed. And also he told him of the adventures of Sir Galahad, Sir Percival, and Sir Bors, which that he knew by the letter of the dead maiden, and also as Sir Galahad had told him.

'Now would God', said the King, 'that they were all three here.'

'That shall never be,' said Sir Lancelot, 'for two of them shall ye never see; but one of them shall come home again.'

Now leaveth this tale and speaketh of Sir Galahad.

Of Sir Galahad

Now saith the tale that Sir Galahad rode many journeys in vain; and at [18] the last he came to the abbey where King Mordrains* was, and when he heard that, he thought he would abide to see him. And so upon the morn, when he had heard Mass, Sir Galahad came unto King Mordrains; and anon the king saw him, which had lain blind of long time. And then he dressed him against him, and said, 'Sir Galahad, the servant of Jesu Christ and very knight, whose coming I have abided long, now embrace me and let me rest on thy breast, so that I may rest between thine arms. For thou art a clean virgin above all knights, as the flower of the lily in whom virginity is signified; and thou art the rose which is the flower of all good virtue, and in colour of fire. For the fire of the Holy Ghost is taken so in thee that my flesh which was all dead of oldness is become again young.'

When Sir Galahad heard his words, then he embraced him and all his body. Then said he, 'Fair Lord Jesu Christ, now I have my will, now I require Thee, in this point that I am in, Thou come and visit me.'

And anon Our Lord heard his prayer, and therewith the soul departed from the body. And then Sir Galahad put him in the earth as a king ought to be; and so departed, and came into a perilous forest where he found the well the which boiled with great waves, as the tale telleth before. And as soon as Sir Galahad set his hand thereto, it ceased, so that it burned no more, and anon the heat departed away. And cause why that it burned, it was a sign of lechery, that was that time much used; but that heat might not abide his pure virginity. And so this was taken in the country for a miracle, and so ever after was it called Galahad's well.*

And so he rode five days till that he came to the Maimed King. And [19] ever followed Sir Percival the five days where he had been; and so one told him how the adventures of Logris were achieved. So on a day it befell that he came out of a great forest, and there met they at traverse with Sir Bors, which rode alone—it is no rede to ask if they were glad. And so he saluted them, and they yielded to him honour and good adventure, and each told other how they had sped.

at traverse] crossing their path   no rede] pointless

Then said Bors, 'It is more than a year and a half that I lay ten times where men dwelled, but in wild forests and in mountains; but God was ever my comfort.'

Then rode they a great while till that they came to the castle of Carbonek. And when they were entered within, King Pelles knew them; so there was great joy, for he wist well by their coming that they had fulfilled the Sangrail.*

And anon alit a voice among them, and said, 'They that ought not to sit at the table of Our Lord Jesu Christ, avoid hence, for now there shall very knights be fed.'

So they went thence, all save King Pelles and Eliazar his son, which were holy men, and a maid which was his niece; and so these three knights and these three were there—else were no more. And anon they saw knights all armed that came in at the hall door and did off their helms and arms, and said unto Sir Galahad, 'Sir, we have hied right much for to be with you at this table where the holy meat shall be departed.'

Then said he, 'Ye be welcome; but of whence be ye?' So three of them said they were of Gaul, and other three said they were of Ireland, and other three said they were of Denmark.

And so as they sat thus there came out a bed of tree from a chamber, which four gentlewomen brought; and in the bed lay a good man sick, and had a crown of gold upon his head. And there in the midst of the palace they set him down, and went again.

Then he lifted up his head and said, 'Sir Galahad, good knight, ye be right welcome; for much have I desired your coming, for in such pain and in such anguish I have suffered long. But now I trust to God the term is come that my pain shall be allayed and I soon pass out of this world, so as it was promised me long ago.'

And therewith a voice said, 'There be two among you that be not in the quest of the Sangrail, and therefore depart.'

[20]   Then King Pelles and his son departed. And therewith beseemed them that there came an old man and four angels from heaven, clothed in likeness of a bishop, and had a cross in his hand; and these four angels bore him up in a chair, and set him down before the table of silver whereupon the Sangrail was. And it seemed that he had in the

very] true   the holy meat shall be departed] the Eucharist shall be divided
bed of tree] a wooden litter

midst of his forehead letters which said, 'See you here Joseph, the first bishop of Christendom, the same which Our Lord succoured in the city of Sarras in the spiritual palace.'

Then the knights marvelled, for that bishop was dead more than three hundred years before.

'Ah, knights,' said he, 'marvel not, for I was sometime an earthly man.'

So with that they heard the chamber door open, and there they saw angels; and two bore candles of wax, and the third bore a towel, and the fourth a spear which bled marvellously, that the drops fell within a box which he held with his other hand. And anon they set the candles upon the table, and the third the towel upon the vessel, and the fourth the holy spear even upright upon the vessel. And then the bishop made semblant as though he would have gone to the sacring of a Mass, and then he took an oblay which was made in likeness of bread. And at the lifting up there came a figure in likeness of a child, and the visage was as red and as bright as any fire, and smote himself into the bread, that they all saw it that the bread was formed of a fleshly man.* And then he put it into the holy vessel again, and then he did that longed to a priest to do Mass.

And then he went to Sir Galahad and kissed him, and bade him go and kiss his fellows; and so he did anon.

'Now,' said he, 'the servants of Jesu Christ, ye shall be fed afore this table with sweet meats that never knights yet tasted.' And when he had said, he vanished away. And they set them at the table in great dread, and made their prayers.

Then looked they and saw a man come out of the holy vessel, that had all the signs of the passion of Jesu Christ bleeding all openly, and said, 'My knights and my servants and my true children, which be come out of deadly life into the spiritual life, I will now no longer cover me from you, but ye shall see now a part of my secrets and of my hidden things. Now hold and receive the high order and meat which ye have so much desired.'

Then took He Himself the holy vessel and came to Sir Galahad; and he kneeled down and he received his Saviour. And after him so received all his fellows; and they thought it so sweet that it was marvellous to tell.

oblay] wafer

Then said He to Sir Galahad, 'Son, wotest thou what I hold betwixt my hands?'

'Nay,' said he, 'but if Ye tell me.'

'This is,' said He, 'the holy dish wherein I ate the lamb on Easter Day.* And now hast thou seen that thou most desired to see; but yet hast thou not seen it so openly as thou shalt see it in the city of Sarras in the spiritual palace. Therefore thou must go hence and bear with thee this holy vessel; for this night it shall depart from the realm of Logris, and it shall never more be seen here. And knowest thou wherefore? For it is not served nor worshipped to its right by them of this land, for they be turned to evil living; and therefore I shall disinherit them of the honour which I have done them. And therefore go ye three unto the sea, where ye shall find your ship ready; and with you take the sword with the strange girdles, and no more with you but Sir Percival and Sir Bors. Also I will that ye take with you of this blood of this spear for to anoint the Maimed King, both his legs and his body, and he shall have his health.'

'Sir,' said Galahad, 'why shall not these other fellows go with us?'

'For this cause: for right as I departed my apostles one here and another there, so I will that ye depart. And two of you shall die in my service, and one of you shall come again and tell tidings.' Then gave He them His blessing and vanished away.

[21]   And Sir Galahad went anon to the spear which lay upon the table, and touched the blood with his fingers, and came after to the Maimed King and anointed his legs and his body. And therewith he clothed him anon, and started upon his feet out of his bed as a whole man, and thanked God that He had healed him. And anon he left the world and yielded himself to a place of religion of white monks, and was a full holy man.

And that same night about midnight came a voice among them which said, 'My sons and not my chief sons, my friends and not my enemies, go ye hence where ye hope best to do, and as I bade you do.'

'Ah, thanked be Thou, Lord, that Thou wilt vouchsafe to call us Thy sons. Now may we well prove that we have not lost our pains.'

And anon in all haste they took their harness and departed. But the three knights of Gaul—one of them hight Claudine, King Claudas' son, and the other two were great gentlemen—then prayed Sir Galahad to each of them, that and they came to King Arthur's court, 'to salute my lord Sir Lancelot, my father, and them all of the Round Table'—if they came on that part, not to forget it.

Right so departed Sir Galahad, and Sir Percival and Sir Bors with him. And so they rode three days, and then they came to a rivage and found the ship whereof the tale speaketh of before. And when they came to the board they found in the midst the table of silver which they had left with the Maimed King, and the Sangrail which was covered with red samite. Then were they glad to have such things in their fellowship, and so they entered and made great reverence thereto.

And Sir Galahad fell on his knees and prayed long time to Our Lord, that at what time he asked, he might pass out of this world. And so long he prayed till a voice said, 'Sir Galahad, thou shalt have thy request; and when thou askest the death of thy body thou shalt have it, and then shalt thou have the life of thy soul.'

Then Sir Percival heard him a little, and prayed him of fellowship that was between them wherefore he asked such things.

'Sir, that shall I tell you,' said Sir Galahad. 'This other day when we saw a part of the adventures of the Sangrail, I was in such joy of heart that I trow never earthly man was. And therefore I wot well, when my body is dead my soul shall be in great joy to see the Blessed Trinity every day, and the majesty of Our Lord Jesu Christ.'

And so long were they in the ship that they said to Sir Galahad, 'Sir, in this bed ye ought to lie, for so saith the letters.' And so he laid him down and slept a great while. And when he awoke he looked before him and saw the city of Sarras; and as they would have landed, they saw the ship wherein Sir Percival had put his sister in.

'Truly,' said Sir Percival, 'in the name of God, well hath my sister held us covenant.'

Then took they out of the ship the table of silver, and he took it to Sir Percival and to Sir Bors to go before, and Sir Galahad came behind, and right so they went into the city. And at the gate of the city they saw an old man crooked; and anon Sir Galahad called him and bade him, 'Help to bear this heavy thing!'

'Truly,' said the old man, 'it is ten years ago that I might not go but with crutches.'

'Care thou not,' said Sir Galahad, 'arise up and show thy good will.'

And so he assayed, and found himself as whole as ever he was. Then ran he to the table, and took one part against Galahad. Anon rose there a great noise in the city, that a cripple was made whole by marvellous knights that entered into the city.

rivage] shore   took] gave

Then anon after, the three knights went to the water, and brought up into the palace Sir Percival's sister, and buried her as richly as they ought a king's daughter.

And when the king of that country knew that and saw that fellowship—his name was Estorause—he asked them of whence they were, and what thing it was that they had brought upon the table of silver. And they told him the truth of the Sangrail, and the power which God had set there. Then this king was a great tyrant and was come of the line of paynims, and took them and put them in prison in a deep hole. [22] But as soon as they were there Our Lord sent them the Sangrail, through whose grace they were always filled while they were in prison.

So at the year's end it befell that this king lay sick, and felt that he should die. Then he sent for the three knights, and they came before him; and he cried them mercy of that he had done to them, and they forgave him goodly, and he died anon.

When the king was dead all the city stood dismayed, and wist not who might be their king. Right so as they were in counsel, there came a voice down among them and bade them choose the youngest knight of three to be their king: 'For he shall well maintain you and all yours.'

So they made Sir Galahad king by all the assent of the whole city, and else they would have slain him. And when he was come to his land, he let make above the table of silver a chest of gold and of precious stones that covered the holy vessel; and every day early these three knights would come before it and make their prayers.

Now at the year's end, and the self Sunday after that Sir Galahad had borne the crown of gold, he arose up early and his fellows, and came to the palace; and saw before them the holy vessel, and a man kneeling on his knees in likeness of a bishop that had about him a great fellowship of angels, as it had been Jesu Christ Himself. And then he arose and began a Mass of Our Lady. And so he came to the sacring, and anon made an end.

He called Sir Galahad unto him and said, 'Come forth, the servant of Jesu Christ, and thou shalt see that thou hast much desired to see.'

And then he began to tremble right hard when the deadly flesh began to behold the spiritual things. Then he held up his hands toward heaven and said, 'Lord, I thank Thee, for now I see that that hath been

paynims] pagans   come to his land] had assumed the rule   sacring] moment of consecration   deadly flesh] mortal body

my desire many a day. Now, my blessed Lord, I would not live in this wretched world no longer, if it might please Thee, Lord.'

And therewith the good man took Our Lord's body betwixt his hands and proffered it to Sir Galahad, and he received it right gladly and meekly.

'Now wotest thou what I am?' said the good man.

'Nay, sir,' said Sir Galahad.

'I am Joseph, the son of Joseph of Arimathea, which Our Lord hath sent thee to bear thee fellowship. And wotest thou wherefore He hath sent me more than any other? For thou hast resembled me in two things: that thou hast seen the marvels of the Sangrail; and for thou hast been a clean maid, as I have been and am.'

And when he had said these words, Sir Galahad went to Sir Percival and kissed him, and commended him to God. And so he went to Sir Bors and kissed him, and commended him to God, and said, 'My fair lord, salute me unto my lord Sir Lancelot, my father, and as soon as ye see him, bid him remember of this world unstable.'

And therewith he kneeled down before the table and made his prayers; and so suddenly departed his soul to Jesu Christ, and a great multitude of angels bore it up to heaven even in the sight of his two fellows.

Also these two knights saw come from heaven a hand, but they saw not the body. And so it came right to the vessel and took it and the spear, and so bore it up to heaven. And sithen was there never man so hardy to say that he had seen the Sangrail.

So when Sir Percival and Sir Bors saw Sir Galahad dead, they made as much sorrow as ever did men; and if they had not been good men they might lightly have fallen in despair. And so people of the country and city, they were right heavy. But so he was buried; and as soon as he was buried Sir Percival yielded him to a hermitage out of the city, and took religious clothing. And Sir Bors was always with him, but he changed never his secular clothing, for that he purposed him to go again into the realm of Logris. [23]

Thus a year and two months lived Sir Percival in the hermitage a full holy life, and then passed out of the world. Then Sir Bors let bury him by his sister and by Sir Galahad in the spiritualities.

So when Sir Bors saw that he was in so far countries as in the parts of Babylon, he departed from the city of Sarras, and armed him and

yielded him] withdrew   spiritualities] consecrated ground came to the sea, and entered into a ship. And so it befell him by good adventure he came unto the realm of Logris; and so he rode apace till he came to Camelot, where the King was. And then was there made great joy of him in all the court, for they weened he had been lost forasmuch as he had been so long out of the country.

And when they had eaten, the King made great clerks to come before him, for cause they should chronicle of the high adventures of the good knights. So when Sir Bors had told him of the high adventures of the Sangrail such as had befallen him and his three fellows, which were Sir Lancelot, Percival, and Sir Galahad and himself, then Sir Lancelot told the adventures of the Sangrail that he had seen. And all this was made in great books, and put up in almeries at Salisbury.

And anon Sir Bors said to Sir Lancelot, 'Sir Galahad, your own son, saluted you by me, and after you my lord King Arthur and all the whole court, and so did Sir Percival; for I buried them both with mine own hands in the city of Sarras. Also, Sir Lancelot, Sir Galahad prayed you to remember of this unsure world, as ye behight him when ye were together more than half a year.'

'This is true,' said Sir Lancelot. 'Now I trust to God his prayer shall avail me.' Then Sir Lancelot took Sir Bors in his arms and said, 'Cousin, ye are right welcome to me, for ye and I shall never depart asunder whilst our lives may last.'

'Sir,' said he, 'as ye will, so will I.'*

Thus endeth the tale of the Sangrail, that was briefy drawn out of French, which is a tale chronicled for one of the truest and of the holiest that is in this world; by Sir Thomas Malory, knight. O blessed Jesu, help him through His might. Amen.

almeries] repositories   behight] promised

THE TALE OF SIR LANCELOT
AND QUEEN GUENIVERE

So after the quest of the Sangrail was fulfilled, and all knights that were left alive were come home again unto the Table Round, as the Book of the Sangrail maketh mention, then was there great joy in the court; and in especial King Arthur and Queen Guenivere made great joy of the remnant that were come home. And passing glad was the King and the Queen of Sir Lancelot and of Sir Bors, for they had been passing long away in the quest of the Sangrail.

Then, as the book saith, Sir Lancelot began to resort unto Queen Guenivere again, and forgot the promise and the perfection that he made in the quest. For, as the book saith, had not Sir Lancelot been in his privy thoughts and in his mind so set inwardly to the Queen as he was in seeming outward to God, there had no knight passed him in the quest of the Sangrail, but ever his thoughts were privily on the Queen. And so they loved together more hotter than they did beforehand, and had many such privy draughts together that many in the court spoke of it, and in especial Sir Agravain, Sir Gawain's brother, for he was ever open-mouthed.

So it befell that Sir Lancelot had many resorts of ladies and damosels that daily resorted unto him to be their champion: in all such matters of right Sir Lancelot applied him daily to do for the pleasure of Our Lord Jesu Christ. And ever as much as he might he withdrew him from the company of Queen Guenivere for to eschew the slander and noise, wherefore the Queen waxed wroth with Sir Lancelot.

So on a day she called him to her chamber, and said thus 'Sir Lancelot, I see and feel daily that thy love beginneth to slacken, for ye have no joy to be in my presence, but ever ye are out of this court. And quarrels and matters ye have nowadays for ladies, maidens, and gentlewomen, more than ever ye were wont to have beforehand.'

'Ah, madam,' said Sir Lancelot, 'in this ye must hold me excused, for divers causes. One is, I was but late in the quest of the Sangrail, and I thank God of His great mercy, and never of my deserving, that I saw in that my quest as much as ever saw any sinful man living, and so was it told me. And if that I had not had my privy thoughts to return to your love again as I do, I had seen as great mysteries as ever saw my son Sir Galahad, Percival, or Sir Bors. And therefore, madam, I was but late in that quest, and wit you well, madam, it may not be yet lightly forgotten the high service in whom I did my diligent labour.

'Also, madam, wit you well that there be many men speak of our love in this court and have you and me greatly in await, as this Sir Agravain and Sir Mordred. And madam, wit you well I dread them more for your sake than for any fear I have of them myself, for I may happen to escape and rid myself in a great need, where, madam, ye must abide all that will be said unto you. And then if that ye fall in any distress through wilful folly, then is there no other help but by me and my blood. And wit you well, madam, the boldness of you and me will bring us to shame and slander; and that were me loath to see you dishonoured. And that is the cause I take upon me more for to do for damosels and maidens than ever I did before, that men should understand my joy and my delight is my pleasure to have ado for damosels and maidens.'

[2] All this while the Queen stood still and let Sir Lancelot say what he would. And when he had all said she burst out weeping, and so she sobbed and wept a great while. And when she might speak she said, 'Sir Lancelot, now I well understand that thou art a false recreant knight and a common lecher, and lovest and holdest other ladies, and of me thou hast disdain and scorn. For wit thou well, now I understand thy falsehood I shall never love thee more. And look thou be never so hardy to come in my sight; and right here I discharge thee this court, that thou never come within it, and I forfend thee my fellowship, and upon pain of thy head that thou see me nevermore.'

Right so Sir Lancelot departed with great heaviness, that uneath he might sustain himself for great dole-making. Then he called Sir Bors, Ector de Maris, and Sir Lionel, and told them how the Queen had forfended him the court, and so he was in will to depart into his own country.

'Fair sir,' said Sir Bors de Ganis, 'ye shall not depart out of this land by my advice; for ye must remember you what ye are, and renowned the most noblest knight of the world, and many great matters ye have in hand. And women in their hastiness will do oftentimes that, after, them sore repenteth. And therefore by my advice ye shall take your horse and ride to the good hermit here beside Windsor, that sometime

in await] under watch   blood] kin   forfend] forbid

was a good knight: his name is Sir Brastias. And there shall ye abide till that I send you word of better tidings.'

'Brother,' said Sir Lancelot, 'wit you well I am full loath to depart out of this realm, but the Queen hath defended me so highly, that me seemeth she will never be my good lady as she hath been.'

'Say ye never so,' said Sir Bors, 'for many times or this she hath been wroth with you, and after that she was the first repented it.'

'Ye say well,' said Lancelot, 'for now will I do by your counsel, and take my horse and my harness and ride to the hermit Sir Brastias; and there will I repose me till I hear some manner of tidings from you. But, fair brother, in that ye can, get me the love of my lady Queen Guenivere.'

'Sir,' said Sir Bors, 'ye need not to move me of such matters, for well ye wot I will do what I may to please you.'

And then Sir Lancelot departed suddenly, and no creature wist where he was become but Sir Bors. So when Sir Lancelot was departed, the Queen outward made no manner of sorrow in showing, to none of his blood nor to no other; but wit ye well, inwardly, as the book saith, she took great thought, but she bore it out with a proud countenance as though she felt no thought nor danger.

So the Queen let make a privy dinner in London unto the knights of [3] the Round Table, and all was for to show outward that she had as great joy in all other knights of the Round Table as she had in Sir Lancelot. So there was all only at that dinner Sir Gawain and his brethren, that is for to say Sir Agravain, Sir Gaheris, Sir Gareth, and Sir Mordred. Also there was Sir Bors de Ganis, Sir Blamor de Ganis, Sir Bleoberis de Ganis, Sir Galihud, Sir Galihodin, Sir Ector de Maris, Sir Lionel, Sir Palomides, Sir Safer his brother, Sir La Cote Mal Taillé, Sir Persant, Sir Ironside, Sir Brandiles, Sir Kay le Seneschal, Sir Mador de la Porte, Sir Patrise (a knight of Ireland), Sir Aliduke, Sir Ascamore, and Sir Pinel le Savage, which was cousin to Sir Lamorak de Gales, the good knight that Sir Gawain and his brethren slew by treason.

And so these four and twenty knights should dine with the Queen in a privy place by themselves, and there was made a great feast of all manner of dainties. But Sir Gawain had a custom that he used daily at meat and at supper, that he loved well all manner of fruit, and in especial apples and pears. And therefore whosoever dined or feasted

defended me so highly] barred me so absolutely

Sir Gawain would commonly purvey for good fruit for him, and so did the Queen: for to please Sir Gawain she let purvey for him all manner of fruit, for Sir Gawain was a passing hot knight of nature.* And this Sir Pinel hated Sir Gawain because of his kinsman Sir Lamorak's death; and therefore for pure envy and hate, Sir Pinel empoisoned certain apples for to empoison Sir Gawain.

So this was well yet unto the end of meat; and so it befell by misfortune a good knight, Sir Patrise, which was cousin unto Sir Mador de la Porte, took an apple, for he was enchafed with heat of wine, and it mishapped him to take a poisoned apple. And when he had eaten it he swelled sore till he brast, and there Sir Patrise fell down suddenly dead among them.

Then every knight leapt from the board ashamed and enraged for wrath out of their wits, for they wist not what to say; considering Queen Guenivere made the feast and dinner, they had all suspicion unto her.

'My lady, the Queen,' said Sir Gawain, 'madam, wit you that this dinner was made for me and my fellows. And for all folks that know my condition understand that I love well fruit, now I see well I had near been slain. Therefore, madam, I dread me lest ye will be shamed.'

Then the Queen stood still, and was so sore abashed that she wist not what to say.

'This shall not so be ended,' said Sir Mador de la Porte, 'for here have I lost a full noble knight of my blood; and therefore upon this shame and despite I will be revenged to the utterance.' And there openly Sir Mador appealed the Queen of the death of his cousin Sir Patrise.

Then stood they all still, that none would speak a word against him; for they all had great suspicion unto the Queen because she let make that dinner. And the Queen was so abashed that she could no other ways do, but wept so heartily that she fell in a swoon. So with this noise and cry came to them King Arthur, and when he wist of the trouble he was a passing heavy man.

[4]   And ever Sir Mador stood still before the King and appealed the Queen of treason; for the custom was such at that time that all manner of shameful death was called treason.

'Fair lords,' said King Arthur, 'me repenteth of this trouble, but the

utterance] utmost, i.e. death   appealed] accused

case is so I may not have ado in this matter, for I must be a rightful judge.* And that repenteth me that I may not do battle for my wife, for, as I deem, this deed came never by her. And therefore I suppose she shall not be all distained, but that some good knight shall put his body in jeopardy for my queen rather than she should be burnt in a wrong quarrel. And therefore, Sir Mador, be not so hasty, for pardieu it may happen she shall not be all friendless. And therefore desire thou thy day of battle, and she shall purvey her of some good knight that shall answer you; or else it were to me great shame, and to all my court.'

'My gracious lord,' said Sir Mador, 'ye must hold me excused, for though ye be our king, in that degree ye are but a knight as we are, and ye are sworn unto knighthood as well as we be; and therefore I beseech you that ye be not displeased, for there is none of the four and twenty knights that were bidden to this dinner but all they have great suspicion unto the Queen. What say ye all, my lords?' said Sir Mador.

Then they answered by and by and said they could not excuse the Queen; for why she made the dinner, and either it must come by her or by her servants.

'Alas,' said the Queen, 'I made this dinner for a good intent, and never for no evil; so Almighty Jesu me help in my right, as I was never purposed to do such evil deeds, and that I report me unto God.'

'My lord the King,' said Sir Mador, 'I require you as ye be a righteous king, give me my day that I may have justice.'

'Well,' said the King, 'this day fifteen days, look thou be ready armed on horseback in the meadow beside Winchester. And if it so fall that there be any knight to encounter against you, there may you do your best, and God speed the right. And if it so befall that there be no knight ready at that day, then must my queen be burned; and there she shall be ready to have her judgement.'

'I am answered,' said Sir Mador. And every knight yode where him liked.

So when the King and the Queen were together, the King asked the Queen how this case befell. Then the Queen said, 'Sir, as Jesu be my help,' she wist not how nor in what manner.

'Where is Sir Lancelot?' said King Arthur. 'And he were here he would not grudge to do battle for you.'

---

distained] dishonoured   report me unto] say before

'Sir,' said the Queen, 'I wot not where he is, but his brother and his kinsmen deem that he be not within this realm.'

'That me repenteth,' said King Arthur, 'for and he were here he would soon stint this strife. Well, then, I will counsel you', said the King, 'that ye go unto Sir Bors and pray him for to do battle for you for Sir Lancelot's sake; and upon my life he will not refuse you. For well I see,' said the King, 'that none of the four and twenty knights that were at your dinner where Sir Patrise was slain will do battle for you, nor none of them will say well of you; and that shall be great slander to you in this court. But now I miss Sir Lancelot, for and he were here he would soon put me in my heart's ease. What aileth you,' said the King, 'that ye cannot keep Sir Lancelot upon your side? For wit you well,' said the King, 'who that hath Sir Lancelot upon his party hath the most man of worship in this world upon his side. Now go your way,' said the King unto the Queen, 'and require Sir Bors to do battle for you for Sir Lancelot's sake.'

[5]   So the Queen departed from the King, and sent for Sir Bors into the chamber; and when he came she besought him of succour.

'Madam,' said he, 'what would ye that I did? For I may not with my worship have ado in this matter, because I was at the same dinner, for dread that any of those knights would have me in suspicion. Also, Madam,' said Sir Bors, 'now miss ye Sir Lancelot, for he would not have failed you in your right nor in your wrong, for when ye have been in right great dangers he hath succoured you. And now ye have driven him out of this country, by whom ye and all we were daily worshipped—therefore, madam, I marvel how ye dare for shame to require me to do any thing for you, in so much ye have chased him out of your court by whom we were up borne and honoured.'

'Alas, fair knight,' said the Queen, 'I put me wholly in your grace, and all that is amiss I will amend as ye will counsel me.' And therewith she kneeled down upon both her knees and besought Sir Bors to have mercy upon her, 'Or else I shall have a shameful death, and thereto I never offended.'

Right so came King Arthur, and found the Queen kneeling; and then Sir Bors took her up and said, 'Madam, ye do me great dishonour.'

'Ah, gentle knight,' said the King, 'have mercy upon my queen,

worshipped] brought honour

courteous knight, for I am now certain she is untruly defamed. And therefore, courteous knight,' the King said, 'promise her to do battle for her, I require you for the love ye owe unto Sir Lancelot.'

'My lord,' said Sir Bors, 'ye require me the greatest thing that any man may require me; and wit you well, if I grant to do battle for the Queen I shall wrath many of my fellowship of the Table Round. But as for that,' said Sir Bors, 'I will grant for my lord Sir Lancelot's sake and for your sake, I will at that day be the Queen's champion unless that there come by adventure a better knight than I am to do battle for her.'

'Will ye promise me this,' said the King, 'by your faith?'

'Yea sir,' said Sir Bors, 'of that I shall not fail you, nor her, but if there came a better knight than I am: then shall he have the battle.'

Then was the King and the Queen passing glad, and so departed, and thanked him heartily.

Then Sir Bors departed secretly upon a day and rode unto Sir Lancelot there as he was with Sir Brastias, and told him of all this adventure.

'Ah Jesu,' Sir Lancelot said, 'this is come happily as I would have it. And therefore I pray you make you ready to do battle, but look that ye tarry till ye see me come as long as ye may. For I am sure Sir Mador is a hot knight when he is enchafed, for the more ye suffer him the hastier will he be to battle.'

'Sir,' said Sir Bors, 'let me deal with him. Doubt ye not ye shall have all your will.'

So departed Sir Bors from him and came to the court again. Then was it noised in all the court that Sir Bors should do battle for the Queen; wherefore many knights were displeased with him, that he would take upon him to do battle in the Queen's quarrel, for there were but few knights in all the court but they deemed the Queen was in the wrong and that she had done that treason. So Sir Bors answered thus to his fellows of the Table Round, 'Wit you well, my fair lords, it were shame to us all and we suffered to see the most noble queen of the world to be shamed openly, considering her lord and our lord is the man of most worship christened, and he hath ever worshipped us all in all places.'

Many answered him again, 'As for our most noble King Arthur, we love him and honour him as well as ye do; but as for Queen Guenivere, we love her not, because she is a destroyer of good knights.'

'Fair lords,' said Sir Bors, 'me seemeth ye say not as ye should say, for never yet in my days knew I never nor heard say that ever she was a destroyer of good knights. But at all times as far as ever I could know she was a maintainer of good knights; and ever she hath been large and free of her goods to all good knights, and the most bounteous lady of her gifts and her good grace that ever I saw or heard speak of. And therefore it were shame to us all and to our most noble king's wife, whom we serve, and we suffered her to be shamefully slain. And wit you well,' said Sir Bors, 'I will not suffer it, for I dare say so much, for the Queen is not guilty of Sir Patrise's death; for she owed him never no evil will, nor none of the four and twenty knights that were at that dinner, for I dare say for good love she bade us to dinner and not for no mal engine. And that I doubt not shall be proved hereafter, for howsoever the game goeth, there was treason among us.'

Then some said to Sir Bors, 'We may well believe your words.' And so some were well pleased, and some were not.

[6]   So the day came on fast until the eve that the battle should be. Then the Queen sent for Sir Bors and asked him how he was disposed.

'Truly, madam,' said he, 'I am disposed in like wise as I promised you, that is to say I shall not fail you, unless there by adventure come a better knight than I am to do battle for you; then, madam, I am of you discharged of my promise.'

'Will ye', said the Queen, 'that I tell my lord the King thus?'

'Do as it pleaseth you, madam.'

Then the Queen yode unto the King and told the answer of Sir Bors.

'Well, have ye no doubt', said the King, 'of Sir Bors, for I call him now that is living one of the noblest knights of the world, and most perfect man.'

And thus it passed on till the morrow; and so the King and the Queen and all manner of knights that were there at that time drew them unto the meadow beside Winchester where the battle should be. And so when the King was come with the Queen and many knights of the Table Round, so the Queen was then put in the constable's ward, and a great fire made about an iron stake, that and Sir Mador de la Porte had the better, she should there be burned. For such custom was used in those days, for favour, love, nor affinity there should be none other but righteous judgement, as well upon a king as upon a knight, and as well upon a queen as upon another poor lady.*

---

large] generous   mal engine] evil trickery   affinity] powerful connections

So this meanwhile came in Sir Mador de la Porte, and took his oath before the King how that the Queen did this treason unto his cousin Sir Patrise. 'And unto my oath I will prove it with my body, hand for hand, who that will say the contrary.'

Right so came in Sir Bors de Ganis, and said that as for Queen Guenivere, 'she is in the right, and that will I make good that she is not culpable of this treason that is put upon her.'

'Then make thee ready,' said Sir Mador, 'and we shall prove whether thou be in the right or I.'

'Sir Mador,' said Sir Bors, 'wit you well, I know you for a good knight; not for that I shall not fear you so greatly but I trust to God I shall be able to withstand your malice. But thus much have I promised my lord Arthur and my lady the Queen, that I shall do battle for her in this cause to the utterest, unless that there come a better knight than I am and discharge me.'

'Is that all?' said Sir Mador, 'Either come thou off and do battle with me, or else say nay.'

'Take your horse,' said Sir Bors, 'and as I suppose, I shall not tarry long but ye shall be answered.'

Then either departed to their tents and made them ready to horse-back as they thought best. And anon Sir Mador came into the field with his shield on his shoulder and his spear in his hand, and so rode about the place crying unto King Arthur, 'Bid your champion come forth, and he dare!'

Then was Sir Bors ashamed, and took his horse and came to the lists' end. And then was he ware where came from a wood there fast by a knight all armed upon a white horse, with a strange shield of strange arms; and he came driving all that his horse might run. And so he came to Sir Bors, and said thus: 'Fair knight, I pray you be not displeased, for here must a better knight than ye are have this battle, therefore I pray you withdraw you. For wit you well, I have had this day a right great journey, and this battle ought to be mine; and so I promised you when I spoke with you last. And with all my heart I thank you of your good will.'

Then Sir Bors rode unto King Arthur and told him how there was a knight come that would have the battle to fight for the Queen.

'What knight is he?' said the King.

driving] spurring

'I wot not,' said Sir Bors, 'but such covenant he made with me to be here this day. Now my lord,' said Sir Bors, 'here I am discharged.'

[7] Then the King called to that knight, and asked him if he would fight for the Queen.

Then he answered and said, 'Sir, therefore came I hither. And therefore, sir king, tarry me no longer; for anon as I have finished this battle I must depart hence, for I have to do many battles elsewhere. For wit you well,' said that knight, 'this is dishonour to you and to all knights of the Round Table, to see and know so noble a lady and so courteous as Queen Guenivere is, thus to be rebuked and shamed amongst you.'

Then they all marvelled what knight that might be that so took the battle upon him, for there was not one that knew him but if it were Sir Bors.

Then said Sir Mador de la Porte unto the King, 'Now let me wit with whom I shall have ado.'

And then they rode to the lists' end, and there they couched their spears and ran together with all their mights; and Sir Mador's spear broke all to pieces, but the other's spear held, and bore Sir Mador's horse and all backward to the earth a great fall. But mightily and deliverly he avoided his horse from him, and put his shield before him and drew his sword, and bade the other knight alight and do battle with him on foot.

Then that knight descended down from his horse, and put his shield before him and drew his sword; and so they came eagerly unto battle, and either gave other many sad strokes, tracing and traversing and foining together with their swords as it were wild boars, thus fighting nigh an hour; for this Sir Mador was a strong knight, and mightily proved in many strong battles. But at the last this knight smote Sir Mador grovelling upon the earth, and he stepped near him to have pulled Sir Mador flatling upon the ground; and therewith Sir Mador arose, and in his rising he smote that knight through the thick of the thighs that the blood brast out fiercely. And when he felt himself so wounded and saw his blood, he let him arise upon his feet; and then he gave him such a buffet upon the helm that he fell to the earth flatling, and therewith he strode to him to have pulled off his helm off his head. And so Sir Mador prayed that knight to save his life, and so he yielded him as overcome, and released the Queen of his quarrel.

'I will not grant thee thy life,' said that knight, 'only that thou freely release the Queen for ever, and that no mention be made upon Sir Patrise's tomb that ever Queen Guenivere consented to that treason.'

'All this shall be done,' said Sir Mador. 'I clearly discharge my quarrel for ever.'

Then the knights parters of the lists took up Sir Mador and led him to his tent, and the other knight went straight to the stair-foot where sat King Arthur. And by that time was the Queen come to the King, and either kissed other heartily. And when the King saw that knight, he stooped down to him and thanked him, and in like wise did the Queen; and the King prayed him to put off his helmet and to repose him and to take a sop of wine. And then he put off his helmet to drink, and then every knight knew him that it was Sir Lancelot. And anon as the King wist that, he took the Queen in his hand, and yode unto Sir Lancelot and said, 'Sir, grantmercy of your great travail that ye have had this day for me and for my queen.'

'My lord,' said Sir Lancelot, 'wit you well I ought of right ever in your quarrel and in my lady the Queen's quarrel to do battle; for ye are the man that gave me the high order of knighthood, and that day my lady, your Queen, did me worship, and else had I been shamed; for that same day that ye made me knight, through my hastiness I lost my sword, and my lady your queen found it and lapped it in her train, and gave me my sword when I had need thereto, and else had I been shamed among all knights.* And therefore, my lord Arthur, I promised her at that day ever to be her knight in right or in wrong.'

'Grantmercy,' said the King, 'for this journey! And wit you well,' said the King, 'I shall acquit your goodness.'

And evermore the Queen beheld Sir Lancelot, and wept so tenderly that she sank almost to the ground for sorrow that he had done to her so great kindness where she showed him great unkindness. Then the knights of his blood drew unto him, and there either of them made great joy of other. And so came all the knights of the Table Round that were there at that time, and welcomed him. And then Sir Mador was healed through leechcraft, and Sir Lancelot was healed of his plaie; and so there was made great joy, and many mirths were made in that court.

knights parters] marshals   sop of wine] a cup of wine with bread in it
lapped it in her train] wrapped it in the skirt of her dress   journey] day's work
acquit] repay   plaie] wound

[8]   And so it befell that the Damosel of the Lake that hight Nenive, which wedded the good knight Sir Pelleas, and so she came to the court; for ever she did great goodness unto King Arthur and to all his knights through her sorcery and enchantments. And so when she heard how the Queen was grieved for the death of Sir Patrise, then she told it openly that she was never guilty; and there she disclosed by whom it was done, and named him, Sir Pinel; and for what cause he did it, there it was openly known and disclosed, and so the Queen was excused. And this knight Sir Pinel fled unto his country, and was openly known that he empoisoned the apples at that feast to that intent to have destroyed Sir Gawain, because Sir Gawain and his brethren destroyed Sir Lamorak de Gales, which Sir Pinel was cousin unto.

Then was Sir Patrise buried in the church of Westminster in a tomb, and thereupon was written: 'Here lieth Sir Patrise of Ireland, slain by Sir Pinel le Savage, that empoisoned apples to have slain Sir Gawain. And by misfortune Sir Patrise ate one of the apples, and then suddenly he brast.' Also there was written upon the tomb that Queen Guenivere was appealed of treason of the death of Sir Patrise by Sir Mador de la Porte; and there was made mention how Sir Lancelot fought with him for Queen Guenivere and overcame him in plain battle. All this was written upon the tomb of Sir Patrise in excusing of the Queen.

And then Sir Mador sued daily and long to have the Queen's good grace; and so by the means of Sir Lancelot he caused him to stand in the Queen's good grace, and all was forgiven.

Thus it passed until Our Lady Day of the Assumption. Within fifteen days of that feast the King let cry a great jousts and a tournament that should be at that day at Camelot, otherwise called Winchester; and the King let cry that he and the King of Scots would joust against all the world. And when this cry was made, thither came many good knights.*

So King Arthur made him ready to depart to his jousts, and would have had the Queen with him; but at that time she would not, she said, for she was sick and might not ride.

'That me repenteth,' said the King, 'for these seven years ye saw not such a noble fellowship together, except the Whitsuntide when Sir Galahad departed from the court.'

Our Lady Day of the Assumption] 15 August   Within fifteen days] i.e. a fortnight before

'Truly,' said the Queen, 'ye must hold me excused: I may not be there.'

And many deemed the Queen would not be there because of Sir Lancelot; for he would not ride with the King, for he said that he was not whole of the plaie of Sir Mador, wherefore the King was heavy and passing wroth; and so he departed toward Winchester with his fellowship. And so by the way the King lodged at a town that was called Ascolat,* that is in English Guildford, and there the King lay in the castle.

So when the King was departed, the Queen called Sir Lancelot unto her and said thus: 'Sir, ye are greatly to blame thus to hold you behind my lord. What will your enemies and mine say and deem? "See how Sir Lancelot holdeth him ever behind the King, and so the Queen doth also, for that they would have their pleasure together." And thus will they say,' said the Queen.

'Have ye no doubt, madam,' said Sir Lancelot, 'I allow your wit; it is [9] of late come since ye were waxed so wise. And therefore, madam, at this time I will be ruled by your counsel, and this night I will take my rest, and tomorrow betimes I will take my way toward Winchester. But wit you well,' said Sir Lancelot unto the Queen, 'at that jousts I will be against the King, and against all his fellowship.'

'Sir, ye may there do as ye list,' said the Queen, 'but by my counsel ye shall not be against your king and your fellowship, for there be full many hardy knights of your blood.'

'Madam,' said Sir Lancelot, 'I shall take the adventure that God will give me.'

And so upon the morn early he heard Mass and dined, and so he took his leave of the Queen and departed. And then he rode so much unto the time he came to Ascolat; and there it happened him that in the eveningtide he came to an old baron's place that hight Sir Barnard of Ascolat. And as Sir Lancelot entered into his lodging, King Arthur espied him as he did walk in a garden beside the castle: he knew him well enough.

'Well, sirs,' said King Arthur unto his knights that were by him beside the castle, 'I have now espied one knight,' he said, 'that will play his play at the jousts, I undertake.'

'Who is that?' said the knights.

---

allow] acknowledge   it is of late come since ye were waxed so wise] it is a recent innovation that you have become so sensible

'At this time ye shall not wit for me,' said the King, and smiled, and went to his lodging.

So when Sir Lancelot was in his lodging and unarmed in his chamber, the old baron Sir Barnard came to him and welcomed him in the best manner; but he knew not Sir Lancelot.

'Fair sir,' said Sir Lancelot to his host, 'I would pray you to lend me a shield that were not openly known, for mine is well known.'

'Sir,' said his host, 'ye shall have your desire, for me seemeth ye be one of the likeliest knights that ever I saw, and therefore, sir, I shall show you friendship. And sir, wit you well I have two sons that were but late made knights, and the eldest hight Sir Tirry; and he was hurt that same day he was made knight, and he may not ride. And his shield ye shall have, for that is not known I dare say but here, and in no place else.' And his younger son hight Sir Lavain; 'and if it please you, he shall ride with you unto that jousts, for he is of his age strong and wight. For much my heart giveth unto you that ye should be a noble knight; and therefore I pray you to tell me your name,' said Sir Barnard.

'As for that,' said Sir Lancelot, 'ye must hold me excused as at this time; and if God give me grace to speed well at the jousts, I shall come again and tell you my name. But I pray you, in any wise let me have your son Sir Lavain with me, and that I may have his brother's shield.'

'Sir, all this shall be done,' said Sir Barnard.

So this old baron had a daughter that was called that time the Fair Maiden of Ascolat; and ever she beheld Sir Lancelot wonderfully. And as the book saith, she cast such a love unto Sir Lancelot that she could never withdraw her love, wherefore she died; and her name was Elaine la Blanche.

So thus, as she came to and fro she was so hot in love that she besought Sir Lancelot to wear upon him at the jousts a token of hers.

'Damosel,' said Sir Lancelot, 'and if I grant you that, ye may say that I do more for your love than ever I did for lady or gentlewoman.'

Then he remembered himself that he would go to the jousts disguised; and because he had never before borne no manner of token of no damosel, he bethought him to bear a token of hers, that none of his blood thereby might know him. And then he said, 'Fair maiden, I will grant you to wear a token of yours upon my helmet. And therefore, what is it?—show ye it me.'

wight] muscular

'Sir,' she said, 'it is a red sleeve of mine of scarlet, well embroidered with great pearls.' And so she brought it him.

So Sir Lancelot received it, and said, 'Never did I erst so much for no damosel.'

Then Sir Lancelot betook the fair maiden his shield in keeping, and prayed her to keep it until time that he came again. And so that night he had merry rest and great cheer, for this damosel Elaine was ever about Sir Lancelot all the while she might be suffered.

So upon a day, on the morn, King Arthur and all his knights [10] departed, for there the King had tarried three days to abide his noble knights. And so when the King was ridden, Sir Lancelot and Sir Lavain made them ready to ride, and either of them had white shields, and the red sleeve Sir Lancelot let carry with him; and so they took their leave at Sir Barnard the old baron, and at his daughter the fair maiden. And then they rode so long till that they came to Camelot, that time called Winchester; and there was great press of kings, dukes, earls, and barons, and many noble knights. But there Sir Lancelot was lodged privily by the means of Sir Lavain with a rich burgess, that no man in that town was ware what they were. And so they reposed them there till Our Lady Day of the Assumption, that the great jousts should be.

So when trumpets blew unto the field, and King Arthur was set on high upon a chaflet to behold who did best—but as the French book saith, the King would not suffer Sir Gawain to go from him, for never had Sir Gawain the better and Sir Lancelot were in the field, and many times was Sir Gawain rebuked so when Sir Lancelot was in the field in any jousts disguised—then some of the kings, as King Angwish of Ireland and the King of Scots, were that time turned to be upon the side of King Arthur. And then the other party was the King of Northgales, and the King with the Hundred Knights, and the King of Northumberland, and Sir Galahalt the Haut Prince. But these three kings and this duke were passing weak to hold against Arthur's party, for with him were the noblest knights of the world.

So then they withdrew them, either party from other, and every man made him ready in his best manner to do what he might. Then

---

betook] entrusted to   all the while she might be suffered] as long as she was allowed   chaflet] platform

Sir Lancelot made him ready, and put the red sleeve upon his helmet and fastened it fast. And so Sir Lancelot and Sir Lavain departed out of Winchester privily, and rode unto a little leaved wood behind the party that held against King Arthur's party; and there they held them still till the parties smote together.*

And there began a great medley; and fifteen knights of the Round Table with more other came in together, and beat aback the King of Northumberland and the King of Northgales. When Sir Lancelot saw this as he hoved in the little leaved wood, then he said unto Sir Lavain, 'See yonder is a company of good knights, and they hold them together as boars that were chased with dogs.'

'That is truth,' said Sir Lavain.

[11]   'Now,' said Sir Lancelot, 'and ye will help a little, ye shall see the yonder fellowship that chaseth now these men on our side, that they shall go as fast backward as they went forward.'

'Sir, spare ye not for my part,' said Sir Lavain, 'for I shall do what I may.'

Then Sir Lancelot and Sir Lavain came in at the thickest of the press, and there Sir Lancelot smote down Sir Brandiles, Sir Sagramore, Sir Dodinas, Sir Kay, Sir Griflet; and all this he did with one spear. And Sir Lavain smote down Sir Lucan the Butler and Sir Bedivere. And then Sir Lancelot got another spear, and there he smote down Sir Agravain and Sir Gaheris, Sir Mordred, Sir Meliot de Logris; and Sir Lavain smote down Sir Ozanna le Coeur Hardi. And then the knights of the Table Round withdrew them aback, after they had gotten their horses as well as they might.

'Ah, mercy Jesu,' said Sir Gawain, 'what knight is yonder that doth so marvellous deeds in that field?'

'I wot what he is,' said the King, 'but as at this time I will not name him.'

'Sir,' said Sir Gawain, 'I would say it were Sir Lancelot by his riding and his buffets that I see him deal; but ever me seemeth it should not be he for that he beareth the red sleeve upon his helmet, for I wist him never bear token at no jousts of lady nor gentlewoman.'

'Let him be,' said King Arthur, 'he will be better known and do more or ever he depart.'

Then the party that was against King Arthur were well comforted,

hoved] waited

and then they held them together that beforehand were sore rebuked. Then Sir Bors, Sir Ector de Maris, and Sir Lionel called unto them the knights of their blood; and so these knights of Sir Lancelot's kin thrust in mightily, for they were all noble knights. And they of great hate and despite thought to rebuke that noble knight Sir Lancelot and Sir Lavain, for they knew them not. And so they came hurling together, and smote down many knights of Northgales and of Northumberland. And when Sir Lancelot saw them fare so, he got a great spear in his hand; and there encountered with him all at once Sir Bors, Sir Ector, and Sir Lionel, and they three smote him at once with their spears, and with force of themselves they smote Sir Lancelot's horse reverse to the earth. And by misfortune Sir Bors smote Sir Lancelot through the shield into the side, and the spear broke, and the head left still in the side.

When Sir Lavain saw his master lie on the ground, he ran to the King of Scots and smote him to the earth; and by great force he took his horse and brought him to Sir Lancelot, and maugre them all he made him to mount upon that horse. And then Sir Lancelot got a spear in his hand, and there he smote Sir Bors, horse and man, to the earth; and in the same wise he served Sir Ector and Sir Lionel, and Sir Lavain smote down Sir Blamor de Ganis. And then Sir Lancelot drew his sword, for he felt himself so sore hurt that he weened there to have had his death.

And by this was Sir Bors horsed again and in came with Sir Ector and Sir Lionel, and all they three smote with their swords upon Sir Lancelot's helmet. And when he felt their buffets, and with that his wound grieved him grievously, then he thought to do what he might while he could endure. And then he gave Sir Bors such a buffet that he made him bow his head passing low; and therewith he rased off his helm and might have slain him; but when he saw his visage, so pulled him down, and in the same wise he served Sir Ector and Sir Lionel. For as the book saith, he might have slain them, but when he saw their visages his heart might not serve him thereto, but left them there. And there Sir Lancelot with his sword smote down and pulled down, as the French book saith, more than thirty knights, and the most part were of the Table Round. And there Sir Lavain did full well that day, for he smote down ten knights of the Table Round.

pulled him down] i.e. from his horse

[12]   'Mercy Jesu,' said Sir Gawain unto King Arthur, 'I marvel what knight that he is with the red sleeve.'

'Sir,' said King Arthur, 'he will be known or ever he depart.'

And then the King blew unto lodging, and the prize was given by heralds unto the knight with the white shield that bore the red sleeve. Then came the King of Northgales, and the King of Northumberland, and the King with the Hundred Knights, and Sir Galahalt the Haut Prince, and said unto Sir Lancelot, 'Fair knight, God you bless, for much have ye done for us this day; and therefore we pray you that ye will come with us, that ye may receive the honour and the prize as ye have worshipfully deserved it.'

'Fair lords,' said Sir Lancelot, 'wit you well, if I have deserved thanks I have sore bought it; and that me repenteth, for I am never likely to escape with the life. Therefore, my fair lords, I pray you that ye will suffer me to depart where me liketh, for I am sore hurt. And I take no force of no honour, for I had liever repose me than to be lord of all the world.'

And therewith he groaned piteously, and rode a great gallop away from them until he came under a wood's eaves. And when he saw that he was from the field nigh a mile, that he was sure he might not be seen, then he said with a high voice and with a great groan, 'Ah, gentle knight, Sir Lavain, help me that this truncheon were out of my side, for it sticketh so sore that it nigh slayeth me.'

'Ah, my own lord,' said Sir Lavain, 'I would fain do that might please you, but I dread me sore and I pull out the truncheon that ye shall be in peril of death.'

'I charge you,' said Sir Lancelot, 'as ye love me, draw it out.'

And therewith he descended from his horse, and right so did Sir Lavain. And forthwith he drew the truncheon out of his side; and he gave a great shriek and a grisly groan that the blood brast out nigh a pint at once, that at the last he sank down upon his arse, and so swooned down pale and deadly.

'Alas,' said Sir Lavain, 'what shall I do?' And then he turned Sir Lancelot into the wind, and so he lay there nigh half an hour as he had been dead.

And so at the last Sir Lancelot cast up his eyes and said, 'Ah, Sir Lavain, help me that I were on my horse, for here is fast by within

take no force of] care nothing for

these two miles a gentle hermit that some time was a full noble knight and a great lord of possessions. And for great goodness he hath taken him to willing poverty and forsaken mighty lands, and his name is Sir Baudwin of Britain; and he is a full noble surgeon and a good leech. Now let see and help me up that I were there, for ever my heart giveth me that I shall never die of my cousin germain's hands.'

And then with great pain Sir Lavain helped him upon his horse; and then they rode a great gallop together, and ever Sir Lancelot bled that it ran down to the earth. And so by fortune they came to a hermitage was under a wood, and a great cliff on the other side, and a fair water running under it. And then Sir Lavain beat on the gate with the butt of his spear and cried fast, 'Let in, for Jesu's sake.' And anon there came a fair child to them, and asked them what they would.

'Fair son,' said Sir Lavain, 'go and pray thy lord the hermit for God's sake to let in here a knight that is full sore wounded. And this day, tell thy lord, I saw him do more deeds of arms than ever I heard say that any man did.'

So the child went in lightly, and then he brought the hermit which was a passing likely man. When Sir Lavain saw him, he prayed him for God's sake of succour.

'What knight is he?' said the hermit. 'Is he of the house of King Arthur, or not?'

'I wot not,' said Sir Lavain, 'what is he, nor what is his name; but well I wot I saw him do marvellously this day as of deeds of arms.'

'On whose party was he?' said the hermit.

'Sir,' said Sir Lavain, 'he was this day against King Arthur, and there he won the prize of all the knights of the Round Table.'

'I have seen the day,' said the hermit, 'I would have loved him the worse because he was against my lord King Arthur, for sometime I was one of the fellowship; but now I thank God I am otherwise disposed. But where is he? Let me see him.'

Then Sir Lavain brought the hermit to him. And when the hermit [13] beheld him as he sat leaning upon his saddle-bow ever bleeding piteously, and ever the knight hermit thought that he should know him; but he could not bring him to knowledge because he was so pale for bleeding.

'What knight are ye,' said the hermit, 'and where were ye born?'

cousin germain's] first cousin's

'My fair lord,' said Sir Lancelot, 'I am a stranger and a knight adventurous, that laboureth throughout many realms for to win worship.'

Then the hermit avised him better, and saw by a wound on his cheek that he was Sir Lancelot.

'Alas,' said the hermit, 'mine own lord, why lain you your name from me? Pardieu, I ought to know you of right, for ye are the most noblest knight of the world, for well I know you for Sir Lancelot.'

'Sir,' said he, 'sith ye know me, help me and ye may, for God's sake, for I would be out of this pain at once either to death or to life.'

'Have ye no doubt,' said the hermit, 'for ye shall live and fare right well.'

And so the hermit called to him two of his servants, and so they bore him into the hermitage and lightly unarmed him and laid him in his bed. And then anon the hermit staunched his blood, and made him to drink good wine, that he was well revigored and knew himself. For in those days it was not the guise as it is nowadays, for there were no hermits in those days but that they had been men of worship and of prowess, and those hermits held great households and refreshed people that were in distress.

Now turn we unto King Arthur, and leave we Sir Lancelot in the hermitage. So when the kings were come together on both parties and the great feast should be held, King Arthur asked the King of Northgales and their fellowship where was that knight that bore the red sleeve.

'Let bring him before me, that he may have his laud and honour and the prize, as it is right.'

Then spoke Sir Galahalt the Haut Prince and the King with the Hundred Knights and said, 'We suppose that knight is mischieved so that he is never likely to see you nor none of us all, and that is the greatest pity that ever we wist of any knight.'

'Alas,' said King Arthur, 'how may this be? is he so sore hurt? But what is his name?' said King Arthur.

'Truly,' said they all, 'we know not his name, nor from whence he came, nor whither he would.'

'Alas,' said the King, 'this is the worst tidings that came to me these seven years, for I would not for all the lands I wield to know and wit it were so that that noble knight were slain.'

avised] looked at his face   lain] conceal

'Sir, know ye ought of him?' said they all.

'As for that,' said King Arthur, 'whether I know him or not, ye shall not know for me what man he is; but Almighty Jesu send me good tidings of him.' And so said they all.

'By my head,' said Sir Gawain, 'if it so be that the good knight be so sore hurt, it is great damage and pity to all this land, for he is one of the noblest knights that ever I saw in a field handle spear or sword. And if he may be found I shall find him, for I am sure he is not far from this country.'

'Sir, ye bear you well', said King Arthur, 'and ye find him, unless that he be in such a plight that he may not wield himself.'

'Jesu defend,' said Sir Gawain, 'but wit well, I shall know what he is and I may find him.'

Right so Sir Gawain took a squire with him upon hackneys, and rode all about Camelot within six or seven miles, but so he came again and could hear no word of him. Then within two days King Arthur and all the fellowship returned unto London again. And so as they rode by the way, it happened Sir Gawain to lodge at Ascolat with Sir Barnard, there as was Sir Lancelot lodged. And so as Sir Gawain was in his chamber to repose him, Sir Barnard, the old baron, came in to him, and his daughter Elaine, to cheer him and to ask him what tidings, and who did best at the tournament of Winchester.

'So God me help,' said Sir Gawain, 'there were two knights that bore two white shields, but one of them bore a red sleeve upon his head, and certainly he was the best knight that ever I saw joust in field. For I dare say,' said Sir Gawain, 'that one knight with the red sleeve smote down forty knights of the Table Round, and his fellow did right well and worshipfully.'

'Now blessed be God,' said this Fair Maiden of Ascolat, 'that that knight sped so well! For he is the man in the world that I first loved, and truly he shall be last that ever I shall love.'

'Now, fair maiden,' said Sir Gawain, 'is that good knight your love?'

'Certainly, sir,' she said, 'he is my love.'

'Then know ye his name?' said Sir Gawain.

'Nay, truly, sir,' said the damosel, 'I know not his name nor from whence he came; but to say that I love him, I promise God and you I love him.'

'How had ye knowledge of him first?' said Sir Gawain.

---

ye bear you well] you will do well   may not wield himself] is disabled

[14]   Then she told him as ye have heard before, and how her father betook him her brother to do him service, and how her father lent him her brother's, Sir Tirry's, shield; 'And here with me he left his own shield.'

'For what cause did he so?' said Sir Gawain.

'For this cause,' said the damosel, 'for his shield was full well known among many noble knights.'

'Ah, fair damosel,' said Sir Gawain, 'please it you to let me have a sight of that shield.'

'Sir,' she said, 'it is in my chamber covered with a case, and if ye will come with me ye shall see it.'

'Not so,' said Sir Barnard to his daughter, 'but send ye for that shield.'*

So when the shield was come Sir Gawain took off the case, and when he beheld that shield he knew anon that it was Sir Lancelot's shield and his own arms.

'Ah, Jesu mercy,' said Sir Gawain, 'now is my heart more heavier than ever it was before.'

'Why?' said this maid Elaine.

'For I have a great cause,' said Sir Gawain. 'Is that knight that owneth this shield your love?'

'Yea, truly,' she said, 'my love is he. God would that I were his love!'

'So God me speed,' said Sir Gawain, 'fair damosel, ye have right, for and he be your love, ye love the most honourable knight of the world, and the man of most worship.'

'So me thought ever,' said the damosel, 'for never or that time loved I never erst no knight that ever I saw.'

'God grant,' said Sir Gawain, 'that either of you may rejoice other, but that is in a great adventure. But truly,' said Sir Gawain unto the damosel, 'ye may say ye have a fair grace, for why I have known that noble knight these four and twenty years, and never or that day I—nor no other knight, I dare make good—saw never, nor heard say, that ever he bore token or sign of no lady, gentlewoman, nor maiden at no jousts nor tournament. And therefore, fair maiden, ye are much beholden to him to give him thanks. But I dread me,' said Sir Gawain, 'that ye shall never see him in this world, and that is as great pity as ever was of any earthly man.'

'Alas,' said she, 'how may this be? is he slain?'

betook] entrusted   adventure] jeopardy

'I say not so,' said Sir Gawain, 'but wit you well he is grievously wounded, by all manner of signs, and more likelier to be dead than to be alive. And wit you well he is the noble knight Sir Lancelot, for by this shield I know him.'

'Alas,' said the Fair Maiden of Ascolat, 'how may this be, and what was his hurt?'

'Truly,' said Sir Gawain, 'the man in the world that loved him best hurt him. And I dare say,' said Sir Gawain, 'and that knight that hurt him knew the very certainty that he had hurt Sir Lancelot, it were the most sorrow that ever came to his heart.'

'Now, fair father,' said then Elaine, 'I require you give me leave to ride and seek him, or else I wot well I shall go out of my mind. For I shall never stint till that I find him and my brother, Sir Lavain.'

'Do ye as it liketh you,' said her father, 'for me sore repents of the hurt of that noble knight.'

Right so the maid made her ready and departed before Sir Gawain, making great dole. Then on the morn Sir Gawain came to King Arthur, and told him all how he had found Sir Lancelot's shield in the keeping of the Fair Maiden of Ascolat.

'All that knew I beforehand,' said King Arthur, 'and that caused me I would not suffer you to have ado at the great jousts; for I espied him when he came unto his lodging full late in the evening into Ascolat. But great marvel have I,' said King Arthur, 'that ever he would bear any sign of any damosel, for or now I never heard say nor knew that ever he bore any token of no earthly woman.'

'By my head, sir,' said Sir Gawain, 'the Fair Maiden of Ascolat loveth him marvellously well; what it meaneth I cannot say. And she is ridden after to seek him.'

So the King and all came to London, and there Gawain openly disclosed it to all the court that it was Sir Lancelot that jousted best. And when Sir Bors heard that, wit you well he was a heavy man, and so were all his kinsmen. But when the Queen wist that it was Sir Lancelot that bore the red sleeve of the Fair Maiden of Ascolat, she was nigh out of her mind for wrath; and then she sent for Sir Bors de Ganis in all the haste that might be. So when Sir Bors was come before the Queen, she said, 'Ah, Sir Bors, have ye not heard say how falsely Sir Lancelot hath betrayed me?' [15]

'Alas, madam,' said Sir Bors, 'I am afraid he hath betrayed himself and us all.'

'No force,' said the Queen, 'though he be destroyed, for he is a false traitor knight.'

'Madam,' said Sir Bors, 'I pray you say ye no more so, for wit you well I may not hear such language of him.'

'Why so, Sir Bors?' said she. 'Should I not call him traitor when he bore the red sleeve upon his head at Winchester at the great jousts?'

'Madam,' said Sir Bors, 'that sleeve-bearing repents me, but I dare say he did bear it to no evil intent; but for this cause he bore the red sleeve, that none of his blood should know him. For or then we nor none of us all never knew that ever he bore token or sign of maiden, lady, nor gentlewoman.'

'Fie on him,' said the Queen, 'yet, for all his pride and bobaunce, for there ye proved yourself better man than he.'

'Nay, madam, say ye never more so, for he beat me and my fellows, and might have slain us and he had willed.'

'Fie on him,' said the Queen, 'for I heard Sir Gawain say before my lord Arthur that it were marvel to tell the great love that is between the Fair Maiden of Ascolat and him.'

'Madam,' said Sir Bors, 'I may not warn Sir Gawain to say what it pleaseth him; but I dare say, as for my lord Sir Lancelot, that he loveth no lady, gentlewoman, nor maiden, but as he loveth all alike much. And therefore, madam,' said Sir Bors, 'ye may say what ye will, but wit you well I will haste me to seek him, and find him wheresoever he be; and God send me good tidings of him.'

And so leave we them there, and speak we of Sir Lancelot that lay in great peril.

And so as this fair maiden Elaine came to Winchester she sought there all about, and by fortune Sir Lavain her brother was ridden to sport him to enchafe his horse. And anon as this maiden Elaine saw him she knew him, and then she cried aloud to him; and when he heard her he came to her, and anon with that she asked her brother, 'How doth my lord Sir Lancelot?'

'Who told you, sister, that my lord's name was Sir Lancelot?'

Then she told him how Sir Gawain by his shield knew him. So they rode together till that they came to the hermitage, and anon she alit. So Sir Lavain brought her in to Sir Lancelot; and when she saw him lie so

---

force] matter   that sleeve-bearing repents me] I regret he carried that sleeve
bobaunce] boasting   warn] forbid   enchafe] exercise

sick and pale in his bed she might not speak, but suddenly she fell down to the earth in a swoon, and there she lay a great while. And when she was relieved, she shrieked and said, 'My lord Sir Lancelot, alas, why lie ye in this plight?' And then she swooned again.

And then Sir Lancelot prayed Sir Lavain to take her up, 'and bring her hither to me'. And when she came to herself Sir Lancelot kissed her and said, 'Fair maiden, why fare ye thus?—for ye put me to more pain. Wherefore make ye no such cheer, for and ye be come to comfort me ye be right welcome; and of this little hurt that I have I shall be right hastily whole, by the grace of God. But I marvel', said Sir Lancelot, 'who told you my name.'

And so this maiden told him all how Sir Gawain was lodged with her father, 'and there by your shield he discovered your name'.

'Alas,' said Sir Lancelot, 'that repenteth me that my name is known, for I am sure it will turn unto anger.'

And then Sir Lancelot compassed in his mind that Sir Gawain would tell Queen Guenivere how he bore the red sleeve, and for whom; that he wist well would turn unto great anger.

So this maiden Elaine never went from Sir Lancelot, but watched him day and night, and did such attendance to him that the French book saith there was never woman did never more kindlier for man.

Then Sir Lancelot prayed Sir Lavain to make aspies in Winchester for Sir Bors if he came there, and told him by what tokens he should know him—by a wound in his forehead. 'For I am sure,' said Sir Lancelot, 'that Sir Bors will seek me, for he is the same good knight that hurt me.'

Now turn we unto Sir Bors de Ganis, that came unto Winchester to [16] seek after his cousin Sir Lancelot. And so when he came to Winchester, Sir Lavain laid watch for Sir Bors; and anon he had warning of him, and so he found him. And anon he saluted him and told him from whence he came.

'Now, fair knight,' said Sir Bors, 'ye be welcome! And I require you that ye will bring me to my lord Sir Lancelot.'

'Sir,' said Sir Lavain, 'take your horse, and within this hour ye shall see him.'

So they departed and came to the hermitage. And when Sir Bors saw Sir Lancelot lie in his bed dead pale and discoloured, anon

relieved] recovered   to make aspies] have watch kept

Sir Bors lost his countenance, and for kindness and pity he might not speak, but wept tenderly a great while. But when he might speak he said thus:

'Ah, my lord, Sir Lancelot, God you bless, and send you hasty recovering! For full heavy am I of my misfortune and of my unhappiness, for now I may call myself unhappy. And I dread me that God is greatly displeased with me, that he would suffer me to have such a shame for to hurt you that are all our leader and all our worship; and therefore I call myself unhappy. Alas, that ever such a caitiff knight as I am should have power by unhappiness to hurt the most noblest knight of the world! Where I so shamefully set upon you and over-charged you, and where ye might have slain me, ye saved me; and so did not I, for I and all our blood did to you their utterance. I marvel', said Sir Bors, 'that my heart or my blood would serve me! Wherefore, my lord Sir Lancelot, I ask you mercy.'

'Fair cousin,' said Sir Lancelot, 'ye be right welcome. And wit you well, overmuch ye say for the pleasure of me—which pleaseth me nothing, for why I have the same I sought, for I would with pride have overcome you all. And there in my pride I was near slain, and that was in my own fault, for I might have give you warning of my being there, and then had I had no hurt. For it is an old-said saw, there is hard battle there as kin and friends do battle either against other, for there may be no mercy, but mortal war. Therefore, fair cousin,' said Sir Lancelot, 'let this language overpass, and all shall be welcome that God sendeth. And let us leave off thy matter and speak of some rejoicing, for this that is done may not be undone; and let us find a remedy how soon that I may be whole.'

Then Sir Bors leaned upon his bedside, and told Sir Lancelot how the Queen was passing wroth with him, 'because ye wore the red sleeve at the great jousts'. And there Sir Bors told him all how Sir Gawain discovered it—'by your shield, that ye left with the Fair Maiden of Ascolat'.

'Then is the Queen wroth?' said Sir Lancelot. 'Therefore am I right heavy; but I deserved no wrath, for all that I did was because I would not be known.'

'Sir, right so excused I you,' said Sir Bors, 'but all was in vain, for she said more largelier to me than I say to you now. But sir, is this she,' said

unhappiness] evil destiny   all our leader] i.e. leader of us all   over-
charged] overbore   old-said saw] traditional saying

Sir Bors, 'that is so busy about you, that men call the Fair Maiden of Ascolat?'

'For sooth, she it is,' said Sir Lancelot, 'that by no means I cannot put her from me.'

'Why should ye put her from you?' said Sir Bors, 'for she is a passing fair damosel, and well beseen and well taught. And would God, fair cousin,' said Sir Bors, 'that ye could love her—but as to that I may not nor dare not counsel you. But I see well,' said Sir Bors, 'by her diligence about you that she loveth you entirely.'

'That me repents,' said Sir Lancelot.

'Well,' said Sir Bors, 'she is not the first that hath lost her pain upon you, and that is the more pity.' And so they talked of many more things.

And so within three or four days Sir Lancelot waxed big and light.

Then Sir Bors told Sir Lancelot how there was sworn a great tour-   [17] nament betwixt King Arthur and the King of Northgales, that should be upon All Hallowmas Day beside Winchester.

'Is that truth?' said Sir Lancelot. 'Then shall ye abide with me still a little while until that I be whole, for I feel myself reasonably big and strong.'

'Blessed be God,' said Sir Bors.

Then were they there nigh a month together, and ever this maiden Elaine did ever her diligence and labour night and day unto Sir Lancelot, that there was never child nor wife more meeker to father and husband than was this Fair Maiden of Ascolat; wherefore Sir Bors was greatly pleased with her. So upon a day, by the assent of Sir Lavain, Sir Bors, and Sir Lancelot, they made the hermit to seek in woods for divers herbs, and so Sir Lancelot made fair Elaine to gather herbs for him to make him a bain. So in the meanwhile Sir Lancelot made Sir Lavain to arm him at all pieces; and there he thought to assay himself upon horseback with a spear, whether he might wield his armour and his spear for his hurt or not. And so when he was upon his horse he stirred him freshly, and the horse was passing lusty and frick because he was not laboured of a month before. And then Sir Lancelot bade Sir Lavain give him that great spear, and so Sir Lancelot couched that spear in the rest, and the courser leapt mightily when he felt the spurs; and he that was upon him was the noblest horseman of the world, strained him

beseen] behaved   big and light] strong and vigorous   All Hallowmas] All Saints' (1 November)   bain] bath   frick] mettlesome   strained him] exerted himself

mightily and stably, and kept still the spear in the rest. And therewith
Sir Lancelot strained himself so straitly with so great force to get the
courser forward that the bottom of his wound brast both within and
without; and therewith the blood came out so fiercely that he felt himself so feeble that he might not sit upon his horse. And then Sir
Lancelot cried unto Sir Bors, 'Ah, Sir Bors and Sir Lavain, help, for I
am come to my end.' And therewith he fell down on the one side to the
earth like a dead corpse.

And then Sir Bors and Sir Lavain came unto him with sorrow-
making out of measure. And so by fortune this maiden Elaine heard
their mourning; and then she came, and when she found Sir Lancelot
there armed in that place she cried and wept as she had been wood.
And then she kissed him, and did what she might to awake him; and
then she rebuked her brother and Sir Bors, and called them false
traitors, and said, 'Why would ye take him out of his bed? for and he
die, I will appeal you of his death.'

And so with that came the hermit, Sir Baudwin of Britain; and when
he found Sir Lancelot in that plight he said but little, but wit you well
he was wroth. But he said, 'Let us have him in.' And anon they bore
him into the hermitage and unarmed him, and laid him in his bed; and
evermore his wound bled piteously, but he stirred no limb of him.
Then the knight hermit put a thing* in his nose and a little deal of
water in his mouth, and then Sir Lancelot waked of his swoon; and
then the hermit staunched his bleeding. And when Sir Lancelot might
speak, he asked why he put his life so in jeopardy.

'Sir,' said Sir Lancelot, 'because I weened I had been strong enough.
And also Sir Bors told me that there should be at Hallowmas a great
jousts betwixt King Arthur and the King of Northgales; and therefore
I thought to assay myself, whether I might be there or not.'

'Ah, Sir Lancelot,' said the hermit, 'your heart and your courage
will never be done until your last day. But ye shall do now by my counsel. Let Sir Bors depart from you, and let him do at that tournament
what he may. And by the grace of God,' said the knight hermit, 'by that
the tournament be done and he come hither again, sir, ye shall be
whole, so that ye will be governed by me.'

[18]   Then Sir Bors made him ready to depart from him; and Sir Lancelot
said, 'Fair cousin, Sir Bors, recommend me unto all those ye ought

straitly] severely   appeal] accuse

recommend me unto. And I pray you, enforce yourself at that jousts that ye may be best, for my love; and here shall I abide you at the mercy of God till your again-coming.'

And so Sir Bors departed and came to the court of King Arthur, and told him in what place he left Sir Lancelot.

'That me repents,' said the King, 'but since he shall have his life we all may thank God.'

And then Sir Bors told the Queen what jeopardy Sir Lancelot was in when he would assay his horse. 'And all that he did was for the love of you, because he would have been at this tournament.'

'Fie on him, recrayed knight,' said the Queen, 'for wit you well I am right sorry and he shall have his life.'

'Madam, his life shall he have,' said Sir Bors, 'and who that would otherwise, except you, madam, we that be of his blood would help to shorten their lives. But madam,' said Sir Bors, 'ye have been often-times displeased with my lord Sir Lancelot, but at all times at the end ye found him a true knight.' And so he departed.

And then every knight of the Round Table that were there that time present made them ready to that jousts at All Hallowmas, and thither drew many knights of divers countries.* And so that day Sir Gawain did great deeds of arms, and began first; and the heralds numbered that Sir Gawain smote down twenty knights. Then Sir Bors de Ganis came in the same time, and he was numbered he smote down twenty knights; and therefore the prize was given betwixt them both, for they began first and longest endured. Also Sir Gareth, as the book saith, did that day great deeds of arms, for he smote down and pulled down thirty knights; but when he had done those deeds he tarried not but so departed, and therefore he lost his prize. And Sir Palomides did great deeds of arms that day, for he smote down twenty knights, but he departed suddenly, and men deemed that he and Sir Gareth rode together to some manner adventures.

So when this tournament was done Sir Bors departed, and rode till he came to Sir Lancelot, his cousin; and then he found him walking on his feet, and there either made great joy of other. And so he told Sir Lancelot of all the jousts like as ye have heard.

'I marvel', said Sir Lancelot, 'that Sir Gareth, when he had done such deeds of arms, that he would not tarry.'

---

enforce] exert   again-coming] return   recrayed] recreant

'Sir, thereof we marvelled all,' said Sir Bors, 'for but if it were you, or the noble knight Sir Tristram, or the good knight Sir Lamorak de Gales, I saw never knight bear down so many knights and smite down in so little a while as did Sir Gareth; and anon as he was gone we all wist not where he became.'

'By my head,' said Sir Lancelot, 'he is a noble knight, and a mighty man and well-breathed; and if he were well assayed,' said Sir Lancelot, 'I would deem he were good enough for any knight that beareth the life. And he is gentle, courteous and right bounteous, meek, and mild; and in him is no manner of mal engine, but plain, faithful, and true.'

So then they made them ready to depart from the hermitage. And so upon a morn they took their horses, and this Elaine la Blanche with them; and when they came to Ascolat there were they well lodged, and had great cheer of Sir Barnard, the old baron, and of Sir Tirry, his son. And so upon the morn when Sir Lancelot should depart, fair Elaine brought her father with her, and Sir Lavain, and Sir Tirry, and thus she said:

[19]   'My lord Sir Lancelot, now I see ye will depart from me. Now, fair knight and courteous knight,' said she, 'have mercy upon me, and suffer me not to die for your love.'

'Why, what would you that I did?' said Sir Lancelot.

'Sir, I would have you to my husband,' said Elaine.

'Fair damosel, I thank you heartily,' said Sir Lancelot. 'But truly,' said he, 'I cast me never to be wedded man.'

'Then, fair knight,' said she, 'will ye be my paramour?'

'Jesu defend me,' said Sir Lancelot, 'for then I rewarded your father and your brother full evil for their great goodness.'

'Alas then,' said she, 'I must die for your love.'

'Ye shall not do so,' said Sir Lancelot, 'for wit you well, fair maiden, I might have been married and I had would, but I never applied me yet to be married. But because, fair damosel, that ye love me as ye say ye do, I will for your good will and kindness show to you some goodness— that is this: that wheresoever ye will set your heart upon some good knight that will wed you, I shall give you together a thousand pounds yearly to you and to your heirs. This much will I give you, fair maiden, for your kindness; and always while I live to be your own knight.'

'Sir, of all this,' said the maiden, 'I will none, for but if ye will wed

mal engine] deceit   cast me] intend   and I had would] if I had wished

me, or to be my paramour at the least, wit you well, Sir Lancelot, my good days are done.'

'Fair damosel,' said Sir Lancelot, 'of these two things ye must pardon me.'

Then she shrieked shrilly and fell down in a swoon; and then women bore her into her chamber, and there she made overmuch sorrow. And then Sir Lancelot would depart, and there he asked Sir Lavain what he would do.

'Sir, what should I do,' said Sir Lavain, 'but follow you, but if ye drive me from you or command me to go from you?'

Then came Sir Barnard to Sir Lancelot and said to him, 'I cannot see but that my daughter will die for your sake.'

'Sir, I may not do withal,' said Sir Lancelot, 'for that me sore repenteth; for I report me to yourself that my proffer is fair. And me repenteth', said Sir Lancelot, 'that she loveth me as she doth, for I was never the causer of it; for I report me unto your son, I never early nor late proffered her bounty nor fair behests. And as for me,' said Sir Lancelot, 'I dare do that a knight should do, and say that she is a clean maiden for me, both for deed and will. For I am right heavy of her distress, for she is a full fair maiden, good and gentle and well taught.'

'Father,' said Sir Lavain, 'I dare make good she is a clean maiden as for my lord Sir Lancelot; but she doth as I do, for sithen I saw first my lord Sir Lancelot, I could never depart from him, nor nought I will and I may follow him.'

Then Sir Lancelot took his leave; and so they departed, and came to Winchester. And when King Arthur wist that Sir Lancelot was come whole and sound, the King made great joy of him, and so did Sir Gawain and all the knights of the Round Table except Sir Agravain and Sir Mordred. Also Queen Guenivere was wood wroth with Sir Lancelot, and would by no means speak with him, but estranged herself from him; and Sir Lancelot made all the means that he might for to speak with the Queen, but it would not be.

Now speak we of the Fair Maiden of Ascolat, that made such sorrow day and night that she never slept, ate, nor drank, and ever she made her complaint unto Sir Lancelot. So when she had thus endured ten days, that she feebled so that she must needs pass out of this world,

---

may not do withal] cannot help it   report me] appeal for confirmation
nor nought I will and I may] I desire nothing so long as I am able to

then she shrove her clean, and received her Creator. And ever she complained still upon Sir Lancelot. Then her ghostly father bade her leave such thoughts.

Then she said, 'Why should I leave such thoughts? Am I not an earthly woman? And all the while the breath is in my body I may complain me, for my belief is that I do no offence, though I love an earthly man, unto God; for He formed me thereto, and all manner of good love cometh of God, and other than good love loved I never Sir Lancelot du Lake. And I take God to record, I loved never none but him, nor never shall, of earthly creatures; and a clean maiden I am for him and for all others. And sithen it is the sufferance of God that I shall die for so noble a knight, I beseech the High Father of Heaven have mercy upon me and my soul, and upon my innumerable pains that I suffer may be allegiance of part of my sins. For sweet Lord Jesu,' said the fair maiden, 'I take God to record I was never to Thee great offender, nor against Thy laws, but that I loved this noble knight Sir Lancelot out of measure. And of myself, good Lord, I had no might to withstand the fervent love, wherefore I have my death.'

And then she called her father Sir Barnard and her brother Sir Tirry, and heartily she prayed her father that her brother might write a letter like as she did indite; and so her father granted her. And when the letter was written word by word like as she devised it, then she prayed her father that she might be watched until she were dead. 'And while my body is hot let this letter be put in my right hand, and my hand bound fast to the letter until that I be cold; and let me be put in a fair bed with all the richest clothes that I have about me, and so let my bed and all my richest clothes be led with me in a chariot unto the next place where the Thames is. And there let me be put within a barget, and but one man with me such as ye trust to steer me thither, and that my barget be covered with black samite over and over. And thus, father, I beseech you let it be done.'

So her father granted her faithfully all things should be done like as she had devised; then her father and her brother made great dole for her. And when this was done, anon she died. And when she was dead the corpse and the bed all was led the next way unto the Thames, and

shrove her clean] purified herself by confession   Creator] i.e. the Eucharist
ghostly father] spiritua father (i.e. confessor)   sufferance] will   alle-
giance] alleviation   indite] compose   barget] small boat

there a man and the corpse and all things as she had devised was put in the Thames. And so the man steered the barget unto Westminster, and there it rubbed and rolled a great while to and fro or any man espied it.

So by fortune King Arthur and Queen Guenivere were talking [20] together at a window, and so as they looked into the Thames they espied that black barget, and had marvel what it meant. Then the King called Sir Kay and showed it him.

'Sir,' said Sir Kay, 'wit you well there is some new tidings.'

'Therefore go ye thither,' said the King to Sir Kay, 'and take with you Sir Brandiles and Sir Agravain, and bring me ready word what is there.'

Then these three knights departed and came to the barget and went in; and there they found the fairest corpse lying in a rich bed that ever they saw, and a poor man sitting in the barget's end, and no word would speak. So these three knights returned unto the King again and told him what they found.

'That fair corpse will I see,' said the King.

And so the King took the Queen by the hand and went thither. Then the King made the barget to be held fast, and then the King and the Queen went in with certain knights with them; and there he saw the fairest woman lie in a rich bed, covered unto her middle with many rich clothes, and all was of cloth of gold. And she lay as she had smiled.

Then the Queen espied the letter in her right hand, and told the King. Then the King took it and said, 'Now am I sure this letter will tell us what she was, and why she is come hither.'

So then the King and the Queen went out of the barget, and so commanded a certain to wait upon the barget. And so when the King was come to his chamber, he called many knights about him, and said that he would wit openly what was written within that letter. Then the King broke it and made a clerk to read it, and this was the intent of the letter:

'Most noble knight, my lord Sir Lancelot, now hath death made us two at debate for your love. And I was your lover, that men called the Fair Maiden of Ascolat. Therefore unto all ladies I make my moan; yet for my soul ye pray and bury me at the least, and offer ye my mass-penny;* this is my last request. And a clean maiden I died, I take God to witness. And pray for my soul, Sir Lancelot, as thou art peerless.'

---

a certain to wait upon] a certain number to guard   broke it] broke the seal

This was all the substance in the letter. And when it was read, the King, the Queen, and all the knights wept for pity of the doleful complaints. Then was Sir Lancelot sent for, and when he was come King Arthur made the letter to be read to him. And when Sir Lancelot heard it word by word, he said, 'My lord Arthur, wit you well I am right heavy of the death of this fair lady. And God knoweth I was never causer of her death by my willing, and that will I report me unto her own brother that here is, Sir Lavain. I will not say nay,' said Sir Lancelot, 'but that she was both fair and good, and much I was beholden unto her; but she loved me out of measure.'

'Sir,' said the Queen, 'ye might have showed her some bounty and gentleness which might have preserved her life.'

'Madam,' said Sir Lancelot, 'she would no other ways be answered but that she would be my wife or else my paramour, and of these two I would not grant her. But I proffered her, for her good love that she showed me, a thousand pounds yearly to her and to her heirs, and to wed any manner of knight that she could find best to love in her heart. For, madam,' said Sir Lancelot, 'I love not to be constrained to love; for love must only arise of the heart's self, and not by no constraint.'

'That is truth, sir,' said the King. 'And with many knights, love is free in himself and never will be bound; for where he is bound, he looseth himself.' Then said the King unto Sir Lancelot, 'Sir, it will be your worship that ye oversee that she be interred worshipfully.'

'Sir,' said Sir Lancelot, 'that shall be done as I can best devise.'

And so many knights yode thither to behold that fair dead maiden. And so upon the morn she was interred richly, and Sir Lancelot offered her mass-penny; and all the knights of the Table Round that were there at that time offered with Sir Lancelot. And then the poor man went again with the barget.

Then the Queen sent for Sir Lancelot, and prayed him of mercy for why that she had been wroth with him causeless.

'This is not the first time', said Sir Lancelot, 'that ye have been displeased with me causeless, but, madam, ever I must suffer you. But what sorrow that I endure, ye take no force.'

So this passed on all that winter, with all manner of hunting and hawking; and jousts and tourneys were many betwixt many great lords.

---

went again] returned   take no force] do not care

And ever in all places Sir Lavain got great worship, that he was nobly famed among many knights of the Table Round.

Thus it passed on till Christmas, and then every day there was jousts [21] made for a diamond: who that jousted best should have a diamond. But Sir Lancelot would not joust but if it were at a great jousts cried. But Sir Lavain jousted there all the Christmas passingly well, and was best praised, for there were but few that did so well; wherefore all manner of knights deemed that Sir Lavain should be made knight of the Table Round at the next feast of Pentecost.

So at after Christmas King Arthur let call unto him many knights, and there they advised together to make a party and a great tournament and jousts.* And the cry was made that the day of jousts should be beside Westminster upon Candlemas Day, whereof many knights were glad, and made them ready to be at that jousts in the freshest manner.

Then Queen Guenivere sent for Sir Lancelot, and said thus: 'I warn you that ye ride no more in no jousts nor tournaments but that your kinsmen may know you; and at these jousts that shall be ye shall have of me a sleeve of gold. And I pray you for my sake to force yourself there, that men may speak you worship. But I charge you as ye will have my love, that ye warn your kinsmen that ye will bear that day the sleeve of gold upon your helmet.'

'Madam,' said Sir Lancelot, 'it shall be done.' And either made great joy of other.

And when Sir Lancelot saw his time he told Sir Bors that he would depart, and no more with him but Sir Lavain, unto the good hermit that dwelled in the forest of Windsor whose name was Sir Brastias; and there he thought to repose him and to take all the rest that he might, because he would be fresh at that day of jousts. So Sir Lancelot and Sir Lavain departed, that no creature wist where he was become but the noble men of his blood. And when he was come to the hermitage, wit you well he had great cheer. And so daily Sir Lancelot used to go to a well by the hermitage, and there he would lie down and see the well spring and burble, and sometimes he slept there.

So at that time there was a lady that dwelled in that forest, and she was a great huntress, and daily she used to hunt; and ever she bore her

---

but if it were at a great jousts cried] except at a formal joust proclaimed by heralds
warn] forbid   force] exert

bow with her, and no men went never with her, but always women. And they were all shooters and could well kill a deer at the stalk and at the trist;* and they daily bore bows, arrows, horns, and wood knives, and many good dogs they had, both for the string and for abait. So it happened the lady the huntress had abaited her dog for the bow at a barren hind;* and so she took the flight over hedges and woods, and ever this lady and part of her women coasted the hind and checked it by the noise of the hound, to have met with the hind at some water. And so it happened that the hind came to the same well there as Sir Lancelot was sleeping and slumbering.

And so the hind, when she came to the well, for heat she went to soil, and there she lay a great while; and the dog came after and cast about, for she had lost the very perfect feute of the hind. Right so came that lady the huntress, that knew by her dog that the hind was at the soil by that well; and there she came straight and found the hind. And anon as she had spied her she put a broad arrow in her bow and shot at the hind; and so she overshot the hind, and so by misfortune the arrow smote Sir Lancelot in the thick of the buttock, over the barbs. When Sir Lancelot felt himself so hurt he whirled up woodly, and saw the lady that had smitten him. And when he knew she was a woman, he said thus: 'Lady or damosel, whatsoever ye be, in an evil time bore ye this bow: the devil made you a shooter.'

[22]　　'Now mercy, fair sir,' said the lady, 'I am a gentlewoman that useth here in this forest hunting, and God knoweth I saw you not; but as here was a barren hind at the soil in this well, and I weened I had done well, but my hand swerved.'

'Alas,' said Sir Lancelot, 'ye have mischieved me.'

And so the lady departed. And Sir Lancelot as he might pulled out the arrow, and left the head still in his buttock, and so he went weakly unto the hermitage evermore bleeding as he went. And when Sir Lavain and the hermit espied that Sir Lancelot was so sore hurt, wit you well they were passing heavy; but Sir Lavain wist not how that he was hurt nor by whom, and then were they wroth out of measure. And so with great pain the hermit got out the arrowhead out of Sir Lancelot's buttock, and much of his blood he shed. And the wound was passing sore, and unhappily smitten, for it was in such a place that he might not sit in no saddle.

for the string and for abait] on the leash and for setting on　　coasted] followed
soil] wallowing-place　　　feute] trail　　　unhappily] unfortunately

'Ah, mercy, Jesu,' said Sir Lancelot, 'I may call myself the most unhappy man that liveth, for ever when I would fainest have worship there befalleth me ever some unhappy thing. Now so Jesu me help,' said Sir Lancelot, 'and if no man would but God, I shall be in the field on Candlemas Day at the jousts, whatsoever fall of it.' So all that might be gotten to heal Sir Lancelot was had.

So when the day was come Sir Lancelot let devise that he was arrayed, and Sir Lavain and their horses, as they had been Saracens; and so they departed and came nigh to the field.

And King Arthur himself came into the field with two hundred knights, and the most part were knights of the Round Table that were all proved noble men; and there were old knights set on scaffolds for to judge with the Queen who did best.

Then they blew unto the field. And there the King of Northgales [23] encountered with the King of Scots, and there the King of Scots had a fall; and the King of Ireland smote down King Uriens; and the King of Northumberland smote down King Howell of Brittany; and Sir Galahalt the Haut Prince smote down Duke Chalance of Clarence. And then King Arthur was wood wroth and ran to the King with the Hundred Knights, and so King Arthur smote him down; and after with that same spear he smote down other three knights, and then his spear broke, and did passingly well. And so therewith came in Sir Gawain and Sir Gaheris, Sir Agravain and Sir Mordred, and there each of them smote down a knight, and Sir Gawain smote down four knights. And then there began a great melée, for then came in the knights of Sir Lancelot's blood and Sir Gareth and Sir Palomides with them, and many knights of the Round Table; and they began to hold the four kings and the mighty duke so hard that they were nigh discomfited. But this Sir Galahalt the Haut Prince was a noble knight, and by his mighty prowess of arms he held the knights of the Table Round strait.

So all this doing saw Sir Lancelot, and then he came into the field with Sir Lavain with him as it had been thunder. And then anon Sir Bors and the knights of his blood espied Sir Lancelot anon, and said unto them all, 'I warn you beware of him with the sleeve of gold upon his head, for he is himself my lord Sir Lancelot.' And for great goodness Sir Bors warned Sir Gareth.

let devise] invented a scheme   held . . . strait] pressed them hard

'Sir, I am well paid', said Sir Gareth, 'that I may know him.'

'But who is he', said they all, 'that rideth with him in the same array?'

'Sir, that is the good and gentle knight Sir Lavain,' said Sir Bors.

So Sir Lancelot encountered with Sir Gawain, and there by force Sir Lancelot smote down Sir Gawain and his horse to the earth. And so he smote down Sir Agravain and Sir Gaheris, and also he smote down Sir Mordred, and all this was with one spear. And then met Sir Lancelot with Sir Palomides, and there Sir Palomides had a fall. And so Sir Lancelot, or ever he stinted, and as fast as he might get spears, he smote down thirty knights, and the most part were knights of the Round Table. And ever the knights of his blood withdrew them, and made them ado in other places where Sir Lancelot came not.

And then King Arthur was wroth when he saw Sir Lancelot do such deeds; and then the King called unto him Sir Gawain, Sir Gaheris, Sir Agravain, Sir Mordred, Sir Kay, Sir Griflet, Sir Lucan the Butler, Sir Bedivere, Sir Palomides, and Sir Safer his brother; and so the King with these nine knights made them ready to set upon Sir Lancelot and upon Sir Lavain. And all this espied Sir Bors and Sir Gareth.

'Now I dread me sore,' said Sir Bors, 'that my lord Sir Lancelot will be hard matched.'

'Now by my head,' said Sir Gareth, 'I will ride unto my lord Sir Lancelot for to help him, whatsoever me betide, for he is the same man that made me knight.'

'Sir, ye shall not do so,' said Sir Bors, 'by my counsel, unless that ye were disguised.'

'Sir, ye shall see me soon disguised,' said Sir Gareth. And therewith he had espied a Welsh knight where he was to repose him, for he was sore hurt before of Sir Gawain. And unto him Sir Gareth rode, and prayed him of his knighthood to lend him his shield for his.

'I will well,' said the Welsh knight.

And when Sir Gareth had his shield (the book saith it was green, with a maiden which seemed in it), then Sir Gareth came driving unto Sir Lancelot all that ever he might, and said, 'Sir knight, take keep to thyself, for yonder cometh King Arthur with nine noble knights with him to put you to a rebuke; and so I am come to bear you fellowship for the old love ye have showed unto me.'

paid] satisfied   seemed] appeared

'Grantmercy,' said Sir Lancelot.

'But sir,' said Sir Gareth, 'encounter ye with Sir Gawain, and I shall encounter with Sir Palomides; and let Sir Lavain match with the noble King Arthur. And when we have delivered them, let us three hold us sadly together.'

So then came in King Arthur with his nine knights with him, and Sir Lancelot encountered with Sir Gawain and gave him such a buffet that the arson of his saddle brast, and Sir Gawain fell to the earth. Then Sir Gareth encountered with Sir Palomides, and he gave him such a buffet that both his horse and he dashed to the earth. Then encountered King Arthur with Sir Lavain, and there either of them smote other to the earth, horse and all, that they lay both a great while. Then Sir Lancelot smote down Sir Agravain, and Sir Gaheris, and Sir Mordred; and Sir Gareth smote down Sir Kay, Sir Safer, and Sir Griflet. And then Sir Lavain was horsed again, and he smote down Sir Lucan the Butler and Sir Bedivere; and then there began great throng of good knights.

Then Sir Lancelot hurtled here and there, and rased and pulled off helms, that at that time there might none sit him a buffet with spear nor with sword. And Sir Gareth did such deeds of arms that all men marvelled what knight he was with the green shield, for he smote down that day and pulled down more than thirty knights. And as the French book saith, Sir Lancelot marvelled when he beheld Sir Gareth do such deeds what knight he might be. And Sir Lavain smote and pulled down more than twenty knights. And yet for all this Sir Lancelot knew not Sir Gareth; for and Sir Tristram de Lyonesse or Sir Lamorak de Gales had been alive, Sir Lancelot would have deemed he had been one of them twain.

So this tournament and jousts endured long, till it was near night, [24] for the knights of the Round Table relieved ever unto King Arthur; for the King was wroth out of measure that he and his knights might not prevail that day.

Then Sir Gawain said to the King, 'Sir, I marvel where are all this day Sir Bors de Ganis and his fellowship of Sir Lancelot's blood, that all this day they be not about you. And therefore I deem it is for some cause,' said Sir Gawain.

---

delivered] dealt with	sadly] steadily	arson] saddle-bow
sit] withstand	relieved] rallied	

'By my head,' said Sir Kay, 'Sir Bors is yonder all this day upon the right hand of this field, and there he and his blood do more worshipfully than we do.'

'It may well be,' said Sir Gawain, 'but I dread me ever of guile; for on pain of my life, that same knight with the red sleeve of gold is himself Sir Lancelot, for I see well by his riding and by his great strokes; and the other knight in the same colours is the good young knight Sir Lavain. And that knight with the green shield is my brother Sir Gareth, and yet he hath disguised himself, for no man shall make him be against Sir Lancelot, because he made him knight.'

'By my head,' said King Arthur, 'nephew, I believe you. And therefore now tell me what is your best counsel.'

'Sir,' said Sir Gawain, 'my counsel is to blow unto lodging; for and he be Sir Lancelot du Lake, and my brother Sir Gareth with him, with the help of that good young knight Sir Lavain, trust me truly it will be no boot to strive with them but if we should fall ten or twelve upon one knight—and that were no worship, but shame.'

'Ye say truth,' said the King. 'It were shame for us, so many as we be, to set upon them any more. For wit ye well,' said King Arthur, 'they be three good knights, and namely that knight with the sleeve of gold.'

And anon they blew unto lodging. But forthwith King Arthur let send unto the four kings and to the mighty duke, and prayed them that the knight with the sleeve of gold depart not from them, but that the King may speak with him. Then forthwith King Arthur alit and unarmed him, and took a little hackney and rode after Sir Lancelot, for ever he had espy upon him. And so he found him among the four kings and the duke; and there the King prayed them all unto supper, and they said they would with good will. And when they were unarmed, King Arthur knew Sir Lancelot, Sir Gareth, and Sir Lavain.

'Ah, Sir Lancelot,' said King Arthur, 'this day ye have heated me and my knights.'

And so they yode unto King Arthur's lodging all together, and there was a great feast and great revel. And the prize was given unto Sir Lancelot, for by heralds they named him that he had smitten down fifty knights, and Sir Gareth five and thirty knights, and Sir Lavain four and twenty. Then Sir Lancelot told the King and the Queen how

blow unto lodging] sound a trumpet to have the knights return to their lodgings
namely] especially

the lady huntress shot him in the forest of Windsor, in the buttock, with a broad arrow, and how the wound was that time six inches deep and alike long.

Also King Arthur blamed Sir Gareth because he left his fellowship and held with Sir Lancelot.

'My lord,' said Sir Gareth, 'he made me knight, and when I saw him so hard bestead, me thought it was my worship to help him. For I saw him do so much deeds of arms, and so many noble knights against him, that when I understood that he was Sir Lancelot du Lake I shamed to see so many good knights against him alone.'

'Now truly,' said King Arthur unto Sir Gareth, 'ye say well, and worshipfully have ye done, and to yourself great worship. And all the days of my life,' said King Arthur unto Sir Gareth, 'wit you well I shall love you and trust you the more better. For ever it is,' said King Arthur, 'a worshipful knight's deed to help and succour another worshipful knight when he seeth him in danger; for ever a worshipful man will be loath to see a worshipful man shamed. And he that is of no worship and meddleth with cowardice, never shall he show gentleness nor no manner of goodness where he seeth a man in danger, for then will a coward never show mercy. And always a good man will do ever to another man as he would be done to himself.'

So then there were made great feasts unto kings and dukes, and revel, game, and play, and all manner of noblesse was used. And he that was courteous, true, and faithful to his friend was that time cherished.

And thus it passed on from Candlemas until after Easter, that the [25] month of May was come, when every lusty heart beginneth to blossom and to burgeon. For like as trees and herbs burgeoneth and and flourisheth in May, in like wise every lusty heart that is any manner of lover springeth, burgeoneth, buddeth, and flourisheth in lusty deeds. For it giveth unto all lovers courage, that lusty month of May, in some thing to constrain him to some manner of thing more in that month than in any other month, for diverse causes: for then all herbs and trees reneweth a man and woman, and in like wise lovers calleth to their mind old gentleness and old service, and many kind deeds that were forgotten by negligence.

For like as winter rasure doth alway erase and deface green summer, so fareth it by unstable love in man and woman. For in many persons

rasure] destruction

there is no stability; for we may see all day, for a little blast of winter's rasure, anon we shall deface and lay apart true love for little or nought, that cost much thing. This is no wisdom nor no stability, but it is feebleness of nature and great disworship, whosoever useth this.

Therefore, like as May month flowereth and flourisheth in every man's garden, so in like wise let every man of worship flourish his heart in this world, first unto God, and next unto the joy of them that he promised his faith unto. For there was never worshipful man nor worshipful woman, but they loved one better than another; and worship in arms may never be foiled. But first reserve the honour to God, and secondly thy quarrel must come of thy lady. And such love I call virtuous love.

But nowadays men cannot love seven night but they must have all their desires. That love may not endure by reason; for where they be soon accorded and hasty, heat soon cooleth. And right so fareth the love nowadays, soon hot, soon cold—this is no stability. But the old love was not so; for men and women could love together seven years, and no lecherous lusts were betwixt them, and then was love truth and faithfulness. And so in like wise was used such love in King Arthur's days. Wherefore I liken love nowadays unto summer and winter; for like as the one is cold and the other is hot, so fareth love nowadays. And therefore all ye that be lovers, call unto your remembrance the month of May, like as did Queen Guenivere; for whom I make here a little mention, that while she lived she was a true lover, and therefore she had a good end.

So it befell in the month of May, Queen Guenivere called unto her ten
knights of the Table Round, and she gave them warning that early
upon the morn she would ride on maying into woods and fields beside
Westminster: 'And I warn you that there be none of you but he be well
horsed, and that ye all be clothed all in green, either in silk or in cloth;
and I shall bring with me ten ladies, and every knight shall have a lady
by him. And every knight shall have a squire and two yeomen, and I
will that all be well horsed.'

So they made them ready in the freshest manner. And these were the
names of the knights: Sir Kay le Seneschal, Sir Agravain, Sir Brandiles,
Sir Sagramore le Desirous, Sir Dodinas le Savage, Sir Ozanna le
Coeur Hardi, Sir Ladinas of the Forest Savage, Sir Persant of Inde,
Sir Ironside that was called the Knight of the Red Launds, and
Sir Pelleas the lover. And these ten knights made them ready in the
freshest manner to ride with the Queen.

And so upon the morn or it were day, in a May morning, they took
their horses with the Queen and rode on maying in woods and meadows
as it pleased them, in great joy and delights; for the Queen had cast to
have been again with King Arthur at the furthest by ten of the clock,
and so was that time her purpose.

Then there was a knight which hight Sir Meliagaunt, and he was
son unto King Bagdemagus; and this knight had that time a castle of
the gift of King Arthur within seven miles of Westminster. And this
knight Sir Meliagaunt loved passing well Queen Guenivere, and so
had he done long and many years. And the book saith he had lain in
wait for to steal away the Queen, but evermore he forbore for because
of Sir Lancelot; for in no wise he would meddle with the Queen and
Sir Lancelot were in her company, or else and he were nearhand.

And that time was such a custom that the Queen rode never without
a great fellowship of men of arms about her, and they were many good
knights, and the most part were young men that would have worship;
and they were called the Queen's Knights. And never in no battle,
tournament, nor jousts, they bore none of them no manner of knowledging of their own arms, but plain white shields, and thereby they
were called the Queen's Knights. And when it happed any of them to
be of great worship by his noble deeds, then at the next feast of Pentecost, if there were any slain or dead—as there was no year that there

---

or else and he were nearhand] or if he were nearby

failed but there were some dead—then was there chosen in his stead that was dead, the most men of worship that were called the Queen's Knights. And thus they came up first before they were renowned men of worship, both Sir Lancelot and all the remnant of them.

But this knight, Sir Meliagaunt, had espied the Queen well and her purpose, and how Sir Lancelot was not with her, and how she had no men of arms with her but the ten noble knights all arrayed in green for maying. Then he purveyed him twenty men of arms and a hundred archers for to distress the Queen and her knights, for he thought that time was best season to take the Queen.

[2]   So as the Queen was out on maying with all her knights, which were bedashed with herbs, mosses, and flowers in the freshest manner, right so there came out of a wood Sir Meliagaunt with eight score men, all harnessed as they should fight in a battle of arrest, and bade the Queen and her knights abide, for maugre their heads they should abide.

'Traitor knight,' said Queen Guenivere, 'what cast thou to do? Wilt thou shame thyself? Bethink thee how thou art a king's son and a knight of the Table Round, and thou thus to be about to dishonour the noble king that made thee knight!—thou shamest all knighthood and thyself and me. And I let thee wit thou shalt never shame me, for I had liever cut my own throat in twain rather than thou should dishonour me.'

'As for all this language,' said Sir Meliagaunt, 'be as it be may, for wit you well, madam, I have loved you many a year, and never or now could I get you at such avail; and therefore I will take you as I find you.'

Then spoke all the ten noble knights at once and said, 'Sir Meliagaunt, wit thou well thou art about to jeopardy thy worship to dishonour, and also ye cast to jeopardy your persons, howbeit we be unarmed and ye have us at a great advantage, for it seemeth by you that ye have laid watch upon us. But rather than ye should put the Queen to a shame and us all, we had as lief to depart from our lives; for and we other ways did, we were shamed for ever.'

Then said Sir Meliagaunt, 'Dress you as well ye can, and keep the Queen!'

Then the ten knights of the Round Table drew their swords, and these others let run at them with their spears; and the ten knights

---

in his stead that was dead] to fill the place of the dead man   bedashed] bedecked
battle of arrest] raid   cast] plot

manly abode them, and smote away their spears that no spear did them no harm. Then they lashed together with swords, and anon Sir Kay, Sir Sagramore, Sir Agravain, Sir Dodinas, Sir Ladinas, and Sir Ozanna were smitten to the earth with grimly wounds. Then Sir Brandiles and Sir Persant, Sir Ironside and Sir Pelleas fought long, and they were sore wounded; for these ten knights, or ever they were laid to the ground, slew forty men of the boldest and the best of them.

So when the Queen saw her knights thus dolefully wounded, and needs must be slain at the last, then for pity and sorrow she cried and said, 'Sir Meliagaunt, slay not my noble knights, and I will go with thee upon this covenant, that thou save them and suffer them no more to be hurt; with this, that they be led with me wheresoever thou leadest me. For I will rather slay myself than I will go with thee, unless that these noble knights may be in my presence.'

'Madam,' said Sir Meliagaunt, 'for your sake they shall be led with you into my own castle, with that ye will be ruled, and ride with me.'

Then the Queen prayed the four knights to leave their fighting, and she and they would not part.

'Madam,' said Sir Pelleas, 'we will do as ye do, for as for me I take no force of my life nor death.'

For as the French book saith, Sir Pelleas gave such buffets there that no armour might hold him.

Then by the Queen's commandment they left battle and dressed the [3] wounded knights on horseback, some sitting and some overthwart their horses, that it was pity to behold. And then Sir Meliagaunt charged the Queen and all her knights that none of her fellowship should depart from her; for full sore he dreaded Sir Lancelot du Lake, lest he should have any knowledging. And all this espied the Queen, and privily she called unto her a child of her chamber which was swiftly horsed, of a great advantage.

'Now go thou,' said she, 'when thou seest thy time, and bear this ring unto Sir Lancelot du Lake, and pray him as he loveth me that he will see me and rescue me, if ever he will have joy of me. And spare not thy horse,' said the Queen, 'neither for water nor for land.'

So this child espied his time, and lightly he took his horse with spurs and departed as fast as he might. And when Sir Meliagaunt saw him so flee, he understood that it was by the Queen's commandment for to

with this] on this condition   hold] resist   of a great advantage] by a great deal

warn Sir Lancelot. Then they that were best horsed chased him and shot at him, but from them all the child went deliverly.

And then Sir Meliagaunt said unto the Queen, 'Madam, ye are about to betray me, but I shall ordain for Sir Lancelot that he shall not come lightly at you.'

And then he rode with her and all the fellowship in all the haste that they might. And so by the way Sir Meliagaunt laid in ambush of the best archers that he had thirty to await upon Sir Lancelot, charging them that if they saw such a manner of knight come by the way upon a white horse, 'that in any wise ye slay his horse, but in no manner have ye ado with him bodily, for he is over hard to be overcome.'

So this was done, and they were come to his castle. But in no wise the Queen would never let none of the ten knights and her ladies out of her sight, but always they were in her presence. For the book saith, Sir Meliagaunt durst make no masteries for dread of Sir Lancelot, insomuch he deemed that he had warning.

So when the child was departed from the fellowship of Sir Meliagaunt, within a while he came to Westminster, and anon he found Sir Lancelot. And when he had told his message and delivered him the Queen's ring, 'Alas,' said Sir Lancelot, 'now am I shamed for ever, unless that I may rescue that noble lady from dishonour.'

Then eagerly he asked his arms; and ever the child told Sir Lancelot how the ten knights fought marvellously, and how Sir Pelleas, Sir Ironside, Sir Brandiles, and Sir Persant of Inde fought strongly, but namely Sir Pelleas, there might no harness hold him; and how they all fought till they were laid to the earth; and how the Queen made appointment for to save their lives and to go with Sir Meliagaunt.

'Alas,' said Sir Lancelot, 'that most noble lady, that she should be so destroyed! I had liever', said Sir Lancelot, 'than all France, that I had been there well armed.'

So when Sir Lancelot was armed and upon his horse, he prayed the child of the Queen's chamber to warn Sir Lavain how suddenly he was departed, and for what cause. 'And pray him as he loveth me, that he will hie him after me; and that he stint not until he come to the castle where Sir Meliagaunt abideth, for there', said Sir Lancelot, 'he shall hear of me, and I be a man living.'

[4] Then Sir Lancelot rode as fast as he might; and the book saith he

---

masteries] deeds of oppression   namely] especially   appointment] terms took the water at Westminster Bridge, and made his horse swim over the Thames unto Lambeth. And so within a while he came to the same place there as the ten noble knights fought with Sir Meliagaunt; and then Sir Lancelot followed the track until that he came to a wood, and there was a strait way. And there the thirty archers bade Sir Lancelot turn again and follow no longer that track.

'What commandment have ye,' said Sir Lancelot, 'to cause me that am a knight of the Round Table to leave my right way?'

'This way shalt thou leave, or else thou shalt go it on thy foot; for wit thou well thy horse shall be slain.'

'That is little mastery,' said Sir Lancelot, 'to slay my horse; but as for myself, when my horse is slain, I give right nought of you, not and ye were five hundred more.'

So then they shot Sir Lancelot's horse, and smote him with many arrows. And then Sir Lancelot avoided his horse and went on foot; but there were so many ditches and hedges betwixt them and him that he might not meddle with none of them.

'Alas, for shame,' said Sir Lancelot, 'that ever one knight should betray another knight. But it is an old-said saw, "A good man is never in danger but when he is in the danger of a coward." '

Then Sir Lancelot walked on a while, and was sore encumbered of his armour, his shield, and his spear; wit you well, he was full sore annoyed, and full loath he was for to leave anything that longed unto him, for he dreaded sore the treason of Sir Meliagaunt. Then by fortune there came a chariot that came thither to fetch wood.

'Say me, carter,' said Sir Lancelot, 'what shall I give thee to suffer me to leap into thy chariot, and that thou wilt bring me unto a castle within these two miles?'

'Thou shalt not enter into this chariot,' said the carter, 'for I am sent for to fetch wood.'

'Unto whom?' said Sir Lancelot.

'Unto my lord, Sir Meliagaunt,' said the carter.

'And with him would I speak,' said Sir Lancelot.

'Thou shalt not go with me,' said the carter.

Then Sir Lancelot leapt to him, and gave him backward with his

---

give right nought of you] am not concerned about you   meddle] reach to fight
danger of a coward] in the power of a coward   annoyed] troubled   chariot] cart

gauntlet a rearmain that he fell to the earth stark dead. Then the other carter, his fellow, was afraid, and weened to have gone the same way; and then he said, 'Fair lord, save my life, and I shall bring you where ye will.'

'Then I charge thee,' said Sir Lancelot, 'that thou drive me and this chariot unto Sir Meliagaunt's gate.'

'Then leap ye up into the chariot,' said the carter, 'and ye shall be there anon.'

So the carter drove on a great gallop, and Sir Lancelot's horse followed the chariot with more than forty arrows in him.

And more than an hour and a half Dame Guenivere was awaiting in a bay window; then one of her ladies espied an armed knight standing in a chariot.

'Ah, see, madam,' said the lady, 'where rides in a chariot a goodly armed knight, and we suppose he rideth unto hanging.'*

'Where?' said the Queen.

Then she espied by his shield that it was Sir Lancelot; and then was she ware where came his horse after that chariot, and ever he trod his guts and his paunch under his feet.

'Alas,' said the Queen, 'now I may prove and see that well is that creature that hath a trusty friend. Ah,' said Queen Guenivere, 'I see well that ye were hard bestead when ye ride in a chariot.' And then she rebuked that lady that likened Sir Lancelot to ride in a chariot to hanging. 'Forsooth, it was foul mouthed,' said the Queen, 'and evil likened, so for to liken the most noble knight of the world unto such a shameful death. Ah, Jesu defend him and keep him,' said the Queen, 'from all mischievous end.'

So by this was Sir Lancelot come to the gates of that castle, and there he descended down, and cried, that all the castle might ring, 'Where art thou, thou false traitor, Sir Meliagaunt, and knight of the Table Round? Come forth, thou traitor knight, thou and thy fellowship with thee! For here I am, Sir Lancelot du Lake, that shall fight with you all.'

And therewith he bore the gate wide open upon the porter, and smote him under the ear with his gauntlet, that his neck brast in two pieces.

[5]   When Sir Meliagaunt heard that Sir Lancelot was come, he ran

---

rearmain] backward blow with the hand   awaiting] watching

unto the Queen and fell upon his knee, and said, 'Mercy, madam, now I put me wholly in your good grace.'

'What ails you now?' said Queen Guenivere. 'Pardieu, I might well wit that some good knight would revenge me, though my lord King Arthur knew not of this your work.'

'Ah, madam,' said Sir Meliagaunt, 'all this that is amiss on my part shall be amended right as yourself will devise, and wholly I put me in your grace.'

'What would ye that I did?' said the Queen.

'Madam, I would no more,' said Sir Meliagaunt, 'but that ye would take all in your own hands, and that ye will rule my lord Sir Lancelot. And such cheer as may be made him in this poor castle, ye and he shall have, until tomorrow, and then may ye and all they return again unto Westminster; and my body and all that I have I shall put in your rule.'

'Ye say well,' said the Queen, 'and better is peace than evermore war, and the less noise the more is my worship.'

Then the Queen and her ladies went down unto Sir Lancelot, that stood wood wroth out of measure to abide battle; and ever he said, 'Thou traitor knight, come forth!'

Then the Queen came unto him and said, 'Sir Lancelot, why be ye so moved?'

'Ah, madam,' said Sir Lancelot, 'why ask ye me that question? For me seemeth ye ought to be more wroth than I am, for ye have the hurt and the dishonour. For wit you well, madam, my hurt is but little in regard for the slaying of a mare's son, but the despite grieveth me much more than all my hurt.'

'Truly,' said the Queen, 'ye say truth. But heartily I thank you,' said the Queen, 'but ye must come in with me peaceably, for all thing is put in my hand, and all that is amiss shall be amended; for the knight full sore repents him of this misadventure that is befallen him.'

'Madam,' said Sir Lancelot, 'sith it is so that ye be accorded with him, as for me I may not gainsay it, howbeit Sir Meliagaunt hath done full shamefully to me, and cowardly. And, madam,' said Sir Lancelot, 'and I had wist that ye would have been so lightly accorded with him, I would not have made such haste unto you.'

'Why say ye so?' said the Queen. 'Do ye forthink yourself of your good deeds? Wit you well,' said the Queen, 'I accorded never with him

noise] loose talk   forthink yourself] regret

for no favour nor love that I had unto him, but of wisdom to lay down every shameful noise.'

'Madam,' said Sir Lancelot, 'ye understand full well I was never willing nor glad of shameful slander nor noise. And there is neither king, queen, nor knight that beareth the life, except my lord King Arthur and you, madam, that should let me but I should make Sir Meliagaunt's heart full cold or ever I departed from hence.'

'That wot I well,' said the Queen, 'but what will ye more? Ye shall have all thing ruled as ye list to have it.'

'Madam,' said Sir Lancelot, 'so ye be pleased, as for my part ye shall soon please me.'

Right so the Queen took Sir Lancelot by the bare hand, for he had put off his gauntlet, and so she went with him to her chamber; and then she commanded him to be unarmed. And then Sir Lancelot asked the Queen where were her ten knights that were wounded with her. Then she showed them unto him, and there they made great joy of the coming of Sir Lancelot, and he made great sorrow of their hurts. And there Sir Lancelot told them how cowardly and traitorly he set archers to slay his horse, and how he was fain to put himself in a chariot. And thus they complained each to other; and full fain they would have been revenged, but they kept the peace because of the Queen.

Then, as the French book saith, Sir Lancelot was called many days after le Chevalier de Chariot, and so he did many deeds and great adventures. And so we leave off here of le Chevalier de Chariot, and turn we to this tale.

So Sir Lancelot had great cheer with the Queen; and then he made a promise with the Queen that the same night he should come to a window outward toward a garden—and that window was barred with iron—and there Sir Lancelot promised to meet her when all folks were asleep.

So then came Sir Lavain driving to the gates, saying, 'Where is my lord Sir Lancelot?' And anon he was sent for; and when Sir Lavain saw Sir Lancelot, he said, 'Ah, my lord, I found how ye were hard bestead, for I have found your horse that is slain with arrows.'

'As for that,' said Sir Lancelot, 'I pray you, Sir Lavain, speak ye of other matters, and let this pass, and right it another time and we may.'

of wisdom to lay down every shameful noise] to suppress wisely every breath of scandal   let me but I should make] stop me from making   driving] spurring

Then the knights that were hurt were searched, and soft salves were laid to their wounds; and so it passed on till supper time, and all the cheer that might be made them there was done unto the Queen and all her knights. And when season was, they went unto their chambers, but in no wise the Queen would not suffer her wounded knights to be from her, but that they were laid in withdraughts* by her chamber upon beds and pallets, that she might herself see unto them that they wanted nothing.

So when Sir Lancelot was in his chamber which was assigned unto him, he called unto him Sir Lavain, and told him that night he must speak with his lady, Queen Guenivere.

'Sir,' said Sir Lavain, 'let me go with you and it please you, for I dread me sore of the treason of Sir Meliagaunt.'

'Nay,' said Sir Lancelot, 'I thank you, but I will have nobody with me.'

Then Sir Lancelot took his sword in his hand, and privily went to the place where he had espied a ladder beforehand; and that he took under his arm and bore it through the garden, and set it up to the window. And anon the Queen was there ready to meet him; and then they made their complaints to other of many diverse things. And then Sir Lancelot wished that he might have come in to her.

'Wit you well,' said the Queen, 'I would as fain as ye that ye might come in to me.'

'Would ye so, madam,' said Sir Lancelot, 'with your heart, that I were with you?'

'Yea, truly,' said the Queen.

'Then shall I prove my might,' said Sir Lancelot, 'for your love.'

And then he set his hands upon the bars of iron, and pulled at them with such a might that he brast them clean out of the stone walls; and therewith one of the bars of iron cut the brawn of his hands throughout to the bone. And then he leapt into the chamber to the Queen.

'Make ye no noise,' said the Queen, 'for my wounded knights lie here fast by me.'

So, to pass upon this tale, Sir Lancelot went to bed with the Queen and took no force of his hurt hand, but took his pleasance and his liking until it was the dawning of the day; for wit you well, he slept not, but watched. And when he saw his time that he might tarry no longer, he took his leave and departed at the window, and put it together as well as he might again, and so departed unto his own chamber; and there he told Sir Lavain how that he was hurt. Then Sir Lavain dressed his hand and put upon it a glove, that it should not be espied. And so they lay long abed in the morning till it was nine of the clock. Then Sir Meliagaunt went to the Queen's chamber, and found her ladies there ready clothed.

'Ah, Jesu mercy,' said Sir Meliagaunt, 'what ails you, madam, that ye sleep this long?'

And therewith he opened the curtain for to behold her; and then was he ware where she lay, and all the headsheet, pillow, and oversheet was all be-bled of the blood of Sir Lancelot and of his hurt hand. When Sir Meliagaunt espied that blood, then he deemed in her that she was false to the King, and that some of the wounded knights had lain by her all that night.

'Ha, madam,' said Sir Meliagaunt, 'now I have found you a false traitress unto my lord Arthur; for now I prove well it was not for nought that ye laid these wounded knights within the bounds of your chamber, therefore I will call you of treason before my lord King Arthur. And now I have proved you, madam, with a shameful deed; and that they be all false, or some of them, I will make it good, for a wounded knight this night hath lain by you.'

'That is false,' said the Queen, 'that I will report me unto them.'

But when the ten knights heard of Sir Meliagaunt's words, then they spoke all at once and said, 'Sir Meliagaunt, thou falsely beliest my lady the Queen, and that we will make good upon thee, any of us. Now choose which thou list of us, when we are whole of the wounds thou gavest us.'

'Ye shall not; away with your proud language, for here ye may all see that a wounded knight this night hath lain by the Queen.'

Then they all looked, and were sore ashamed when they saw that blood; and wit you well Sir Meliagaunt was passing glad that he had the Queen at such advantage, for he deemed by that to hide his own treason. And so in this rumour came in Sir Lancelot, and found them at a great affray.

[7]   'What array is this?' said Sir Lancelot.

Then Sir Meliagaunt told them what he had found, and so he showed him the Queen's bed.

'Now truly,' said Sir Lancelot, 'ye did not your part, nor knightly, to

report me] appeal for confirmation   rumour] disturbance touch a queen's bed while it was drawn, and she lying therein.* And I dare say,' said Sir Lancelot, 'my lord King Arthur himself would not have displayed her curtains, she being within her bed, unless that it had pleased him to have lain him down by her. And therefore, Sir Meliagaunt, ye have done unworshipfully and shamefully to yourself.'

'Sir, I wot not what ye mean,' said Sir Meliagaunt, 'but well I am sure there hath one of her hurt knights lain with her this night; and that will I prove with my hands, that she is a traitress unto my lord King Arthur.'

'Beware what ye do,' said Lancelot, 'for and ye say so and will prove it, it will be taken at your hands.'

'My lord Sir Lancelot,' said Sir Meliagaunt, 'I rede you beware what ye do; for though ye are never so good a knight, as I wot well ye are renowned the best knight of the world, yet should ye be advised to do battle in a wrong quarrel, for God will have a stroke in every battle.'

'As for that,' said Sir Lancelot, 'God is to be dreaded! But as to that I say nay plainly, that this night there lay none of these ten knights wounded with my lady Queen Guenivere; and that will I prove with my hands, that ye say untruly in that. Now what say ye?' said Sir Lancelot.

'Thus I say,' said Sir Meliagaunt, 'here is my glove that she is a traitress unto my lord King Arthur, and that this night one of the wounded knights lay with her.'

'Well, sir, and I receive your glove,' said Sir Lancelot.

And anon they were sealed with their signets, and delivered unto the ten knights.

'At what day shall we do battle together?' said Sir Lancelot.

'This day eight days,' said Sir Meliagaunt, 'in the field beside Westminster.'

'I am agreed,' said Sir Lancelot.

'But now,' said Sir Meliagaunt, 'sithen it is so that we must needs fight together, I pray you, as ye be a noble knight, await me with no treason nor no villainy the meanwhile, nor none for you.'

'So God me help,' said Sir Lancelot, 'ye shall right well wit that I was never of no such conditions, for I report me to all knights that ever

---

displayed] drawn back   it will be taken at your hands] your challenge will be
taken up   rede] advise   be advised] take careful thought

have known me, I fared never with no treason, nor I loved never the fellowship of him that fared with treason.'

'Then let us go unto dinner,' said Sir Meliagaunt, 'and after dinner the Queen and ye may ride all unto Westminster.'

'I will well,' said Sir Lancelot.

Then Sir Meliagaunt said unto Sir Lancelot, 'Sir, pleaseth you to see the estures of this castle?'

'With a good will,' said Sir Lancelot.

And then they went together from chamber to chamber, for Sir Lancelot dreaded no perils; for ever a man of worship and of prowess dreads but little of perils, for they ween that every man be as they be—but ever he that fareth with treason putteth often a true man in great danger. And so it befell upon Sir Lancelot that dreaded no peril, as he went with Sir Meliagaunt he trod on a trap and the board rolled, and there Sir Lancelot fell down more than ten fathom into a cave full of straw. And then Sir Meliagaunt departed and made no fare, no more than he that wist not where he was.

And when Sir Lancelot was thus missed they marvelled where he was become; and then the Queen and many of them deemed that he was departed as he was wont to do, suddenly. For Sir Meliagaunt made suddenly to put aside Sir Lavain's horse, that they might all understand that Sir Lancelot was departed suddenly, so that it passed on till after dinner. And then Sir Lavain would not stint until that he had horse-litters for the wounded knights, that they might be carried in them, and so with the Queen, both ladies and gentlewomen, they rode unto Westminster. And there the knights told how Sir Meliagaunt had appealed the Queen of high treason and how Sir Lancelot received the glove of him, 'and this day eight days they shall do battle before you'.

'By my head,' said King Arthur, 'I am afraid Sir Meliagaunt hath charged himself with a great charge! But where is Sir Lancelot?' said the King.

'Sir, we wot not where he is, but we deem he is ridden to some adventure as he is ofttimes wont to do, for he had Sir Lavain's horse.'

'Let him be,' said the King, 'for he will be found, but if he be trapped with some treason.'

[8]   Thus leave we Sir Lancelot lying within that cave in great pain; and every day there came a lady and brought him his meat and his drink,

estures] rooms   ten fathom] sixty feet (twenty metres)   fare] fuss and wooed him to have lain by her. And ever the noble knight Sir Lancelot said her nay.

Then said she, 'Sir, ye are not wise, for ye may never out of this prison but if ye have my help. And also your lady, Queen Guenivere, shall be burnt in your default, unless that ye be there at the day of battle.'

'God defend', said Sir Lancelot, 'that she should be burnt in my default. And if it be so', said Sir Lancelot, 'that I may not be there, it shall be well understood, both at the King and at the Queen and with all men of worship, that I am dead, sick, or in prison, for all men that know me will say for me that I am in some evil case and I be not that day there. And thus well I understand that there is some good knight, either of my blood or some other that loves me, that will take my quarrel in hand. And therefore,' said Sir Lancelot, 'wit you well ye shall not fear me; and if there were no more women in all this land but ye, yet shall not I have ado with you.'

'Then are ye shamed,' said the lady, 'and destroyed for ever.'

'As for world's shame, now Jesu defend me; and as for my distress, it is welcome whatsoever it be that God sends me.'

So she came to him again the same day that the battle should be, and said, 'Sir Lancelot, bethink you, for ye are too hard-hearted. And therefore, and ye would but once kiss me, I should deliver you and your armour, and the best horse that was within Sir Meliagaunt's stable.'

'As for to kiss you,' said Sir Lancelot, 'I may do that and lose no worship. And wit you well, and I understood there were any disworship for to kiss you, I would not do it.'

And then he kissed her; and anon she got him up unto his armour, and when he was armed she brought him to a stable where stood twelve good coursers, and bade him to choose of the best. Then Sir Lancelot looked upon a white courser, and that liked him best; and anon he commanded him to be saddled with the best saddle of war, and so it was done. Then he got his own spear in his hand and his sword by his side; and then he commended the lady unto God, and said, 'Lady, for this day's deed I shall do you service if ever it lie in my power.'

Now leave we here Sir Lancelot, all that ever he might gallop, and [9] speak we of Queen Guenivere that was brought to a fire to be burnt; for Sir Meliagaunt was sure, him thought, that Sir Lancelot should not be

fear] frighten

at that battle, and therefore he ever cried upon Sir Arthur to do him justice, or else bring forth Sir Lancelot. Then was the King and all the court full sore abashed and shamed that the Queen should be burnt in the default of Sir Lancelot.

'My lord King Arthur,' said Sir Lavain, 'ye may understand that it is not well with my lord Sir Lancelot, for and he were alive, so he be not sick or in prison, wit you well he would have been here; for never heard ye that ever he failed yet his part for whom he should do battle for. And therefore,' said Sir Lavain, 'my lord King Arthur, I beseech you that ye will give me licence to do battle here this day for my lord and master, and for to save my lady the Queen.'

'Grantmercy, gentle Sir Lavain,' said King Arthur, 'for I dare say all that Sir Meliagaunt putteth upon my lady the Queen is wrong; for I have spoken with all the ten wounded knights, and there is not one of them, and he were whole and able to do battle, but he would prove upon Sir Meliagaunt's body that it is false that he putteth upon my queen.'

'And so shall I,' said Sir Lavain, 'in the defence of my lord Sir Lancelot, and ye will give me leave.'

'And I give you leave,' said King Arthur, 'and do your best, for I dare well say there is some treason done to Sir Lancelot.'

Then was Sir Lavain armed and horsed, and deliverly at the lists' end he rode to perform his battle. And right as the heralds should cry, 'Lessez les aller,'* right so came Sir Lancelot driving with all the might of his horse. And then King Arthur cried, 'Whoa!' and 'Abide!'

And then was Sir Lancelot called before King Arthur, and there he told openly before the King all how that Sir Meliagaunt had served him first and last. And when the King and Queen and all the lords knew of the treason of Sir Meliagaunt they were all ashamed on his behalf. Then was the Queen sent for, and set by the King in the great trust of her champion.

And then Sir Lancelot and Sir Meliagaunt dressed them together with spears as thunder, and there Sir Lancelot bore him quite over his horse's croup. And then Sir Lancelot alit and dressed his shield on his shoulder and took his sword in his hand, and so they dressed to each other and smote many great strokes together. And at the last Sir Lancelot smote him such a buffet upon the helmet that he fell on the one side to the earth.

driving] galloping

And then he cried upon him loud and said, 'Most noble knight Sir Lancelot, save my life, for I yield me unto you, and I require you, as ye be a knight and fellow of the Table Round, slay me not, for I yield me as overcome. And whether I shall live or die I put me in the King's hands and yours.'

Then Sir Lancelot wist not what to do, for he had had liever than all the goods in the world that he might be revenged upon him. So Sir Lancelot looked upon the Queen, if he might espy by any sign or countenance what she would have done. And anon the Queen wagged her head upon Sir Lancelot, as who saith, 'Slay him.' And full well knew Sir Lancelot by her signs that she would have him dead.

Then Sir Lancelot bade him, 'Arise, for shame, and perform this battle with me to the utterance.'

'Nay,' said Sir Meliagaunt, 'I will never arise until that ye take me as yielded and recreant.'

'Well, I shall proffer you a large proffer,' said Sir Lancelot, 'that is for to say I shall unarm my head and my left quarter of my body, all that may be unarmed as for that quarter, and I will let bind my left hand behind me where it shall not help me, and right so I shall do battle with you.'

Then Sir Meliagaunt started up and said on high, 'Take heed, my lord Arthur, of this proffer, for I will take it, and let him be disarmed and bound according to his proffer.'

'What say ye?' said King Arthur unto Sir Lancelot. 'Will ye abide by your proffer?'

'Yea, my lord,' said Sir Lancelot, 'for I will never go from that I have once said.'

Then the knights parters of the field disarmed Sir Lancelot, first his head and then his left arm and his left side, and they bound his left arm fast to his left side behind his back, without shield or anything; and anon they yode together. Wit you well there was many a lady and many a knight marvelled that Sir Lancelot would jeopardy himself in such wise.

Then Sir Meliagaunt came with sword all on high, and Sir Lancelot showed him openly his bare head and the bare left side; and when he weened to have smitten him upon the bare head, then lightly he avoided the left leg and the left side, and put his hand and his sword to

knights parters of the field] marshals of the lists

that stroke, and so put it aside with great sleight. And then with great force Sir Lancelot smote him on the helmet such a buffet that the stroke carved the head in two parts. Then there was no more to do, but he was drawn out of the field.

And at the great instance of the knights of the Table Round, the King suffered him to be interred, and the mention made upon him who slew him and for what cause he was slain. And then the King and the Queen made more of Sir Lancelot, and more he was cherished than ever he was beforehand.

[10] Then as the French book maketh mention,* there was a good knight in the land of Hungary whose name was Sir Urry; and he was an adventurous knight, and in all places where he might hear of any adventurous deeds and of worship, there would he be. So it happened in Spain there was an earl, and his son's name was called Sir Alpheus; and at a great tournament in Spain this Sir Urry, knight of Hungary, and Sir Alpheus of Spain encountered together for very envy, and so either undertook other to the utterance. And by fortune this Sir Urry slew Sir Alpheus, the earl's son of Spain; but this knight that was slain had given Sir Urry, or ever he were slain, seven great wounds, three on the head and three on his body and one upon his left hand. And this Sir Alpheus had a mother which was a great sorceress; and she, for the despite of her son's death, wrought by her subtle crafts that Sir Urry should never be whole, but ever his wounds should one time fester and another time bleed, so that he should never be whole until the best knight of the world had searched his wounds. And thus she made her avaunt, wherethrough it was known that this Sir Urry should never be whole.

Then his mother let make a horse litter, and put him therein with two palfreys carrying him; and then she took with him his sister, a full fair damosel whose name was Filelolie, and a page with them to keep their horses; and so they led Sir Urry through many countries. For as the French book saith, she led him so seven years through all lands christened, and never could find no knight that might ease her son. So she came into Scotland and into the bounds of England; and by fortune she came unto the feast of Pentecost unto King Arthur's court, that at that time was held at Carlisle. And when she came there, she made it to be openly known how that she was come into that land for to heal her son.

avaunt] boast

Then King Arthur let call that lady and ask her the cause why she brought that hurt knight into that land.

'My most noble king,' said that lady, 'wit you well I brought him hither to be healed of his wounds, that of all these seven years might never be whole.' And thus she told the King, and where he was wounded and with whom, and how his mother discovered it in her pride how she had wrought by enchantment that he should never be whole until the best knight of the world had searched his wounds. 'And so I have passed all the lands christened through to have him healed, except this land; and if I fail here in this land, I will never take more pain upon me, and that is great pity, for he was a good knight and of great noblesse.'

'What is his name?' said King Arthur.

'My good and gracious lord,' she said, 'his name is Sir Urry of the Mount.'

'In good time,' said the King, 'and sithen ye are come into this land, ye are right welcome. And wit you well, here shall your son be healed and ever any Christian man may heal him. And for to give all other men of worship courage, I myself will assay to handle your son, and so shall all the kings, dukes, and earls that be here present at this time; not presuming upon me that I am so worthy to heal your son by my deeds, but I will courage other men of worship to do as I will do.'

And then the King commanded all the kings, dukes, and earls and all noble knights of the Round Table that were there that time present to come into the meadow of Carlisle. And so at that time there were but a hundred and ten of the Round Table, for forty knights were that time away.* And so here we must begin at King Arthur, as is kindly to begin at him that was that time the most man of worship christened.

Then King Arthur looked upon Sir Urry, and he thought he was a [11] full likely man when he was whole. And then the King made to take him down off the litter and laid him upon the earth, and anon there was laid a cushion of gold that he should kneel upon.

And then King Arthur said, 'Fair knight, me rueth of thy hurt; and for to courage all other knights, I will pray thee softly to suffer me to handle thy wounds.'

'My most noble christened king, do as ye list,' said Sir Urry, 'for I am at the mercy of God, and at your commandment.'

---

discovered] revealed   kindly] in accordance with nature   me rueth of]
I pity

So then King Arthur softly handled him, and then some of his wounds renewed upon bleeding.

Then King Clariance of Northumberland searched, and it would not be. And then Sir Barrant le Apres that was called the King with the Hundred Knights, he assayed and failed. So did King Uriens of the land of Gore; so did King Angwish of Ireland, and so did King Nentres of Garlot. So did King Carados of Scotland; so did the duke Sir Galahalt, the Haut Prince; so did Duke Chalance of Clarence; so did the Earl of Ulbawes; so did the Earl Lambaile; so did the Earl Aristance.

Then came in Sir Gawain with his three sons, Sir Gingalin, Sir Florence, and Sir Lovell—these two were begotten upon Sir Brandiles' sister—and all they failed. Then came in Sir Agravain, Sir Gaheris, and Sir Mordred, and the good knight Sir Gareth that was of very knighthood worth all the brethren.

So came in the knights of Sir Lancelot's kin, but Sir Lancelot was not that time in the court, for he was that time upon his adventures. Then Sir Lionel, Sir Ector de Maris, Sir Bors de Ganis, Sir Blamor de Ganis, Sir Bleoberis de Ganis, Sir Gahalantine, Sir Galihodin, Sir Menaduke, Sir Villiars the Valiant, Sir Hebes le Renowne—all these were of Sir Lancelot's kin, and all they failed.

Then came in Sir Sagramore le Desirous, Sir Dodinas le Savage, Sir Dinadan, Sir Breunor le Noir that Sir Kay named La Cote Mal Taillé, and Sir Kay le Seneschal; Sir Kay l'Estrange, Sir Meliot de Logris, Sir Petipace of Winchelsea, Sir Galleron of Galway, Sir Melion of the Mountain, Sir Cardok, Sir Uwain le Avoutres, and Sir Ozanna le Coeur Hardi. Then came in Sir Ascamore and Sir Grummor Grummorson; Sir Crosselm; Sir Severause le Breuse, that was called a passing strong knight—for as the book saith, the chief Lady of the Lake feasted Sir Lancelot and Sir Severause le Breuse, and when she had feasted them both at sundry times she prayed them to give her a done, and anon they granted her. And then she prayed Sir Severause that he would promise her never to do battle against Sir Lancelot, and in the same wise she prayed Sir Lancelot never to do battle against Sir Severause, and so either promised her. For the French book saith that Sir Severause had never courage nor great lust to do battle against no man but if it were against giants, and against dragons and wild beasts.

done] boon

So leave we this matter, and speak we of them that at the King's request were at the high feast as knights of the Round Table for to search Sir Urry. And to this intent the King did it, to wit which was the most noblest knight among them all.

Then came in Sir Agloval, Sir Dornar, and Sir Tor that was begotten upon the cowherd's wife (but he was begotten before Aries wedded her; and King Pellinore begat them all—first Sir Tor; Sir Agloval; Sir Dornar; Sir Lamorak, the most noblest knight alone of them that ever was in King Arthur's days as for a worldly knight; and Sir Percival that was peerless, except Sir Galahad, in holy deeds, but they died in the quest of the Sangrail).

Then came in Sir Griflet le Fils de Dieu; Sir Lucan the Butler; Sir Bedivere, his brother; Sir Brandiles; Sir Constantine, Sir Cador's son of Cornwall, that was king after Arthur's days; and Sir Clegis, Sir Sadok, Sir Dinas le Seneschal de Cornwall, Sir Fergus, Sir Driant, Sir Lambegus, Sir Clarrus of Cleremont, Sir Clodrus, Sir Hectimere; Sir Edward of Caernarvon, Sir Dinas, Sir Priamus which was christened by means of Sir Tristram the noble knight, and these three were brethren; Sir Helian le Blanc that was son unto Sir Bors, for he begot him upon King Brandegoris' daughter; and Sir Brian de Listinoise; Sir Gauter, Sir Reynold, Sir Gillimer, were three brethren which Sir Lancelot won upon a bridge in Sir Kay's arms; Sir Gumret le Petit; Sir Bellenger le Beau, that was son to the good knight Sir Alexander le Orphelin, that was slain by the treason of King Mark.

Also that traitor king slew the noble knight Sir Tristram, as he sat harping before his lady La Belle Isode, with a trenchant glaive, for whose death was the most wailing of any knight that ever was in King Arthur's days; for there was never none so bewailed as was Sir Tristram and Sir Lamorak, for they were with treason slain, Sir Tristram by King Mark, and Sir Lamorak by Sir Gawain and his brethren.

And this Sir Bellenger revenged the death of his father Sir Alexander, and Sir Tristram, for he slew King Mark. And La Belle Isode died swooning upon the corpse* of Sir Tristram, whereof was great pity. And all that were with King Mark which were of assent of the death of Sir Tristram were slain, as Sir Andret and many others.

Then came Sir Hebes, Sir Morganor, Sir Sentrail, Sir Suppinabiles; Sir Belliance le Orgulous, that the good knight Sir Lamorak

trenchant glaive] sharp sword

won in plain battle; Sir Neroveus and Sir Plenorius, two good knights that Sir Lancelot won; Sir Damas; Sir Harry le Fils Lake; Sir Herminde, brother to King Hermance, for whom Sir Palomides fought at the Red City with two brethren; and Sir Selises of the Dolorous Tower; Sir Edward of Orkney; Sir Ironside, that was called the noble Knight of the Red Launds that Sir Gareth won for the love of Dame Lyonesse; Sir Arrok; Sir Degrevant*; Sir Degrave sans Villainy that fought with the giant of the Black Lowe; Sir Epinogris, that was the King's son of Northumberland; Sir Pelleas, that loved the lady Ettard (and he had died for her sake had not been one of the ladies of the lake whose name was Dame Nenive, and she wedded Sir Pelleas; and she saved him ever after, that he was never slain by her days, and he was a full noble knight); and Sir Lamiel of Cardiff that was a great lover, Sir Plaine de Fors, Sir Melias de l'Isle, Sir Borre le Coeur Hardi that was King Arthur's son, Sir Mador de la Porte, Sir Colgrevance, Sir Hervis de la Forest Savage; Sir Marrok, the good knight that was betrayed by his wife, for she made him seven year a werewolf; Sir Persant, Sir Pertolepe his brother that was called the Green Knight, and Sir Perimones, brother unto them both, which was called the Red Knight, that Sir Gareth won when he was called Beaumains.

All these hundred knights and ten searched Sir Urry's wounds by the commandment of King Arthur.

[12]   'Mercy Jesu,' said King Arthur, 'where is Sir Lancelot du Lake, that he is not here at this time?'

And thus, as they stood and spoke of many things, there one espied Sir Lancelot that came riding toward them, and anon they told the King.

'Peace,' said the King, 'let no man say nothing until he be come to us.'

So when Sir Lancelot had espied King Arthur, he descended down from his horse and came to the King and saluted him and them all. And anon as the damsel, Sir Urry's sister, saw Sir Lancelot, she roamed to her brother there as he lay in his litter, and said, 'Brother, here is come a knight that my heart giveth greatly unto.'

'Fair sister,' said Sir Urry, 'so doth my heart light greatly against him, and my heart giveth me more unto him more than to all these that have searched me.'

Then said King Arthur unto Sir Lancelot, 'Sir, ye must do as we have done,' and told him what they had done, and showed him them all that had searched him.

'Jesu defend me,' said Sir Lancelot, 'while so many noble kings and knights have failed, that I should presume upon me to achieve that all ye, my lords, might not achieve.'

'Ye shall not choose,' said King Arthur, 'for I command you to do as we all have done.'

'My most renowned lord,' said Sir Lancelot, 'I know well I dare not nor may not disobey you; but and I might or durst, wit you well I would not take upon me to touch that wounded knight in that intent that I should pass all other knights—Jesu defend me from that shame.'

'Sir, ye take it wrong,' said King Arthur, 'for ye shall not do it for no presumption, but for to bear us fellowship in so much as ye be a fellow of the Round Table. And wit you well,' said King Arthur, 'and ye prevail not and heal him, I dare say there is no knight in this land that may heal him. And therefore I pray you, do as we have done.'

And then all the kings and knights for the most part prayed Sir Lancelot to search him. And then the wounded knight, Sir Urry, set him up weakly, and said unto Sir Lancelot, 'Now, courteous knight, I require thee for God's sake heal my wounds, for methinks ever sithen ye came here my wounds grieve me not so much as they did.'

'Ah, my fair lord,' said Sir Lancelot, 'Jesu would that I might help you! For I shame sore with myself that I should be thus required, for never was I able in worthiness to do so high a thing.'

Then Sir Lancelot kneeled down by the wounded knight, saying, 'My lord Arthur, I must do your commandment, which is sore against my heart.'

And then he held up his hands and looked unto the east, saying secretly unto himself, 'Now blessed Father and Son and Holy Ghost, I beseech Thee of Thy mercy that my simple worship and honesty be saved; and Thou blessed Trinity, Thou mayst give me power to heal this sick knight by the great virtue and grace of Thee, but, good Lord, never of myself.'

And then Sir Lancelot prayed Sir Urry to let him see his head. And then, devoutly kneeling, he ransacked the three wounds that they bled a little; and forthwith the wounds fair healed, and seemed as they had been whole seven years. And in like wise he searched his body of other three wounds, and they healed in like wise. And then the last of all he searched his hand, and anon it fair healed. Then King Arthur and all

---

and I might or durst] if I could or dared   ransacked] searched

the kings and knights kneeled down and gave thankings and loving unto God and unto His blessed Mother. And ever Sir Lancelot wept as he had been a child that had been beaten.

Then King Arthur let ravish priests and clerks in the most devoutest wise to bring in Sir Urry into Carlisle, with singing and loving to God. And when this was done, the King let clothe him in rich manner; and then were there but few better made knights in all the court, for he was passingly well made and bigly. Then King Arthur asked Sir Urry how he felt himself.

'Ah, my good and gracious lord, I felt myself never so lusty.'

'Then will ye joust and do any arms?' said King Arthur.

'Sir, and I had all that longed unto jousts I would be soon ready.'

[13]　　Then King Arthur made a party of a hundred knights to be against a hundred; and so upon the morn they jousted for a diamond, but there jousted none of the dangerous knights. And so, for to shorten this tale, Sir Urry and Sir Lavain jousted best that day, for there was none of them but he overthrew and pulled down thirty knights. And then, by assent of all the kings and lords, Sir Urry and Sir Lavain were made knights of the Table Round. And then Sir Lavain cast his love unto Dame Filelolie, Sir Urry's sister, and then they were wedded with great joy. And so King Arthur gave to each of them a barony of lands.

And this Sir Urry would never go from Sir Lancelot, but he and Sir Lavain waited evermore upon him. And they were in all the court accounted for good knights, and full desirous in arms; and many noble deeds they did, for they would have no rest, but ever sought upon their deeds.

Thus they lived in all that court with great noblesse and joy long time. But every night and day Sir Agravain, Sir Gawain's brother, awaited Queen Guenivere and Sir Lancelot to put them both to a rebuke and a shame.

And so I leave here of this tale, and overleap great books of Sir Lancelot, what great adventures he did when he was called le Chevalier de Chariot. For as the French book saith, because of despite that knights and ladies called him 'the knight that rode in the chariot' like as he were judged to the gibbet, therefore in the despite of all them that named him so, he was carried in a chariot a twelvemonth; for but little after

loving] praise　　　　let ravish] had fetched　　　　sought upon their deeds] strove
after action　　　　　chariot] i.e. cart

that he had slain Sir Meliagaunt in the Queen's quarrel, he never of a twelvemonth came on horseback.* And as the French book saith, he did that twelvemonth more than forty battles. And because I have lost the very matter of le Chevalier du Chariot, I depart from the tale of Sir Lancelot; and here I go unto the morte Arthur, and that caused Sir Agravain.*

And here on the other side followeth the most piteous tale of the Morte Arthur sans guerdon, par le chevalier Sir Thomas Malory, knight. Jesu, aide-le pour votre bonne merci.* Amen.

morte] death [of]

THE DEATH OF ARTHUR

[xx.i]   In May, when every heart flourisheth and burgeoneth—for as the season is lusty to behold and comfortable, so man and woman rejoiceth and gladdeth of summer coming with his fresh flowers, for winter with his rough winds and blasts causeth lusty men and women to cower and to sit by fires—so this season it befell in the month of May a great anger and unhappy, that stinted not till the flower of chivalry of the world was destroyed and slain. And all was long upon two unhappy knights which were named Sir Agravain and Sir Mordred, that were brethren unto Sir Gawain; for this Sir Agravain and Sir Mordred had ever a privy hate unto the Queen, Dame Guenivere, and to Sir Lancelot. And daily and nightly they ever watched upon Sir Lancelot.

So it misfortuned Sir Gawain and all his brethren were in King Arthur's chamber, and then Sir Agravain said thus openly, and not in no counsel, that many knights might hear,

'I marvel that we all be not ashamed both to see and to know how Sir Lancelot lieth daily and nightly by the Queen; and all we know well that it is so, and it is shamefully suffered of us all that we should suffer so noble a king as King Arthur is to be shamed.'

Then spoke Sir Gawain and said, ' Brother Sir Agravain, I pray you and charge you, move no such matters no more before me; for wit you well, I will not be of your counsel.'

'So God me help,' said Sir Gaheris and Sir Gareth, 'we will not be knowing of your deeds.'

'Then will I,' said Sir Mordred.

'I believe you well,' said Sir Gawain, 'for ever unto all unhappiness, Sir, ye will grant. And I would that ye left all this, and make you not so busy! For I know', said Sir Gawain, 'what will fall of it.'

'Fall whatsoever fall may,' said Sir Agravain, 'I will disclose it to the King.'

'Not by my counsel,' said Sir Gawain. 'For and there arise war and wrack betwixt Sir Lancelot and us, wit you well, brother, there will many knights and great lords hold with Sir Lancelot. Also, brother

long upon] on account of   not in no counsel] not confidentially   wrack]
strife

Sir Agravain,' said Sir Gawain, 'ye must remember how oftentimes Sir Lancelot hath rescued the King and the Queen; and the best of us all had been full cold at the heart root had not Sir Lancelot been better than we, and that hath he proved himself full oft. And as for my part,' said Sir Gawain, 'I will never be against Sir Lancelot for one day's deed: that was when he rescued me from King Carados of the Dolorous Tower, and slew him and saved my life. Also, brother Sir Agravain and Sir Mordred, in like wise Sir Lancelot rescued you both, and three score and two, from Sir Tarquin.* And therefore, brother, methinks such noble deeds and kindness should be remembered.'

'Do as ye list,' said Sir Agravain, 'for I will lain it no longer.'

So with these words came in Sir Arthur.

'Now, brother,' said Sir Gawain, 'stint your strife.'

'That will I not,' said Sir Agravain and Sir Mordred.

'Well, will ye so?' said Sir Gawain. 'Then God speed you, for I will not hear of your tales, neither be of your counsel.'

'No more will I,' said Sir Gaheris.

'Neither I,' said Sir Gareth, 'for I shall never say evil by that man that made me knight.'

And therewith they three departed, making great dole.

'Alas!' said Sir Gawain and Sir Gareth. 'Now is this realm wholly destroyed and mischieved, and the noble fellowship of the Round Table shall be disparbled.' So they departed; and then King Arthur [2] asked them what noise they made.

'My lord,' said Sir Agravain, 'I shall tell you, for I may keep it no longer. Here is I and my brother Sir Mordred broke unto my brother Sir Gawain, Sir Gaheris, and to Sir Gareth—for this is all, to make it short: we know all that Sir Lancelot holdeth your queen, and hath done long. And we be your sister's sons; we may suffer it no longer. And all we wot that ye should be above Sir Lancelot; and ye are the king that made him knight, and therefore we will prove it that he is a traitor to your person.'

'If it be so,' said the King, 'wit you well, he is none other; but I would be loath to begin such a thing but I might have proofs of it. For Sir Lancelot is a hardy knight, and all ye know that he is the best knight among us all; and but if he be taken with the deed he will fight with him

---

lain] conceal   disparbled] broken up   but if he be taken with the deed]
unless he is taken red-handed

that bringeth up the noise, and I know no knight that is able to match him. Therefore, and it be sooth as ye say, I would that he were taken with the deed.'

For as the French book saith, the King was full loath that such a noise should be upon Sir Lancelot and his queen. For the King had a deeming of it; but he would not hear thereof, for Sir Lancelot had done so much for him and for the Queen so many times that, wit you well, the King loved him passingly well.

'My lord,' said Sir Agravain, 'ye shall ride tomorrow an-hunting; and doubt ye not, Sir Lancelot will not go with you. And so, when it draweth toward night, ye may send the Queen word that ye will lie out all that night, and so ye may send for your cooks. And then, upon pain of death, that night we shall take him with the Queen, and we shall bring him unto you quick or dead.'

'I will well,' said the King. 'Then I counsel you to take with you sure fellowship.'

'Sir,' said Sir Agravain, 'my brother Sir Mordred and I will take with us twelve knights of the Round Table.'

'Beware,' said King Arthur, 'for I warn you, ye shall find him wight.'

'Let us deal,' said Sir Agravain and Sir Mordred.

So on the morn King Arthur rode an-hunting and sent word to the Queen that he would be out all that night. Then Sir Agravain and Sir Mordred got to them twelve knights, and hid themselves in a chamber in the castle of Carlisle. And these were their names: Sir Colgrevance, Sir Mador de la Porte, Sir Gingalin, Sir Meliot de Logris, Sir Petipace of Winchelsea, Sir Galleron of Galloway, Sir Melion de la Mountain, Sir Ascamore, Sir Gromore Somer Jour,* Sir Curselain, Sir Florence, and Sir Lovell. So these twelve knights were with Sir Mordred and Sir Agravain, and all they were of Scotland,* or else of Sir Gawain's kin, or well-willers to his brother.

So when the night came, Sir Lancelot told Sir Bors how he would go that night and speak with the Queen.

'Sir,' said Sir Bors, 'ye shall not go this night by my counsel.'

'Why?' said Sir Lancelot.

'Sir, for I dread me ever of Sir Agravain, that waiteth upon you daily to do you shame, and us all. And never gave my heart against no going that ever ye went to the Queen so much as now, for I mistrust that the

___
wight| strong

King is out this night from the Queen because peradventure he hath laid some watch for you and the Queen; therefore I dread me sore of some treason.'

'Have ye no dread,' said Sir Lancelot, 'for I shall go and come again and make no tarrying.'

'Sir,' said Sir Bors, 'that me repents, for I dread me sore that your going this night shall wrath us all.'

'Fair nephew,' said Sir Lancelot, 'I marvel me much why ye say thus, sithen the Queen hath sent for me; and wit you well, I will not be so much a coward, but she shall understand I will see her good grace.'

'God speed you well,' said Sir Bors, 'and send you sound and safe again!'

So Sir Lancelot departed and took his sword under his arm; and so he walked in his mantle, that noble knight, and put himself in great jeopardy, and so he passed on till he came to the Queen's chamber. And so lightly he was had into the chamber; for as the French book saith, the Queen and Sir Lancelot were together. And whether they were abed or at other manner of disports, me list not thereof make no mention, for love that time was not as love is nowadays. But thus as they were together, there came Sir Agravain and Sir Mordred with twelve knights with them of the Round Table, and they said with great crying and scaring voice, 'Thou traitor Sir Lancelot, now art thou taken!' And thus they cried with a loud voice, that all the court might hear it. And these fourteen knights were armed at all points, as they should fight in a battle. [3]

'Alas!' said Queen Guenivere, 'now are we mischieved both.'

'Madam,' said Sir Lancelot, 'is there here any armour within your chamber that might cover my body withal? And if there be any, give it me, and I shall soon stint their malice, by the grace of God!'

'Now truly,' said the Queen, 'I have no armour, neither helm, shield, sword nor spear, wherefore I dread me sore our long love is come to a mischievous end. For I hear by their noise there be many noble knights, and well I wot they be surely armed; and against them ye may make no resistance, wherefore ye are likely to be slain, and then shall I be burnt. For and ye might escape them,' said the Queen, 'I would not doubt but that ye would rescue me, in what danger that I ever stood in.'

'Alas,' said Sir Lancelot, 'in all my life thus was I never bestead, that I should be thus shamefully slain for lack of my armour.'

wrath] injure

But ever Sir Agravain and Sir Mordred cried, 'Traitor knight, come out of the Queen's chamber, for wit thou well thou art beset so that thou shalt not escape!'

'Ah, Jesu mercy!' said Sir Lancelot. 'This shameful cry and noise I may not suffer! For better were death at once than thus to endure this pain.' Then he took the Queen in his arms and kissed her and said, 'Most noblest Christian queen, I beseech you, as ye have ever been my special good lady, and I at all times your poor knight and true unto my power, and as I never failed you in right nor in wrong sithen the first day King Arthur made me knight, that ye will pray for my soul if that I be slain. For well I am assured that Sir Bors, my nephew, and all the remnant of my kin, with Sir Lavain and Sir Urry, that they will not fail you to rescue you from the fire. And therefore, mine own lady, comfort yourself, whatsoever come of me, that ye go with Sir Bors, my nephew; and they all will do you all the pleasure that they may, and ye shall live like a queen upon my lands.'

'Nay, Sir Lancelot, nay!' said the Queen, 'wit thou well that I will never live long after thy days.* But and ye be slain, I will take my death as meekly as ever did martyr take his death for Jesu Christ's sake.'

'Well, madam,' said Sir Lancelot, 'sith it is so that the day is come that our love must depart, wit you well I shall sell my life as dear as I may. And a thousandfold,' said Sir Lancelot, 'I am more heavier for you than for myself. And now I had liever than to be lord of all Christendom that I had sure armour upon me, that men might speak of my deeds or ever I were slain.'

'Truly,' said the Queen, 'and it might please God, I would that they would take me and slay me and suffer you to escape.'

'That shall never be,' said Sir Lancelot. 'God defend me from such a shame! But Jesu Christ, be Thou my shield and mine armour.'

[4]   And therewith Sir Lancelot wrapped his mantle about his arm well and surely; and by then they had got a great form out of the hall, and therewith they all rushed at the door.

'Now, fair lords,' said Sir Lancelot, 'leave your noise and your rushing, and I shall set open this door; and then may ye do with me what it liketh you.'

'Come off,' then said they all, 'and do it, for it availeth thee not to

form] bench (to use as a battering-ram)

strive against us all. And therefore let us into this chamber, and we shall save thy life—until thou come to King Arthur.'

Then Sir Lancelot unbarred the door, and with his left hand he held it open a little that but one man might come in at once. And so there came striding a good knight, a much man and a large, and his name was called Sir Colgrevance of Gore. And he with a sword struck at Sir Lancelot mightily; and so he put aside the stroke, and gave him such a buffet upon the helmet that he fell grovelling dead within the chamber door. Then Sir Lancelot with great might drew the knight within the chamber door. And then Sir Lancelot, with help of the Queen and her ladies, he was lightly armed in Colgrevance's armour. And ever stood Sir Agravain and Sir Mordred crying, 'Traitor knight, come forth out of the Queen's chamber!'

'Sirs, leave your noise,' said Sir Lancelot, 'for wit you well, Sir Agravain, ye shall not prison me this night. And therefore, and ye do by my counsel, go ye all from this chamber door and make you no such crying and such manner of slander as ye do. For I promise you by my knighthood, and ye will depart and make no more noise, I shall tomorrow appear before you all and before the King; and then let it be seen which of you all, or else ye all, that will deprave me of treason. And there shall I answer you as a knight should, that hither I came to the Queen for no manner of mal engine; and that will I prove and make it good upon you with my hands.'

'Fie upon thee, traitor!' said Sir Agravain and Sir Mordred, 'for we will have thee maugre thy head, and slay thee and we list—for we let thee wit we have the choice of King Arthur to save thee or slay thee.'

'Ah, sirs,' said Sir Lancelot, 'is there no other grace with you? Then keep yourself!'

And then Sir Lancelot set all open the chamber door, and mightily and knightly he strode in among them; and anon at the first stroke he slew Sir Agravain, and anon after twelve of his fellows—within a while he had laid them down cold to the earth, for there was none of the twelve knights might stand Sir Lancelot one buffet. And also he wounded Sir Mordred, and therewith he fled with all his might.

And then Sir Lancelot returned again unto the Queen and said, 'Madam, now wit you well, all our true love is brought to an end, for now will King Arthur ever be my foe. And therefore, madam, and it

deprave] accuse   mal engine] evil purpose

like you that I may have you with me, I shall save you from all manner adventures dangerous.'

'Sir, that is not best,' said the Queen, 'me seemeth, for now ye have done so much harm, it will be best that ye hold you still with this. And if ye see that tomorrow they will put me to death, then may ye rescue me as ye think best.'

'I will well,' said Sir Lancelot. 'For have ye no doubt, while I am a man living I shall rescue you.' And then he kissed her, and either of them gave other a ring. And so the Queen he left there, and went unto his lodging.

[5]   When Sir Bors saw Sir Lancelot, he was never so glad of his home-coming.

'Jesu mercy,' said Sir Lancelot, 'why be ye all armed? What meaneth this?'

'Sir,' said Sir Bors, 'after ye were departed from us, we all that be of your blood, and your well-willers, were so a-dreamed that some of us leapt out of our beds naked, and some in their dreams caught naked swords in their hands. And therefore,' said Sir Bors, 'we deemed there was some great strife on hand; and so we deemed that ye were betrapped with some treason, and therefore we made us thus ready, what need that ever ye were in.'

'My fair nephew,' said Sir Lancelot unto Sir Bors, 'now shall ye wit all, that this night I was more hard bestead than ever I was days of my life; and thanked be God, I am myself escaped their danger.' And so he told them all how and in what manner, as ye have heard beforehand. 'And therefore, my fellows,' said Sir Lancelot, 'I pray you all that ye will be of heart good, and help me in what need that ever I stand, for now is war come to us all.'

'Sir,' said Sir Bors, 'all is welcome that God sendeth us. And as we have taken much weal with you and much worship, we will take the woe with you as we have taken the weal.'

And therefore they said, all the good knights, 'Look ye take no dis-comfort; for there is no bands of knights under heaven but we shall be able to grieve them as much as they us, and therefore discomfort not yourself by no manner. And we shall gather together all that we love and that love us, and what that ye will have done shall be done. And therefore let us take the woe and the joy together.'

weal] happiness, well-being

'Grantmercy,' said Sir Lancelot, 'of your good comfort, for in my great distress, fair nephew, ye comfort me greatly. But thus, my fair nephew, I would that ye did, in all haste that ye may, for it is far past day: that ye will look in their lodgings that be lodged nigh here about the King, which will hold with me and which will not, for now I would know which were my friends from my foes.'

'Sir,' said Sir Bors, 'I shall do my pain, and or it be seven of the clock I shall wit of such as ye have done for who that will hold with you.'

Then Sir Bors called unto him Sir Lionel, Sir Ector de Maris, Sir Blamor de Ganis, Sir Gahalantine, Sir Galihodin, Sir Galihud, Sir Menaduke, Sir Villiars the Valiant, Sir Hebes le Renowne, Sir Lavain, Sir Urry of Hungary, Sir Neroveus, Sir Plenorius (for these two were knights that Sir Lancelot won upon a bridge, and therefore they would never be against him); and Sir Harry le Fils Lake, and Sir Selises of the Dolorous Tower, Sir Melias de l'Isle, and Sir Bellenger le Beau that was Sir Alexander le Orphelin's son—because his mother was kin unto Sir Lancelot, he held with him. So came Sir Palomides and Sir Safer, his brother; Sir Clegis, Sir Sadok, Sir Dinas, and Sir Clarrus of Cleremont. So these four-and-twenty knights drew them together; and by then they were armed and on horseback, they promised Sir Lancelot to do what he would. Then there fell to them, what of North Wales and of Cornwall, for Sir Lamorak's sake and Sir Tristram's sake, to the number of four score knights.

Then spoke Sir Lancelot, 'Wit you well, I have been ever since I came to this court well-willed unto my lord Arthur, and unto my lady Queen Guenivere unto my power. And this night, because my lady the Queen sent for me to speak with her—I suppose it was made by treason; how be it, I dare largely excuse her person, notwithstanding I was there nearhand slain, but as Jesu provided for me.' And then that noble knight Sir Lancelot told them how he was hard bestead in the Queen's chamber, and how and in what manner he escaped from them. 'And therefore wit you well, my fair lords, I am sure there is but war unto me and to mine, and for cause I have slain this night Sir Agravain, Sir Gawain's brother, and at the least twelve of his fellows. And for this cause now am I sure of mortal war, for these knights were sent by King Arthur to betray me. And therefore the King will in this heat and malice judge the Queen unto burning, and that may not I suffer that she

done for] helped   fell to] fell in with   heat] anger should be burned for my sake. For and I may be heard and suffered and so taken, I will fight for the Queen, that she is a true lady unto her lord. But the King, in his heat, I dread will not take me as I ought to be taken.'

[6]   'My lord Sir Lancelot,' said Sir Bors, 'by my advice, ye shall take the woe with the weal; and sithen it is fallen as it is, I counsel you to keep yourself—for and ye will keep yourself, there is no fellowship of knights christened that shall do you wrong. And also I will counsel you, my lord, that my lady Queen Guenivere, and she be in any distress, in so much as she is in pain for your sake, that ye knightly rescue her; for and ye did any otherwise, all the world would speak you shame to the world's end. Insomuch as ye were taken with her, whether ye did right or wrong, it is now your part to hold with the Queen, that she be not slain and put to a mischievous death; for and she so die, the shame shall be evermore yours.'

'Now Jesu defend me from shame,' said Sir Lancelot, 'and keep and save my lady the Queen from villainy and shameful death, and that she never be destroyed in my default!* Wherefore, my fair lords, my kin and my friends,' said Sir Lancelot, 'what will ye do?'

And anon they all said with one voice, 'We will do as ye will do.'

'Then I put this case unto you,' said Sir Lancelot, 'that my lord King Arthur by evil counsel will tomorrow in his heat put my lady the Queen unto the fire, and there to be burned. Then, I pray you, counsel me what is best for me to do.'

Then they said all at once with one voice, 'Sir, us thinks best that ye knightly rescue the Queen: insomuch as she shall be burned, it is for your sake. And it is to suppose, and ye might be handled, ye should have the same death, or else a more shamefuller death. And, sir, we say all that ye have rescued her from her death many times for other men's quarrels; therefore it seemeth it is more your worship that ye rescue the Queen from this quarrel, insomuch that she hath it for your sake.'

Then Sir Lancelot stood still and said, 'My fair lords, wit you well I would be loath to do that thing that should dishonour you or my blood, and wit you well I would be full loath that my lady the Queen should die such a shameful death. But and it be so that ye will counsel me to rescue her, I must do much harm or I rescue her, and peradventure

taken] understood   handled] taken

I shall destroy there some of my best friends. And if so be that I may win the Queen away, where shall I keep her?'

'Sir, that shall be the least care of us all,' said Sir Bors. 'For how did the most noble knight Sir Tristram? By your good will kept he not with him La Belle Isode near three years in Joyous Gard, the which was done by your althers advice? And that same place is your own, and in like wise ye may do and ye list, and take the Queen knightly away with you if so be that the King will judge her to be burned. And in Joyous Gard may ye keep her long enough until the heat be passed of the King. And then it may fortune you to bring the Queen again to the King with great worship, and peradventure ye shall have then thanks for your bringing home where others may happen to have magré.'

'That is hard for to do,' said Sir Lancelot, 'for by Sir Tristram I may have a warning. For when by means of treaty Sir Tristram brought again La Belle Isode unto King Mark from Joyous Gard, look ye now what befell in the end, how shamefully that false traitor King Mark slew him as he sat harping before his lady, La Belle Isode—with a grounden glaive he thrust him in behind to the heart; which grieveth me sore', said Sir Lancelot, 'to speak of his death, for all the world may not find such another knight.'

'All this is truth,' said Sir Bors, 'but there is one thing shall courage you and us all. Ye know well that King Arthur and King Mark were never like of conditions, for there was never yet man that ever could prove King Arthur untrue of his promise.'

But so to make short tale, they were all condescended that for better or for worse, if so were that the Queen were brought on that morn to the fire, shortly they all would rescue her. And so, by the advice of Sir Lancelot, they put them all in a wood as nigh Carlisle as they might, and there they abode still to wit what the King would do.

Now turn we again, that when Sir Mordred was escaped from [7] Sir Lancelot, he got his horse and came to King Arthur sore wounded and all for-bled, and there he told the King all how it was, and how they were all slain save himself alone.

your althers advice] the advice of you all   may happen to have magré] may turn out to be in disfavour   grounden glaive] sharpened sword   like of conditions] similar in character   condescended] agreed   all for-bled] having lost much blood

'Ah, Jesu mercy! how may this be?' said the King. 'Took ye him in the Queen's chamber?'

'Yea, so God me help,' said Sir Mordred, 'there we found him unarmed. And anon he slew Sir Colgrevance and armed him in his armour.' And so he told the King from the beginning to the ending.

'Jesu mercy,' said the King, 'he is a marvellous knight of prowess. And alas,' said the King, 'me sore repenteth that ever Sir Lancelot should be against me, for now I am sure the noble fellowship of the Round Table is broken for ever, for with him will many a noble knight hold. And now it is fallen so', said the King, 'that I may not with my worship but my Queen must suffer death'—and was sore moved.

So then there was made great ordinance in this ire, and the Queen must needs be judged to the death. And the law was such in those days, that whosoever they were, of what estate or degree, if they were found guilty of treason* there should be none other remedy but death, and either the mainour or the taking with the deed should be causer of their hasty judgement. And right so was it ordained for Queen Guenivere: because Sir Mordred was escaped sore wounded, and the death of thirteen knights of the Round Table, these proofs and experiences caused King Arthur to command the Queen to the fire, and there to be burned.

Then spoke Sir Gawain and said, 'My lord Arthur, I would counsel you not to be over hasty, but that ye would put it in respite this judgement of my lady the Queen, for many causes. One is this: though it were so that Sir Lancelot were found in the Queen's chamber, yet it might be so that he came thither for no evil. For ye know, my lord,' said Sir Gawain, 'that my lady the Queen hath oftentimes been greatly beholden unto Sir Lancelot, more than to any other knight, for oftentimes he hath saved her life and done battle for her when all the court refused the Queen. And peradventure she sent for him for goodness and for no evil, to reward him for his good deeds that he had done to her in times past. And peradventure my lady the Queen sent for him to that intent, that Sir Lancelot should have come privily to her, weening that it had been best in eschewing of slander; for oftentimes we do many things that we ween be for the best, and yet peradventure it turneth to the worst. For I dare say,' said Sir Gawain, 'my lady your

---

I may not with my worship] I cannot honourably do otherwise   mainour]
incriminating circumstances   causer of their hasty judgement] sufficient
reason for an immediate sentence

Queen is to you both good and true. And as for Sir Lancelot, I dare say he will make it good upon any knight living that will put upon him villainy or shame, and in like wise he will make good for my lady the Queen.'

'That I believe well,' said King Arthur. 'But I will not that way work with Sir Lancelot, for he trusteth so much upon his hands and his might that he doubteth no man. And therefore for my queen he shall never more fight, for she shall have the law. And if I may get Sir Lancelot, wit you well he shall have as shameful a death.'

'Jesu defend me,' said Sir Gawain, 'that I never see it nor know it.'

'Why say you so?' said King Arthur. 'For pardieu, you have no cause to love him, for this last night past he slew your brother Sir Agravain, a full good knight. And almost he had slain your other brother, Sir Mordred; and also there he slew thirteen noble knights. And also remember you, Sir Gawain, he slew two sons of yours, Sir Florence and Sir Lovell.'

'My lord,' said Sir Gawain, 'of all this I have a knowledge, which of their deaths sore repents me. But in so much as I gave them warning and told my brother and my sons beforehand what would fall in the end, and in so much as they would not do by my counsel, I will not meddle me thereof, nor revenge me nothing of their deaths, for I told them there was no boot to strive with Sir Lancelot. How be it, I am sorry of the death of my brother and of my two sons; but they are the causers of their own death, for oftentimes I warned my brother Sir Agravain, and I told him of the perils.'

Then said King Arthur unto Sir Gawain, 'Make you ready, I pray you, in your best armour, with your brethren Sir Gaheris and Sir Gareth, to bring my queen to the fire and there to have her judgement.' [8]

'Nay, my most noble king,' said Sir Gawain, 'that will I never do! For wit you well I will never be in that place where so noble a queen as is my lady Dame Guenivere shall take such a shameful end. For wit you well,' said Sir Gawain, 'my heart will not serve me for to see her die; and it shall never be said that ever I was of your counsel for her death.'

Then said the King unto Sir Gawain, 'Suffer your brethren Sir Gaheris and Sir Gareth to be there.'

'My lord,' said Sir Gawain, 'wit you well they will be loath to be there present because of many adventures that is like to fall; but they are young, and full unable to say you nay.'

doubteth] fears

Then spoke Sir Gaheris and the good knight Sir Gareth unto King Arthur, 'Sir, ye may well command us to be there, but wit you well it shall be sore against our will. But and we be there by your strait commandment, ye shall plainly hold us there excused: we will be there in peaceable wise, and bear no harness of war upon us.'

'In the name of God,' said the King, 'then make you ready, for she shall have soon her judgement.'

'Alas,' said Sir Gawain, 'that ever I should endure to see this woeful day!'

So Sir Gawain turned him and wept heartily, and so he went into his chamber. And so the Queen was led forth without Carlisle, and anon she was despoiled into her smock. And then her ghostly father was brought her, to be shriven of her misdeeds. Then was there weeping and wailing and wringing of hands of many lords and ladies; but there were but few in comparison that would bear any armour for to strengthen the death of the Queen.

Then was there one that Sir Lancelot had sent unto, which went to espy what time the Queen should go unto her death. And anon as he saw the Queen despoiled into her smock and shriven, then he gave Sir Lancelot warning anon. Then was there but spurring and plucking up of horses, and right so they came unto the fire. And who that stood against them, there were they slain, full many a noble knight: for there was slain Sir Belliance le Orgulous, Sir Segwarides, Sir Griflet, Sir Brandiles, Sir Agloval, Sir Tor; Sir Gauter, Sir Gillimer, Sir Reynold, three brethren; and Sir Damas, Sir Priamus, Sir Kay l'Estrange, Sir Driant, Sir Lambegus, Sir Herminde; Sir Pertolepe and Sir Perimones, two brethren which were called the Green Knight and the Red Knight. And so in this rushing and hurling, as Sir Lancelot thrang here and there, it misfortuned him to slay Sir Gaheris and Sir Gareth, the noble knight, for they were unarmed and unwares. As the French book saith, Sir Lancelot smote Sir Gaheris and Sir Gareth upon the brain-pans, where through that they were slain in the field; how be it, in very truth, Sir Lancelot saw them not. And so they were found dead among the thickest of the press.

Then Sir Lancelot, when he had thus done, and slain and put to flight all that would withstand him, then he rode straight unto Queen Guenivere and made cast a kirtle and a gown upon her, and then he

ghostly father] spiritual father, i.e. confessor   strengthen] enforce

made her to be set behind him, and prayed her to be of good cheer. Now wit you well, the Queen was glad that she was at that time escaped from the death, and then she thanked God and Sir Lancelot. And so he rode his way with the Queen, as the French book saith, unto Joyous Gard, and there he kept her as a noble knight should. And many great lords and many good knights were sent him, and many full noble knights drew unto him. When they heard that King Arthur and Sir Lancelot were at debate, many knights were glad, and many were sorry of their debate.

Now turn we again unto King Arthur, that when it was told him how [9] and in what manner the Queen was taken away from the fire, and when he heard of the death of his noble knights, and in especial Sir Gaheris and Sir Gareth—then he swooned for very pure sorrow. And when he awoke of his swoon, then he said,

'Alas, that ever I bore crown upon my head, for now have I lost the fairest fellowship of noble knights that ever Christian king held together. Alas, my good knights be slain and gone away from me, that now within these two days I have lost nigh forty knights, and also the noble fellowship of Sir Lancelot and his blood; for now may I never more hold them together with my worship. Now alas, that ever this war began! Now, fair fellows,' said the King, 'I charge you that no man tell Sir Gawain of the death of his two brethren, for I am sure,' said the King, 'when he heareth tell that Sir Gareth is dead, he will go nigh out of his mind. Mercy Jesu,' said the King, 'why slew he Sir Gaheris and Sir Gareth? for I dare say as for Sir Gareth, he loved Sir Lancelot of all men earthly.'

'That is truth,' said some knights, 'but they were slain in the hurling, as Sir Lancelot thrang in the thickest of the press; and as they were unarmed, he smote them and wist not whom that he smote,* and unhappily they were slain.'

'Well, said Arthur, 'the death of them will cause the greatest mortal war that ever was; for I am sure that when Sir Gawain knoweth hereof, that Sir Gareth is slain, I shall never have rest of him till I have destroyed Sir Lancelot's kin and himself both, or else he to destroy me. And therefore,' said the King, 'wit you well, my heart was never so heavy as it is now. And much more am I sorrier for my good knights' loss than for the loss of my fair queen; for queens I might have enough, but such a fellowship of good knights shall never be together in no company. And now I dare say,' said King Arthur, 'there was never Christian king that ever held such a fellowship together. And alas, that ever Sir Lancelot and I should be at debate! Ah, Agravain, Agravain,' said the King, 'Jesu forgive it thy soul, for thy evil will that thou hadst, and Sir Mordred thy brother, unto Sir Lancelot, hath caused all this sorrow.' And ever among these complaints the King wept and swooned.

Then came there one to Sir Gawain and told how the Queen was led away with Sir Lancelot, and nigh four-and-twenty knights slain.

'Ah, Jesu save me my two brethren,' said Sir Gawain. 'For full well wist I', said Sir Gawain, 'that Sir Lancelot would rescue her, or else he would die in that field; and to say the truth, he were not of worship but if he had rescued the Queen, insomuch as she should have been burned for his sake. And as in that,' said Sir Gawain, 'he hath done but knightly, and as I would have done myself and I had stood in like case. But where are my brethren?' said Sir Gawain. 'I marvel that I see not of them.'

Than said that man, 'Truly, Sir Gaheris and Sir Gareth be slain.'

'Jesu defend!' said Sir Gawain. 'For all this world I would not that they were slain, and in especial my good brother Sir Gareth.'

'Sir,' said the man, 'he is slain, and that is great pity.'

'Who slew him?' said Sir Gawain.

'Sir Lancelot,' said the man, 'slew them both.'

'That may I not believe,' said Sir Gawain, 'that ever he slew my good brother Sir Gareth, for I dare say my brother loved him better than me and all his brethren and the King both. Also I dare say, and Sir Lancelot had desired my brother Sir Gareth with him, he would have been with him against the King and us all. And therefore I may never believe that Sir Lancelot slew my brethren.'

'Verily, sir,' said the man, 'it is noised that he slew him.'

[10]   'Alas,' said Sir Gawain, 'now is my joy gone!' And then he fell down and swooned, and long he lay there as he had been dead. And when he arose out of his swoon he cried out sorrowfully and said, 'Alas!' And forthwith he ran unto the King, crying and weeping, and said, 'Ah, my uncle, King Arthur, my good brother Sir Gareth is slain, and so is my brother Sir Gaheris, which were two noble knights.'

Then the King wept and he both, and so they fell on swooning. And when they were revived, then spoke Sir Gawain and said, 'Sir, I will go and see my brother Sir Gareth.'

'Sir, ye may not see him,' said the King, 'for I caused him to be interred and Sir Gaheris both, for I well understood that ye would make overmuch sorrow, and the sight of Sir Gareth should have caused your double sorrow.'

'Alas, my lord,' said Sir Gawain, 'how slew he my brother Sir Gareth? I pray you tell me.'

'Truly,' said the King, 'I shall tell you as it hath been told me. Sir Lancelot slew him and Sir Gaheris both.'

'Alas,' said Sir Gawain, 'they bore no arms against him, neither of them both.'

'I wot not how it was,' said the King, 'but as it is said, Sir Lancelot slew them in the thick press and knew them not. And therefore let us shape a remedy for to revenge their deaths.'

'My king, my lord, and mine uncle,' said Sir Gawain, 'wit you well, now I shall make you a promise which I shall hold by my knighthood, that from this day forward I shall never fail Sir Lancelot until that one of us have slain the other; and therefore I require you, my lord and king, dress you unto the wars, for wit you well, I will be revenged upon Sir Lancelot. And therefore, as ye will have my service and my love, now haste ye thereto and assay your friends.* For I promise unto God,' said Sir Gawain, 'for the death of my brother Sir Gareth, I shall seek Sir Lancelot throughout seven kings' realms, but I shall slay him, or else he shall slay me.'

'Sir, ye shall not need to seek him so far,' said the King, 'for as I hear say, Sir Lancelot will abide me and us all within the castle of Joyous Gard; and much people draweth unto him, as I hear say.'

'That may I right well believe,' said Sir Gawain. 'But my lord,' he said, 'assay your friends, and I will assay mine.'

'It shall be done,' said the King, 'and as I suppose, I shall be big enough to drive him out of the biggest tower of his castle.'

So then the King sent letters and writs throughout all England, both the length and the breadth, for to summon all his knights. And so unto King Arthur drew many knights, dukes, and earls, that he had a great host; and when they were assembled the King informed them how Sir Lancelot had bereft him his queen. Then the King and all his host made them ready to lay siege about Sir Lancelot where he lay within Joyous Gard. And anon Sir Lancelot heard thereof and purveyed him of many good knights; for with him held many knights, some for his own sake and some for the Queen's sake. Thus they were on both parties well furnished and garnished of all manner of things that longed unto the war.

But King Arthur's host was so great that Sir Lancelot's host would not abide him in the field; for he was full loath to do battle against the King. But Sir Lancelot drew him unto his strong castle with all manner of victual plenty, and as many noble men as he might suffice within the town and the castle. Then came King Arthur with Sir Gawain with a great host, and laid siege all about Joyous Gard, both the town and the castle, and there they made strong war on both parties. But in no wise Sir Lancelot would ride out of the castle of long time, and neither he would not suffer none of his good knights to issue out, neither of the town nor of the castle, until fifteen weeks were past.

[11]   So it fell upon a day that Sir Lancelot looked over the walls and spoke on high unto King Arthur and to Sir Gawain, 'My lords both, wit you well all this is in vain that ye make at this siege, for here win ye no worship, but magré and dishonour; for and it list me to come myself out and my good knights, I should full soon make an end of this war.'

'Come forth,' said King Arthur unto Sir Lancelot, 'and thou darest! And I promise I shall meet thee in the midst of this field.'

'God defend me,' said Sir Lancelot, 'that ever I should encounter with the most noble king that made me knight.'

'Now fie upon thy fair language!' said the King, 'for wit thou well and trust it, I am thy mortal foe, and ever will to my death day; for thou hast slain my good knights and full noble men of my blood, that shall I never recover again. Also thou hast lain by my queen and held her many winters, and sithen, like a traitor, taken her away from me by force.'

'My most noble lord and king,' said Sir Lancelot, 'ye may say what ye will, for ye wot well, with yourself I will not strive. But thereas ye say that I have slain your good knights, I wot well that I have done so; and that me sore repenteth. But I was forced to do battle with them in saving of my life, or else I must have suffered them to have slain me. And as for my lady Queen Guenivere: except your person of your highness and my lord Sir Gawain, there is no knight under heaven that dare make it good upon me that ever I was traitor unto your person. And where it please you to say that I have held my lady your queen years and winters, unto that I shall ever make a large answer, and prove it upon

magré] ill will

any knight that beareth the life, except your person and Sir Gawain, that my lady Queen Guenivere is as true a lady unto your person as is any lady living unto her lord; and that will I make good with my hands. How be it, it hath liked her good grace to have me in favour and cherish me more than any other knight; and unto my power again I have deserved her love, for oftentimes, my lord, ye have consented that she should have been burned and destroyed in your heat, and then it fortuned me to do battle for her, and or I departed from her adversary they confessed their untruth, and she full worshipfully excused. And at such times, my lord Arthur,' said Sir Lancelot, 'ye loved me and thanked me when I saved your queen from the fire; and then ye promised me for ever to be my good lord, and now me thinketh ye reward me evil for my good service. And my lord, me seemeth I had lost a great part of my worship in my knighthood and I had suffered my lady your queen to have been burned, insomuch as she should have been burned for my sake. For sithen I have done battles for your queen in other quarrels, then in my own quarrel me seemeth now I had more right to do battle for her in her right quarrel. And therefore, my good and gracious lord,' said Sir Lancelot, 'take your queen unto your good grace, for she is both true and good.'

'Fie on thee, false recrayed knight!' said Sir Gawain, 'for I let thee wit, my lord, my uncle King Arthur, shall have his queen and thee both, maugre thy visage, and slay you both and save you whether it please him.'

'It may well be,' said Sir Lancelot. 'But wit thou well, my lord Sir Gawain, and me list to come out of this castle, ye should win me and the queen more harder than ever ye won a strong battle.'

'Now fie on thy proud words!' said Sir Gawain. 'As for my lady the Queen, wit thou well I will never say her shame. But thou false and recrayed knight,' said Sir Gawain, 'what cause hadst thou to slay my good brother Sir Gareth, that loved thee more than me and all my kin? And alas, thou madest him knight with thine own hands! Why slewest thou him that loved thee so well?'

'For to excuse me,' said Sir Lancelot, 'it booteth me not; but by Jesu and by the faith that I owe unto the high order of knighthood, I would with as good a will have slain my nephew Sir Bors de Ganis. And alas, that ever I was so unhappy,' said Sir Lancelot, 'that I had not seen Sir Gareth and Sir Gaheris.'

---

recrayed] recreant   booteth] avails

'Thou liest, recrayed knight,' said Sir Gawain, 'thou slewest him in the despite of me, and therefore wit thou well, Sir Lancelot, I shall make war upon thee, and all the while that I may live be thine enemy.'

'That me repents,' said Sir Lancelot, 'for well I understand it booteth me not to seek no accord while ye, Sir Gawain, are so mischievously set. And if ye were not, I would not doubt to have the good grace of my lord King Arthur.'

'I believe well, false recrayed knight, for thou hast many long days overled me and us all, and destroyed many of our good knights.'

'Sir, ye say as it pleaseth you,' said Sir Lancelot, 'yet may it never be said on me and openly proved that ever I by forecast of treason slew no good knight, as ye, my lord Sir Gawain, have done; and so did I never but in my defence, that I was driven thereto in saving of my life.'

'Ah, thou false knight,' said Sir Gawain, 'that thou meanest by Sir Lamorak. But wit thou well I slew him!'

'Sir, ye slew him not yourself,'* said Sir Lancelot, 'for it had been overmuch for you, for he was one of the best knights christened of his age; and it was great pity of his death.'

[12] 'Well, well, Sir Lancelot,' said Sir Gawain, 'sithen thou upbraidest me of Sir Lamorak, wit thou well I shall never leave thee till I have thee at such avail that thou shalt not escape my hands.'

'I trust you well enough,' said Sir Lancelot, 'and ye may get me, I get but little mercy.'

But the French book saith, King Arthur would have taken his queen again and to have been accorded with Sir Lancelot; but Sir Gawain would not suffer him by no manner of mean. And so Sir Gawain made many men to blow upon Sir Lancelot, and so all at once they called him false recrayed knight. But when Sir Bors de Ganis, Sir Ector de Maris, and Sir Lionel heard this outcry, they called unto them Sir Palomides and Sir Lavain and Sir Urry, with many more knights of their blood, and all they went unto Sir Lancelot and said thus:

'My lord, wit you well we have great scorn of the great rebukes that we have heard Sir Gawain say unto you; wherefore we pray you and charge you, as ye will have our service, keep us no longer within these walls; for we let you wit plainly, we will ride into the field and do battle

overled] oppressed   forecast of] conspiracy to commit   I trust . . . and ye may get me] I am quite sure that if you can lay hands on me   blow upon] insult

with them. For ye fare as a man that were afraid; and for all your fair speech it will not avail you, for wit you well, Sir Gawain will never suffer you to accord with King Arthur. And therefore fight for your life and right, and ye dare.'

'Alas,' said Sir Lancelot, 'for to ride out of this castle and to do battle I am full loath.'

Then Sir Lancelot spoke on high unto King Arthur and Sir Gawain, 'My lord, I require you and beseech you, sithen that I am thus required and conjured to ride into the field, that neither you, my lord King Arthur, nor you, Sir Gawain, come not into the field.'

'What shall we do, then?' said Sir Gawain. 'Is not this the King's quarrel to fight with thee? And also it is my quarrel to fight with thee, because of the death of my brother Sir Gareth.'

'Then must I needs unto battle,' said Sir Lancelot. 'Now wit you well, my lord Arthur and Sir Gawain, ye will repent it whensoever I do battle with you.'

And so then they departed either from other; and then either party made them ready on the morn for to do battle, and great purveyance was made on both sides. And Sir Gawain let purvey many knights for to wait upon Sir Lancelot, for to overset him and to slay him; and on the morn at undern King Arthur was ready in the field with three great hosts. And then Sir Lancelot's fellowship came out at the three gates in full good array. And Sir Lionel came in the foremost battle, and Sir Lancelot came in the middle, and Sir Bors came out at the third gate; and thus they came in order and rule as full noble knights. And ever Sir Lancelot charged all his knights in any wise to save King Arthur and Sir Gawain.

Then came forth Sir Gawain from the King's host, and proffered to [13] joust. And Sir Lionel was a fierce knight, and lightly he encountered with him, and there Sir Gawain smote Sir Lionel throughout the body, that he dashed to the earth like as he had been dead. And then Sir Ector de Maris and other more bore him into the castle. And anon there began a great stour, and much people were slain. And ever Sir Lancelot did what he might to save the people on King Arthur's party; for Sir Bors and Sir Palomides and Sir Safer overthrew many knights, for they were deadly knights, and Sir Blamor de Ganis and Sir Bleoberis with Sir Bellenger le Beau—these six knights did much harm. And

battle] battalion   stour] battle

ever was King Arthur about Sir Lancelot to have slain him, and ever Sir Lancelot suffered him and would not strike again. So Sir Bors encountered with King Arthur; and Sir Bors smote him, and so he alit and drew his sword and said to Sir Lancelot, 'Sir, shall I make an end of this war?'—for he meant to have slain him.

'Not so hardy,' said Sir Lancelot, 'upon pain of thy head, that thou touch him no more! For I will never see that most noble king that made me knight neither slain nor shamed.' And therewith Sir Lancelot alit off his horse and took up the King and horsed him again, and said thus: 'My lord the king, for God's love, stint this strife, for ye get here no worship and I would do my utterance. But always I forbear you, and ye nor none of yours forbear not me. And therefore, my lord, I pray you remember what I have done in many places, and now am I evil rewarded.'

So when King Arthur was on horseback he looked on Sir Lancelot; then the tears burst out of his eyes, thinking of the great courtesy that was in Sir Lancelot more than in any other man. And therewith the King rode his way and might no longer behold him, saying to himself, 'Alas, alas, that yet this war began!'

And then either party of the battles withdrew them to repose them, and buried the dead and searched the wounded men, and laid to their wounds soft salves; and thus they endured that night till on the morn. And on the morn by undern they made them ready to do battle; and then Sir Bors led the vanguard. So upon the morn there came Sir Gawain as breme as any boar, with a great spear in his hand.

And when Sir Bors saw him, he thought to revenge his brother Sir Lionel of the despite Sir Gawain gave him the other day. And so, as they that knew either other, fewtered their spears, and with all their might of their horses and themselves, so fiercely they met together and so feloniously that either bore other through, and so they fell both to the bare earth. And then the battle joined, and there was much slaughter on both parties.

Then Sir Lancelot rescued Sir Bors and sent him into the castle; but neither Sir Gawain nor Sir Bors died not of their wounds, for they were well helped. Then Sir Lavain and Sir Urry prayed Sir Lancelot

---

for ye get here ... do my utterance] you would get no honour here if I did my deadly best   breme] fierce

to do his pain, 'And fight as they do, for we see that ye forbear and spare, and that doth us much harm; and therefore we pray you, spare not your enemies no more than they do you.'

'Alas,' said Sir Lancelot, 'I have no heart to fight against my lord Arthur, for ever me seemeth I do not as I ought to do.'

'My lord,' said Sir Palomides, 'though ye spare them never so much, all this day they will never can you thank; and if they may get you at avail, you are but a dead man.'

So when Sir Lancelot understood that they said him truth, then he strained himself more than he did beforehand; and because his nephew Sir Bors was sore wounded, he pained himself the more. And so within a little while, by evensong time, Sir Lancelot's party the better stood, for their horses went in blood past the fetlocks, there were so many people slain. And then for very pity Sir Lancelot withheld his knights, and suffered King Arthur's party to withdraw them aside. And so he withdrew his meinie into the castle; and either party buried the dead and put salve unto the wounded men. So when Sir Gawain was hurt, they on King Arthur's party were not so orgulous as they were beforehand to do battle.

So of this war that was between King Arthur and Sir Lancelot it was noised through all Christian realms; and so it came at last by relation unto the Pope. And then the Pope took consideration of the great goodness of King Arthur and of the high prowess of Sir Lancelot, that was called the most noblest knight of the world. Wherefore the Pope called unto him a noble clerk that at that time was there present—the French book saith it was the Bishop of Rochester; and the Pope gave him bulls under lead and sent them unto the King, charging him upon pain of interdicting of all England* that he take his queen again and accord with Sir Lancelot.

So when this bishop was come unto Carlisle he showed the [14] King his bulls; and when the King understood them, he wist not what to do, but full fain he would have been accorded with Sir Lancelot. But Sir Gawain would in no wise suffer the King to accord with Sir Lancelot; but as for the Queen, he consented. So the bishop had of the King his great seal and his assurance, as he was a true

can you thank] express thanks   get you at avail] get advantage of you
meinie] company of followers   orgulous] over-confident

and anointed king, that Sir Lancelot should go safe and come safe, and that the Queen should not be said unto of the King nor of none other for nothing done of time past; and of all these appointments the bishop brought with him sure writing to show unto Sir Lancelot. So when the bishop was come to Joyous Gard, there he showed Sir Lancelot how he came from the Pope with writing unto King Arthur and unto him. And there he told him the perils if he withheld the Queen from the King.

'Sir, it was never in my thought', said Sir Lancelot, 'to withhold the Queen from my lord Arthur. But I keep her for this cause: insomuch as she should have been burned for my sake, me seemed it was my part to save her life and put her from that danger till better recovery might come. And now I thank God,' said Sir Lancelot, 'that the Pope hath made her peace. For God knoweth,' said Sir Lancelot, 'I will be a thousandfold more gladder to bring her again than ever I was of her taking away, with this: I may be sure to come safe and go safe, and that the Queen shall have her liberty, and never for nothing that hath been surmised before this time that she never from this stand in no peril. For else,' said Sir Lancelot, 'I dare adventure me to keep her from a harder shower than ever yet I had.'

'Sir, it shall not need you,' said the bishop, 'to dread thus much. For wit you well, the Pope must be obeyed; and it were not the Pope's worship, nor my poor honesty, to know you distressed nor the Queen, neither in peril nor shamed.' And then he showed Sir Lancelot all his writing both from the Pope and King Arthur.

'This is sure enough,' said Sir Lancelot, 'for full well I dare trust my lord's own writing and his seal, for he was never shamed of his promise. Therefore,' said Sir Lancelot unto the bishop, 'ye shall ride unto the King before, and recommend me unto his good grace; and let him have knowledging that this same day eight days, by the grace of God, I myself shall bring the Queen unto him. And then say ye to my most redoubted king that I will say largely for the Queen, that I shall none except for dread nor for fear but the King himself and and my lord Sir Gawain; and that is for the King's love more than for himself.'

So the bishop departed and came to the King to Carlisle, and told him all how Sir Lancelot answered him; so that made the tears fall out

said unto] upbraided   with this] on this condition   never for nothing . . .
stand in no peril] that she shall not in the future be in danger on account of any conjectures made in the past   shower] storm   say largely for] offer an open challenge on behalf of

at the King's eyes. Then Sir Lancelot purveyed him a hundred knights, and all well clothed in green velvet, and their horses trapped in the same to the heels; and every knight held a branch of olive in his hand in tokening of peace. And the Queen had four-and-twenty gentle-women following her in the same wise; and Sir Lancelot had twelve coursers following him, and on every courser sat a young gentleman, and all they were arrayed in white velvet with sarpes of gold about their quarters, and the horses trapped in the same wise down to the heels, with many owches set with stones and pearls in gold to the number of a thousand. And in the same wise was the Queen arrayed and Sir Lancelot in the same, of white cloth of gold tissue. And right so as ye have heard, as the French book maketh mention, he rode with the Queen from Joyous Gard to Carlisle; and so Sir Lancelot rode throughout Carlisle and so into the castle, that all men might behold them. And there was many a weeping eye. And then Sir Lancelot him-self alit and voided his horse, and took down the Queen, and so led her where King Arthur was in his seat. And Sir Gawain sat before him, and many other great lords. So when Sir Lancelot saw the King and Sir Gawain, then he led the Queen by the arm, and then he kneeled down and the Queen both.

Wit you well, then was there many a bold knight with King Arthur that wept as tenderly as they had seen all their kin dead before them. So the King sat still and said no word.

And when Sir Lancelot saw his countenance, he arose up and pulled up the Queen with him, and thus he said full knightly:*

'My most redoubted King, ye shall understand, by the Pope's com-mandment and yours I have brought to you my lady the Queen, as right requireth. And if there be any knight, of what degree that ever he be of, except your person, that will say or dare say but that she is true and clean to you, I here myself, Sir Lancelot du Lake, will make it good upon his body that she is a true lady unto you. [15]

'But sir, liars ye have listened, and that hath caused great debate betwixt you and me. For time hath been, my lord Arthur, that ye were greatly pleased with me when I did battle for my lady your queen; and full well ye know, my most noble king, that she hath been put to great

sarpes of gold about their quarters] chains of gold round their hips   owches]
ornamental clasps   clean] pure

wrong or this time. And sithen it pleased you at many times that I should fight for her; and therefore me seemeth, my good lord, I had more cause to rescue her from the fire when she should have been burned for my sake. For they that told you those tales were liars, and so it fell upon them; for by likelihood, had not the might of God been with me, I might never have endured with fourteen knights and they armed and before purposed, and I unarmed and not purposed, for I was sent for unto my lady, your queen, I wot not for what cause. But I was not so soon within the chamber door, but anon Sir Agravain and Sir Mordred called me traitor and false recrayed knight.'

'By my faith, they called thee right!' said Sir Gawain.

'My lord Sir Gawain,' said Sir Lancelot, 'in their quarrel they proved not themselves the best, neither in the right.'

'Well, well, Sir Lancelot,' said the King, 'I have given you no cause to do to me as ye have done, for I have worshipped you and yours more than any other knights.'

'My lord,' said Sir Lancelot, 'so ye be not displeased, ye shall under-stand that I and mine have done you oftentimes better service than any other knights have done, in many divers places; and where ye have been full hard bestead, divers times I have rescued you from many dangers; and ever unto my power I was glad to please you and my lord Sir Gawain. In jousts and in tournaments and in battles set, both on horseback and on foot, I have often rescued you, and you, my lord Sir Gawain, and many more of your knights in many divers places. For now I will make avaunt,' said Sir Lancelot, 'I will that ye all wit that as yet I never found no manner of knight but that I was over hard for him and I had done my utterance, God grant mercy!* How be it I have been matched with good knights, as Sir Tristram and Sir Lamorak, but ever I had favour unto them and a deeming what they were; and I take God to record, I never was wroth nor greatly heavy with no good knight and I saw him busy and about to win worship, and glad I was ever when I found a good knight that might anything endure me on horseback and on foot.

'How be it, Sir Carados of the Dolorous Tower was a full noble knight and a passing strong man. And that wot ye, my lord Sir Gawain; for he might well be called a noble knight when he by fine force pulled you out of your saddle and bound you overthwart before him to his

---

recrayed | recreant   make avaunt] boast

saddle-bow, and there, my lord Sir Gawain, I rescued you and slew him before your sight. Also I found your brother Sir Gaheris, and Sir Tarquin leading him bound before him; and there also I rescued your brother and slew Sir Tarquin, and delivered three score and four of my lord Arthur's knights out of his prison. And now I dare say,' said Sir Lancelot, 'I met never with so strong a knight, nor so well-fighting, as was Sir Carados and Sir Tarquin, for they and I fought to the uttermost. And therefore,' said Sir Lancelot unto Sir Gawain, 'me seemeth ye ought of right to remember this; for and I might have your good will, I would trust to God for to have my lord Arthur's good grace.'

'Sir, the King may do as he will,' said Sir Gawain. 'But wit thou well, [16] Sir Lancelot, thou and I shall never be accorded while we live; for thou hast slain three of my brethren, and two of them thou slew traitorously and piteously, for they bore no harness against thee, nor none would do.'

'Sir, God would they had been armed!' said Sir Lancelot, 'for then had they been alive. And for Gareth, I loved no kinsman I had more than I loved him; and ever while I live,' said Sir Lancelot, 'I will bewail Sir Gareth's death, not all only for the great fear I have of you, but for many causes which cause me to be sorrowful. One is that I made him knight. Another is, I wot well he loved me above all other knights. And the third is, he was passing noble and true, courteous and gentle and well-conditioned. The fourth is, I wist well, anon as I heard that Sir Gareth was dead, I knew well that I should never after have your love, my lord Sir Gawain, but everlasting war betwixt us. And also I wist well that ye would cause my noble lord King Arthur for ever to be my mortal foe. And as Jesu be my help, and by my knighthood, I slew never Sir Gareth nor his brother by my willing; but alas that ever they were unarmed that unhappy day!

'But this much I shall offer me to you,' said Sir Lancelot, 'if it may please the King's good grace and you, my lord Sir Gawain. I shall first begin at Sandwich, and there I shall go in my shirt barefoot; and at every ten miles' end I shall found and gar make a house of religious, of what order that ye will assign me, with a whole convent to sing and read day and night in especial for Sir Gareth's sake and Sir Gaheris', and this shall I perform from Sandwich unto Carlisle. And every house shall have sufficient livelihood; and this shall I perform while that

gar make] have established

I have any livelihood in Christendom. And there is none of all these religious places but they shall be performed, furnished, and garnished with all things as a holy place ought to be. And this were fairer and more holier and more perfect to their souls than ye, my most noble king, and you, Sir Gawain, to war upon me, for thereby shall ye get no avail.'

Then all the knights and ladies that were there wept as they were mad, and the tears fell on King Arthur's cheeks.

'Sir Lancelot,' said Sir Gawain, 'I have right well heard thy language and thy great proffers. But wit thou well, let the King do as it pleaseth him, I will never forgive thee my brothers' death, and in especial the death of my brother Sir Gareth. And if my uncle King Arthur will accord with thee, he shall lose my service; for wit thou well,' said Sir Gawain, 'thou art both false to the King and to me.'

'Sir,' said Sir Lancelot, 'he beareth not the life that may make it good! And ye, Sir Gawain, will charge me with so high a thing, ye must pardon me, for then needs must I answer you.'

'Nay, nay,' said Sir Gawain. 'We are past that as at this time; and that causeth the Pope, for he hath charged my uncle the King that he shall take again his queen, and to accord with thee, Sir Lancelot, as for this season, and therefore thou shalt go safe as thou came. But in this land thou shalt not abide past fifteen days, such summons I give thee; for so the King and we were condescended and accorded or thou came. And else,' said Sir Gawain, 'wit thou well, thou should not have come here but if it were maugre thy head. And if it were not for the Pope's commandment,' said Sir Gawain, 'I should do battle with thee, with my own hands, body for body, and prove it upon thee that thou hast been both false unto my uncle King Arthur and to me both; and that shall I prove on thy body when thou art departed from hence, wheresoever that I find thee.'

[17]   Then Sir Lancelot sighed, and therewith the tears fell on his cheeks; and then he said thus: 'Most noblest Christian realm, whom I have loved above all other realms, and in thee have I got a great part of my worship! And now that I shall depart in this wise, truly me repents that ever I came in this realm, that I should be thus shamefully banished, undeserved and causeless. But fortune is so variant and the wheel so

---

he beareth not . . . make it good] no man alive is able to prove that [in combat] condescended] agreed

mutable that there is no constant abiding; and that may be proved by many old chronicles, as of noble Hector of Troy and Alexander the mighty conqueror, and many more other. When they were most in their royalty, they alighted passing low.* And so fareth it by me,' said Sir Lancelot, 'for in this realm I had worship, and by me and mine all the whole Round Table hath been increased more in worship than ever it was by any of you all. And therefore wit thou well, Sir Gawain, I may live upon my lands as well as any knight that here is. And if ye, my most redoubted King, will come upon my lands with Sir Gawain to war upon me, I must endure you as well as I may. But as to you, Sir Gawain, if that ye come there, I pray you charge me not with treason nor felony, for and ye do, I must answer you.'

'Do thou thy best,' said Sir Gawain, 'and therefore hie thee fast that thou were gone. And wit thou well, we shall soon come after, and break thy strongest castle that thou hast upon thy head.'

'It shall not need that,' said Sir Lancelot, 'for and I were as orgulous set as ye are, wit you well I should meet you in midst of the field.'

'Make thou no more language,' said Sir Gawain, 'but deliver the Queen from thee, and pick thee lightly out of this court.'

'Well,' said Sir Lancelot, 'and I had wist of this short coming, I would have advised me twice or that I had come here. For and the Queen had been so dear unto me as ye noise her, I durst have kept her from the fellowship of the best knights under heaven.'

And then Sir Lancelot said unto Queen Guenivere in hearing of the King and them all, 'Madam, now I must depart from you and this noble fellowship for ever; and sithen it is so, I beseech you to pray for me, and I shall pray for you. And tell ye me and if ye be hard bestead by any false tongues; but lightly my good lady, send me word, and if any knight's hands under the heaven may deliver you by battle, I shall deliver you.'

And therewith Sir Lancelot kissed the Queen, and then he said all openly, 'Now let see whatsoever he be in this place that dare say the Queen is not true unto my lord Arthur: let see who will speak, and he dare speak.' And therewith he brought the Queen to the King.

And then Sir Lancelot took his leave and departed; and there was neither king, duke, earl, baron, nor knight, lady, nor gentlewoman, but all they wept as people out of their mind, except Sir Gawain. And

orgulous set] arrogantly minded   pick thee lightly] get yourself speedily

when this noble knight Sir Lancelot took his horse to ride out of Carlisle, there was sobbing and weeping for pure dole of his departing. And so he took his way to Joyous Gard; and then ever after he called it the Dolorous Tower. And thus departed Sir Lancelot from the court for ever.

And so when he came to Joyous Gard, he called his fellowship unto him and asked them what they would do. Then they answered all wholly together with one voice, they would do as he would do.

'Then, my fair fellows,' said Sir Lancelot, 'I must depart out of this most noble realm; and now I shall depart it grieveth me sore, for I shall depart with no worship, for a flemed man departeth never out of a realm with no worship. And that is to me great heaviness, for ever I fear after my days that men shall chronicle upon me that I was flemed out of this land. And else, my fair lords, be ye sure, and I had not dreaded shame, my lady Queen Guenivere and I should never have parted.'

Then spoke noble knights—as Sir Palomides and Sir Safer his brother, and Sir Bellenger le Beau and Sir Urry with Sir Lavain, with many other—'Sir, and ye will so be disposed to abide in this land, we will never fail you; and if ye list not abide in this land, there is none of the good knights that here be that will fail you, for many causes. One is, all we that be not of your blood shall never be welcome unto the court; and sithen it liked us to take a part with you in your distress in this realm, wit you well, it shall like us as well to go in other countries with you, and there to take such part as ye do.'

'My fair lords,' said Sir Lancelot, 'I well understand you, and as I can, I thank you. And ye shall understand, such livelihood as I am born unto I shall part with you in this manner of wise: that is for to say, I shall part all my livelihood and all my lands freely among you, and myself will have as little as any of you. For have I sufficient that may long unto my person, I will ask no other riches nor array; and I trust to God to maintain you on my lands as well as ever ye were maintained.'

Then spoke all the knights at once, 'Have he shame that will leave you! For we all understand, in this realm will be never quiet, but ever debate and strife, now the fellowship of the Round Table is broken. For by the noble fellowship of the Round Table was King Arthur upborne, and by their noblesse the King and all the realm was ever in quiet and

flemed man] a man forced to flee   all we that be not of your blood] i.e. even
those of us who are not related to you

rest; and a great part', they said all, 'was because of your most noblesse, Sir Lancelot.'

'Now truly, I thank you all of your good saying, how be it I wot well [18] that in me was not all the stability of this realm, but in that I might I did my devoir. And well I am sure, I knew many rebellions in my days that by me and mine were peaced; and that I trow we all shall hear of in short space, and that me sore repenteth. For ever I dread me', said Sir Lancelot, 'that Sir Mordred will make trouble, for he is passing envious, and applieth him much to trouble.'

And so they were accorded to depart with Sir Lancelot to his lands; and to make short this tale, they trussed and paid all that would ask them. And wholly a hundred knights departed with Sir Lancelot at once, and made their vows they would never leave him for weal nor for woe. And so they shipped at Cardiff, and sailed unto Benwick (some men call it Bayonne, and some men call it Beaune, where the wine of Beaune is). But to say the sooth, Sir Lancelot, and his nephews, was lord of all France and of all the lands that longed unto France; he and his kindred rejoiced it all through Sir Lancelot's noble prowess. And then he stuffed and furnished and garnished all his noble towns and castles. Then all the people of the lands came unto Sir Lancelot on foot and hands. And so when he had established all those countries, he shortly called a parliament, and there he crowned Sir Lionel king of France. And Sir Bors he crowned him king of all King Claudas' lands; and Sir Ector de Maris, Sir Lancelot's younger brother, he crowned him king of Benwick and king of all Guienne, which was Sir Lancelot's own lands, and he made Sir Ector prince of them all. And thus he departed his lands and advanced all his noble knights.* And first he advanced them of his blood, as Sir Blamor, he made him duke of Limousin in Guienne; and Sir Bleoberis, he made him duke of Poitiers; and Sir Gahalantine, he made him duke of Auvergne; and Sir Galihodin, he made him duke of Saintonge; and Sir Galihud, he made him earl of Périgord; and Sir Menaduke, he made him earl of Rouergue; and Sir Villiars the Valiant, he made him earl of Béarn; and Sir Hebes le Renowne, he made him earl of Comminges; and Sir Lavain, he made him earl of Armagnac; and Sir Urry, he made him earl of Astarac; and Sir Neroveus, he made him earl of Pardiac; and Sir Plenorius, he made him earl of Foix; and Sir Selises of the Dolorous Tower, he made him earl of Marsan; and Sir Melias de l'Isle, he made him earl of Tursan; and Sir Bellenger le Beau, he made him earl of the Landes; and Sir Palomides, he made him duke of Provence; and Sir Safer, he made him duke of Languedoc. And Sir Clegis, he gave him the earldom of Agen; and Sir Sadok, he gave him the earldom of Sarlat; and Sir Dinas le Seneschal, he made him duke of Anjou; and Sir Clarrus, he made him duke of Normandy. Thus Sir Lancelot rewarded his noble knights, and many more that me seemeth it were too long to rehearse.

[19] So leave we Sir Lancelot in his lands, and his noble knights with him; and return we again unto King Arthur and unto Sir Gawain, that made a great host ready to the number of three score thousand, and all thing was made ready for shipping to pass over the sea to war upon Sir Lancelot and upon his lands. And so they shipped at Cardiff; and there King Arthur made Sir Mordred chief ruler of all England. And also he put the Queen under his governance, because Sir Mordred was King Arthur's son, he gave him the rule of his land and of his wife. And so the King passed the sea and landed upon Sir Lancelot's lands, and there he burned and wasted through the vengeance of Sir Gawain all that they might overrun.

So when this word was come unto Sir Lancelot, that King Arthur and Sir Gawain were landed upon his lands and made full great destruction and waste—then spoke Sir Bors and said, 'My lord Sir Lancelot, it is shame that we suffer them thus to ride over our lands. For wit you well, suffer ye them as long as ye will, they will do you no favour and they may handle you.'

Then said Sir Lionel that was ware and wise, 'My lord Sir Lancelot, I will give you this counsel: let us keep our strong walled towns until they have hunger and cold, and blow on their nails. And then let us freshly set upon them and shred them down as sheep in a fold, that ever after aliens may take example how they land upon our lands.'*

Then spoke King Bagdemagus to Sir Lancelot and said, 'Sir, your courtesy will shend us all, and your courtesy hath waked all this sorrow; for and they thus override our lands, they shall by process bring us all to nought, while we thus in holes us hide.'

Then said Sir Galihud unto Sir Lancelot, 'Sir, here be knights come

handle] get hold of   blow on their nails] i.e. to warm their hands   shend] destroy

of kings' blood, that will not long droop and dare within these walls. Therefore give us leave, like as we be knights, to meet them in the field, and we shall so deal with them that they shall curse the time that ever they came into this country.'

Then spoke seven brethren of North Wales which were seven noble knights (for a man might seek seven kings' lands or he might find such seven knights), and these seven noble knights said all at once, 'Sir Lancelot, for Christ's sake let us ride out with Sir Galihud, for we were never wont to cower in castles nor in noble towns.'

Then spoke Sir Lancelot, that was master and governor of them all, and said, 'My fair lords, wit you well I am full loath to ride out with my knights for shedding of Christian blood; and yet my lands, I understand, be full bare for to sustain any host a while, for the mighty wars that whilom King Claudas made upon this country, and upon my father King Ban and on my uncle King Bors. How be it, we will as at this time keep our strong walls. And I shall send a messenger unto King Arthur a treaty for to take; for better is peace than always war.'

So Sir Lancelot sent forth a damosel with a dwarf with her, requiring King Arthur to leave his warring upon his lands; and so she started upon a palfrey, and the dwarf ran by her side. And when she came to the pavilion of King Arthur, there she alit; and there met her a gentle knight, Sir Lucan the Butler, and said, 'Fair damosel, come ye from Sir Lancelot du Lake?'

'Yea, sir,' she said, 'therefore came I hither, to speak with my lord the King.'

'Alas,' said Sir Lucan, 'my lord Arthur would accord with Sir Lancelot, but Sir Gawain will not suffer him.' And then he said, 'I pray to God, damosel, that ye may speed well, for all we that be about the King would that Lancelot did best of any knight living.' And so with this, Sir Lucan led the damosel to the King where he sat with Sir Gawain, for to hear what she would say.

So when she had told her tale, the water ran out of the King's eyes. And all the lords were full glad for to advise the King to be accorded with Sir Lancelot, save all only Sir Gawain. And he said, 'My lord, my uncle, what will ye do? Will ye now turn again, now ye are passed this far upon your journey? All the world will speak of you villainy and shame.'

dare] lurk   for] for fear of   whilom] a while ago

'Now,' said King Arthur, 'wit you well, Sir Gawain, I will do as ye advise me. And yet me seemeth,' said King Arthur, 'his fair proffers were not good to be refused. But sithen I am come so far upon this journey, I will that ye give the damosel her answer; for I may not speak to her for pity, for her proffers be so large.'

[20]   Then Sir Gawain said unto the damosel, 'Thus say ye to Sir Lancelot, that it is waste labour now to sue to my uncle; for tell him, and he would have made any labour for peace, he should have made it or this time, for tell him, now it is too late. And say to him that I, Sir Gawain, so send him word, that I promise him by the faith that I owe to God and to knighthood, I shall never leave him till he hath slain me or I him.'

And so the damosel wept and departed; and so there was many a weeping eye. And then Sir Lucan brought the damosel to her palfrey, and so she came to Sir Lancelot where he was among all his knights.

And when Sir Lancelot had heard her answer, then the tears ran down by his cheeks. And then his noble knights came about him and said, 'Sir Lancelot, wherefore make ye such cheer? Now think what ye are and what men we are, and let us noble knights match them in midst of the field.'

'That may be lightly done,' said Sir Lancelot, 'but I was never so loath to do battle; and therefore I pray you, sirs, as you love me, be ruled at this time as I will have you. For I will always flee that noble king that made me knight; and when I may no further, I must needs defend me. And that will be more worship for me and us all than to compare with that noble king whom we have all served.'

Then they held their language, and that night they took their rest. And upon the morning early, in the dawning of the day, as the knights looked out, they saw the city of Benwick besieged round about, and began fast to set up ladders. And they within kept them out of the town and beat them mightily from the walls.

Than came forth Sir Gawain, well armed upon a stiff steed, and he came before the chief gate with his spear in his hand, crying, 'Where art thou, Sir Lancelot? Is there none of all your proud knights that dare break a spear with me?'

Then Sir Bors made him ready and came forth out of the town. And there Sir Gawain encountered with Sir Bors, and at that time he smote

compare] contend   ladders] i.e. to storm the walls   stiff] strong him down from his horse, and almost he had slain him. And so Sir Bors was rescued and borne into the town.

Then came forth Sir Lionel and thought to revenge him, and either fewtered their spears and so ran together, and there they met dispiteously. But Sir Gawain had such a grace that he smote Sir Lionel down, and wounded him there passingly sore; and then Sir Lionel was rescued and borne into the town. And thus Sir Gawain came every day, and failed not but that he smote down one knight or other. So thus they endured half a year, and much slaughter was of people on both parties.

Then it befell upon a day that Sir Gawain came before the gates armed at all pieces, on a noble horse, with a great spear in his hand. And then he cried with loud voice and said, 'Where art thou now, thou false traitor Sir Lancelot? Why holdest thou thyself within holes and walls, like a coward? Look out, thou false traitor knight, and here I shall revenge upon thy body the death of my three brethren.'

And all this language heard Sir Lancelot every deal. Then his kin and his knights drew about him, and all they said at once unto Sir Lancelot, 'Sir, now you must defend you like a knight, or else ye be shamed for ever; for now ye be called upon treason,* it is time for you to stir, for ye have slept overlong and suffered overmuch.'

'So God me help,' said Sir Lancelot, 'I am right heavy at Sir Gawain's words, for now he chargeth me with a great charge; and therefore I wot as well as ye, I must needs defend me, or else to be recreant.'

Then Sir Lancelot bade saddle his strongest horse, and bade let fetch his arms and bring all to the tower of the gate. And then Sir Lancelot spoke on high unto the King and said, 'My lord Arthur, and noble king that made me knight, wit you well, I am right heavy for your sake that ye thus sue upon me; and always I forbear you, for and I would be vengeable I might have met you in midst the field or this time, and there to have made your boldest knights full tame. And now I have forborne you and suffered you half a year, and Sir Gawain, to do what ye would do. And now I may no longer suffer to endure, but needs must I defend myself in so much as Sir Gawain hath becalled me of treason; which is greatly against my will that ever I should fight against any of your blood. But now I may not forsake it, for I am driven thereto as a beast to a bay.'

sue] follow hard   becalled] accused   a beast to a bay] a cornered animal
forced to defend itself

Then Sir Gawain said unto Sir Lancelot, 'And thou darest do battle, leave thy babbling and come off, and let us ease our hearts!'

Then Sir Lancelot armed him and mounted upon his horse, and either of them got great spears in their hands. And so the host without stood still all apart. And the noble knights of the city came a great number, that when King Arthur saw the number of men and knights he marvelled and said to himself, 'Alas that ever Sir Lancelot was against me, for now I see that he hath forborne me.'

And so the covenant was made, there should no man nigh them nor deal with them till the one were dead or yielded.

[21] Then Sir Lancelot and Sir Gawain departed a great way asunder; and then they came together with all their horses' mights as fast as they might run, and either smote other in midst of their shields. But the knights were so strong and their spears so big that their horses might not endure their buffets, and so their horses fell to the earth. And then they avoided their horses and dressed their shields before them. Then they came together and gave many sad strokes on divers places of their bodies, that the blood brast out on many sides.

Then had Sir Gawain such a grace and gift that a holy man had given him, that every day in the year from undern till high noon, his might increased those three hours as much as thrice his strength; and that caused Sir Gawain to win great honour. And for his sake, King Arthur made an ordinance that all manner of battles for any quarrels that should be done before King Arthur should begin at undern. And all was done for Sir Gawain's love, that by likelihood, if Sir Gawain were on the one party, he should have the better in battle while his strength endured three hours. But there were that time but few knights living that knew this advantage that Sir Gawain had, but King Arthur all only.

So Sir Lancelot fought with Sir Gawain. And when Sir Lancelot felt his might evermore increase, Sir Lancelot wondered and dreaded him sore to be shamed; for as the French book saith, he weened, when he felt Sir Gawain double his strength, that he had been a fiend and no earthly man. Wherefore Sir Lancelot traced and traversed, and covered himself with his shield, and kept his might and his breath during three hours. And that while Sir Gawain gave him many sad brunts, that all knights that beheld Sir Lancelot marvelled how he might

sad brunts] grievous blows

endure him; but full little understood they that travail that Sir Lancelot had to endure him. And then when it was past noon, Sir Gawain's strength was gone, and he had no more but his own might.

When Sir Lancelot felt him so come down, then he stretched him up and strode near Sir Gawain, and said thus: 'Now I feel ye have done your worst! And now, my lord Sir Gawain, I must do my part, for many great and grievous strokes I have endured you this day with great pain.' And so Sir Lancelot doubled his strokes, and gave Sir Gawain such a stroke upon the helmet that sidelong he fell down upon his one side; and Sir Lancelot withdrew from him.

'Why withdrawest thou thee?' said Sir Gawain. 'Turn again, false traitor knight, and slay me outright, for and thou leave me thus, anon as I am whole I shall do battle with thee again.'

'Sir,' said Sir Lancelot, 'I shall endure you, by God's grace! But wit thou well, Sir Gawain, I will never smite a felled knight.'

And so Sir Lancelot departed and went unto the city. And Sir Gawain was borne unto King Arthur's pavilion, and anon leeches were brought unto him of the best and searched and salved him with soft ointments. And then Sir Lancelot said, 'Now have good day, my lord the King, for wit you well, ye win no worship at these walls. For and I would my knights out bring,* there should many a doughty man die. And therefore, my lord Arthur, remember you of old kindness, and howsoever I fare, Jesu be your guide in all places.'

'Now alas,' said the King, 'that ever this unhappy war began! For ever [22] Sir Lancelot forbeareth me in all places, and in like wise my kin; and that is seen well this day, what courtesy he showed my nephew Sir Gawain.' Then King Arthur fell sick for sorrow of Sir Gawain, that he was so sore hurt, and because of the war betwixt him and Sir Lancelot.

So after that, they on King Arthur's party kept the siege with little war without; and they within kept their walls, and defended them when need was.

Thus Sir Gawain lay sick and unsound three weeks in his tents with all manner of leechcraft that might be had. And as soon as Sir Gawain might go and ride, he armed him at all points and bestrode a stiff courser and got a great spear in his hand, and so he came riding before the chief gate of Benwick. And there he cried on high and said, 'Where art thou, Sir Lancelot? Come forth, thou false traitor knight and

leechcraft] medical skill

recrayed, for I am here, Sir Gawain, that will prove this that I say upon thee!'

And all this language Sir Lancelot heard, and said thus: 'Sir Gawain, me repents of your foul saying, that ye will not cease your language. For ye wot well, Sir Gawain, I know your might, and all that ye may do. And well ye wot, Sir Gawain, ye may not greatly hurt me.'

'Come down, traitor knight,' said he, 'and make it good the contrary with thy hands! For it mishapped me the last battle to be hurt of thy hands, therefore wit thou well I am come this day to make amends, for I ween this day to lay thee as low as thou laidest me.'

'Jesu defend me,' said Sir Lancelot, 'that ever I be so far in your danger as ye have been in mine, for then my days were done. But, Sir Gawain,' said Sir Lancelot, 'ye shall not think that I shall tarry long. But sithen that ye unknightly call me thus of treason, ye shall have both your hands full of me.'

And then Sir Lancelot armed him at all points and mounted upon his horse, and got a great spear in his hand and rode out at the gate; and both their hosts were assembled, of them without and within, and stood in array full manly. And both parties were charged to hold them still to see and behold the battle of these two noble knights; and then they laid their spears in their rests and so came together as thunder. And Sir Gawain broke his spear in a hundred pieces to his hand; and Sir Lancelot smote him with a greater might, that Sir Gawain's horse's feet raised, and so the horse and he fell to the earth. Then Sir Gawain deliverly avoided his horse, and put his shield before him and eagerly drew his sword; and bade Sir Lancelot 'Alight, traitor knight!' and said, 'If a mare's son hath failed me, wit thou well a king's son and a queen's son shall not fail thee.'

Then Sir Lancelot avoided his horse and dressed his shield before him and drew his sword; and so they came eagerly together and gave many sad strokes, that all men on both parties had wonder. But when Sir Lancelot felt Sir Gawain's might so marvellously increase, he then withheld his courage and his wind, and so he kept him under cover of his might and of his shield; he traced and traversed here and there to break Sir Gawain's strokes and his courage. And ever Sir Gawain enforced himself with all his might and power to destroy Sir Lancelot, for, as the French book saith, ever as Sir Gawain's might increased, right so increased his wind and his evil will. And thus he did great pain unto Sir Lancelot three hours, that he had much ado to defend him.

And when the three hours were past, that he felt Sir Gawain was come home to his own proper strength, then Sir Lancelot said,

'Sir, now I have proved you twice that ye are a full dangerous knight and a wonderful man of might, and many wondrous deeds have ye done in your days, for by your might increasing ye have deceived many a full noble knight. And now I feel that ye have done your mighty deeds, now wit you well I must do my deeds.'

And then Sir Lancelot strode near Sir Gawain and doubled his strokes; and ever Sir Gawain defended him mightily. But nevertheless, Sir Lancelot smote such a stroke upon his helm, and upon the old wound, that Sir Gawain sank down and swooned. And anon as he awoke he waved and foined at Sir Lancelot as he lay, and said, 'Traitor knight, wit thou well I am not yet slain. Therefore come thou near me, and perform this battle to the utterance!'

'I will no more do than I have done,' said Sir Lancelot, 'for when I see you on foot I will do battle upon you all the while I see you stand upon your feet; but to smite a wounded man that may not stand, God defend me from such a shame.'

And then he turned his way toward the city, and Sir Gawain ever-more calling him traitor knight, and said, 'Traitor knight, wit thou well, Sir Lancelot, when I am whole I shall do battle with thee again, for I shall never leave thee till the one of us be slain.'

Thus as this siege endured, and as Sir Gawain lay sick nearhand a month; and when he was well recovered, and ready within three days to do battle again with Sir Lancelot; right so came tidings unto King Arthur from England that made King Arthur and all his host to remove.

As Sir Mordred was ruler of all England, he let make letters as though [XXI.1] that they had come from beyond the sea, and the letters specified that King Arthur was slain in battle with Sir Lancelot. Wherefore Sir Mordred made a parliament and called the lords together, and there he made them to choose him king; and so was he crowned at Canterbury, and held a feast there fifteen days. And afterward he drew him unto Winchester, and there he took Queen Guenivere and said plainly that he would wed her, which was his uncle's wife and his father's wife. And so he made ready for the feast, and a day prefixed that they should be wedded, wherefore Queen Guenivere was passing heavy; but she durst not discover her heart, but spoke fair and agreed to Sir Mordred's will.

And anon she desired of Sir Mordred to go to London to buy all manner of things that longed to the bridal; and because of her fair speech, Sir Mordred trusted her and gave her leave. And so when she came to London she took the Tower of London, and suddenly in all haste possible she stuffed it with all manner of victual, and well garnished it with men, and so kept it.

And when Sir Mordred wist this, he was passing wroth out of measure; and short tale to make, he laid a mighty siege about the Tower and made many assaults, and threw engines unto them and shot great guns.* But all might not prevail, for Queen Guenivere would never, for fair speech nor for foul, never trust unto Sir Mordred to come in his hands again.

Then came the Bishop of Canterbury, which was a noble clerk and a holy man, and thus he said unto Sir Mordred: 'Sir, what will ye do? Will ye first displease God, and sithen shame yourself and all knighthood? For is not King Arthur your uncle, and no further but your mother's brother, and upon her he himself begot you, upon his own sister? therefore how may ye wed your own father's wife? And therefore, sir,' said the bishop, 'leave this opinion, or else I shall curse you with book, bell, and candle.'*

'Do thou thy worst,' said Sir Mordred, 'and I defy thee.'

'Sir,' said the bishop, 'wit you well I shall not fear me to do that me ought to do. And also ye noise that my lord Arthur is slain, and that is not so; and therefore ye will make a foul work in this land.'

'Peace, thou false priest,' said Sir Mordred, 'for and thou chafe me any more, I shall strike off thy head.'

So the bishop departed, and did the cursing in the most orgulest wise that might be done; and then Sir Mordred sought the Bishop of Canterbury for to have slain him. Then the bishop fled and took part of his goods with him, and went nigh unto Glastonbury; and there he was a priest hermit in a chapel, and lived in poverty and in holy prayers, for well he understood that mischievous war was at hand.

Then Sir Mordred sought upon Queen Guenivere by letters and sondes, and by fair means and foul means, to have her to come out of the Tower of London; but all this availed nought, for she answered him

---

engines] missiles hurled from siege-engines   chafe] anger   most
orgulest] most impressive   sought upon] pressed   sondes] messengers

shortly, openly and privily, that she had liever slay herself than to be married with him.

Then came there word unto Sir Mordred that King Arthur had raised the siege from Sir Lancelot and was coming homeward with a great host to be avenged upon Sir Mordred; wherefore Sir Mordred made writs unto all the barony of this land, and much people drew unto him. For then was the common voice among them that with King Arthur was never other life but war and strife, and with Sir Mordred was great joy and bliss. Thus was King Arthur depraved and evil said of. And many there were that King Arthur had brought up of nought, and given them lands, that might not then say him a good word. Lo ye all Englishmen, see ye not what a mischief was here? For he that was the most king and noblest knight of the world, and most loved the fellowship of noble knights, and by him they all were upheld, and yet might not these Englishmen hold them content with him. Lo, thus was the old custom and usages of this land; and men say that we of this land have not yet lost that custom. Alas, this is a great default of us Englishmen, for there may nothing please us no term.*

And so fared the people at that time; they were better pleased with Sir Mordred than they were with the noble King Arthur, and much people drew unto Sir Mordred and said they would abide with him for better and for worse. And so Sir Mordred drew with a great host to Dover, for there he heard say that King Arthur would arrive, and so he thought to beat his own father from his own lands. And the most part of all England held with Sir Mordred, the people were so new-fangle.

And so as Sir Mordred was at Dover with his host, so came King [2] Arthur with a great navy of ships and galleys and carracks. And there was Sir Mordred ready awaiting upon his landing, to let his own father to land upon the land that he was king over. Then there was launching of great boats and small, and full of noble men of arms; and there was much slaughter of gentle knights, and many a full bold baron was laid full low on both parties. But King Arthur was so courageous that there might no manner of knight let him to land, and his knights fiercely followed him; and so they landed maugre Sir Mordred's head and all his power, and put Sir Mordred aback and all his people.

depraved] denigrated   brought up of nought] raised from nothing   most
king] greatest king   new-fangle] fickle   carracks] cargo ships used in
sea-battles   let] prevent

So when this battle was done, King Arthur let search his people that were hurt and dead. And then was noble Sir Gawain found in a great boat, lying more than half dead. When King Arthur knew that he was laid so low, he went unto him and so found him; and there the King made great sorrow out of measure and took Sir Gawain in his arms, and thrice he there swooned. And then when he was waked, King Arthur said, 'Alas, Sir Gawain, my sister's son, here now thou liest, the man in the world that I loved most, and now is my joy gone; for now, my nephew Sir Gawain, I will discover me unto you, that in your person and in Sir Lancelot I most had my joy and my affiance. And now have I lost my joy of you both, wherefore all my earthly joy is gone from me.'

'Ah, mine uncle,' said Sir Gawain, 'now I will that ye wit that my death-day be come; and all I may wite mine own hastiness and my wilfulness, for through my wilfulness I was causer of my own death. For I was this day hurt and smitten upon my old wound that Sir Lancelot gave me, and I feel myself that I must needs be dead by the hour of noon.* And through me and my pride ye have all this shame and disease, for had that noble knight Sir Lancelot been with you, as he was and would have been, this unhappy war had never been begun, for he through his noble knighthood and his noble blood held all your cankered enemies in subjection and danger. And now,' said Sir Gawain, 'ye shall miss Sir Lancelot. But alas that I would not accord with him! And therefore, fair uncle, I pray you that I may have paper, pen, and ink, that I may write unto Sir Lancelot a letter written with my own hand.'

So when paper, pen, and ink was brought, then Sir Gawain was set up weakly by King Arthur (for he was shriven a little before); and then he took his pen and wrote thus, as the French book maketh mention:

'Unto thee, Sir Lancelot, flower of all noble knights that ever I heard of or saw by my days, I, Sir Gawain, King Lot's son of Orkney and sister's son unto the noble King Arthur, send thee greeting, letting thee to have knowledge that the tenth day of May I was smitten upon the old wound that thou gave me before the city of Benwick, and through that wound I am come to my death-day. And I will that all the world wit that I, Sir Gawain, knight of the Table Round, sought my death, and not

discover me] confess   affiance] trust   wite] blame

through thy deserving, but my own seeking. Wherefore I beseech thee, Sir Lancelot, to return again unto this realm, and see my tomb and pray some prayer more or less for my soul. And this same day that I wrote this same sedle, I was hurt to the death, which wound was first given of thy hand, Sir Lancelot; for of a more nobler man might I not be slain.

'Also, Sir Lancelot, for all the love that ever was betwixt us, make no tarrying, but come over the sea in all the goodly haste that ye may with your noble knights, and rescue that noble king that made thee knight; for he is full straitly bestead with a false traitor, which is my half-brother Sir Mordred. For he hath crowned himself king, and would have wedded my lady Queen Guenivere, and so had he done had she not kept the Tower of London with strong hand. And so the tenth day of May last past, my lord King Arthur and we all landed upon them at Dover, and there he put that false traitor Sir Mordred to flight; and so there it misfortuned me to be smitten upon the stroke that ye gave me of old. And the date of this letter was written but two hours and a half before my death, written with my own hand, and subscribed with part of my heart's blood. And therefore I require thee, most famous knight of the world, that thou wilt see my tomb.'

And then he wept and King Arthur both, and swooned. And when they were awaked both, the King made Sir Gawain to receive his sacrament. And then Sir Gawain prayed the King for to send for Sir Lancelot, and to cherish him above all other knights. And so at the hour of noon Sir Gawain yielded up the ghost.

And then the King let inter him in a chapel within Dover Castle; and there yet all men may see the skull of him, and the same wound is seen that Sir Lancelot gave in battle.

Then was it told the King that Sir Mordred had pitched a new field upon Barham Down. And so upon the morn King Arthur rode thither to him, and there was a great battle betwixt them and much people were slain on both parties. But at the last King Arthur's party stood best, and Sir Mordred and his party fled unto Canterbury. And then [3] the King let search all the downs for his knights that were slain, and interred them; and salved them with soft salves that full sore were wounded.

sedle] short letter   pitched a new field] encamped ready for battle

Then much people drew unto King Arthur, and then they said that Sir Mordred warred upon King Arthur with wrong. And anon King Arthur drew him with his host down by the seaside westward toward Salisbury. And there was a day assigned betwixt King Arthur and Sir Mordred, that they should meet upon a down beside Salisbury and not far from the seaside, and this day was assigned on Monday after Trinity Sunday; whereof King Arthur was passing glad that he might be avenged upon Sir Mordred.

Then Sir Mordred raised much people about London, for they of Kent, Sussex, and Surrey, Essex, Suffolk, and Norfolk held the most part with Sir Mordred; and many a full noble knight drew unto him, and also to the King. But they that loved Sir Lancelot drew unto Sir Mordred.

So upon Trinity Sunday at night, King Arthur dreamed a wonderful dream; and in his dream him seemed that he sat upon a chaflet in a chair, and the chair was fast to a wheel, and thereupon sat King Arthur in the richest cloth of gold that might be made. And the King thought there was under him, far from him, a hideous deep black water, and therein was all manner of serpents and worms and wild beasts, foul and horrible. And suddenly the King thought that the wheel turned upside down, and he fell among the serpents, and every beast took him by a limb. And then the King cried as he lay in his bed, 'Help, help!'

And then knights, squires, and yeomen awaked the King, and then he was so amazed that he wist not where he was. And then so he waked until it was nigh day, and then he fell on slumbering again, not sleeping nor thoroughly waking.

So the King seemed verily that there came Sir Gawain unto him with a number of fair ladies with him. So when King Arthur saw him, he said, 'Welcome, my sister's son! I weened ye had been dead, and now I see thee alive, much am I beholden unto almighty Jesu. Ah, fair nephew, what be these ladies that hither be come with you?'

'Sir,' said Sir Gawain, 'all these be ladies for whom I have fought when I was man living, and all these are those that I did battle for in righteous quarrels; and God hath given them that grace at their great prayer, because I did battle for them for their right, that they should bring me hither unto you. Thus much hath God given me leave, for to warn you of your death; for and ye fight tomorrow with Sir Mordred

chaflet] platform

as ye both have assigned, doubt ye not ye shall be slain, and the most part of your people on both parties. And for the great grace and goodness that almighty Jesu hath unto you, and for pity of you and many more other good men there shall be slain, God hath sent me to you of His special grace to give you warning that in no wise ye do battle tomorrow, but that ye take a treaty for a month day, and proffer you largely so that tomorrow ye put in a delay. For within a month shall come Sir Lancelot with all his noble knights, and rescue you worshipfully, and slay Sir Mordred and all that ever will hold with him.'

Then Sir Gawain and all the ladies vanished; and anon the King called upon his knights, squires, and yeomen, and charged them wightly to fetch his noble lords and wise bishops unto him. And when they were come, the King told them of his vision, that Sir Gawain had told him and warned him that and he fought on the morn he should be slain. Then the King commanded Sir Lucan the Butler and his brother Sir Bedivere the bold, with two bishops with them, and charged them in any wise to take a treaty for a month day with Sir Mordred, 'and spare not, proffer him lands and goods as much as ye think reasonable.'

So then they departed, and came to Sir Mordred where he had a grim host of a hundred thousand; and there they entreated Sir Mordred long time. And at the last Sir Mordred was agreed for to have Cornwall and Kent by King Arthur's days, and after that all England, after the days of King Arthur.

Then were they condescended that King Arthur and Sir Mordred [4] should meet betwixt both their hosts, and each of them should bring fourteen persons; and so they came with this word unto Arthur. Then said he, 'I am glad that this is done'; and so he went into the field.

And when King Arthur should depart, he warned all his host that and they see any sword drawn, 'Look ye come on fiercely, and slay that traitor Sir Mordred, for in no wise trust him.'

In like wise Sir Mordred warned his host, that 'and ye see any manner of sword drawn, look that ye come on fiercely, and so slay all that ever before you standeth; for in no wise I will not trust for this treaty.' And in the same wise said Sir Mordred unto his host, 'for I know well my father will be avenged upon me'.

proffer you largely] offer generous terms   wightly] quickly   condescended] agreed

And so they met as their appointment was, and were agreed and accorded thoroughly; and wine was fetched, and they drank together. Right so came out an adder of a little heath bush, and it stung a knight in the foot. And so when the knight felt him so stung, he looked down and saw the adder; and anon he drew his sword to slay the adder, and thought no other harm. And when the host on both parties saw that sword drawn, then they blew beams, trumpets, and horns, and shouted grimly; and so both hosts dressed them together. And King Arthur took his horse and said, 'Alas, this unhappy day!' and so rode to his party; and Sir Mordred in like wise.

And never since was there seen a more dolefuller battle in no Christian land; for there was but rushing and riding, foining and striking, and many a grim word was there spoken of either to other, and many a deadly stroke. But ever King Arthur rode throughout the battle of Sir Mordred many times, and did full nobly as a noble king should do, and at all times he fainted never. And Sir Mordred did his devoir that day, and put himself in great peril.

And thus they fought all the long day, and never stinted till the noble knights were laid to the cold earth. And ever they fought still till it was near night, and by then was there a hundred thousand laid dead upon the earth. Then was King Arthur wood wroth out of measure, when he saw his people so slain from him. And so he looked about him, and could see no more of all his host and good knights left no more alive but two knights; the one was Sir Lucan the Butler, and his brother Sir Bedivere, and yet they were full sore wounded.

'Jesu mercy,' said the King, 'where are all my noble knights become? Alas, that ever I should see this doleful day! For now', said King Arthur, 'I am come to my end. But would to God', said he, 'that I wist now where were that traitor Sir Mordred, that hath caused all this mischief.'

Then King Arthur looked about, and was ware where stood Sir Mordred leaning upon his sword among a great heap of dead men.

'Now give me my spear,' said King Arthur unto Sir Lucan, 'for yonder I have espied the traitor that all this woe hath wrought.'

'Sir, let him be,' said Sir Lucan, 'for he is unhappy; and if ye pass this unhappy day ye shall be right well revenged. And, good lord, remember ye of your night's dream, and what the spirit of Sir Gawain

beams] bugles   fainted] shrank   devoir] duty

told you tonight, and yet God of His great goodness hath preserved you hitherto. And for God's sake, my lord, leave off this, for blessed be God, ye have won the field; for yet we be here three alive, and with Sir Mordred is not one alive. And therefore if ye leave off now, this wicked day of destiny is past.'

'Now tide me death, tide me life,' said the King, 'now I see him yonder alone he shall never escape my hands, for at a better avail shall I never have him.'

'God speed you well,' said Sir Bedivere.

Then the King got his spear in both his hands and ran toward Sir Mordred, crying and saying, 'Traitor, now is thy death-day come!'

And when Sir Mordred saw King Arthur, he ran unto him with his sword drawn in his hand; and there King Arthur smote Sir Mordred under the shield with a foin of his spear, throughout the body, more than a fathom. And when Sir Mordred felt that he had his death's wound, he thrust himself with the might that he had up to the bur of King Arthur's spear; and right so he smote his father, King Arthur, with his sword holding in both his hands, upon the side of the head, that the sword pierced the helmet and the tay of the brain. And therewith Mordred dashed down stark dead to the earth.

And noble King Arthur fell in a swoon to the earth, and there he swooned oftentimes. And Sir Lucan and Sir Bedivere ofttimes heaved him up, and so weakly betwixt them they led him to a little chapel not far from the sea; and when the King was there, he thought him reasonably eased. Then heard they people cry in the field.

'Now go thou, Sir Lucan,' said the King, 'and do me to wit what betokens that noise in the field.'

So Sir Lucan departed, for he was grievously wounded in many places. And so as he yode, he saw and hearkened by the moonlight how that pillagers and robbers were come into the field to pillage and to rob many a full noble knight of brooches and bees, and of many a good ring and many a rich jewel. And who that were not dead all out, there they slew them for their harness and their riches.

When Sir Lucan understood this work, he came to the King as soon as he might, and told him all what he had heard and seen.

'Therefore by my rede,' said Sir Lucan, 'it is best that we bring you to some town.'

---

tide] betide, let come   avail] advantage   a fathom] six feet (two metres)
bur] butt   tay] outermost layer   bees] arm- or neck-ring

[5]   'I would it were so,' said the King, 'but I may not stand, my head works so. Ah, Sir Lancelot,' said King Arthur, 'this day have I sore missed thee. And alas that ever I was against thee, for now have I my death, whereof Sir Gawain warned me in my dream.'

Then Sir Lucan took up the King the one part, and Sir Bedivere the other part, and in the lifting up the King swooned; and in the lifting Sir Lucan fell in a swoon, that part of his guts fell out of his body, and therewith the noble knight's heart brast. And when the King awoke, he beheld Sir Lucan how he lay foaming at the mouth, and part of his guts lay at his feet.

'Alas,' said the King, 'this is to me a full heavy sight, to see this noble duke so die for my sake; for he would have helped me, that had more need of help than I. Alas that he would not complain him, for his heart was so set to help me! Now Jesu have mercy upon his soul.'

Then Sir Bedivere wept for the death of his brother.

'Now leave this mourning and weeping, gentle knight,' said the King, 'for all this will not avail me; for wit thou well, and I might live myself, the death of Sir Lucan would grieve me evermore. But my time passeth on fast,' said the King. 'Therefore,' said King Arthur unto Sir Bedivere, 'take thou here Excalibur, my good sword, and go with it to yonder water's side; and when thou comest there, I charge thee throw my sword in that water, and come again and tell me what thou seest there.'

'My lord,' said Sir Bedivere, 'your commandment shall be done, and lightly bring you word again.'

So Sir Bedivere departed, and by the way he beheld that noble sword; and the pommel and the haft was all precious stones. And then he said to himself, 'If I throw this rich sword in the water, thereof shall never come good, but harm and loss.' And then Sir Bedivere hid Excalibur under a tree. And so as soon as he might he came again unto the King, and said he had been at the water, and had thrown the sword into the water.

'What saw thou there?' said the King.

'Sir,' he said, he saw nothing but waves and winds.

'That is untruly said of thee,' said the King. 'And therefore go thou lightly again, and do my commandment; as thou art to me lief and dear, spare not, but throw it in.'

Then Sir Bedivere returned again, and took the sword in his hand; and yet him thought sin and shame to throw away that noble sword. And so eft he hid the sword, and returned again, and told the King that he had been at the water and done his commandment.

'What sawest thou there?' said the King.

'Sir,' he said, 'I saw nothing but waters wap and waves wan.'*

'Ah, traitor unto me and untrue,' said King Arthur, 'now hast thou betrayed me twice! Who would ween that thou that hast been to me so lief and dear, and also named so noble a knight, that thou would betray me for the riches of the sword? But now go again lightly, for thy long tarrying putteth me in great jeopardy of my life, for I have taken cold. And but if thou do now as I bid thee, if ever I may see thee, I shall slay thee with my own hands; for thou wouldst for my rich sword see me dead.'

Then Sir Bedivere departed, and went to the sword and lightly took it up, and so he went unto the water's side; and there he bound the girdle about the hilts, and threw the sword as far into the water as he might. And there came an arm and a hand above the water and took it and clutched it, and shook it thrice and brandished, and then vanished with the sword into the water. So Sir Bedivere came again to the King, and told him what he saw.

'Alas,' said the King, 'help me hence, for I dread me I have tarried over long.'

Then Sir Bedivere took the King upon his back, and so went with him to the water's side. And when they were there, even fast by the bank hoved a little barge with many fair ladies in it, and among them all was a queen. And all they had black hoods, and all they wept and shrieked when they saw King Arthur.

'Now put me into that barge,' said the King.

And so he did softly; and there received him three ladies with great mourning. And so they set them down, and in one of their laps King Arthur laid his head. And then the queen said, 'Ah, my dear brother, why have ye tarried so long from me? Alas, this wound on your head hath caught over-much cold.'

And anon they rowed from the land, and Sir Bedivere beheld all those ladies go from him. Then Sir Bedivere cried and said, 'Ah, my lord Arthur, what shall become of me, now ye go from me and leave me here alone among mine enemies?'

eft] again   wap] lap   wan] darken   hoved] floated

'Comfort thyself,' said the King, 'and do as well as thou mayest, for in me is no trust for to trust in. For I will into the vale of Avilion to heal me of my grievous wound; and if thou hear never more of me, pray for my soul.'*

But ever the queen and ladies wept and shrieked, that it was pity to hear. And as soon as Sir Bedivere had lost the sight of the barge, he wept and wailed, and so took the forest and went all that night. And in [6] the morning he was ware betwixt two holts hoar, of a chapel and a hermitage. Then was Sir Bedivere fain, and thither he went; and when he came into the chapel, he saw where lay a hermit grovelling on all fours, fast there by a tomb was new graven. When the hermit saw Sir Bedivere he knew him well, for he was but little before Bishop of Canterbury, that Sir Mordred flemed.

'Sir,' said Sir Bedivere, 'what man is there here interred that ye pray so fast for?'

'Fair son,' said the hermit, 'I wot not verily, but by deeming. But this same night at midnight, here came a number of ladies, and brought here a dead corpse, and prayed me to inter him; and here they offered a hundred tapers, and they gave me a thousand bezants.'

'Alas,' said Sir Bedivere, 'that was my lord King Arthur, which lieth here graven in this chapel.'

Then Sir Bedivere swooned; and when he awoke he prayed the hermit that he might abide with him still, there to live with fasting and prayers. 'For from hence will I never go,' said Sir Bedivere, 'by my will, but all the days of my life here to pray for my lord Arthur.'

'Sir, ye are welcome to me,' said the hermit, 'for I know you better than ye ween that I do: for ye are Sir Bedivere the bold, and the full noble duke Sir Lucan the Butler was your brother.'

Then Sir Bedivere told the hermit all as ye have heard before. And so he beleft with the hermit that was beforehand Bishop of Canterbury, and there Sir Bedivere put upon him poor clothes, and served the hermit full lowly in fasting and in prayers.

Thus of Arthur I find no more written in books that be authorized, nor more of the very certainty of his death heard I never read, but thus was he led away in a ship wherein were three queens; that one was King Arthur's sister, Queen Morgan le Fay, the other was the Queen of Northgales, and the third was the Queen of the Waste Lands. Also

| holts hoar] grey woods | flemed] forced to flee | deeming] supposition |
| bezants] gold coins | graven] buried | beleft] remained |

there was Dame Nenive, the chief lady of the lake, which had wedded Pelleas the good knight, and this lady had done much for King Arthur. And this Dame Nenive would never suffer Sir Pelleas to be in no place where he should be in danger of his life, and so he lived to the uttermost of his days with her in great rest.

Now more of the death of King Arthur could I never find, but that these ladies brought him to his grave; and such one was interred there which the hermit bore witness, that sometime was Bishop of Canterbury. But yet the hermit knew not in certain that he was verily the body of King Arthur; for this tale Sir Bedivere, a knight of the Table Round, made it to be written.

Yet some men say in many parts of England that King Arthur is not [7] dead, but had by the will of Our Lord Jesu into another place; and men say that he shall come again, and he shall win the Holy Cross.* Yet I will not say that it shall be so; but rather I would say, here in this world he changed his life. But many men say that there is written upon the tomb this:

Hic iacet Arthurus, rex quondam rexque futurus.*

And thus leave I here Sir Bedivere with the hermit, that dwelled that time in a chapel beside Glastonbury, and there was his hermitage. And so they lived in prayers and fastings and great abstinence.

And when Queen Guenivere understood that King Arthur was dead and all the noble knights, Sir Mordred, and all the remnant, then she stole away with five ladies with her, and so she went to Amesbury;* and there she let make herself a nun, and wore white clothes and black, and great penance she took upon her as ever did sinful woman in this land. And never creature could make her merry; but ever she lived in fasting, prayers, and alms-deeds, that all manner of people marvelled how virtuously she was changed.

Now leave we the Queen in Amesbury, a nun in white clothes and black, and there she was abbess and ruler as reason would. And now turn we from her, and speak we of Sir Lancelot du Lake.

When he heard in his country that Sir Mordred was crowned king [8] in England, and made war against King Arthur, his own father, and would let him to land in his own land; also it was told him how

let] prevent

Sir Mordred had laid a siege about the Tower of London, because the Queen would not wed him—then was Sir Lancelot wroth out of measure, and said to his kinsmen,

'Alas, that double traitor Sir Mordred, now me repenteth that ever he escaped my hands, for much shame hath he done unto my lord Arthur. For I feel by this doleful letter that Sir Gawain sent me, on whose soul Jesu have mercy, that my lord Arthur is full hard bestead. Alas,' said Sir Lancelot, 'that ever I should live to hear of that most noble king that made me knight thus to be overset with his subject in his own realm! And this doleful letter that my lord Sir Gawain hath sent me before his death, praying me to see his tomb, wit you well his doleful words shall never go from my heart, for he was a full noble knight as ever was born. And in an unhappy hour was I born that ever I should have that mishap to slay first Sir Gawain, Sir Gaheris the good knight, and my own friend Sir Gareth that was a full noble knight. Now, alas, I may say I am unhappy that ever I should do thus, and yet, alas, might I never have hap to slay that traitor, Sir Mordred.'

'Now leave your complaints,' said Sir Bors, 'and first revenge you of the death of Sir Gawain, on whose soul Jesu have mercy, and it will be well done that ye see his tomb. And secondly, that ye revenge my lord Arthur and my lady Queen Guenivere.'

'I thank you,' said Sir Lancelot, 'for ever ye will my worship.'

Then they made them ready in all haste that might be, with ships and galleys, with him and his host to pass into England. And so at the last he came to Dover; and there he landed with seven kings, and the number was hideous to behold.

Then Sir Lancelot spered of men of Dover where was the King become. And anon the people told him how he was slain and Sir Mordred too, with a hundred thousand that died upon a day; and how Sir Mordred gave King Arthur the first battle there at his landing, and there was Sir Gawain slain; and upon the morn Sir Mordred fought with the King on Barham Down, and there the King put Sir Mordred to the worse.

'Alas,' said Sir Lancelot, 'this is the heaviest tidings that ever came to my heart. Now, fair sirs,' said Sir Lancelot, 'show me the tomb of Sir Gawain.'

And anon he was brought into the castle of Dover, and so they

spered] enquired

showed him the tomb. Then Sir Lancelot kneeled down by the tomb and wept, and prayed heartily for his soul. And that night he let make a dole for all that would come of the town or of the country: they had as much flesh and fish and wine and ale, and every man and woman he dealt twelve pence, come whoso would. Thus with his own hand dealt he this money, in a mourning gown; and ever he wept heartily, and prayed the people to pray for the soul of Sir Gawain. And on the morn all the priests and clerks that might be gotten in the country and in the town were there, and sang Masses of requiem. And there offered first Sir Lancelot, and he offered a hundred pounds; and then the seven kings offered, and each of them offered forty pounds. Also there was a thousand knights, and each of them offered a pound; and the offering dured from the morn to night. And Sir Lancelot lay two nights upon his tomb in prayers and in doleful weeping.

Then on the third day, Sir Lancelot called the kings, dukes, and earls, with the barons and all his noble knights, and said thus: 'My fair lords, I thank you all of your coming into this country with me. But wit you well, all we are come too late, and that shall repent me while I live; but against death may no man rebel. But sithen it is so,' said Sir Lancelot, 'I will myself ride and seek my lady, Queen Guenivere; for as I hear say she hath had great pain and much disease, and I hear say that she is fled into the west. And therefore ye all shall abide me here, and but if I come again within these fifteen days, take your ships and your fellowship and depart into your country, for I will do as I say you.'

Then came Sir Bors and said, 'My lord Sir Lancelot, what think ye for to do now for to ride in this realm? Wit you well ye shall find few friends.' [9]

'Be as be may as for that,' said Sir Lancelot. 'Keep you still here, for I will forth on my journey, and no man nor child shall go with me.'

So it was no boot to strive, but he departed and rode westerly, and there he sought seven or eight days; and at the last he came to a nunnery. And anon Queen Guenivere was ware of Sir Lancelot as she walked in the cloister; and anon as she saw him there she swooned thrice, that all ladies and gentlewomen had work enough to hold the Queen from the earth.

So when she might speak, she called her ladies and gentlewomen to her, and then she said thus: 'Ye marvel, fair ladies, why I make this fare.

dole] memorial almsgiving   disease] hardship   it was no boot to strive] opposition was useless

Truly,' she said, 'it is for the sight of yonder knight that yonder standeth; wherefore I pray you call him hither to me.'

Then Sir Lancelot was brought before her; then the Queen said to all those ladies, 'Through this same man and me hath all this war been wrought, and the death of the most noblest knights of the world; for through our love that we have loved together is my most noble lord slain. Therefore, Sir Lancelot, wit thou well I am set in such a plight to get my soul health; and yet I trust through God's grace and through His Passion of His wounds wide, that after my death I may have a sight of the blessed face of Christ Jesu, and at Doomsday to sit on His right side; for as sinful as ever I was, now are saints in heaven. And therefore, Sir Lancelot, I require thee and beseech thee heartily, for all the love that ever was betwixt us, that thou never see me no more in the visage. And I command thee, on God's behalf, that thou forsake my company; and to thy kingdom look thou turn again, and keep well thy realm from war and wrack. For as well as I have loved thee heretofore, my heart will not serve now to see thee, for through thee and me is the flower of kings and knights destroyed. And therefore go thou to thy realm, and there take ye a wife and live with her with joy and bliss. And I pray thee heartily to pray for me to the everlasting Lord that I may amend my misliving.'

'Now, my sweet madam,' said Sir Lancelot, 'would ye that I should turn again unto my country, and there to wed a lady? Nay, madam, wit you well, that shall I never do, for I shall never be so false unto you of that I have promised. But the self destiny that ye have taken you to, I will take me to, for the pleasure of Jesu; and ever for you I cast me specially to pray.'

'Ah, Sir Lancelot, if ye will do so and hold thy promise! But I may never believe you,' said the Queen, 'but that ye will turn to the world again.'

'Well, madam,' said he, 'ye say as it pleaseth you, for yet wist ye me never false of my promise. And God defend but I should forsake the world as ye have done, for in the quest of the Sangrail I had that time forsaken the vanities of the world had not your love been. And if I had done so at that time with my heart, will, and thought, I had passed all the knights that ever were in the Sangrail except Sir Galahad,* my son.

on His right side] i.e. with those who are saved   self] same   cast me] intend

And therefore, lady, sithen ye have taken you to perfection, I must needs take me to perfection, of right. For I take record of God, in you I have had mine earthly joy; and if I had found you now so disposed, I had cast me to have had you into mine own realm. But sithen I find you thus disposed, I ensure you faithfully, I will ever take me to penance and pray while my life lasteth, if that I may find any hermit, either grey or white,* that will receive me. Wherefore, madam, I pray you kiss me, and never no more.' [10]

'Nay,' said the Queen, 'that shall I never do, but abstain you from such works.' And they departed; but there was never so hard a hearted man but he would have wept to see the dolour that they made, for there was lamentation as they had been stung with spears. And many times they swooned, and the ladies bore the Queen to her chamber. And Sir Lancelot awoke, and went and took his horse, and rode all that day and all night in a forest, weeping.

And at last he was ware of a hermitage and a chapel stood betwixt two cliffs; and then he heard a little bell ring to Mass, and thither he rode and alit and tied his horse to the gate, and heard Mass, and he that sang Mass was the Bishop of Canterbury. Both the bishop and Sir Bedivere knew Sir Lancelot, and they spoke together after Mass; but when Sir Bedivere had told his tale all whole, Sir Lancelot's heart almost brast for sorrow. And Sir Lancelot threw his arms abroad and said, 'Alas, who may trust this world?'

And then he kneeled down on his knee, and prayed the bishop to shrive him and assoil him; and then he besought the bishop that he might be his brother. Then the bishop said, 'I will gladly,' and there he put a habit upon Sir Lancelot. And there he served God day and night with prayers and fastings.

Thus the great host abode at Dover. And then Sir Lionel took fifteen lords with him, and rode to London to seek Sir Lancelot; and there Sir Lionel was slain, and many of his lords. Then Sir Bors de Ganis made the great host for to go home again; and Sir Bors, Sir Ector de Maris, Sir Blamor, Sir Bleoberis, with more other of Sir Lancelot's kin, took on them to ride all England overthwart and endlong to seek Sir Lancelot.

shrive him and assoil] hear his confession and absolve   brother] i.e. fellow
hermit

So Sir Bors by fortune rode so long till he came to the same chapel where Sir Lancelot was; and so Sir Bors heard a little bell knell that rang to Mass, and there he alit and heard Mass. And when Mass was done, the bishop, Sir Lancelot, and Sir Bedivere came to Sir Bors; and when Sir Bors saw Sir Lancelot in that manner clothing, then he prayed the bishop that he might be in the same suit. And so there was a habit put upon him, and there he lived in prayers and fasting. And within half a year, there was come Sir Galihud, Sir Galihodin, Sir Blamor, Sir Bleoberis, Sir Villiars, Sir Clarrus, and Sir Gahalantine. So all these seven noble knights there abode still; and when they saw Sir Lancelot had taken him to such perfection, they had no lust to depart, but took such a habit as he had.

Thus they endured in great penance six years; and then Sir Lancelot took the habit of priesthood of the bishop, and a twelve-month he sang Mass. And there was none of these other knights but they read in books, and helped for to sing Mass, and rang bells, and did lowly all manner of service. And so their horses went where they would, for they took no regard of no worldly riches; for when they saw Sir Lancelot endure such penance in prayers and fastings, they took no force what pain they endured, for to see the noblest knight of the world take such abstinence that he waxed full lean.

And thus upon a night there came a vision to Sir Lancelot, and charged him, in remission of his sins, to haste him unto Amesbury: 'And by then thou come there, thou shalt find Queen Guenivere dead. And therefore take thy fellows with thee and purvey them of a horse bier, and fetch thou the corpse of her, and bury her by her husband, the noble King Arthur.' So this vision came to Sir Lancelot thrice in one night.

[11]   Then Sir Lancelot rose up or day, and told the hermit.

'It were well done', said the hermit, 'that ye made you ready, and that ye disobey not the vision.'

Then Sir Lancelot took his seven fellows with him, and on foot they yede from Glastonbury to Amesbury, the which is little more than thirty miles. And thither they came within two days, for they were weak and feeble to go. And when Sir Lancelot was come to Amesbury within the nunnery, Queen Guenivere died but half an hour before. And the ladies told Sir Lancelot that Queen Guenivere told them all or

in the same suit] clothed likewise   took no force] cared nothing

she passed, that Sir Lancelot had been priest near a twelvemonth, 'And hither he cometh as fast as he may to fetch my corpse; and beside my lord, King Arthur, he shall bury me.' Wherefore the Queen said in hearing of them all, 'I beseech Almighty God that I may never have power to see Sir Lancelot with my worldly eyes.' 'And thus,' said all the ladies, 'was ever her prayer these two days, till she was dead.'

Then Sir Lancelot saw her visage, but he wept not greatly, but sighed. And so he did all the observance of the service himself, both the dirge,* and on the morn he sang Mass. And there was ordained a horse bier; and so with a hundred torches ever burning about the corpse of the Queen, and ever Sir Lancelot with his seven fellows went about the horse bier singing and reading many a holy orison, and frankincense upon the corpse incensed.

Thus Sir Lancelot and his seven fellows went on foot from Amesbury unto Glastonbury; and when they were come to the chapel and the hermitage, there she had a dirge with great devotion, and on the morn the hermit that sometime was Bishop of Canterbury sang the Mass of requiem with great devotion. And Sir Lancelot was the first that offered, and then all his eight fellows. And then she was wrapped in cered cloth of Rennes, from the top to the toe, in thirtyfold; and after she was put in a web of lead, and then in a coffin of marble. And when she was put in the earth, Sir Lancelot swooned and lay long still, while the hermit came and awaked him, and said, 'Ye be to blame, for ye displease God with such manner of sorrow-making.'

'Truly,' said Sir Lancelot, 'I trust I do not displease God, for He knoweth my intent. For my sorrow was not, nor is not, for any rejoicing of sin, but my sorrow may never have end. For when I remember of her beauty and of her noblesse, that was both with her king and with her, so when I saw his corpse and her corpse so lie together, truly my heart would not serve to sustain my careful body. Also when I remember me how by my fault, my orgule, and my pride that they were both laid full low, that were peerless that ever was living of Christian people—wit you well,' said Sir Lancelot, 'this remembered of their kindness and my unkindness sank so to my heart, that I might not sustain myself.' So the French book maketh mention.

cered] waxed   web] wrapping   careful] sorrowful   orgule] overweening

[12]   Then Sir Lancelot never after ate but little meat, nor drank, till he was dead; for then he sickened more and more, and dried and dwindled away. For the bishop nor none of his fellows might not make him to eat, and little he drank, that he was waxen by a cubit shorter than he was, that the people could not know him. For evermore, day and night, he prayed, but sometime he slumbered a broken sleep; ever he was lying grovelling on the tomb of King Arthur and Queen Guenivere. And there was no comfort that the bishop, nor Sir Bors, nor none of his fellows could make him, it availed not.

So within six weeks after, Sir Lancelot fell sick and lay in his bed; and then he sent for the bishop that there was hermit, and all his true fellows. Then Sir Lancelot said with dreary steven, 'Sir bishop, I pray you give to me all my rites that longeth to a Christian man.'

'It shall not need you,' said the hermit and all his fellows, 'it is but heaviness of your blood, ye shall be well mended by the grace of God tomorrow.'

'My fair lords,' said Sir Lancelot, 'wit you well my careful body will into the earth, I have warning more than now I will say;* therefore give me my rites.'

So when he was houselled and eneled, and had all that a Christian man ought to have, he prayed the bishop that his fellows might bear his body to Joyous Gard—some men say it was Alnwick, and some men say it was Bamborough—'howbeit,' said Sir Lancelot, 'me repenteth sore, but I made my vow some time, that in Joyous Gard I would be buried. And because of breaking of my vow, I pray you all, lead me thither.' Then there was weeping and wringing of hands among his fellows.

So at a season of the night they all went to their beds, for they all lay in one chamber. And so after midnight, against day, the bishop that was hermit, as he lay in his bed asleep, he fell upon a great laughter. And therewith the fellowship awoke and came to the bishop, and asked him what he ailed.

'Ah, Jesu mercy,' said the bishop, 'why did ye wake me? I was never in all my life so merry and so well at ease.'

'Wherefore?' said Sir Bors.

'Truly,' said the bishop, 'here was Sir Lancelot with me with more

cubit] a forearm's length   steven] voice   houselled and eneled] given the Eucharist and extreme unction

angels than ever I saw men in one day. And I saw the angels heave up Sir Lancelot unto heaven, and the gates of heaven opened against him.'

'It is but dretching of swevens,' said Sir Bors, 'for I doubt not Sir Lancelot aileth nothing but good.'

'It may well be,' said the bishop. 'Go ye to his bed, and then shall ye prove the sooth.'

So when Sir Bors and his fellows came to his bed, they found him stark dead; and he lay as he had smiled, and the sweetest savour about him that ever they felt.* Then was there weeping and wringing of hands, and the greatest dole they made that ever made men. And on the morn the bishop did his Mass of requiem; and after, the bishop and all the nine knights put Sir Lancelot in the same horse bier that Queen Guenivere was laid in before that she was buried. And so the bishop and they all together went with the body of Sir Lancelot daily till they came to Joyous Gard, and ever they had a hundred torches burning about him. And so within fifteen days they came to Joyous Gard; and there they laid his corpse in the body of the choir, and sang and read many psalters and prayers over him and about him. And ever his visage was laid open and naked, that all folks might behold him. For such was the custom in those days, that all men of worship should so lie with open visage till that they were buried. And right thus as they were at their service, there came Sir Ector de Maris that had seven years sought all England, Scotland, and Wales seeking his brother Sir Lancelot.

And when Sir Ector heard such noise and light in the choir of Joyous Gard, he alit and put his horse from him, and came into the choir, and there he saw men sing and weep; and all they knew Sir Ector, but he knew not them. [13]

Then went Sir Bors unto Sir Ector, and told him how there lay his brother Sir Lancelot, dead; and then Sir Ector threw his shield, sword, and helm from him. And when he beheld Sir Lancelot's visage, he fell down in a swoon. And when he woke, it were hard any tongue to tell the doleful complaints that he made for his brother.

'Ah, Lancelot,' he said, 'thou were head of all Christian knights! And now I dare say,' said Sir Ector, 'thou, Sir Lancelot, there thou liest, that thou were never matched of earthly knight's hand. And thou

dretching of swevens] troubling dreams

were the courteoust knight that ever bore shield; and thou were the truest friend to thy lover that ever bestrode horse; and thou were the truest lover of a sinful man that ever loved woman; and thou were the kindest man that ever struck with sword; and thou were the goodliest person that ever came among press of knights. And thou was the meekest man and the gentlest that ever ate in hall among ladies, and thou were the sternest knight to thy mortal foe that ever put spear in the rest.'

Then there was weeping and dolour out of measure.

Thus they kept Sir Lancelot's corpse aloft fifteen days, and then they buried it with great devotion. And then at leisure they went all with the Bishop of Canterbury to his hermitage, and there they were together more than a month.

Then Sir Constantine, that was Sir Cador's son of Cornwall, was chosen king of England; and he was a full noble knight, and worshipfully he ruled this realm. And then this King Constantine sent for the Bishop of Canterbury, for he heard say where he was; and so he was restored unto his bishopric, and left that hermitage. And Sir Bedivere was there ever still hermit to his life's end.

Then Sir Bors de Ganis, Sir Ector de Maris, Sir Gahalantine, Sir Galihud, Sir Galihodin, Sir Blamor, Sir Bleoberis, Sir Villiars le Valiant, Sir Clarrus of Cleremont, all these knights drew them to their countries—howbeit King Constantine would have had them with him, but they would not abide in this realm. And there they all lived in their countries as holy men. And some English books make mention that they went never out of England after the death of Sir Lancelot, but that was but favour of makers. For the French book maketh mention, and is authorized, that Sir Bors, Sir Ector, Sir Blamor, and Sir Bleoberis went into the Holy Land there as Jesu Christ was quick and dead, and anon as they had established their lands. For the book saith, so Sir Lancelot commanded them for to do or ever he passed out of this world. And these four knights did many battles upon the miscreants or Turks;* and there they died upon a Good Friday for God's sake.

Here is the end of the whole book of King Arthur, and of his noble knights of

---

favour of makers] authorial partiality   anon as they had established their lands] as soon as they had arranged for the rule of their lands

the Round Table, that when they were whole together there was ever a hundred and forty. And here is the end of the death of Arthur. I pray you, all gentlemen and gentlewomen that readeth this book of Arthur and his knights from the beginning to the ending, pray for me while I am alive, that God send me good deliverance, and when I am dead, I pray you all pray for my soul.

For this book was ended the ninth year of the reign of King Edward the Fourth,* by Sir Thomas Malory, knight, as Jesu help him for His great might, as he is the servant of Jesu both day and night.*

APPENDIX
CAXTON'S PREFACE

After that I had accomplished and finished divers histories, as well of contemplation as of other historical and worldly acts of great conquerors and princes, and also certain books of examples and doctrine, many noble and divers gentlemen of this realm of England came and demanded me, many and ofttimes, wherefore that I have not done made and imprinted the noble history of the Sangrail, and of the most renowned Christian king, first and chief of the three best Christian and worthy, King Arthur, which ought most to be remembered among us English men before all other Christian kings.

For it is noteworthily known through the universal world that there be nine worthy and the best that ever were, that is to wit, three paynims, three Jews, and three Christian men.* As for the paynims, they were before the Incarnation of Christ, which were named: the first, Hector of Troy, of whom the history is common both in ballad and in prose; the second, Alexander the Great; and the third, Julius Caesar, Emperor of Rome, of whom the histories be well-known and had. And as for the three Jews, which also were before the Incarnation of our Lord, of whom the first was Duke Joshua, which brought the children of Israel into the land of behest; the second David, King of Jerusalem; and the third Judas Maccabaeus—of these three the Bible rehearseth all their noble histories and acts. And sith the said Incarnation have been three noble Christian men installed and admitted through the universal world into the number of the nine best and worthy, of whom was first the noble Arthur, whose noble acts I purpose to write in this present book here following. The second was Charlemagne, or Charles the Great, of whom the history is had in many places both in French and in English; and the third and last was Godfrey of Bouillon, of whose acts and life I made a book unto the excellent prince and king of noble memory, King Edward the Fourth.*

The said noble gentlemen instantly required me to imprint the history of the said noble king and conqueror, King Arthur, and of his

---

done made] had made   paynims] pagans   behest] promise

knights, with the history of the Sangrail, and of the death and ending of the said Arthur, affirming that I ought rather to imprint his acts and noble feats, than of Godfrey of Bouillon or any of the other eight, considering that he was a man born within this realm, and king and emperor of the same; and that there be in French divers and many noble volumes of his acts, and also of his knights. To whom I answered, that divers men hold opinion that there was no such Arthur; and that all such books as be made of him be but feigned and fables, because that some chronicles make of him no mention nor remember him nothing, nor of his knights.*

Whereto they answered, and one in special said that in him that should say or think that there was never such a king called Arthur might well be aretted great folly and blindness; for he said that there were many evidences of the contrary. First, ye may see his sepulchre in the monastery of Glastonbury;* and also in *Polychronicon*,* in the fifth book the sixth chapter, and in the seventh book the twenty-third chapter, where his body was buried, and after found and translated into the said monastery. Ye shall see also in the history of Boccaccio, in his book *De casu principum*,* part of his noble acts, and also of his fall. Also Galfridus in his Brutish book* recounteth his life. And in divers places of England many remembrances be yet of him and shall remain perpetually, and also of his knights. First in the Abbey of Westminster, at Saint Edward's shrine, remaineth the print of his seal in red wax closed in beryl, in which is written 'Patricius Arthurus, Britannie, Gallie, Germanie, Dacie, Imperator.'* Item in the castle of Dover ye may see Gawain's skull and Craddock's mantle;* at Winchester, the Round Table;* in other places, Lancelot's sword and many other things. Then all these things considered, there can no man reasonably gainsay but there was a king of this land named Arthur. For in all places, Christian and heathen, he is reputed and taken for one of the nine worthy, and the first of the three Christian men. And also he is more spoken of beyond the sea, more books made of his noble acts than there be in England: as well in Dutch, Italian, Spanish, and Greek, as in French. And yet of record remain in witness of him in Wales, in the town of Camelot, the great stones and marvellous works of iron lying under the ground, and royal vaults, which divers now living hath seen.* Wherefore it is a marvel why he is no more renowned in his own

aretted] presumed   translated] removed   Dutch] German country, save only it accordeth to the word of God, which saith that no man is accepted for a prophet in his own country.

Then, all these things foresaid alleged, I could not well deny but that there was such a noble king named Arthur, and reputed one of the nine worthy, and first and chief of the Christian men. And many noble volumes be made of him and of his noble knights in French, which I have seen and read beyond the sea, which be not had in our maternal tongue; but in Welsh be many and also in French—and some in English, but nowhere nigh all. Wherefore, such as have late been drawn out briefly into English I have after the simple cunning that God hath sent to me, under the favour and correction of all noble lords and gentlemen, enprised to imprint a book of the noble histories of the said King Arthur and of certain of his knights, after a copy unto me delivered; which copy Sir Thomas Malory did take out of certain books of French, and reduced it into English.

And I, according to my copy, have done set it in imprint, to the intent that noble men may see and learn the noble acts of chivalry, the gentle and virtuous deeds that some knights used in those days, by which they came to honour; and how they that were vicious were punished and oft put to shame and rebuke; humbly beseeching all noble lords and ladies, with all other estates, of what estate or degree they be of, that shall see and read in this said book and work, that they take the good and honest acts in their remembrance, and to follow the same; wherein they shall find many joyous and pleasant histories, and noble and renowned acts of humanity, gentleness, and chivalries. For herein may be seen noble chivalry, courtesy, humanity, friendliness, hardiness, love, friendship, cowardice, murder, hate, virtue, and sin. Do after the good and leave the evil, and it shall bring you to good fame and renown.

And for to pass the time this book shall be pleasant to read in; but for to give faith and belief that all is true that is contained herein, ye be at your liberty. But all is written for our doctrine,* and for to beware that we fall not to vice nor sin, but to exercise and follow virtue, by which we may come and attain to good fame and renown in this life, and after this short and transitory life, to come unto everlasting bliss in heaven: the which he grant us that reigneth in heaven, the blessed Trinity. Amen.*

cunning] knowledge   enprised] undertaken   estates] social ranks

EXPLANATORY NOTES

FROM THE MARRIAGE OF KING UTHER UNTO KING ARTHUR

How Uther Pendragon begot the noble conqueror King Arthur

The opening and closing leaves of the manuscript are missing, so the beginning and ending are here transcribed from Caxton's print. His spelling of names (Ulfius, Brastias, Merlin) is retained as standard. The main title to this opening series of episodes is taken from Malory's conclusion to them (the end of Caxton's Book IV, see p. 81); the subheading comes from Caxton's summary of the contents of his Book I, since any indication as to what heading Malory himself might have given it is missing. Malory's source for these opening sections of his work is the French prose romance known as the *Suite de Merlin*; Vinaver accordingly named this part of the work *Merlin* in his edition.

3 [*I. 1*]: book and chapter numbers are taken from Caxton, and are included here for ease of both reference within the text and cross-reference to other editions. Book numbers are repeated at the top of the page.

5 *the four Evangelists*: i.e. the Gospels, which were commonly copied as a separate book.

6 *King Lot of Lothian and of Orkney*: King Lot—named Loth by some other writers—is the originary legendary ruler of Lothian, hence the sharing of name between king and country. Scotland was divided into a number of independent kingdoms, Lothian among them, until the process of unification began in the ninth century. The Isles of Orkney, which in terms of the modern political configuration of Europe appear too remote to accord a ruler much power, were much more important in the early Middle Ages, since they served as the nexus of travel and communications between the Viking kingdom of Norway and the extensive Norse holdings in Scotland, northern Britain, and Ireland, finally reaching their peak of prosperity at around the time that the French prose romances of Arthur were being composed. They did not become a Scottish possession until the fifteenth century. Lot's sons are always referred to as being 'of Orkney': the designation carried weight as well as a touch of exoticism for a medieval reader.

that his wife nourish yours: it was common practice for babies to be suckled by a wet-nurse of a lower rank: for royal children this would normally be a lady of knightly class. Sir Ector's wife is to suckle Arthur, while her own child, Kay, will be fostered by 'another woman'.

8 *made them clean of their life*: i.e. sought absolution for their sins.

the French book maketh no mention: Malory often makes such references to omissions in his sources when he wants to put forward an unauthorized narrative detail or opinion of his own; they do not necessarily signal actual omissions. Here his aim is to increase the sense of topographical authenticity. St Paul's was in Malory's time the largest church within the City of London, and the seat of the bishops of London—as indeed it still is, though the church Malory knew was destroyed in the Great Fire of 1666.

9 *to swear upon a book*: i.e. a book of God's word, such as the Gospels (see note to p. 5 above) or a service book; or possibly, since the scene takes place 'in the greatest church of London', an entire Bible—Bibles, being hand-copied on to parchment or vellum (sheep- and calf-skin), were bulky, expensive, and generally found only in larger religious institutions.

10 *will ye be my good and gracious lord*: 'good lordship' carried a formal meaning in Malory's time of political protection; it indicates a relationship of service from the vassal in return for support from the king. Although it would appear to provide a feudal bond, in the Wars of the Roses and at the end of the *Morte* 'good lordship' in fact generates factions that help to split the country.

11 *Candlemas*: 2 February, the Feast of the Purification of the Virgin, when Christ was presented in the Temple and His mother supposedly underwent the ritual of 'churching' carried out after childbirth. Candlemas derives its name from the blessing of and procession with candles that forms the distinctive part of the ritual of the Mass for the day. It was the fourth most important feast day of the late-medieval liturgical year, after the Passion and Resurrection (Easter), the Nativity (Christmas), and the descent of the Holy Spirit (Pentecost or Whitsuntide, seven weeks after Easter): Pentecost is generally the occasion for the largest annual feast of Arthur's court.

12 *seneschal . . . constable . . . chamberlain*: the 'seneschal of England' was responsible for the management of the king's own estates and for the running of the royal household; the constable was commander-in-chief after the king himself, and substituted for the king in his absence (as Baudwin does when Arthur goes overseas to pursue his war against the Emperor Lucius); the chamberlain controlled access to the king and therefore held a key position of political power.

receive no gifts of a beardless boy that was come of low blood: the giving and receiving of gifts was fraught with social and political significance in the Middle Ages. The kings' refusal to accept those Arthur sends them indicates not only their rejection of his status as fellow sovereign, but that they will not acknowledge him even as part of their own 'community of honour' on account of his low birth.

13 *well victualled*: i.e. had food-supplies sufficient to withstand a long siege. Starvation was as likely a reason as military defeat for a castle or town to surrender.

he is no bastard: if Igraine's husband had still been alive, Arthur would have been begotten in adultery, and would therefore, according to canon law, necessarily be illegitimate. As he is begotten after she is widowed, and born after her marriage to his father, he is Uther's legitimate child.

witch: witches were defined as being servants of the devil and able to make use of diabolical powers; Merlin himself was supposedly the son of a devil and a mortal woman. The term was applied to men as well as women; charges of witchcraft were indeed more likely to be brought against men. Such charges were, however, rare in the Middle Ages; witch-hunting on a large scale, predominantly aimed against women, was just beginning to get under way in continental Europe in Malory's time, but it did not have a significant impact in England until well into the sixteenth century. It was a Renaissance phenomenon, not a medieval one.

14 *his sword Excalibur*: there is a confusion here: Excalibur is the name of the sword Arthur receives from the lake later in the book.

15 *come and see*: the first surviving leaf of the manuscript begins at this point.

18 *that ever they heard or saw*: a short section is omitted, in which twenty-one knights attack the eleven kings.

19 *he did write all the battles . . . of Arthur's court*: the stress on there being early written authorities for the deeds of Arthur and his knights is intended to enhance the historical veracity of the work: it is not enough that they happened, action must also be recorded as text. Malory seems to have regarded himself as a chronicler in the same tradition.

Merlin: this is the first of many instances in the manuscript where Merlin (spelled 'Merlion' in Winchester: 'Merlin' is the form used by Caxton and generally elsewhere) is abbreviated to an initial M. Both the scribes who share the writing of the manuscript make the abbreviation, although no other name is so treated; it is sometimes, as here, associated with disguise on Merlin's part, but by no means always. The use of initials was common for the most frequently used names in the French prose romances (G for 'Gauvain'; T for 'Tristan' in the 1489 print of *Tristan*); and indeed a manuscript of Malory's source, the *Suite du Merlin*, which was in England in the fifteenth century and may have been the one actually used by Malory, abbreviates Merlin similarly. It is extraordinary, however, that this abbreviation should have survived through Malory's translation and one or more copyings, especially when Merlin appears too seldom for scribal speed and convenience to be the reason here: one wonders if it indicates a reluctance on the part of the scribes to write out in full the name of an enchanter who had some claim to continuing power—Merlin never actually dies, and his prophecies were still current as late as the seventeenth century.

20 *always he was against him*: a short passage is omitted, in which four knights are sent to protect Benwick.

21 *as any was then living*: a passage is omitted in which the eleven kings take protective measures against the Saracens.

in the beast's belly . . . in the beast's belly: this is the first example in the manuscript of an eyeskip error in the copying, where the scribe omits the words between the two occurrences of 'belly'. Caxton's own exemplar contained the missing words, which are supplied from his print.

24 *here is my glove . . . will say the contrary*: the offer of a glove as a challenge, for any opponent to take up, is an indication of the seriousness of the issue: it was especially associated in the later Middle Ages with political issues and charges of treason, as here.

28 *recreant*: 'recreant' need mean no more than 'overcome', but it was also recognized as being one of the most opprobrious terms in Middle English: Malory uses it to indicate everything that is the opposite of knightliness, with connotations of falsehood, cowardice, and giving up on the challenge of adventure and quest. Pellinore is inviting Arthur not just to yield, but to accept defamation.

31 *as it rehearseth afterwards . . . Morte Arthur*: the story of Mordred's coming to court is in fact never told, either by Malory or any of his sources. Malory does, in any case, change the story significantly: in the particular French source he is using here, Arthur orders all the children born in May to be sent to him, and it is the ship sent by King Lot containing Mordred that is lost with all lives except the baby's. His name is known because of an inscription on the cradle in which he is washed ashore, and he is brought up as Sagramore's foster-brother. Arthur considers killing all the remaining children, but instead has them set adrift in a pilotless boat for God to determine their fate, and they come ashore safely. It is not uncommon in medieval literature and legend for a child of incest to be cast to sea in a small vessel (it was prescribed in early Irish law), for God to determine whether it should survive; one of the most widely known of such legends concerned Gregorius, the future Pope Gregory. Not every such child was preserved on account of its potential sanctity, however: a similar legend also existed about Judas, the betrayer of Christ, who is the more appropriate comparison here. It seems to be Malory's own unique variant on the motif that the fairly born children should die in the course of such an episode while the incestuous child and future traitor survives.

The Tale of Balin and Balan

The title is taken from the explicit at the end of the tale. An opening summary of the story so far is omitted.

This section has a double purpose, to complete the story of King Roince, and to act as a kind of Book of Prophecies, in rather the way that the Old Testament was read in the Middle Ages and later as prefiguring the New. This makes for a number of digressive episodes that have little logic so far as the main narrative of Balin and Balan is concerned, and the lack of logic is compounded by the fact that not all the prophecies are consistent with Malory's later narratives. I have accordingly omitted some material, indicated in the notes below.

37 *Then the King buried her richly*: a passage is omitted in which Merlin denounces the damosel; this is followed by a subsidiary story in which Balin is pursued by a knight named Lanceor and kills him in combat, whereupon his lady Colombe kills herself with Lanceor's sword. The continuation of the story after the meeting of Balin with Balan (below, Caxton chapters 6

and 7) is also omitted, where King Mark and Merlin, who happen to be passing, make a tomb for the dead lovers. Merlin predicts Lancelot and Tristram's combat at the tomb, Tristram's adultery with Isode, and Balin's wounding of King Pellam.

and wept for joy and pity: the following passage is slightly abbreviated.

40 *till Nero and his people were destroyed*: some details of the battle are omitted.

41 *others were buried in a great rock*: details of the burial are omitted, along with some rather perfunctory prophecies of Merlin's; a further item of explication is omitted from the end of the chapter.

44 *now it sticketh in thy body*: short omission.

45 *which Joseph of Arimathea brought into this land*: it was believed that Joseph of Arimathea had first brought Christianity to England; the legend is summarized in the course of the *Tale of the Sangrail*, below, where Galahad's healing of King Pellam, the Maimed King, is also recounted (though an alternative account of his maiming is given at XVII.5). The title of 'the Haut [high] Prince' strictly speaking belongs to a character named Galahalt, but it is frequently given to the Galahad of the Grail.

which Longius smote Our Lord with to the heart: the reference is to a legend that grew up around the Biblical account of the piercing of the side of the crucified Christ (John 19:34): the soldier in question, named Longius or Longinus, was blind, and had his hand guided by another soldier. The blood flowing from Christ's side healed his blindness.

he was passing fain: there follows an episode, here omitted, in which Balin attempts to help a lover named Garnish, with disastrous results.

[*17*]: from here until Merlin takes Balin's sword is supplied from Caxton, as a leaf is missing from the Winchester MS.

47 *that unhappy sword*: 'unhappy' is a strong word in Malory, meaning 'doomed' or 'doom-bearing', almost 'accursed'. Used here about Balin's sword, it suggests that the whole history of the sword recounted earlier in the *Tale* has been leading up to this moment.

48 *the dolorous stroke*: other activities of Merlin are omitted.

Camelot, that is in English called Winchester: the identification was due to the presence of the Round Table at Winchester, the existence of which Caxton notes in his Preface (for the history of its construction, see note on p. 565 below).

The Wedding of King Arthur

This section is divided off from the previous one in the manuscript by a line of space and a large capital. The heading is taken from the explicit at the end.

52 *a lean mare*: no knight would ever ride a mare. Their status is indicated by the fact that one is ridden by the Ploughman in the General Prologue to Chaucer's *Canterbury Tales*.

53 *milk my kine . . . half by force he had my maidenhood*: Andreas Capellanus, in his late-twelfth-century treatise on love, notoriously recommended the use of a modicum of force to overcome a peasant girl's modesty. The figure in such stories in French is commonly a shepherdess; that she should be a milkmaid is a distinctively English variation, which makes its first recorded appearance here. Later versions of the motif include the lyric 'Hey trolly lolly lo, maid, whither go you?', from the court of Henry VIII, and the nursery rhyme (bowdlerized from an earlier ballad), 'Where are you going to, my pretty maid?—I'm going a milking, sir, she said.'

55 *bring again the white hart*: Tor and Pellinore are also given charges to recover the brachet and the lady. The adventures of Gawain that follow are framed by two further encounters omitted here. Winchester erroneously omits Gawain's release of the greyhounds at the start of chapter 7; this is supplied from Caxton.

57 *thus endeth the adventure of Sir Gawain . . . at the marriage of Arthur*: this injunction to Gawain has little consequence in the rest of Malory's work until Arthur's vision of the dead Gawain at the very end (XXI.3), though it bears an obvious relation to the reputation of the French Gawain as a ladies' man and a less obvious relationship to the English Gawain's reputation as the exemplar of courtesy. The adventures of Tor and Pellinore, omitted here, interpose at this point between Gawain's return and the oath of knighthood.

both old and young: the oath sworn by the knights of the Round Table is closely similar to the charge given the new knights in the fifteenth-century ceremonial for creating knights of the Order of the Bath. The 'certain points that longeth unto this high and worshipful order of knighthood' there include, after injunctions to be faithful to God and the king: 'Ye shall sustain widows in their right at every time they will require you, and maidens in their virginity, and help them and soccour them with your goods . . . Also ye shall sit in no place where that any judgement should be given wrongfully against anybody to your knowledge. Also ye shall not suffer no murderers nor extortioners of the king's people in the country where ye dwell, but with your power ye shall let do take them [have them captured] and put them into the hands of justice.' (From Viscount Dillon, 'A Manuscript Collection of Ordinances of Chivalry of the Fifteenth Century', *Archaeologia*, 57:1 (1900), 27–70 (67–8).)

Of Nenive and Morgan le Fay

There is no heading in the manuscript, although this section starts a new folio after a gap of half a page; and the explicit at the end concludes the whole series of episodes so far. Caxton's summary runs, 'How Merlin was besotted, and of war made to King Arthur', which covers only the first three of his twenty-nine chapters. The present heading is editorial, based on the main events of the abbreviated narrative given here.

59 *he was a devil's son*: according to the story first recounted by Geoffrey of

Monmouth in his *History of the Kings of Britain*, Merlin was the son of an incubus (a devil who copulates with mortal women in their sleep).

60 *rode long in a forest*: short omission.

65 *he drew blood on Arthur*: it is very hard to make a knight appear heroic when he has supernatural help. That Arthur is given Excalibur marks him out as special; that he should prove his heroism fighting against the magic sword with nothing but his own courage and strength proves his prowess as no magic could. The wonder that one expects to attach to the supernatural is therefore transferred to Arthur himself.

69 *a palfrey . . . a courser*: a palfrey is a horse used for recreational riding; a courser is a war-horse.

72 *now may we go where we will*: Morgan's capture of a knight named Manessen is omitted.

74 *Gawain and Uwain decide to go separate ways*: Malory provides a larger frame story for the episode that follows. Gawain and Uwain meet up with Sir Marhalt, and the three of them find three damosels, of 60, 30, and 15 years of age. They decide to separate to seek adventures, each accompanied by one of the damosels (Gawain, to his delight, gets the 'youngest and the fairest'), and to meet again in a year and a day. The damosels play little part in the adventures. Malory recounts Marhalt's and Uwain's adventures, which follow Gawain's, more perfunctorily than his; I give only Gawain's.

[*19/20*]: Caxton's numbering gets confused at chapters 18/19; this chapter is accordingly numbered 19 or 20 in different editions, and so on to the end of Caxton's Book IV.

75 *he maketh no resistance*: a short interruption to the main narrative is omitted here.

80 *so it rehearseth in the book of the French*: there follow a few sentences of somewhat misleading summary of later events.

81 *That God send him good recovery, amen!*: this is the first mention of Malory's being a prisoner. The invitation to the reader to seek further adventures in other books suggests that Malory started with this part of the work and without any intention of continuing; but his chronological cross-referencing to Lancelot and Tristram would seem to indicate that he already had the structure of the whole work in mind, as the *Suite du Merlin* does not contain such a reference.

THE NOBLE TALE BETWIXT KING ARTHUR AND LUCIUS THE EMPEROR OF ROME

The title is taken from the colophon at the end of the section, p. 94. Malory is here using an English source, the alliterative *Morte Arthure*, composed *c*.1400; his version still preserves many of the alliterating lines—see note to p. 86 below. The poem survives in a single manuscript, in which Arthur's epitaph, in the same form that Malory gives, is copied immediately following the end of the poem itself; but Malory appears to have been working from a different copy, since his version incorporates some alliterative lines not found in the extant manuscript. The dialect in which the poem is written is both earlier and more northern than Malory's own, and it incorporates a good deal of specialist alliterative vocabulary. As Malory's rewriting preserves many of these features, this section requires heavier glossing than the rest of his text, and modernization presents particular problems. I have modernized word order on a handful of occasions where the original presents particular difficulty, and more rarely excised a phrase where the meaning is especially obscure.

Caxton's print offers a rather different version of this section, substantially shorter than the one given in the manuscript. He may himself have rewritten Malory's text; or he may have had a copy that was already substantially abbreviated, possibly even a revision made by Malory himself. The version I give here is also much abbreviated, but by cutting whole sections rather than through the sentence-by-sentence slimming that characterizes Caxton.

Although chapter numbers are given as a rough finding guide, the wide differences between the texts of the manuscript and the print make them less precisely helpful here than elsewhere.

83 *Helena's son of England was Emperor of Rome*: Geoffrey of Monmouth had popularized an earlier legend that Helena, mother of the Emperor Constantine and supposed finder of the True Cross, was British by birth. The capture of Rome by Belinus and Brennius ('Sir Beline and Sir Brine') is largely Geoffrey's invention.

   we have evidence enough to the empire of whole Rome: Arthur's other counsellors advise him similarly (omitted here). That he consults his knights before taking action marks his rule as good kingship rather than tyranny.

83–4 *Watling Street*: the Roman road (reputedly built by Belinus) from the Channel ports to the upper Severn, much of it now the A2 and A5.

85 *many giants of Genoa*: the association of giants with Genoa probably has less to do with folklore than with the demands of alliteration, j- initial sounds being comparatively scarce in English.

   with my good knights: the Emperor's assembly of his forces is omitted.

   I shall thoroughly destroy it: the Emperor's further plans are omitted.

   Sir Constantine, that after was king after Arthur's days: the story followed by the alliterative *Morte* is that of the historical tradition based on Geoffrey of Monmouth, in which Mordred is made regent in Arthur's absence; Malory, following the romance tradition, holds over the making of Mordred regent until the war against Lancelot. It is therefore Malory himself who substitutes Baudwin and Constantine at this point, but it is curious that he does so with what looks like a retained alliterative line: 'For to counsel and comfort Sir Cador's son of Cornwall.'

   Sir Lancelot was passing wroth: this is one of the most striking of Malory's cross-referencing interpolations that offer parallel chronologies for the various stories he tells: see X. 22 (pp. 238–9).

86 *that falleth for the war*: some details of the embarkation are omitted.

flying on wing out of the west parts: compare the passage in the alliterative *Morte Arthure* on which this is based:

> The king was in a grete cogge with knightes full many,
> In a cabane enclosed, clenlich arrayed;
> Within on a rich bed restes a little,
> And with the swogh of the se in swefning he fell.
> Him dremed of a dragon, dredful to behold,
> Come drivand over the deep to drenchen his pople,
> Even walkand out of the West landes.

87 *nigh of thy blood*: Malory follows the tradition that identifies Howell, or Hoel, as son of a sister of Uther Pendragon, therefore Arthur's cousin. Geoffrey of Monmouth describes him as Arthur's nephew.

88 *Sir Bedivere*: in this section, and occasionally elsewhere, the name is spelt 'Bedwere'; I have standardized to 'Bedivere' as that is Malory's (or the scribe's) preferred form at the end of the work, where he appears in his most famous episode of throwing Excalibur into the lake.

90 *this corsaint*: Arthur is joking that the giant is St Michael himself, patron saint of St Michael's Mount; a 'corsaint' (*corps saint*, holy body) is a saint's body or relics such as might be worshipped at a shrine.

91 *all the commons of this country may behold it*: the heads of malefactors were commonly displayed above city gates. Two short passages of further instructions relating to the giant's treasure are omitted.

thank ye God . . . and no man else: compare Henry V's instruction after the battle of Agincourt, some fifty years before Malory was writing, to give the glory to God alone.

92 *war is at hand*: a short summary of the defeat is omitted.

93 *many good towns*: an episode follows in which Gawain overcomes a pagan knight named Sir Priamus. Priamus assists Arthur's knights in a skirmish, and after being christened is made a knight of the Round Table.

that for us all on the Rood died: Arthur may be announcing his intention to make a pilgrimage to Jerusalem, or, more likely in view of his intention of taking 'good men of arms' with him, to go on crusade to recover the Holy Land for the Christians, as the last survivors of the Round Table do after the deaths of Arthur and Lancelot. If a 'historical' Arthur of the fifth or sixth century had gone to Palestine, however, he would have found that it was part of the Christian Byzantine Empire. The need for a crusade was an urgent issue in Malory's time, but in order to attempt to stem the Turkish advance across the Mediterranean rather than to reconquer the Holy Land.

as the romance tells: the romance in fact tells nothing of the sort: in the alliterative *Morte Arthure*, as in Geoffrey of Monmouth, Arthur is recalled by the news of Mordred's usurpation before he is crowned (a sequence of events that helps to avoid the issue of why Arthur does not appear as emperor in histories of the Roman Empire). The only other text to have

Arthur crowned as emperor is John Hardyng's metrical *Chronicle*, composed just before Malory was writing and which he could possibly have known.

93 *to part betwixt you even*: i.e. they are to take possession of him as prisoner and divide equally between them the ransom paid for his release.

ever be his own: Sir Priamus is also rewarded, with the duchy of Lorraine: see the first note to p. 93 above.

A NOBLE TALE OF SIR LANCELOT DU LAKE

The title is taken from the explicit to the tale. Sir Lancelot has as yet played little part in the work, but from this point forwards he takes over from Arthur as its hero. His adventures were told at the greatest length in the *Lancelot* section of the French prose Vulgate Cycle, where it is his love for Guenivere that is the primary focus of interest. Malory here selects just three short episodes from this, and those show him in a chivalric rather than an amatory light; Lancelot's insistence that knights errant should not love *par amours* is Malory's own addition, and is typical of his shift of emphasis in his own version from sexual love to knightliness. The repeated accusations that he does indeed love Guenivere, however, both give substance to the reader's own foreknowledge of the story and foreshadow its later development.

The three episodes occur at a late point in the original, after the moment when Lancelot rides in a cart to rescue Guenivere; Malory does not recount this episode until near the end of his own work, after the Grail Quest (XIX.1–9). A few passages bear close verbal resemblances to another French romance, the non-Vulgate *Perlesvaus*.

99 *an abbey of white monks*: i.e. Cistercian monks, who wore white habits. This is the monastic order most frequently cited in the French Vulgate Cycle, especially in the *Quest of the Holy Grail*: see note to p. 321 below.

112 *lodged together in one bed*: it was normal practice to share beds in the Middle Ages; illustrations of hospitals show even the sick lying two to a bed. In fourteenth-century France a member of a sect that required him to get up in the middle of the night to pray was required by his fellow-travellers to sleep on the outside of the communal bed in the inns where they stayed, so that he would disturb them less. The richest or highest ranking might sleep alone if they chose, but the 'old gentlewoman' seems not to have the wealth to offer such a luxury.

departed and thanked his host: an encounter between Lancelot and three knights is omitted, as is their arrival at court at the end of the book (p. 118).

114 *many fair rich shields turned upside down*: the implication is that the knights have been overcome and killed, and their reputations dishonoured: displaying a shield upside down is an insult to the bearer of the arms it carries.

116 *the fair Périgord falcon*: both Winchester and Caxton read 'falcon Perigot', which suggests a resistance to the obvious easy correction 'peregrine'.

'Périgord' (the area around Périgueux, in the Dordogne) seems a reasonable guess, though it does not seem to have been particularly noted for its falcons. Perigot could be a proper name, but no other animal is given a name by Malory—not even the horses, which are often named in other romances.

118 *he had escaped that hard adventure*: there follows an incident in which Sir Lancelot fails to save a lady from her jealous husband, named Sir Pedivere.

THE TALE OF SIR GARETH OF ORKNEY

The heading is taken from the colophon. Malory's source for this section is unknown, though there are a number of analogues in both French and English; it is possible that he made it up himself on the model of these. One such analogue in French that he certainly knew, since he includes it later in his own work, is the story of the young knight nicknamed La Cote Mal Taillé, 'the ill-fitting coat', which occurs in the course of the prose *Tristan*; because of its similarity to the story of Gareth, and because it forms a largely self-contained digression within the *Tristram*, it has become one of the victims of abbreviation in this edition. An English metrical romance based on a French original, entitled *Lybeaus Desconus*—'le bel inconnu', the fair unknown—tells a somewhat similar story, this time about Gawain's son Gingalin. Another English romance, *Ipomadon*, has its unrecognized hero travel and fight in the company of a scornful damosel, and makes much of its hero's fighting in a tournament in different colours of armour. The attractive portrayal of Gawain up until the very end of the tale argues for an English source, whether a lost romance or Malory himself.

120 *the fairest hands that ever man saw*: the fair hands are an indication of his true nature, since they are a sign of someone not used to manual labour. Sir Kay nicknames the young man more truly than he knows.

121 *fostered up in some abbey . . . and hither he is come for his sustenance*: the association of monasteries with good food is a recurrent item of medieval satire; Chaucer's Monk is another example. The speech as given here summarizes an original conversation that makes reference to the similar story of La Cote Mal Taillé.

126 *set him at a side board, and set himself before him*: as distinguished visitors, Gareth and the damosel would normally be seated with their host at the high table on the dais. When the damosel objects to Beaumains' being placed above her—that is, given precedence of honour in the order of seating—the knight moves himself as well as Beaumains to one of the lower tables, so acceding to her wishes without dishonouring his other guest.

132 *the good knight Sir Lamorak*: Sir Lamorak is to be one of the key characters of the *Book of Sir Tristram*, and of the working out of the whole history of the Round Table; it is significant that the first thing that we should be told about his actions (his existence was earlier mentioned, with approval, by Merlin in I.24) is that he is a 'good knight'. His introduction here marks

Malory's concern to make his work a 'whole book': other adventures of Arthur's knights are happening simultaneously offstage, and will come to the fore when their turn comes to be told.

135 *lest ye shall catch some hurt . . . the siege about my lady*: this is the first speech in which the damosel addresses Beaumains by the courtly or polite *you*, rather than the familiar or insulting *thou* used to inferiors, enemies, or (on very rare occasions in Malory) intimates.

136 *in war or in peace*: the phrase is a technical one from the world of fifteenth-century chivalry: 'in war' indicated combat potentially until one combatant was dead or disabled, 'in peace' a purely friendly encounter.

137 *to do Sir Persant such a shame*: a man's honour (his reputation and standing in the eyes of the world and himself) depended in part on the honour (unblemished chastity) of the female members of his family. Sir Persant offers Gareth the most precious gift he can, in the shape of the body of his daughter, despite the cost to himself. Although daughters were officially at their father's disposal in the Middle Ages and beyond, the offer here seems to have wandered into the narrative from a different culture—except, of course, that the key point is Gareth's chivalric refusal.

142 *hale and ho*: this was cited as the typical shipman's call for centuries, and occurs later as a refrain in sea-shanties. It seems to have been used as a chant to co-ordinate the sailors' pulling on the ropes that raised and lowered the sails.

a horn . . . of an elephant's bone: a horn made from an elephant tusk had high heroic associations beyond its mere size: Roland, at the battle of Ronces-valles, was equipped with an 'olifaunt'.

150 *my fellow*: 'fellow' is used by Malory as a mode of address both to inferiors and between knights: there seems to be something of a suggestion here that the dwarf is in full chivalric 'fellowship' with Gareth.

156 *[25/6]*: Caxton's chapter numbering skips one at this point; other editors accordingly use one or other of the two numberings.

158 *the Assumption of Our Lady*: 15 August. The feast, one of the leading Marian festivals of the medieval church, celebrated the belief, developed by the sixth century, that the Virgin had been taken up bodily into heaven.

160 *the knights of either party rescued other*: some details of the tournament are omitted, here and later.

163 *ye would not have smitten me so*: the manuscript reads 'would have smitten'; the 'not' is imported from Caxton. The scribe omits another 'not' just below.

167 *that hated Sir Gareth*: this paragraph foreshadows the events of the *Book of Sir Tristram*, with which the *Tale of Sir Gareth* intersects chronologically—witness the presence of Tristram at the tournament. See in particular X.58 below. The character of Gawain changes radically in different sections of

Malory's work to correspond with the very different portraits of him drawn
by his various sources: see the Introduction, pp. xvi–xvii, and the headnote
to this tale.

168 *and it were better*: other offers of service are omitted.

none that were wedded should joust at that feast: the request is premissed on
the high rates of injury and mortality in tournaments: Dame Lyonesse
wants to preserve husbands (including Gareth) for their wives (including
herself). An account of the tournament is omitted.

THE BOOK OF SIR TRISTRAM DE LYONESSE

The great French prose *Tristan* was one of the most widely known of all the
Arthurian romances in the late Middle Ages, and had largely replaced the earlier, simpler love story. The prose romance provided Malory with what he
needed for the great central section of his own Arthuriad in a way that the earlier
version could not have done: it gives an extended narrative of what happens to
the fellowship of the Round Table between Arthur's military victories and
the Grail Quest. The parallelism of the stories of Tristram and Lancelot has a
double ancestry: the story of Lancelot was originally modelled in part on that of
Tristan, and then Tristan's own story was reworked to bring in ideas and motifs
from the *Lancelot*. Malory makes the most of the opportunities this offers to ele-
vate Lancelot as the leading knight of the Round Table: Lancelot is the ideal by
which Tristram measures himself.

The French *Tristan* survives in a large number of manuscripts, and a print of
1489 for which the manuscript copytext is no longer extant (there is a modern
facsimile of this edition). No single surviving manuscript represents the text as
Malory appears to have known it; his version is at times closest to the print, presumably because its text was based on a manuscript similar to the one he himself
used. The first modern edition, in multiple volumes, is now available, but
only parts of this correlate closely with Malory's text. The original *Tristan* is
about six times the length of Malory's, and in some versions has an extension
that includes the Grail quest as well. Malory reverts to the Vulgate Cycle for
his own Grail section, but incorporates the begetting and birth of Galahad
from the interlaced narrative of the *Tristan* (which had itself borrowed the
episode from the prose *Lancelot*).

Malory's *Book of Sir Tristram* contains a number of more or less self-
contained narratives—those of Sir La Cote Mal Taillé, Alexander the Orphan,
and Sir Palomides' adventures at the Red City—that are omitted in this edition.
Malory was also writing for a readership with an insatiable appetite for the
details of tournaments, of which there are a great many; these are here cut
heavily, partly in order to highlight the events of the extraordinary tournament
at Lonazep, when the personal and social tensions within the broader Arthurian
fellowship and in Tristram's own group begin to express themselves in a violence
at odds with the ostensible ceremony of the occasion. The adventures contained
in the *Tristram* are in some ways the archetypal ones of the Arthurian world, of
knights meeting in forest glades to engage in fierce combat, of quests undertaken

and diverted into further quests. Reading the *Tristram* complete, however, can begin to seem itself like an endless digression; I have concentrated on the main threads of the continuing story of the fellowship, and the processes that first show it beginning to break.

Caxton divided the *Tristram* into some 200 chapters, themselves divided into five books of widely varying lengths; Vinaver offers a fifteen-part division based on the individual stories. The manuscript contains thirty-eight large capitals, occasionally with a blank line preceding them; the breaks in the narrative in this edition follow those divisions.

169 *Here beginneth . . . King Mark of Cornwall*: this neat heading to the 'first book' does not announce any consistent structural division: Malory's 'second book' seems to correspond to a volume of his French exemplar, or the exemplar of that, and is divided from the first in the middle of a speech. The 'third book' connects Tristram's adventures to the Grail, and Malory changes to a different source at that point.

both good and fair: Malory here inserts a short summary of Arthur's reign.

171 *Sir Tristram*: on a handful of occasions Tristram is called 'Sir' in the manuscript even before he has been knighted; as it tends to happen when he is acting in the most chivalric fashion, it is possibly deliberate.

172 *the book of Sir Tristram*: the most famous English medieval hunting treatise, compiled by Dame Julian Barnes or Berners, cites Sir Tristram as its authority. 'Beasts of venery' are the noblest beasts to hunt, and include the red deer (the largest native English species), the hare, and the boar; 'beasts of chase' include the fallow and roe deer; 'vermin' include the badger, wild cat, and otter. Foxes can appear in either of the last two categories—most often as beasts of chase, but vixens frequently figure as vermin.

174 *as the book saith, she died*: the scribe made a marginal note in the manuscript at this point: 'How the King of France's daughter sent to Sir Tristram a fair brachet.' That the hunting-dog is taken as more noteworthy than her dying for love is probably not so far at odds with Malory's own priorities.

176 *now I see him*: Tristram is inexperienced in the restricted vision of a helmet.

180 *good ladyship*: the term acknowledges Isode's feudal support (see note to p. 10); 'better lady', later in the conversation, implies something more.

182 *that won the Dolorous Gard*: this is a famous exploit from early in Lancelot's career that Malory does not include in his own redaction. The castle was renamed 'Joyous Gard' after Lancelot had liberated it from its previous tyrannical owner.

183 *made a bain for Sir Tramtrist*: baths were highly regarded by the upper classes for much of the Middle Ages, and carried none of the modern associations of indignity. In Malory's time, particularly distinguished visitors might be welcomed at court with a bath; the Order of the Bath testifies to their knightly associations.

188 *love was there none*: a further episode involving Segwarides' wife and

Sir Bleoberis is omitted, as is a later reference to it when Tristram and Bleoberis encounter (VIII.22, p. 192).

190 *the king departed unto his lodging*: an encounter between Sir Tristram and Breunis sans Pité is omitted.

195 *days of their life*: some miscellaneous adventures in the course of the voyage are omitted. The section just below this, of Lancelot's rescue of Gawain, forms the last part of these.

197 *maiden and lady unto La Belle Isode*: Malory handles this episode very differently from his French source. There, Brangwain, who is still a virgin, is substituted for Isode in her marriage-bed, and Isode herself plots Brangwain's death for fear she will reveal what has happened. Malory cuts the substitution, and gives the two women a relationship of 'fellowship' analogous to that between good knights.

198 *ye shall have your desire that I promised you*: Caxton makes this part of Palomides' speech: 'But before my lord *your* husband, there shall ye know that *I will* have *my* desire that *ye* have promised *me*.'

if she were hasty . . . that she performed her promise: the manuscript reads 'And if I were hasty . . .'; Caxton reads, 'And if ye were hasty . . . that ye performed your promise', so that the whole speech is addressed to Isode. I take it that Mark makes the second part of the speech as a general statement: 'Even if she were rash in granting whatever request he might wish to ask, I would want her to keep her promise.'

201 *I would be loath that he should die a Saracen*: 'Saracen' would normally indicate a Moslem; here it means little more than 'unchristened'. The point is that Sir Palomides would go straight to Hell when he died: baptism was believed to be a condition for salvation.

202 *to take and devour him*: there follows a short quarrel between Tristram and King Mark.

207 *Isode les Blanches Mains*: in the French, Tristram agrees to marry this second Isode after he has been overheard sighing over his love for an unspecified 'Isode' and his intentions mistaken. Malory's omission loses the naturalistic point of the two women's sharing the same name, but the doubling remains typical of his own work and of Arthurian romance in general.

208 *better than ever he did*: omitted here are some adventures of Sir Lamorak, which form the end of Caxton's Book VIII, and the largely self-contained story of Sir La Cote Mal Taillé, 'the ill-fitting coat', from the start of Book IX, which is similar in outline to the story of Sir Gareth.

211 [*16/17*]: there is confusion over the chapter numbering in Caxton at this point; from here on, the lower number is that of the Penguin edition, the higher is Vinaver's. Some intervening adventures are also omitted at this point.

213 *Sir Gingalin, Sir Gawain's son*: Sir Gingalin is the hero of *Lybeaus Desconus*,

'the fair unknown', which is a possible analogue for the *Tale of Sir Gareth*. He is also named in *The Wedding of Sir Gawain and Dame Ragnell*, on which see *The Death of King Arthur*, note to p. 470 below.

214 *made him like a fool*: there follows an episode in which Sir Dagonet, King Arthur's fool, comes across the mad Tristram in the forest without knowing who he is, and warns King Mark about him.

218 *first and last*: I omit Tristram's references to other episodes cut in this edition.

222 *the man of most worship in the world*: short omission.

223 *he lay still*: there are some short omissions between this point and the damosel's arrival at the old kight's house, below.

225 *Then was Sir Palomides ashamed*: an account is omitted of how ten of Arthur's knights, including Lancelot, determine to find Sir Tristram; they undergo various adventures, at this point in the text and after Tristram has been imprisoned by Sir Darras (chapters 36/7–39/40, below). A further short repetitive episode is omitted from the middle of 39/40.

when sickness toucheth a prisoner's body . . . then hath he cause to wail and to weep: this is one of the most explicit autobiographical passages in the work, where Malory makes an addition to his French source to comment feelingly from what was presumably his own experience.

226 *the sheep would suffer the wolf to be in peace*: both the manuscript and Caxton read, 'the wolf would suffer the sheep to be in peace': but Dinadan is casting Tristram as the wolf who may attack the sheep Palomides if he is provoked.

And so they peaced themselves: short omission.

227 *here will we depart in sunder*: there follow the adventures of Sir Dinadan, who overcomes Sir Breunis sans Pité; and of Sir Tristram, who carries a shield given him by Morgan le Fay before Arthur at the tournament at the Hard Roche, the shield bearing an emblematic device of a knight standing on the heads of a king and queen. He maintains his anonymity throughout the tournament.

229 *where Merlin set the perron*: the 'perron' is generally taken to mean a large stone; to be consistent with the story as told in the *Tale of Balin*, it would refer to the tomb on which Merlin wrote a prophecy of the combat between Lancelot and Tristram (see *Balin*, note to p. 37). Chivalric challengers at passages at arms, *pas d'armes*, in continental Europe in the fifteenth century frequently set themselves up beside a 'perron' to take on all comers: in such cases the word probably denoted a pillar erected to announce their whereabouts and purpose.

231 *then the King made great dole*: a passage is omitted in which King Arthur identifies the hostile protagonist of some earlier adventures as Lancelot.

Welcome . . . ye are welcome to this court: this speech of Arthur's, like the other accounts of Tristram's contributions to the art of hunting, is Malory's addition to his French source.

232 *turn we unto King Mark*: a reprise of Tristram's combat with Marhalt is omitted before this sentence. There follows a large capital and a line space, and the next section starts with a reprise of who Tristram is and why King Mark dislikes him.

234 *for while the truncheon of the spear stuck in his body he spoke*: Amant remains alive, and therefore able to speak, so long as the broken spear stays lodged in the wound. Death, as often in Malory, results from the rush of bleeding caused by its removal.

235 *three miles English*: weights and measures were standardized in England in the Middle Ages, in contrast to France. The commonest French measurement of distance, the league, had six official standards, ranging between about 4 and 6 kilometres (2½ to 4 miles).

236 *a broken love day between them*: a love day was a day appointed for reconciling quarrels; a 'broken' one indicates that the promises of peace are not kept.

238 *good lord*: i.e. feudal protector and supporter.

239 *to slay Sir Tristram*: a folio is missing from the manuscript at this point; the text is supplied from Caxton. The page-break that follows is based on the announcement of the new direction of the narrative.

241 *my father's death is not revenged*: this speech is an addition of Malory's to his source, but it misrepresents the story as he has told it: King Lot was indeed killed by King Pellinore.

243 *great damage*: 'great damage' is inserted from Caxton.

a passing good knight: a short passage is omitted in which Dinadan meets Palomides.

246 *any other instrument*: an omission here includes mention of a new character named Elyas; the manuscript proceeds to rename the minstrel as Elyas by confusion.

Sir Dinadan can make wonderly well, and ill where he should make evil: i.e. Dinadan can compose wonderfully good poetry, which is also wonderfully insulting poetry where he intends to make mischief.

those lords that I bear the arms of: it was a common practice in the fifteenth century for minstrels or players patronized by a nobleman to travel around the country giving performances in return for lodging and a small payment. Presumably, in view of King Mark's reply, such minstrels enjoyed the same rights of licensed speech as fools in the age of Shakespeare.

in that country: there follows a large inset story, of King Mark and another nephew of his, Alexander the Orphan.

249 *where he was become*: Sir Tristram is here released and rapidly re-imprisoned; this edition conflates the two episodes.

the realm of Logris, that is this land: Logris was the area of Britain supposedly given by the legendary Trojan founder of Britain, Brutus, to his son

Locrine, from whom it takes its name. As Malory indicates, it corresponded roughly to England.

251 *all manner of game*: See note to p. 172 above. A list of hunting terms and horn calls is omitted.

251 *bearing his shield and his spear*: various encounters between knights of the Round Table and Sir Breunis sans Pité are omitted. The following encounter between Tristram and Dinadan is abbreviated.

255 *God*: Caxton reads 'the devil'.

259 *his kin about him*: Sir Palomides at this point successfully undertakes an adventure in the Red City, and returns to meet up with the others.

260 *to ride toward Lonazep*: their jousts on the journey are omitted.

261 *The tournament gets under way*: the account of the tournament that follows is considerably abbreviated.

263 *sleeping in his bed*: an episode is omitted in which King Arthur determines to set eyes on La Belle Isode, and is unhorsed by Sir Palomides.

271 *that other . . . is my lord Sir Lancelot*: it is common for knights not to recognize each other face to face, as they so often meet fully armed; damosels and ladies, by contrast, recognize faces. Dinadan's recognition of Arthur and Lancelot shows not only that he has spent more time at Arthur's court than Tristram, but that he enjoys a social intimacy with the knights of the court rather than just a relationship of combat.

278 *that day fifteen days*: some short omissions follow.

279 *Sir Tristram could never meet with Sir Palomides*: such a deferral of closure is typical of romance, and in particular of the interlaced structure elaborated in the prose romances. The story of Sir Tristram and Sir Palomides is concluded after the inset story of Lancelot and Elaine, at the end of Caxton's Book XII.

280 *letters . . . of recommendation*: i.e. recommending themselves to him; late-medieval letters typically began with a formula such as 'My right worshipful lord, I recommend me unto you . . .'

281 *of Sir Galahad . . . how he was begotten*: this section of the work occurs as an extended episode within the larger story of Tristram. The opening is marked by a large capital in the Winchester manuscript, but not by a page-break. The heading is taken from the introductory transition formula, 'Now . . . speak we of . . .'

283 *should beget a pucel*: a *pucel* (usually found in the feminine form *pucelle*) is a virgin. The point is that Galahad is preordained to remain a virgin throughout his life; marriage was sometimes praised most highly in the Middle Ages as being the source of virgins, and some similar justification seems to be implied for the scheming of King Pelles.

284 *that I have loved*: 'lived' is the more predictable expression, and is given by Caxton. 'Loved' suggests that Lancelot identifies his honour with his love

for the Queen, and now he is shamed (has lost his honour) by betraying his love; I retain it as an interesting reading. (The alternative interpretation that suggests itself to a modern reader, 'alas that I have spent so long making love', is less likely in terms of Middle English usage of the verb 'love'.)

285 *owe me your good will*: this is one of a number of passages for which there is no precedent in Malory's source, which urge both sympathy for Elaine and the poignancy of their relationship: she could be the ideal wife for Lancelot if he were not already committed to Guenivere.

the Lady of the Lake confirmed him Sir Lancelot du Lake: the story is recounted in the French Prose *Lancelot*, but is not given by Malory. There follows an episode, omitted in this edition, in which Sir Bors comes to the castle of Corbenic and undergoes a series of enigmatic encounters and visions.

King Arthur had . . . won much of his lands: Malory goes to some trouble to locate his various stories chronologically in relation to each other; this passage confirms that what we have been reading is in effect a flashback to the earlier days of the Round Table.

286 *King*: Caxton reads 'Queen': that reading would suggest possibly just that Guenivere is in charge of the accommodation arrangements for the ladies, or else that she wants to keep Elaine under her eye. The King would have overall charge of accommodation, and might himself wish to honour Elaine by placing her so close to the Queen.

288 *clattered as a jay*: jays were often kept as pets and taught to speak.

And therefore alas . . . the best knight of the world: the last part of this speech (which, along with the following exchange between the women, is original to Malory), is as close as he ever comes to criticizing Lancelot's love for Guinevere; but even here the criticism is formulated entirely in personal terms, as grief for the people concerned rather than as a moral principle.

290 *Now fie on your weeping . . . that be of his blood*: this speech is another of Malory's additions, and is typical of his insistence on Lancelot's supremacy.

291 *where they should meet*: there follow the adventures of Sir Percival with his brother Sir Agloval and Sir Persides.

293 *Of Sir Lancelot, that suffered . . . many sharp showers*: the division is marked in the manuscript by a clear line and a large capital. The heading is taken from the transition formula that follows.

302 *to the city of Corbin*: a short adventure of Sir Bors' is omitted.

303 *It hath cost my lady the queen twenty thousand pound the seeking of you*: it is Malory's addition to put a price-tag on the search for Lancelot. The modern equivalent would be about twenty million pounds.

the best man of his kin, except one: Elaine underestimates her son: he proves himself the best of all knights, not excluding his father.

304 *of Sir Tristram and of Sir Palomides*: again, the heading is taken from the opening words of the next section.

305 *that I would hold so noble a knight as ye are from his worship*: knights are crit-
icized in a number of romances for just the kind of uxurious failure of attention to chivalry that Isode fears, most famously in Chrétien de Troyes' *Erec
et Enide*.

309 *here is no rehearsal of the third book*: the numbering presumably refers to volumes of Malory's French source. It may be that Malory did not have access
to the 'third book' of the French *Tristan*, which contains a version of the
Grail story; or he may have made the choice to work from the Vulgate
Queste del Saint Graal instead.

THE NOBLE TALE OF THE SANGRAIL

Malory's tale of the Sangrail ('saint graal', holy grail) is based on the French
Queste del Saint Graal, one of the sections of the great thirteenth-century Vulgate Cycle. Malory's adaptation is generally fairly close, though his own version,
as usual, is considerably abbreviated from the original: he generally concentrates
on the narratives of the questing knights and greatly cuts down the generous
quantities of exegetical material and religious allegory found in the French.
More notable is his change of emphasis from the French. There, the object of
this section of the cycle is to show the limitations of earthly chivalry by comparison with the requirements of God, and by so doing to prepare for the fall of the
Round Table through the revelation of Lancelot's sexual sin. Galahad is accordingly the hero of the French, and Lancelot's failure is the central moral lesson.
In Malory's version, Lancelot and Galahad share the central place, and the
emphasis falls much more on how close Lancelot comes to achieving the quest
than on his failure.

310 *At the vigil of Pentecost . . . heard their service*: the 'vigil of Pentecost' is Whit
Saturday, the day before Pentecost itself. Although the hearing of Mass
receives emphasis throughout Malory's work as one of the duties of every
Christian, the opening of the Grail Quest with religious observance is particularly appropriate. Pentecost was the most important feast day of the
Christian year after Easter and Christmas, and here brings with it its full
religious charge as the day when the Holy Ghost came down among the
apostles (Acts 2); the knights are similarly 'lighted of the grace of the
Holy Ghost' when the Holy Grail makes its first appearance.

312 *not . . . sit at your meat or that ye have seen some adventure*: Arthur's refusal to
eat until he had seen some adventure is the starting-point for a number of
Arthurian romances, most famously *Sir Gawain and the Green Knight*,
though the feast on that occasion is Christmas rather than Pentecost.

314 *King Pecheur*: the name is derived from 'le roi pecheur', the Fisher King
who appears in the earliest version of the Grail legend by Chrétien de
Troyes, in which Percival, not Galahad, is the chosen knight. The *Queste
del Saint Graal* identifies the fisher king as the father of King Pelles, therefore Galahad's great-grandfather.

317 *such meats and drinks as he best loved in this world*: the Grail may have its

origins in Celtic legends of a magic horn of plenty; the identification of it with the cup of the Last Supper was a late innovation, in the French prose version that Malory is translating.

321 *Of Sir Galahad*: this and the following text divisions are marked in the manuscript by large capitals. The headings are taken from the narrative transitions that announce the next subject at the close the preceding section, or, as in this instance, sign off the action at its end.

a white abbey: an abbey of white-habited Cistercian monks. The *Queste del Saint Graal* may have been written under Cistercian influence.

323 *Mordrains*: in the French, Mordrains is not a separate character but the name taken by Evelake after baptism.

. . . many marvellous deeds: the history of Galahad's shield (here abbreviated to about half its length in Malory's original) is part of the pre-Arthurian history of the Grail that had expanded to become a complete romance in itself, in the *Estoire del Saint Graal* of Robert de Boron. The *Estoire* had already been translated into English before Malory, by the Londoner Henry Lovelich, as *The History of the Holy Grail* (*c*.1425); he converts the French prose into loose couplet form. Three much-abbreviated versions of the legend of Joseph of Arimathea were printed early in the sixteenth century. That he was believed to have been the apostle to the British had some propaganda value in the Middle Ages, as giving England a Christian history earlier than Scotland or most other European countries. For the role of the Biblical Joseph, see John 19: 38–42.

the white knight vanished away: the adventures of a would-be Grail knight are omitted.

328 *I will . . . show you my life if it please you*: i.e. make a full confession. The emphasis on individual private confession in the *Queste del Saint Graal*, which is carried over into Malory's version, may be due to the fact that it had been made a universal requirement for all believers only in 1215, shortly before the composition of the *Queste*.

in prison before the Incarnation of Our Lord Jesu Christ: the 'prison' is Hell: the reference is to the doctrine that all the souls of mankind were taken by the devil before the Redemption, but that Christ 'harrowed Hell' between His Crucifixion and Resurrection and led the good souls out to Heaven.

330 *King Pecheur's house*: that is, in the house of King Pelles, King Pecheur's son: for the incident referred to here, see XI.2.

332 *he had loved a queen*: Lancelot's avoidance of naming Guenivere accords with the requirements of confession: the penitent must confess his own sins, not implicate others.

333 *the fig tree . . . that had leaves and no fruit*: the reference is to Mark 11: 13–14.

335 *after your departing . . . she died*: Percival's leaving of his mother at the point of death is of major significance in Chrétien's version of the Grail story, but has become very much attenuated by this stage of its history. There is a

Middle English stanzaic version in which the mother is brought back to health after being dosed with medicine from a spoon.

336 *no earthly man's hand*: the recluse's explanation of the symbolism of the Round Table is omitted. Malory himself cuts out a lengthy passage in the French in which she recounts the derivation of the Round Table from the table of the Last Supper (see in particular Luke 22: 13–20) by way of Joseph of Arimathea's table of the Holy Grail: Malory insistently regards Arthur's fellowship as having earthly value in its own right.

336 *he heard a clock smite*: in the French Percival hears a chapel bell tolling: mechanical clocks were invented between the time of the writing of the French *Queste* and Malory's version. Early clocks struck the hour but had no dial or hands.

338 *on foot, crying*: Percival's first attempt to get a horse is omitted.

he made a sign of the cross in his forehead: making the sign of the cross becomes, in the Grail quest, a way of opening a direct channel for God's power into the world. Here, it frees Percival from the horse, and later from the fiend in the guise of a woman; and Lancelot is enabled to pass the lions (XVII.14). Balin's crossing of himself, by contrast, conveys no active power whatsoever (II.17).

341 *And she that rode on the serpent . . . put away his power*: the devil is symbolized by both the serpent and the horse, both of which Percival has killed: the serpent in what appeared to be a non-allegorical battle, the horse when he made the sign of the cross. The woman riding the serpent symbolizes the Old (Jewish) Law; she is represented as being in confederation with the devil (the serpent) because it was held that the devil had hardened the hearts of the Jews against the New Law of Christ.

342 *He hideth Him not unto his words*: Percival is citing Christ's promise from Matthew 7: 7–8.

343 *he made me so fair and clear . . . I ought to have had*: the story identifies the lady as Lucifer, created by God as the fairest of all the angels, but who rebelled through pride and was cast out to Hell.

344 *rove himself through the thigh that the blood started about him*: a wound in the thigh was a common euphemism for castration. Whether or not one reads Percival's wounding of himself in this way, his action clearly seems intended to recall the idea of Matthew 19: 12, widely cited in the Middle Ages as a text in favour of clerical celibacy, 'There be eunuchs which have made themselves eunuchs for the kingdom of heaven's sake. He that is able to receive it, let him receive it.' The text was customarily read as moral rather than literal: the early Greek theologian Origen received fame, or notoriety, for actually putting it into practice. The Maimed King's wound in the thigh has been read by comparative mythologists as a metonym for the infertility of the Waste Land. The version Malory follows in fact separates the two motifs: on the Maimed King's wounding, see XVII.7 below; on the desolating of the Waste Land, Malory offers two accounts, in one of

which it is the result of Balin's 'dolorous stroke' of King Pellam in II.16, and in the other the result of an unconnected 'dolorous stroke' in a tangential story omitted in this edition, XVII.3.

346 *God save you*: an encounter between the hermit and a loquacious fiend is omitted.

349 *a window that she might see up to the altar*: it was common for women recluses to be enclosed in a cell adjoining a church, so that they could see the celebration of Mass. Her interpretation of Lancelot's encounter that follows is slightly abbreviated.

350 *that hight Mortaise*: Vinaver's emendation, confirmed both by the French source and by the naming of the river when Lancelot's adventures are resumed later. The manuscript reads 'and an high mortays', Caxton 'and an high mountain'.

351 *if one thing were not . . . the more pain upon him*: the 'one thing' is Lancelot's affair with the Queen: without that, Gawain suggests, he would be supreme in the Grail quest. As it is, he will do no better than the rest of the knights unless he goes to extraordinary efforts—which of course he does.

352 *viand*: the manuscript and Caxton read 'wind': P. J. C. Field's emendation.

set him upon an ass: some details of Ector's vision and its later exposition (XVI.5) are omitted.

355 *God would not ride . . . an ass betokeneth meekness*: the reference is to Christ's entry into Jerusalem, Matthew 21: 2–7; the moral interpretation is given in verse 5: 'Behold, thy King cometh unto thee, meek, and sitting upon an ass.'

357 *a scarlet coat . . . the quest of the Sangrail*: the French stipulates that Bors must put on another garment under the scarlet one—presumably a hair shirt or similar garment to mortify the flesh, though that is not stated. The unpenitential-sounding scarlet coat therefore conceals Bors' humility from the world, so that he cannot be given credit for it or take pride in it.

359 *the one would have benome . . . touched not one another*: Caxton's reading (largely adopted by Vinaver) suggests that one flower threatens to corrupt the other, in accordance with the episode of the intended rape that follows. The manuscript reading opposes the rescue of Lionel (the tree) to the prevention of the corruption of both lovers (the flowers), an interpretation supported by the fact that in the French *Queste* the 'good man' occupies the chair between the tree and the flowers.

362 *I shall succour this maid*: Sir Bors' choice now seems odd, since life too once lost cannot be got again. In the Middle Ages, however, virginity was commonly regarded as carrying spiritual as well as physical qualities: virgin saints could suffer horrendous tortures, but God always saved them from rape. Canon law acknowledged the avoidance of rape as the only justification for suicide, despite the arguments of theologians of the status of St Augustine on the primacy of an unspotted will over the pollution of the body; rape could be regarded literally as a fate worse than death.

364 *the love of the vainglory of the world*: the argument is that Sir Bors' profession of chastity is a kind of pride, which must be resisted.

365 *he had liever they all had lost their souls than he his soul*: suicide, other than to avoid rape, was regarded as incurring damnation: see note to p. 362 above.

366 *the blood that the great fowl bled raised the chicks from death to life*: the symbolism is familiar in iconography, where the bird representing Christ is specified as a pelican. The image of its piercing its breast to revive its chicks with its blood is known as 'a pelican in its piety'; it is found, for instance, as the emblem of Corpus Christi College, Cambridge. (If the chicks are regarded as the central characters, the same image can betoken filial ingratitude—hence John of Gaunt's lines in Shakespeare's *Richard II*, on Richard's killing of his uncle: 'That blood already, like the pelican, | Hast thou tapped out and drunkenly caroused.')

366 *I am black*: 'I am black but comely': Song of Songs 1: 5. That the text refers to the Church was the standard interpretation. On the Old Law, see note to p. 341 above.

377 *save only to you*: Percival's sister tells two stories from the history of the ship that are omitted here, one at this point, one after the end of the next paragraph.

the Maimed King: the Maimed King is in fact the father of Pelles, therefore the great-grandfather of Galahad, and is elsewhere given the name King Pellam or Pecheur. Since the account of his maiming given here is different from that of the maiming of Pellam given in *The Tale of Balin*, I have not corrected the name or the detail of family relationships. The confusion occurs in part because Malory is trying to reduce the number of characters found in the French *Queste*: there, the king who is wounded is a new character who is at war with the father of the Maimed King.

378 *bade him know his wife fleshly as nature required*: there was some debate in the Middle Ages as to whether Adam and Eve had sex before the Fall: the injunction to 'Be fruitful and multiply' was given them in Paradise, but their first recorded act of sex (in which Cain was begotten, not, as is implied here, Abel) took place after their expulsion (Genesis 1: 28, 4: 1). It is in keeping with the whole ethos of the Grail quest that there should have been no sexual activity in Paradise; the French gives a disquisition on the supreme virtue of virginity at this point, which Malory, typically, cuts. God's ensuing command to Adam to make love to his wife is in keeping with the doctrine of Christian marriage, but that was regarded by the celibacy lobby very much as second best.

he despised them in his books: Solomon's denial that there was such a thing as a good woman (Ecclesiastes 7: 27–9) was notorious in the Middle Ages, and was frequently quoted and (as here) challenged. Many of the defences are put into the mouths of women: other examples are Chaucer's Proserpina, in *The Merchant's Tale*, and Prudence, the wife of *The Tale of Melibee*.

if heaviness come to a man by a woman . . . that woman shall be born of thy lineage: the references are to Eve and to the Virgin Mary.

a man which shall be a maid . . . Duke Joshua, thy brother-in-law: the choice of words suggests that this is a prophecy of Christ, of whom Joshua was taken to be a foreshadowing; in fact, as the next chapter shows, it refers to Galahad. The overlap between Galahad and Christ is not, of course, accidental.

380 *Now here is a wonderful tale of King Solomon and of his wife*: the line is set off as a heading in the manuscript: whether as part of the apparatus of presentation, or as part of the speech, is unclear—quite possibly both at once.

382 *vengeance is not ours, but to Him which hath power thereof*: 'Vengeance is mine; I will repay, saith the Lord' (Romans 12: 19).

383 *Long have I abided . . . as ye be*: the moment echoes Simeon's *Nunc dimittis* (Luke 2: 29), when he prays for death after beholding the infant Christ; Mordrains makes a somewhat similar speech just before his own death, chapter 18 below. Both episodes are part of the chain associating Galahad with Christ.

384 *as he ought to be*: an emblematic episode follows concerning the Evangelists and the Resurrection.

386 *let me go as adventure will lead me*: a number of saints' legends similarly record the placing of the saint's corpse in an unsteered boat, to be taken by God to the place where it is to lie in accordance with divine will; hence Percival's sister's conviction as to where its destination is to be.

388 *He that fed . . . so was he fed*: Exodus 16. Stories of rudderless boats frequently note biblical parallels for God's feeding of the passenger: compare, for instance, Chaucer's story of Custance in *The Man of Law's Tale*.

389 *marvellous strange*: the bottom quarter of the leaf is torn away in the manuscript; the missing portions of the lines are supplied from Caxton.

391 *it seemed to Sir Lancelot . . . to the people*: what is being described here is the priest's elevation of the Host to show to the congregation at the Mass, only with its theological meaning rendered visible: the figure placed between the priest's hands is Christ Himself, Who is embodied in the Mass wafer. The two figures who place the third between the priest's hands are the Father and the Holy Ghost.

395 *King Mordrains*: Mordrains and Evelake are two different names for the same person in the French (see note to p. 323 above); this is therefore the same blind king that Percival has encountered in XIV.3, who is awaiting Galahad's appearance for his healing and death.

Galahad's well: holy wells were often associated with virginity: St Winifred's Well at the pilgrimage site of Holywell in Clwyd sprang up where Winifred was martyred by a would-be rapist. A further adventure with an associate of Joseph of Arimathea's is omitted.

396 *they had fulfilled the Sangrail*: Sir Galahad proceeds to mend a sword that was broken when Joseph of Arimathea was wounded.

397 *he took an oblay . . . fleshly man*: this is transubstantiation made visible: the

substance of the Mass wafer is seen to change into the Body of Christ. The doctrine, first defined in the ninth century but made official dogma only in 1215, shortly before the writing of the French *Queste del Saint Graal*, caused recurrent difficulties during the Middle Ages, and was rejected by a number of heretical movements (and at the Reformation); miracle stories such as this were designed to promote acceptance of the doctrine.

398 *I ate the lamb on Easter Day*: in fact, the day of the Passover, the 'last supper' that is re-enacted in the Eucharist (Matthew 26:17–30).

402 *so will I*: it is Malory's innovation, in keeping with the focus of his whole compilation on Lancelot, to re-introduce him here at the end of the Grail.

through His might: the last thirteen words are written in larger letters, and may be intended to be read as a rhyming tag:

> By Sir Thomas Malory, knight.
> O blessed Jesu, help him through His might.

THE TALE OF SIR LANCELOT AND QUEEN GUENIVERE

In the conclusion to Book XIX, Malory refers to this whole section as 'the tale of Sir Lancelot'. I have added Guenivere both as giving a fair idea of its contents and to distinguish it from the earlier 'tales of Sir Lancelot'. Malory is here using two sources concurrently: the French prose *Mort le Roi Artu*, and its English adaptation, the stanzaic *Morte Arthur*. Malory disentangles the various episodes from the interlacing found in both sources, but he largely follows the English in his selection of incidents (the main exception being Lancelot's wounding by a hunter, XVIII.21–2, which appears in the French but not the English). The only surviving manuscript of the English poem was copied around Malory's own time; the original is likely to have been composed at the beginning of the fifteenth century. This romance, in common with the whole English Arthurian tradition before Malory himself, offers a much more favourable reading of Gawain than do Malory's French sources.

There is one major interpolation from a different source, and that is the story of Guenivere's abduction by Meliagaunt. This is first found in one of the earliest French Arthurian romances, the *Chevalier de la Charrette* of Chrétien de Troyes, and was retold in the prose *Lancelot*, but Malory's precise source here is uncertain. The introduction of this episode here is both an indication of his originality in shaping his vision of the Arthurian legends, and crucial for defining the part played by the lovers' adultery in the destruction of Arthur's realm (see Introduction, p. xv).

Two further episodes, the tournament in which Gareth changes sides in order to fight with Lancelot (XVIII.23–4, with its concluding encomium on love, 25), and the healing of Sir Urry (XIX.10–13), have no known sources.

406 *fruit . . . a passing hot knight of nature*: medieval nutrition theory recommended certain foods to counterbalance predominant physical humours or temperaments: fruit was cooling, therefore appropriate for a 'hot' choleric nature such as Gawain's.

407 *I must be a rightful judge*: the first duty of a king, undertaken in his coronation oath, was to uphold the law. Arthur's obligation to enforce justice has to take precedence over support for his wife, just as later he has to support Gawain in a legally correct quarrel against Lancelot.

410 *such custom was used . . . another poor lady*: there is a strong contrast implied here with the system of justice in Malory's own day, when association with an affinity—the power group assembled by a great magnate—was particularly important in obtaining a favourable verdict, as the lord could often pack the jury with other members of his affinity.

413 *that day my lady . . . shamed among all knights*: the episode is recounted in the French Prose *Lancelot*.

414 *thither came many good knights*: a short list of the knights is omitted.

415 *Ascolat*: the more familiar 'Astolat' is Caxton's spelling. The manuscript initially most often reads 'Ascolot', but later settles into 'Ascalat' as its preferred form.

418 *the parties smote together*: the following account of the tournament is slightly abbreviated.

424 *Not so . . . send ye for that shield*: a caring medieval father will not allow his daughter to take a knight up to her bedchamber, and especially not one with the reputation of Sir Gawain. (In the French, Gawain propositions her.)

430 *a thing*: presumably a herb of some kind, to act like smelling salts.

431 *many knights of divers countries*: a list of participating knights is omitted.

435 *mass-penny*: the mass-penny is the offering given to the priest to perform requiem masses for the soul of the dead; the sum given was often considerably more than a penny.

437 *a great tournament and jousts*: details of the parties are omitted here and from the course of the tournament.

438 *at the stalk and at the trist*: i.e. by stalking them or when the deer were driven out by beaters. In the French *Mort le Roi Artu*, the hunter is the king's huntsman, and there is no mention of women; presumably the all-women team of huntresses is derived from some version of the story of Diana, though Malory's precise source is unknown. Ovid, the obvious ultimate source for such matters, was the Classical author best known in the Middle Ages, and there were abundant retellings of and allusions to the myths contained in the *Metamorphoses* in both English and French. Some of those concerning Diana are summarized, for instance, in Chaucer's description of the goddess's temple in *The Knight's Tale*.

abaited her dog for the bow at a barren hind: the huntress sets her dog on the trail of a female deer so that it can drive the animal out to where it can be shot with the bow; when the deer retreats into the water beside the well, the hound loses the scent.

450 *he rideth unto hanging*: condemned felons were taken to be hanged in a cart; it was unheard of for a knight to adopt such a mode of transport.

453 *they were laid in withdraughts*: a 'withdraught' is a small corner room or recess off a larger chamber; an example is still extant in Magdalene College, Cambridge, where the master occupied the larger chamber and his pupils the satellite recesses.

455 *to touch a queen's bed . . . and she lying therein*: the private space in a medieval household was not the bedroom but the curtained bed.

458 *Lessez les aller*: this is the heralds' cry to the knights to let their horses run; as a traditional phrase of chivalric etiquette, it kept its original French form.

460 *as the French book maketh mention*: there is in fact no known source for this section, and it would be unlikely that a French version, if any existed, would have placed the story of Sir Urry here: Malory's interjection at this point of Lancelot's own personal miracle, immediately after his one explicit act of adultery in the whole work, makes it very clear that in his version God is not displeased with Lancelot. The Vulgate Cycle offers a much simpler moral cause-and-effect relationship between the shortcomings of earthly chivalry (as embodied in Lancelot's adultery and shown up in the Grail Quest) and the downfall of the Round Table. Malory reshapes his narrative towards the much more tragic structure of the destruction of the good.

461 *there were but a hundred and ten . . . that time away*: the magnificent roll-call that follows offers in miniature a portrait of the knights of the Round Table and their deeds. Many of the knights have been heard of before in the course of the work, and their stories told; others have their deeds recounted only here; some are never mentioned elsewhere. One major incident, the death of Sir Tristram, receives its fullest narration here. The passage summarizes the histories of the individual members of the fellowship, and gives a glimpse of a hinterland of further adventures that could also have been recounted—an abundance of further unwritten romances. There is a sense in which this passage, far more than the tournament before the Grail Quest, gives a last sight of the fellowship 'all whole together', despite the absentees—or because of them, since they are away fulfilling their knightly function of adventure. (Two duplicated names are removed.)

463 *corpse*: both Caxton and Winchester read 'cross'; it seems more plausible that Malory wrote 'cors', corpse. This is certainly how she meets her death in the French, where Tristram's final mighty embrace of her as he dies ends her own life too.

464 *Sir Degrevant*: Sir Degrevant is the hero of an independent Middle English romance, in which he is described as a knight of the Round Table. He does not figure in the mainstream Arthurian stories, and presumably Malory includes him because of his own acquaintance with the romance.

467 *as the French book saith . . . came on horseback*: Malory here summarizes the prose version of the story. In the original *Chevalier de la Charette* by Chrétien de Troyes, Lancelot's ride in the cart is a single incident, undertaken after his horse has been killed.

that caused Sir Agravain: this uncompromising ascription of the blame for Arthur's death to Agravain, rather than to any failing on the part of earthly chivalry in general or of Lancelot in particular, is a recurrent theme in the rest of the work (only with the name of Mordred frequently coupled with his brother), and again is Malory's own. The change in emphasis suggests that the previous remark, on losing the rest of the story of Lancelot, may be disingenuous. It might be true; it could be no more than a variant on Malory's frequent remarks on abridging his sources (the effect is certainly the same, to produce a much tighter narrative structure); or Malory may have wished to avoid a further digression on the way to his conclusion, so that Lancelot's miracle remains in the forefront of his readers' minds.

the most piteous tale . . . votre bonne merci: 'the most piteous tale of the death of Arthur without redress, by the knight Sir Thomas Malory. Jesus of Your mercy help him.' The colophon is the only indication of a section break.

THE DEATH OF ARTHUR

The title adopted for this section is that given at the end of the work rather than the French 'Morte Arthur' given at the close of the preceding section. The *Mort le Roi Artu* is very much the minor partner to the English source for this final part of the work: the two cover much the same material, but the stanzaic English version provides Malory with a much tighter narrative structure, the inspiration for some of his best phrasing (concerning, for instance, the responses to the death of Gareth, the final battle, and the throwing of Excalibur into the water), and also the entire episode of Lancelot and Guenivere's final meeting in the nunnery.

469 *he rescued me from King Carados . . . from Sir Tarquin*: see *The Book of Sir Tristram*, VIII.28, for the rescue of Gawain from Sir Carados, and *The Tale of Sir Lancelot*, VI.7–9, for the rescue of Agravain from Sir Tarquin, Carados' brother. The reminder of Lancelot's previous adventures is typical of the way Malory brings the whole history of the Round Table to bear on its destruction.

470 *Sir Gromore Somer Jour:* this knight makes an appearance as the opponent of Arthur in *The Wedding of Sir Gawain and Dame Ragnell*, where he is the brother of Dame Ragnell (and therefore in due course the brother-in-law of Gawain and uncle of Gingalin, who is there identified as Gawain's son by Ragnell). The work is a late-fifteenth-century rhyming romance, the author of which describes himself at the end as being a prisoner. On the basis of that, and the reappearance of the name Gromore Somer Jour in Malory's known work, P. J. C. Field has suggested that Malory may have been the author of *The Wedding* too. Sir Gromore is presumably intended to be the same character as the Grummor Grummorson mentioned at the healing of Sir Urry.

all they were of Scotland: knights of Scotland would be likely to support the sons of Lot of Lothian and Orkney, the leading Scottish king of the work.

472 *wit thou well . . . after thy days*: this is the one occasion in the work when

the Queen slips into the intimate *thou* with Lancelot (as distinct from her angry usage of the word in her quarrel over Elaine the mother of Galahad); it contrasts strikingly with the insulting *thou* being shouted at Lancelot from outside the door. He invariably addresses her with the respectful *you*.

476 *in my default*: this is the most ambiguous of several instances where 'default' may mean either 'fault' or 'lack': Guenivere may be destroyed because of Lancelot's past actions ('for my sake'), or if he fails to rescue her. Malory may have intended both meanings to be present.

478 *treason*: treason was a very fluid term at the time when the Arthurian romances were taking shape, but any kind of betrayal of one's overlord could fall within the definition. Guenivere's adultery amounts to both a betrayal of Arthur and a risk to the succession, itself defined as high treason; under the Statute of Treasons of 1352, anyone who violated the wife or eldest daughter of the king committed treason. This is the basis of Arthur's charge of treason against Lancelot in chapter 11, but presumably not Gawain's in chapter 20: see note to p. 501 below.

481 *as they were unarmed, he . . . wist not whom that he smote*: knights normally identify each other by the coats of arms on their shields; as Gaheris and Gareth are unarmed, Lancelot fails to recognize them.

483 *My king . . . assay your friends*: the formulations Gawain uses—'my king, my lord, and mine uncle . . . as ye will have my service and my love'—allow Arthur no room for manœuvre. It is not that despite being king he is ordered about by a subject, but *because* he is king (and therefore bound to uphold both the law and feudal obligations) that Gawain can compel him to do what he wishes. As king, he has to uphold a legally just quarrel (Gareth and Gaheris were unlawfully killed while they were acting under Arthur's orders); as Gawain's lord, he has to uphold Gawain in his quarrels just as Gawain has given him his own 'service and love'; and as his uncle, it is his blood-feud as much as it is Gawain's. Arthur must 'assay his friends', test his followers to see who will support him rather than Lancelot, in preparation for the war that is to follow.

486 *ye slew him not yourself*: i.e. by yourself: it needed the combined efforts of Gawain, Gaheris, Agravain, and Mordred to overcome Sir Lamorak—see X.58.

489 *interdicting of all England*: an interdiction is the laying of a whole country under excommunication, so that no ecclesiastical functions may be performed, from the regular church services to christenings or the last rites.

491 *thus he said full knightly*: the extent of Lancelot's speeches here is Malory's own—one of the few places in the work where he generously extends the French (the stanzaic English *Morte*, typically, is very laconic). Everywhere else in the work Lancelot has been able to fight in his own defence; here, he has to rely on eloquence—though it is an eloquence backed with reminders of what he can do by way of prowess.

492 *God grant mercy*: the phrase is balanced between piety and threat—between thanks to God (the common Anglo-Norman *grand merci*) and 'God have mercy upon them'.

495 *fortune is so variant . . . they alighted passing low*: the turning of the wheel of Fortune, to cast down by an inescapable process those who climbed highest, was a commonplace of medieval thought. In the alliterative *Morte Arthure*, used by Malory as his source for his account of Arthur's conquest of the Roman Empire, Arthur himself has a dream that shows those of the Nine Worthies who precede him, including Hector and Alexander, falling from the wheel (cf. XXI.3). On the Worthies, see Caxton's Preface, pp. 528–9.

497 *he departed his lands and advanced all his noble knights*: there is the barest hint for this episode in the sources, with no general distribution of lands. The places listed are all genuine, and show some knowledge of the detailed geography of central and southern France. Attempts have been made to construct elements of a biography for Malory from this, but he could as easily have derived knowledge of the names of some of the more obscure places from acquaintances or other sources as from first-hand experience. The English had been involved in active military campaigns in France throughout the earlier decades of the century, and links through trade, travel, and ecclesiastical connections were commonplace.

498 *Then said Sir Lionel . . . land upon our lands*: this whole series of speeches is derived from the English stanzaic *Morte Arthur*, where each occupies one stanza. The closeness of Malory's borrowing shows up particularly strongly in Lionel's speech:

> Lionel speaks in that tide,
> That was of war wise and bold:
> 'Lordings, yet I rede we bide
> And our worthy walls hold:
> Let them prick [spur] with all their pride
> Till they have caught both hunger and cold,
> Then we shall out upon them ride,
> And shred them down as sheep in fold.'

501 *treason*: Gawain's accusation of treason against Lancelot is presumably not based on his adultery with the Queen, since he refuses to countenance such charges. The Statute of Treasons included among its definitions the levying of war on the king in his own kingdom; Gawain may be taking Lancelot's attack on the party accompanying the Queen to the stake as such an act. He does not, however, specify any particular act as treasonable; it is the accusation itself that matters, not the detail of the charge.

503 *Now have good day . . . my knights out bring*: the rhythm, inversion of word order and rhyme are a relic of the stanzaic *Morte Arthur*:

> But have good day, my lord the king,
> And your doughty knightes all;
> Wendeth home and leave your warring;

> Ye win no worship at this wall.
> And I would my knights out bring,
> I wot full sore rue it ye shall.

506 *shot great guns*: the guns are Malory's addition. Cannon were first used in siege warfare in the early fourteenth century, a hundred years after the writing of the prose *Mort le Roi Artu*.

book, bell, and candle: these were the chief instruments in the ritual of excommunication.

507 *men say that we of this land . . . please us no term*: the reference is presumably to the fluctuating loyalties accorded to the Lancastrian and Yorkist claimants to the English throne during the Wars of the Roses.

508 *I must needs be dead by the hour of noon*: given that Gawain's strength normally increases until the hour of noon, its ebbing is doubled in effect by this prophecy of the hour of his death (a prophecy which also enables him to give the timing of his letter, below).

515 *What sawest thou there? . . . waves wan*: the whole passage is closely based on the stanzaic *Morte*; compare here:

> 'What saw thou there?' then said the King,
> 'Tell me now, if thou can.'
> 'Certes, sir,' he said, 'no thing
> But waters deep and waves wan.'

516 *Comfort thyself . . . pray for my soul*: this passage inspires one of Tennyson's closest adaptations of Malory, in his own *Passing of Arthur*:

> Comfort thyself; what comfort is in me?
> I have lived my life, and that which I have done
> May He within Himself make pure! but thou,
> If thou shouldst never see my face again,
> Pray for my soul . . .
> I am going a long way
> With these thou seest—if indeed I go—
> For all my mind is clouded with a doubt—
> To the island-valley of Avilion . . .
> Where I will heal me of my grievous wound.

It is symptomatic of the different emphasis Tennyson gives to the Arthurian legends that he should find the most detailed inspiration in a speech of loss and nostalgia rather than in the scenes of action.

517 *he shall win the Holy Cross*: presumably, to recover for Christianity the scene of the Crucifixion and the rest of the Holy Land by the ultimate successful crusade. The Cross itself was believed to have been found by St Helena in the fourth century, and fragments of it had been distributed across Christendom.

Hic iacet Arthurus, rex quondam rexque futurus: 'Here lies Arthur, king once, king to be.' The line forms a leonine hexameter, i.e. a line with a medial rhyme of the kind common in medieval Latin poetry. Epitaphs for Arthur exist in many variants; the one said to have been found on a cross above Arthur's tomb in Glastonbury (where Malory locates the hermitage) when it was excavated in 1191 read 'Hic iacet sepultus inclitus rex Arturius in insula Avalonia', 'Here lies buried the renowned King Arthur in the isle of Avalon'. Modern research has tended to confirm that the Glastonbury monks did indeed find an early princely burial. The wording Malory gives for the epitaph is found at the end of the sole surviving copy of the alliterative *Morte Arthure* in the Lincoln Thornton manuscript and as a gloss to Arthur's English epitaph in Lydgate's *Fall of Princes* (see John Withrington in *Arthurian Literature* 7 (1987), 103–44).

517 *Amesbury*: there was a Benedictine nunnery at Amesbury in Malory's time.

520 *except Sir Galahad*: the Winchester manuscript has lost its final leaves, its last words being the catchwords for the next leaf, 'except Sir'. The rest of the text is taken from Caxton's print.

521 *grey or white*: the terms were most commonly used about the Franciscan (grey) and Carmelite (white) friars; 'white monks' were Cistercians, as in the Book of the Grail.

523 *dirge*: this is part of the Office of the Dead, so called from the opening word of the antiphon: 'Dirige, Domine, deus meus, in conspectu tuo viam meam', 'O Lord my God, direct my way in Thy sight'.

524 *I have warning more than now I will say*: those close to sanctity were often represented as knowing the time of their deaths.

525 *the sweetest savour about him that ever they felt*: the 'odour of sanctity' that distinguishes the corpse of the saint.

526 *the miscreants or Turks*: 'miscreants' means literally 'misbelievers'— Moslems. The advance of the Turks represented the greatest danger to Christian Europe in Malory's lifetime: Constantinople had fallen in 1453, and Belgrade, Rhodes, and the eastern Mediterranean were all threatened.

527 *the ninth year of the reign of King Edward the Fourth*: i.e. 4 March 1469 to 4 March 1470. In the course of this year, Malory was excluded for the second time from a general pardon.

    as Jesu help him . . . both day and night: the last two clauses again look like a doggerel couplet, as at the end of the *Sangrail*. Caxton's own colophon follows, and reads: 'Thus endeth this noble and joyous book entitled Le Morte Darthur. Notwithstanding it treateth of the birth, life, and acts of the said King Arthur, of his noble knights of the Round Table, their marvellous quests and adventures, the achieving of the Sangrail, and in the end the dolorous death and departing out of this world of them all. Which book was reduced into English by Sir Thomas Malory, knight, as before is said, and by me divided into twenty-one books, chaptered and imprinted, and finished in the abbey Westminster the last day of July the year of Our Lord 1485. Caxton me fieri fecit [Caxton had me made].'

APPENDIX: CAXTON'S PREFACE

This preface, prefixed by Caxton to his edition of the *Morte*, gives an invaluable insight into how Malory's work might have been understood in the late fifteenth century, both as to its historicity and its moral value (literature was supposed to instruct and to entertain, and to entertain primarily in order to make its moral teaching palatable—a problematic demand here given the nature of much of the material). Also notable is Caxton's promotion of England and the English language through the printing of an Arthuriad in English to match that in French. It is not known whether the 'many noble and divers gentlemen' who he claims urged him to print such a work actually existed, or if they are an advertiser's fiction; Earl Rivers, brother-in-law to Edward IV, who had a close relationship with Caxton, has been suggested as a possibility.

528 *there be nine worthy . . . three Christian men*: the tradition of the 'nine worthies' that Caxton rehearses here was especially popular in the fifteenth and sixteenth centuries. It is referred to in numerous romances, provided the subject of many pageants (including one in Shakespeare's *Love's Labour's Lost*), and spawned various offspring, such as the nine female worthies and the nine worthies of the City of London.

Godfrey of Bouillon . . . King Edward the Fourth: Godfrey of Bouillon was one of the leaders of the First Crusade, which captured Jerusalem from the Saracens in 1099, and he became its first ruler. Caxton printed not only his history but also one of Charlemagne; his Arthur completes the trio of Christian worthies. Edward IV died in 1483, two years before the printing of the *Morte*.

529 *divers men hold opinion . . . nor of his knights*: Arthur was generally (though not universally) accepted within Britain as having had a historical existence. Scepticism was much more widespread in continental Europe, where the lack of evidence to corroborate his supposed conquests, in particular over the Emperor Lucius, was frequently pointed out.

Glastonbury: Geoffrey of Monmouth had stated that Arthur was buried at Avalon, which was commonly identified with Glastonbury. The supposed grave of Arthur was found there in 1191. Malory makes the same identification of Arthur's burial place.

Polychronicon: a mid-fourteenth-century universal history written in Latin by the monk Ranulph Higden, and translated into English in 1387 by John Trevisa. Higden is one of the historians who expresses reservations as to the historicity of Arthur's foreign conquests.

Boccaccio, in his book 'De casu principum': Boccaccio's *De casibus virorum illustrium*, 'On the falls of great men' (*c*.1360), was widely known throughout Europe and had been translated into English by John Lydgate. He too was something of a sceptic as to Arthur's exploits, and offered them as a moral example to be avoided.

Galfridus in his Brutish book: Geoffrey (Galfridus) of Monmouth was the first to give shape and coherence to the earlier legends of Arthur, in his

History of the Kings of Britain (see Introduction). Histories that followed the same model were known as 'Brutus books' or *Bruts*, after the legendary founder of Britain.

Patricius Arthurus, Britannie, Gallie, Germanie, Dacie, Imperator: 'Lord Arthur, emperor of Britain, Gaul, Germany, and Denmark' (Dacia being a common term in medieval Latin for Denmark—not, as in classical Latin, Transylvania, which would make the territorial claims excessive even by the most jingoistic standards). The seal does not survive.

Gawain's skull and Craddock's mantle: Malory recounts Gawain's death from head wounds at Dover in Book XXI. The story of the chastity-testing mantle, which only Craddock's wife was able to wear, survives in a number of medieval versions in various European languages; the earliest English text, *The Boy and the Mantle*, is contained in the Percy Folio Manuscript, a seventeenth-century compilation that contains a number of ballads and romances of fifteenth-century origins. In an earlier English reference to the story in the fourteenth-century *Scalachronicon*, the mantle is said to have been made into a chasuble preserved at Glastonbury. As the ballad claims that the mantle fitted 'between two nut-shells', its loss is hardly surprising.

at Winchester, the Round Table: the Round Table, still on display in Winchester Great Hall, was probably made by Edward I in the late thirteenth century. The present decoration, with place-names for twenty-four knights, post-dates Malory by some forty years.

in Wales, in the town of Camelot . . . now living hath seen: Caxton's placing of Camelot in Wales conflicts with Malory's identification of it with Winchester. He may be thinking of Caerleon, where Geoffrey of Monmouth has Arthur hold a plenary court, and where there are substantial archaeological ruins (actually Roman, though they had no way of knowing that), including an amphitheatre. Still impressive, the remains would have been even more massive in the fifteenth century.

530 *all is written for our doctrine*: based on Romans 15: 4, which could be taken as giving biblical approval to all literature regardless of the topic.

Amen: Caxton follows this preface with an outline of his book and chapter divisions.

INDEX OF CHARACTERS

Roman numerals indicate discussion in the Introduction; significant entries in the commentary are marked with an asterisk.

	Classical Literary Criticism
	Greek Lyric Poetry
ARISTOTLE	The Nicomachean Ethics
	Physics
	Politics
CAESAR	The Civil War
	The Gallic War
CATULLUS	The Poems of Catullus
EURIPIDES	Medea, Hippolytus, Electra, and Helen
HERODOTUS	The Histories
HOMER	The Iliad
	The Odyssey
HORACE	The Complete Odes and Epodes
JUVENAL	The Satires
MARCUS AURELIUS	The Meditations
OVID	The Love Poems
	Metamorphoses
	Sorrows of an Exile
PETRONIUS	The Satyricon
PLATO	Defence of Socrates, Euthyphro, and Crito
	Republic
PLAUTUS	Four Comedies
SOPHOCLES	Antigone, Oedipus the King, and Electra
VIRGIL	The Aeneid
	The Eclogues and Georgics

The Oxford World's Classics Website

www.worldsclassics.co.uk

- Information about new titles
- Explore the full range of Oxford World's Classics
- Links to other literary sites and the main OUP webpage
- Imaginative competitions, with bookish prizes
- Peruse *Compass*, the Oxford World's Classics magazine
- Articles by editors
- Extracts from Introductions
- A forum for discussion and feedback on the series
- Special information for teachers and lecturers

www.worldsclassics.co.uk

American Literature

British and Irish Literature

Children's Literature

Classics and Ancient Literature

Colonial Literature

Eastern Literature

European Literature

History

Medieval Literature

Oxford English Drama

Poetry

Philosophy

Politics

Religion

The Oxford Shakespeare

A complete list of Oxford Paperbacks, including Oxford World's Classics, OPUS, Past Masters, Oxford Authors, Oxford Shakespeare, Oxford Drama, and Oxford Paperback Reference, is available in the UK from the Academic Division Publicity Department, Oxford University Press, Great Clarendon Street, Oxford OX2 6DP.

In the USA, complete lists are available from the Paperbacks Marketing Manager, Oxford University Press, 198 Madison Avenue, New York, NY 10016.

Oxford Paperbacks are available from all good bookshops. In case of difficulty, customers in the UK can order direct from Oxford University Press Bookshop, Freepost, 116 High Street, Oxford OX1 4BR, enclosing full payment. Please add 10 per cent of published price for postage and packing.